7.95

CONCEPTS
OF
LITERATURE

PRENTICE-HALL INTERNATIONAL, INC., *London*
PRENTICE-HALL OF AUSTRALIA, PTY. LTD., *Sydney*
PRENTICE-HALL OF CANADA, LTD., *Toronto*
PRENTICE-HALL OF INDIA PRIVATE LTD., *New Delhi*
PRENTICE-HALL OF JAPAN, INC., *Tokyo*

CONCEPTS
OF
LITERATURE

JAMES WILLIAM JOHNSON
University of Rochester

PRENTICE-HALL, Inc.   Englewood Cliffs, N. J.

PRENTICE-HALL ENGLISH LITERATURE SERIES

Maynard Mack, editor

© 1970 by PRENTICE-HALL, INC., Englewood Cliffs, N. J.

13-166199-X

Library of Congress Catalog Card No.: 70–97923

Current printing (*last number*): 10   9   8   7   6   5   4   3   2   1

Printed in the United States of America

ACKNOWLEDGMENTS

For prose works included in this anthology, permissions to reprint and copyrights are
acknowledged on the title pages of the selections. For permission to use the following poems,
I herewith acknowledge the cooperation of the publishers of these authors:

W. H. Auden, "A Walk after Dark" from COLLECTED SHORTER POEMS 1927–1957,
by W. H. Auden. © 1966 by W. H. Auden. Reprinted by permission of Random House, Inc.

E. E. Cummings, "Space being(don't forget to remember)Curved"   Copyright, 1931, 1959,
by E. E. Cummings. Reprinted from his volume POEMS 1923–1954 by permission of
Harcourt, Brace & World, Inc. "my sweet old etcetera" Copyright, 1926, by Horace
Liveright; copyright, 1954, by E. E. Cummings. Reprinted from POEMS 1923–1954 by
permission of Harcourt, Brace & World, Inc. and Faber and Faber Ltd. "my father moved
through dooms of love"   Copyright, 1940, by E. E. Cummings. Reprinted from his volume
POEMS 1923–1954 by permission of Harcourt, Brace & World, Inc. and Faber and Faber
Ltd. "if there are any heavens" Copyright, 1931, 1959, by E. E. Cummings. Reprinted
from his volume POEMS 1923–1954 by permission of Harcourt, Brace & World, Inc. and
Faber and Faber Ltd.

for REED,
Who knows bees and cowslip bells

Contents

vii

II
PERSPECTIVES
ON
REALITY   53

III
EMPIRICAL
REALITIES

Narrative Fictions   446

Contents

Rhetorical and Prosodic

DEFINITION

CLASSIFICATION

COMPARISON AND CONTRAST

ILLUSTRATION

DESCRIPTION AND DETAILS

CHARACTERIZATION

PROCESS

CAUSE AND EFFECT

EXPOSITION

ANALYSIS

ARGUMENTATION AND REASONING

Contents

Thematic

THE NATURE OF THE UNIVERSE

THE WORLD AROUND US

LIFE AND DEATH

AFFAIRS OF THE SPIRIT

THE WAYS OF THE MIND

VARIETIES OF LOVE

THE EDUCATIONAL PROCESS

LANGUAGE AND LITERATURE

OUR CLASSICAL HERITAGE

MAN AMONG HIS KIND

THE NEGRO IN AMERICA

THE FAMILY UNIT

DEFINING THE SELF

I
THEORIES
OF
THOUGHT
AND
LITERATURE

Introduction

When you encounter the word, *literature,* what do you think of? Everything that is written or printed, from laundry lists to *War and Peace*? A particular kind of literary composition distinguished for its "fine" or "beautiful" use of words, works of the imagination, or works that deal with testable "truth"? Does "literature" include stories and songs that pass from mouth to ear through oral tradition and are not recorded? And is a *play* or *drama* a species of literature, even though it is meant to be acted rather than read? If you begin to consider these questions, you may see that defining "literature" is less simple than you may have thought.

In its root meaning, as well as general application, literature is everything that is written down in alphabetical characters or "letters." Thus, we say a man is "lettered" or "literate," if he is able to read; and we likewise refer to the writer as "the man of letters." In its broadest application, "literature" would be anything consisting of words on paper, from I.O.U. notes to the *Tibetan Book of the Dead.*

Most of us, however, think of "literature" as much more exclusive than that on the one hand and more inclusive on the other. "Literature" would *not* include government pamphlets on hoof and mouth disease but it *would* include such ballads as "The Wife of Usher's Well" or folk tales and epic poems. It might appear, then, that "literature" is understood to signify "creative" or "imaginative" compositions and not factual writing. Yet this arbitrary distinction does not work very well, for many of the acknowledged masterpieces of literature include factual elements, in part or in whole: Chesterfield's *Letters,* Boswell's *Life of Johnson,* or John Hersey's *Hiroshima.* And besides such kinds of factual writing as letters, biography, autobiography, and history, "literature" may even include the writings of social and natural scientists, such as Sir James Frazer and George Gamow. Obviously, we must either redefine "creative" and "imaginative" to describe the process by which scientists as well as poets shape their ideas into words or else we must define "literature" in terms other than a disjunction between "fiction" and "fact."

There is one other common principle by which "literature" is sometimes established as a category: style. In other languages, what we call "literature" in English is distinguished by the excellent employment of words, its verbal techniques. Thus in French, *belles lettres* refers to accomplished writing of many kinds, fictional *and* factual. It is "fine" writing, not in the sense of being "pretty" combinations of words or bouquets of purple prose; it is the best use of words to express the particular ideas with which the writer is concerned. It is the most appropriate adaptation of style to the demands of the writer's thought process. Another French phase—*le style, c'est l'homme même,* "style is the man himself"— is another way of indicating that excellent writing is a fusion of the writer's conception and his knowledge of language into the best or most accurate or most effective pattern of words.

Of course, it is possible to define "literature" quite simply as "verbal compositions" and stop there. But if we want to comprehend to our own advantage the fullness of a writer's intellectual scope and the unique manner in which he conveys his ideas, we have to accustom ourselves to reading the "verbal composition" as a simultaneous combination of conception and expression.

Every written composition is the product and embodiment of a human mind in action. Through his senses, the writer experiences life; and his mind orders, arranges, and evaluates his experiences even as our minds do. Through his faculties, both intuitive and empirical (or imaginative and logical), he "conceives" patterns of experience that are meaningful to him; and because he is a man accomplished at formulating his experiences in *words,* the writer embodies in the formal patterns of syntax his conceptual processes. He may conceive of human experience in predominantly intuitive ways that are not testable by scientific methods of weighing and observing and measuring; if so, his literary composition will be a "fictional" creation, though it may still be "true" emotionally or aesthetically. Or the writer may conceive experience in terms of observable and testable sense data; in this case, his writing will appear empirically demonstrable or "factual." Again, it may be true—or it may not. A sonnet describing the feeling of romantic love may be "true" whereas a psychological report on clinical or statistical data about love may not. As human beings conceive experience, there are many forms of "truth" and neither the intuitive nor the logical way of thinking has a pre-emptive claim to the true. We must remember that much of what seems to be scientific "fact" is actually a form of intuitive truth: a "hypothesis" or "theorem" or "postulate". E equals mc^2; is that a "fact"? Is it empirically "true" or "false"?

What men write, then, depends on how they think and feel, what they experience and observe, what they consider significant, and how capable they are of using words and word-systems to convey their conceptions to others. In every literary product—every "verbal composition"—there will be intuitive and empirical, emotional and logical, fictional and factual components, arranged into discernible word patterns of one kind or another. It is possible to sort out various literary works by *classifying* them: primarily by their word patterns or *forms* but also by their subject matter, intention, tone, techniques, or a combination of all these. For example, written works might be classified according to their prosody as either prose or poetry, then go on to be subdivided by method as argumentative, expository, descriptive, and narrative (in the case of prose) and lyric, narrative, and dramatic (in the case of poetry). Such categories by form and technique may assist the reader to see the immediate, surface qualities of a specific composition: to identify it as an argument or a dramatic monologue and thus measure it beside other instances of its kind. But there are some disadvantages to approaching literature generally and a particular work in this fashion exclusively. It can raise too artificial distinctions based on secondary characteristics or keep the reader from seeing the very real, inner similarities between such apparently unlike ways of conceiving experience as the historian's and playwright's or the anthropologist's and storyteller's.

In the coming pages, therefore, although the literary selections are grouped according to more or less conventional *genres* (or literary "families"), the overall arrangement of the works is established to suggest some basic resemblances, as well as differences, between various kinds of writing and to encourage the student to see that in their various approaches to life's experiences, *all* writers confront many of the same problems in putting their conceptions into words.

In the section immediately below, "Theories of Thought and Literature," experts from different fields—psychology, philosophy, literary history and criticism, communications—deal with some basic questions about the nature of thought and the processes of conceptualization, how ideas transform into written language, and the connection between the writer's experience and the reader's. Section II, "Perspectives on Reality," presents a variety of compositions that show how writers define their relationship to themselves, other people, and the world we commonly inhabit: from the most personal and private versions of experience (the diary or journal) to the most impersonal and public (history).

With some ideas established in Sections I and II on why and how writers conceive experience as they do and what possible perspectives they can take as a vantage point to define their views, the readings in Section III emphasize the kinds of writing that depend most directly or heavily on an empirical approach to knowledge; those in Section IV then stress the intuitive approach.

In each section, the readings are grouped by a principle form or genre; throughout the collections, however, common subjects and themes appear and reappear, taking various shapes from the nature of the thought processes that treat them as well as the formal concerns of the work that deals with them. By using the questions at the end of each section, the student can pursue his exploration into the common concerns and the particular differences among literary works of disparate persuasions as thoroughly as he has the time for.

Initially, "literature" may be defined as "verbal composition which fuses conceptual process with syntactic patterns in such a way as to link the writer and reader, significantly and effectively, with a shared experience." With this working definition as a start, the reader can proceed to the body of writing before him, ready to expand and qualify his understanding of "literature" even as he experiences a wide variety of it, increasing (hopefully) his enjoyment and appreciation as he discovers ways of treating it critically.

WILLIAM JAMES

Reverie, Inference, and Reasoning

We talk of man being the rational animal; and the traditional intellectualist philosophy has always made a great point of treating the brutes as wholly irrational creatures. Nevertheless, it is by no means easy to decide just what is meant by reason, or how the peculiar thinking process called reasoning differs from other thought-sequences which may lead to similar results.

Much of our thinking consists of trains of images suggested one by another, of a sort of spontaneous reverie of which it seems likely enough that the higher brutes should be capable. This sort of thinking leads nevertheless to

REVERIE, INFERENCE, AND REASONING: From *The Principles of Psychology* (1902). Reprinted by permission of Holt, Rinehart and Winston, Inc., Publishers.

rational conclusions, both practical and theoretical. The links between the terms are either "contiguity" or "similarity," and with a mixture of both these things we can hardly be very incoherent. As a rule, in this sort of irresponsible thinking, the terms which fall to be coupled together are empirical concretes, not abstractions. A sunset may call up the vessel's deck from which I saw one last summer, the companions of my voyage, my arrival into port, etc.; or it may make me think of solar myths, of Hercules's and Hector's funeral pyres, of Homer and whether he could write, of the Greek alphabet, etc. If habitual contiguities predominate, we have a prosaic mind; if rare contiguities, or similarities, have free play, we call the person fanciful, poetic, or witty. But the thought as a rule is of matters taken in their entirety. Having been thinking of one, we find later that we are thinking of another, to which we have been lifted along, we hardly know how. If an abstract quality figures in the procession, it arrests our attention but for a moment, and fades into something else; and is never very abstract.

Thus, in thinking of the sun-myths, we may have a gleam of admiration at the gracefulness of the primitive human mind, or a moment of disgust at the narrowness of modern interpreters. But, in the main, we think less of qualities than of whole things, real or possible, just as we may experience them.

The upshot of it may be that we are reminded of some practical duty: we write a letter to a friend abroad, or we take down the lexicon and study our Greek lesson. Our thought is rational, and leads to a rational act, but it can hardly be called reasoning in a strict sense of the term.

There are other shorter flights of thought, single couplings of terms which suggest one another by association, which approach more to what would commonly be classed as acts of reasoning proper. Those are where a present sign suggests an unseen, distant, or future reality. Where the sign and what it suggests are both concretes which have been coupled together on previous occasions, the inference is common to both brutes and men, being really nothing more than association by contiguity. *A* and *B*, dinner bell and dinner, have been experienced in immediate succession. Hence *A* no sooner falls upon the sense than *B* is anticipated, and steps are taken to meet it. The whole education of our domestic beasts, all the cunning added by age and experience to wild ones, and the greater part of our human knowingness consists in the ability to make a mass of inferences of this simplest sort. Our "perceptions," or recognitions of what objects are before us, are inferences of this kind. We feel a patch of color, and we say "a distant house," a whiff of odor crosses us, and we say "a skunk," a faint sound is heard, and we call it "a railroad train." Examples are needless; for such inferences of sensations not presented form the staple and tissue of our perceptive life, and our Chapter XIX was full of them, illusory or veracious. They have been called *unconscious inferences*. Certainly we are commonly unconscious that we are inferring at all. The sign and the signified melt into what seems to us the object of a single pulse of thought....

THUS, THERE ARE TWO
GREAT POINTS IN REASONING:

First, an extracted character is taken as equivalent to the entire datum from which it comes; and,

Second, the character thus taken suggests a certain consequence more obviously than it was suggested by the total datum as it originally came.

1. Suppose I say, when offered a piece of cloth, "I won't buy that; it looks as if it would fade," meaning merely that something about it suggests the idea of fading to my mind—my judgment, though possibly correct, is not reasoned, but purely empirical; but, if I can say that into the color there enters a certain dye which I know to be chemically unstable, and that *therefore* the color will fade, my judgment is reasoned. The notion of the dye which is one of the parts of the cloth, is the connecting link between the latter and the notion of fading. So, again, an uneducated man will expect from past experience to see a piece of ice melt if placed near the fire, and the tip of his finger look coarse if he views it through a convex glass. In neither of these cases could the result be anticipated without full previous acquaintance with the entire phenomenon. It is not a result of reasoning.

But a man who should conceive heat as a mode of motion, and liquefaction as identical with increased motion of molecules; who should know that curved surfaces bend light-rays in special ways, and that the apparent size of anything is connected with the amount of the "bend" of its light-rays as they enter the eye— such a man would make the right inferences for all these objects, even though he had never in his life had any concrete experience of them; and he would do this because the ideas which we have above supposed him to possess would mediate in his mind between the phenomena he starts with and the conclusions he draws. But these ideas or reasons for his conclusions are all mere extracted portions or circumstances singled out from the mass of characters which make up the entire phenomena. The motions which form heat, the bending of the light-waves, are, it is true, excessively recondite ingredients; the hidden pendulum I spoke of above is less so; and the sticking of a door on its sill in the earlier example would hardly be so at all. But each and all agree in this, that they bear a *more evident relation* to the conclusion than did the immediate data in their full totality.

The difficulty is, in each case, to extract from the immediate data that particular ingredient which shall have this very evident relation to the conclusion. Every phenomenon or so-called "fact" has an infinity of aspects or properties, as we have seen, amongst which the fool, or man with little sagacity, will inevitably go astray. But no matter for this point now. The first thing is to have seen that every possible case of reasoning involves the extraction of a particular partial aspect of the phenomena thought about, and that whilst Empirical Thought simply associates phenomena in their entirety, Reasoned Thought couples them by the conscious use of this extract.

2. And, now, to prove the second point: Why are the couplings, consequences, and implications of extracts more evident and obvious than those of entire phenomena? For two reasons.

First, the extracted characters are more general than the concretes, and the connections they may have are, therefore, more familiar to us, having been more often met in our experience. Think of heat as motion, and whatever is true of motion will be true of heat; but we have had a hundred experiences of motion for every one of heat. Think of the rays passing through this lens as bending towards the perpendicular, and you substitute for the comparatively unfamiliar lens the very familiar notion of a particular change in direction of a line, of which notion every day brings us countless examples.

The other reason why the relations of the extracted characters are so evident is that their properties are so *few*, compared with the properties of the whole, from which we derived

them. In every concrete total the characters and their consequences are so inexhaustibly numerous that we may lose our way among them before noticing the particular consequence it behooves us to draw. But, if we are lucky enough to single out the proper character, we take in, as it were, by a single glance all its possible consequences. Thus the character of scraping the sill has very few suggestions, prominent among which is the suggestion that the scraping will cease if we raise the door; whilst the entire refractory door suggests an enormous number of notions to the mind.

Take another example. I am sitting in a railroad car, waiting for the train to start. It is winter, and the stove fills the car with pungent smoke. The brakeman enters, and my neighbor asks him to "stop that stove smoking." He replies that it will stop entirely as soon as the car begins to move. "Why so?" asks the passenger. "It *always* does," replies the brakeman. It is evident from this "always" that the connection between car moving and smoke stopping was a purely empirical one in the brakeman's mind, bred of habit. But, if the passenger had been an acute reasoner, he, with no experience of what that stove always did, might have anticipated the brakeman's reply, and spared his own question. Had he singled out of all the numerous points involved in a stove's not smoking the one special point of smoke pouring freely out of the stovepipe's mouth, he would, probably, owing to the few associations of that idea, have been immediately reminded of the law that a fluid passes more rapidly out of a pipe's mouth if another fluid be at the same time streaming over that mouth; and then the rapid draught of air over the stovepipe's mouth, which is one of the points involved in the car's motion, would immediately have occurred to him.

Thus a couple of extracted characters, with a couple of their few and obvious connections, would have formed the reasoned link in the passenger's mind between the phenomena, smoke stopping and car moving, which were only linked as wholes in the brakeman's mind.

Such examples may seem trivial, but they contain the essence of the most refined and transcendental theorizing. The reason why physics grows more deductive the more the fundamental properties it assumes are of a mathematical sort, such as molecular mass or wavelength, is that the immediate consequences of these notions are so few that we can survey them all at once, and promptly pick out those which concern us.

Sagacity; or the Perception of the Essence

To reason, then, we must be able to extract characters—not *any* characters, but the right characters for our conclusion. If we extract the wrong character, it will not lead to that conclusion. Here, then, is the difficulty: *How are characters extracted, and why does it require the advent of a genius in many cases before the fitting character is brought to light?* Why cannot anybody reason as well as anybody else? Why does it need a Newton to notice the law of the squares, a Darwin to notice the survival of the fittest? To answer these questions we must begin a new research, and see how our insight into facts naturally grows.

All our knowledge at first is vague. When we say that a thing is vague, we mean that it has no subdivisions *ab intra*, nor precise limitations *ab extra*; but still all the forms of thought may apply to it. It may have unity, reality, externality, extent, and what not—*thinghood*, in a word, but thinghood only as a whole. In this vague way, probably, does the room appear to the babe who first begins to be conscious of it as something other than his moving nurse. It has no subdivisions in his mind, unless, perhaps, the window is able to attract his separate notice. In this vague way, certainly, does every entirely new experience appear to the adult. A library, a museum, a machine shop, are mere confused wholes to the uninstructed, but the machinist, the antiquary, and the bookworm perhaps hardly notice the whole at all, so eager are they to pounce upon the details. Familiarity has in them bred discrimination. Such vague terms as "grass," "mould," and "meat" do not exist for the botanist or the anatomist. They know too much about grasses, moulds, and muscles. A certain person said to Charles Kingsley, who was showing him the dissection of a caterpillar, with its exquisite viscera, "Why, I thought it was nothing but skin and squash!" A layman present at a shipwreck, a battle, or a fire is helpless. Discrimination has been so little awakened in him by experience that his consciousness leaves no single point of the complex situation accented and standing out for him to begin to act upon. But the sailor, the fireman, and the general know directly at what corner to take up the business. They "see into the situation"—that is, they analyze it—with their first glance. It is full of delicately differenced ingredients which their education has little by little brought to their consciousness, but of which the novice gains no clear idea....We dissociate the elements of originally vague totals by attending to them or noticing them alternately, of course. But what determines which element we shall attend to first? There are two immediate and obvious answers: first, our practical or instinctive interests; and, second, our aesthetic interests. The dog singles out of any situation its smells, and the horse its sounds, because they may reveal facts of practical moment, and are instinctively exciting to these several creatures. The infant notices the candle-flame or the window, and ignores the rest of the room, because those objects give him a vivid pleasure. So, the country boy dissociates the blackberry, the chestnut, and the wintergreen, from the vague mass of other shrubs and trees, for their practical uses, and the savage is delighted with the beads, the bits of looking glass, brought by an exploring vessel, and gives no heed to the features of the vessel itself, which is too much beyond his sphere. These aesthetic and practical interests, then, are the weightiest factors in making particular ingredients stand out in high relief. What they lay their accent on, that we notice; but what they are in themselves, we cannot say. We must content ourselves here with simply accepting them as irreducible ultimate factors in determining the way our knowledge grows.

Now, a creature which has few instinctive impulses, or interests, practical or aesthetic, will dissociate few characters, and will, at best, have limited reasoning powers; whilst one whose interests are very varied will reason much better. Man, by his immensely varied instincts, practical wants, and aesthetic feelings, to which every sense contributes, would, by dint of these alone, be sure to dissociate vastly more characters than any other animal; and accordingly we find that the lowest savages reason incomparably better than the highest brutes. . . .

Man is known again as "the talking animal"; and language is assuredly a capital distinction between man and brute. But it may readily be shown how this distinction merely flows from those we have pointed out, easy dissociation of a representation into its ingredients, and association by similarity.

Language is a system of *signs*, different from the things signified, but able to suggest them.

No doubt brutes have a number of such signs. When a dog yelps in front of a door, and his master, understanding his desire, opens it, the dog may, after a certain number of repetitions, get to repeat in cold blood a yelp which was at first the involuntary interjectional expression of strong emotion. The same dog may be taught to "beg" for food, and afterwards come to do so deliberately when hungry. The dog also learns to understand the signs of men, and the word "rat" uttered to a terrier suggests exciting thoughts of the rat-hunt. If the dog had the varied impulse to vocal utterance which some other animals have, he would probably repeat the word "rat" whenever he spontaneously happened to think of a rat-hunt—he no doubt does have it as an auditory image, just as a parrot calls out different words spontaneously from its repertory, and having learned the name

of a given dog will utter it on the sight of a different dog. In each of these separate cases the particular sign *may* be consciously noticed by the animal, as distinct from the particular thing signified, and will thus, so far as it goes, be a true manifestation of language. But when we come to man we find a great difference. *He has a deliberate intention to apply a sign to everything.* The linguistic impulse is with him generalized and systematic. For things hitherto unnoticed or unfelt, he *desires* a sign before he has one. Even though the dog should possess his "yelp" for this thing, his "beg" for that, and his auditory image "rat" for a third thing, the matter with him rests there. If a fourth thing interests him for which no sign happens already to have been learned, he remains tranquilly without it and goes no further. But the man *postulates* it, its absence irritates him, and he ends by inventing it. *This* GENERAL PURPOSE *constitutes, I take it, the peculiarity of human speech, and explains its prodigious development.* . . .

But, now, since nature never makes a jump, it is evident that we should find the lowest men occupying in this respect an intermediate position between the brutes and the highest men. And so we do. Beyond the analogies which their own minds suggest by breaking up the literal sequence of their experience, there is a whole world of analogies which they can appreciate when imparted to them by their betters, but which they could never excogitate alone. This answers the question why Darwin and Newton had to be waited for so long. The flash of similarity between an apple and the moon, between the rivalry for food in nature and the rivalry for man's selection, was too recondite to have occurred to any but exceptional minds. *Genius, then,* as has been already said, *is identical with the possession of similar association to an extreme degree.* Professor Bain says: "This I count the leading fact of genius. I consider it quite impossible to afford any explanation of intellectual originality except on the supposition of unusual energy on this point." Alike in the arts, in literature, in practical affairs, and in science, association by similarity is the prime condition of success.

But as, according to our view, there are two stages in reasoned thought, one where similarity merely *operates* to call up cognate thoughts, and another farther stage, where the bond of identity between the cognate thoughts is *noticed; so minds of genius may be divided into two main sorts, those who notice the bond and those who merely obey it.* The first are the abstract reasoners, properly so called, the men of science, and philosophers—the analysts, in a word; the latter are the poets, the critics—the artists, in a word, the men of intuitions. These judge rightly, classify cases, characterize them by the most striking analogic epithets, but go no further. At first sight it might seem that the analytic mind represented simply a higher intellectual stage, and that the intuitive mind represented an arrested stage of intellectual development; but the difference is not so simple as this. Professor Bain has said that a man's advance to the scientific stage (the stage of noticing and abstracting the bond of similarity) may often be due to an *absence* of certain emotional sensibilities. The sense of color, he says, may no less determine a mind away from science than it determines it toward painting. There must be a penury in one's interest in the details of particular forms in order to permit the forces of the intellect to be concentrated on what is common to many forms. In other words, supposing a mind fertile in the suggestion of analogies, but, at the same time, keenly interested in the particulars of each suggested image, that mind would be far less apt to single out the particular character which called up the analogy than one whose interests were less generally lively. A certain richness of the aesthetic nature may, therefore, easily keep one in the intuitive stage. All the poets are examples of this. Take Homer:

> Ulysses, too, spied round the house to see if any man were still alive and hiding, trying to get away from gloomy death. He found them all fallen in the blood and dirt, and in such number as the fish which the fishermen to the low shore, out of the foaming sea, drag with their meshy nets. These all, sick for the ocean water, are strewn around the sands, while the blazing sun takes their life from them. So there the suitors lay strewn round on one another.

Or again:

> "And as when a Mæonian or a Carian woman stains ivory with purple to be a check-piece for horses, and it is kept in the chamber, and many horsemen have prayed to bear it off; but it is kept a treasure for a king, both a trapping for his horse and a glory to the driver—in such wise were thy stout thighs, Menelaos, and legs and fair ankles stained with blood.

A man in whom all the accidents of an analogy rise up as vividly as this, may be excused for not attending to the ground of the analogy. But he need not on that account be deemed intellectually the inferior of a man of drier mind, in whom the ground is not as liable to be eclipsed by the general splendor. Rarely are both sorts of intellect, the splendid and the analytic, found in conjunction. Plato among philosophers, and M. Taine, who cannot quote a child's saying without describing the "*voix chantante, étonnée, heureuse*" in which it is uttered, are only exceptions whose strangeness proves the rule.

An often-quoted writer has said that Shakespeare possessed more *intellectual power* than any one else that ever lived. If by this he meant the power to pass from given premises to right or congruous conclusions, it is no doubt true. The abrupt transitions in Shakespeare's thought astonish the reader by their unexpectedness no less than they delight him by their fitness. Why, for instance, does the death of Othello so stir the spectator's blood and leave him with a sense of reconcilement? Shakespeare himself could very likely not say why; for his invention, though rational, was not ratiocinative. Wishing the curtain to fall upon a reinstated Othello, that speech about the turbaned Turk suddenly simply flashed across him as the right end of all that went before. The dry critic who comes after can, however, point out the subtle bonds of identity that guided Shakespeare's pen through that speech to the death of the Moor. Othello is sunk in ignominy, lapsed from his height at the beginning of the play. What better way to rescue him at last from this abasement than to make him for an instant identify himself in memory with the old Othello of better days, and then execute justice on his present disowned body, as he used then to smite all enemies of the State? But Shakespeare, whose mind supplied these means, could probably not have told why they were so effective.

But though this is true, and though it would be absurd in an absolute way to say that a given analytic mind was superior to any intuitional one, yet it is none the less true that the former *represents* the higher stage. Men, taken historically, reason by analogy long before they have learned to reason by abstract characters. Association by similarity and true reasoning may have identical results. If a philosopher wishes to prove to you why you should do a certain thing, he may do so by using abstract considerations exclusively; a savage will prove the same by reminding you of a similar case in which you notoriously do as he now proposes, and this with no ability to state the *point* in which the cases are similar. In all primitive literature, in all savage oratory, we find persuasion carried on exclusively by parables and similes, and travellers in savage countries readily adopt the native custom. Take, for example, Dr. Livingstone's argument with the negro conjuror. The missionary was trying to dissuade the savage from his fetichistic ways of invoking rain. "You see," said he, "that, after all your operations, sometimes it rains and sometimes it does not, exactly as when you have not operated at all." "But," replied the sorcerer, "it is just the same with you doctors; you give your remedies, and sometimes the patient gets well and sometimes he dies, just as when you do nothing at all." To that the pious missionary replied: "The doctor does his duty, after which God performs the cure if it pleases Him." "Well," rejoined the savage, "it is just so with me. I do what is necessary to procure rain, after which God sends it or withholds it according to His pleasure."

This is the stage in which proverbial philosophy reigns supreme. "An empty sack can't stand straight" will stand for the reason why a man with debts may lose his honesty; and "a bird in the hand is worth two in the bush" will serve to back up one's exhortations to prudence. Or we answer the question: "Why is snow white?" by saying, "For the same reason that soapsuds or whipped eggs are white"— in other words, instead of giving the *reason* for a fact, we give another *example* of the same fact. This offering a similar instance, instead of a reason, has often been criticized as one of the forms of logical depravity in men. But manifestly it is not a perverse act of thought, but only an incomplete one. Furnishing parallel cases is the necessary first step towards abstracting the reason imbedded in them all.

As it is with reasons, so it is with words. The first words are probably always names of entire things and entire actions, of extensive coherent groups. A new experience in the primitive man can only be talked about by him in terms of the old experiences which have received names. It reminds him of certain ones from among them, but the *points* in which it agrees with them are neither named nor dissociated. Pure similarity must work before the abstraction can work which is based upon it. The first adjectives will therefore probably be total nouns embodying the striking character. The primeval man will say, not "the bread is hard," but "the bread is stone"; not "the face is round," but "the face is moon"; not "the fruit is sweet," but "the fruit is sugarcane." The first words are thus neither particular nor general, but *vaguely* concrete; just as we speak of an "oval" face, a "velvet" skin, or an "iron" will, without meaning to connote any other attributes of the adjective-noun than those in which it *does* resemble the noun it is used to qualify. After a while certain of these adjectively-used nouns come only to signify the particular quality for whose sake they are oftenest used; the *entire thing* which they originally meant receives another name, and they become true abstract and general terms.

Oval, for example, with us suggests *only* shape. The first abstract qualities thus formed are, no doubt, qualities of one and the same sense found in different objects—as big, sweet; next analogies between different senses, as "sharp" of taste, "high" of sound, etc.; then analogies of motor combinations, or form of relation, as simple, confused, difficult, reciprocal, relative, spontaneous, etc. The extreme degree of subtlety in analogy is reached in such cases as when we say certain English art critics' writing reminds us of a close room in which pastilles have been burning, or that the mind of certain Frenchmen is like old Roquefort cheese. Here language utterly fails to hit upon the basis of resemblance.

Over immense departments of our thought we are still, all of us, in the savage state. Similarity operates in us, but abstraction has not taken place. We know what the present case is like, we know what it reminds us of, we have an intuition of the right course to take, if it be a practical matter. But analytic thought has made no tracks, and we cannot justify ourselves to others. In ethical, psychological, and aesthetic matters, to give a clear reason for one's judgment is universally recognized as a mark of rare genius. The helplessness of uneducated people to account for their likes and dislikes is often ludicrous. Ask the first Irish girl why she likes this country better or worse than her home, and see how much she can tell you. But if you ask your most educated friend why he prefers Titian to Paul Veronese, you will hardly get more of a reply; and you will probably get absolutely none if you inquire why Beethoven reminds him of Michaelangelo, or how it comes that a bare figure with unduly flexed joints, by the latter, can so suggest the moral tragedy of life. His thought obeys a *nexus*, but cannot name it. And so it is with all those judgments of *experts*, which even though unmotived are so valuable. Saturated with experience of a particular class of materials, an expert intuitively feels whether a newly-reported fact is probable or not, whether a proposed hypothesis is worthless or the reverse. He instinctively knows that, in a novel case, this

and not that will be the promising course of action. The well-known story of the old judge advising the new one never to give reasons for his decisions, "the decisions will probably be right, the reasons will surely be wrong," illustrates this. The doctor will feel that the patient is doomed, the dentist will have a premonition that the tooth will break, though neither can articulate a reason for his foreboding. The reason lies imbedded, but not yet laid bare, in all the countless previous cases dimly suggested by the actual one, all calling up the same conclusion, which the adept thus finds himself swept on to, he knows not how or why.

NORMAN O. BROWN

The Disease Called Man

There is one word which, if we only understand it, is the key to Freud's thought. That word is "repression." The whole edifice of psychoanalysis, Freud said, is based upon the theory of repression. Freud's entire life was devoted to the study of the phenomenon he called repression. The Freudian revolution is that radical revision of traditional theories of human nature and human society which becomes necessary if repression is recognized as a fact. In the new Freudian perspective, the essence of society is repression of the individual, and the essence of the individual is repression of himself.

The best way to explore the notion of repression is to review the path which led Freud to his hypothesis. Freud's breakthrough was the discovery of meaningfulness in a set of phenomena theretofore regarded, at least in scientific circles, as meaningless: first, the "mad" symptoms of the mentally deranged; second, dreams; and third, the various phenomena gathered together under the title of the psychopathology of everyday life, including slips of the tongue, errors, and random thoughts.

Now in what sense does Freud find meaningfulness in neurotic symptoms, dreams, and errors? He means, of course, that these phenomena are determined and can be given a causal explanation. He is rigorously insisting on unequivocal allegiance to the principle of psychic determinism; but he means much more than that. For if it were possible to explain these phenomena on behavioristic principles, as the result of superficial associations of ideas, then they would have a cause but no meaning. Meaningfulness means expression of a purpose or an intention. The crux of Freud's discovery is that neurotic symptoms, as well as the dreams and errors of everyday life, do have meaning, and that the meaning of "meaning" has to be radically revised because they have meaning. Since the purport of these purposive expressions is generally unknown to the person whose purpose they express, Freud is driven to embrace the paradox that there are in a human being purposes of which he knows nothing, involuntary purposes, or, in more technical Freudian language, "unconscious ideas." From this point of view a new world of psychic reality is opened up, of whose inner nature we are every bit as ignorant as we are of the reality of the external world, and of which our ordinary conscious observation tells us no more than our sense organs are able to report to us of the external world. Freud can thus define psychoanalysis as "nothing more than the discovery of the unconscious in mental life."

But the Freudian revolution is not limited to the hypothesis of an unconscious psychic life in the human being in addition to his conscious life. The other crucial hypothesis is that some unconscious ideas in a human being are incapable of becoming conscious to him in the ordinary way, because they are strenuously disowned and resisted by the conscious self. From this point of view Freud can say that "the whole of psychoanalytic theory is in fact built up on the perception of the resistance exerted by the patient when we try to make him conscious of his unconscious." The dynamic relation between the unconscious and the conscious life is one of conflict, and psychoanalysis is from top to bottom a science of mental conflict.

The realm of the unconscious is established in the individual when he refuses to admit into his conscious life a purpose or desire which he has, and in doing so establishes in himself a psychic force opposed to his own idea. This rejection by the individual of a purpose or idea, which nevertheless remains his, is repression. "The essence of repression lies simply in the function of rejecting or keeping something out of consciousness." Stated in more general terms, the essence of repression lies in the refusal of the human being to recognize the realities of his human nature. The fact that the repressed purposes nevertheless remain his is shown by dreams and neurotic symptoms, which represent an irruption of the unconscious into consciousness, producing not indeed a pure image of the unconscious, but a compromise between the two conflicting systems, and thus exhibiting the reality of the conflict.

Thus the notion of the unconscious remains an enigma without the theory of repression; or, as Freud says, "We obtain our theory of the unconscious from the theory of repression." To put it another way, the unconscious is "the dynamically unconscious repressed." Repression is the key word in the whole system; the word is chosen to indicate a structure dynamically based on psychic conflict. Freud illustrates the nature of psychic repression by a series of metaphors and analogies drawn from the social phenomena of war, civil war, and police action.

From neurotic symptoms, dreams, and errors to a general theory of human nature may seem like a long step. Granting that it is a long step, Freud could argue that he is entitled to explore the widest possible application of a hypothesis derived from a narrow field. He could take the offensive and claim that traditional theories of human nature must be regarded as unsatisfactory because they have nothing to say about these peripheral phenomena. What theory of human nature, except Freud's, does have anything significant to say about dreams or insanity? And are dreams and insanity really negligible factors on the periphery of human life?

But the truth of the matter is that Freud maintains that to go from neurotic symptoms, dreams, and errors, to a new theory of human nature in general involves no further step at all. For the evidence on which the hypothesis of the repressed unconscious is based entails the conclusion that it is a phenomenon present in all human beings. The psychopathological phenomena of everyday life, although trivial from a practical point of view, are theoretically important because they show the intrusion of unconscious intentions into our everyday and supposedly normal behavior.

Even more theoretically important are dreams. For dreams, also "normal" phenomena, exhibit in detail not only the existence of the unconscious but also the dynamics of its repression (the dream-censorship). But since the same dynamics of repression explained neurotic symptoms, and since the dreams of neurotics, which are a clue to the meaning of their symptoms, differ neither in structure nor in content from the dreams of normal people, the conclusion is that a dream is itself a neurotic symptom. We are all therefore neurotic. At least dreams show that the difference between neurosis and health prevails only by day; and since the psychopathology of everyday life exhibits the same dynamics, even the waking life of the "healthy" man is pervaded by innumerable symptom-formations. Between "normality" and "abnormality" there is no qualitative but only a quantitative difference, based largely on the practical question of whether our neurosis is serious enough to incapacitate us for work.

Or perhaps we are closer to the Freudian point of view if we give a more paradoxical formulation; the difference between "neurotic" and "healthy" is only that the "healthy" have a socially usual form of neurosis. At any rate, to quote a more technical and cautious formulation of the same theorem, Freud says that from the study of dreams we learn that the neuroses make use of a mechanism already in existence as a normal part of our psychic structure, not of one that is newly created by some morbid disturbance or other.

Thus Freud's first paradox, the existence of a repressed unconscious, necessarily implies the second and even more significant paradox, the universal neurosis of mankind. Here is the *pons asinorum* of psychoanalysis. Neurosis is not an occasional aberration; it is not just in other people; it is in us, and in us all the time. It is in the psychoanalyst: Freud discovered the Oedipus complex, which he regarded as the root of all neurosis, by self-analysis. *The Interpretation of Dreams* is one of the great applications and extensions of the Socratic maxim, "Know thyself." Or, to put it another way, the doctrine of the universal neurosis of mankind is the psychoanalytical analogue of the theological doctrine of original sin.

The crucial point in Freud's basic hypothesis is the existence of psychic conflict; the hypothesis cannot be meaningfully formulated without some further specification of the nature of the conflict and the conflicting forces. Now Freud made repeated analyses of the fundamental psychic conflict, at several different levels and from several points of view. Let us at this point try to abstract the common core from these various accounts.

In our first description of Freud's theory of repression we used the word "purpose" to designate that which is repressed into the unconscious. This excessively vague word conceals a fundamental Freudian axiom. The psychic conflict which produces dreams and neuroses is not generated by intellectual problems but by purposes, wishes, desires. Freud's frequent use of the term "unconscious idea" can be misleading here. But as Freud says,

> We remain on the surface so long as we treat only of memories and ideas. The only valuable things in psychic life are, rather, the emotions. All psychic forces are significant only through their aptitude to arouse emotions. Ideas are repressed only because they are bound up with releases of emotions, which are not to come about; it would be more correct to say that repression deals with the emotions, but these are comprehensible to us only in their tie-up with ideas.

Freud is never tired of insisting that dreams are in essence wish fulfillments, expressions of repressed unconscious wishes, and neurotic symptoms likewise.

Now if we take "desire" as the most suitably abstract of this series of terms, it is a Freudian axiom that the essence of man consists, not, as Descartes maintained, in thinking, but in desiring. Plato (and, *mutatis mutandis*, Aristotle) identified the *summum bonum* for man with contemplation; since the *telos* or end is the basic element in definition, this amounts to saying that the essence of man is contemplation. But ambiguously juxtaposed with this doctrine of man as contemplator is the Platonic doctrine of Eros, which, as elaborated by Plato in the *Symposium* and the *Phaedrus*, suggests that the fundamental quest of man is to find a satisfactory object for his love. A similar ambiguity between man as contemplator and man as lover is to be found in Spinoza and Hegel. The turning point in the Western tradition comes in the reaction to Hegel. Feuerbach, followed by Marx, calls for the abandonment of the contemplative tradition in favor of what he calls "practical-sensuous activity"; the meaning of this concept, and its relation to Freud, would take us far afield. But Schopenhauer, in his notion of the primacy of will—however much he may undo his own notion by his search for an escape from the primacy of the will—is a landmark, seceding from the great, and really rather insane, Western tradition that the goal of mankind is to become as contemplative as possible. Freudian psychology eliminates the category of pure contemplation as nonexistent. Only a wish, says

Freud, can possibly set our psychic apparatus in motion.

With this notion of desire as the essence of man is joined a definition of desire as energy directed toward the procurement of pleasure and avoidance of pain. Hence Freud can say, "Our entire psychical activity is bent upon procuring pleasure and avoiding pain, is automatically regulated by the pleasure-principle." Or, "It is simply the pleasure-principle which draws up the programme of life's purpose." At this level of analysis, the pleasure-principle implies no complicated hedonistic theory nor any particular theory as to the sources of pleasure. It is an assumption taken from common sense, and means much the same as Aristotle's dictum that all men seek happiness: Freud says that the goal of the pleasure-principle is happiness.

But man's desire for happiness is in conflict with the whole world. Reality imposes on human beings the necessity of renunciation of pleasures; reality frustrates desire. The pleasure-principle is in conflict with the reality-principle, and this conflict is the cause of repression. Under the conditions of repression the essence of our being lies in the unconscious, and only in the unconscious does the pleasure-principle reign supreme. Dreams and neurotic symptoms show that the frustrations of reality cannot destroy the desires which are the essence of our being: the unconscious is the unsubdued and indestructible element in the human soul. The whole world may be against it, but still man holds fast to the deep-rooted, passionate striving for a positive fulfillment of happiness.

The conscious self, on the other hand, which by refusing to admit a desire into consciousness institutes the process of repression, is, so to speak, the surface of ourselves mediating between our inner real being and external reality. The nucleus of the conscious self is that part of the mind or system in the mind which receives perceptions from the external world. This nucleus acquires a new dimension through the power of speech, which makes it accessible to the process of education and acculturation. The conscious self is the organ of adaptation to the environment and to the culture. The conscious self, therefore, is governed not by the pleasure-principle but by the principle of adjustment to reality, the reality-principle.

From this point of view dreams and neurotic symptoms, which we previously analyzed as produced by the conflict between the conscious and unconscious systems, can also be analyzed as produced by the conflict between the pleasure-principle and the reality-principle. On the one hand, dreams, neurotic symptoms, and all other manifestations of the unconscious, such as fantasy, represent in some degree or other a flight or alienation from a reality which is found unbearable. On the other hand, they represent a return to the pleasure-principle; they are substitutes for pleasures denied by reality. In this compromise between the two conflicting systems, the pleasure desired is reduced or distorted or even transformed to pain. Under the conditions of repression, under the domination of the reality-principle, the pursuit of pleasure is degraded to the status of a symptom.

But to say that reality or the reality-principle causes repression defines the problem rather than solves it. Freud sometimes identifies the reality-principle with the "struggle for existence," as if repression could be ultimately explained by some objective economic necessity to work. But man makes his own reality and various kinds of reality (and various compulsions to work) through the medium of culture or society. It is therefore more adequate to say that society imposes repression, though even this formula in Freud's early writings is connected with the inadequate idea that society, in imposing repression, is simply legislating the demands of objective economic necessity. This naïve and rationalistic sociology stands, or rather falls, with Freud's earlier version of psychoanalysis. The later Freud, as we shall see, in his doctrine of anxiety is moving toward the position that man is the animal which represses himself and which creates culture or society in order to

repress himself. Even the formula that society imposes repression poses a problem rather than solves it; but the problem it poses is large. For if society imposes repression, and repression causes the universal neurosis of mankind, it follows that there is an intrinsic connection between social organization and neurosis. Man the social animal is by the same token the neurotic animal. Or, as Freud puts it, man's superiority over the other animals is his capacity for neurosis, and his capacity for neurosis is merely the obverse of his capacity for cultural development.

Freud therefore arrives at the same conclusion as Nietzsche ("the disease called man"), but by a scientific route, by a study of the neuroses. Neurosis is an essential consequence of civilization or culture. Here again is a harsh lesson in humility, which tender-minded critics and apostles of Freud evade or suppress. We must be prepared to analyze clinically as a neurosis not only the foreign culture we dislike, but also our own.

LIONEL TRILLING

Art and Neurosis

The question of the mental health of the artist has engaged the attention of our culture since the beginning of the Romantic Movement. Before that time it was commonly said that the poet was "mad," but this was only a manner of speaking, a way of saying that the mind of the poet worked in different fashion from the mind of the philosopher; it had no real reference to the mental hygiene of the man who was the poet. But in the early nineteenth century, with

ART AND NEUROSIS: From *The Liberal Imagination* by Lionel Trilling. Copyright 1945 by Lionel Trilling. Reprinted by permission of The Viking Press, Inc.

the development of a more elaborate psychology and a stricter and more literal view of mental and emotional normality, the statement was more strictly and literally intended. So much so, indeed, that Charles Lamb, who knew something about madness at close quarters and a great deal about art, undertook to refute in his brilliant essay, "On the Sanity of True Genius," the idea that the exercise of the imagination was a kind of insanity. And some eighty years later, the idea having yet further entrenched itself, Bernard Shaw felt called upon to argue the sanity of art, but his cogency was of no more avail than Lamb's. In recent years the connection between art and mental illness has been formulated not only by those who are openly or covertly hostile to art, but also and more significantly by those who are most intensely partisan to it. The latter willingly and even eagerly accept the idea that the artist is mentally ill and go on to make his illness a condition of his power to tell the truth.

This conception of artistic genius is indeed one of the characteristic notions of our culture. I should like to bring it into question. To do so is to bring also into question certain early ideas of Freud's and certain conclusions which literary laymen have drawn from the whole tendency of the Freudian psychology. From the very start it was recognized that psychoanalysis was likely to have important things to say about art and artists. Freud himself thought so, yet when he first addressed himself to the subject he said many clumsy and misleading things. I have elsewhere and at length tried to separate the useful from the useless and even dangerous statements about art that Freud has made. To put it briefly here, Freud had some illuminating and even beautiful insights into certain particular works of art which made complex use of the element of myth. Then, without specifically undertaking to do so, his *Beyond the Pleasure Principle* offers a brilliant and comprehensive explanation of our interest in tragedy. And what is of course most important of all—it is a point to which I shall return—Freud, by the whole

tendency of his psychology, establishes the *naturalness* of artistic thought. Indeed, it is possible to say of Freud that he ultimately did more for our understanding of art than any other writer since Aristotle; and this being so, it can only be surprising that in his early work he should have made the error of treating the artist as a neurotic who escapes from reality by means of "substitute gratifications."

As Freud went forward he insisted less on this simple formulation. Certainly it did not have its original force with him when, at his seventieth birthday celebration, he disclaimed the right to be called the discoverer of the unconscious, saying that whatever he may have done for the systematic understanding of the unconscious, the credit for its discovery properly belonged to the literary masters. And psychoanalysis has inherited from him a tenderness for art which is real although sometimes clumsy, and nowadays most psychoanalysts of any personal sensitivity are embarrassed by occasions which seem to lead them to reduce art to a formula of mental illness. Nevertheless Freud's early belief in the essential neuroticism of the artist found an all too fertile ground—found, we might say, the very ground from which it first sprang, for, when he spoke of the artist as a neurotic, Freud was adopting one of the popular beliefs of his age. Most readers will see this belief as the expression of the industrial rationalization and the bourgeois philistinism of the nineteenth century. In this they are partly right. The nineteenth century established the basic virtue of "getting up at eight, shaving close at a quarter-past, breakfasting at nine, going to the City at ten, coming home at half-past five, and dining at seven." The Messrs. Podsnap who instituted this scheduled morality inevitably decreed that the arts must celebrate it and nothing else. "Nothing else to be permitted to these... vagrants the Arts, on pain of excommunication. Nothing else To Be—anywhere!" We observe that the virtuous day ends with dinner—bed and sleep are naturally not part of the Reality that Is, and nothing must be set forth which will, as

Mr. Podsnap put it, bring a Blush to the Cheek of a Young Person.

The excommunication of the arts, when it was found necessary, took the form of pronouncing the artist mentally degenerate, a device which eventually found its theorist in Max Nordau. In the history of the arts this is new. The poet was always known to belong to a touchy tribe—*genus irritabile* was a tag anyone would know—and ever since Plato the process of the inspired imagination, as we have said, was thought to be a special one of some interest, which the similitude of madness made somewhat intelligible. But this is not quite to say that the poet was the victim of actual mental aberration. The eighteenth century did not find the poet to be less than other men, and certainly the Renaissance did not. If he was a professional, there might be condescension to his social status, but in a time which deplored all professionalism whatever, this was simply a way of asserting the high value of poetry, which ought not to be compromised by trade. And a certain good nature marked even the snubbing of the professional. At any rate, no one was likely to identify the poet with the weakling. Indeed, the Renaissance ideal held poetry to be, like arms or music, one of the signs of manly competence.

The change from this view of things cannot be blamed wholly on the bourgeois or philistine public. Some of the "blame" must rest with the poets themselves. The Romantic poets were as proud of their art as the vaunting poets of the sixteenth century, but one of them talked with an angel in a tree and insisted that Hell was better than Heaven and sexuality holier than chastity; another told the world that he wanted to lie down like a tired child and weep away this life of care; another asked so foolish a question as "Why did I laugh tonight?"; and yet another explained that he had written one of his best poems in a drugged sleep. The public took them all at their word—they were not as other men. Zola, in the interests of science, submitted himself to examination by fifteen psychiatrists and agreed with their conclusion that his genius

had its source in the neurotic elements of his temperament. Baudelaire, Rimbaud, Verlaine found virtue and strength in their physical and mental illness and pain. W. H. Auden addresses his "wound" in the cherishing language of a lover, thanking it for the gift of insight it has bestowed. "Knowing you," he says, "has made me understand." And Edmund Wilson in his striking phrase, "the wound and the bow," has formulated for our time the idea of the characteristic sickness of the artist, which he represents by the figure of Philoctetes, the Greek warrior who was forced to live in isolation because of the disgusting odor of a suppurating wound and who yet had to be sought out by his countrymen because they had need of the magically unerring bow he possessed.

The myth of the sick artist, we may suppose, has established itself because it is of advantage to the various groups who have one or another relation with art. To the artist himself the myth gives some of the ancient powers and privileges of the idiot and the fool, half-prophetic creatures, or of the mutilated priest. That the artist's neurosis may be but a mask is suggested by Thomas Mann's pleasure in representing his untried youth as "sick" but his successful maturity as senatorially robust. By means of his belief in his own sickness, the artist may the more easily fulfill his chosen, and assigned, function of putting himself into connection with the forces of spirituality and morality; the artist sees as insane the "normal" and "healthy" ways of established society, while aberration and illness appear as spiritual and moral health if only because they controvert the ways of respectable society.

Then too, the myth has its advantage for the philistine—a double advantage. On the one hand, the belief in the artist's neuroticism allows the philistine to shut his ears to what the artist says. But on the other hand it allows him to listen. For we must not make the common mistake—the contemporary philistine does want to listen, at the same time that he wants to shut his ears. By supposing that the artist has an interesting but not always reliable relation to reality, he is able to contain (in the military sense) what the artist tells him. If he did not want to listen at all, he would say "insane"; with "neurotic," which hedges, he listens when he chooses.

And in addition to its advantage to the artist and to the philistine, we must take into account the usefulness of the myth to a third group, the group of "sensitive" people, who, although not artists, are not philistines either. These people form a group by virtue of their passive impatience with philistinism, and also by virtue of their awareness of their own emotional pain and uncertainty. To these people the myth of the sick artist is the institutional sanction of their situation; they seek to approximate or acquire the character of the artist, sometimes by planning to work or even attempting to work as the artist does, always by making a connection between their own powers of mind and their consciousness of "difference" and neurotic illness.

The early attempts of psychoanalysis to deal with art went on the assumption that, because the artist was neurotic, the content of his work was also neurotic, which is to say that it did not stand in a correct relation to reality. But nowadays, as I have said, psychoanalysis is not likely to be so simple in its transactions with art. A good example of the psychoanalytical development in this respect is Dr. Saul Rosenzweig's well-known essay, "The Ghost of Henry James." This is an admirable piece of work, marked by accuracy in the reporting of the literary fact and by respect for the value of the literary object. Although Dr. Rosenzweig explores the element of neurosis in James's life and work, he nowhere suggests that this element in any way lessens James's value as an artist or moralist. In effect he says that neurosis is a way of dealing with reality which, in real life, is uncomfortable and uneconomical, but that this judgment of neurosis in life cannot mechanically be transferred to works of art upon which neurosis has had its influence. He nowhere implies that a

work of art in whose genesis a neurotic element may be found is for that reason irrelevant or in any way diminished in value. Indeed, the manner of his treatment suggests, what is of course the case, that every neurosis deals with a real emotional situation of the most intensely meaningful kind.

Yet as Dr. Rosenzweig brings his essay to its close, he makes use of the current assumption about the causal connection between the psychic illness of the artist and his power. His investigation of James, he says, "reveals the aptness of the Philoctetes pattern." He accepts the idea of "the sacrificial roots of literary power" and speaks of "the unhappy sources of James's genius." "The broader application of the inherent pattern," he says, "is familiar to readers of Edmund Wilson's recent volume *The Wound and the Bow*.... Reviewing the experience and work of several well-known literary masters, Wilson discloses the sacrificial roots of their power on the model of the Greek legend. In the case of Henry James, the present account...provides a similar insight into the unhappy sources of his genius...."

This comes as a surprise. Nothing in Dr. Rosenzweig's theory requires it. For his theory asserts no more than that Henry James, predisposed by temperament and family situation to certain mental and emotional qualities, was in his youth injured in a way which he believed to be sexual; that he unconsciously invited the injury in the wish to identify himself with his father, who himself had been similarly injured—"castrated": A leg had been amputated—and under strikingly similar circumstances; this resulted for the younger Henry James in a certain pattern of life and in a preoccupation in his work with certain themes which more or less obscurely symbolize his sexual situation. For this I think Dr. Rosenzweig makes a sound case. Yet I submit that this is not the same thing as disclosing the roots of James's power or discovering the sources of his genius. The essay which gives Edmund Wilson's book its title and cohering principle does not explicitly say that the roots of power are sacrificial and that the source of genius is unhappy. Where it is explicit, it states only that "genius and disease, like strength and mutilation, may be inextricably bound up together," which of course, on its face, says no more than that personality is integral and not made up of detachable parts; and from this there is no doubt to be drawn the important practical and moral implication that we cannot judge or dismiss a man's genius and strength because of our awareness of his disease or mutilation. The Philoctetes legend in itself does not suggest anything beyond this. It does not suggest that the wound is the price of the bow, or that without the wound the bow may not be possessed or drawn. Yet Dr. Rosenzweig has accurately summarized the force and, I think, the intention of Mr. Wilson's whole book; its several studies do seem to say that effectiveness in the arts does depend on sickness.

An examination of this prevalent idea might well begin with the observation of how pervasive and deeply rooted is the notion that power may be gained by suffering. Even at relatively high stages of culture the mind seems to take easily to the primitive belief that pain and sacrifice are connected with strength. Primitive beliefs must be treated with respectful alertness to their possible truth and also with the suspicion of their being magical and irrational, and it is worth noting on both sides of the question, and in the light of what we have said about the ambiguous relation of the neurosis to reality, that the whole economy of the neurosis is based exactly on this idea of the *quid pro quo* of sacrificial pain: the neurotic person unconsciously subscribes to a system whereby he gives up some pleasure or power, or inflicts pain on himself in order to secure some other power or some other pleasure.

In the ingrained popular conception of the relation between suffering and power there are actually two distinct although related ideas. One is that there exists in the individual a fund of power which has outlets through various organs or faculties, and that if its outlet through one organ or faculty be prevented, it will flow to increase the force or sensitivity of another. Thus it is popularly believed that the sense of touch is intensified in the blind not so much by the will of the blind person to adapt himself to the necessities of his situation, as, rather, by a sort of mechanical redistribution of power. And this idea would seem to explain, if not the origin of the ancient mutilation of priests, then at least a common understanding of their sexual sacrifice.

The other idea is that a person may be taught by, or proved by, the endurance of pain. There will easily come to mind the ritual suffering that is inflicted at the tribal initiation of youths into full manhood or at the admission of the apprentice into the company of journeyman adepts. This idea in sophisticated form found its way into high religion at least as early as Aeschylus, who held that man achieves knowledge of God through suffering, and it was from the beginning an important element of Christian thought. In the nineteenth century the Christianized notion of the didactic suffering of the artist went along with the idea of his mental degeneration and even served as a sort of countermyth to it. Its doctrine was that the artist, a man of strength and health, experienced and suffered, and thus learned both the facts of life and his artistic craft. "I am the man, I suffered, I was there," ran his boast, and he derived his authority from the knowledge gained through suffering.

There can be no doubt that both these ideas represent a measure of truth about mental and emotional power. The idea of didactic suffering expresses a valuation of experience and of steadfastness. The idea of natural compensation for the sacrifice of some faculty also says something that can be rationally defended: one cannot be and do everything and the wholehearted absorption in any enterprise, art for example, means that we must give up other possibilities, even parts of ourselves. And there is even a certain validity to the belief that the individual has a fund of undifferentiated energy which presses the harder upon what outlets are available to it when it has been deprived of the normal number.

Then, in further defense of the belief that artistic power is connected with neurosis, we can say that there is no doubt that what we call mental illness may be the source of psychic knowledge. Some neurotic people, because they are more apprehensive than normal people, are able to see more of certain parts of reality and to see them with more intensity. And many neurotic or psychotic patients are in certain respects in closer touch with the actualities of the unconscious than are normal people. Further, the expression of a neurotic or psychotic conception of reality is likely to be more intense than a normal one.

Yet when we have said all this, it is still wrong, I believe, to find the root of the artist's power and the source of his genius in neurosis. To the idea that literary power and genius spring from pain and neurotic sacrifice there are two major objections. The first has to do with the assumed uniqueness of the artist as a subject of psychoanalytical explanation. The second has to do with the true meaning of power and genius.

One reason why writers are considered to be more available than other people to psychoanalytical explanation is that they tell us what is going on inside them. Even when they do not make an actual diagnosis of their malaises or describe "symptoms," we must bear it in mind that it is their profession to deal with fantasy in some form or other. It is the nature of the writer's job that he exhibit his unconscious. He may disguise it in various ways, but disguise is not concealment. Indeed, it may be said that the more a writer takes pains with his work to remove it from the personal and subjective, the more—and not the less—he will express his true unconscious, although not what passes with most for the unconscious.

Further, the writer is likely to be a great hand at personal letters, diaries, and autobiographies: indeed, almost the only good autobiographies are those of writers. The writer is more aware of what happens to him or goes on in him and often

finds it necessary or useful to be articulate about his inner states, and prides himself on telling the truth. Thus, only a man as devoted to the truth of the emotions as Henry James was would have informed the world, despite his characteristic reticence, of an accident so intimate as his. We must not of course suppose that a writer's statements about his intimate life are equivalent to true statements about his unconscious, which, by definition, he doesn't consciously know; but they may be useful clues to the nature of an entity about which we can make statements of more or less cogency, although never statements of certainty; or they at least give us what is surely related to a knowledge of his unconscious —that is, an insight into his personality.[1]

But while the validity of dealing with the writer's intellectual life in psychoanalytical terms is taken for granted, the psychoanalytical explanation of the intellectual life of scientists is generally speaking not countenanced. The old myth of the mad scientist, with the exception of an occasional mad psychiatrist, no longer exists. The social position of science requires that it should cease, which leads us to remark that those partisans of art who insist on explaining artistic genius by means of psychic imbalance are in effect capitulating to the dominant mores which hold that the members of the respectable professions are, however dull they may be, free from neurosis. Scientists, to continue with them as the best example of the respectable professions, do not usually give us the clues to their personalities which writers habitually give. But no one

[1] I am by no means in agreement with the statements of Dr. Edmund Bergler about "the" psychology of the writer, but I think that Dr. Bergler has done good service in warning us against taking at their face value a writer's statements about himself, the more especially when they are "frank." Thus, to take Dr. Bergler's notable example, it is usual for biographers to accept Stendhal's statements about his open sexual feelings for his mother when he was a little boy, feelings which went with an intense hatred of his father. But Dr. Bergler believes that Stendhal unconsciously used his consciousness of his love of his mother and of his hatred of his father to mask an unconscious love of his father, which frightened him. ("Psychoanalysis of Writers and of Literary Productivity," in *Psychoanalysis and the Social Sciences*, Vol. 1.)

who has ever lived observantly among scientists will claim that they are without an unconscious or even that they are free from neurosis. How often, indeed, it is apparent that the devotion to science, if it cannot be called a neurotic manifestation, at least can be understood as going very cozily with neurotic elements in the temperament, such as, for example, a marked compulsiveness. Of scientists as a group we can say that they are less concerned with the manifestations of personality, their own or others', than are writers as a group. But this relative indifference is scarcely a sign of normality—indeed, if we choose to regard it with the same sort of eye with which the characteristics of writers are regarded, we might say the indifference to matters of personality is in itself a suspicious evasion.

It is the basic assumption of psychoanalysis that the acts of *every* person are influenced by the forces of the unconscious. Scientists, bankers, lawyers, or surgeons, by reason of the traditions of their professions, practice concealment and conformity; but it is difficult to believe that an investigation according to psychoanalytical principles would fail to show that the strains and imbalances of their psyches are not of the same frequency as those of writers, and of similar kind. I do not mean that everybody has the same troubles and identical psyches, but only that there is no special category for writers.[2]

If this is so, and if we still want to relate the writer's power to his neurosis, we must be willing to relate all intellectual power to neurosis. We must find the roots of Newton's power in his emotional extravagances, and the roots of Darwin's power in his sorely neurotic temperament, and the roots of Pascal's mathematical genius in the impulses which drove him to extreme religious masochism—I choose but the classic examples. If we make the neurosis-

power equivalence at all, we must make it in every field of endeavor. Logician, economist, botanist, physicist, theologian—no profession may be so respectable or so remote or so rational as to be exempt from the psychological interpretation.[3]

Further, not only power but also failure or limitation must be accounted for by the theory of neurosis, and not merely failure or limitation in life but even failure or limitation in art. Thus it is often said that the warp of Dostoevsky's

[2] Dr. Bergler believes that there is a particular neurosis of the writers, based on an oral masochism which makes them the enemy of the respectable world, courting poverty and persecution. But a later development of Dr. Bergler's theory of oral masochism makes it *the* basic neurosis, not only of writers but of everyone who is neurotic.

[3] In his interesting essay, "Writers and Madness," in *Partisan Review*, January-February 1947, William Barrett has taken issue with this point and has insisted that a clear distinction is to be made between the relation that exists between the scientist and his work and the relation that exists between the artist and his work. The difference, as I understand it, is in the claims of the ego. The artist's ego makes a claim upon the world which is personal in a way that the scientist's is not, for the scientist, although he does indeed want prestige and thus "responds to one of the deepest urges of his ego, it is only that his prestige may come to attend his person through the public world of other men; and it is not in the end his own being that is exhibited or his own voice that is heard in the learned report to the Academy." Actually, however, as is suggested by the sense which mathematicians have of the *style* of mathematical thought, the creation of the abstract thinker is as deeply involved as the artist's—see *An Essay on the Psychology of Invention in the Mathematical Field* by Jacques Hadamard, Princeton University Press, 1945—and he quite as much as the artist seeks to impose *himself*, to *express* himself. I am of course not maintaining that the processes of scientific thought are the same as those of artistic thought, or even that the scientist's creation is involved with his total personality *in the same way* that the artist's is—I am maintaining only that the scientist's creation is as *deeply* implicated with his total personality as is the artist's.

This point of view seems to be supported by Freud's monograph on Leonardo. One of the problems that Freud sets himself is to discover why an artist of the highest endowment should have devoted himself more and more to scientific investigation, with the result that he was unable to complete his artistic enterprises. The particular reasons for this that Freud assigns need not be gone into here; all that I wish to suggest is that Freud understands these reasons to be the working out of an inner conflict, the attempt to deal with the difficulties that have their roots in the most primitive situations. Leonardo's scientific investigations were as necessary and "compelled" and they constituted as much of a claim on the whole personality as anything the artist undertakes; and so far from being carried out for the sake of public prestige, they were largely private and personal and were thought by the public of his time to be something very like insanity.

mind accounts for the brilliance of his psychological insights. But it is never said that the
same warp of Dostoevsky's mind also accounted
for his deficiency in insight. Freud, who greatly
admired Dostoevsky, although he did not like
him, observed that "his insight was entirely
restricted to the workings of the abnormal
psyche. Consider his astounding helplessness
before the phenomenon of love; he really
only understands either crude, instinctive desire
or masochistic submission or love from pity."[4]
This, we must note, is not merely Freud's
comment on the extent of the province which
Dostoevsky chose for his own, but on his failure
to understand what, given the province of his
choice, he might be expected to understand.

And since neurosis can account not only for
intellectual success and for failure or limitation
but also for mediocrity, we have most of society
involved in neurosis. To this I have no objection
—I think most of society is indeed involved in
neurosis. But with neurosis accounting for so
much, it cannot be made exclusively to account
for one man's literary power.

We have now to consider what is meant by
genius when its source is identified as the
sacrifice and pain of neurosis.

In the case of Henry James, the reference to
the neurosis of his personal life does indeed tell
us something about the latent intention of his
work and thus about the reason for some large
part of its interest for us. But if genius and its
source are what we are dealing with, we must
observe that the reference to neurosis tells us
nothing about James's passion, energy, and
devotion, nothing about his architectonic skill,
nothing about the other themes that were important to him which are not connected with his
unconscious concern with castration. We cannot,
that is, make the writer's inner life exactly
equivalent to his power of expressing it. Let us
grant for the sake of argument that the literary
genius, as distinguished from other men, is the
victim of a "mutilation" and that his fantasies

[4] From a letter quoted in Theodor Reik's *From Thirty
Years With Freud*, p. 175.

are neurotic.[5] It does not then follow as the
inevitable next step that his ability to express
these fantasies and to impress us with them is
neurotic, for that ability is what we mean by his
genius. Anyone might be injured as Henry
James was, and even respond within himself to
the injury as James is said to have done, and
yet not have his literary power.

The reference to the artist's neurosis tells us
something about the material on which the
artist exercises his powers, and even something
about his reasons for bringing his powers into
play, but it does not tell us anything about the
source of his power, it makes no causal connection between them and the neurosis. And if we
look into the matter, we see that there is in fact
no causal connection between them. For, still
granting that the poet is uniquely neurotic,
what is surely not neurotic, what indeed
suggests nothing but health, is his power of using
his neuroticism. He shapes his fantasies, he
gives them social form and reference. Charles
Lamb's way of putting this cannot be improved.
Lamb is denying that genius is allied to insanity;
for "insanity" the modern reader may substitute "neurosis." "The ground of the mistake,"
he says, "is, that men, finding in the raptures of
the higher poetry a condition of exaltation, to
which they have no parallel in their own experience, besides the spurious resemblance of it
in dreams and fevers, impute a state of dreami-
ness and fever to the poet. But the true poet
dreams being awake. He is not possessed by his
subject but has dominion over it…. Where he
seems most to recede from humanity, he will be
found the truest to it. From beyond the scope of
nature if he summon possible existences, he
subjugates them to the law of her consistency.
He is beautifully loyal to that sovereign

[5] I am using the word *fantasy*, unless modified, in a
neutral sense. A fantasy, in this sense, may be distinguished
from the representation of something that actually exists,
but it is not opposed to "reality" and not an "escape"
from reality. Thus the idea of a rational society, of the
image of a good house to be built, as well as the story of
something that could never really happen, is a fantasy.
There may be neurotic or nonneurotic fantasies.

directress, when he appears most to betray and desert her.... Herein the great and the little wits are differenced; that if the latter wander ever so little from nature or natural existence, they lose themselves and their readers.... They do not create, which implies shaping and consistency. Their imaginations are not active—for to be active is to call something into act and form— but passive as men in sick dreams."

The activity of the artist, we must remember, may be approximated by many who are themselves not artists. Thus, the expressions of many schizophrenic people have the intense appearance of creativity and an inescapable interest and significance. But they are not works of art, and although Van Gogh may have been schizophrenic he was in addition an artist. Again, as I have already suggested, it is not uncommon in our society for certain kinds of neurotic people to imitate the artist in his life and even in his ideals and ambitions. They follow the artist in everything except successful performance. It was, I think, Otto Rank who called such people half-artists and confirmed the diagnosis of their neuroticism at the same time that he differentiated them from true artists.

Nothing is so characteristic of the artist as his power of shaping his work, of subjugating his raw material, however aberrant it be from what we call normality, to the consistency of nature. It would be possible to deny that whatever disease or mutilation the artist may suffer is an element of his production which has its effect on every part of it, but disease and mutilation are available to us all—life provides them with prodigal generosity. What marks the artist is his power to shape the material of pain we all have.

At this point, with our recognition of life's abundant provision of pain, we are at the very heart of our matter, which is the meaning we may assign to neurosis and the relation we are to suppose it to have with normality. Here Freud himself can be of help, although it must be admitted that what he tells us may at first seem somewhat contradictory and confusing.

Freud's study of Leonardo da Vinci is an attempt to understand why Leonardo was unable to pursue his artistic enterprises, feeling compelled instead to advance his scientific investigations. The cause of this Freud traces back to certain childhood experiences not different in kind from the experiences which Dr. Rosenzweig adduces to account for certain elements in the work of Henry James. And when he has completed his study Freud makes this *caveat*: "Let us expressly emphasize that we have never considered Leonardo as a neurotic.... We no longer believe that health and disease, normal and nervous, are sharply distinguished from each other. We know today that neurotic symptoms are substitutive formations for certain repressive acts which must result in the course of our development from the child to the cultural man, that we all produce such substitutive formations, and that only the amount, intensity, and distribution of these substitutive formations justify the practical conception of illness...." The statement becomes the more striking when we remember that in the course of his study Freud has had occasion to observe that Leonardo was both homosexual and sexually inactive. I am not sure that the statement that Leonardo was not a neurotic is one that Freud would have made at every point in the later development of psychoanalysis, yet it is in conformity with his continuing notion of the genesis of culture. And the *practical*, the quantitative or economic, conception of illness he insists on in a passage in the *Introductory Lectures*. "The neurotic symptoms," he says, "...are activities which are detrimental, or at least useless, to life as a whole; the person concerned frequently complains of them as obnoxious to him or they involve suffering and distress for him. The principal injury they inflict lies in the expense of energy they entail, and, besides this, in the energy needed to combat them. Where the symptoms are extensively developed, these two kinds of effort may exact such a price that the person suffers a very serious impoverishment in available mental energy which consequently disables him for all the important tasks of life. This result depends principally upon the amount of energy taken up in this way; therefore you will see that 'illness' is essentially a practical conception. But if you look at the matter from a theoretical point of view and ignore this question of degree, you can very well see that we are all ill, i.e., neurotic; for the conditions required for symptom-formation are demonstrable also in normal persons."

We are all ill: the statement is grandiose, and its implications—the implications, that is, of understanding the totality of human nature in the terms of disease—are vast. These implications have never been properly met (although I believe that a few theologians have responded to them), but this is not the place to attempt to meet them. I have brought forward Freud's statement of the essential sickness of the psyche only because it stands as the refutation of what is implied by the literary use of the theory of neurosis to account for genius. For if we are ill, and if, as I have said, neurosis can account for everything, for failure and mediocrity—"a very serious impoverishment of available mental energy"—as well as for genius, it cannot uniquely account for genius.

This, however, is not to say that there is no connection between neurosis and genius, which would be tantamount, as we see, to saying that there is no connection between human nature and genius. But the connection lies wholly in a particular and special relation which the artist has to neurosis.

In order to understand what this particular and special connection is we must have clearly in mind what neurosis is. The current literary conception of neurosis as a *wound* is quite misleading. It inevitably suggests passivity, whereas, if we follow Freud, we must understand a neurosis to be an *activity*, an activity with a purpose, and a particular kind of activity, a *conflict*. This is not to say that there are no abnormal mental states which are not conflicts. There are; the struggle between elements of the unconscious may never be instituted in the first

place, or it may be called off. As Freud says in a passage which follows close upon the one I last quoted, "If regressions do not call forth a prohibition on the part of the ego, no neurosis results; the libido succeeds in obtaining a real, although not a normal, satisfaction. But if the ego ... is not in agreement with these regressions, conflict ensues." And in his essay on Dostoevsky Freud says that "there are no neurotic complete masochists," by which he means that the ego which gives way completely to masochism (or to any other pathological excess) has passed beyond neurosis; the conflict has ceased, but at the cost of the defeat of the ego, and now some other name than that of neurosis must be given to the condition of the person who thus takes himself beyond the pain of the neurotic conflict. To understand this is to become aware of the curious complacency with which literary men regard mental disease. The psyche of the neurotic is not equally complacent; it regards with the greatest fear the chaotic and destructive forces it contains, and it struggles fiercely to keep them at bay.[6]

We come then to a remarkable paradox: We are all ill, but we are ill in the service of health, or ill in the service of life, or, at the very least, ill in the service of life-in-culture. The form of the mind's dynamics is that of the neurosis, which

[6] In the article to which I refer in note 3, William Barrett says that he prefers the old-fashioned term "madness" to "neurosis." But it is not quite for him to choose—the words do not differ in fashion but in meaning. Most literary people, when they speak of mental illness, refer to neurosis. Perhaps one reason for this is that the neurosis is the most benign of the mental ills. Another reason is surely that psychoanalytical literature deals chiefly with the neurosis, and its symptomatology and therapy have become familiar; psychoanalysis has far less to say about psychosis, for which it can offer far less therapeutic hope. Further, the neurosis is easily put into a causal connection with the social maladjustments of our time. Other forms of mental illness of a more severe and degenerative kind are not so widely recognized by the literary person and are often assimilated to neurosis with a resulting confusion. In the present essay I deal only with the conception of neurosis, but this should not be taken to imply that I believe that other pathological mental conditions, including actual madness, do not have relevance to the general matter of the discussion.

is to be understood as the ego's struggle against being overcome by the forces with which it coexists, and the strategy of this conflict requires that the ego shall incur pain and make sacrifices of itself, at the same time seeing to it that its pain and sacrifice be as small as they may.

But this is characteristic of all minds: no mind is exempt except those which refuse the conflict or withdraw from it; and we ask wherein the mind of the artist is unique. If he is not unique in neurosis, is he then unique in the significance and intensity of his neurosis? I do not believe that we shall go more than a little way toward a definition of artistic genius by answering this question affirmatively. A neurotic conflict cannot ever be either meaningless or merely personal; it must be understood as exemplifying cultural forces of great moment, and this is true of any neurotic conflict at all. To be sure, some neuroses may be more interesting than others, perhaps because they are fiercer or more inclusive; and no doubt the writer who makes a claim upon our interest is a man who by reason of the energy and significance of the forces in struggle within him provides us with the largest representation of the culture in which we, with him, are involved; his neurosis may thus be thought of as having a connection of concomitance with his literary powers. As Freud says in the Dostoevsky essay, "the neurosis...comes into being all the more readily the richer the complexity which has to be controlled by his ego." Yet even the rich complexity which his ego is doomed to control is not the definition of the artist's genius, for we can by no means say that the artist is preeminent in the rich complexity of elements in conflict within him. The slightest acquaintance with the clinical literature of psychoanalysis will suggest that a rich complexity of struggling elements is no uncommon possession. And that same literature will also make it abundantly clear that the devices of art—the most extreme devices of poetry, for example—are not particular to the mind of the artist but are characteristic of mind itself.

But the artist is indeed unique in one respect, in the respect of his relation to his neurosis. He is what he is by virtue of his successful objectification of his neurosis, by his shaping it and making it available to others in a way which has its effect upon their own egos in struggle. His genius, that is, may be defined in terms of his faculties of perception, representation, and realization, and in these terms alone. It can no more be defined in terms of neurosis than can his power of walking and talking, or his sexuality. The use to which he puts his power, or the manner and style of his power, may be discussed with reference to his particular neurosis, and so may such matters as the untimely diminution or cessation of its exercise. But its essence is irreducible. It is, as we say, a gift.

We are all ill: but even a universal sickness implies an idea of health. Of the artist we must say that whatever elements of neurosis he has in common with his fellow mortals, the one part of him that is healthy, by any conceivable definition of health, is that which gives him the power to conceive, to plan, to work, and to bring his work to a conclusion. And if we are all ill, we are ill by a universal accident, not by a universal necessity, by a fault in the economy of our powers, not by the nature of the powers themselves. The Philoctetes myth, when it is used to imply a causal connection between the fantasy of castration and artistic power, tells us no more about the source of artistic power than we learn about the source of sexuality when the fantasy of castration is adduced, for the fear of castration may explain why a man is moved to extravagant exploits of sexuality, but we do not say that his sexual power itself derives from his fear of castration; and further the same fantasy may also explain impotence or homosexuality. The Philoctetes story, which has so established itself among us as explaining the source of the artist's power, is not really an explanatory myth at all; it is a moral myth having reference to our proper behavior in the circumstances of the universal accident. In its juxtaposition of the wound and the bow, it tells us that we must be aware that weakness does not preclude strength nor strength weakness. It is therefore not irrelevant to the artist, but when we use it we will do well to keep in mind the other myths of the arts, recalling what Pan and Dionysius suggest of the relation of art to physiology and superabundance, remembering that to Apollo were attributed the bow and the lyre, two strengths together, and that he was given the lyre by its inventor, the baby Hermes—that miraculous infant who, the day he was born, left his cradle to do mischief: and the first thing he met with was a tortoise, which he greeted politely before scooping it from its shell, and, thought and deed being one with him, he contrived the instrument to which he sang "the glorious tale of his own begetting." These were gods, and very early ones, but their myths tell us something about the nature and source of art even in our grim, late human present.

CARL G. JUNG

The Personal and the Collective Unconscious

In Freud's view, as most people know, the contents of the unconscious are limited to infantile tendencies which are repressed because of their incompatible character. Repression is a process that begins in early childhood under the moral influence of the environment and lasts throughout life. Through analysis the repressions are removed and the repressed wishes made conscious.

THE PERSONAL AND THE COLLECTIVE UNCONSCIOUS: From *The Collected Works of C. G. Jung,* translated by R. F. C. Hull. Vol. VII, *Two Essays on Psychoanalytical Psychology.* Bollingen Series XX.7. Copyright 1953 and second edition 1966 by Bollingen Foundation, New York. Distributed by Princeton University Press.

According to this theory, the unconscious contains only those parts of the personality which could just as well be conscious and are in fact suppressed only through upbringing. Although from one point of view the infantile tendencies of the unconscious are the most conspicuous, it would nonetheless be incorrect to define or evaluate the unconscious entirely in these terms. The unconscious has still another side to it: it includes not only repressed contents, but also all psychic material that lies below the threshold of consciousness. It is impossible to explain the subliminal nature of all this material on the principle of repression; otherwise, through the removal of repressions, a man would acquire a phenomenal memory which would thenceforth forget nothing.

We therefore emphatically say that in addition to the repressed material the unconscious contains all those psychic components that have fallen below the threshold, including subliminal sense-perceptions. Moreover we know, from abundant experience as well as for theoretical reasons, that the unconscious also contains components that have *not yet* reached the threshold of consciousness. These are the seeds of future conscious contents. Equally we have reason to suppose that the unconscious is never at rest in the sense of being inactive, but is continually engaged in grouping and regrouping its contents. Only in pathological cases can this activity be regarded as completely autonomous; normally it is coordinated with the conscious mind in a compensatory relationship.

It is to be assumed that all these contents are personal in so far as they are acquired during the individual's life. Since this life is limited, the number of acquired contents in the unconscious must also be limited. This being so, it might be thought possible to empty the unconscious either by analysis or by making a complete inventory of unconscious contents, on the ground that the unconscious cannot produce anything more than is already known and accepted in the conscious mind. We should also have to infer, as already indicated, that if one could stop the descent of conscious contents into the unconscious by doing away with repression, unconscious productivity would be paralysed. This is possible only to a very limited extent, as we know from experience. We urge our patients to hold fast to repressed contents that have been reassociated with consciousness, and to assimilate them into their plan of life. But this procedure, as we may daily convince ourselves, makes no impression on the unconscious, since it calmly continues to produce dreams and fantasies which, according to Freud's original theory, must arise from personal repressions. If in such cases we pursue our observations systematically and without prejudice, we shall find material which, although similar in form to the previous personal contents, yet seems to contain allusions that go far beyond the personal sphere....

There are present in every individual, besides his personal memories, the great "primordial" images, as Jacob Burckhardt once aptly called them, the inherited powers of human imagination as it was from time immemorial. The fact of this inheritance explains the truly amazing phenomenon that certain motifs from myths and legends repeat themselves the world over in identical forms. It also explains why it is that our mental patients can reproduce exactly the same images and associations that are known to us from the old texts. I give some examples of this in my book *Symbols of Transformation*. In so doing I do not by any means assert the inheritance of ideas, but only of the possibility of such ideas, which is something very different.

In this further stage of treatment, then, when fantasies are produced which no longer rest on personal memories, we have to do with the manifestations of a deeper layer of the unconscious where the primordial images common to humanity lie sleeping. I have called these images or motifs "archetypes," also "dominants" of the unconscious. For a further elucidation of the idea I must refer the reader to the relevant literature.

This discovery means another step forward in our understanding: the recognition, that is, of two layers in the unconscious. We have to distinguish between a personal unconscious and an impersonal or transpersonal unconscious. We speak of the latter also as the collective unconscious, because it is detached from anything personal and is entirely universal, and because its contents can be found everywhere, which is naturally not the case with the personal contents. The personal unconscious contains lost memories, painful ideas that are repressed (i.e., forgotten on purpose), subliminal perceptions, by which are meant sense-perceptions that were not strong enough to reach consciousness, and finally, contents that are not yet ripe for consciousness. It corresponds to the figure of the shadow so frequently met with in dreams.

The primordial images are the most ancient and the most universal "thought-forms" of humanity. They are as much feelings as thoughts; indeed, they lead their own independent life rather in the manner of part-souls, as can easily be seen in those philosophical or Gnostic systems which rely on awareness of the unconscious as the source of knowledge. The idea of angels, archangels, "principalities and powers" in St. Paul, the archons of the Gnostics, the heavenly hierarchy of Dionysius the Areopagite, all come from the perception of the relative autonomy of the archetypes....

The greatest and best thoughts of man shape themselves upon these primordial images as upon a blueprint. I have often been asked where the archetypes of primordial images come from. It seems to me that their origin can only be explained by assuming them to be deposits of the constantly repeated experiences of humanity. One of the commonest and at the same time most impressive experiences is the apparent movement of the sun every day. We certainly cannot discover anything of the kind in the unconscious, so far as the known physical process is concerned. What we do find, on the other hand, is the myth of the sun-hero in all its countless modifications. It is this myth, and not the physical process, that forms the sun archetype. The same can be said of the phases of the moon. The archetype is a kind of readiness to produce over and over again the same or similar mythical ideas. Hence it seems as though what is impressed upon the unconscious were exclusively the subjective fantasy-ideas aroused by the physical process. Therefore we may take it that archetypes are recurrent impressions made by subjective reactions. Naturally this assumption only pushes the problem further back without solving it. There is nothing to prevent us from assuming that certain archetypes exist even in animals, that they are grounded in the peculiarities of the living organism itself and are therefore direct expressions of life whose nature cannot be further explained. Not only are the archetypes, apparently, impressions of ever-repeated typical experiences, but, at the same time, they behave empirically like agents that tend towards the repetition of these same experiences. For when an archetype appears in a dream, in a fantasy, or in life, it always brings with it a certain influence or power by virtue of which it either exercises a numinous or a fascinating effect, or impels to action.

"No mortal mind can plumb the depths of nature"—nor even the depths of the unconscious. We do know, however, that the unconscious never rests. It seems to be always at work, for even when asleep we dream. There are many people who declare that they never dream, but the probability is that they simply do not remember their dreams. It is significant that people who talk in their sleep mostly have no recollection either of the dream which started them talking, or even of the fact that they dreamed at all. Not a day passes but we make some slip of the tongue, or something slips our memory which at other times we know perfectly well, or we are seized by a mood whose cause we cannot trace, etc. These things are all symptoms of some consistent unconscious activity which becomes directly visible at night in dreams, but only occasionally breaks through the inhibitions imposed by our daytime consciousness.

So far as our present experience goes, we can lay it down that the unconscious processes stand in a compensatory relation to the conscious mind. I expressly use the word "compensatory" and not the word "opposed," because conscious and unconscious are not necessarily in opposition to one another, but complement one another to form a totality, which is the *self*. According to this definition the self is a quantity that is superordinate to the conscious ego. It embraces not only the conscious but also the unconscious psyche, and is therefore, so to speak, a personality which we *also* are. It is easy enough to think of ourselves as possessing part-souls. Thus we can, for instance, see ourselves as a persona without too much difficulty. But it transcends our powers of imagination to form a clear picture of what we are as a self, for in this operation the part would have to comprehend the whole. There is little hope of our ever being able to reach even approximate consciousness of the self, since however much we may make conscious there will always exist an indeterminate and indeterminable amount of unconscious material which belongs to the totality of the self. Hence the self will always remain a superordinate quantity.

The unconscious processes that compensate the conscious ego contain all those elements that are necessary for the self-regulation of the psyche as a whole. On the personal level, these are the not consciously recognized personal motives which appear in dreams, or the meanings of daily situations which we have overlooked, or conclusions we have failed to draw, or effects we have not permitted, or criticisms we have spared ourselves. But the more we become conscious of ourselves through self-knowledge, and act accordingly, the more the layer of the personal unconscious that is superimposed on the collective unconscious will be diminished. In this way there arises a consciousness which is no longer imprisoned in the petty, oversensitive, personal world of the ego, but participates freely in the wider world of objective interests. This widened consciousness is no longer that touchy, egotistical bundle of personal wishes, fears, hopes, and ambitions which always has to be compensated or corrected by unconscious counter-tendencies; instead, it is a function of relationship to the world of objects, bringing the individual into absolute, binding, and indissoluble communion with the world at large. The complications arising at this stage are no longer egotistic wish-conflicts, but difficulties that concern others as much as oneself. At this stage it is fundamentally a question of collective problems, which have activated the collective unconscious because they require collective rather than personal compensation. We can now see that the unconscious produces contents which are valid not only for the person concerned, but for others as well, in fact for a great many people and possibly for all.

The Elgonyi, natives of the Elgon forests, of central Africa, explained to me that there are two kinds of dreams: the ordinary dream of the little man, and the "big vision" that only the great man has, e.g., the medicine man or chief. Little dreams are of no account, but if a man has a "big dream" he summons the whole tribe in order to tell it to everybody.

How is a man to know whether his dream is a "big" or a "little" one? He knows it by an instinctive feeling of significance. He feels so overwhelmed by the impression it makes that he would never think of keeping the dream to himself. He *has* to tell it, on the psychologically correct assumption that it is of general significance. Even with us the collective dream has a feeling of importance about it that impels communication. It springs from a conflict of relationship and must therefore be built into our conscious relations, because it compensates these and not just some inner personal quirk.

The processes of the collective unconscious are concerned not only with the more or less personal relations of an individual to his family or to a wider social group, but with his relations to society and to the human community in general. The more general and impersonal the condition that releases the unconscious reaction,

the more significant, bizarre, and overwhelming will be the compensatory manifestation. It impels not just private communication, but drives people to revelations and confessions, and even to a dramatic representation of their fantasies.

I will explain by an example how the unconscious manages to compensate relationships. A somewhat arrogant gentleman once came to me for treatment. He ran a business in partnership with his younger brother. Relations between the two brothers were very strained, and this was one of the essential causes of my patient's neurosis. From the information he gave me, the real reason for the tension was not altogether clear. He had all kinds of criticisms to make of his brother, whose gifts he certainly did not show in a very favourable light. The brother frequently came into his dreams, always in the role of a Bismarck, Napoleon, or Julius Caesar. His house looked like the Vatican or Yildiz Kiosk. My patient's unconscious evidently had the need to exalt the rank of the younger brother. From this I concluded that he was setting himself too high and his brother too low. The further course of analysis entirely justified this inference.

Another patient, a young woman who clung to her mother in an extremely sentimental way, always had very sinister dreams about her. She appeared in the dreams as a witch, as a ghost, as a pursuing demon. The mother had spoilt her beyond all reason and had so blinded her by tenderness that the daughter had no conscious idea of her mother's harmful influence. Hence the compensatory criticism exercised by the unconscious.

I myself once happened to put too low a value on a patient, both intellectually and morally. In a dream I saw a castle perched on a high cliff, and on the topmost tower was a balcony, and there sat my patient. I did not hesitate to tell her this dream at once, naturally with the best results.

We all know how apt we are to make fools of ourselves in front of the very people we have unjustly underrated. Naturally the case can also be reversed, as once happened to a friend of mine. While still a callow student he had written to Virchow, the pathologist, craving an audience with "His Excellency." When, quaking with fear, he presented himself and tried to give his name, he blurted out, "My name is Virchow." Whereupon His Excellency, smiling mischievously, said, "Ah! So your name is Virchow too?" The feeling of his own nullity was evidently too much for the unconscious of my friend, and in consequence it instantly prompted him to present himself as equal to Virchow in grandeur.

In these more personal relations there is of course no need for any very collective compensations. On the other hand, the figures employed by the unconscious in our first case are of a definitely collective nature: they are universally recognized heroes. Here there are two possible interpretations: Either my patient's younger brother is a man of acknowledged and far-reaching collective importance, or my patient is overestimating his own importance not merely in relation to his brother but in relation to everybody else as well. For the first assumption there was no support at all, while for the second there was the evidence of one's own eyes. Since the man's extreme arrogance affected not only himself, but a far wider social group, the compensation availed itself of a collective image.

The same is true of the second case. The "witch" is a collective image; hence we must conclude that the blind dependence of the young woman applied as much to the wider social group as it did to her mother personally. This was indeed the case, in so far as she was still living in an exclusively infantile world, where the world was identical with her parents. These examples deal with relations within the personal orbit. There are, however, impersonal relations which occasionally need unconscious compensation. In such cases collective images appear with a more or less mythological character. Moral, philosophical, and religious problems are, on account of their universal validity, the most likely to call for mythological compensation. In the aforementioned novel by H. G. Wells we find a classical type of compensation: Mr. Preemby, a midget personality, discovers that he is really a reincarnation of Sargon, King of Kings. Happily, the genius of the author rescues poor old Sargon from pathological absurdity, and even gives the reader a chance to appreciate the tragic and eternal meaning in this lamentable affray. Mr. Preemby, a complete nonentity, recognizes himself as the point of intersection of all ages past and future. This knowledge is not too dearly bought at the cost of a little madness, provided that Preemby is not in the end devoured by that monster of a primordial image—which is in fact what nearly happens to him.

The universal problem of evil and sin is another aspect to our impersonal relations to the world. Almost more than any other, therefore, this problem produces collective compensations. One of my patients, aged sixteen, had as the initial symptom of a severe compulsion neurosis the following dream:

> He is walking along an unfamiliar street. It is dark, and he hears steps coming behind him. With a feeling of fear he quickens his pace. The footsteps come nearer, and his fear increases. He begins to run. But the footsteps seem to be overtaking him. Finally he turns round, and there he sees the devil. In deathly terror he leaps into the air and hangs there suspended.

This dream was repeated twice, a sign of its special urgency.

It is a notorious fact that the compulsion neuroses, by reason of their meticulousness and ceremonial punctilio, not only have the surface appearance of a moral problem but are indeed brim-full of inhuman beastliness and ruthless evil, against whose integration the otherwise very delicately organized personality puts up a desperate struggle. This explains why so many things have to be performed in ceremonially "correct" style, as though to counteract the evil hovering in the background. After this dream the neurosis started, and its essential feature was that the patient had, as he put it, to keep himself in a "provisional" or "uncontaminated" state of purity. For this purpose he either severed or made "invalid" all contact with the world and with everything that reminded him of the transitoriness of human existence, by means of lunatic formalities, scrupulous cleansing ceremonies, and the anxious observance of innumerable rules and regulations of an un- believable complexity. Even before the patient had any suspicion of the hellish existence that lay before him, the dream showed him that if he wanted to come down to earth again there would have to be a pact with evil.

Elsewhere I have described a dream that illustrates the compensation of a religious problem in a young theological student. He was involved in all sorts of difficulties of belief, a not uncommon occurrence in the man of today. In his dream he was the pupil of the "white magician," who, however, was dressed in black. After having instructed him up to a certain point, the white magician told him that they now needed the "black magician." The black magician appeared, but clad in a white robe. He declared that he had found the keys of paradise, but needed the wisdom of the white magician in order to understand how to use them. This dream obviously contains the problem of opposites which, as we know, has found in Taoist philosophy a solution very different from the views prevailing in the West. The figures employed by the dream are imper- sonal collective images corresponding to the nature of the impersonal religious problem. In contrast to the Christian view, the dream stresses the relativity of good and evil in a way that immediately calls to mind the Taoist symbol of Yin and Yang.

We should certainly not conclude from these compensations that, as the conscious mind becomes more deeply engrossed in universal problems, the unconscious will bring forth correspondingly far-reaching compensations. There is what one might call a legitimate and an illegitimate interest in impersonal problems. Excursions of this kind are legitimate only when

they arise from the deepest and truest needs of the individual; illegitimate when they are either mere intellectual curiosity or a flight from un- pleasant reality. In the latter case the un- conscious produces all too human and purely personal compensations, whose manifest aim is to bring the conscious mind back to ordinary reality. People who go illegitimately mooning after the infinite often have absurdly banal dreams which endeavour to damp down their ebullience. Thus, from the nature of the compensation, we can at once draw conclusions as to the seriousness and rightness of the conscious strivings.

There are certainly not a few people who are afraid to admit that the unconscious could ever have "big" ideas. They will object, "But do you really believe that the unconscious is capable of offering anything like a constructive criticism of our Western mentality?" Of course, if we take the problem intellectually and impute rational intentions to the unconscious, the thing becomes absurd. But it would never do to foist our conscious psychology upon the un- conscious. Its mentality is an instinctive one; it has no differentiated functions, and it does not "think" as we understand "thinking." It simply creates an image that answers to the conscious situation. This image contains as much thought as feeling, and is anything rather than a product of rationalistic reflection. Such an image would be better described as an artistic vision. We tend to forget that a problem like the one which underlies the dream last men- tioned cannot, even to the conscious mind of the dreamer, be an intellectual problem, but is profoundly emotional. For a moral man the ethical problem is a passionate question which has its roots in the deepest instinctual processes as well as in his most idealistic aspirations. The problem for him is devastatingly real. It is not surprising, therefore, that the answer likewise springs from the depths of his nature. The fact that everyone thinks his psychology is the measure of all things, and, if he also happens to be a fool, will inevitably think that such a problem is beneath his notice, should not trouble the psychologist in the least, for he has to take things objectively, as he finds them, without twisting them to fit his subjective suppositions. The richer and more capacious natures may legitimately be gripped by an impersonal problem, and to the extent that this is so, their unconscious can answer in the same style. And just as the conscious mind can put the question, "Why is there this frightful conflict between good and evil?," so the unconscious can reply, "Look closer! Each needs the other. The best, just because it is the best, holds the seed of evil, and there is nothing so bad but good can come of it."

It might then dawn on the dreamer that the apparently insoluble conflict is, perhaps, a prejudice, a frame of mind conditioned by time and place. The seemingly complex dream-image might easily reveal itself as plain, instinctive common sense, as the tiny germ of a rational idea, which a maturer mind could just as well have thought consciously. At all events Chinese philosophy thought of it ages ago. The singularly apt, plastic configuration of thought is the prerogative of that primitive, natural spirit which is alive in all of us and is only obscured by a one-sided conscious development. If we consider the unconscious compensations from this angle, we might justifiably be accused of judging the unconscious too much from the conscious standpoint. And indeed, in pursuing these reflections, I have always started from the view that the unconscious simply reacts to the conscious contents, albeit in a very significant way, but that it lacks initiative. It is, however, far from my intention to give the impression that the unconscious is merely reactive in all cases. On the contrary, there is a host of experiences which seem to prove that the unconscious is not only spontaneous but can actually take the lead. There are innumerable cases of people who lingered on in a pettifogging unconsciousness, only to become neurotic in the end. Thanks to the neurosis contrived by the unconscious, they are shaken out of their apathy,

and this in spite of their own laziness and often desperate resistance.

Yet it would, in my view, be wrong to suppose that in such cases the unconscious is working to a deliberate and concerted plan and is striving to realize certain definite ends. I have found nothing to support this assumption. The driving force, so far as it is possible for us to grasp it, seems to be in essence only an urge towards self-realization. If it were a matter of some general teleological plan, then all individuals who enjoy a surplus of unconsciousness would necessarily be driven towards higher consciousness by an irresistible urge. That is plainly not the case. There are vast masses of the population who, despite their notorious unconsciousness, never get anywhere near a neurosis. The few who are smitten by such a fate are really persons of the "higher" type who, for one reason or another, have remained too long on a primitive level. Their nature does not in the long run tolerate persistence in what is for them an unnatural torpor. As a result of their narrow conscious outlook and their cramped existence they save energy; bit by bit it accumulates in the unconscious and finally explodes in the form of a more or less acute neurosis. This simple mechanism does not necessarily conceal a "plan." A perfectly understandable urge towards self-realization would provide a quite satisfactory explanation. We could also speak of a retarded maturation of the personality.

Since it is highly probable that we are still a long way from the summit of absolute consciousness, presumably everyone is capable of wider consciousness, and we may assume accordingly that the unconscious processes are constantly supplying us with contents which, if consciously recognized, would extend the range of consciousness. Looked at in this way, the unconscious appears as a field of experience of unlimited extent. If it were merely reactive to the conscious mind, we might aptly call it a psychic mirror-world. In that case, the real source of all contents and activities would lie in the conscious mind, and there would be absolutely nothing in the unconscious except the distorted reflections of conscious contents. The creative process would be shut up in the conscious mind, and anything new would be nothing but conscious invention or cleverness. The empirical facts give the lie to this. Every creative man knows that spontaneity is the very essence of creative thought. Because the unconscious is not just a reactive mirror-reflection, but an independent, productive activity, its realm of experience is a self-contained world, having its own reality, of which we can only say that it affects us as we affect it—precisely what we say about our experience of the outer world. And just as material objects are the constituent elements of this world, so psychic factors constitute the objects of that other world.

The idea of psychic objectivity is by no means a new discovery. It is in fact one of the earliest and most universal achievements of humanity: it is nothing less than the conviction as to the concrete existence of a spirit-world. The spirit-world was certainly never an invention in the sense that fire-boring was an invention; it was far rather the experience, the conscious accept-ance of a reality in no way inferior to that of the material world. I doubt whether primitives exist anywhere who are not acquainted with magical influence or a magical substance. ("Magical" is simply another word for "psychic.") It would also appear that practically all primitives are aware of the existence of spirits. "Spirit" is a psychic fact. Just as we distinguish our own bodiliness from bodies that are strange to us, so primitives—if they have any notion of "souls" at all—distinguish between their own souls and the spirits, which are felt as strange and as "not belonging." They are objects of outward perception, whereas their own soul (or one of several souls where a plurality is assumed), though believed to be essentially akin to the spirits, is not usually an object of so-called sensible perception. After death the soul (or one of the plurality of souls) becomes a spirit which survives the dead man, and often it shows a marked deterioration of character that partly

contradicts the notion of personal immortality. The Bataks, of Sumatra, go so far as to assert that the people who were good in this life turn into malign and dangerous spirits. Nearly every-thing that the primitives say about the tricks which the spirit play on the living, and the general picture they give of the *revenants*, corresponds down to the last detail with the phenomena established by spiritualistic ex-perience. And just as the communications from the "Beyond" can be seen to be the activities of broken-off bits of the psyche, so these primitive spirits are manifestations of unconscious com-plexes. The importance that modern psychology attaches to the "parental complex" is a direct continuation of primitive man's experience of the dangerous power of the ancestral spirits. Even the error of judgment which leads him unthinkingly to assume that the spirits are realities of the external world is carried on in our assumption (which is only partially correct) that the real parents are responsible for the parental complex. In the old trauma theory of Freudian psychoanalysis, and in other quarters as well, this assumption even passed for a scientific explanation. (It was in order to avoid this confusion that I advocated the term "parental imago.")

The simple soul is of course quite unaware of the fact that his nearest relations, who exercise immediate influence over him, create in him an image which is only partly a replica of them-selves, while its other part is compounded of elements derived from himself. The imago is built up of parental influences plus the specific reactions of the child; it is therefore an image that reflects the object with very considerable qualifications. Naturally, the simple soul believes that his parents are as he sees them. The image is unconsciously projected, and when the parents die, the projected image goes on working as though it were a spirit existing on its own. The primitive then speaks of parental spirits who return by night (*revenants*), while the modern man calls it a father or mother complex.

The more limited a man's field of consciousness is, the more numerous the psychic contents (imagos) which meet him as quasi-external apparitions, either in the form of spirits, or as magical potencies projected upon living people (magicians, witches, etc.). At a rather higher stage of development, where the idea of the soul already exists, not all the imagos continue to be projected (where this happens, even trees and stones talk), but one or the other complex has come near enough to consciousness to be felt as no longer strange, but as somehow "belonging." Nevertheless, the feeling that it "belongs" is not at first sufficiently strong for the complex to be sensed as a subjective content of consciousness. It remains in a sort of no man's land between conscious and unconscious, in the half-shadow, in part belonging or akin to the conscious subject, in part an autonomous being, and meeting consciousness as such. At all events it is not necessarily obedient to subjective intentions, it may even be of a higher order, more often than not a source of inspiration or warning, or of "supernatural" information. Psychologically such a content could be explained as a partly autonomous complex that is not yet fully integrated. The archaic souls, the *ba* and *ka* of the Egyptians, are complexes of this kind. At a still higher level, and particularly among the civilized peoples of the West, this complex is invariably of the feminine gender...a fact for which deeper and cogent reasons are not lacking.

NORTHROP FRYE

The Archetypes of Literature

Every organized body of knowledge can be learned progressively; and experience shows that there is also something progressive about

THE ARCHETYPES OF LITERATURE: Originally from *The Kenyon Review* (Winter, 1951). Reprinted by the kind permission of the author.

the learning of literature. Our opening sentence has already got us into a semantic difficulty. Physics is an organized body of knowledge about nature, and a student of it says that he is learning physics, not that he is learning nature. Art, like nature, is the subject of a systematic study, and has to be distinguished from the study itself, which is criticism. It is therefore impossible to "learn literature": one learns about it in a certain way, but what one learns, transitively, is the criticism of literature. Similarly, the difficulty often felt in "teaching literature" arises from the fact that it cannot be done: the criticism of literature is all that can be directly taught. So while no one expects literature itself to behave like a science, there is surely no reason why criticism, as a systematic and organized study, should not be, at least partly, a science. Not a "pure" or "exact" science, perhaps, but these phrases form part of a nineteenth-century cosmology which is no longer with us. Criticism deals with the arts and may well be something of an art itself, but it does not follow that it must be unsystematic. If it is to be related to the sciences too, it does not follow that it must be deprived of the graces of culture.

Certainly criticism as we find it in learned journals and scholarly monographs has every characteristic of a science. Evidence is examined scientifically; previous authorities are used scientifically; fields are investigated scientifically; texts are edited scientifically. Prosody is scientific in structure; so is phonetics; so is philology. And yet in studying this kind of critical science the student becomes aware of a centrifugal movement carrying him away from literature. He finds that literature is the central division of the "humanities," flanked on one side by history and on the other by philosophy. Criticism so far ranks only as a subdivision of literature; and hence, for the systematic mental organization of the subject, the student has to turn to the conceptual framework of the historian for events, and to that of the philosopher for ideas. Even the more centrally placed critical sciences, such as textual editing, seem to be part of a "background" that recedes into history or some other nonliterary field. The thought suggests itself that the ancillary critical disciplines may be related to a central expanding pattern of systematic comprehension which has not yet been established, but which, if it were established, would prevent them from being centrifugal. If such a pattern exists, then criticism would be to art what philosophy is to wisdom and history to action.

Most of the central area of criticism is at present, and doubtless always will be, the area of commentary. But the commentators have little sense, unlike the researchers, of being contained within some sort of scientific discipline: they are chiefly engaged, in the words of the gospel hymn, in brightening the corner where they are. If we attempt to get a more comprehensive idea of what criticism is about, we find ourselves wandering over quaking bogs of generalities, judicious pronouncements of value, reflective comments, perorations to works of research, and other consequences of taking the large view. But this part of the critical field is so full of pseudo-propositions, sonorous nonsense that contains no truth and no falsehood, that it obviously exists only because criticism, like nature, prefers a waste space to an empty one.

The term "pseudo-proposition" may imply some sort of logical positivist attitude on my own part. But I would not confuse the significant proposition with the factual one; nor should I consider it advisable to muddle the study of literature with a schizophrenic dichotomy between subjective-emotional and objective-descriptive aspects of meaning, considering that in order to produce any literary meaning at all one has to ignore this dichotomy. I say only that the principles by which one can distinguish a significant from a meaningless statement in criticism are not clearly defined. Our first step, therefore, is to recognize and get rid of meaningless criticism: that is, talking about literature in a way that cannot help to build up a systematic structure of knowledge. Casual value-judgments

belong not to criticism but to the history of taste, and reflect, at best, only the social and psychological compulsions which prompted their utterance. All judgments in which the values are not based on literary experience but are sentimental or derived from religious or political prejudice may be regarded as casual. Sentimental judgments are usually based either on nonexistent categories or antitheses ("Shakespeare studied life, Milton books") or on a visceral reaction to the writer's personality. The literary chitchat which makes the reputations of poets boom and crash in an imaginary stock exchange is pseudo-criticism. That wealthy investor Mr. Eliot, after dumping Milton on the market, is now buying him again; Donne has probably reached his peak and will begin to taper off; Tennyson may be in for a slight flutter but the Shelley stocks are still bearish. This sort of thing cannot be part of any systematic study, for a systematic study can only progress: whatever dithers or vacillates or reacts is merely leisure-class conversation.

We next meet a more serious group of critics who say: the foreground of criticism is the impact of literature on the reader. Let us, then, keep the study of literature centripetal, and base the learning process on a structural analysis of the literary work itself. The texture of any great work of art is complex and ambiguous, and in unravelling the complexities we may take in as much history and philosophy as we please, if the subject of our study remains at the center. If it does not, we may find that in our anxiety to write about literature we have forgotten how to read it.

The only weakness in this approach is that it is conceived primarily as the antithesis of centrifugal or "background" criticism, and so lands us in a somewhat unreal dilemma, like the conflict of internal and external relations in philosophy. Antitheses are usually resolved, not by picking one side and refuting the other, or by making eclectic choices between them, but by trying to get past the antithetical way of stating the problem. It is right that the first effort of critical apprehension should take the form of a rhetorical or structural analysis of a work of art. But a purely structural approach has the same limitation in criticism that it has in biology. In itself it is simply a discrete series of analyses based on the mere existence of the literary structure, without developing any explanation of how the structure came to be what it was and what its nearest relatives are. Structural analysis brings rhetoric back to criticism, but we need a new poetics as well, and the attempt to construct a new poetics out of rhetoric alone can hardly avoid a mere complication of rhetorical terms into a sterile jargon. I suggest that what is at present missing from literary criticism is a coordinating principle, a central hypothesis which, like the theory of evolution in biology, will see the phenomena it deals with as parts of a whole. Such a principle, though it would retain the centripetal perspective of structural analysis, would try to give the same perspective to other kinds of criticism too.

The first postulate of this hypothesis is the same as that of any science: the assumption of total coherence. The assumption refers to the science, not to what it deals with. A belief in an order of nature is an inference from the intelligibility of the natural sciences; and if the natural sciences ever completely demonstrated the order of nature they would presumably exhaust their subject. Criticism, as a science, is totally intelligible; literature, as the subject of a science, is, so far as we know, an inexhaustible source of new critical discoveries, and would be even if new works of literature ceased to be written. If so, then the search for a limiting principle in literature in order to discourage the development of criticism is mistaken. The assertion that the critic should not look for more in a poem than the poet may safely be assumed to have been conscious of putting there is a common form of what may be called the fallacy of premature teleology. It corresponds to the assertion that a natural phenomenon is as it is because Providence in its inscrutable wisdom made it so.

Simple as the assumption appears, it takes a long time for a science to discover that it is in fact a totally intelligible body of knowledge. Until it makes this discovery it has not been born as an individual science, but remains an embryo within the body of some other subject. The birth of physics from "natural philosophy" and of sociology from "moral philosophy" will illustrate the process. It is also very approximately true that the modern sciences have developed in the order of their closeness to mathematics. Thus physics and astronomy assumed their modern form in the Renaissance, chemistry in the nineteenth century, biology in the nineteenth, and the social sciences in the twentieth. If systematic criticism, then, is developing only in our day, the fact is at least not an anachronism.

We are now looking for classifying principles lying in an area between two points that we have fixed. The first of these is the preliminary effort of criticism, the structural analysis of the work of art. The second is the assumption that there is such a subject as criticism, and that it makes, or could make, complete sense. We may next proceed inductively from structural analysis, associating the data we collect and trying to see larger patterns in them. Or we may proceed deductively, with the consequences that follow from postulating the unity of criticism. It is clear, of course, that neither procedure will work indefinitely without correction from the other. Pure induction will get us lost in haphazard guessing; pure deduction will lead to inflexible and oversimplified pigeonholing. Let us now attempt a few tentative steps in each direction, beginning with the inductive one.

II

The unity of a work of art, the basis of structural analysis, has not been produced solely by the unconditioned will of the artist, for the artist is only its efficient cause: it has form, and consequently a formal cause. The fact that revision is possible, that the poet makes changes not because he likes them better but because they are better, means that poems, like poets, are born and not made. The poet's task is to deliver the poem in as uninjured a state as possible, and if the poem is alive, it is equally anxious to be rid of him, and screams to be cut loose from his private memories and associations, his desire for self-expression, and all the other navel-strings and feeding tubes of his ego. The critic takes over where the poet leaves off, and criticism can hardly do without a kind of literary psychology connecting the poet with the poem. Part of this may be a psychological study of the poet, though this is useful chiefly in analysing the failures in his expression, the things in him which are still attached to his work. More important is the fact that every poet has his private mythology, his own spectroscopic band or peculiar formation of symbols, of much of which he is quite unconscious. In works with characters of their own, such as dramas and novels, the same psychological analysis may be extended to the interplay of characters, though of course literary psychology would analyse the behavior of such characters only in relation to literary convention.

There is still before us the problem of the formal cause of the poem, a problem deeply involved with the question of genres. We cannot say much about genres, for criticism does not know much about them. A good many critical efforts to grapple with such words as "novel" or "epic" are chiefly interesting as examples of the psychology of rumor. Two conceptions of the genre, however, are obviously fallacious, and as they are opposite extremes, the truth must lie somewhere between them. One is the pseudo-Platonic conception of genres as existing prior to and independently of creation, which confuses them with mere conventions of form like the sonnet. The other is that pseudo-biological conception of them as evolving species which turns up in so many surveys of the "development" of this or that form.

We next inquire for the origin of the genre,

and turn first of all to the social conditions and cultural demands which produced it—in other words to the material cause of the work of art. This leads us into literary history, which differs from ordinary history in that its containing categories, "Gothic," "Baroque," "Romantic," and the like are cultural categories, of little use to the ordinary historian. Most literary history does not get as far as these categories, but even so we know more about it than about most kinds of critical scholarship. The historian treats literature and philosophy historically; the philosopher treats history and literature philosophically; and the so-called "history of ideas" approach marks the beginning of an attempt to treat history and philosophy from the point of view of an autonomous criticism.

But still we feel that there is something missing. We say that every poet has his own peculiar formation of images. But when so many poets use so many of the same images, surely there are much bigger critical problems involved than biographical ones. As Mr. Auden's brilliant essay *The Enchafèd Flood* shows, an important symbol like the sea cannot remain within the poetry of Shelley or Keats or Coleridge: it is bound to expand over many poets into an archetypal symbol of literature. And if the genre has a historical origin, why does the genre of drama emerge from medieval religion in a way so strikingly similar to the way it emerged from Greek religion centuries before? This is a problem of structure rather than origin, and suggests that there may be archetypes of genres as well as of images.

It is clear that criticism cannot be systematic unless there is a quality in literature which enables it to be so, an order of words corresponding to the order of nature in the natural sciences. An archetype should be not only a unifying category of criticism, but itself a part of a total form, and it leads us at once to the question of what sort of total form criticism can see in literature. Our survey of critical techniques has taken us as far as literary history. Total literary history moves from the primitive to the sophisticated, and here we glimpse the possibility of seeing literature as a complication of a relatively restricted and simple group of formulas that can be studied in primitive culture. If so, then the search for archetypes is a kind of literary anthropology, concerned with the way that literature is informed by pre-literary categories such as ritual, myth and folk tale. We next realize that the relation between these categories and literature is by no means purely one of descent, as we find them reappearing in the greatest classics—in fact there seems to be a general tendency on the part of great classics to revert to them. This coincides with a feeling that we have all had: that the study of mediocre works of art, however energetic, obstinately remains a random and peripheral form of critical experience, whereas the profound masterpiece seems to draw us to a point at which we can see an enormous number of converging patterns of significance. Here we begin to wonder if we cannot see literature, not only as complicating itself in time, but as spread out in conceptual space from some unseen center.

This inductive movement towards the archetype is a process of backing up, as it were, from structural analysis, as we back up from a painting if we want to see composition instead of brushwork. In the foreground of the grave-digger scene in *Hamlet*, for instance, is an intricate verbal texture, ranging from the puns of the first clown to the *danse macabre* of the Yorick soliloquy, which we study in the printed text. One step back, and we are in the Wilson Knight and Spurgeon group of critics, listening to the steady rain of images of corruption and decay. Here too, as the sense of the place of this scene in the whole play begins to dawn on us, we are in the network of psychological relationships which were the main interest of Bradley. But after all, we say, we are forgetting the genre: *Hamlet* is a play, and an Elizabethan play. So we take another step back into the Stoll and Shaw group and see the scene conventionally as part of its dramatic context. One

step more, and we can begin to glimpse the archetype of the scene, as the hero's *Liebestod* and first unequivocal declaration of his love, his struggle with Laertes and the sealing of his own fate, and the sudden sobering of his mood that marks the transition to the final scene, all take shape around a leap into and return from the grave that has so weirdly yawned open on the stage.

At each stage of understanding this scene we are dependent on a certain kind of scholarly organization. We need first an editor to clean up the text for us, then the rhetorician and philologist, then the literary psychologist. We cannot study the genre without the help of the literary social historian, the literary philosopher and the student of the "history of ideas," and for the archetype we need a literary anthropologist. But now that we have got our central pattern of criticism established, all these interests are seen as converging on literary criticism instead of receding from it into psychology and history and the rest. In particular, the literary anthropologist who chases the source of the Hamlet legend from the pre-Shakespeare play to Saxo, and from Saxo to nature-myths, is not running away from Shakespeare: he is drawing closer to the archetypal form which Shakespeare recreated. A minor result of our new perspective is that contradictions among critics, and assertions that this and not that critical approach is the right one, show a remarkable tendency to dissolve into unreality. Let us now see what we can get from the deductive end.

III

Some arts move in time, like music; others are presented in space, like painting. In both cases the organizing principle is recurrence, which is called rhythm when it is temporal and pattern when it is spatial. Thus we speak of the rhythm of music and the pattern of painting; but later, to show off our sophistication, we may begin to speak of the rhythm of painting and the pattern of music. In other words, all arts may be conceived both temporally and spatially. The score of a musical composition may be studied all at once; a picture may be seen as the track of an intricate dance of the eye. Literature seems to be intermediate between music and painting: its words form rhythms which approach a musical sequence of sounds at one of its boundaries, and form patterns which approach the hieroglyphic or pictorial image at the other. The attempts to get as near to these boundaries as possible form the main body of what is called experimental writing. We may call the rhythm of literature the narrative, and the pattern, the simultaneous mental grasp of the verbal structure, the meaning or significance. We hear or listen to a narrative, but when we grasp a writer's total pattern we "see" what he means.

The criticism of literature is much more hampered by the representational fallacy than even the criticism of painting. That is why we are apt to think of narrative as a sequential representation of events in an outside "life," and of meaning as a reflection of some external "idea." Properly used as critical terms, an author's narrative is his linear movement; his meaning is the integrity of his completed form. Similarly an image is not merely a verbal replica of an external object, but any unit of a verbal structure seen as part of a total pattern or rhythm. Even the letters an author spells his words with form part of his imagery, though only in special cases (such as alliteration) would they call for critical notice. Narrative and meaning thus become respectively, to borrow musical terms, the melodic and harmonic contexts of the imagery.

Rhythm, or recurrent movement, is deeply founded on the natural cycle, and everything in nature that we think of as having some analogy with works of art, like the flower or the bird's song, grows out of a profound synchronization between an organism and the rhythms of its environment, especially that of the solar year. With animals some expressions of synchronization, like the mating dances of birds, could

almost be called rituals. But in human life a ritual seems to be something of a voluntary effort (hence the magical element in it) to recapture a lost rapport with the natural cycle. A farmer must harvest his crop at a certain time of year, but because this is involuntary, harvesting itself is not precisely a ritual. It is the deliberate expression of a will to synchronize human and natural energies at that time which produces the harvest songs, harvest sacrifices and harvest folk customs that we call rituals. In ritual, then, we may find the origin of narrative, a ritual being a temporal sequence of acts in which the conscious meaning or significance is latent: it can be seen by an observer, but is largely concealed from the participators themselves. The pull of ritual is toward pure narrative, which, if there could be such a thing, would be automatic and unconscious repetition. We should notice too the regular tendency of ritual to become encyclopedic. All the important recurrences in nature, the day, the phases of the moon, the seasons and solstices of the year, the crises of existence from birth to death, get rituals attached to them, and most of the higher religions are equipped with a definitive total body of rituals suggestive, if we may put it so, of the entire range of potentially significant actions in human life.

Patterns of imagery, on the other hand, or fragments of significance, are oracular in origin, and derive from the epiphanic moment, the flash of instantaneous comprehension with no direct reference to time, the importance of which is indicated by Cassirer in *Myth and Language*. By the time we get them, in the form of proverbs, riddles, commandments and etiological folk tales, there is already a considerable element of narrative in them. They too are encyclopedic in tendency, building up a total structure of significance, or doctrine, from random and empiric fragments. And just as pure narrative would be unconscious act, so pure significance would be an incommunicable state of consciousness, for communication begins by constructing narrative.

The myth is the central informing power that gives archetypal significance to the ritual and archetypal narrative to the oracle. Hence the myth *is* the archetype, though it might be convenient to say myth only when referring to narrative, and archetype when speaking of significance. In the solar cycle of the day, the seasonal cycle of the year, and the organic cycle of human life, there is a single pattern of significance, out of which myth constructs a central narrative around a figure who is partly the sun, partly vegetative fertility and partly a god or archetypal human being. The crucial importance of this myth has been forced on literary critics by Jung and Frazer in particular, but the several books now available on it are not always systematic in their approach, for which reason I supply the following table of its phases:

1. The dawn, spring and birth phase. Myths of the birth of the hero, of revival and resurrection, of creation and (because the four phases are a cycle) of the defeat of the powers of darkness, winter and death. Subordinate characters: the father and the mother. The archetype of romance and of most dithyrambic and rhapsodic poetry.

2. The zenith, summer, and marriage or triumph phase. Myths of apotheosis, of the sacred marriage, and of entering into Paradise. Subordinate characters: the companion and the bride. The archetype of comedy, pastoral and idyll.

3. The sunset, autumn and death phase. Myths of fall, of the dying god, of violent death and sacrifice and of the isolation of the hero. Subordinate characters: the traitor and the siren. The archetype of tragedy and elegy.

4. The darkness, winter and dissolution phase. Myths of the triumph of these powers; myths of floods and the return of chaos, of the defeat of the hero, and Götterdämmerung myths. Subordinate characters: the ogre and the witch. The archetype of satire (see, for instance, the conclusion of *The Dunciad*).

The quest of the hero also tends to assimilate the oracular and random verbal structures, as we can see when we watch the chaos of local legends that results from prophetic epiphanies consolidating into a narrative mythology of departmental gods. In most of the higher religions this in turn has become the same central quest-myth that emerges from ritual, as the Messiah myth became the narrative structure of the oracles of Judaism. A local flood may beget a folktale by accident, but a comparison of flood stories will show how quickly such tales become examples of the myth of dissolution. Finally, the tendency of both ritual and epiphany to become encyclopedic is realized in the definitive body of myth which constitutes the sacred scriptures of religions. These sacred scriptures are consequently the first documents that the literary critic has to study to gain a comprehensive view of his subject. After he has understood their structure, then he can descend from archetypes to genres, and see how the drama emerges from the ritual side of myth and lyric from the epiphanic or fragmented side, while the epic carries on the central encyclopedic structure.

Some words of caution and encouragement are necessary before literary criticism has clearly staked out its boundaries in these fields. It is part of the critic's business to show how all literary genres are derived from the quest-myth, but the derivation is a logical one within the science of criticism: the quest-myth will constitute the first chapter of whatever future handbooks of criticism may be written that will be based on enough organized critical knowledge to call themselves "introductions" or "outlines" and still be able to live up to their titles. It is only when we try to expound the derivation chronologically that we find ourselves writing pseudo-prehistorical fictions and theories of mythological contract. Again, because psychology and anthropology are more highly developed sciences, the critic who deals with this kind of material is bound to appear, for some time, a dilettante of those subjects. These two phases of criticism are largely undeveloped in comparison with literary history and rhetoric, the reason being the later development of the sciences they are related to. But the fascination which *The Golden Bough* and Jung's book on libido symbols have for literary critics is not based on dilettantism, but on the fact that these books are primarily studies in literary criticism, and very important ones.

In any case the critic who is studying the principles of literary form has a quite different interest from the psychologist's concern with states of mind or the anthropologist's with social institutions. For instance: the mental response to narrative is mainly passive; to significance mainly active. From this fact Ruth Benedict's *Patterns of Culture* develops a distinction between "Apollonian" cultures based on obedience to ritual and "Dionysiac" ones based on a tense exposure of the prophetic mind to epiphany. The critic would tend rather to note how popular literature which appeals to the inertia of the untrained mind puts a heavy emphasis on narrative values, whereas a sophisticated attempt to disrupt the connection between the poet and his environment produces the Rimbaud type of *illumination*, Joyce's solitary epiphanies, and Baudelaire's conception of nature as a source of oracles. Also how literature, as it develops from the primitive to the self-conscious, shows a gradual shift of the poet's attention from narrative to significant values, this shift of attention being the basis of Schiller's distinction between naïve and sentimental poetry.

The relation of criticism to religion, when they deal with the same documents, is more complicated. In criticism, as in history, the divine is always treated as a human artifact. God for the critic, whether he finds him in *Paradise Lost* or the Bible, is a character in a human story; and for the critic all epiphanies are explained, not in terms of the riddle of a possessing god or devil, but as mental phenomena closely associated in their origin with dreams. This once established, it is then necessary to say that nothing in criticism or art compels the critic to take the attitude of ordinary waking consciousness towards the dream or the god. Art deals not with the real but with the conceivable; and criticism, though it will eventually have to have some theory of conceivability, can

never be justified in trying to develop, much less assume, any theory of actuality. It is necessary to understand this before our next and final point can be made.

We have identified the central myth of literature, in its narrative aspect, with the quest-myth. Now if we wish to see this central myth as a pattern of meaning also, we have to start with the workings of the subconscious where the epiphany originates, in other words in the dream. The human cycle of waking and dreaming corresponds closely to the natural cycle of light and darkness, and it is perhaps in this correspondence that all imaginative life begins. The correspondence is largely an antithesis: it is in daylight that man is really in the power of darkness, a prey to frustration and weakness; it is in the darkness of nature that the "libido" or conquering heroic self awakes. Hence art, which Plato called a dream for awakened minds, seems to have as its final cause the resolution of the antithesis, the mingling of the sun and the hero, the realizing of a world in which the inner desire and the outward circumstance coincide. This is the same goal, of course, that the attempt to combine human and natural power in ritual has. The social function of the arts, therefore, seems to be closely connected with visualizing the goal of work in human life. So in terms of significance, the central myth of art must be the vision of the end of social effort, the innocent world of fulfilled desires, the free human society. Once this is understood, the integral place of criticism among the other social sciences, in interpreting and systematizing the vision of the artist, will be easier to see. It is at this point that we can see how religious conceptions of the final cause of human effort are as relevant as any others to criticism.

The importance of the god or hero in the myth lies in the fact that such characters, who are conceived in human likeness and yet have more power over nature, gradually build up the vision of an omnipotent personal community beyond an indifferent nature. It is this community which the hero regularly enters in his apotheosis. The world of this apotheosis thus begins to pull away from the rotary cycle of the quest in which all triumph is temporary. Hence if we look at the quest-myth as a pattern of imagery, we see the hero's quest first of all in terms of its fulfillment. This gives us our central pattern of archetypal images, the vision of innocence which sees the world in terms of total human intelligibility. It corresponds to, and is usually found in the form of, the vision of the unfallen world or heaven in religion. We may call it the comic vision of life, in contrast to the tragic vision, which sees the quest only in the form of its ordained cycle.

We conclude with a second table of contents, in which we shall attempt to set forth the central pattern of the comic and tragic visions. One essential principle of archetypal criticism is that the individual and the universal forms of an image are identical, the reasons being too complicated for us just now. We proceed according to the general plan of the game of Twenty Questions, or, if we prefer, of the Great Chain of Being:

1. In the comic vision the *human* world is a community, or a hero who represents the wish fulfillment of the reader. The archetype of images of symposium, communion, order, friendship and love. In the tragic vision the human world is a tyranny or anarchy, or an individual or isolated man, the leader with his back to his followers, the bullying giant of romance, the deserted or betrayed hero. Marriage or some equivalent consummation belongs to the comic vision; the harlot, witch and other varieties of Jung's "terrible mother" belong to the tragic one. All divine, heroic, angelic or other superhuman communities follow the human pattern.

2. In the comic vision the *animal* world is a community of domesticated animals, usually a flock of sheep, or a lamb, or one of the gentler birds, usually a dove. The archetype of pastoral images. In the tragic vision the animal world is seen in terms of beasts and birds of prey, wolves, vultures, serpents, dragons and the like.

3. In the comic vision the *vegetable* world is a garden, grove or park, or a tree of life, or a rose or lotus. The archetype of Arcadian images, such as that of Marvell's green world or of Shakespeare's forest comedies. In the tragic vision it is a sinister forest like the one in *Comus* or at the opening of the *Inferno,* or a heath or wilderness, or a tree of death.

4. In the comic vision the *mineral* world is a city, or one building or temple, or one stone, normally a glowing precious stone—in fact the whole comic series, especially the tree, can be conceived as luminous or fiery. The archetype of geometrical images: the "starlit dome" belongs here. In the tragic vision the mineral world is seen in terms of deserts, rocks and ruins, or of sinister geometrical images like the cross.

5. In the comic vision the *unformed* world is a river, traditionally fourfold, which influenced the Renaissance image of the temperate body with its four humors. In the tragic vision this world usually becomes the sea, as the narrative myth of dissolution is so often a flood myth. The combination of the sea and beast images gives us the leviathan and similar water monsters.

Obvious as this table looks, a great variety of poetic images and forms will be found to fit it. Yeats's "Sailing to Byzantium," to take a famous example of the comic vision at random, has the city, the tree, the bird, the community of sages, the geometrical gyre and the detachment from the cyclic world. It is, of course, only the general comic or tragic context that determines the interpretation of any symbol: this is obvious with relatively neutral archetypes like the island, which may be Prospero's island or Circe's.

Our tables are, of course, not only elementary but grossly oversimplified, just as our inductive approach to the archetype was a mere hunch. The important point is not the deficiencies of either procedure, taken by itself, but the fact that, somewhere and somehow, the two are clearly going to meet in the middle. And if they do meet, the ground plan of a systematic and comprehensive development of criticism has been established.

MARSHALL McLUHAN

The Spoken Word
and the Written Word

The Spoken Word:
Flower of Evil?

A few seconds from a popular disk-jockey show were typed out as follows:

> That's Patty Baby and that's the girl with the dancing feet and that's Freddy Cannon there on the David Mickie Show in the night time oohbah scubadoo how are you booboo. Next we'll be Swinging on a Star and sssshhhwwoooo and sliding on a moonbeam.
>
> Waaaaaaa how about the...one of the goodest guys with you...this is lovable kissable D.M. in the p.m. at 22 minutes past nine o'clock there, aahhrightie, we're gonna have a Hitline, all you have to do is call WAlnut 5-1151, WAlnut 5-1151, tell them what number it is on the Hitline.

Dave Mickie alternately soars, groans, swings, sings, solos, intones, and scampers, always reacting to his own actions. He moves entirely in the spoken rather than the written area of experience. It is in this way that audience participation is created. The spoken word involves all of the senses dramatically, though highly literate people tend to speak as connectedly and causally as possible. The sensuous involvement natural to cultures in which literacy is not the ruling form of experience is sometimes indicated in travel guides, as in this item from a guide to Greece:

> You will notice that many Greek men seem to spend a lot of time counting the beads of what appear to be amber rosaries. But these have no religious significance. They are *komboloia* or "worry beads," a legacy from the Turks, and Greeks click them on land, on the sea, in the air to ward off that insupportable silence which

THE SPOKEN WORD AND THE WRITTEN WORD: From *Understanding Media: The Extensions of Man* by Marshall McLuhan. Copyright © 1964 by Marshall McLuhan. Used by permission of McGraw-Hill Book Company.

threatens to reign whenever conversation lags. Shepherds do it, cops do it, stevedores and merchants in their shops do it. And if you wonder why so few Greek women wear beads, you'll know it's because their husbands have preempted them for the simple pleasure of clicking. More aesthetic than thumb-twiddling, less expensive than smoking, this Queeg-like obsession indicates a tactile sensuousness characteristic of a race which has produced the western world's greatest sculpture....

Where the heavy visual stress of literacy is lacking in a culture, there occurs another form of sensuous involvement and cultural appreciation that our Greek guide explains whimsically:

> ...do not be surprised at the frequency with which you are patted, petted and prodded in Greece. You may end up feeling like the family dog...in an affectionate family. This propensity to pat seems to us a tactile extension of the avid Greek curiosity noted before. It's as though your hosts are trying to find out what you are made of.

The widely separate characters of the spoken and written words are easy to study today when there is ever closer touch with nonliterate societies. One native, the only literate member of his group, told of acting as reader for the others when they received letters. He said he felt impelled to put his fingers to his ears while reading aloud, so as not to violate the privacy of their letters. This is interesting testimony to the values of privacy fostered by the visual stress of phonetic writing. Such separation of the senses, and of the individual from the group, can scarcely occur without the influence of phonetic writing. The spoken word does not afford the extension and amplification of the visual power needed for habits of individualism and privacy.

It helps to appreciate the nature of the spoken word to contrast it with the written form. Although phonetic writing separates and extends the visual power of words, it is comparatively crude and slow. There are not many ways of writing "tonight," but Stanislavsky used to ask his young actors to pronounce and stress it fifty different ways while the audience wrote down the different shades of feeling and meaning expressed. Many a page of prose and many a narrative has been devoted to expressing what was, in effect, a sob, a moan, a laugh, or a piercing scream. The written word spells out in sequence what is quick and implicit in the spoken word.

Again, in speech we tend to react to each situation that occurs, reacting in tone and gesture even to our own act of speaking. But writing tends to be a kind of separate or specialist action in which there is little opportunity or call for reaction. The literate man or society develops the tremendous power of acting in any matter with considerable detachment from the feelings or emotional involvement that a nonliterate man or society would experience.

Henri Bergson, the French philosopher, lived and wrote in a tradition of thought in which it was and is considered that language is a human technology that has impaired and diminished the values of the collective unconscious. It is the extension of man in speech that enables the intellect to detach itself from the vastly wider reality. Without language, Bergson suggests, human intelligence would have remained totally involved in the objects of its attention. Language does for intelligence what the wheel does for the feet and the body. It enables them to move from thing to thing with greater ease and speed and ever less involvement. Language extends and amplifies man but it also divides his faculties. His collective consciousness or intuitive awareness is diminished by this technical extension of consciousness that is speech.

Bergson argues in *Creative Evolution* that even consciousness is an extension of man that dims the bliss of union in the collective unconscious. Speech acts to separate man from man, and mankind from the cosmic unconscious. As an extension or uttering (outering) of all our senses at once, language has always been held to be man's richest art form, that which distinguishes him from the animal creation.

If the human ear can be compared to a radio receiver that is able to decode electromagnetic waves and recode them as sound, the human voice may be compared to the radio transmitter in being able to translate sound into electro-magnetic waves. The power of the voice to shape air and space into verbal patterns may well have been preceded by a less specialized expression of cries, grunts, gestures, and commands, of song and dance. The patterns of the senses that are extended in the various languages of men are as varied as styles of dress and art. Each mother tongue teaches its users a way of seeing and feeling the world, and of acting in the world, that is quite unique.

Our new electric technology that extends our senses and nerves in a global embrace has large implications for the future of language. Electric technology does not need words any more than the digital computer needs numbers. Electricity points the way to an extension of the process of consciousness itself, on a world scale, and without any verbalization whatever. Such a state of collective awareness may have been the pre-verbal condition of men. Language as the technology of human extension, whose powers of division and separation we know so well, may have been the "Tower of Babel" by which men sought to scale the highest heavens. Today computers hold out the promise of a means of instant translation of any code or language into any other code or language. The computer, in short, promises by technology a Pentecostal condition of universal understanding and unity. The next logical step would seem to be, not to translate, but to bypass languages in favor of a general cosmic consciousness which might be very like the collective unconscious dreamt of by Bergson. The condition of "weightlessness," that biologists say promises a physical immortality, may be paralleled by the condition of speechlessness that could confer a perpetuity of collective harmony and peace.

The Written Word:
An Eye for an Ear

Prince Modupe wrote of his encounter with the written word in his West African days:

> The one crowded space in Father Perry's house was his bookshelves. I gradually came to

understand that the marks on the pages were *trapped words*. Anyone could learn to decipher the symbols and turn the trapped words loose again into speech. The ink of the print trapped the thoughts; they could no more get away than a *doomboo* could get out of a pit. When the full realization of what this meant flooded over me, I experienced the same thrill and amazement as when I had my first glimpse of the bright lights of Konakry. I shivered with the intensity of my desire to learn to do this wondrous thing myself.

In striking contrast to the native's eagerness, there are the current anxieties of civilized man concerning the written word. To some Westerners the written or printed word has become a very touchy subject. It is true that there is more material written and printed and read today than ever before, but there is also a new electric technology that threatens this ancient technology of literacy built on the phonetic alphabet. Because of its action in extending our central nervous system, electric technology seems to favor the inclusive and participational spoken word over the specialist written word. Our Western values, built on the written word, have already been considerably affected by the electric media of telephone, radio, and TV. Perhaps that is the reason why many highly literate people in our time find it difficult to examine this question without getting into a moral panic. There is the further circumstance that, during his more than two thousand years of literacy, Western man has done little to study or to understand the effects of the phonetic alphabet in creating many of his basic patterns of culture. To begin now to examine the question may, therefore, seem too late.

Suppose that, instead of displaying the Stars and Stripes, we were to write the words "American flag" across a piece of cloth and to display that. While the symbols would convey the same meaning, the effect would be quite different. To translate the rich visual mosaic of the Stars and Stripes into written form would be to deprive it of most of its qualities of corporate image and of experience, yet the abstract literal bond would remain much the same. Perhaps this illustration will serve to suggest the change the tribal man experiences when he becomes literate. Nearly all the emotional and corporate family feeling is eliminated from his relationship with his social group. He is emotionally free to separate from the tribe and to become a civilized individual, a man of visual organization who has uniform attitudes, habits, and rights with all other civilized individuals.

The Greek myth about the alphabet was that Cadmus, reputedly the king who introduced the phonetic letters into Greece, sowed the dragon's teeth, and they sprang up armed men. Like any other myth, this one capsulates a prolonged process into a flashing insight. The alphabet meant power and authority and control of military structures at a distance. When combined with papyrus, the alphabet spelled the end of the stationary temple bureaucracies and the priestly monopolies of knowledge and power. Unlike prealphabetic writing, which with its innumerable signs was difficult to master, the alphabet could be learned in a few hours. The acquisition of so extensive a knowledge and so complex a skill as prealphabetic writing represented, when applied to such unwieldy materials as brick and stone, insured for the scribal caste a monopoly of priestly power. The easier alphabet and the light, cheap, transportable papyrus together effected the transfer of power from the priestly to the military class. All this is implied in the myth about Cadmus and the dragon's teeth, including the fall of the city states, the rise of empires and military bureaucracies.

In terms of the extensions of man, the theme of the dragon's teeth in the Cadmus myth is of the utmost importance. Elias Canetti in *Crowds and Power* reminds us that the teeth are an obvious agent of power in man, and especially in many animals. Languages are filled with testimony to the grasping, devouring power and precision of teeth. That the power of letters as agents of aggressive order and precision should be expressed as extensions of the dragon's teeth is natural and fitting. Teeth are emphatically visual in their lineal order. Letters are not only like teeth visually, but their power to put teeth into the business of empire-building is manifest in our Western history.

The phonetic alphabet is a unique technology. There have been many kinds of writing, pictographic and syllabic, but there is only one phonetic alphabet in which semantically meaningless letters are used to correspond to semantically meaningless sounds. This stark division and parallelism between a visual and an auditory world was both crude and ruthless, culturally speaking. The phonetically written word sacrifices worlds of meaning and perception that were secured by forms like the hieroglyph and the Chinese ideogram. These culturally richer forms of writing, however, offered men no means of sudden transfer from the magically discontinuous and traditional world of the tribal word into the cool and uniform visual medium. Many centuries of ideogrammic use have not threatened the seamless web of family and tribal subtleties of Chinese society. On the other hand, a single generation of alphabetic literacy suffices in Africa today, as in Gaul two thousand years ago, to release the individual initially, at least, from the tribal web. This fact has nothing to do with the *content* of the alphabetized words; it is the result of the sudden breach between the auditory and the visual experience of man. Only the phonetic alphabet makes such a sharp division in experience, giving to its user an eye for an ear, and freeing him from the tribal trance of resonating word magic and the web of kinship.

It can be argued, then, that the phonetic alphabet, alone, is the technology that has been the means of creating "civilized man"—the separate individuals equal before a written code of law. Separateness of the individual, continuity of space and of time, and uniformity of codes are the prime marks of literate and civilized societies. Tribal cultures like those of the Indian and the Chinese may be greatly superior to the Western cultures, in the range and delicacy of their perceptions and expression. However, we are not here concerned with the question of values, but with the configurations of societies. Tribal cultures cannot entertain the possibility of the individual or of the separate citizen. Their ideas of spaces and times are neither continuous nor uniform, but compassional and compressional in their intensity. It is in its power to extend patterns of visual uniformity and continuity that the "message" of the alphabet is felt by cultures.

As an intensification and extension of the visual function, the phonetic alphabet diminishes the role of the other senses of sound and touch and taste in any literate culture. The fact that this does not happen in cultures such as the Chinese, which use nonphonetic scripts, enables them to retain a rich store of inclusive perception in depth of experience that tends to become eroded in civilized cultures of the phonetic alphabet. For the ideogram is an inclusive *gestalt*, not an analytic dissociation of senses and functions like phonetic writing.

The achievements of the Western world, it is obvious, are testimony to the tremendous values of literacy. But many people are also disposed to object that we have purchased our structure of specialist technology and values at too high a price. Certainly the lineal structuring of rational life by phonetic literacy has involved us in an interlocking set of consistencies that are striking enough to justify a much more extensive inquiry than that of the present chapter. Perhaps there are better approaches along quite different lines; for example, consciousness is regarded as the mark of a rational being, yet there is nothing lineal or sequential about the total field of awareness that exists in any moment of consciousness. Consciousness is not a verbal process. Yet during all our centuries of phonetic literacy we have favored the chain of inference as the mark of logic and reason. Chinese writing, in contrast, invests each ideogram with a total intuition of being and reason that allows only a small role to visual sequence as a mark of mental effort and organization. In Western literate society it is still plausible and acceptable to say that something "follows" from something, as if there were some cause at work that makes such a sequence. It was David Hume who, in the eighteenth century, demonstrated that there is no causality indicated in any sequence, natural or logical. The sequential is merely additive, not causative. Hume's argument, said Immanuel Kant, "awoke me from my dogmatic slumber." Neither Hume nor Kant, however, detected the hidden cause of our Western bias toward sequence as "logic" in the all-pervasive technology of the alphabet. Today in the electric age we feel as free to invent nonlineal logics as we do to make non-Euclidean geometries. Even the assembly line, as the method of analytic sequence for mechanizing every kind of making and production, is nowadays yielding to new forms.

Only alphabetic cultures have ever mastered connected lineal sequences as pervasive forms of psychic and social organization. The breaking up of every kind of experience into uniform units in order to produce faster action and change of form (applied knowledge) has been the secret of Western power over man and nature alike. That is the reason why our Western industrial programs have quite involuntarily been so militant, and our military programs have been so industrial. Both are shaped by the alphabet in their technique of transformation and control by making all situations uniform and continuous. This procedure, manifest even in the Graeco-Roman phase, became more intense with the uniformity and repeatability of the Gutenberg development.

Civilization is built on literacy because literacy is a uniform processing of a culture by a visual sense extended in space and time by the alphabet. In tribal cultures, experience is arranged by a dominant auditory sense-life that represses visual values. The auditory sense, unlike the cool and neutral eye, is hyper-esthetic and delicate and all-inclusive. Oral cultures act and react at the same time. Phonetic culture endows men with the means of repressing their feelings and emotions when engaged in action. To act without reacting, without involvement, is the peculiar advantage of Western literate man.

The story of *The Ugly American* describes the endless succession of blunders achieved by visual and civilized Americans when confronted with the tribal and auditory cultures of the East. As a civilized UNESCO experiment, running water —with its lineal organization of pipes—was installed recently in some Indian villages. Soon the villagers requested that the pipes be removed, for it seemed to them that the whole social life of the village had been impoverished when it was no longer necessary for all to visit the communal well. To us the pipe is a convenience. We do not think of it as culture or as a product of literacy, any more than we think of literacy as changing our habits, our emotions, or our perceptions. To nonliterate people, it is perfectly obvious that the most commonplace conveniences represent total changes in culture.

The Russians, less permeated with the patterns of literate culture than Americans, have much less difficulty in perceiving and accommodating the Asiatic attitudes. For the West, literacy has long been pipes and taps and streets and assembly lines and inventories. Perhaps most potent of all as an expression of literacy is our system of uniform pricing that penetrates distant markets and speeds the turnover of commodities. Even our ideas of cause and effect in the literate West have long been in the form of things in sequence and succession, an idea that strikes any tribal or auditory culture as quite ridiculous, and one that has lost its prime place in our own new physics and biology.

All the alphabets in use in the Western world, from that of Russia to that of the Basques, from that of Portugal to that of Peru, are derivatives of the Graeco-Roman letters. Their unique separation of sight and sound from semantic and verbal content made them a most radical technology for the translation and homogenization of cultures. All other forms of writing had served merely one culture, and had served to separate that culture from others. The phonetic letters alone could be used to translate, albeit crudely, the sounds of any language into one-and-the-same visual code. Today, the effort of the Chinese to use our phonetic letters to translate their language has run into special problems in the wide tonal variations and meanings of similar sounds. This has led to the practice of fragmenting Chinese monosyllables into polysyllables in order to eliminate tonal ambiguity. The Western phonetic alphabet is now at work transforming the central auditory features of the Chinese language and culture in order that China can also develop the lineal and visual patterns that give central unity and aggregate uniform power to Western work and organization. As we move out of the Gutenberg era of our own culture, we can more readily discern its primary features of homogeneity, uniformity, and continuity. These were the characteristics that gave the Greeks and Romans their easy ascendancy over the nonliterate barbarians. The barbarian or tribal man, then as now, was hampered by cultural pluralism, uniqueness, and discontinuity.

To sum up, pictographic and hieroglyphic writing as used in Babylonian, Mayan, and Chinese cultures represents an extension of the visual sense for storing and expediting access to human experience. All of these forms give pictorial expression to oral meanings. As such, they approximate the animated cartoon and are extremely unwieldy, requiring many signs for the infinity of data and operations of social action. In contrast, the phonetic alphabet, by a few letters only, was able to encompass all languages. Such an achievement, however, involved the separation of both signs and sounds from their semantic and dramatic meanings. No other system of writing had accomplished this feat.

The same separation of sight and sound and meaning that is peculiar to the phonetic alphabet also extends to its social and psychological effects. Literate man undergoes much separation of his imaginative, emotional, and sense life, as Rousseau (and later the Romantic poets and philosophers) proclaimed long ago. Today the mere mention of D. H. Lawrence will serve to recall the twentieth-century efforts made to bypass literate man in order to recover human "wholeness." If Western literate man undergoes much dissociation of inner sensibility from his use of the alphabet, he also wins his personal freedom to dissociate himself from clan and family. This freedom to shape an individual career manifested itself in the ancient world in military life. Careers were open to talents in Republican Rome, as much as in Napoleonic France, and for the same reasons. The new literacy had created an homogeneous and malleable milieu in which the mobility of armed groups and of ambitious individuals, equally, was as novel as it was practical.

Questions for Review

1. What does William James mean by *reverie*? By *unconscious inferences*? How is each of these thought processes related to our empirical (i.e., *sense*) experiences?

2. What does James describe as the process of *reasoning* and how is it connected with facts? What meaning does James give to the term, *fact*?

3. Explain James's theory of the relationship of genius to the ability to perceive similarities. Why do some men possess this ability while others do not?

4. Summarize James's theory of the difference between the *abstract* or *analytical* thinker and the *intuitive* or *artistic* thinker. Do they tend to be average or typical men? Explain. Which does James consider the superior—the analytical or the intuitive mind?

5. How does James relate the development of words and language to his theory of the three kinds of thought: reverie, inference, and reasoning? Does thought deal more with concrete or abstract concepts as it moves from reverie to reasoning? Does language become more or less concrete as it develops?

6. Put into your own words James's main points about the way in which kinds of thinking are reflected in types of intelligence and in the uses of language.

7. N. O. Brown's précis of Freud's psychological system establishes a number of theories similar in purpose to those of James but quite unlike in nature. For instance, contrast Brown's unconscious ideas with James's unconscious inferences. Would James agree with the Freudian belief that desire or the wish for pleasure and not the striving for reasonable contemplation is the basis of human life?

8. What are the implications in terms of thought and reasoning of Freud's theory that everyone is neurotic? Is the artist necessarily more or less neurotic than everyone else?

9. Would you say that literature as a whole is more concerned with the *pleasure principle* or the *reality principle?* Is it a form of "a flight or alienation from a reality which is found unbearable" or is it a form of "the struggle for existence"?

10. According to Brown's essay, is the use of language or words more a function of the individual's neurosis or a means of adjusting to the reality-principle? What does this suggest about the writer and his motivations?

11. Lionel Trilling's essay, "Art and Neurosis," departs from the same Freudian theories as does N. O. Brown's "The Disease Called Man." Does Trilling's summary of Freud's principles differ in any way from Brown's summary?

12. Summarize Trilling's argument from the assumption that all men are neurotic to his conclusion that the writer is not to be distinguished from his fellow men on the basis of neurosis only.

13. What, according to Trilling's essay, explains the widespread belief among the members of society at large that writers are "mad" or "insane"? Do you agree with this explanation?

14. Compare Trilling's ideas of the role of fantasy in the thought processes with Brown's. Is fantasy similar to what James called "reverie"?

15. If the artist is capable, as Trilling asserts, of mastering his neuroses and turning them to his own and social benefit, does this make him healthier and more normal than the so-called "normal man"? Explain.

16. How does the theory of universal neurosis help to explain the interest of readers in literature?

17. Trilling asserts that neurosis does not explain *why* the genius is able to compose a great work whereas other neurotics cannot. Does he suggest a possible cause for the genius's ability to compose?

18. What is Trilling's view of the relative neuroticism of the scientist and the poet? Does one tend to be more neurotic than the other? (Note especially footnote 3 to the essay.)

19. Carl Jung, the author of "The Personal and the Collective Unconscious," began as a follower of Sigmund Freud's but went on to develop his own psychological theories of the unconscious. What does Jung mean by *myth?* Compare his use of the term with that of James, Brown, and Trilling.

20. How does the theory of the collective unconscious help to explain why literature exercises an appeal for its readers?

21. How is the "big dream" and the dreamer's compulsion to tell it related to the writer's perception of archetypal truths and his motive for writing?

22. Summarize Jung's views of the collective unconscious, its discovery through feeling rather than rationalistic reflection, and its relation to the artistic vision.

23. Does Jung consider the real world (the material world apparent to our senses) more true than the spirit world (that of dreams and feelings)? Is one more properly the source of literature than the other?

24. Northrop Frye's "The Archetypes of Literature" is obviously indebted to Jung's theories for its assumptions. Frye confines himself in this essay solely to the kind of literature called "fictional." Would his comments apply equally to the literature called "factual"? Why?

25. What aspects of human experience

(laborious, recreational, religious, and so forth) does Frye use to establish his archetypal cycles? Are these activities more effectively dealt with in one kind of writing than in another?

26. In his statement that the composition (poem) cries to be cut off from the writer, does Frye seem to subscribe to the Freudian thesis of art as neurosis or to the Jamesian thesis of art as truth intuitively determined?

27. Does this essay make clear the principle Frye uses to determine which written works are "literature" and which are not?

28. What does Marshall McLuhan mean by the statement, "Many a page of prose and many a narrative has been devoted to expressing what was, in effect, a sob, a moan, a laugh, or a piercing scream"? What does he suggest about the relationship between sense experience and literature?

29. Does McLuhan agree with Bergson's idea of the connection between the "collective unconscious" and language? Does the meaning of "collective unconscious" in this essay differ from that in Carl Jung's?

30. McLuhan suggests that instantaneous electronic communication of the spoken word will lead to the increased community of men but that the fact man is literate tends to isolate him, thus separating him from other men. Do these ideas contradict each other?

31. All of the theories given here indicate some sort of antithesis (*conscious* vs. *unconscious; reasonable* vs. *imaginative; pleasure principle* vs. *reality principle; community* vs. *isolation*). How does this theory of antithesis affect the opinions about sensation and expression, or experience and language? Is the antithesis a valid one or not?

Questions for Discussion and Writing

1. Some of the writers above believe that thought derives from man's rational (logical or reasonable) nature whereas others believe thought stems from his irrational (emotional or nonlogical) nature. Are these two beliefs entirely hostile to each other or can they be reconciled?

2. Is it valid to say that the literature of science is rational and the literature of the humanities is irrational or emotional? Is this differentiation useful or true?

3. Can the writer be considered more a man whose thought processes depend on feeling than one whose thought is rational or analytical?

4. Is language a more suitable means of conveying analytical thought than intuitive truth?

5. Read the group of essays by scientists on p. 288 ff. explaining how they think and the group by poets on p. 388 ff. and discuss the following problems:

    A. Is the scientist really less emotionally concerned with his ideas than the poet or the philosopher? Is scientific thinking any less imaginative or creative than poetic or philosophical thinking? Is the scientific process substantially different from the poetic process?

    B. What differences, if any, are there between the way the poet thinks, according to Wordsworth, and the way a scientist thinks, according to Conant? Compare Wallace Stevens's conception of order in the mind with Leacock's criticism of scientific errors.

    C. If Freud is correct in saying that all men are neurotic, and if Danzig is right about the number system being the extension of man, then is all scientific theory neurotic?

    D. William James, J. B. Conant, and Marianne Moore all describe in words their conception of the human mind and how it acts. Compare and contrast the language they use to communicate their conceptions. Which writer uses the most abstract words, and which the most concrete? What conclusions can you draw about the language of science and that of poetry?

II
PERSPECTIVES ON REALITY

The Private Utterance

The question of why men choose to write down their formulations of experience has engrossed not only critics; it has been a matter of great concern to writers themselves. In the daily records kept by men, women, and even children, the vital problems of literature and life have been pondered from 161 A.D. and before, to the present. In the personal records of a Roman Emperor, a Scottish rake, and a young Jewish girl are to be found some provocative meditations about the relationship between life and literature. Furthermore, in the kind of writing known as the journal or diary—the "daily" record—a writer must confront and solve the basic difficulties involved in transmitting concepts to paper and in verbalizing states of mind. He must choose some experiences and reject others, combine and correlate ideas and emotions, indicate the passing of time, and define his double role as a writer and the reader of what he has written. Since the journal is almost always composed in private, if not in secret, the writer is also his own reader, possibly his only one. He is conveying experiences to himself, formulating ideas for his personal use or benefit. It is the journal or diary, therefore, that introduces the student to the fundamental problems of a writer while it reveals an author's drives and desires.

MARCUS AURELIUS

Some Daily Reminders

1. Remember to put yourself in mind every morning, that before night it will be your luck to meet with some busybody, with some ungrateful, abusive fellow, with some knavish, envious, or unsociable churl or other. Now all this perverseness in them proceeds from their ignorance of good and evil; and since it has fallen to my share to understand the natural beauty of a good action, and the deformity of an ill one—since I am satisfied the person disobliging is of kin to me, and though we are not just of the same flesh and blood, yet our minds are nearly related, being both extracted from the Deity—I am likewise convinced that no man can do me a real injury, because no man can force me to misbehave myself, nor can I find it in my heart to hate or to be angry with one of my own nature and family. For we are all made for mutual assistance, as the feet, the hands, and the eyelids, as the rows of the upper and under teeth, from whence it follows that clashing and opposition is perfectly unnatural. Now such an unfriendly disposition is implied in resentment and aversion.

2. This being of mine, all there is of it, consists of flesh, breath, and the ruling part. Away with your books then. Suffer not your mind any more to be distracted. It is not permitted. As for your body, value it no more than if you were just expiring. For what is it? Nothing but a little blood and bones; a piece of network, wrought out of nerves, veins, and arteries twisted together. In the next place, consider what sort of thing your breath is; why, only a little air, and that not constant, but every moment let out of your lungs and sucked in again. The third part of your composition is the ruling part. Now con-

sider thus: You are an old man: Do not suffer this noble part of you under servitude any longer. Let it not be moved by the springs of selfish passions; let it not quarrel with fate, be uneasy at the present, or afraid of the future.

3. Providence shines clearly through the works of the gods; even the works of chance are not without dependence on Nature, being only an effect of that chain of causes which are under a providential regulation. Indeed, all things flow from this fountain; besides, there is necessity, and the interest of the whole universe, of which you are a part. Now, that which is both the product and support of universal Nature, must by consequence be serviceable to every part of it; but the world subsists upon change, and is preserved by the mutation of the simple elements, and also of things mixed and compounded, and what it loses one way it gets another. Let these reflections satisfy you, and make them your rule to live by. As for books, cast away your thirst after them, that you may not die complaining, but go off in good humor, and heartily thank the gods for what you have had.

4. Remember how often you have postponed minding your interest, and let slip those opportunities the gods have given you. It is now high time to consider what sort of world you are part of, and from what kind of governor of it you are descended; that you have a set period assigned you to act in, and unless you improve it to brighten and compose your thoughts, it will quickly run off with you, and be lost beyond recovery.

5. Take care always to remember that you are a man and a Roman; and let every action be done with perfect and unaffected gravity, humanity, freedom, and justice. And be sure you entertain no fancies, which may give check to these qualities. This is possible, if you will but perform every action as though it were your last; if your appetites and passions do not cross upon your reason; if you keep clear of rashness, and have nothing of insincerity and self-love to infect you, and do not complain of your destiny. You see what a few points a man has to gain in

---

SOME DAILY REMINDERS: From the *Meditations*. Translated by Jeremy Collier.

order to attain to a godlike way of living; for he that comes thus far, performs all which the immortal powers will require of him.

6. Continue to dishonour yourself, my soul! Neither will you have much time left to do yourself honour. For the life of each man is almost up already; and yet, instead of paying a due regard to yourself, you place your happiness in the souls of other men.

7. Do not let accidents disturb, or outward objects engross your thoughts, but keep your mind quiet and disengaged, that you may be at leisure to learn something good, and cease rambling from one thing to another. There is likewise another sort of roving to be avoided; for some people are busy and yet do nothing; they fatigue and wear themselves out, and yet aim at no goal, nor propose any general end of action or design.

8. A man can rarely be unhappy by being ignorant of another's thoughts; but he that does not attend to the motions of his own is certainly unhappy.

9. These reflections ought always to be at hand: to consider well the nature of the universe and my own nature, together with the relation betwixt them, and what kind of part it is, of what kind of whole; and that no mortal can hinder me from acting and speaking conformably to the being of which I am a part.

10. Theophrastus, in comparing the degrees of faults (as men would commonly distinguish them), talks like a philosopher when he affirms that those instances of misbehaviour which proceed from desire are greater than those of which anger is the occasion. For a man that is angry seems to quit his hold of reason unwillingly and with pain, and start out of rule before he is aware. But he that runs riot out of desire, being overcome by pleasure, loses all hold on himself, and all manly restraint. Well, then, and like a philosopher, he said that he of the two is the more to be condemned that sins with pleasure than he that sins with grief. For the first looks like an injured person, and is vexed, and, as it were, forced into a passion; whereas the other

begins with inclination, and commits the fault through desire.

11. Manage all your actions, words, and thoughts accordingly, since you may at any moment quit life. And what great matter is the business of dying? If the gods are in being, you can suffer nothing, for they will do you no harm. And if they are not, or take no care of us mortals —why, then, a world without either gods or Providence is not worth a man's while to live in. But, in truth, the being of the gods, and their concern in human affairs, is beyond dispute. And they have put it entirely in a man's power not to fall into any calamity properly so-called. And if other misfortunes had been really evils, they would have provided against them too, and furnished man with capacity to avoid them. But how can that which cannot make the man worse make his life so? I can never be persuaded that the universal Nature neglected these matters through want of knowledge, or, having that, yet lacked the power to prevent or correct the error; or that Nature should commit such a fault, through want of power or skill, as to suffer things, really good and evil, to happen promiscuously to good and bad men. Now, living and dying, honour and infamy, pleasure and pain, riches and poverty—all these things are the common allotment of the virtuous and vicious, because they have nothing intrinsically noble or base in their nature; and, therefore, to speak properly, are neither good nor bad.

12. Consider how quickly all things are dissolved and resolved; the bodies and substances themselves into the matter and substance of the world, and their memories into its general age and time. Consider, too, the objects of sense, particularly those which charm us with pleasure, frighten us with pain, or are most admired for empty reputation. The power of thought will show a man how insignificant, despicable, and paltry these things are, and how soon they wither and die. It will show him what those people are upon whose fancy and good word the being of fame depends: also the nature of death, which, if once abstracted from the pomp and terror of

the idea, will be found nothing more than a pure natural action. Now he that dreads the course of nature is a very child; but this is not only a work of nature, but is also profitable to her. Lastly, we should consider how we are related to the Deity, and in what part of our being, and in what condition of that part.

13. Nothing can be more unhappy than the curiosity of that man that ranges everywhere, and digs into the earth, as the poet says, for discovery; that is wonderfully busy to force by conjecture a passage into other people's thoughts, but does not consider that it is sufficient to reverence and serve the divinity within himself. And this service consists in this, that a man keep himself pure from all violent passion, and evil affection, from all rashness and vanity, and from all manner of discontent towards gods or men. For as for the gods, their administration ought to be revered upon the score of excellency; and as for men, their actions should be well taken for the sake of common kindred. Besides, they are often to be pitied for their ignorance of good and evil; which incapacity of discerning between moral qualities is no less a defect than that of a blind man, who cannot distinguish between white and black.

14. Though you were to live three thousand, or, if you please, thirty thousand of years, yet remember that no man can lose any other life than that which he now lives, neither is he possessed of any other than that which he loses. Whence it follows that the longest life, as we commonly speak, and the shortest, come all to the same reckoning. For the present is of the same duration everywhere. Everybody's loss, therefore, is of the same bigness, and reaches no further than to a point of time, for no man is capable of losing either the past or the future; for how can one be deprived of what he has not? So that under this consideration there are two notions worth remembering. One is, that Nature treads in a circle, and has much the same face through the whole course of eternity. And therefore it signifies not at all whether a man stands gazing here an hundred, or two hundred, or an infinity of years; for all that he gets by it is only to see the same sights so much the oftener. The other hint is, that when the longest and shortest-lived persons come to die, their loss is equal; they can but lose the present as being the only thing they have; for that which he has not, no man can be truly said to lose.

15. Monimus, the Cynic philosopher, used to say that all things were but opinion. Now this saying may undoubtedly prove serviceable, provided one accepts it only as far as it is true.

16. There are several different ways by which a man's soul may do violence to itself; first of all, when it becomes an abscess, and, as it were, an excrescence on the universe, as far as in it lies. For to be vexed at anything that happens is a separation of ourselves from nature, in some part of which the natures of all other things are contained. Second, it falls under the same misfortune when it hates any person, or goes against him, with an intention of mischief, which is the case of the angry and revengeful. Third, it wrongs itself when it is overcome by pleasure or pain. Fourth, when it makes use of art, tricking, and falsehood, in word or action. Fifth, when it does not know what it would be at in a business, but runs on without thought or design, whereas even the least undertaking ought to be aimed at some end. Now the end of rational beings is to be governed by the law and reason of the most venerable city and constitution.

17. The extent of human life is but a point; its substance is in perpetual flux, its perceptions dim, and the whole composition of the body tending to corruption. The soul is but a whirl, fortune not to be guessed at, and fame undiscerning—in a word, that which belongs to the body is a flowing river, and what the soul has is but dream and bubble. Life is but a campaign, or course of travels, and after-fame is oblivion. What is it, then, that will stick by a man? Why, nothing but philosophy. Now, this consists in keeping the divinity within us from injury and disgrace, superior to pleasure and pain, doing nothing at random, without any dissembling and pretence, and independent of the motions

of another. Farther, philosophy brings the mind to take things as they fall, and acquiesce in their distribution, inasmuch as all events proceed from the same cause with itself; and, above all, to have an easy prospect of death, as being nothing more than a dissolving of the elements of which each thing is composed. Now, if the elements themselves are never the worse for running off one into another, what if they should all change and be dissolved Why should any man be concerned at the consequence? All this is but Nature's method; now, Nature never does any mischief.

WRITTEN AT CARNUNTUM.

SAMUEL PEPYS

The Winter of 1660-61

December 1660

DECEMBER 1ST.   This morning observing some things to be laid up not as they should be by my girl, I took a broom and basted her till she cried extremely, which made me vexed; but, before I went out, I left her appeased.

4TH.   To the Duke of York, and he took us into his closet, and we did open to him our project of stopping the growing charge of the fleet, by paying them in hand one moiety, and the other four months hence. This he do like. This day the Parliament voted that the bodies of Oliver, Ireton, Bradshaw, and Thomas Pride, should be taken up out of their graves in the Abbey, and drawn to the gallows, and there hanged and buried under it: which (methinks) do trouble me that a man of so great courage as

---

THE WINTER OF 1660–61: From the *Diary*. First printed in 1825.

he was should have that dishonour, though otherwise he might deserve it enough.

5TH.   After dinner went to the New Theatre, and there I saw *The Merry Wives of Windsor* acted—the humours of the country gentleman and the French doctor very well done, but the rest but very poorly, and Sir J. Falstaff as bad as any.

12TH.   To the Exchequer, and did give my mother Bowyer a visit, and her daughters, the first time that I did see them since I went last to sea. My father did offer me six pieces of gold, in lieu of six pounds that he borrowed of me the other day, but it went against me to take it of him, and therefore did not. Home and to bed, reading myself asleep, while the wench sat mending my breeches by my bedside.

20TH.   This day I hear that the Princess Royal has the smallpox.

21ST.   They told me that this is St. Thomas's, and that, by an old custom, this day the Exchequer men had formerly, and do intend this night, to have a supper; which, if I could, I promised to come to, but did not. To my Lady's and dined with her: but told me how dangerously ill the Princess Royal is: and that this morning she was said to be dead. But she hears that she hath married herself to young Jermyn, which is worse than the Duke of York's marrying the Chancellor's daughter, which is now publicly owned.

22ND.   Went to the Sun Tavern on Fish Street hill, to a dinner of Captain Teddiman's, where was my Lord Inchiquin (who seems to be a very fine person), Sir W. Pen, Captain Cuttance, and one Mr. Lawrence (a fine gentleman, now going to Algiers), and other good company, where we had a very fine dinner, good music, and a great deal of wine. I very merry. Went to bed: my head aching all night.

31ST.   In Paul's Churchyard I bought the play of *Henry the Fourth*, and so went to the new Theatre and saw it acted; but my expectation being too great, it did not please me, as otherwise I believe it would; and my having a book I believe did spoil it a little. That being done, I went to my Lord's, where I found him private at cards with my Lord Lauderdale and some persons of honour, my boy taking a cat home with him from my Lord's, which Sarah had given him for my wife, we being much troubled with mice. At Whitehall we inquiring for a coach, there was a Frenchman with one eye that was going my way, so he and I hired the coach between us, and he set me down in Fenchurch Street. Strange how the fellow, without asking, did tell me all what he was, and how he had run away from his father, and come into England to serve the King, and now going back again, etc.

1661

At the end of the last and the beginning of this year I do live in one of the houses belonging to the Navy Office, as one of the principal officers, and have done now about half-a-year; my family being myself, my wife, Jane, Will, Hewer, and Wayneman, my girl's brother. Myself in constant good health, and in a most handsome and thriving condition. Blessed be Almighty God for it! As to things of State— The King settled, and loved of all. The Duke of York matched to my Lord Chancellor's daughter, which do not please many. The Queen upon her return to France with the Princess Henrietta. The Princess of Orange lately dead, and we into new mourning for her. We have been lately frighted with a great plot, and many taken up on it, and the fright not quite over. The Parliament, which had done all this great good to the King, beginning to grow factious, the King did dissolve it December 29th last, and another likely to be chosen speedily. I take myself now to be worth £300 clear in money, and all my goods, and all manner of debts paid, which are none at all.

January 1661

JANUARY 1ST.   Comes in my brother Thomas, and after him my father, Dr. Thomas Pepys, my uncle Fenner and his two sons (Anthony's only child dying this morning, yet he was so civil to come, and was pretty merry) to breakfast; and I had for them a barrel of oysters, a dish of neat's tongues, and a dish of anchovies, wine of all sorts, and Northdown ale. We were very merry till about eleven o'clock, and then they went away. At noon I carried my wife by coach to my cousin Thomas Pepys, where we, with my father, Dr. Thomas, cousin Stradwick, Scott, and their wives dined. Here I saw first his second wife, which is a very respectful woman; but his dinner a sorry, poor dinner for a man of his estate, there being nothing but ordinary meat in it. To-day the King dined at a lord's two doors from us. Mr. Moore and I went to Mr. Pierce's; in our way seeing the Duke of York bring his Lady to-day to wait upon the Queen, the first time that ever she did since that business; and the Queen is said to receive her now with much respect and love; and there he cast up the fees, and I told the money, by the same token the £100 bag, after I had told it, fell all about the room, and I fear I have lost some of it. Supped with them and Mr. Pierce, the purser, and his wife and mine, where we had a calf's head carboned, but it was raw—we could not eat it—and a good hen. But she is such a slut that I do not love her victuals. . . .

7TH.   This morning news was brought to me to my bedside that there had been a great stir in the City this night by the Fanatics, who had been up and killed six or seven men, but all are fled. My Lord Mayor and the whole City had been in arms, about 40,000. Tom and I and my wife to the theatre, and there saw *The Silent Woman*. Among other things here, Kinaston, the boy, had the good turn to appear in three shapes: first, as a poor woman in ordinary clothes, to please Morose; then in fine clothes, as a gallant; and in them was clearly the prettiest woman in the whole house; and lastly, as a man; and then likewise did appear the handsomest man in the house.

9TH. Waked in the morning about six o'clock by people running up and down in Mr. Davis's house, talking that the Fanatics were up in arms in the City. And so I rose and went forth; where in the street I found everybody in arms at the doors. So I returned (though with no good courage at all, but that I might not seem to be afraid) and got my sword and pistol, which, however, I had no powder to charge; and went to the door, where I found Sir R. Ford, and with him I walked up and down as far as the Exchange, and there I left him. In our way the streets full of train-bands, and great stories what mischief these rogues have done; and I think near a dozen had been killed this morning on both sides. The shops shut, and all things in trouble. Home to my lute till late, and then to bed, there being strict guards all night in the city, though most of the enemies, they say, are killed or taken.

12TH. With Colonel Slingsby and a friend of his, Major Waters (a deaf and most amorous melancholy gentleman, who is under a despair in love, as the Colonel told me, which makes him bad company, though a most good-natured man), by water to Redriffe, and so on foot to Deptford. We fell to choosing four captains to command the guards, and choosing the place where to keep them, and other things in order thereunto. Never till now did I see the great authority of my place, all the captains of the fleet coming cap in hand to us. I went home with Mr. Davis, storekeeper (whose wife is ill, and so I could not see her), and was there most princelike lodged, with so much respect and honour, that I was at a loss how to behave myself.

19TH. To the Comptroller's, and with him by coach to Whitehall; in our way meeting Venner and Pritchard upon a sledge, who with two more Fifth-Monarchy men were hanged

to-day, and the two first drawn and quartered. Went to the theatre, where I saw *The Lost Lady*, which do not please me much. Here I was troubled to be seen by four of our office clerks, which sat in the half-crown box, and I in the 1s. 6d. From thence by link, and bought two mouse-traps of Thomas Pepys, the turner.

21ST. To Westminster Hall, to the Commissioners for paying off the Army and Navy, where the Duke of Albemarle was; and we sat with our hats on, and did discourse about paying off the ships, and do find that they do intend to undertake it without our help; and we are glad of it, for it is a work that will much displease the poor seamen, and so we are glad to have no hand in it. It is strange what weather we have had all this winter; no cold at all; but the ways are dusty, and the flies fly up and down, and the rose-bushes are full of leaves; such a time of the year as was never known in this world before here. This day many more of the Fifth-Monarchy men were hanged.

22ND. I met with Dr. Thomas Fuller; he tells me of his last and great book that is coming out: that is, the History of all the Families in England; and could tell me more of my own than I knew myself. And also to what perfection he hath now brought the art of memory; that he did lately to four eminently great scholars dictate together in Latin, upon different subjects of their proposing, faster than they were able to write, till they were tired; and that the best way of beginning a sentence, if a man should be out and forget his last sentence (which he never was), that then his last refuge is to begin with an "Utcunque."

29TH. To Mr. Turner's house, where the Comptroller, Sir William Batten, and Mr. Davis, and their ladies; and here we had a most neat little but costly and genteel supper. After that, a great deal of impertinent mirth by Mr. Davis, and some catches, and so broke up, and going away, Mr. Davis's eldest son took up my old Lady Slingsby in his arms, and carried her to the coach, and is said to be able to carry three of the biggest men that were in the company, which I wonder at.

February 1661

FEBRUARY 4TH.   To the tavern, where Sir William Pen, and the Comptroller, and several others were, men and women; and we had a very great and merry dinner; and after dinner the Comptroller began some sports, among others, the naming of people round, and afterwards demanding questions of them that they are forced to answer their names to, which do make very good sport. And here I took pleasure to take forfeits of the ladies who would not do their duty by kissing of them; among others a pretty lady, who I found afterwards to be wife to Sir William Batten's son. We sat late, talking with my Lady and others, and Dr. Whistler, who I found good company and a very ingenious man; so home and to bed.

10TH.   (Lord's day.) Took physic all day, and, God forgive me, did spend it in reading of some little French romances. At night my wife and I did please ourselves talking of our going into France, which I hope to effect this summer.

15TH.   Making up my accounts for my Lord tomorrow; and that being done, I found myself to be clear (as I think) £350 in the world, besides my goods in my house, and all things paid for.

18TH.   In the afternoon my wife and I and Mrs. Martha Batten, my Valentine, to the Exchange, and there upon a pair of embroidered and six pair of plain white gloves I laid out 40s. upon her. Then we went to a mercer's at the end of Lombard Street, and there she bought a suit of lutestring for herself; and so home. It is much talked that the King is already married to the niece of the Prince de Ligne, and that he hath two sons already by her; which I am sorry to hear; but yet am gladder that it should be so than that the Duke of York and his family should come to the Crown, he being a professed friend to the Catholics.

23RD.   To the playhouse, and there saw *The Changeling*, the first time it hath been acted these twenty years, and it takes exceedingly. Besides, I see the gallants do begin to be tired with the vanity and pride of the theatre actors, who are indeed grown very proud and rich. I also met with the Comptroller, who told me how it was easy for us all, the principal officers, and proper for us, to labour to get into the next Parliament; and would have me to ask the Duke's letter, but I shall not endeavour it. This is now 28 years that I am born. And blessed be God, in a state of full content, and a great hope to be a happy man in all respects, both to myself and friends.

JAMES BOSWELL

A Crisis in Identity

Introduction

The ancient philosopher certainly gave a wise counsel when he said, "Know thyself." For surely this knowledge is of all the most important. I might enlarge upon this. But grave and serious declamation is not what I intend at present. A man cannot know himself better than by attending to the feelings of his heart and to his external actions, from which he may with tolerable certainty judge "what manner of person he is." I have therefore determined to keep a daily journal in which I shall set down my various sentiments and my various conduct, which will be not only useful but very agreeable. It will give me a habit of application and im-

A CRISIS IN IDENTITY: From *Boswell's London Journal*, 1762–63, edited by F. A. Pottle. Copyright © 1950 by Yale University. Used by permission of McGraw-Hill Book Company.

prove me in expression; and knowing that I am to record my transactions will make me more careful to do well. Or if I should go wrong, it will assist me in resolutions of doing better. I shall here put down my thoughts on different subjects at different times, the whims that may seize me and the sallies of my luxuriant imagination. I shall mark the anecdotes and the stories that I hear, the instructive or amusing conversations that I am present at, and the various adventures that I may have.

I was observing to my friend Erskine that a plan of this kind was dangerous, as a man might in the openness of his heart say many things and discover many facts that might do him great harm if the journal should fall into the hands of my enemies. Against which there is no perfect security. "Indeed," said he, "I hope there is no danger at all; for I fancy you will not set down your robberies on the highway, or the murders that you commit. As to other things there can be no harm." I laughed heartily at my friend's observation, which was so far true. I shall be upon my guard to mention nothing that can do harm. Truth shall ever be observed, and these things (if there should be any such) that require the gloss of falsehood shall be passed by in silence. At the same time I may relate things under borrowed names with safety that would do much mischief if particularly known.

In this way I shall preserve many things that would otherwise be lost in oblivion. I shall find daily employment for myself, which will save me from indolence and help to keep off the spleen, and I shall lay up a store of entertainment for my after life. Very often we have more pleasure in reflecting on agreeable scenes that we have been in than we had from the scenes themselves. I shall regularly record the business or rather the pleasure of every day. I shall not study much correctness, lest the labour of it should make me lay it aside altogether. I hope it will be of use to my worthy friend Johnston, and that while he laments my personal absence, this journal may in some measure supply that defect and make him happy.

MONDAY 15 NOVEMBER. Elated with the thoughts of my journey to London, I got up. I called upon my friend Johnston, but found he was not come from the country, which vexed me a little, as I wished to bid him cordially adieu. However, I excused him to myself, and as Cairnie told me that people never took leave in France, I made the thing sit pretty easy. I had a long serious conversation with my father and mother. They were very kind to me. I felt parental affection was very strong towards me; and I felt a very warm filial regard for them. The scene of being a son setting out from home for the wide world and the idea of being my own master, pleased me much. I parted with my brother Davy, leaving him my best advices to be diligent at his business as a banker and to make rich and be happy....

FRIDAY 26 NOVEMBER. I waited on Lord Adam Gordon, who was very polite. I liked to see a Colonel of the Guards in his elegant house. I was much difficulted about lodgings. A variety I am sure I saw, I dare say fifty. I was amused in this way. At last I fixed in Downing Street, Westminster. I took a lodging up two pair of stairs with the use of a handsome parlour all the forenoon, for which I agreed to pay forty guineas a year, but I took it for a fortnight first, by way of a trial. I also made bargain that I should dine with the family whenever I pleased, at a shilling a time. My landlord was Mr. Terrie, chamber-keeper to the Office for Trade and Plantations. He was originally from the Shire of Moray. He had a wife but no children. The street was a genteel street, within a few steps of the Parade; near the House of Commons, and very healthful. I went to Mr. Cochrane, my banker, and received £25, my allowance every six weeks.

I then dined with Lord Eglinton. Lord Elibank was there, a man of great genius, great knowledge, and much whim, and Sir James Macdonald, a remarkable young man of good parts and great application. So that he knows a great deal. Also Sir Simeon Stuart, much of a gentleman. We had much ingenious talk. But

I am dull, and cannot recollect it. Before this I saw *The Witches*, a pantomime. I felt composed, serene, happy.

SATURDAY 27 NOVEMBER.   I walked into the City and ordered a remaining parcel of my *Cub* to be sent to Donaldson. I then breakfasted at Child's Coffee-house, read the political papers, and had some chat with citizens. On Sunday I had called at the Inner Temple for my old friend Temple, but did not find him. This day I called again. He was out of town. I longed to see him.

I then went to Lord Eglinton's. Finding him very obliging, I was glad to take the benefit of it. He carried me to Covent Garden in a coach and bid me wait in the Bedford Coffee-house till he sent for me. In a few minutes the famous Mr. Beard of Covent Garden Theatre came for me and carried me up a great many steps to a handsome room above the theatre, in which was met the Beefsteak Club, a society which has subsisted these thirty years. The room where it met was once burnt. The Gridiron (in Scotch, *brander*) was almost consumed, but a thin image of it remained entire. That they have fixed in the stucco in the roof. The president sits in a chair under a canopy, above which you have in golden letters, *Beef and Liberty*. We were entertained by the Club. Lord Sandwich was in the chair, a jolly, hearty, lively man. It was a very mixed society: Lord Eglinton, Mr. Beard, Colonel West of the Guards, Mr. Havard the actor, Mr. Churchill the poet, Mr. Wilkes the author of *The North Briton*, and many more. We had nothing to eat but beefsteaks, and had wine and punch in plenty and freedom. We had a number of songs.

Lord Eglinton and I talked a little privately. He imagined me much in the style that I was three years ago: raw, curious, volatile, credulous. He little knew the experience I had got and the notions and the composure that I had obtained by reflection. "My Lord," said I, "I am now a little wiser." "Not so much as you think," said he. "For, as a boy who has just learned the alphabet

when he begins to make out words thinks himself a great master of reading, so the little advance you have made in prudence appears very great, as it is so much before what you was formerly." I owned that there was some justice in what he said. And I hoped that a little diffidence would help to keep me safe. I told him I was sorry that my dedication without leave to the Duke of York had been ill-taken, and I insisted that he should make it up and bring us together, which he half-assented to.

My Lord's character is very particular. He is a man of uncommon genius for everything: strong good sense, great quickness of apprehension and liveliness of fancy, with a great deal of humour. He was neglected in his education, so that his knowledge from books is superficial. Yet he has picked up an infinite variety of knowledge from conversation. He has at the same time a flightiness, a reverie and absence of mind, with a disposition to downright trifling. Pope's lines may be applied to him:

With too much quickness ever to be taught;
With too much thinking to have common thought.

He is very selfish and deceitful, yet he has much good nature and affection. He now declared to me that he liked me as well as ever. And I believe he spoke truth. For I have such an opinion of myself as to imagine that nobody can be more agreeable company to him. Yet I kept aloof in some measure, and, finding myself too fond of him, I pulled the reins hard.

We parted at seven. I went to my lodging in Downing Street and put up my things, then went and saw the King and Queen pass from the Opera, and then saw the Guards drawn up in the court of the Palace while the moon shone and showed their splendour. I was all gentle felicity, and thought on an Edinburgh Saturday passed in a variety of amusing scenes. I had now got a genteel violet-coloured frock suit. I went home, sat a while with my landlord and landlady. They made too much work about me. I went to bed.

SUNDAY 28 NOVEMBER.   I breakfasted with

Mr. Douglas. I went to St. James's Church and heard service and a good sermon on "By what means shall a young man learn to order his ways," in which the advantages of early piety were well displayed. What a curious, inconsistent thing is the mind of man! In the midst of divine service I was laying plans for having women, and yet I had the most sincere feelings of religion. I imagine that my want of belief is the occasion of this, so that I can have all the feelings. I would try to make out a little consistency this way. I have a warm heart and a vivacious fancy. I am therefore given to love, and also to piety or gratitude to GOD, and to the most brilliant and showy method of public worship.

I then walked in the Park and went home to dinner, which was just a good joint of veal and a pudding. This they told me was their usual fare, which I approved of. I found my landlord rather too free. Therefore I carried myself with reserve and something of state.

At six I went to Mr. Sheridan's. He had been at Court and was splendidly dressed. He met me at the door with a cordial warmth. I felt a little out, as his plan for me of the Temple was changed. He is a man of great genius and understands propriety of speech better than anybody. But he is rather too much of an enthusiast in favour of his darling study. He has read much and seen much and is very good company. I was introduced to Mrs. Sheridan, a woman of very homely looks, but very sensible and very clever, as appears from her *Memoirs of Miss Sidney Bidulph*. I let myself appear by degrees, and I found that I was agreeable to her, which flattered me a good deal.

I asked for Mr. Samuel Johnson. Sheridan said he now could not bear him, because he had taken a pension of three hundred a year from the Court, by the particular interest of Lord Bute, and yet he still railed against the royal family and the Scots minister. I said I imagined he put it upon this: that the pension was not a *favour* but a reward *due* to his merit, and therefore he would show still the same principles of opposition freely and openly. "No, Sir," said he. "Johnson took it as a favour; waited on Lord Bute, said he could not find an English word to express what he felt, and was therefore obliged to have recourse to the French: 'I am *pénétré* with his Majesty's goodness.' This being the case, his business was to be silent; or, if called upon to give his opinion, to say, 'Gentlemen, my sentiments are just the same that they were. But an obligation forbids me to say much.'" It hurt me to find Sheridan abusing a man for whom I have heard him profess the greatest regard. He added, "The bearish manners of Johnson were insupportable without the idea of his having a good heart. But since he has been made the object of royal favour, his character has been sifted and is bad." I drank tea and coffee and was very well. I came home and went to bed. . . .

I thought my present lodgings too dear, and therefore looked about and found a place in Crown Street, Westminster, an obscure street but pretty lodgings at only £22 a year. Much did I ruminate with regard to lodgings. Sometimes I considered that a fine lodging denoted a man of great fashion, but then I thought that few people would see it and therefore the expense would be hid, whereas my business was to make as much show as I could with my small allowance. I thought that an elegant place to come home to was very agreeable and would inspire me with ideas of my own dignity; but then I thought it would be hard if I had not a proportionable show in other things, and that it was better to come gradually to a fine place than from a fine to a worse. I therefore resolved to take the Crown Street place, and told my present landlord that I intended to leave him. He told me that he was very sorry, and that he would allow me to make my own terms rather than quit his house; for he was in such circumstances that he was not obliged to let lodgings for bread, and that as I was extremely agreeable to the family, he begged I would stay, and he would let me have my three rooms for £30. I thanked him for his good opinion of me, but told him that economy at present was my object, although I was very happy in his house; and that I could not ask him to let me have three rooms in a genteel street as cheap as two in an obscure one. He paused a while and then told me that I should have them at the same price. He only begged that I would not mention it, as he certainly let them below value. I therefore struck a bargain and settled myself for a year.

I do think this a very strong proof of my being agreeable. For here was I, a perfect stranger to my landlord, who showed so great regard for me. I thought my seeking a lodging was like seeking a wife. Sometimes I aimed at one of two guineas a week, like a rich lady of quality. Sometimes at one guinea, like a knight's daughter; and at last fixed on £22 a year, like the daughter of a good gentleman of moderate fortune. Now when fixed, I felt very comfortable, having got rid of the inconstant roving disposition of a bachelor as to lodging. However, I hope my choice of a wife will be more elegant. I hope that shall not be in haste. When I strolled in high spirits through London, full of gay expectation, I considered how much happier I was than if I had been married last year to Miss Colquhoun or Miss Bruce, and been a poor regular animal tied down to one. I thanked Johnston for his kind advices.

WEDNESDAY 1 DECEMBER. The Duke of Queensberry was now come to town. I had called once or twice, but had never found him. Mrs. Douglas told me that Old Quant the porter would do nothing without the silver key. I therefore called today, and chatting a little with the surly dog, "Mr. Quant," said I, "I give you a great deal of trouble"; bowed and smiled, and put half a crown into his hand. He told me the Duke would be glad to see me next morning at nine.

On Tuesday I wanted to have a silver-hilted sword, but upon examining my pockets as I walked up the Strand, I found that I had left the most of my guineas at home and had not enough to pay for it with me. I determined to make a

trial of the civility of my fellow-creatures, and what effect my external appearance and address would have. I accordingly went to the shop of Mr. Jefferys, sword-cutter to his Majesty, looked at a number of his swords, and at last picked out a very handsome one at five guineas. "Mr. Jefferys," said I, "I have not money here to pay for it. Will you trust me?" "Upon my word Sir," said he, "you must excuse me. It is a thing we never do to a stranger." I bowed genteelly and said, "Indeed, Sir, I believe it is not right." However, I stood and looked at him, and he looked at me. "Come, Sir," cried he, "I will trust you." "Sir," said I, "if you had not trusted me, I should not have bought it from you." He asked my name and place of abode, which I told him. I then chose a belt, put the sword on, told him I would call and pay it tomorrow, and walked off. I called this day and paid him. "Mr. Jefferys," said I, "there is your money. You paid me a very great compliment. I am much obliged to you. But pray don't do such a thing again. It is dangerous." "Sir," said he, "we know our men. I would have trusted you with the value of a hundred pounds." This I think was a good adventure and much to my honour. . . .

This afternoon I was surprised with the arrival of Lady Betty Macfarlane, Lady Anne Erskine, Captain Erskine, and Miss Dempster, who were come to the Red Lion Inn at Charing Cross. It seems Lady Betty had written to the Laird that if he would not come down, she would come up; and upon his giving her an indolent answer, like a woman of spirit, she put her resolution in practice. I immediately went to them.

To tell the plain truth, I was vexed at their coming. For to see just the plain *hamely* Fife family hurt my grand ideas of London. Besides, I was now upon a plan of studying polite reserved behaviour, which is the only way to keep up dignity of character. And as I have a good share of pride, which I think is very proper and even noble, I am hurt with the taunts of ridicule and am unsatisfied if I do not feel myself something of a superior animal. This has always been my favourite idea in my best moments. Indeed, I have been obliged to deviate from it by a variety of circumstances. After my wild expedition to London in the year 1760, after I got rid of the load of serious reflection which then burthened me, by being always in Lord Eglinton's company, very fond of him, and much caressed by him, I became dissipated and thoughtless. When my father forced me down to Scotland, I was at first very low-spirited, although to appearance very high. I afterwards from my natural vivacity endeavoured to make myself easy; and like a man who takes to drinking to banish care, I threw myself loose as a heedless, dissipated, rattling fellow who might say or do every ridiculous thing. This made me sought after by everybody for the present hour, but I found myself a very inferior being; and I found many people presuming to treat me as such, which notwithstanding of my appearance of undiscerning gaiety, gave me much pain. I was, in short, a character very different from what GOD intended me and I myself chose. I remember my friend Johnston told me one day after my return from London that I had turned out different from what he imagined, as he thought I would resemble Mr. Addison. I laughed and threw out some loud sally of humour, but the observation struck deep. Indeed, I must do myself the justice to say that I always resolved to be such a man whenever my affairs were made easy and I got upon my own footing. For as I despaired of that, I endeavoured to lower my views and just to be a good-humoured comical being, well liked either as a waiter, a common soldier, a clerk in Jamaica, or some other odd out-of-the-way sphere. Now, when my father at last put me into an independent situation, I felt my mind regain its native dignity. I felt strong dispositions to be a Mr. Addison. Indeed, I had accustomed myself so much to laugh at everything that it required time to render my imagination solid and give me just notions of real life and of religion. But I hoped by degrees to attain to some degree of propriety. Mr. Addison's character in sentiment, mixed with a little of the gaiety of Sir Richard Steele and the manners of Mr. Digges, were the ideas which I aimed to realize.

Indeed, I must say that Digges has more or as much of the deportment of a man of fashion as anybody I ever saw; and he keeps up this so well that he never once lessened upon me even on an intimate acquaintance, although he is now and then somewhat melancholy, under which it is very difficult to preserve dignity; and this I think is particularly to be admired in Mr. Digges. Indeed, he and I never came to familiarity, which is justly said to beget contempt. The great art of living easy and happy in society is to study proper behaviour, and even with our most intimate friends to observe politeness; otherwise we will insensibly treat each other with a degree of rudeness, and each will find himself despised in some measure by the other. As I was therefore pursuing this laudable plan, I was vexed at the arrival of the Kellie family, with whom when in Scotland I had been in the greatest familiarity. Had they not come for a twelvemonth, I should have been somewhat established in my address, but as I had been but a fortnight from them, I could not without the appearance of strong affectation appear much different from what they had seen me. I accordingly was very free, but rather more silent, which they imputed to my dullness, and roasted me about London's not being agreeable to me. I bore it pretty well, and left them ....

FRIDAY 25 FEBRUARY. I continued in exceeding high spirits. Variety of fine cheering ideas glanced athwart my blest imagination, ideas which gave me exquisite sensations at the time but which are so very nice that they elude endeavours to paint them. A man of similar feelings with me may conceive them. The law scheme appeared in another light. I considered it as bringing me back to a situation that I had long a rooted aversion to. That my father might agree to let me be upon the footing of independence, but when he had me under his eye, he would not be able to keep to it. I considered that I would at once embark myself for all my life in a labyrinth of care, and that my mind would be harassed with vexation. That the notion of being of consequence was not much, for that just now I knew from experience that just by strength of imagination I could strut about and think myself as great as any man. That the Guards was a situation of life that had always appeared most enchanting to me, as I could in that way enjoy all the elegant pleasures of the gay world, and by living in the Metropolis and having plenty of time, could pursue what studies and follow what whims I pleased, get a variety of acquaintances of all kinds, get a number of romantic adventures, and thus have my satisfaction of life. That if a man who is born to a fortune cannot make himself easier and freer than those who are not, he gains nothing. That if I should suddenly relinquish my favourite schemes, I should deservedly be considered as a man of no stability but inconstant and wavering with every breath. I considered that at present I was not a fair judge of a question of so much importance; that by a long course of confinement and medicine my animal spirits were necessarily tamed and my relish for pleasure and amusement and whim evaporated. That the mere satisfaction of ease after a situation of pain and the happy prospect of a recovery of health had elevated me too much and made me imagine nothing too difficult for me to compass. That indeed I had laboured hard, but it had been in writing my journal, letters, and essays, which were all works chiefly of the imagination. But that I would find it very irksome to sit for hours hearing a heavy agent explain a heavy cause, and then to be obliged to remember and repeat distinctly the dull story, probably of some very trivial affair. I considered that when I should again go about and mix in the hurry and bustle of life and have my spirits agitated with a variety of brilliant scenes, this dull legal scheme would appear in its usual colours.

Such were my reasonings upon both sides of this question, which are, in my own opinion, very ingenious. It is strange to consider that the same man who could waver so much could produce them. I was somewhat uneasy at the consideration of my indetermined state of mind, which argues a degree of imbecility. I wished for some of my sincerely affectionate friends to whom I might unbosom myself, and whose kind counsel might relieve and direct me. I had much ado to keep myself from mentioning the thing to people who must laugh at me and had not my interest deeply at heart. However, I resolved to keep my own counsel, and I was sure it was a thing that nobody would suspect. I was anxious a little about my commission, and thought I should be disappointed in it and become peevish and turn a sort of misanthrope. But I summoned up more cheerful ideas and imagined that my noble Countess was pushing for me. At any rate, I determined to give it a year's run; and after that time I would be fully able to judge what to think of great people and what plan of life I should pursue....

FRIDAY 11 MARCH. Dempster took me into the House of Commons. The novelty of being in the High Court of Parliament which I had heard so much about pleased me exceedingly. My respect for it was greatly abated by seeing that it was such a tumultuous scene. Yet I felt an ambition to be a speaker there. I wish that may be the case. It must afford very high satisfaction to make a figure as an orator before an assembly of so much consequence. At night I was at Lady Northumberland's. She said that she had as yet only seen Lord Granby in public, but would not forget me. She spoke rather slightly, and I imagined she had no more thoughts of serving me. I was really depressed.

SATURDAY 12 MARCH. This was one of the blackest days that I ever passed. I was most miserably melancholy. I thought I would get no commission, and thought that a grievous misfortune, and that I was very ill used in life. I ruminated of hiding myself from the world. I thought of going to Spain and living there as a silent morose Don. Or of retiring to the sweeter climes of France and Italy. But then I considered that I wanted money. I then thought of having obscure lodgings, and actually looked up and down the bottom of Holborn and towards Fleet Ditch for an out-of-the-way place. How very absurd are such conceits! Yet they are common. When a man is out of humour, he thinks he will vex the world by keeping away from it, and that he will be greatly pitied; whereas in truth the world are too busy about themselves to think of him, and "out of sight, out of mind."

I again went to my good Child's, which gave me some comfort. I felt a warmth of heart to it after so long an absence. I then dined at Lord Eglinton's. Sir James and Lord Advocate were there. I was very dreary. I had lost all relish of London. I thought I saw the nothingness of all sublunary enjoyments. I was cold and spiritless.

I went to Lady Betty's. Lady Anne only was at home. She gave me some tea and we chatted gently. Then the rest came in. I valued them, as they were to go for Scotland on Monday. I stayed supper, after which we talked of death, of theft, robbery, murder, and ghosts. Lady Betty and Lady Anne declared seriously that at Allanbank they were disturbed two nights by something walking and groaning in the room, which they afterwards learnt was haunted. This was very strong. My mind was now filled with a real horror instead of an imaginary one. I shuddered with apprehension. I was frightened to go home. Honest Erskine made me go with him, and kindly gave the half of his bed, in which, though a very little one, we passed the silent watches in tranquillity.

SUNDAY 13 MARCH. I got up rather out of order. I am very easily disconcerted. I could never submit with patience to the inconveniences of a marching corps. The want of my own bed and my own nightcap, and being confined to stretch myself in a small space, hurt my cogitations. We went over to Lady Betty's immediately, and breakfast relieved me. As I was rather in bad frame, and as it was the last

day of the ladies' being in London, I stayed at home from church. Erskine and I took a walk to Covent Garden, and I carried him to Southampton Street and showed him the house in which I first paid my addresses to the Paphian Queen, where I first experienced the melting and transporting rites of Love. We then returned to dinner, after which the ladies went out, and the afternoon was passed round the fire by Macfarlane, myself, Erskine, and the Laird of Spottiswoode, a very curious exhibition. He is quite a *braid-Scots man*. His conversation was diverting from being so very unlike anything that I have heard for a good time. He is half-brother to Macfarlane, and they have a great similarity. They are both crammed with knowledge of families and places in Scotland, and have both a sort of greasy drollery. In the evening I walked early and quietly home, and felt a most comfortable degree of sensation upon getting into my neat warm bed and resigning myself to repose....

TUESDAY 2 AUGUST. I should have mentioned yesterday that I dined with Coutts, where we were very merry. Friday the fifth of this month was now fixed as the day of my departure. I had taken leave of Dr. Pringle, and had all my letters of recommendation and other things prepared. Mr. Johnson did me the honour to come and see me at my chambers this forenoon. Dempster too came in.

Johnson said that he always felt an inclination to do nothing. I said it was strange to think that the most indolent man in Britain had written the most laborious work, *The English Dictionary*. He said he took ten years to do it; but that if he had applied properly, he might have done it in three.

In the afternoon he carried me to drink tea with Miss Williams, who has a snug lodging in Bolt Court, Fleet Street. I found her a facetious, agreeable woman, though stone-blind. I was cheerful, and well received. He then carried me to what he called his walk, which is a paved long court overshadowed by some trees in a neighbouring garden. There he advised me when fixed in a place abroad to read with a keenness after knowledge, and to read every day an hour at Greek. And when I was moving about, to read diligently the great book of mankind. We supped at the Turk's Head. I was somewhat melancholy, but it went off. Mr. Johnson filled my mind with so many noble and just sentiments that the Demon of Despondency was driven away.

WEDNESDAY 3 AUGUST.   I should have mentioned that on Monday night, coming up the Strand, I was tapped on the shoulder by a fine fresh lass. I went home with her. She was an officer's daughter, and born at Gibraltar. I could not resist indulging myself with the enjoyment of her. Surely, in such a situation, when the woman is already abandoned, the crime must be alleviated, though in strict morality, illicit love is always wrong.

I last night sat up again, but I shall do so no more, for I was very stupid today and had a kind of feverish headache. At night Mr. Johnson and I supped at the Turk's Head. He talked much for restoring the Convocation of the Church of England to its full powers, and said that religion was much assisted and impressed on the mind by external pomp. My want of sleep sat heavy upon me, and made me like to nod, even in Mr. Johnson's company. Such must be the case while we are united with flesh and blood.

THURSDAY 4 AUGUST.   This is now my last day in London before I set out upon my travels, and makes a very important period in my journal. Let me recollect my life since this journal began. Has it not passed like a dream? Yes, but I have been attaining a knowledge of the world. I came to town to go into the Guards. How different is my scheme now! I am now upon a less pleasurable but a more rational and lasting plan. Let me pursue it with steadiness and I may be a man of dignity. My mind is strangely agitated. I am happy to think of going upon my travels and seeing the diversity

of foreign parts; and yet my feeble mind shrinks somewhat at the idea of leaving Britain in so very short a time from the moment in which I now make this remark. How strange must I feel myself in foreign parts. My mind too is gloomy and dejected at the thoughts of leaving London, where I am so comfortably situated and where I have enjoyed most happiness. However, I shall be the happier for being abroad, as long as I live. Let me be manly. Let me commit myself to the care of my merciful Creator.

THE END OF MY JOURNAL BEFORE MY TRAVELS.

DOROTHY WORDSWORTH

An Episode of Daffodils

[MARCH 23RD,] TUESDAY.   A mild morning. William worked at *The Cuckow* poem. I sewed beside him. After dinner he slept, I read German, and, at the closing-in of day, went to sit in the orchard—he came to me, and walked backwards and forwards. We talked about C. Wm. repeated the poem to me. I left him there, and in 20 minutes he came in, rather tired with attempting to write. He is now reading Ben Jonson. I am going to read German. It is about 10 o'clock, a quiet night. The fire flutters, and the watch ticks. I hear nothing else save the breathing of my Beloved, and he now and then pushes his book forward, and turns over a leaf. Fletcher is not come home. No letter from C.

[MARCH 24TH,] WEDNESDAY.   We walked to Rydale for letters. It was a beautiful spring morning—warm, and quiet with mists. We found a letter from M. H. I made a vow that

AN EPISODE OF DAFFODILS: From *Journals of Dorothy Wordsworth*, edited by Helen Darbishire, published by Oxford University Press. Reprinted by their permission.

we would not leave this country for G. Hill— Sara and Tom not being going to the Wolds. I wrote to Mary in the evening. I went to bed after dinner. William walked out and wrote [to] Peggy Ashburner—I rose better. Wm. altered *The Butterfly* as we came from Rydale.

[MARCH 25TH,] THURSDAY. We did not walk though it was a fine day—[? old] Mrs. Simpson drank tea with us. No letter from Coleridge.

[MARCH 26TH,] FRIDAY. A beautiful morning. William wrote to Annette, then worked at *The Cuckow*. I was ill and in bad spirits—After dinner I sate 2 hours in the orchard. William and I walked together after tea, first to the top of White Moss, then to Mr. Olliff's. I left Wm. and while he was absent wrote out poems. I grew alarmed, and went to seek him—I met him at Mr. Olliff's. He has been trying, without success, to alter a passage—in *Silver How* poem. He had written a conclusion just before he went out. While I was getting into bed, he wrote *The Rainbow*.

[MARCH 27TH,] SATURDAY. A divine morning. At breakfast William wrote part of an ode. Mr. Olliff sent the dung and Wm. went to work in the garden. We sate all day in the orchard.

[MARCH 28TH,] SUNDAY. We went to Keswick. Arrived wet to skin. A letter from Mary. C. was not tired with walking to meet us. I lay down after dinner with a bad headach.

[MARCH 29TH,] MONDAY. A cold day. I went down to Miss Crosthwaite's to unpack the box— Wm. and C. went to Armathwaite—a letter from S. H.—had headach, I lay till after tea. Conversation with Mrs. Coleridge.

MARCH 30TH, TUESDAY. We went to Calvert's. I was somewhat better though not well.

MARCH 31ST, WEDNESDAY. Very unwell. We walked to Portinscale, lay upon the turf, and saw into the Vale of Newlands up to Borrowdale, and down to Keswick—a soft Venetian view. I returned better. Calvert and Wilkinsons dined

with us. I walked with Mrs. W. to the Quaker's meeting, met Wm., and we walked in the field together.

APRIL 1ST, THURSDAY. Mrs. C., Wm., C. and I went to the How—a pleasant morning. We came home by Portinscale—sate for some time on the hill.

[APRIL] 2ND, FRIDAY. Wm. and I sate all the morning in the field. I nursed Derwent. Drank tea with the Miss Cockins.

[APRIL] 3RD, SATURDAY. Wm. went on to Skiddaw with C. We dined at Calvert's. Fine day.

[APRIL] 4TH, SUNDAY. We drove in the gig to Water End—I walked down to Coleridge's. Mrs. C. came to Greta Bank to tea. Wm. walked down with Mrs. C. I repeated his verses to them. We sate pleasantly enough after supper.

[APRIL] 5TH, MONDAY. We came to Eusemere. Coleridge walked with us to Threlkeld— reached Eusemere to tea. The schoolmistress at Dacre and her scholars. Mrs. C. at work in the garden—she met us.

APRIL 6TH, TUESDAY. Mrs. C., Wm. and I walked to Waterside. Wm. and I walked together in the evening towards Dalemain—the moon and stars.

[APRIL] 7TH, WEDNESDAY. Wm.'s birthday. Wm. went to Middleham. I walked 6 miles with him. It rained a little, but a fine day. Broth to supper, and went soon to bed.

[APRIL] 8TH, THURSDAY. Mrs. C. and I walked to Woodside. We slept after dinner on the sofa—sate up till $\frac{1}{2}$ past 10. Mrs. C. tired. I wrote to M. H. in the morning, to Sara in the evening.

[APRIL] 9TH, FRIDAY. Mrs. C. planting. Sent off letters. A windy morning—rough lake—sun shines—very cold—a windy night. Walked in Dunmallet, marked our names on a tree.

[APRIL] 10TH, SATURDAY. Very cold—a stormy night, wrote to C. A letter from Wm. and S. H.

[APRIL] 11TH, SUNDAY. Very stormy and cold. I did not walk.

[APRIL] 12TH, MONDAY. Had the mantua-maker. The ground covered with snow. Walked to T. Wilkinson's and sent for letters. The woman brought me one from William and Mary. It was a sharp, windy night. Thomas Wilkinson came with me to Barton, and questioned me like a catechizer all the way. Every question was like the snapping of a little thread about my heart— I was so full of thought of my half-read letter and other things. I was glad when he left me. Then I had time to look at the moon while I was thinking over my own thoughts. The moon travelled through the clouds, tinging them yellow as she passed along, with two stars near her, one larger than the other. These stars grew or diminished as they passed from, or went into, the clouds. At this time William, as I found the next day, was riding by himself between Middleham and Barnard Castle, having parted from Mary. I read over my letter when I got to the house. Mr. and Mrs. C. were playing at cards.

APRIL 13TH, TUESDAY. I had slept ill and was not well and obliged to go to bed in the afternoon—Mrs. C. waked me from sleep with a letter from Coleridge. After tea I went down to see the bank and walked along the Lakeside to the field where Mr. Smith thought of building his house. The air was become still, the lake was of a bright slate colour, the hills darkening. The bays shot into the low fading shores. Sheep resting. All things quiet. When I returned Jane met me—*William* was come. The surprise shot through me. He looked well, but he was tired and went soon to bed after a dish of tea.

APRIL 14TH, WEDNESDAY. William did not rise till dinner time. I walked with Mrs. C. I was ill, out of spirits, disheartened. Wm. and I took a long walk in the rain.

[APRIL] 15TH, THURSDAY. It was a threatening, misty morning, but mild. We set off after dinner from Eusemere. Mrs. Clarkson went a short way with us, but turned back. The wind was furious, and we thought we must have returned. We first rested in the large boat-house, then under a furze bush opposite Mr. Clarkson's. Saw the plough going in the field. The wind seized our breath. The Lake was rough. There was a boat by itself floating in the middle of the bay below Water Millock. We rested again in the Water Millock Lane. The hawthorns are black and green, the birches here and there greenish, but there is yet more of purple to be seen on the twigs. We got over into a field to avoid some cows—people working. A few primroses by the roadside—woodsorrel flower, the anemone, scentless violets, strawberries, and that starry, yellow flower which Mrs. C. calls pile wort. When we were in the woods beyond Gowbarrow Park we saw a few daffodils close to the water-side. We fancied that the lake had floated the seeds ashore, and that the little colony had so sprung up. But as we went along there were more and yet more; and at last, under the boughs of the trees, we saw that there was a long belt of them along the shore, about the breadth of a country turnpike road. I never saw daffodils so beautiful. They grew among the mossy stones about and about them; some rested their heads upon these stones as on a pillow for weariness; and the rest tossed and reeled and danced, and seemed as if they verily laughed with the wind, that blew upon them over the lake; they looked so gay, ever glancing, ever changing. This wind blew directly over the lake to them. There was here and there a little knot, and a few stragglers a few yards higher up; but they were so few as not to disturb the simplicity, unity, and life of that one busy highway. We rested again and again. The bays were stormy, and we heard the waves at different distances, and in the middle of the water, like the sea. Rain came on—we were wet when we reached Luff's, but we called in. Luckily all was chearless and gloomy, so we faced the storm—we *must* have been wet if we had waited —put on dry clothes at Dobson's. I was very kindly treated by a young woman, the landlady looked sour, but it is her way. She gave us a goodish supper, excellent ham and potatoes. We paid 7/- when we came away. William was sitting by a bright fire when I came downstairs. He soon made his way to the library, piled up in a corner of the window. He brought out a volume of Enfield's *Speaker*, another miscellany, and an odd volume of Congreve's plays. We had a glass of warm rum and water. We enjoyed ourselves, and wished for Mary. It rained and blew, when we went to bed. N. B. Deer in Gowbarrow Park like skeletons.

ANNE FRANK

The Two Annes

Saturday, 20th June, 1942

I haven't written for a few days, because I wanted first of all to think about my diary. It's an odd idea for someone like me to keep a diary; not only because I have never done so before, but because it seems to me that neither I—nor for that matter anyone else—will be interested in the unbosomings of a thirteen-year-old schoolgirl. Still, what does that matter? I want to write, but more than that, I want to bring out all kinds of things that lie buried deep in my heart.

There is a saying that "paper is more patient than man"; it came back to me on one of my slightly melancholy days, while I sat chin in hand, feeling too bored and limp even to make up my mind whether to go out or stay at home. Yes, there is no doubt that paper is patient and

as I don't intend to show this cardboard-covered notebook, bearing the proud name of "diary," to anyone, unless I find a real friend, boy or girl, probably nobody cares. And now I come to the root of the matter, the reason for my starting a diary: it is that I have no such real friend.

Let me put it more clearly, since no one will believe that a girl of thirteen feels herself quite alone in the world, nor is it so. I have darling parents and a sister of sixteen. I know about thirty people whom one might call friends—I have strings of boy friends, anxious to catch a glimpse of me and who, failing that, peep at me through mirrors in class. I have relations, aunts and uncles, who are darlings too, a good home, no—I don't seem to lack anything. But it's the same with all my friends, just fun and games, nothing more. I can never bring myself to talk of anything outside the common round. We don't seem to be able to get any closer, that is the root of the trouble. Perhaps I lack confidence, but anyway, there it is, a stubborn fact and I don't seem to be able to do anything about it.

Hence, this diary. In order to enhance in my mind's eye the picture of the friend for whom I have waited so long, I don't want to set down a series of bald facts in a diary like most people do, but I want this diary itself to be my friend, and I shall call my friend Kitty. No one will grasp what I'm talking about if I begin my letters to Kitty just out of the blue, so, albeit unwillingly, I will start by sketching in brief the story of my life.

My father was 36 when he married my mother, who was then 25. My sister Margot was born in 1926 in Frankfort-on-Main. I followed on 12th June, 1929, and, as we are Jewish, we emigrated to Holland in 1933, where my father was appointed Managing Director of Travies N.V. This firm is in close relationship with the firm of Kolen & Co. in the same building, of which my father is a partner.

The rest of our family, however, felt the full impact of Hitler's anti-Jewish laws, so life was filled with anxiety. In 1938 after the pogroms, my two uncles (my mother's brothers) escaped to the U.S.A. My old grandmother came to us, she was then 73. After May, 1940, good times rapidly fled: first the war, then the capitulation, followed by the arrival of the Germans. That is when the sufferings of us Jews really began. Anti-Jewish decrees followed each other in quick succession. Jews must wear a yellow star, Jews must hand in their bicycles, Jews are banned from trams and are forbidden to drive. Jews are only allowed to do their shopping between three and five o'clock and then only in shops which bear the placard "Jewish shop." Jews must be indoors by eight o'clock and cannot even sit in their own gardens after that hour. Jews are forbidden to visit theatres, cinemas, and other places of entertainment. Jews may not take part in public sports. Swimming baths, tennis courts, hockey fields, and other sports grounds are all prohibited to them. Jews may not visit Christians. Jews must go to Jewish schools, and many more restrictions of a similar kind.

So we could not do this and were forbidden to do that. But life went on in spite of it all. Jopie used to say to me: "You're scared to do anything, because it may be forbidden." Our freedom was strictly limited. Yet things were still bearable.

Granny died in January, 1942; no one will ever know how much she is present in my thoughts and how much I love her still.

In 1934 I went to school at the Montessori Kindergarten and continued there. It was at the end of the school year, I was in form 6B, when I had to say good-bye to Mrs. K. We both wept, it was very sad. In 1941 I went, with my sister Margot, to the Jewish Secondary School, she into the fourth form and I into the first.

So far everything is all right with the four of us and here I come to the present day.

Saturday, 7th November, 1942

Dear Kitty,

Mummy is frightfully irritable and that always seems to herald unpleasantness for me.

Is it just chance that Daddy and Mummy never rebuke Margot and that they always drop on me for everything? Yesterday evening, for instance: Margot was reading a book with lovely drawings in it; she got up and went upstairs, put the book down ready to go on with it later. I wasn't doing anything, so picked up the book and started looking at the pictures. Margot came back, saw "her" book in my hands, wrinkled her forehead and asked for the book back. Just because I wanted to look a little farther on, Margot got more and more angry. Then Mummy joined in: "Give the book to Margot; she was reading it," she said. Daddy came into the room. He didn't even know what it was all about, but saw the injured look on Margot's face and promptly dropped on me: "I'd like to see what you'd say if Margot ever started looking at one of your books!" I gave way at once, laid the book down and left the room—offended, as they thought. It so happened I was neither offended nor cross, just miserable. It wasn't right of Daddy to judge without knowing what the squabble was about. I would have given Margot the book myself, and much more quickly, if Mummy and Daddy hadn't interfered. They took Margot's part at once, as though she were the victim of some great injustice.

It's obvious that Mummy would stick up for Margot; she and Margot always do back each other up. I'm so used to that that I'm utterly indifferent to both Mummy's jawing and Margot's moods.

I love them; but only because they are Mummy and Margot. With Daddy it's different. If he holds Margot up as an example, approves of what she does, praises and caresses her, then something gnaws at me inside, because I adore Daddy. He is the one I look up to. I don't love anyone in the world but him. He doesn't notice that he treats Margot differently from me. Now Margot is just the prettiest, sweetest, most beautiful girl in the world. But all the same I feel I have some right to be taken seriously too. I have always been the dunce, the ne'er-do-well of the family, I've always had to pay double for my deeds, first with the scolding and then again because of the way my feelings are hurt. Now I'm not satisfied with this apparent favouritism any more. I want something from Daddy that he is not able to give me.

I'm not jealous of Margot, never have been. I don't envy her good looks or her beauty. It is only that I long for Daddy's real love: not only as his child, but for me—Anne, myself.

I cling to Daddy because it is only through him that I am able to retain a remnant of family feeling. Daddy doesn't understand that I need to give vent to my feelings over Mummy sometimes. He doesn't want to talk about it; he simply avoids anything which might lead to remarks about Mummy's failings. Just the same Mummy, and her failings, are something I find harder to bear than anything else. I don't know how to keep it all to myself. I can't always be drawing attention to her untidiness, her sarcasm, and her lack of sweetness, neither can I believe that I'm always in the wrong.

We are exact opposites in everything; so naturally we are bound to run up against each other. I don't pronounce judgment on Mummy's character, for that is something I can't judge. I only look at her as a mother, and she just doesn't succeed in being that to me; I have to be my own mother. I've drawn myself apart from them all; I am my own skipper and later on I shall see where I come to land. All this comes about particularly because I have in my mind's eye an image of what a perfect mother and wife should be; and in her whom I must call "Mother" I find no trace of that image.

I am always making resolutions not to notice Mummy's bad example, I want to see only the good side of her and to seek in myself what I cannot find in her. But it doesn't work; and the worst of it is that neither Daddy nor Mummy understands this gap in my life, and I blame them for it. I wonder if anyone can ever succeed in making their children absolutely content.

Sometimes I believe that God wants to try me, both now and later on; I must become good through my own efforts, without examples and without good advice. Then later on I shall be all the stronger.

Who besides myself will ever read these letters? From whom but myself shall I get comfort? I need comforting often, as I so frequently feel weak and dissatisfied with myself; my shortcomings are too great. I know this, and every day I try to improve myself, again and again.

My treatment varies so much. One day Anne is so sensible and is allowed to know everything; and the next day I hear that Anne is just a silly little goat who doesn't know anything at all and imagines that she's learnt a wonderful lot from books. I'm not a baby or a spoilt darling any more, to be laughed at, whatever she does. I have my own views, plans and ideas, though I can't put them into words yet. Oh, so many things bubble up inside me as I lie in bed, having to put up with people I'm fed up with, who always misinterpret my intentions. That's why in the end I always come back to my diary. That is where I start and finish, because Kitty is always patient. I'll promise her that I shall persevere, in spite of everything, and find my own way through it all, and swallow my tears. I only wish I could see the results already or occasionally receive encouragement from someone who loves me.

Don't condemn me; remember rather that sometimes I too can reach bursting-point.

Yours, ANNE

Thursday, 19th November, 1942

Dear Kitty,

Dussel is a very nice man, just as we had all imagined. Of course he thought it was all right to share my little room.

Quite honestly I'm not so keen that a stranger should use my things, but one must be prepared to make some sacrifices for a good cause, so I shall make my little offering with a good will.

"If we can save someone, then everything else is of secondary importance," says Daddy, and he's absolutely right.

The first day that Dussel was here, he immediately asked me all sorts of questions: When does the charwoman come? When can one use the bathroom? When is one allowed to use the lavatory? You may laugh, but these things are not so simple in a hiding-place. During the day we mustn't make any noise that might be heard downstairs; and if there is some stranger—such as the charwoman for example—then we have to be extra careful. I explained all this carefully to Dussel. But one thing amazed me: he is very slow in the uptake. He asks everything twice over and still doesn't seem to remember. Perhaps that will wear off in time, and it's only that he's thoroughly upset by the sudden change.

Apart from that, all goes well. Dussel has told us a lot about the outside world, which we have missed for so long now. He had very sad news. Countless friends and acquaintances have gone to a terrible fate. Evening after evening the green and grey army lorries trundle past. The Germans ring at every front door to inquire if there are any Jews living in the house. If there are, then the whole family has to go at once. If they don't find any, they go on to the next house. No one has a chance of evading them unless one goes into hiding. Often they go round with lists, and only ring when they know they can get a good haul. Sometimes they let them off for cash—so much per head. It seems like the slave hunts of olden times. But it's certainly no joke; it's much too tragic for that. In the evenings when it's dark, I often see rows of good, innocent people accompanied by crying children, walking on and on, in charge of a couple of these chaps, bullied and knocked about until they almost drop. No one is spared—old people, babies, expectant mothers, the sick—each and all join in the march of death.

How fortunate we are here, so well cared for and undisturbed. We wouldn't have to worry about all this misery were it not that we are so anxious about all those dear to us whom we can no longer help.

I feel wicked sleeping in a warm bed, while my dearest friends have been knocked down or have fallen into a gutter somewhere out in the cold night. I get frightened when I think of close friends who have now been delivered into the hands of the cruellest brutes that walk the earth. And all because they are Jews!

Yours, ANNE

Friday, 20th November, 1942

Dear Kitty,
  None of us really knows how to take it all. The news about the Jews had not really penetrated through to us until now, and we thought it best to remain as cheerful as possible. Every now and then, when Miep lets out something about what has happened to a friend, Mummy and Mrs. Van Daan always begin to cry, so Miep thinks it better not to tell us any more. But Dussel was immediately plied with questions from all sides, and the stories he told us were so gruesome and dreadful that one can't get them out of one's mind.

Yet we shall still have our jokes and tease each other, when these horrors have faded a bit in our minds. It won't do us any good, or help those outside, to go on being as gloomy as we are at the moment. And what would be the object of making our "Secret Annexe" into a "Secret Annexe of Gloom"? Must I keep thinking about those other people, whatever I am doing? And if I want to laugh about something, should I stop myself quickly and feel ashamed that I am cheerful? Ought I then to cry the whole day long? No, that I can't do. Besides, in time this gloom will wear off.

Added to this misery there is another, but of a purely personal kind; and it pales into insignificance beside all the wretchedness I've just told you about. Still, I can't refrain from telling you that lately I have begun to feel deserted. I am surrounded by too great a void. I never used to feel like this, my fun and amusements, and my girl friends completely filled my thoughts. Now I either think about unhappy things, or about myself. And at long last I have made the discovery that Daddy, although he's such a darling, still cannot take the place of my entire little world of bygone days. But why do I bother you with such foolish things? I'm very ungrateful, Kitty; I know that. But it often makes my head swim if I'm jumped upon too much, and then on top of that have to think about all those other miseries!

Yours, ANNE

Saturday, 28h November, 1942

Dear Kitty,

We have used too much electricity, more than our ration. Result: the utmost economy and the prospect of having it cut off. No light for a fortnight; a pleasant thought, that, but who knows, perhaps it won't happen after all! It's too dark to read in the afternoons after four or half past. We pass the time in all sorts of crazy ways: asking riddles, physical training in the dark, talking English and French, criticising books. But it all begins to pall in the end. Yesterday evening I discovered something new: to peer through a powerful pair of field-glasses into the lighted rooms of the houses at the back. In the daytime we can't allow even as much as a centimetre's chink to appear between our curtains, but it can't do any harm after dark. I never knew before that neighbours could be such interesting people. At any rate, ours are. I found one couple having a meal, one family was in the act of taking a cine-film; and the dentist opposite was just attending to an old lady, who was awfully scared.

It was always said about Mr. Dussel that he could get on wonderfully with children and that he loved them all. Now, he shows himself in his true colours: a stodgy, old-fashioned disciplin-arian, and preacher of long-drawn-out sermons on manners.

As I have the unusual good fortune (!) to share my bedroom—alas, a small one—with His Lordship, and as I'm generally considered to be the most badly behaved of the three young people, I have a lot to put up with and have to pretend to be deaf in order to escape the old, much repeated tickings-off and warnings. All this wouldn't be too bad, if he wasn't such a frightful sneak and he didn't pick on Mummy of all people to sneak to every time. When I've already just had a dose from him, Mummy goes over it all again, so I get a gale aft as well as forward. Then, if I'm really lucky, I'm called on to give an account of myself to Mrs. Van Daan and then I get a veritable hurricane!

Honestly, you needn't think it's easy to be the "badly brought-up" central figure of a hyper-critical family in hiding. When I lie in bed at night and think over the many sins and short-comings attributed to me, I get so confused by it all that I either laugh or cry: it depends what sort of mood I am in.

Then I fall asleep with a stupid feeling of wishing to be different from what I am or from what I want to be; perhaps to behave differently from the way I want to behave, or do behave. Oh, heavens above, now I'm getting you in a muddle too. Forgive me, but I don't like crossing things out, and in these days of paper shortage we are not allowed to throw paper away. Therefore I can only advise you not to read the last sentence again, and certainly not to try to understand it, because you won't succeed anyhow!

Yours, ANNE

Wednesday, 13th January, 1943

Dear Kitty,

Everything has upset me again this morning, so I wasn't able to finish a single thing properly.

It is terrible outside. Day and night more

of those poor miserable people are being dragged off, with nothing but a rucksack and a little money. On the way they are deprived even of these possessions. Families are torn apart, the men, women and children all being separated. Children coming home from school find that their parents have disappeared. Women return from shopping to find their homes shut up and their families gone.

The Dutch people are anxious too, their sons are being sent to Germany. Everyone is afraid.

And every night hundreds of 'planes fly over Holland and go to German towns, where the earth is ploughed up by their bombs, and every hour hundreds and thousands of people are killed in Russia and Africa. No one is able to keep out of it, the whole globe is waging war and although it is going better for the Allies, the end is not yet in sight.

And as for us, we are fortunate. Yes, we are luckier than millions of people. It is quiet and safe here, and we are, so to speak, living on capital. We are even so selfish as to talk about "after the war," brighten up at the thought of having new clothes and new shoes, whereas we really ought to save every penny, to help other people, and save what is left from the wreckage after the war.

The children here run about in just a thin blouse and clogs; no coat, no hat, no stockings, and no one helps them. Their tummies are empty, they chew an old carrot to stay the pangs, go from their cold homes out into the cold street and, when they get to school, find themselves in an even colder classroom. Yes, it has even got so bad in Holland that countless children stop the passers-by and beg for a piece of bread. I could go on for hours about all the suffering the war has brought, but then I would only make myself more dejected. There is nothing we can do but wait as calmly as we can till the misery comes to an end. Jews and Christians wait, the whole earth waits; and there are many who wait for death.

Yours, ANNE

Saturday, 30th January, 1943

Dear Kitty,

I'm boiling with rage, and yet I mustn't show it. I'd like to stamp my feet, scream, give Mummy a good shaking, cry, and I don't know what else, because of the horrible words, mocking looks and accusations which are levelled at me repeatedly every day, and find their mark, like shafts from a tightly strung bow, and which are just as hard to draw from my body.

I would like to shout to Margot, Van Daan, Dussel—and Daddy too—"Leave me in peace, let me sleep one night at least without my pillow being wet with tears, my eyes burning and my head throbbing. Let me get away from it all, preferably away from the world!" But I can't do that, they mustn't know my despair, I can't let them see the wounds which they have caused, I couldn't bear their sympathy and their kind-hearted jokes, it would only make me want to scream all the more. If I talk, everyone thinks I'm showing off; when I'm silent they think I'm ridiculous; rude if I answer, sly if I get a good idea, lazy if I'm tired, selfish if I eat a mouthful more than I should, stupid, cowardly, crafty, etc. etc. The whole day long I hear nothing else but that I am an insufferable baby, and although I laugh about it and pretend not to take any notice, I *do* mind. I would like to ask God to give me a different nature, so that I didn't put everyone's back up. But that can't be done. I've got the nature that has been given to me and I'm sure it can't be bad. I do my very best to please everybody, far more than they'd ever guess. I try to laugh it all off, because I don't want to let them see my trouble. More than once, after a whole string of undeserved rebukes, I have flared up at Mummy: "I don't care what you say anyhow. Leave me alone: I'm a hopeless case anyway." Naturally, I was then told I was rude and was virtually ignored for two days; and then, all at once, it was quite forgotten, and I was treated like everyone else again. It is impossible for me to be all sugar one day and spit venom the next. I'd rather choose the golden mean (which is not so golden), keep my thoughts to myself and try for *once* to be just as disdainful to them as they are to me. Oh, if only I could!

Yours, ANNE

Saturday, 4th March, 1944

Dear Kitty,

This is the first Saturday for months and months that hasn't been boring, dreary and dull. And Peter is the cause.

This morning I went to the attic to hang up my apron, when Daddy asked whether I'd like to stay and talk some French. I agreed. First we talked French, and I explained something to Peter; then we did some English. Daddy read out loud to us from Dickens and I was in the seventh heaven, because I sat on Daddy's chair very close to Peter.

I went downstairs at eleven o'clock. When I came upstairs again at half-past eleven, he was already waiting for me on the stairs. We talked until a quarter to one. If, as I leave the room, he gets a chance after a meal, for instance, and if no one can hear, he says: "Good-bye, Anne, see you soon."

Oh, I am so pleased! I wonder if he is going to fall in love with me after all? Anyway, he is a very nice fellow and no one knows what lovely talks I have with him!

Mrs. Van Daan quite approves when I go and talk to him, but she asked today teasingly, "Can I really trust you two up there together?"

"Of course," I protested. "Really, you quite insult me!"

From morn till night I look forward to seeing Peter.

Yours, ANNE

Monday, 6th March, 1944

Dear Kitty,

I can tell by Peter's face that he thinks just as much as I do, and when Mrs. Van Daan yester-day evening said scoffingly, "The thinker!" I was irritated. Peter flushed and looked very embarrassed, and I was about to explode.

Why can't these people keep their mouths shut?

You can't imagine how horrible it is to stand by and see how lonely he is and yet not be able to do anything. I can so well imagine, just as if I were in his place, how desperate he must feel sometimes in quarrels and in love. Poor Peter, he needs love very much!

When he said he didn't need any friends how harsh the words sounded to my ears. Oh, how mistaken he is! I don't believe he meant it a bit.

He clings to his solitude, to his affected indifference and his grown-up ways, but it's just an act, so as never, never to show his real feelings. Poor Peter, how long will he be able to go on playing this rôle? Surely a terrible outburst must follow as the result of this superhuman effort?

Oh, Peter, if only I could help you, if only you would let me! Together we could drive away your loneliness and mine!

I think a lot, but I don't say much. I am happy if I see him and if the sun shines when I'm with him. I was very excited yesterday; while I was washing my hair, I knew that he was sitting in the room next to ours. I couldn't do anything about it; the more quiet and serious I feel inside, the more noisy I become outwardly.

Who will be the first to discover and break through this armour? I'm glad after all that the Van Daans have a son and not a daughter, my conquest could never have been so difficult, so beautiful, so good, if I had not happened to hit on someone of the opposite sex.

Yours, ANNE

P.S.—You know that I'm always honest with you, so I must tell you that I actually live from one meeting to the next. I keep hoping to discover that he too is waiting for me all the time and I'm thrilled if I notice a small shy advance from his side. I believe he'd like to say a lot just like I would; little does he know that it's just his clumsiness that attracts me.

Yours, ANNE

Tuesday, 7th March, 1944

Dear Kitty,

If I think now of my life in 1942, it all seems so unreal. It was quite a different Anne who enjoyed that heavenly existence to the Anne who has grown wise within these walls. Yes, it was a heavenly life. Boy friends at every turn, about twenty friends and acquaintances of my own age, the darling of nearly all the teachers, spoilt from top to toe by Mummy and Daddy, lots of sweets, enough pocket money, what more could one want?

You will certainly wonder by what means I got round all these people. Peter's word "attractiveness" is not altogether true. All the teachers were entertained by my cute answers, my amusing remarks, my smiling face, and my questioning looks. That is all I was—a terrible flirt, coquettish and amusing. I had one or two advantages, which kept me rather in favour. I was industrious, honest and frank. I would never have dreamt of cribbing from anyone else. I shared my sweets generously, and I wasn't conceited.

Wouldn't I have become rather forward with so much admiration? It was a good thing that in the midst of, at the height of, all this gaiety, I suddenly had to face reality, and it took me at least a year to get used to the fact that there was no more admiration forthcoming.

How did I appear at school? As one who thought of new jokes and pranks, always "king of the castle," never in a bad mood, never a cry-baby. No wonder everyone cycled with me, and was nice.

Now I look back at that Anne as an amusing, but very superficial girl, who has nothing to do with the Anne of today. Peter said quite rightly about me: "If ever I saw you, you were always surrounded by two or more boys and a whole troupe of girls. You were always laughing and always the center of everything!"

What is left of this girl? Oh, don't worry, I haven't forgotten how to laugh or to answer back readily. I'm just as good, if not better at criticising people, and I can still flirt if... I wish. That's not it though, I'd like that sort of life again for an evening, a few days, or even a week; the life which seems so carefree and gay. But at the end of that week, I should be dead-beat and would be only too thankful to listen to anyone who began to talk about something sensible. I don't want followers, but friends, admirers who fall not for a flattering smile but for what one does and for one's character.

I know quite well that the circle around me would be much smaller. But what does that matter, as long as one still keeps a few sincere friends?

Yet I wasn't entirely happy in 1942 in spite of everything; I often felt deserted, but because I was on the go the whole day long, I didn't think about it and enjoyed myself as much as I could. Consciously or unconsciously, I tried to drive away the emptiness I felt with jokes and pranks. Now I think seriously about life and what I have to do. One period of my life is over for ever. The carefree schooldays are gone, never to return.

I don't even long for them any more; I have outgrown them, I can't just only enjoy myself as my serious side is always there.

I look upon my life up till the New Year, as it were, through a powerful magnifying-glass. The sunny life at home, then coming here in 1942, the sudden change, the quarrels, the bickerings. I couldn't understand it, I was taken by surprise, and the only way I could keep up some dignity was by being impertinent.

The first half of 1943: my fits of crying, the loneliness, how I slowly began to see all my faults and shortcomings, which are so great and which seemed much greater then. During the day I deliberately talked about anything and everything that was farthest from my thoughts, tried to draw Pim to me; but couldn't. Alone I had to face the difficult task of changing myself, to stop the everlasting reproaches, which were so oppressive and which reduced me to such terrible despondency.

Things improved slightly in the second half of the year, I became a young woman and was treated more like a grown-up. I started to think, and write stories, and came to the conclusion that the others no longer had the right to throw me about like an india-rubber ball. I wanted to change in accordance with my own desires. But *one* thing that struck me even more was when I realised that even Daddy would never become my confidant over everything. I didn't want to trust anyone but myself any more.

At the beginning of the New Year: the second great change, my dream…. And with it I discovered my longing, not for a girl friend, but for a boy friend. I also discovered my inward happiness and my defensive armour of superficiality and gaiety. In due time I quietened down and discovered my boundless desire for all that is beautiful and good.

And in the evening, when I lie in bed and end my prayers with the words, "I thank you, God, for all that is good and dear and beautiful," I am filled with joy. Then I think about "the good" of going into hiding, of my health and with my whole being of the "dearness" of Peter, of that which is still embryonic and impressionable and which we neither of us dare to name or touch, of that which will come some time; love, the future, happiness and of "the beauty" which exists in the world; the world, nature, beauty and all, all that is exquisite and fine.

I don't think then of all the misery, but of the beauty that still remains. This is one of the things that Mummy and I are so entirely different about. Her counsel when one feels melancholy is: "Think of all the misery in the world and be thankful that you are not sharing in it!" My advice is: "Go outside, to the fields, enjoy nature and the sunshine, go out and try to recapture happiness in yourself and in God.

Think of all the beauty that's still left in and around you and be happy!"

I don't see how Mummy's idea can be right, because then how are you supposed to behave if you are going through the misery yourself? Then you are lost. On the contrary, I've found that there is always some beauty left—in nature, sunshine, freedom, in yourself; these can all help you. Look at these things, then you find yourself again, and God, and then you regain your balance.

And whoever is happy, will make others happy too. He who has courage and faith will never perish in misery!

Yours, ANNE

Tuesday, 4th April, 1944

Dear Kitty,

For a long time I haven't had any idea of what I was working for any more; the end of the war is so terribly far away, so unreal, like a fairy tale. If the war isn't over by September I shan't go to school any more. Because I don't want to be two years behind. Peter filled my days—nothing but Peter, in dreams and thoughts until Saturday, when I felt so utterly miserable; oh, it was terrible. I was holding back my tears all the while I was with Peter, then laughed with Van Daan over a lemon-punch, was cheerful and excited, but the moment I was alone I knew that I would have to cry my heart out. So, clad in my nightdress, I let myself go and slipped down on to the floor. First I said my long prayer very earnestly, then I cried with my head on my arms, my knees bent up, on the bare floor, completely folded up. One large sob brought me back to earth again, and I quelled my tears because I didn't want them to hear anything in the next room. Then I began trying to talk some courage into myself. I could only say: "I must, I must, I must…." Completely stiff from the unnatural position, I fell against the side of the bed and fought on, until I climbed into bed again just before half-past ten. It was over!

And now it's all over. I must work, so as not to be a fool, to get on, to become a journalist, because that's what I want! I know that I can write, a couple of my stories are good, my descriptions of the "Secret Annexe" are humorous, there's a lot in my diary that speaks, but— whether I have real talent remains to be seen.

"Eva's Dream" is my best fairy-tale, and the queer thing about it is that I don't know where it comes from. Quite a lot of "Cady's Life" is good too, but, on the whole, it's nothing.

I am the best and sharpest critic of my own work. I know myself what is and what is not well written. Anyone who doesn't write doesn't know how wonderful it is; I used to bemoan the fact that I couldn't draw at all, but now I am more than happy that I can at least write. And if I haven't any talent for writing books or newspaper articles, well, then I can always write for myself.

I want to get on; I can't imagine that I would have to lead the same sort of life as Mummy and Mrs. Van Daan and all the women who do their work and are then forgotten. I must have something besides a husband and children, something that I can devote myself to!

I want to go on living even after my death! And therefore I am grateful to God for giving me this gift, this possibility of developing myself and of writing, of expressing all that is in me.

I can shake off everything if I write; my sorrows disappear, my courage is reborn. But, and that is the great question, will I ever be able to write anything great, will I ever become a journalist or a writer? I hope so, oh, I hope so very much, for I can recapture everything when I write, my thoughts, my ideals and my fantasies.

I haven't done anything more to "Cady's Life" for ages; in my mind I know exactly how to go on, but somehow it doesn't flow from my pen. Perhaps I never shall finish it, it may land up in the wastepaper basket, or the fire... that's a horrible idea, but then I think to myself, "at the age of fourteen and with so little experience, how can you write about philosophy?"

So I go on again with fresh courage; I think I shall succeed, because I want to write!

Yours, ANNE

Saturday, 15th July, 1944

Dear Kitty,

We have had a book from the library with the challenging title of: *What do you think of the modern young girl?* I want to talk about this subject today.

The author of this book criticises "the youth of today" from top to toe, without, however, condemning the whole of the young brigade as "incapable of anything good." On the contrary, she is rather of the opinion that if young people wished, they have it in their hands to make a bigger, more beautiful and better world, but that they occupy themselves with superficial things, without giving a thought to real beauty.

In some passages the writer gave me very much the feeling she was directing her criticisms at me, and that's why I want to lay myself completely bare to you for once and defend myself against this attack.

I have one outstanding trait in my character, which must strike anyone who knows me for any length of time, and that is my knowledge of myself. I can watch myself and my actions, just like an outsider. The Anne of every day I can face entirely without prejudice, without making excuses for her, and watch what's good and what's bad about her. This "self-consciousness" haunts me, and every time I open my mouth I know as soon as I've spoken whether "that ought to have been different" or "that was right as it was." There are so many things about myself that I condemn; I couldn't begin to name them all. I understand more and more how true Daddy's words were when he said: "All children must look after their own upbringing." Parents can only give good advice or put them on the right paths, but the final forming of a person's character lies in his own hands.

In addition to this, I have lots of courage, I always feel so strong and as if I can bear a great deal, I feel so free and so young! I was glad when I first realised it, because I don't think I shall easily bow down before the blows that inevitably come to everyone.

But I've talked about these things so often before. Now I want to come to the chapter of "Daddy and Mummy don't understand me." Daddy and Mummy have always thoroughly spoilt me, were sweet to me, defended me and have done all that parents could do. And yet I've felt so frightfully lonely for a long time, so left out, neglected and misunderstood. Daddy tried all he could to check my rebellious spirit, but it was no use, I have cured myself, by seeing for myself what was wrong in my behaviour and keeping it before my eyes.

How is it that Daddy was never any support to me in my struggle, why did he completely miss the mark when he wanted to offer me a helping hand? Daddy tried the wrong methods, he always talked to me as a child who was going through difficult phases. It sounds crazy, because Daddy's the only one who has always taken me into his confidence, and no one but Daddy has given me the feeling that I'm sensible. But there's one thing he's omitted: you see, he hasn't realised that for me the fight to get on top was more important than all else. I didn't want to hear about "symptoms of your age," or "other girls," or "it wears off by itself"; I didn't want to be treated as a girl-like-all-others, but as Anne-on-her-own-merits. Pim didn't understand that. For that matter, I can't confide in anyone, unless they tell me a lot about themselves, and as I know very little about Pim, I don't feel that I can tread upon more intimate ground with him. Pim always takes up the older, fatherly attitude, tells me that he too has had similar passing tendencies. But still he's not able to feel with me like a friend, however hard he tries. These things have made me never mention my views on life nor my well-considered theories to anyone but my diary and, occasionally, to Margot. I concealed from Daddy everything that perturbed me; I never shared my ideals with him. I was aware of the fact that I was pushing him away from me.

I couldn't do anything else. I have acted entirely according to my feelings, but I have acted in the way that was best for my peace of mind. Because I should completely lose my repose and self-confidence, which I have built up so shakily, if, at this stage, I were to accept criticisms of my half-completed task. And I can't do that even from Pim, although it sounds very hard, for not only have I not shared my secret thoughts with Pim but I have often pushed him even further from me, by my irritability.

This is a point that I think a lot about: Why is it that Pim annoys me? So much so that I can hardly bear him teaching me, that his affectionate ways strike me as being put on, that I want to be left in peace and would really prefer it if he dropped me a bit, until I felt more certain in my attitude towards him? Because I still have a gnawing feeling of guilt over that horrible letter that I dared to write him when I was so overwrought. Oh, how hard it is to be really strong and brave in every way!

Yet, this was not my greatest disappointment; no, I ponder far more over Peter than Daddy. I know very well that I conquered him instead of he conquering me. I created an image of him in my mind, pictured him as a quiet, sensitive, lovable boy, who needed affection and friendship. I needed a living person to whom I could pour out my heart; I wanted a friend who'd help to put me on the right road. I achieved what I wanted, and, slowly but surely, I drew him towards me. Finally, when I had made him feel friendly, it automatically developed into an intimacy, which, on second thoughts, I don't think I ought to have allowed.

We talked about the most private things, and yet up till now, we have never touched on those things that filled, and still fill, my heart and soul. I still don't know quite what to make of Peter— is he superficial, or does he still feel shy, even of me? But dropping that, I committed one error in my desire to make a real friendship: I switched over and tried to get at him by developing it into a more intimate relationship, whereas I should have explored all other possibilities. He longs to be loved and I can see that he's beginning to be more and more in love with me. He gets satisfaction out of our meetings, whereas they just have the effect of making me want to try it out with him again. And yet, I don't seem able to touch on the subjects that I'm so longing to bring out into the daylight. I drew Peter towards me, far more than he realises. Now he clings to me, and for the time being, I don't see any way of shaking him off and putting him on his own feet. When I realised that he could not be a friend for my understanding, I thought I would at least try to lift him up out of his narrow-mindedness and make him do something with his youth.

"For in its innermost depths youth is lonelier than old age." I read this saying in some book and I've always remembered it, and found it to be true. Is it true then that grown-ups have a more difficult time here than we do? No. I know it isn't. Older people have formed their opinions about everything, and don't waver before they act. It's twice as hard for us young ones to hold our ground, and maintain our opinions, in a time when all ideals are being shattered and destroyed, when people are showing their worst side, and do not know whether to believe in truth and right and God.

Anyone who claims that the older ones have a more difficult time here, certainly doesn't realise to what extent our problems weigh down on us, problems for which we are probably much too young, but which thrust themselves upon us continually, until, after a long time, we think we've found a solution, but the solution doesn't seem able to resist the facts which reduce it to nothing again. That's the difficulty in these times: ideals, dreams, and cherished hopes rise within us, only to meet the horrible truth and be shattered.

It's really a wonder that I haven't dropped all my ideals because they seem so absurd and impossible to carry out. Yet, I keep them, because in spite of everything I still believe that people are really good at heart. I simply can't build up my hopes on a foundation consisting of confusion, misery, and death. I see the world gradually being turned into a wilderness, I hear the ever-approaching thunder, which will destroy us too, I can feel the sufferings of millions and yet, if I look up into the heavens, I think that it will all come right, that this cruelty too will end, and that peace and tranquillity will return again.

In the meantime, I must uphold my ideals, for perhaps the time will come when I shall be able to carry them out.

Yours, ANNE

Questions for Review

1. What evidence is there in the selection from Marcus Aurelius's *Meditations* given above that the diarist never intended for anyone else to read it?

2. Does Marcus Aurelius give any reasons for keeping this record of his thoughts? Can you suggest any probable reasons, considering the nature of the subject matter?

3. To whom does Marcus appear to be speaking in the *Meditations?* Who is the "you" he addresses? What does this usage indicate about the point of view from which the remarks are given and about Marcus's attitude toward himself?

4. Do you get a very extensive or clear idea of Marcus Aurelius as a social being, or "personality," from his diary? Explain.

5. Samuel Pepys, like Marcus Aurelius, never intended for anyone other than himself to see this record of his life; he even kept his journal in a shorthand that he invented. Is there any obvious reason in the material of the diary for Pepys's desire for total secrecy?

6. To whom does Pepys appear to be speaking in the diary? Compare and contrast his point of view with that of Marcus Aurelius and the other diarists.

7. Do you have a very clear view of Pepys's personality or intellectual character from his diary?

8. What principle(s) of selection appear to determine what Pepys writes in his journal? Is the overall impression of the diary one of unity and coherence or of disjointed chaos?

9. Is Pepys more interested in actions, ideas, or people? Is he concerned with his own states of feeling?

10. Is Pepys more objective toward himself than Marcus Aurelius, Boswell, or Anne Frank?

11. Of the diarists included here, James Boswell is the most explicit in his reasons for keeping a journal. What are the chief reasons he gives and to what extent does his record fulfill his ideas of what his diary can achieve?

12. Boswell declares that he wishes to "know himself." What does he mean? How could keeping a diary aid in self-knowledge— and what kind of knowledge might be imparted in this manner?

13. Boswell is the only diarist in this group who admittedly intended for his writing to be seen by someone else (that is, by his friend Johnston). How does his awareness of a reader affect his selection and presentation of material and color his attitude toward it?

14. Boswell was still a very young man when he started his journal and was much involved in what is now called "an identity crisis." What views of himself does Boswell express in this journal? Is the Narrator Boswell to be distinguished here from the Character Boswell in any basic way? Is Boswell's point of view as an observer and recorder the same throughout the selections here or does it change?

15. Dorothy Wordsworth's Grasmere Journal is a diary of her residence in the Lake District together with her brother William, the poet, and their association with Samuel Taylor Coleridge. From its material, why do you think Dorothy wished to keep a journal? Would she, like Boswell, think it a means to self-knowledge?

16. Is Dorothy Wordsworth's journal more like that of Pepys or of Boswell? Are her interests as a woman significantly different from those of male diarists? If so, how?

17. The entries of the Grasmere Journal are at first very terse and prosaic, and then they grow more expanded and poetic; in fact, the Daffodil Episode is very like William Wordsworth's poem on p. 393 below. How do you account for this shift in interest and style (or diction)?

18. Like Boswell, Anne Frank filled her diary with introspective soliloquies that revealed her identity crisis. What are the "Two Annes" revealed in the diary? Are there more than two?

19. Do Anne Frank's reasons for keeping a diary differ from those of other diarists here? What reasons does she give? Which are the ones unique to her, if any?

20. Would you say that Anne's diary shows a more significant change or development in her thought than the other diaries show in the thoughts of their authors? How do you account for this?

21. Which of the diarists do you consider the one most absorbed with his private self? Which with the world about him? Which with ideas? With other people? How do these concerns affect the character of the writing in each diary?

22. Which of the diaries would be most useful or interesting to each of the following: An historian, a biographer, a social critic, the general reader, and you?

Questions for Discussion and Writing

1. From the evidence contained in the diary selections above, which theory of literary creation would you say best applies: that of William James, Freud, Jung, Frye, McLuhan, or none?

2. Utilizing all the diarists, what characteristics seem to you to distinguish the diary as a literary type? Do these depend primarily on subject matter, diction, form, point of view, or something else?

3. Which of the diarists holds the most objective view toward himself, the most critically harsh, the most self-indulgent, and the most matter-of-fact?

4. Do the diarists here seem to consider themselves unusual people because they write? Does any of the diarists above think himself superior to other people because he writes? Inferior to others? Peculiar or eccentric?

5. What are the reasons for composition that best explain all of the diaries above: desire for fame, a wish for living reputation after death, hope of praise or money, or others?

6. All writers must face the problem of showing the passage of time in their work. In some kinds of literature, the problem of time-sequence, or chronology, is very difficult to solve. Does the diarist seem to have much trouble with chronology? Why or why not? What result does the diarist's reliance on a particular kind of chronological order have on the tension, the emphasis, and the effect of his work?

SECTION TWO

The Private Communication

Like the journal, the personal letter or *epistle* depends for its subject matter on the experiences of the writer; but the fact that he is composing his experiences with a definite reader in mind inevitably affects the intentions and methods of the letter-writer. Even the diarist, writing solely for himself, on occasions objectifies himself as a theoretical reader (as Marcus Aurelius does when he addresses himself) or he invents a nonexistent reader (as Anne Frank does "Kitty") and writes with that "reader" in view. The writer of a letter has some actual reader in mind, as he writes; he selects details, style, and tone in accordance with the nature and interests of his addressee, their mutual attitudes, and the immediate occasion served by the written communication. In some instances—Jonathan Swift's *Journal to Stella* or Boswell's *London Journal* —a diary record may serve as a lengthy, day-by-day epistle. In other instances, the epistle may alter or manipulate the writer's emotions or ideas in order to communicate them. In the change from the secret record to the semiprivate communication, the verbal composition undergoes some significant shifts of emphasis and technique.

PHILIP STANHOPE,
LORD CHESTERFIELD

Two letters to His Son

Bath, 19 October O.S. 1748

Dear Boy,

Having, in my last, pointed out what sort of company you should keep, I will now give you some rules for your conduct in it; rules which my own experience and observation enable me to lay down and communicate to you with some degree of confidence. I have often given you hints of this kind before, but then it has been by snatches; I will now be more regular and methodical. I shall say nothing with regard to your bodily carriage and address, but leave them to the care of your dancing-master, and to your own attention to the best models; remember, however, that they are of consequence.

Talk often, but never long; in that case, if you do not please, at least you are sure not to tire your hearers. Pay your own reckoning, but do not treat the whole company; this being one of the very few cases in which people do not care to be treated, every one being fully convinced that he has wherewithal to pay.

Tell stories very seldom, and absolutely never but where they are very apt, and very short. Omit every circumstance that is not material, and beware of digressions. To have frequent recourse to narrative betrays great want of imagination.

Never hold anybody by the button, or the hand, in order to be heard out; for, if people are not willing to hear you, you had much better hold your tongue than them.

Most long talkers single out some one unfortunate man in company (commonly him whom they observe to be the most silent, or their next neighbour) to whisper, or at least,

in a half voice, to convey a continuity of words to. This is excessively ill-bred, and, in some degree, a fraud; conversation-stock being a joint and common property. But, on the other hand, if one of these unmerciful talkers lays hold of you, hear him with patience, and at least seeming attention, if he is worth obliging; for nothing will oblige him more than a patient hearing, as nothing would hurt him more than either to leave him in the midst of his discourse, or to discover your impatience under your affliction.

Take, rather than give, the tone of the company you are in. If you have parts, you will show them, more or less, upon every subject; and, if you have not, you had better talk sillily upon a subject of other people's than of your own choosing.

Avoid as much as you can, in mixed companies, argumentative polemical conversations; which, though they should not, yet certainly do, indispose, for a time, the contending parties towards each other; and, if the controversy grows warm and noisy, endeavour to put an end to it by some genteel levity or joke. I quieted such a conversation hubbub once, by representing to them that, though I was persuaded none there present would repeat, out of company, what passed in it, yet I could not answer for the discretion of the passengers in the street, who must necessarily hear all that was said.

Above all things, and upon all occasions, avoid speaking of yourself, if it be possible. Such is the natural pride and vanity of our hearts, that it perpetually breaks out, even in people of the best parts, in all the various modes and figures of the egotism.

Some abruptly speak advantageously of themselves, without either pretense or provocation. They are impudent. Others proceed more artfully, as they imagine, and forge accusations against themselves, complain of calumnies which they never heard, in order to justify themselves, by exhibiting a catalogue of their many virtues. "They acknowledge it may, indeed, seem odd, that they should talk in that manner of themselves; it is what they do not like,

---

Two Letters to His Son: From *The Letters of Lord Chesterfield to His Son*. First printed in 1774.

and what they never would have done; no, no tortures should ever have forced it from them, if they had not been thus unjustly and monstrously accused. But, in these cases, justice is surely due to one's self, as well as to others; and, when our character is attacked, we may say, in our own justification, what otherwise we never would have said." This thin veil of modesty drawn before vanity, is much too transparent to conceal it, even from very moderate discernment.

Others go more modestly and more slyly still (as they think) to work; but, in my mind, still more ridiculously. They confess themselves (not without some degree of shame and confusion) into all the cardinal virtues; by first degrading them into weaknesses, and then owning their misfortune, in being made up of those weaknesses. "They cannot see people suffer, without sympathizing with, and endeavouring to help them. They cannot see people want, without relieving them; though, truly, their own circumstances cannot very well afford it. They cannot help speaking truth, though they know all the imprudence of it. In short, they know that, with all these weaknesses, they are not fit to live in the world, much less to thrive in it. But they are now too old to change, and must rub on as well as they can." This sounds too ridiculous and *outré*, almost for the stage; and yet, take my word for it, you will frequently meet with it upon the common stage of the world. And here I will observe, by the bye, that you will often meet with characters in nature so extravagant, that a discreet poet would not venture to set them upon the stage in their true and high colouring.

This principle of vanity and pride is so strong in human nature, that it descends even to the lowest objects; and one often sees people angling for praise, where, admitting all they say to be true (which, by the way, it seldom is), no just praise is to be caught. One man affirms that he has rode post an hundred miles in six hours: probably it is a lie; but supposing it to be true, what then? Why, he is a very good post-boy, that is all. Another asserts, and probably not

without oaths, that he has drank six or eight bottles of wine at a sitting; out of charity, I will believe him a liar; for, if I do not, I must think him a beast.

Such, and a thousand more, are the follies and extravagancies, which vanity draws people into, and which always defeat their own purpose, and, as Waller says upon another subject—

Make the wretch the most despised,
Where most he wishes to be prized.

The only sure way of avoiding these evils is never to speak of yourself at all. But when historically you are obliged to mention yourself, take care not to drop one single word, that can directly or indirectly be construed as fishing for applause. Be your character what it will, it will be known; and nobody will take it upon your own word. Never imagine that anything you can say yourself will varnish your defects, or add lustre to your perfections; but, on the contrary, it may, and nine times in ten will, make the former more glaring, and the latter obscure. If you are silent upon your own subject, neither envy, indignation, nor ridicule will obstruct or allay the applause which you may really deserve; but if you publish your own panegyric, upon any occasion, or in any shape whatsoever, and however artfully dressed or disguised, they will all conspire against you, and you will be disappointed of the very end you aim at.

Take care never to seem dark and mysterious; which is not only a very unamiable character, but a very suspicious one too; if you seem mysterious with others, they will be really so with you, and you will know nothing. The height of abilities is, to have *volto sciolto* and *pensieri stretti*; that is, a frank, open, and ingenuous exterior, with a prudent and reserved interior; to be upon your own guard, and yet, by a seeming natural openness, to put people off theirs. Depend upon it, nine in ten of every company you are in will avail themselves of every indiscreet and unguarded expression of yours, if they can turn it to their own advantage. A prudent reserve is therefore necessary as a seeming openness is prudent. Always look people in the face when you speak to them; the not doing it is thought to imply conscious guilt; besides that, you lose the advantage of observing by their countenances what impression your discourse makes upon them. In order to know people's real sentiments, I trust much more to my eyes than to my ears; for they can say whatever they have a mind I should hear; but they can seldom help looking what they have no intention that I should know.

Neither retail nor receive scandal willingly; for though the defamation of others may for the present gratify the malignity of the pride of our hearts, cool reflection will draw very disadvantageous conclusions from such a disposition; and in the case of scandal, as in that of robbery, the receiver is always thought as bad as the thief.

Mimicry, which is the common and favourite amusement of little low minds, is in the utmost contempt with great ones. It is the lowest and most illiberal of all buffoonery. Pray, neither practise it yourself, nor applaud it in others. Besides that, the person mimicked is insulted; and, as I have often observed to you before, an insult is never forgiven.

I need not, I believe, advise you to adapt your conversation to the people you are conversing with; for I suppose you would not, without this caution, have talked upon the same subject and in the same manner to a minister of state, a bishop, a philosopher, a captain, and a woman. A man of the world must, like the chameleon, be able to take every different hue, which is by no means a criminal or abject, but a necessary complaisance, for it relates only to manners, and not to morals.

One word only as to swearing; and that I hope and believe is more than is necessary. You may sometimes hear some people in good company interlard their discourse with oaths, by way of embellishment, as they think; but you must observe, too, that those who do so are never those who contribute in any degree to give that company the denomination of good company. They are always subalterns, or people of low education; for that practice, besides that it has no one temptation to plead, is as silly and as illiberal as it is wicked.

Loud laughter is the mirth of the mob, who are only pleased with silly things; for true wit or good sense never excited a laugh since the creation of the world. A man of parts and fashion is therefore only seen to smile, but never heard to laugh.

But, to conclude this long letter; all the above-mentioned rules, however carefully you may observe them, will lose half their effect if unaccompanied by the Graces. Whatever you say, if you say it with a supercilious, cynical face, or an embarrassed countenance, or a silly, disconcerted grin, will be ill received. If, into the bargain, *you mutter it, or utter it indistinctly and ungracefully*, it will be still worse received. If your air and address are vulgar, awkward, and *gauche*, you may be esteemed indeed if you have great intrinsic value; but you will never please, and without pleasing you will rise but heavily. Venus, among the ancients, was synonymous with the Graces, who were always supposed to accompany her; and Horace tells us, that even youth, and Mercury, the god of arts and eloquence, would not do without her.

—*Parum comis* sine te Juventas
  Mercuriusque.

They are not inexorable ladies, and may be had if properly and diligently pursued. Adieu!

Bath, 29 October O.S. 1748

Dear Boy,

My anxiety for your success increases in proportion as the time approaches for your taking your part upon the great stage of the world. The audience will form their opinion of you upon your first appearance (making the proper allowance for your inexperience), and so far it will be final, that, though it may vary as to the degrees, it will never totally change. This consideration excites that restless attention with which I am constantly examining how I can best contribute to the perfection of that character in which the least spot or blemish would give me more real concern than I am now capable of feeling upon any other account whatsoever.

I have long since done mentioning your great religious and moral duties, because I could not make your understanding so bad a compliment, as to suppose that you wanted or could receive any new instructions upon those two important points. Mr. Harte, I am sure, has not neglected them; besides, they are so obvious to common sense and reason, that commentators may (as they often do) perplex, but cannot make them clearer. My province, therefore, is to supply by my experience your hitherto inevitable inexperience in the ways of the world. People at your age are in a state of natural ebriety, and want rails and *gardefous* wherever they go, to hinder them from breaking their necks. This drunkenness of youth is not only tolerated, but even pleases, if kept within certain bounds of discretion and decency. Those bounds are the point which it is difficult for the drunken man himself to find out; and there it is that the experience of a friend may not only serve, but save him.

Carry with you, and welcome, into company all the gaiety and spirits, but as little of the giddiness of youth as you can. The former will charm, but the latter will often, though innocently, implacably offend. Inform yourself of the characters and situations of the company before you give way to what your imagination may prompt you to say. There are in all companies more wrong heads than right ones, and many more who deserve than who like censure. Should you therefore expatiate in the praise of some virtue, which some in company notoriously want, or declaim against any vice which others are notoriously infected with, your reflexions, however general and unapplied, will, by being applicable, be thought personal and levelled at those people. This consideration points out to you sufficiently not to be suspicious

and captious yourself, not to suppose that things, because they may be, are therefore meant at you. The manners of well-bred people secure one from those indirect and mean attacks; but if, by chance, a flippant woman or a pert coxcomb lets off anything of that kind, it is much better not to seem to understand, than to reply to it.

Cautiously avoid talking of either your own or other people's domestic affairs. Yours are nothing to them, but tedious; theirs are nothing to you. The subject is a tender one; and it is odds but you touch somebody or other's sore place; for in this case there is no trusting to specious appearances, which may be, and often are, so contrary to the real situations of things between men and their wives, parents and their children, seeming friends, etc., that, with the best intentions in the world, one often blunders disagreeably.

Remember, that the wit, humour, and jokes of most mixed companies are local. They thrive in that particular soil, but will not often bear transplanting. Every company is differently circumstanced, has its particular cant and jargon, which may give occasion to wit and mirth within that circle, but would seem flat and insipid in any other, and therefore will not bear repeating. Nothing makes a man look sillier than a pleasantry not relished or not understood; and if he meets with a profound silence when he expected a general applause, or, what is worse, if he is desired to explain the *bon mot*, his awkward and embarrassed situation is easier imagined than described. *À propos* of repeating; take great care never to repeat (I do not mean here the pleasantries) in one company what you hear in another. Things seemingly indifferent, may, by circulation, have much graver consequences than you would imagine. Besides, there is a general tacit trust in conversation by which a man is obliged not to report anything out of it, though he is not immediately enjoined secrecy. A retailer of this kind is sure to draw himself into a thousand scrapes and discussions, and to be shyly and uncomfortably received wherever he goes.

You will find, in most good company, some people who only keep their place there by a contemptible title enough—these are what we call *very good-natured fellows*, and the French *bons diables*. The truth is, they are people without any parts or fancy, and who, having no will of their own, readily assent to, concur in, and applaud whatever is said or done in the company; and adopt, with the same alacrity, the most virtuous or the most criminal, the wisest or the silliest scheme, that happens to be entertained by the majority of the company. This foolish, and often criminal complaisance, flows from a foolish cause—the want of any other merit. I hope you will hold your place in company by a nobler tenure, and that you will hold it (you can bear a quibble, I believe, yet) *in capite.* Have a will and an opinion of your own, and adhere to them steadily; but then do it with good-humour, good-breeding, and (if you have it) with urbanity; for you have not yet heard enough either to preach or censure.

All other kinds of complaisance are not only blameless, but necessary in good company. Not to seem to perceive the little weaknesses, and the idle but innocent affectations of the company, but even to flatter them in a certain manner, is not only very allowable, but, in truth, a sort of polite duty. They will be pleased with you, if you do; and will certainly not be reformed by you, if you do not. For instance; you will find, in every *groupe* of company, two principal figures, *viz.* the fine lady and the fine gentleman; who absolutely give the law of wit, language, fashion, and taste, to the rest of that society. There is always a strict, and often, for the time being, a tender alliance between these two figures. The lady looks upon her empire as founded upon the divine right of beauty (and full as good a divine right it is, as any king, emperor, or pope can pretend to); she requires, and commonly meets with, unlimited passive obedience. And why should she not meet with it? Her demands go no higher than to have her unquestioned pre-eminence in beauty, wit, and fashion, firmly established. Few sovereigns (by

the way) are so reasonable. The fine gentleman's claims of right are, *mutatis mutandis*, the same; and though, indeed, he is not always a wit *de jure*, yet, as he is the wit *de facto* of that company, he is entitled to a share of your allegiance; and everybody expects, at least, as much as they are entitled to, if not something more. Prudence bids you make your court to these joint sovereigns; and no duty, that I know of, forbids it. Rebellion, here, is exceedingly dangerous, and inevitably punished by banishment, and immediate forfeiture of all your wit, manners, taste, and fashion; as, on the other hand, a cheerful submission, not without some flattery, is sure to procure you a strong recommendation, and most effectual pass, throughout all their, and probably the neighbouring dominions. With a moderate share of sagacity, you will, before you have been half an hour in their company, easily discover these two principal figures; both by the deference which you will observe the whole company pay them, and by that easy, careless, and serene air, which their consciousness of power gives them. As in this case, so in all others, aim always at the highest; get always into the highest company, and address yourself particularly to the highest in it. The search after the unattainable philosopher's stone has occasioned a thousand useful discoveries, which otherwise would never have been made.

What the French justly call *les manières nobles*, are only to be acquired in the very best companies. They are the distinguishing characteristics of men of fashion; people of low education never wear them so close but that some part or other of the original vulgarism appears. *Les manières nobles* equally forbid insolent contempt, or low envy and jealousy. Low people in good circumstances, fine clothes, and equipages, will insolently show contempt for all those who cannot afford as fine clothes, as good an equipage, and who have not (as their term is) as much money in their pockets; on the other hand, they are gnawed with envy, and cannot help discovering it, of those who surpass them in any of these articles, which are far from being sure criterions of merit. They are likewise jealous of being slighted, and, consequently, suspicious and captious; they are eager and hot about trifles, because trifles were, at first, their affairs of consequence. *Les manières nobles* imply exactly the reverse of all this. Study them early; you cannot make them too habitual and familiar to you.

Just as I had written what goes before, I received your letter of the 24th N.S. but I have not received that which you mention from Mr. Harte. Yours is of the kind that I desire, for I want to see your private picture drawn by yourself at different sittings; for though, as it is drawn by yourself, I presume you will take the most advantageous likeness, yet I think I have skill enough in that kind of painting to discover the true features, though ever so artfully coloured or thrown into skilful lights and shades.

By your account of the German play, which I do not know whether I should call tragedy or comedy, the only shining part of it (since I am in a way of quibbling) seems to have been the fox's tail. I presume, too, that the play has had the same fate as the squib, and has gone off no more. I remember a squib much better applied, when it was made the device of the colours of a French regiment of grenadiers; it was represented bursting with this motto under it— *Peream dum luceam.*

I like the description of your *pic-nic*, where I take it for granted that your cards are only to break the formality of a circle, and your *symposion* intended more to promote conversation than drinking. Such an *amicable collision*, as Lord Shaftesbury very prettily calls it, rubs off and smooths those rough corners which mere nature has given to the smoothest of us. I hope some part, at least, of the conversation is in German. *À propos*; tell me—do you speak that language correctly, and do you write it with ease? I have no doubt of your mastering the other modern languages, which are much easier, and occur much oftener; for which reason I desire you will apply most diligently to German while you are in Germany,

that you may speak and write that language most correctly.

I expect to meet Mr. Eliot in London in about three weeks; after which you will see him at Leipsig. Adieu!

DR. SAMUEL JOHNSON

A Letter to Lord Chesterfield

TO THE RIGHT HONOURABLE THE EARL
OF CHESTERFIELD
February 7, 1755.

My Lord,

I have been lately informed, by the proprietor of *The World*, that two papers, in which my Dictionary is recommended to the publick, were written by your Lordship. To be so distinguished, is an honour, which, being very little accustomed to favours from the great, I know not well how to receive, or in what terms to acknowledge.

When, upon some slight encouragement, I first visited your Lordship, I was overpowered, like the rest of mankind, by the enchantment of your address; and could not forbear to wish that I might boast myself *Le vainqueur du vainqueur de la terre*;—that I might obtain that regard for which I saw the world contending; but I found my attendance so little encouraged, that neither pride nor modesty would suffer me to continue it. When I had once addressed your Lordship in publick, I had exhausted all the art of pleasing which a retired and uncourtly scholar can possess. I had done all that I could; and no man is well pleased to have his all neglected, be it ever so little.

Seven years, my Lord, have now past, since I waited in your outward rooms, or was repulsed from your door; during which time I have been pushing on my work through difficulties, of which it is useless to complain, and have brought it, at last, to the verge of publication, without one act of assistance, one word of encouragement, or one smile of favour. Such treatment I did not expect, for I never had a Patron before.

The shepherd in Virgil grew at last acquainted with Love, and found him a native of the rocks.

Is not a Patron, my Lord, one who looks with unconcern on a man struggling for life in the water, and, when he has reached ground, encumbers him with help? The notice which you have been pleased to take of my labours, had it been early, had been kind; but it has been delayed till I am indifferent, and cannot enjoy it; till I am solitary, and cannot impart it; till I am known, and do not want it. I hope it is no very cynical asperity not to confess obligations where no benefit has been received, or to be unwilling that the Publick should consider me as owing that to a Patron, which Providence has enabled me to do for myself.

Having carried on my work thus far with so little obligation to any favourer of learning, I shall not be disappointed though I should conclude it, if less be possible, with less; for I have been long wakened from that dream of hope, in which I once boasted myself with so much exultation, my Lord,

your Lordship's most humble,
most obedient servant,
SAM: JOHNSON

JOHN KEATS

Letters to Fanny

Sunday Night [25 July 1819].

My sweet Girl,
I hope you did not blame me much for not obeying your request of a Letter on Saturday:
we have had four in our small room playing at cards night and morning leaving me no undisturb'd opportunity to write. Now Rice and Martin are gone I am at liberty. Brown to my sorrow confirms the account you give of your ill health. You cannot conceive how I ache to be with you: how I would die for one hour——— for what is in the world? I say you cannot conceive; it is impossible you should look with such eyes upon me as I have upon you: it cannot be. Forgive me if I wander a little this evening, for I have been all day employ'd in a very abstr[a]ct Poem and I am in deep love with you—two things which must excuse me. I have, believe me, not been an age in letting you take possession of me; the very first week I knew you I wrote myself your vassal; but burnt the Letter as the very next time I saw you I thought you manifested some dislike to me. If you should ever feel for Man at the first sight what I did for you, I am lost. Yet I should not quarrel with you, but hate myself if such a thing were to happen—only I should burst if the thing were not as fine as a Man as you are as a Woman. Perhaps I am too vehement, then fancy me on my knees, especially when I mention a part of your Letter which hurt me; you say speaking of Mr Severn "but you must be satisfied in knowing that I admired you much more than your friend." My dear love, I cannot believe there ever was or ever could be any thing to admire in me especially as far as sight goes—I cannot be admired, I am not a thing to be admired. You are, I love you; all I can bring you is a swooning admiration of your Beauty. I hold that place among Men which snubnos'd brunettes with meeting eyebrows do among women—they are trash to me—unless I should find one among them with a fire in her heart like the one that burns in mine. You absorb me in spite of myself—you alone: for I look not forward with any pleasure to what is call'd being settled in the world; I tremble at domestic cares—yet for you I would meet them, though if it would leave you the happier I would rather die than do so. I have two luxuries to brood over in my

walks, your Loveliness and the hour of my death. O that I could have possession of them both in the same minute. I hate the world: it batters too much the wings of my self-will, and would I could take a sweet poison from your lips to send me out of it. From no others would I take it. I am indeed astonish'd to find myself so careless of all cha[r]ms but yours—rememb[e]ring as I do the time when even a bit of ribband was a matter of interest with me. What softer words can I find for you after this—what it is I will not read. Nor will I say more here, but in a Postscript answer any thing else you may have mentioned in your Letter in so many words—for I am distracted with a thousand thoughts. I will imagine you Venus to-night and pray, pray, pray to your star like a He[a]then.

Your's ever, fair Star,
JOHN KEATS

25 College Street [Postmark, 13 October 1819].

My dearest Girl,

This moment I have set myself to copy some verses out fair. I cannot proceed with any degree of content. I must write you a line or two and see if that will assist in dismissing you from my Mind for ever so short a time. Upon my Soul I can think of nothing else. The time is passed when I had power to advise and warn you against the unpromising morning of my Life. My love has made me selfish. I cannot exist without you. I am forgetful of everything but seeing you again—my Life seems to stop there—I see no further. You have absorb'd me. I have a sensation at the present moment as though I was dissolving—I should be exquisitely miserable without the hope of soon seeing you. I should be afraid to separate myself far from you. My sweet Fanny, will your heart never change? My love, will it? I have no limit now to my love.... You[r] note came in just here. I cannot be happier away from you. 'Tis richer

than an Argosy of Pearles. Do not threat me even in jest. I have been astonished that Men could die Martyrs for religion—I have shudder'd at it. I shudder no more—I could be martyr'd for my Religion—Love is my religion—I could die for that. I could die for you. My Creed is Love and you are its only tenet. You have ravish'd me away by a Power I cannot resist; and yet I could resist till I saw you; and even since I have seen you I have endeavoured often "to reason against the reasons of my Love." I can do that no more—the pain would be too great. My love is selfish. I cannot breathe without you.

Yours for ever
JOHN KEATS

Tuesday Morn. [Kentish Town, May 1820].

My dearest Girl,

I wrote a Letter for you yesterday expecting to have seen your mother. I shall be selfish enough to send it though I know it may give you a little pain, because I wish you to see how unhappy I am for love of you, and endeavour as much as I can to entice you to give up your whole heart to me whose whole existence hangs upon you. You could not step or move an eyelid but it would shoot to my heart—I am greedy of you. Do not think of any thing but me. Do not live as if I was not existing—Do not forget me—But have I any right to say you forget me? Perhaps you think of me all day. Have I any right to wish you to be unhappy for me? You would forgive me for wishing it, if you knew the extreme passion I have that you should love me—and for you to love me as I do you, you must think of no one but me, much less write that sentence. Yesterday and this morning I have been haunted with a sweet vision—I have seen you the whole time in your shepherdess dress. How my senses have ached at it! How my heart has been devoted to it! How my eyes have been full of Tears at it! I[n]deed I think a real Love is enough to occupy the widest heart. Your going to town alone, when I heard of it was a shock to me—yet I expected it—*promise me you will not for some time, till I get better*. Promise me this and fill the paper full of the most endearing names. If you cannot do so with good will, do my Love tell me—say what you think—confess if your heart is too much fasten'd on the world. Perhaps then I may see you at a greater distance, I may not be able to appropriate you so closely to myself. Were you to loose a favorite bird from the cage, how would your eyes ache after it as long as it was in sight; when out of sight you would recover a little. Perphaps [sic] if you would, if so it is, confess to me how many things are necessary to you besides me, I might be happier, by being less tantaliz'd. Well may you exclaim, how selfish, how cruel, not to let me enjoy my youth! to wish me to be unhappy! You must be so if you love me—upon my Soul I can be contented with nothing else. If you could really what is call'd enjoy yourself at a Party—if you can smile in peoples faces, and wish them to admire you *now*, you never have [loved] nor ever will love me. I see *life* in nothing but the certainty of your Love—convince me of it my sweetest. If I am not somehow convinc'd I shall die of agony. If we love we must not live as other men and women do—I cannot brook the wolfsbane of fashion and foppery and tattle. You must be mine to die upon the rack if I want you. I do not pretend to say I have more feeling than my fellows—but I wish you seriously to look over my letters kind and unkind and consider whether the Person who wrote them can be able to endure much longer the agonies and uncertainties which you are so peculiarly made to create. My recovery of bodily hea[l]th will be of no benefit to me if you are not all mine when I am well. For God's sake save me—or tell me my passion is of too awful a nature for you. Again God bless you

                                J. K.

No—my sweet Fanny—I am wrong. I do not want you to be unhappy—and yet I do, I must

while there is so sweet a Beauty—my loveliest my darling! Good bye! I Kiss you—O the torments!

Wednesday Morn[in]g. [Kentish Town, 1820; ?5 July.]

My dearest Girl,

I have been a walk this morning with a book in my hand, but as usual I have been occupied with nothing but you: I wish I could say in an agreeable manner. I am tormented day and night. They talk of my going to Italy. 'Tis certain I shall never recover if I am to be so long separate from you: yet with all this devotion to you I cannot persuade myself into any confidence of you. Past experience connected with the fact of my long separation from you gives me agonies which are scarcely to be talked of. When your mother comes I shall be very sudden and expert in asking her whether you have been to Mrs Dilke's, for she might say no to make me easy. I am literally worn to death, which seems my only recourse. I cannot forget what has pass'd. What? nothing with a man of the world, but to me dreadful. I will get rid of this as much as possible. When you were in the habit of flirting with Brown you would have left off, could your own heart have felt one half of one pang mine did. Brown is a good sort of Man—he did not know he was doing me to death by inches. I feel the effect of every one of those hours in my side now; and for that cause, though he has done me many services, though I know his love and friendship for me, though at this moment I should be without pence were it not for his assistance, I will never see or speak to him until we are both old men, if we are to be. I *will* resent my heart having been made a football. You will call this madness. I have heard you say that it was not unpleasant to wait a few years—you have amusements—your mind is away—you have not brooded over one idea as I have, and how should you? You are to me an object intensely desireable—the air I breathe in a room empty of you is unhealthy.

I am not the same to you—no—you can wait—you have a thousand activities—you can be happy without me. Any party, any thing to fill up the day has been enough. How have you pass'd this month? Who[m] have you smil'd with? All this may seem savage in me. You do not feel as I do—you do not know what it is to love—one day you may—your time is not come. Ask yourself how many unhappy hours Keats has caused you in Loneliness. For myself I have been a Martyr the whole time, and for this reason I speak; the confession is forc'd from me by the torture. I appeal to you by the blood of that Christ you believe in: Do not write to me if you have done anything this month which it would have pained me to have seen. You may have altered—if you have not—if you still behave in dancing rooms and other societies as I have seen you—I do not want to live—if you have done so I wish this coming night may be my last. I cannot live without you, and not only you but *chaste you; virtuous you*. The Sun rises and sets, the day passes, and you follow the bent of your inclination to a certain extent—you have no conception of the quantity of miserable feeling that passes through me in a day.—Be serious! Love is not a plaything—and again do not write unless you can do it with a crystal conscience. I would sooner die for want of you than———

Yours for ever
J. KEATS

[*Kentish Town, July 1820?*]

My dearest Fanny,

My head is puzzled this morning, and I scarce know what I shall say though I am full of a hundred things. 'Tis certain I would rather be writing to you this morning, notwithstanding the alloy of grief in such an occupation, than enjoy any other pleasure, with health to boot, unconnected with you. Upon my soul I have loved you to the extreme. I wish you could know the Tenderness with which I continually brood over your different aspects of countenance, action and dress. I see you come down in the morning: I see you meet me at the Window—I see every thing over again eternally that I ever have seen. If I get on the pleasant clue I live in a sort of happy misery, if on the unpleasant 'tis miserable misery. You complain of my illtreating you in word, thought and deed—I am sorry—at times I feel bitterly sorry that I ever made you unhappy—my excuse is that those words have been wrung from me by the sha[r]pness of my feelings. At all events and in any case I have been wrong; could I believe that I did it without any cause, I should be the most sincere of Penitents. I could give way to my repentant feelings now, I could recant all my suspicions, I could mingle with you heart and Soul though absent, were it not for some parts of your Letters. Do you suppose it possible I could ever leave you? You know what I think of myself and what of you. You know that I should feel how much it was my loss and how little yours. My friends laugh at you! I know some of them—when I know them all I shall never think of them again as friends or even acquaintance. My friends have behaved well to me in every instance but one, and there they have become tattlers, and inquisitors into my conduct: spying upon a secret I would rather die than share it with any body's confidence. For this I cannot wish them well, I care not to see any of them again. If I am the Theme, I will not be the Friend of idle Gossips. Good gods what a shame it is our Loves should be so put into the microscope of a Coterie. Their laughs should not affect you (I may perhaps give you reasons some day for these laughs, for I suspect a few people to hate me well enough, *for reasons I know of,* who have pretended a great friendship for me) when in competition with one, who if he never should see you again would make you the Saint of his memory. These Laughers, who do not like you, who envy you for your Beauty, who would have God-bless'd me from you for ever: who were plying me with disencouragements with respect to you eternally. People are revengeful—do not mind them—do nothing but love me—if I knew that for certain life and health will in such event be a heaven, and death itself will be less painful. I long to believe in immortality. I shall never be able to bid you an entire farewell. If I am destined to be happy with you here—how short is the longest Life. I wish to believe in immortality—I wish to live with you for ever. Do not let my name ever pass between you and those laughers, if I have no other merit than the great Love for you, that were sufficient to keep me sacred and un-mentioned in such Society. If I have been cruel and unjust I swear my love has ever been greater than my cruelty which last[s] but a minute whereas my Love come what will shall last for ever. If concession to me has hurt your Pride, god knows I have had little pride in my heart when thinking of you. Your name never passes my Lips—do not let mine pass yours. Those People do not like me. After reading my Letter [if] you even then wish to see me, I am strong enough to walk over—but I dare not. I shall feel so much pain in parting with you again. My dearest love, I am affraid to see you, I am strong, but not strong enough to see you. Will my arm be ever round you again. And if so shall I be obliged to leave you again. My sweet Love! I am happy whilst I believe your first Letter. Let me be but certain that you are mine heart and soul, and I could die more happily than I could otherwise live. If you think me cruel—if you think I have sleighted you—do muse it over again and see into my heart. My Love to you is 'true as truth's simplicity and simpler than the infancy of truth' as I think I once said before. How could I slight you? How threaten to leave you? not in the spirit of a Threat to you—no—but in the spirit of Wretch-edness in myself. My fairest, my delicious, my angel Fanny! do not believe me such a vulgar fellow. I will be as patient in illness and as believing in Love as I am able.

Yours for ever my dearest
JOHN KEATS

EMILY DICKINSON

Letters From a Recluse

7 and 17 May 1850

To Abiah Root

Dear Remembered,

The circumstances under which I write you this morning are at once glorious, afflicting, and beneficial—glorious in *ends,* afflicting in *means,* and *beneficial* I *trust* in *both.* Twin loaves of bread have just been born into the world under my auspices—fine children—the image of their *mother*—and *here* my dear friend is the *glory.*

On the lounge asleep, lies my sick mother, suffering intensely from Acute Neuralgia—except at a moment like this, when kind sleep draws near, and beguiles her, *here* is the *affliction.*

I need not draw the *beneficial* inference—the good I myself derive, the winning the spirit of patience, the genial house-keeping influence stealing over my mind, and soul, you know all these things I would say, and will seem to suppose they are *written,* when indeed they are only *thought.* On Sunday my mother was taken, had been perfectly well before, and could remember no possible imprudence which should have induced the disease, everything has been done, and tho' we think her gradually throwing it off, she still has much suffering. I have always neglected the culinary arts, but attend to them now from necessity, and from a desire to make everything pleasant for father, and Austin. Sickness makes desolation, and "the day is dark, and dreary," but health will come back I hope, and light hearts, and smiling faces. We are sick hardly ever at home, and dont know what to do when it comes, wrinkle our little brows,

LETTERS FROM A RECLUSE: Reprinted by permission of the publishers and the Trustees of Amherst College from Thomas H. Johnson, Editor, *The Letters of Emily Dickinson,* Cambridge, Mass.: The Belknap Press of Harvard University Press, Copyright, 1958, by The President and Fellows of Harvard College.

and stamp our little feet, and our tiny souls get angry, and command it to go away. Mrs. *Brown* will be glad to see it, old-ladies *expect* to die, as for *us*, the young, and active, with all longings "for the strife," *we* to "perish by the road-side, weary with the march of life" no—no my dear "Father Mortality," get out of our way if you please, we will call if we ever want you, Good-morning Sir, ah Good-morning! When I am not at work in the kitchen, I sit by the side of mother, provide for her little wants—and try to cheer, and encourage her. I ought to be glad, and grateful that I *can* do anything now, but I do feel so very lonely, and so anxious to have her cured. I hav'nt repined but *once*, and you shall know all the why. While I washed the dishes at noon in that little "sink-room" of our's, I heard a well-known rap, and a friend I love *so* dearly came and asked me to ride in the woods, the sweet-still woods, and I wanted to exceedingly—I told him I could not go, and he said he was disappointed—he wanted me very much—then the tears came into my eyes, tho' I tried to choke them back, and he said I *could*, and *should* go, and it seemed to me unjust. Oh I struggled with great temptation, and it cost me much of denial, but I think in the end I conquered, not a glorious victory Abiah, where you hear the rolling drum, but a kind of a helpless victory, where triumph would come of itself, faintest music, weary soldiers, nor a waving flag, nor a long-loud shout. I had read of Christ's temptations, and how they were like our own, only he did'nt sin; I wondered if *one* was like mine, and whether it made him angry— I couldnt make up my mind; do you think he ever did?

I went cheerfully round my work, humming a little air till mother had gone to sleep, then cried with all my might, seemed to think I was much abused, that this wicked world was unworthy such devoted, and terrible sufferings, and came to my various senses in great dudgeon at life, and time, and love for affliction, and anguish.

What shall we do my darling, when trial grows more, and more, when the dim, lone light expires, and it's dark, so very dark, and we wander, and know not where, and cannot get out of the forest—whose is the hand to help us, and to lead, and forever guide us, they talk of a "Jesus of Nazareth," will you tell me if it be he?

I presume you have heard from Abby, and know what she now believes—she makes a sweet, girl christian, religion makes her face quite different, calmer, but full of radiance, holy, yet very joyful. She talks of herself quite freely, seems to love Lord Christ most dearly, and to wonder, and be bewildered, at the life she has always led. It all looks black, and distant, and God, and Heaven are near, she is certainly very much changed.

She has told you about things here, how the "still small voice" is calling, and how the people are listening, and believing, and truly obeying— how the place is very solemn, and sacred, and the bad ones slink away, and are sorrowful—not at their wicked lives—but at this strange time, great change. *I* am one of the lingering *bad* ones, and so do *I* slink away, and pause, and ponder, and ponder, and pause, and do work without knowing why—not surely for *this* brief world, and more sure it is not for Heaven—and I ask what this message *means* that they ask for so very eagerly, *you* know of this depth, and fulness, will you *try* to tell me about it?

It's *Friday* my dear Abiah, and that in another week, yet my mission is unfulfilled—and you so sadly neglected, and dont know the reason why. Where do you think I've strayed, and from what new errand returned? I have come from "*to* and *fro*, and walking up, and down" the same place that Satan hailed from, when God asked him where he'd been, but not to illustrate further I tell you I have been dreaming, dreaming a *golden* dream, with eyes all the while wide open, and I guess it's almost morning, and besides I have been at work, providing the "food that perisheth," scaring the timorous dust, and being obedient, and kind. *I* call it kind obedience in the books the Shadows write in, it may have another name. I am yet the Queen of the court, if regalia be dust, and dirt, have three loyal subjects, whom I'd rather relieve from service. Mother is still an invalid tho' a partially restored one—Father and Austin still clamor for food, and I, like a martyr am feeding them. Would'nt you love to see me in these bonds of great despair, looking around my kitchen, and praying for kind deliverance, and declaring by "Omar's beard" I never was in such plight. *My* kitchen I think I called it, God forbid that it was, or shall be my own—God keep me from what they call *households*, except that bright one of "faith"!

Dont be afraid of my imprecations, they never did anyone harm, and they make me feel so cool, and and [*sic*] so very much more comfortable!

Where are you now Abiah, where are your thoughts, and aspirings, where are your young affections, not with the *boots*, and *whiskers; any* with *me* ungrateful, *any* tho' drooping, dying? I presume you are loving your mother, and loving the stranger, and wanderer, visiting the poor, and afflicted, and reaping whole fields of blessings. Save me a *little* sheaf—only a very little one! Remember, and care for me sometimes, and scatter a fragrant flower in this wilderness life of mine by writing me, and by not forgetting, and by lingering longer in prayer, that the Father may bless one more!

Your aff friend,
EMILY

about 6 November 1858

To Dr. and Mrs. J. G. Holland

Dear Hollands,

Good-night! I can't stay any longer in a world of death. Austin is ill of fever. I buried my garden last week—our man, Dick, lost a little girl through the scarlet fever. I thought perhaps that *you* were dead, and not knowing the sexton's address, interrogate the daisies. Ah! dainty—dainty Death! Ah! democratic Death! Grasping the proudest zinnia from my purple garden—then deep to his bosom calling the serf's child!

Say, is he everywhere? Where shall I hide my things? Who is alive? The woods are dead. Is Mrs. H. alive? Annie and Katie—are they below, or received to nowhere?

I shall not tell how short time is, for I was told by lips which sealed as soon as it was said, and the open revere the shut. You were not here in summer. *Summer?* My memory flutters—had I—was there a summer? You should have seen the fields go—gay little entomology! Swift little ornithology! Dancer, and floor, and cadence quite gathered away, and I, a phantom, to you a phantom, rehearse the story! An orator of feather unto an audience of fuzz—and pantomimic plaudits. "Quite as good as a play," indeed!

Tell Mrs. Holland she is mine. Ask her if *vice versa?* Mine is but just the thief's request—"Remember me to-day." Such are the bright chirographies of the "Lamb's Book." Good-night! My ships are in!—My window overlooks the wharf! One yacht, and a man-of-war; two brigs and a schooner! "Down with the topmast! Lay her a' hold, a' hold!"

EMILIE

April 1873?

To Louise and Frances Norcross

Sisters,

I hear robins a great way off, and wagons a great way off, and rivers a great way off, and all appear to be hurrying somewhere undisclosed to me. Remoteness is the founder of sweetness; could we see all we hope, or hear the whole we fear told tranquil, like another tale, there would be madness near. Each of us gives or takes heaven in corporeal person, for each of us has the skill of life. I am pleased by your sweet acquaintance. It is not recorded of any rose that it failed of its bee, though obtained in specific instances through scarlet experience. The career of flowers differs from ours only in inaudibleness. I feel more reverence as I grow for these mute creatures whose suspense or transport may surpass my own. Pussy remembered the judgment, and remained with Vinnie. Maggie preferred her home to "Miggles" and "Oakhurst," so with a few spring touches, nature remains unchanged.

> The most triumphant bird
> I ever knew or met,
> Embarked upon a twig to-day,—
> And till dominion set
> I perish to behold
> So competent a sight—
> And sang for nothing scrutable
> But impudent delight.
> Retired and resumed
> His transitive estate;
> To what delicious accident
> Does finest glory fit!

EMILY

summer 1874

To Louise and Frances Norcross

You might not remember me, dears. I cannot recall myself. I thought I was strongly built, but this stronger has undermined me.

We were eating our supper the fifteenth of June, and Austin came in. He had a despatch in his hand, and I saw by his face we were all lost, though I didn't know how. He said that father was very sick, and he and Vinnie must go. The train had already gone. While horses were dressing, news came he was dead.

Father does not live with us now—he lives in a new house. Though it was built in an hour it is better than this. He hasn't any garden because he moved after gardens were made, so we take him the best flowers, and if we only knew he knew, perhaps we could stop crying....The grass begins after Pat has stopped it.

I cannot write any more, dears. Though it is many nights, my mind never comes home. Thank you each for the love, though I could not notice it. Almost the last tune that he heard was, "Rest from thy loved employ."

EMILY

mid-June 1875

To T. W. Higginson

Dear friend—

Mother was paralyzed Tuesday, a year from the evening Father died. I thought perhaps you would care—

YOUR SCHOLAR

late November 1882

To Louise and Frances Norcross

Dear cousins,

I hoped to write you before, but mother's dying almost stunned my spirit.

I have answered a few inquiries of love, but written little intuitively. She was scarcely the aunt you knew. The great mission of pain had been ratified—cultivated to tenderness by persistent sorrow, so that a larger mother died than had she died before. There was no earthly parting. She slipped from our fingers like a flake gathered by the wind, and is now part of the drift called "the infinite."

We don't know where she is, though so many tell us.

I believe we shall in some manner be cherished by our Maker—that the One who gave us this remarkable earth has the power still farther to surprise that which He has caused. Beyond that all is silence....

Mother was very beautiful when she had died. Seraphs are solemn artists. The illumination that comes but once paused upon her features, and it seemed like hiding a picture to lay her in the grave; but the grass that received my father will suffice his guest, the one he asked at the altar to visit him all his life.

I cannot tell how Eternity seems. It sweeps around me like a sea....Thank you for remembering me. Remembrance—mighty word.

"Thou gavest it to me from the foundation of the world."

Lovingly,
EMILY

late June 1883

To Maria Whitney

Dear Friend,

You are like God. We pray to Him, and He answers "No." Then we pray to Him to rescind the "no," and He don't answer at all, yet "Seek and ye shall find" is the boon of faith.

You failed to keep your appointment with the apple-blossoms—the japonica, even, bore an apple to elicit you, but that must be a silver bell which calls the human heart.

I still hope that you live, and in lands of consciousness.

It is Commencement now. Pathos is very busy.

The past is not a package one can lay away. I see my father's eyes, and those of Mr. Bowles— those isolated comets. If the future is mighty as the past, what may vista be?

With my foot in a sling from a vicious sprain, and reminded of you almost to tears by the week and its witness, I send this sombre word.

The vane defines the wind.

Where we thought you were, Austin says you are not. How strange to change one's sky, unless one's star go with it, but yours has left an astral wake.

Vinnie gives her hand.

Always with love,
EMILY

mid-April 1886

To Charles H. Clark

Thank you, Dear friend—I am better. The velocity of the ill, however, is like that of the snail.

I am glad of your Father's tranquility, and of your own courage.

Fear makes us all martial.

I could hardly have thought it possible that the scholarly Stranger to whom my Father introduced me, could have mentioned my Friend, almost itself a Vision, or have still left a Legend to relate his name.

With the exception of my Sister who never saw Mr. Wadsworth, your Name alone remains.

"Going Home," was he not an Aborigine of the sky? The last time he came in Life, I was with my Lilies and Heliotropes, said my sister to me, "the Gentleman with the deep voice wants to see you, Emily," hearing him ask of the servant. "Where did you come from," I said, for he spoke like an Apparition.

"I stepped from my Pulpit [from] to the Train" was my [*sic*] simple reply, and when I asked "how long," "Twenty Years" said he with inscrutable roguery—but the loved Voice has ceased, and to some one who heard him "Going Home," it was sweet to speak. I am glad his Willie is faithful, of whom he said "the Frogs were his little friends" and I told him they were my Dogs, the last smile that he gave me. Thank you for each circumstance, and tell me all you love to say of what said your lost Brother "The Doctor opened his Heart to Charlie." Excuse me for the Voice, this moment immortal. With my Sister's remembrance,

E. DICKINSON

May 1886

To Louise and Frances Norcross[1]
Little Cousins,
   Called back.

EMILY

FRANZ KAFKA

Dearest Father

Dearest Father:

You asked me recently why I maintain that I am afraid of you. As usual, I was unable to

---

[1] Written the day before her death.

think of any answer to your question, partly for the very reason that I am afraid of you, and partly because an explanation of the grounds for this fear would mean going into far more details than I could even approximately keep in mind while talking. And if I now try to give you an answer in writing, it will still be very incomplete, because even in writing this fear and its consequences hamper me in relation to you and because [anyway] the magnitude of the subject goes far beyond the scope of my memory and power of reasoning....

Compare the two of us: I, to put it in a very much abbreviated form, a Löwy[1] with a certain basis of Kafka, which, however, is not set in motion by the Kafka will to life, business, and conquest, but by a Löwyish spur that urges more secretly, more diffidently, and in another direction, and which often fails to work entirely. You, on the other hand, a true Kafka in strength, health, appetite, loudness of voice, eloquence, self-satisfaction, worldly dominance, endurance, presence of mind, knowledge of human nature, a certain way of doing things on a grand scale, of course also with all the defects and weaknesses that go with all these advantages and into which your temperament and sometimes your hot temper drive you....

However it was, we were so different and in our difference so dangerous to each other that, if anyone had tried to calculate in advance how I, the slowly developing child, and you, the full-grown man, would stand to each other, he could have assumed that you would simply trample me underfoot so that nothing was left of me. Well, that didn't happen. Nothing alive can be calculated. But perhaps something worse happened. And in saying this I would all the time beg of you not to forget that I never, and not even for a single moment, believe any guilt to be on your side. The effect you had on me was the effect you could not help having. But you should stop considering it some particular malice on my part that I succumbed to that effect.

I was a timid child. For all that, I am sure

¹ Löwy was the name of Kafka's mother's family.

I was also obstinate, as children are. I am sure that Mother spoilt me too, but I cannot believe I was particularly difficult to manage; I cannot believe that a kindly word, a quiet taking of me by the hand, a friendly look, could not have got me to do anything that was wanted of me. Now you are after all at bottom a kindly and softhearted person (what follows will not be in contradiction to this, I am speaking only of the impression you made on the child), but not every child has the endurance and fearlessness to go on searching until it comes to the kindliness that lies beneath the surface. You can only treat a child in the way you yourself are constituted, with vigor, noise, and hot temper, and in this case this seemed to you, into the bargain, extremely suitable, because you wanted to bring me up to be a strong brave boy....

There is only one episode in the early years of which I have a direct memory. You may remember it, too. Once in the night I kept on whimpering for water, not, I am certain, because I was thirsty, but probably partly to be annoying, partly to amuse myself. After several vigorous threats had failed to have any effect, you took me out of bed, carried me out onto the *pavlatche* and left me there alone for a while in my nightshirt, outside the shut door. I am not going to say that this was wrong—perhaps at that time there was really no other way of getting peace and quiet that night—but I mention it as typical of your methods of bringing up a child and their effect on me. I dare say I was quite obedient afterwards at that period, but it did me inner harm. What was for me a matter of course, that senseless asking for water, and the extraordinary terror of being carried outside were two things that I, my nature being what it was, could never properly connect with each other. Even years afterwards I suffered from the tormenting fancy that the huge man, my father, the ultimate authority, would come almost for no reason at all and take me out of bed in the night and carry me out onto the *pavlatche*, and that therefore I was such a mere nothing for him.

That then was only a small beginning, but this sense of nothingness that often dominates me (a feeling that is in another respect, admittedly, also a noble and fruitful one) comes largely from your influence. What I would have needed was a little encouragement, a little friendliness, a little keeping open of my road, instead of which you blocked it for me, though of course with the good intention of making me go another road. But I was not fit for that. You encouraged me, for instance, when I saluted and marched smartly, but I was no future soldier, or you encouraged me when I was able to eat heartily or even drink beer with my meals, or when I was able to repeat songs, singing what I had not understood, or prattle to you using your own favorite expressions, imitating you, but nothing of this had anything to do with my future. And it is characteristic that even today you really only encourage me in anything when you yourself are involved in it, when what is at stake is your own sense of self-importance.

At that time, and at that time everywhere, I would have needed encouragement. I was, after all, depressed even by your mere physical presence. I remember, for instance, how we often undressed together in the same bathing hut. There was I, skinny, weakly, slight; you strong, tall, broad. Even inside the hut I felt myself a miserable specimen, and what's more, not only in your eyes but in the eyes of the whole world, for you were for me the measure of all things. But then when we went out of the bathing hut before the people, I with you holding my hand, a little skeleton, unsteady, barefoot on the boards, frightened of the water, incapable of copying your swimming strokes, which you, with the best of intentions, but actually to my profound humiliation, always kept on showing me, then I was frantic with desperation and all my bad experiences in all spheres at such moments fitted magnificently together....

In keeping with that, furthermore, was your intellectual domination. You had worked your way up so far alone, by your own energies, and as a result you had unbounded confidence in your opinion. For me as a child that was not yet so dazzling as later for the boy growing up. From your armchair you ruled the world. Your opinion was correct, every other was mad, wild, *meshugge*, not normal. With all this your self-confidence was so great that you had no need to be consistent at all and yet never ceased to be in the right. It did sometimes happen that you had no opinion whatsoever about a matter and as a result all opinions that were at all possible with respect to the matter were necessarily wrong, without exception. You were capable, for instance, of running down the Czechs, and then the Germans, and then the Jews, and what is more, not only selectively but in every respect, and finally nobody was left except yourself. For me you took on the enigmatic quality that all tyrants have whose rights are based on their person and not on reason. At least so it seemed to me.

Now where I was concerned you were in fact astonishingly often in the right, which was a matter of course in talk, for there was hardly ever any talk between us, but also in reality. Yet this too was nothing particularly incomprehensible; in all my thinking I was, after all, under the heavy pressure of your personality, even in that part of it—and particularly in that—which was not in accord with yours. All these thoughts, seemingly independent of you, were from the beginning loaded with the burden of your harsh and dogmatic judgments; it was almost impossible to endure this, and yet to work out one's thoughts with any measure of completeness and permanence. I am not here speaking of any sublime thoughts, but of every little enterprise in childhood. It was only necessary to be happy about something or other, to be filled with the thought of it, to come home and speak of it, and the answer was an ironical sigh, a shaking of the head, a tapping of the table with one finger: "Is that all you're so worked up about?" or "I wish I had your worries!" or "The things some people have time to think about!" or "What can you buy yourself with that?" or

"What a song and dance about nothing!" Of course, you couldn't be expected to be enthusiastic about every childish triviality, toiling and moiling as you used to. But that wasn't the point. The point was, rather, that you could not help always and on principle causing the child such disappointments, by virtue of your antagonistic nature, and further that this antagonism was ceaselessly intensified through accumulation of its material, that it finally became a matter of established habit even when for once you were of the same opinion as myself, and that finally these disappointments of the child's were not disappointments in ordinary life but, since what it concerned was your person, which was the measure of all things, struck to the very core. Courage, resolution, confidence, delight in this and that, did not endure to the end when you were against whatever it was or even if your opposition was merely to be assumed; and it was to be assumed in almost everything I did....

You have, I think, a gift for bringing up children; you could, I am sure, have been of use to a human being of your own kind with your methods; such a person would have seen the reasonableness of what you told him, would not have troubled about anything else, and would quietly have done things the way he was told. But for me a child everything you shouted at me was positively a heavenly commandment, I never forgot it, it remained for me the most important means of forming a judgment of the world, above all of forming a judgment of you yourself, and there you failed entirely. Since as a child I was together with you chiefly at meals, your teaching was to a large extent teaching about proper behavior at table. What was brought to the table had to be eaten up, there could be no discussion of the goodness of the food—but you yourself often found the food uneatable, called it "this swill," said "that brute" (the cook) had ruined it. Because in accordance with your strong appetite and your particular habit you ate everything fast, hot and in big mouthfuls, the child had to hurry, there

was a somber silence at table, interrupted by admonitions: "Eat first, talk afterwards," or "Faster, faster, faster," or "There you are, you see, I finished ages ago." Bones musn't be cracked with the teeth, but you could. Vinegar must not be sipped noisily, but you could. The main thing was that the bread should be cut straight. But it didn't matter that you did it with a knife dripping with gravy. One had to take care that no scraps fell on the floor. In the end it was under your chair that there were most scraps. At table one wasn't allowed to do anything but eat, but you cleaned and cut your fingernails, sharpened pencils, cleaned your ears with the toothpick. Please, Father, understand me rightly: these would in themselves have been utterly insignificant details, they only became depressing for me because you, the man who was so tremendously the measure of all things for me, yourself did not keep the commandments you imposed on me. Hence the world was for me divided into three parts: into one in which I, the slave, lived under laws that had been invented only for me and which I could, I did not know why, never completely comply with; then into a second world, which was infinitely remote from mine, in which you lived, concerned with government, with the issuing of orders and with annoyance about their not being obeyed; and finally into a third world where everybody else lived happily and free from orders and from having to obey. I was continually in disgrace, either I obeyed your orders, and that was a disgrace, for they applied, after all, only to me, or I was defiant, and that was a disgrace too, for how could I presume to defy you, or I could not obey because, for instance, I had not your strength, your appetite, your skill, in spite of which you expected it of me as a matter of course; this was the greatest disgrace of all. What moved in this way was not the child's reflections, but his feelings....

It was true that Mother was illimitably good to me, but all that was for me in relation to you, that is to say, in no good relation. Mother unconsciously played the part of a beater during a hunt. Even if your method of upbringing might in some unlikely case have set me on my own feet by means of producing defiance, dislike, or even hate in me, Mother canceled that out again by kindness, by talking sensibly (in the maze and chaos of my childhood she was the very pattern of good sense and reasonableness), by pleading for me, and I was again driven back into your orbit, which I might perhaps otherwise have broken out of, to your advantage and to my own. Or it was so that no real reconciliation ever came about, that Mother merely shielded me from you in secret, secretly gave me something, or allowed me to do something, and then where you were concerned I was again the furtive creature, the cheat, the guilty one, who in his worthlessness could only pursue backstairs methods even to get the things he regarded as his right. Of course, I then became used to taking such courses also in quest of things to which, even in my own view, I had no right. This again meant an increase in the sense of guilt.

It is also true that you hardly ever really gave me a whipping. But the shouting, the way your face got red, the hasty undoing of the braces and the laying of them ready over the back of the chair, all that was almost worse for me. It is like when someone is going to be hanged. If he is really hanged, then he's dead and it's all over. But if he has to go through all the preliminaries to being hanged and only when the noose is dangling before his face is told of his reprieve, then he may suffer from it all his life long. Besides, from so many occasions when I had, as you clearly showed you thought, deserved to be beaten, when you were however gracious enough to let me off at the last moment, here again what accumulated was only a huge sense of guilt. On every side I was to blame, I was in debt to you.

You have always reproached me (and what is more either alone or in front of others, you having no feeling for the humiliation of this latter, your children's affairs always being public affairs) for living in peace and quiet, warmth, and abundance, lacking for nothing, thanks to your hard work. I think here of remarks that must positively have worn grooves in my brain, like: "When I was only seven I had to push the barrow from village to village." "We all had to sleep in one room." "We were glad when we got potatoes." "For years I had open sores on my legs from not having enough clothes to wear in winter." "I was only a little boy when I was sent away to Pisek to go into business." "I got nothing from home, not even when I was in the army, even then I was sending money home." "But for all that, for all that—Father was always Father to me. Ah, nobody knows what that means these days! What do these children know of things? Nobody's been through that! Is there any child that understands such things today?" Under other conditions such stories might have been very educational, they might have been a way of encouraging one and strengthening one to endure similar torments and deprivations to those one's father had undergone. But that wasn't what you wanted at all; the situation had, after all, become quite different as a result of all your efforts, and there was no opportunity to distinguish oneself in the world as you had done. Such an opportunity would first of all have had to be created by violence and revolution, it would have meant breaking away from home (assuming one had had the resolution and strength to do so and that Mother wouldn't have worked against it, for her part, with other means). But all that was not what you wanted at all, that you termed ingratitude, extravagance, disobedience, treachery, madness. And so, while on the one hand you tempted me to it by means of example, story, and humiliation, on the other hand you forbade it with the utmost severity....

(Up to this point there is in this letter relatively little I have intentionally passed over in silence, but now and later I shall have to be silent on certain matters that it is still too hard for me to confess—to you and to myself. I say this in order that, if the picture as a whole should be somewhat blurred here and there, you should not believe that what is to blame is any lack of evidence; on the contrary, there is evidence that might well make the picture unbearably stark. It is not easy to strike a median position.) Here, it is enough to remind you of early days. I had lost my self-confidence where you were concerned, and in its place had developed a boundless sense of guilt. (In recollection of this boundlessness I once wrote of someone, accurately: "He is afraid the shame will outlive him, even.") I could not suddenly undergo a transformation when I came into the company of other people; on the contrary, with them I came to feel an even deeper sense of guilt, for, as I have already said, in their case I had to make good the wrongs done them by you in the business, wrongs in which I too had my share of responsibility. Besides, you always, of course, had some objection to make, frankly or covertly, to everyone I associated with, and for this too I had to beg his pardon. The mistrust that you tried to instill into me, at business and at home, towards most people (tell me of any single person who was of importance to me in my childhood whom you didn't at least once tear to shreds with your criticism), this mistrust, which oddly enough was no particular burden to you (the fact was that you were strong enough to bear it, and besides, it was in reality perhaps only a token of the autocrat), this mistrust, which for me as a little boy was nowhere confirmed in my own eyes, since I everywhere saw only people excellent beyond all hope of emulation, in me turned into mistrust of myself and into perpetual anxiety in relation to everything else. There, then, I was in general certain of not being able to escape from you ....

I found equally little means of escape from you in Judaism. Here some escape would, in principle, have been thinkable, but more than that, it would have been thinkable that we might both have found each other in Judaism or even that we might have begun from there in harmony. But what sort of Judaism was it I got from you? In the course of the years I have taken roughly three different attitudes to it.

As a child I reproached myself, in accord with you, for not going to the synagogue enough, for not fasting, and so on. I thought that in this way I was doing a wrong not to myself but to you, and I was penetrated by a sense of guilt, which was, of course, always ready to hand.

Later, as a boy, I could not understand how, with the insignificant scrap of Judaism you yourself possessed, you could reproach me for not (if for no more than the sake of piety, as you put it) making an effort to cling to a similar insignificant scrap. It was indeed really, so far as I could see, a mere scrap, a joke, not even a joke. On four days in the year you went to the synagogue, where you were, to say the least of it, closer to the indifferent than to those who took it seriously, patiently went through the prayers by way of formality, sometimes amazed me by being able to show me in the prayer book the passage that was being said at the moment, and for the rest, so long (and this was the main thing) as I was there in the synagogue I was allowed to hang about wherever I liked. And so I yawned and dozed through the many hours (I don't think I was ever again so bored, except later at dancing lessons) and did my best to enjoy the few little bits of variety there were, as, for instance, when the Ark of the Covenant was opened, which always reminded me of the shooting galleries where a cupboard door would open in the same way whenever one got a bull's-eye, only with the difference that there something interesting always came out and here it was always just the same old dolls with no heads. Incidentally, it was also very frightening for me there, not only, as goes without saying, because of all the people one came into close contact with, but also because you once mentioned, by the way, that I too might be called up to read the Torah. That was something I went in dread of for years. But otherwise I was not fundamentally disturbed in my state of boredom, unless it was by the *bar mizvah*, but that meant no more than some ridiculous learning by heart, in other words, led to nothing but something like the ridiculous passing of an examination, and then, so far as you were con-cerned, by little, not very significant incidents, as when you were called up to read the Torah and came well out of the affair, which to my way of feeling was purely social, or when you stayed on in the synagogue for the prayers for the dead, and I was sent away, which for a long time, obviously because of being sent away and lacking, as I did, any deeper interest, aroused in me the more or less unconscious feeling that what was about to take place was something indecent.—That was how it was in the syna-gogue, and at home it was, if possible, even more poverty-stricken, being confined to the first evening of Passover, which more and more developed into a farce, with fits of hysterical laughter, admittedly under the influence of the growing children. (Why did you have to give way to that influence? Because you brought it about in the first place.) And so there was the religious material that was handed on to me, to which may be added at most the outstretched hand pointing to "the sons of the millionaire Fuchs," who were in the synagogue with their father at the high holidays. How one could do anything better with this material than get rid of it as fast as possible was something I could not understand; precisely getting rid of it seemed to me the most effective act of "piety" one could perform....

I showed no foresight at all with regard to the significance and possibility of a marriage for me; this up to now the greatest terror of my life has come upon me almost completely un-expectedly. The child had developed so slowly, these things were outwardly all too remote from him; now and then the necessity of thinking of them did arise; but that here a permanent, decisive and indeed the most grimly bitter ordeal was imminent was something that could not be recognized. In reality, however, the plans to marry became the most large-scale and hopeful attempt at escape, and then the failure was on a correspondingly large scale, too.

I am afraid that, because in this sphere every-thing I try is a failure, I shall also fail to make

these attempts to marry comprehensible to you. And yet on this depends the success of this whole letter, for in these attempts there was, on the one hand, concentrated everything I had at my disposal in the way of positive forces, and, on the other hand, here there also accumulated, and with downright fury, all the negative forces that I have described....

How, now, was I prepared for this? As badly as possible....

I remember going for a walk one evening with you and Mother; it was on the Josefsplatz near where the Länderbank is today; and I began talking about these interesting things, in a stupidly boastful, superior, proud, cool (that was spurious), cold (that was genuine) and stammering manner, as indeed I usually talked to you, reproaching the two of you for my having been left uninstructed, for the fact that it was my schoolmates who first had to take me in hand, that I had been in the proximity of great dangers (here I was brazenly lying, as was my way, in order to show myself brave, for as a consequence of my timidity I had, except for the usual sexual misdemeanors of city children, no very exact notion of these "great dangers"), but finally hinted that now, fortunately, I knew everything, no longer needed any advice, and that everything was all right. I began talking about this, in any case, mainly because it gave me pleasure at least to talk about it, and then too out of curiosity, and finally too in order somehow to avenge myself on the two of you for something or other. In keeping with your nature you took it quite simply, only saying something to the effect that you could give me some advice about how I could go in for these things without danger....

It is not easy to judge the answer you gave me then; on the one hand, there was, after all, something staggeringly frank, in a manner of speaking, primeval, about it; on the other hand, however, as regards the instruction itself, it was uninhibited in a very modern way. I don't know how old I was at the time, certainly not much over sixteen. It was nevertheless a very remarkable answer for such a boy to be given, and the distance between the two of us is also shown in the fact that this was actually the first direct instruction bearing on real life that I ever received from you. But its real meaning, which sank into my mind even then, but only much later came partly to the surface of my consciousness, was this: what you were advising me to do was, after all, in your opinion and, still far more, in my opinion at that time, the filthiest thing possible. The fact that you were prepared to see to it that physically speaking I should not bring any of the filth home with me was incidental, for in that way you were only protecting yourself, your own household. The main thing was, rather, that you remained outside your own advice, a married man, a pure man, exalted above these things; this was intensified for me at that time probably even more through the fact that marriage too seemed to me to be shameless and hence it was impossible for me to refer the general information I had picked up about marriage to my parents. In this way you became still more pure, rose still higher. The thought that you might perhaps have given yourself similar advice too before marriage was to me utterly unthinkable. So there was almost no smudge of earthly filth on you at all. And precisely you were pushing me, just as though I were predestined to it, down into this filth, with a few frank words. And so if the world consisted only of me and you, a notion I was much inclined to have, then this purity of the world came to an end with you and, by virtue of your advice, the filth began with me....

A similar clash between us took place in quite different circumstances some twenty years later, as a fact horrible, in itself, however, much less damaging—for where was there anything in me, the thirty-six-year-old, that could still be damaged? I am referring to a little discussion on one of the few agitated days after I had informed you of my last marriage project. What you said to me was more or less as follows: "She probably put on some specially chosen blouse, the thing these Prague Jewesses are good at, and straightaway, of course, you made up your mind to marry her. And, what's more, as fast as possible, in a week, tomorrow, today. I can't make you out, after all, you're a grown man, here you are in town, and you can't think of any way of managing but going straight off and marrying the next best girl. Isn't there anything else you can do? If you're frightened, I'll go along with you myself." You put it in more detail and more plainly, but I can no longer recall the particular points, perhaps too things became a little misty before my eyes, I was almost more interested in Mother, as she, though perfectly in agreement with you, nevertheless took something from the table and left the room with it.

You have, I suppose, scarcely ever humiliated me more deeply with words and have never more clearly shown me your contempt. When you spoke to me in a similar way twenty years earlier, looking at it through your eyes one might even have seen in it some respect for the precocious city boy, who in your opinion could already be initiated into life without more ado. Today this consideration could only intensify the contempt, for the boy who was about to take his first leap into life got stuck halfway and seems to you today to be richer by no experience but only more pitiable by twenty years. My deciding on a girl meant nothing at all to you. You had (unconsciously) always kept down my power of decision and now believed (unconsciously) that you knew what it was worth. Of my attempts at escape in other directions you knew nothing, thus you could not know anything, either, of the thought processes that had led me to this attempt to marry, and had to try to guess at them, and your guess was in keeping with your total judgment of me, a guess at the most abominable, crude, and ridiculous thing possible. And you did not for a moment hesitate to say this to me in just such a manner. The shame you inflicted on me with this was nothing to you in comparison to the shame that I would, in your opinion, inflict on your name by this marriage.

Now, as it happens, with regard to my attempts at marriage there is much you can say in reply, and you have indeed done so: you could not have much respect for my decision since I had twice broken the engagement to F. and twice renewed it again, since I had dragged you and Mother to Berlin to celebrate the engagement, and all for nothing, and the like. All this is true—but how did it come about? ...

Here, in the attempt to marry, two seemingly antagonistic elements in my relations with you unite more intensely than anywhere else. Marriage is certainly the pledge of the most acute form of self-liberation and independence. I should have a family, the highest thing that one can achieve, in my opinion, and so too the highest thing you have achieved; I should be your equal; all old and everlastingly new shame and tyranny would now be mere history. That would, admittedly, be like a fairy tale, but precisely there does the questionable element lie. It is too much; so much cannot be achieved ....

If I want to become independent in the particular unhappy relationship in which I stand to you, I must do something that will have, if possible, no relation to you at all; marrying is, it is true, the greatest thing of all and provides the most honorable independence, but it is also at the same time in the closest relation to you ....

I picture this equality that would then arise between us, and which you would be able to understand better than any other form of equality, as so beautiful precisely because I could then be a free, grateful, guiltless, upright son, and you could be an untroubled, untyrannical, sympathetic, contented father. But to this end it would be necessary to make all that has happened be as though it had never happened, which means, we ourselves should have to be cancelled out.

But we being what we are, marrying is barred to me through the fact that it is precisely and peculiarly your most intimate domain. Sometimes I imagine the map of the world spread out flat and you stretched out diagonally across it.

And what I feel then is that only those territories come into question for my life that either are not covered by you or are not within your reach. And, in keeping with the conception that I have of your magnitude, these are not many and not very comforting territories, and above all marriage is not among them ....

Questions for Review

1. Lord Chesterfield's letters have been admired for their elegant style since they were first written in the eighteenth century; however, they have also been condemned for their contents. What relationship is there between Chesterfield's diction and his subject matter?

2. For what purpose(s) does Chesterfield write his letters? Does he explicitly state his purpose(s)?

3. How would you characterize the tone of the letters? What are Chesterfield's attitudes toward himself, toward the behavior of society, and toward his son?

4. Dr. Johnson's letter to Lord Chesterfield on the subject of Chesterfield's patronage of Johnson's *Dictionary* is very famous. How would you account for the critical approval given by so many readers to this letter?

5. What is the tone of Johnson's letter? Does he use irony?

6. Johnson was an expert with words. Examine closely the diction in this letter. Can you find any places where another word can be easily or effectively substituted for the one Johnson used?

7. What is the purpose of this letter? What is its theme?

8. Keats's letters to Fanny Brawne shocked the reading public when they were first published because of their intimacy and their revelation of the poet's private emotions. They are still among the most passionate of epistolary literature. In what ways do Keats's letters resemble a diary?

9. Although Keats is seemingly in a state of constant concern about Fanny's attitudes

and character, do the letters give a clear depiction of her? How would you best describe Keats's attitude toward Fanny? Toward himself? Is Keats actually more interested in his own state of emotion than he is in Fanny as a woman and human being?

10. What tones are to be found in these letters? How would you characterize the overall tone of the correspondence?

11. Emily Dickinson is respected as one of America's greatest poets. Is there evidence in her letters to show that she wrote poetry? Explain.

12. Do facts (i.e., pieces of information) play an important part in Emily Dickinson's letters? Are her letters less factual than those of Keats? Of Chesterfield? Is "factual" a significant term to use in discussing letters critically?

13. Miss Dickinson's letters may seem strangely disjointed in subject matter but closely integrated by her style (tone and diction). Are there other unifying elements besides style?

14. What tone(s) are to be found in the Dickinson letters? Does the tone depend mainly on the subject? Are the tones in the "death" letters different in quality from those in the thank-you notes? How do you account for this?

15. Franz Kafka's letter to his father was never sent and the elder man never read it. Did Kafka apparently intend to send the letter as intent can be seen within the letter itself? Is there any evidence in the letter that would explain why it was not sent?

16. The tone of this letter is, on the surface, very unlike the passionate declamations of Keats or the bursts of emotion by Emily Dickinson. Is Kafka's tone really cold and unemotional? Explain. Similarly, is this letter really one of objective analysis and exposition or is it something else?

17. Is Kafka's depiction of his father to be taken as an accurate description of the man? Why or why not? Does Carl Jung's theory of the imago (see p. 35 above) help us as readers to put Kafka's portrait of his father in perspective?

18. Read Kafka's "fictional" story, "The Judgment" on p. 464. Is the father in the story Kafka's own father? Is the son Kafka himself? Do the characters in the story seem more or less "real" than the two Kafkas? Do you find the letter or story the more interesting and moving?

Questions for Discussion and Writing

1. Basing your answer on the selection of letters above, what would you say are the basic intentions or aims of the letter-writer: to amuse, instruct, persuade, correct, explain, or what?

2. Compare and contrast the purpose of the journal and that of the letter. How do these differences in purpose relate to the differences in form and technique between the two kinds of composition?

3. Would the writer be likely to use the same language in a letter that he uses in a diary? In private conversation? In a public gathering? What guiding principle(s) of diction does a letter-writer follow, insofar as the letters above provide evidence?

4. Are there any kinds of subject matter that would be suitable to a journal but unsuitable for a letter? What principle of determination would operate in this case?

5. What qualities should a letter possess in order to fulfill its intention (or its generic function)?

6. Are letters "fictional" in any important way or are they entirely "factual"? Is their "truth" intuitive rather than empirical?

7. Several of the letter-writers included here are also poets or story tellers. Compare and contrast the use of similar materials in different forms by Keats (pp. 94–98 and 546–547), Kafka (pp. 102–110 and 464–470), and Dickinson (pp. 98–102 and 547).

8. Dr. Johnson remarked on separate occasions that the soul of a man lies bare in his letters and that of all kinds of writing, the letter revealed the least about its

author. Are these two statements compatible or not? Apply one (or both) to the letters of Chesterfield, Keats, and Kafka.

9. Is the letter-writer more spontaneous or more self-conscious than the diarist? Elaborate upon your answer.

10. It is possible to learn more about the mind and character of a man from his journal, his letters, or from what he writes about another man? (Compare Boswell as he is revealed in his various compositions, on pp. 62–70, 166–171, and 172–178, or Chesterfield as he appears in his own letters and in Johnson's above).

SECTION TWO

Public Revelation
of the
Private

Like the diarist and letter writer, the autobiographer uses his own experience as the subject of his composition. Autobiography literally means "to write about one's self," and the autobiographer, like the diarist, is concerned with formulating his experiences in a verbally coherent manner. But the writer of autobiography is unlike the diarist in that he is writing for readers other than himself; and he is unlike the letter writer in that his audience is chiefly composed of people unknown to him. Why would a man choose to write an account of himself for the perusal of strangers? The traditional nomenclature of auto-biographical writing suggests several possibilities: often termed "apology," "confession," or "account," autobiographical literature has on occasion presented the writer defending himself against criticism, justifying his own choices or actions, explaining how he did something or why he did not do it, or even attacking his readers for their inability to understand him and accept his beliefs. The group of essays here embodies all of these approaches—and several others as well. Autobiographical literature is highly diverse in its points of view, styles, methods, and tones; as a literary "type" it has almost as many forms as it has practitioners.

ST. AUGUSTINE

The Sins of My Youth

Thou, then, O Lord my God, who gavest life to this my infancy, furnishing thus with senses (as we see) the frame Thou gavest, compacting its limbs, ornamenting its proportions, and, for its general good and safety, implanting in it all vital functions, Thou commandest me to praise Thee in these things, *to confess unto Thee, and sing unto Thy name, Thou most Highest.* For Thou art God, Almighty and Good, even hadst Thou done nought but only this, which none could do but Thou: whose Unity is the mould of all things; who out of Thy own fairness makest all things fair; and orderest all things by Thy law. This age then, Lord, whereof I have no remembrance, which I take on others' word, and guess from other infants that I have passed, true though the guess be, I am yet loth to count in this life of mine which I live in this world. For no less than that which I spent in my mother's womb, is it hid from me in the shadows of forgetfulness. But if *I was shapen in iniquity, and in sin did my mother conceive me*, where, I beseech Thee, O my God, where, Lord, or when, was I Thy servant guiltless? But, lo! that period I pass by; and what have I now to do with that, of which I can recall no vestige?

Passing hence from infancy, I came to boyhood, or rather it came to me, displacing infancy. Nor did that depart—(for whither went it?)—and yet it was no more. For I was no longer a speechless infant, but a speaking boy. This I remember; and have since observed how I learned to speak. It was not that my elders taught me words (as, soon after, other learning) in any set method; but I, longing by cries and broken accents and various motions of my limbs to express my thoughts, that so I might have my

will, and yet unable to express all I willed, or to whom I willed, did myself, by the understanding which Thou, my God, gavest me, practise the sounds in my memory. When they named any thing, and as they spoke turned towards it, I saw and remembered that they called what they would point out, by the name they uttered. And that they meant this thing and no other, was plain from the motions of their body, the natural language, as it were, of all nations, expressed by the countenance, glances of the eye, gestures of the limbs, and tones of the voice, indicating the affections of the mind, as it pursues, possesses, rejects, or shuns. And thus by constantly hearing words, as they occurred in various sentences, I collected gradually for what they stood; and having broken in my mouth to these signs, I thereby gave utterance to my will. Thus I exchanged with those about me these current signs of our wills, and so launched deeper into the stormy intercourse of human life, yet depending on parental authority and the beck of elders.

O God my God, what miseries and mockeries did I now experience, when obedience to my teachers was proposed to me, as proper in a boy, in order that in this world I might prosper, and excel in tongue-science, which should serve to the "praise of men," and to deceitful riches. Next I was put to school to get learning, in which I (poor wretch) knew not what use there was; and yet, if idle in learning, I was beaten. For this was judged right by our forefathers; and many, passing the same course before us, framed for us weary paths, through which we were fain to pass; multiplying toil and grief upon the sons of Adam. But, Lord, we found that men called upon Thee, and we learnt from them to think of Thee (according to our powers) as of some great One, who, though hidden from our senses, couldst hear and help us. For so I began, as a boy, to pray to Thee, my aid and refuge; and broke the fetters of my tongue to call on Thee, praying Thee, though small, yet with no small earnestness, that I might not be beaten at school. And when Thou heardest me not,

THE SINS OF MY YOUTH: From the *Confessions*, translated by E. B. Pusey.

(*not thereby giving me over to folly*) my elders, yea, my very parents, who yet wished me no ill, mocked my stripes, my then great and grievous ill.

Is there, Lord, any of soul so great, and cleaving to Thee with so intense affection, (for a sort of stupidity will in a way do it); but is there any one, who, from cleaving devoutly to Thee, is endued with so great a spirit, that he can think as lightly of the racks and hooks and other torments, (against which, throughout all lands, men call on Thee with extreme dread,) mocking at those by whom they are feared most bitterly, as our parents mocked the torments which we suffered in boyhood from our masters? For we feared not our torments less; nor prayed we less to Thee to escape them. And yet we sinned, in writing or reading or studying less than was exacted of us. For we wanted not, O Lord, memory or capacity, whereof Thy will gave enough for our age; but our sole delight was play; and for this we were punished by those who yet themselves were doing the like. But elder folks' idleness is called "business"; that of boys, being really the same, is punished by those elders; and none commiserates either boys or men. For will any of sound discretion approve of my being beaten as a boy, because, by playing at ball, I made less progress in studies which I was to learn, only that, as a man, I might play more unbeseemingly? And what else did he, who beat me? who, if worsted in some trifling discussion with his fellow-tutor, was more embittered and jealous than I, when beaten at ball by a play-fellow?

And yet, I sinned herein, O Lord God, the Creator and Disposer of all things in nature, of sin the Disposer only, O Lord my God, I sinned in transgressing the commands of my parents and those of my masters. For what they, with whatever motive, would have me learn, I might afterward have put to good use. For I disobeyed, not from a better choice, but from love of play, loving the pride of victory in my contests, and to have my ears tickled with lying fables, that they might itch the more; the same

curiosity flashing from my eyes more and more, for the shows and games of my elders. Yet those who give these shows are in such esteem, that almost all wish the same for their children, and yet are very willing that they should be beaten, if those very games detain them from the studies, whereby they would have them attain to be the givers of them. Look with pity, Lord, on these things, and deliver us who call upon Thee now; deliver those too who call not on Thee yet, that they may call on Thee, and Thou mayest deliver them.

In boyhood itself, however, (so much less dreaded for me than youth,) I loved not study, and hated to be forced to it. Yet I was forced; and this was well done towards me, but I did not well; for, unless forced, I had not learnt. But no one doth well against his will, even though what he doth be well. Yet neither did they well who forced me, but what was well came to me from Thee, my God. For they were regardless how I should employ what they forced me to learn, except to satiate the insatiate desires of a wealthy beggary, and a shameful glory. But Thou, *by whom the very hairs of our head are numbered*, didst use for my good the error of all who urged me to learn; and my own, who would not learn, Thou didst use for my punishment— a fit penalty for one, so small a boy and so great a sinner. So by those who did not well, Thou didst well for me; and by my own sin Thou didst justly punish me. For Thou hast commanded, and so it is, that ever inordinate affection should be its own punishment.

But why did I so much hate the Greek, which I studied as a boy? I do not yet fully know. For the Latin I loved; not what my first masters, but what the so-called grammarians taught me. For those first lessons, reading, writing, and arithmetic, I thought as great a burden and penalty as any Greek. And yet whence was this too, but from the sin and vanity of this life, because *I was flesh, and a breath that passeth away and cometh not again?* For those first lessons were better certainly, because more certain; by them I obtained, and still retain, the power of reading what I find written, and myself writing what I will; whereas in the others, I was forced to learn the wanderings of one Aeneas, forgetful of my own, and to weep for dead Dido, because she killed herself for love; the while, with dry eyes, I endured my miserable self dying among these things, far from Thee, O my God my life.

For what more miserable than a miserable being who commiserates not himself; weeping the death of Dido for love to Aeneas, but weeping not his own death for want of love to Thee, O God? Thou light of my heart, Thou bread of my inmost soul, Thou Power who givest vigour to my mind, who quickenest my thoughts, I loved Thee not. I committed fornication against Thee, and all around me thus fornicating there echoed "Well done! well done!" *for the friendship of this world is fornication against Thee;* and "Well done! well done!" echoes on till one is ashamed not to be thus a man. And all this I wept not, I who wept for Dido slain, and "seeking by the sword a stroke and wound extreme," myself seeking the while a worse extreme, the extremest and lowest of Thy creatures, having forsaken Thee, earth passing in to the earth. And if forbid to read all this, I was grieved that I might not read what grieved me. Madness like this is thought a higher and a richer learning, than that by which I learned to read and write.

But now, my God, cry Thou aloud in my soul; and let Thy truth tell me, "Not so, not so. Far better was that first study." For, lo, I would readily forget the wanderings of Aeneas and all the rest, rather than how to read and write. But over the entrance of the Grammar School is a veil drawn! true; yet is this not so much an emblem of aught recondite, as a cloak of error. Let not those, whom I no longer fear, cry out against me, while I confess to Thee, my God, whatever my soul will, and acquiesce in the condemnation of my evil ways, that I may love Thy good ways. Let not either buyers or sellers of grammar-learning cry out against me. For if I question them whether it be true, that Aeneas came on a time to Carthage, as the Poet

tells, the less learned will reply that they know not, the more learned that he never did. But should I ask with what letters the name "Aeneas" is written, every one who has learnt this will answer me aright, as to the signs which men have conventionally settled. If, again, I should ask, which might be forgotten with least detriment to the concerns of life, reading and writing or these poetic fictions? Who does not foresee, what all must answer who have not wholly forgotten themselves? I sinned, then, when as a boy I preferred those empty to those more profitable studies, or rather loved the one and hated the other. "One and one, two"; "two and two, four"; this was to me a hateful sing-song: "the wooden horse lined with armed men," and "the burning of Troy," and "Creusa's shade and sad similitude," were the choice spectacle of my vanity.

Why then did I hate the Greek classics, which have the like tales? For Homer also curiously wove the like fictions, and is most sweetly-vain, yet was he bitter to my boyish taste. And so I suppose would Virgil be to Grecian children, when forced to learn him. I learnt many a useful word, but these may as well be as I was Homer. Difficulty, in truth, the difficulty of a foreign tongue, dashed, as it were, with gall all the sweetness of Grecian fable. For not one word of it did I understand, and to make me understand I was urged vehemently with cruel threats and punishments. Time was also, (as an infant,) I knew no Latin; but this I learned without fear of suffering, by mere observation, amid the caresses of my nursery and jests of friends, smiling and sportively encouraging me. This I learned without any pressure of punishment to urge me on, for my heart urged me to give birth to its conceptions, which I could only do by learning words not of those who taught, but of those who talked with me; in whose ears also I gave birth to the thoughts, whatever I conceived. No doubt then, that a free curiosity has more force in our learning these things, than a frightful enforcement. Only this enforcement restrains the rovings of that freedom, through Thy laws, O my God, Thy laws, from the master's cane to the martyr's trials, being able to temper for us a wholesome bitter, recalling us to Thyself from that deadly pleasure which lures us from Thee.

Hear, Lord, my prayer; let not my soul faint under Thy discipline, nor let me faint in confessing unto Thee all Thy mercies, whereby Thou hast drawn me out of all my most evil ways, that Thou mightest become a delight to me above all the allurements which I once pursued; that I may most entirely love Thee, and clasp Thy hand with all my affections, and Thou mayest yet rescue me from every temptation, even unto the end. For, lo, O Lord, my King and my God, for Thy service be whatever useful thing my childhood learned; for Thy service, that I speak—write—read—reckon. For Thou didst grant me Thy discipline, while I was learning vanities; and my sin of delighting in those vanities Thou hast forgiven. In them, indeed, learned in things not vain; and that is the safe path for the steps of youth.

EDWARD GIBBON

An Appraisal of My Life

From my early acquaintance with Lausanne I had always cherished a secret wish that the school of my youth might become the retreat of my declining age. A moderate fortune would secure the blessings of ease, leisure, and independence. The country, the people, the manners, the language, were congenial to my taste, and I might indulge the hope of passing

AN APPRAISAL OF MY LIFE: From *The Autobiography of Edward Gibbon,* edited by Dero A. Saunders. Copyright © 1961. Reprinted by permission of The World Publishing Company.

some years in the domestic society of a friend. After traveling with several English, Mr. Deyverdun was now settled at home in a pleasant habitation, the gift of his deceased aunt. We had long been separated; we had long been silent; yet in my first letter I exposed with the most perfect confidence my situation, my sentiments, and my designs. His immediate answer was a warm and joyful acceptance. The picture of our future life provoked my impatience; and the terms of arrangement were short and simple, as he possessed the property and I undertook the expense of our common house.

Before I could break my English chain it was incumbent on me to struggle with the feelings of my heart, the indolence of my temper, and the opinion of the world, which unanimously condemned this voluntary banishment. In the disposal of my effects, the library, a sacred deposit, was alone excepted. As my post chaise moved over Westminster Bridge I bade a long farewell to the "smoke, the wealth, and the street noise of Rome." My journey, by the direct road through France, was not attended with any accident, and I arrived at Lausanne nearly twenty years after my second departure. Within less than three months the coalition [in Parliament] struck on some hidden rocks: Had I remained on board I should have perished in the general shipwreck.

Since my establishment at Lausanne more than seven years have elapsed, and if every day has not been equally soft and serene, not a day, not a moment, has occurred in which I have repented of my choice. During my absence, a long portion of human life, many changes had happened. My elder acquaintances had left the stage, virgins were ripened into matrons, and children were grown to the age of manhood; but the same manners were transmitted from one generation to another. My friend alone was an inestimable treasure; my name was not totally forgotten, and all were ambitious to welcome the arrival of a stranger and the return of a fellow citizen. The first winter was given to a general embrace, without any nice discrimination of persons and characters. After a more regular settlement, a more accurate survey, I discovered three solid and permanent benefits of my new situation.

1. My personal freedom had been somewhat impaired by the House of Commons and the Board of Trade, but I was now delivered from the chain of duty and dependence, from the hopes and fears of political adventure. My sober mind was no longer intoxicated by the fumes of party, and I rejoiced in my escape as often as I read of the midnight debates which preceded the dissolution of Parliament.

2. My English economy had been that of a solitary bachelor who might afford some occasional dinners. In Switzerland I enjoyed at every meal, at every hour, the free and pleasant conversation of the friend of my youth, and my daily table was always provided for the reception of one or two extraordinary guests. Our importance in society is less a positive than a relative weight. In London I was lost in the crowd. I ranked with the first families of Lausanne, and my style of prudent expense enabled me to maintain a fair balance of reciprocal civilities.

3. Instead of a small house between a street and a stableyard, I began to occupy a spacious and convenient mansion, connected on the north side with the city, and open on the south to a beautiful and boundless horizon. A garden of four acres had been laid out by the taste of Mr. Deyverdun. From the garden a rich scenery of meadows and vineyards descends to the Leman Lake, and the prospect far beyond the lake is crowned by the stupendous mountains of Savoy. My books and my acquaintance had been first united in London, but this happy position of my library in town and country was finally reserved for Lausanne. Possessed of every comfort in this triple alliance, I could not be tempted to change my habitation with the changes of the seasons.

My friends had been kindly apprehensive that I should not be able to exist in a Swiss town at the foot of the Alps after so long conversing with the first men of the first cities of the world. Such lofty connections may attract the curious and gratify the vain. But I am too modest, or too proud, to rate my own value by that of my associates, and whatsoever may be the fame of learning or genius, experience has shown me that the cheaper qualifications of politeness and good sense are of more useful currency in the commerce of life. By many, conversation is esteemed as a theater or a school. But after the morning has been occupied by the labors of the library I wish to unbend rather than to exercise my mind, and in the interval between tea and supper I am far from disdaining the innocent amusement of a game at cards....

My transmigration from London to Lausanne could not be effected without interrupting the course of my historical labors. The hurry of my departure, the joy of my arrival, the delay of my tools, suspended their progress; and a full twelvemonth was lost before I could resume the thread of regular and daily industry. A number of books most requisite and least common had been previously selected; the academical library of Lausanne, which I could use as my own, contains at least the fathers and councils; and I have derived some occasional succor from the public collections of Bern and Geneva.

The fourth volume was soon terminated by an abstract of the controversies of the Incarnation, which the learned Dr. Prideaux was apprehensive of exposing to profane eyes... The pious historian was apprehensive of exposing that incomprehensible mystery to the cavils and objections of unbelievers; and he durst not, "seeing the nature of this book, venture it abroad in so wanton and lewd an age."

In the fifth and sixth volumes the revolutions of the empire and the world are most rapid, various, and instructive; and the Greek or Roman historians are checked by the hostile narratives of the barbarians of the East and the West. It was not till after many designs and many trials that I preferred, as I still prefer, the method of grouping my picture by nations;

and the seeming neglect of chronological order is surely compensated by the superior merits of interest and perspicuity.

The style of the first volume is, in my opinion, somewhat crude and elaborate; in the second and third it is ripened into ease, correctness, and numbers. But in the three last I may have been seduced by the facility of my pen, and the constant habit of speaking one language and writing another may have infused some mixture of Gallic idioms. Happily for my eyes, I have always closed my studies with the day, and commonly with the morning; and a long, but temperate, labor has been accomplished without fatiguing either the mind or body. But when I computed the remainder of my time and my task, it was apparent that, according to the season of publication, the delay of a month would be productive of that of a year. I was now straining for the goal, and in the last winter many evenings were borrowed from the social pleasures of Lausanne. I could now wish that a pause, an interval, had been allowed for a serious revisal.

I have presumed to mark the moment of conception; I shall now commemorate the hour of my final deliverance. It was on the day, or rather, night, of the 27th of June 1787, between the hours of eleven and twelve, that I wrote the last lines of the last page in a summerhouse in my garden. After laying down my pen I took several turns in a *berceau*, or covered walk of acacias, which commands a prospect of the country, the lake, and the mountains. The air was temperate, the sky was serene, the silver orb of the moon was reflected from the waters, and all nature was silent. I will not dissemble the first emotions of joy on recovery of my freedom, and perhaps the establishment of my fame. But my pride was soon humbled, and a sober melancholy was spread over my mind, by the idea that I had taken an everlasting leave of an old and agreeable companion, and that whatsoever might be the future fate of my *History*, the life of the historian must be short and precarious.

I will add two facts, which have seldom occurred in the composition of six, or at least of five, quartos. 1. My first rough manuscript, without any intermediate copy, has been sent to the press. 2. Not a sheet has been seen by any human eyes, excepting those of the author and the printer; the faults and the merits are exclusively my own....

After a quiet residence of four years, during which I had never moved ten miles from Lausanne, it was not without some reluctance and terror that I undertook, in a journey of two hundred leagues, to cross the mountains and the sea. Yet this formidable adventure was achieved without danger or fatigue, and at the end of a fortnight I found myself in Lord Sheffield's house and library, safe, happy, and at home. The character of my friend had recommended him to a seat in Parliament for Coventry, the command of a regiment of light dragoons, and an Irish peerage. The sense and spirit of his political writings have decided the public opinion on the great questions of our commercial interest with America and Ireland....

During the whole time of my residence in England I was entertained at Sheffield Place and in Downing Street by his hospitable kindness, and the most pleasant period was that which I passed in the domestic society of the family....

At Tunbridge, some weeks after the publication of my *History*, I tore myself from the embraces of Lord and Lady Sheffield, and with a young Swiss friend, whom I had introduced to the English world, I pursued the road of Dover and Lausanne. My habitation was embellished in my absence, and the last division of books, which followed my steps, increased my chosen library to the number of six or seven thousand volumes. My seraglio was ample, my choice was free, my appetite was keen. After a full repast on Homer and Aristophanes, I involved myself in the philosophic maze of the writings of Plato, of which the dramatic is perhaps more interesting than the argumentative part; but I stepped aside into every path of inquiry which reading or reflection accidentally opened.

Alas! the joy of my return, and my studious ardor, were soon damped by the melancholy state of my friend Mr. Deyverdun. His health and spirits had long suffered a gradual decline. A succession of apoplectic fits announced his dissolution, and before he expired, those who loved him could not wish for the continuance of his life. The voice of reason might congratulate his deliverance, but the feelings of nature and friendship could be subdued only by time. His amiable character was still alive in my remembrance; each room, each walk was imprinted with our common footsteps; and I should blush at my own philosophy, if a long interval of study had not preceded and followed the death of my friend.

By his last will he left to me the option of purchasing his house and garden or of possessing them during my life on the payment either of a stipulated price or of an easy retribution to his kinsman and heir. I should probably have been tempted by the demon of property if some legal difficulties had not been started against my title. A contest would have been vexatious, doubtful, and invidious; and the heir most gratefully subscribed an agreement which rendered my life possession more perfect, and his future condition more advantageous. Yet I had often revolved the judicious lines in which Pope answers the objections of his longsighted friend:

> Pity to build without or child or wife;
> Why, you'll enjoy it only all your life:
> Well, if the use be mine, does it concern one
> Whether the name belong to Pope or Vernon?

The certainty of my tenure has allowed me to lay out a considerable sum in improvements and alterations. They have been executed with skill and taste, and few men of letters, perhaps, in Europe are so desirably lodged as myself. But I feel, and with the decline of years I shall more painfully feel, that I am alone in paradise. Among the circle of my acquaintance at Lausanne, I have gradually acquired the solid and tender friendship of a respectable family. The four persons of whom it is composed are all endowed with the virtues best adapted to their age and situation, and I am encouraged to love the parents as a brother, and the children as a father. Every day we seek and find the opportunities of meeting; yet even this valuable connection cannot supply the loss of domestic society.

Within the last two or three years our tranquillity has been clouded by the disorders of France. Many families at Lausanne were alarmed and affected by the terrors of an impending bankruptcy; but the revolution, or rather the dissolution of the kingdom, has been heard and felt in the adjacent lands.

I beg leave to subscribe my assent to Mr. Burke's creed on the revolution of France. I admire his eloquence; I approve his politics; I adore his chivalry; and I can almost excuse his reverence for church establishments. I have sometimes thought of writing a dialogue of the dead in which Lucian, Erasmus, and Voltaire should mutually acknowledge the danger of exposing an old superstition to the contempt of the blind and fanatic multitude.

A swarm of emigrants of both sexes, who escaped from the public ruin, has been attracted by the vicinity, the manners, and the language of Lausanne; and our narrow habitations, in town and country, are now occupied by the first names and titles of the departed monarchy. These noble fugitives are entitled to our pity; they may claim our esteem; but they cannot, in their present state of mind and fortune, much contribute to our amusement. Instead of looking down as calm and idle spectators on the theater of Europe, our domestic harmony is somewhat embittered by the infusion of party spirit. Our ladies and gentlemen assume the character of self-taught politicians, and the sober dictates of wisdom and experience are silenced by the clamor of the triumphant *démocrates*.

The fanatic missionaries of sedition have scattered the seeds of discontent in our cities and villages, which have flourished above two hundred and fifty years without fearing the approach of war or feeling the weight of government. Many individuals, and some communities, appear to be infected with the French disease, the wild theories of equal and boundless freedom. But I trust that the body of the people will be faithful to their sovereign and to themselves, and I am satisfied that the failure or success of a revolt would equally terminate in the ruin of the country. While the aristocracy of Berne protects the happiness, it is superfluous to inquire whether it be founded in the rights of man. The economy of the state is liberally supplied without the aid of taxes, and the magistrates *must* reign with prudence and equity, since they are unarmed in the midst of an armed nation....

When I contemplate the common lot of mortality, I must acknowledge that I have drawn a high prize in the lottery of life. The far greater part of the globe is overspread with barbarism or slavery; in the civilized world the most numerous class is condemned to ignorance and poverty; and the double fortune of my birth in a free and enlightened country, in an honorable and wealthy family, is the lucky chance of a unit against millions. The general probability is about three to one that a newborn infant will not live to complete his fiftieth year. I have now passed that age, and may fairly estimate the present value of my existence in the threefold division of mind, body, and estate.

1. The first and indispensable requisite of happiness is a clear conscience, unsullied by the reproach or remembrance of an unworthy action.

> Be this thy brazen shield
> To know no wrong that leads thee to turn pale.

I am endowed with a cheerful temper, a moderate sensibility, and a natural disposition to repose rather than to action; some mischievous appetites and habits have perhaps been corrected by philosophy or time. The love of study, a passion which derives fresh vigor from enjoyment, supplies each day, each hour, with a perpetual source of independent and rational pleasure, and I am not sensible of any decay of the mental faculties. The original soil has been highly improved by labor and manure, but it may be questioned whether some flowers of fancy, some grateful errors, have not been eradicated with the weeds of prejudice.

2. Since I have escaped from the long perils of my childhood, the serious advice of a physician has seldom been requisite. "The madness of superfluous health" I have never known; but my tender constitution has been fortified by time, the play of the animal machine still continues to be easy and regular, and the inestimable gift of the sound and peaceful slumbers of infancy may be imputed both to the mind and body. About the age of forty I was first afflicted with the gout, which in the space of fourteen years has made seven or eight different attacks. Their duration, though not their intensity, appears to increase, and after each fit I rise and walk with less strength and agility than before. But the gout has hitherto been confined to my feet and knees; the pain is never intolerable; I am surrounded by all the comforts that art and attendance can bestow; my sedentary life is amused with books and company; and in each step of my convalescence I pass through a progress of agreeable sensations.

3. I have already described the merits of my society and situation, but these enjoyments would be tasteless and bitter if their possession were not assured by an annual and adequate supply. By the painful method of amputation, my father's debts have been completely discharged. The labor of my pen, the sale of lands, the inheritance of a maiden aunt (Mrs. Hester Gibbon), have improved my property, and it will be exonerated on some melancholy day from the payment of Mrs. Gibbon's jointure. According to the scale of Switzerland I am a rich man, and I am indeed rich, since my income is superior to my expense, and my expense is equal to my wishes. My friends, more especially Lord Sheffield, kindly relieve me

from the cares to which my taste and temper are most adverse. The economy of my house is settled without avarice or profusion. At stated periods all my bills are regularly paid, and in the course of my life I have never been reduced to appear, either as plaintiff or defendant, in a court of justice. Shall I add that, since the failure of my first wishes, I have never entertained any serious thoughts of a matrimonial connection?

I am disgusted with the affectation of men of letters who complain that they have renounced a substance for a shadow and that their fame (which sometimes is no insupportable weight) affords a poor compensation for envy, censure, and persecution. M. d'Alembert relates that, as he was walking in the gardens of Sans Souci with the King of Prussia, Frederick said to him, "Do you see that old woman, a poor weeder, asleep on that sunny bank? She is probably a more happy being than either of us."

The king and the philosopher may speak for themselves; for my part, I do not envy the old woman. My own experience, at least, has taught me a very different lesson. Twenty happy years have been animated by the labor of my *History*, and its success has given me a name, a rank, a character in the world, to which I should not otherwise have been entitled. The freedom of my writings has indeed provoked an implacable tribe; but as I was safe from the stings, I was soon accustomed to the buzzing of the hornets. My nerves are not tremblingly alive, and my literary temper is so happily framed that I am less sensible of pain than of pleasure.

The rational pride of an author may be offended, rather than flattered, by vague indiscriminate praise, but he cannot, he should not, be indifferent to the fair testimonies of private and public esteem. Even his social sympathy may be gratified by the idea that now, in the present hour, he is imparting some degree of amusement or knowledge to his friends in a distant land, that one day his mind will be familiar to the grandchildren of those who are yet unborn. I cannot boast of the friendship or favor of princes. The patronage of English literature has long since been devolved on our booksellers, and the measure of their liberality is the least ambiguous test of our common success. Perhaps the golden mediocrity of my fortune has contributed to fortify my application.

The present is a fleeting moment; the past is no more; and our prospect of futurity is dark and doubtful. This day may *possibly* be my last, but the laws of probability, so true in general, so fallacious in particular, still allow me about fifteen years, and I shall soon enter into the period which, as the most agreeable of his long life, was selected by the judgment and experience of the sage Fontenelle. His choice is approved by the eloquent historian of nature, who fixes our moral happiness to the mature season in which our passions are supposed to be calmed, our duties fulfilled, our ambition satisfied, our fame and fortune established on a solid basis. In private conversation, that great and amiable man added the weight of his own experience, and this autumnal felicity might be exemplified in the lives of Voltaire, Hume, and many other men of letters.

I am far more inclined to embrace than to dispute this comfortable doctrine. I will not suppose any premature decay of the mind or body, but I must reluctantly observe that two causes, the abbreviation of time and the failure of hope, will always tinge with a browner shade the evening of life.

The proportion of a part to the whole is the only standard by which we can measure the length of our existence. At the age of twenty, one year is a tenth, perhaps, of the time which has elapsed within our consciousness and memory. At the age of fifty it is no more than the fortieth, and this relative value continues to decrease till the last sands are shaken by the hand of death. This reasoning may seem metaphysical, but on a trial it will be found satisfactory and just.

The warm desires, the long expectations of youth, are founded on the ignorance of themselves and of the world. They are gradually damped by time and experience, by disappointment and possession; and after the middle season the crowd must be content to remain at the foot of the mountain, while the few who have climbed the summit aspire to descend or expect to fall. In old age the consolation of hope is reserved for the tenderness of parents, who commence a new life in their children; the faith of enthusiasts, who sing hallelujahs above the clouds; and the vanity of authors, who presume the immortality of their name and writings.

THOMAS DE QUINCEY

The Pleasures and Pains of Drug-Taking

The Pleasures of Opium

It is so long since I first took opium, that if it had been a trifling incident in my life, I might have forgotten its date: but cardinal events are not to be forgotten; and from circumstances connected with it, I remember that it must be referred to the autumn of 1804. During that season I was in London, having come thither for the first time since my entrance at college. And my introduction to opium arose in the following way. From an early age I had been accustomed to wash my head in cold water at least once a day: being suddenly seized with toothache, I attributed it to some relaxation caused by an accidental intermission of that practice; jumped out of bed; plunged my head into a basin of cold water; and with hair thus wetted went to sleep. The next morning, as I need hardly say,

THE PLEASURES AND PAINS OF DRUG-TAKING: From *Confessions of an English Opium-Eater,* first published in 1822.

I awoke with excruciating rheumatic pains of the head and face, from which I had hardly any respite for about twenty days. On the twenty-first day, I think it was, and on a Sunday, that I went out into the streets; rather to run away, if possible, from my torments, than with any distinct purpose. By accident I met a college acquaintance who recommended opium. Opium! dread agent of unimaginable pleasure and pain! I had heard of it as I had of manna or of ambrosia, but no further: how unmeaning a sound was it at that time! what solemn chords does it now strike upon my heart! what heartquaking vibrations of sad and happy remembrances! Reverting for a moment to these, I feel a mystic importance attached to the minutest circumstances connected with the place and the time, and the man (if man he was) that first laid open to me the Paradise of Opium-eaters. It was a Sunday afternoon, wet and cheerless: and a duller spectacle this earth of ours has not to show than a rainy Sunday in London. My road homewards lay through Oxford-street; and near "the *stately* Pantheon," (as Mr. Wordsworth has obligingly called it) I saw a druggist's shop. The druggist—unconscious minister of celestial pleasures—as if in sympathy with the rainy Sunday, looked dull and stupid, just as any mortal druggist might be expected to look on a Sunday: and, when I asked for the tincture of opium, he gave it to me as any other man might do: and furthermore, out of my shilling, returned me what seemed to be real copper half-pence, taken out of a real wooden drawer. Nevertheless, in spite of such indications of humanity, he has ever since existed in my mind as the beatific vision of an immortal druggist, sent down to earth on a special mission to myself. And it confirms me in this way of considering him, that, when I next came up to London, I sought him near the stately Pantheon, and found him not: and thus to me, who knew not his name (if indeed he had one) he seemed rather to have vanished from Oxford-street than to have removed in any bodily fashion. The reader may choose to think of him as, possibly, no more than a sublunary druggist: it may be so: but my faith is better: I believe him to have evanesced,[1] or evaporated. So unwillingly would I connect any mortal remembrances with that hour, and place, and creature, that first brought me acquainted with the celestial drug.

Arrived at my lodgings, it may be supposed that I lost not a moment in taking the quantity prescribed. I was necessarily ignorant of the whole art and mystery of opium-taking: and, what I took, I took under every disadvantage. But I took it—and in an hour, oh! heavens! what a revulsion! what an upheaving, from its lowest depths, of the inner spirit! what an apocalypse of the world within me! That my pains had vanished, was now a trifle in my eyes—this negative effect was swallowed up in the immensity of those positive effects which had opened before me—in the abyss of divine enjoyment thus suddenly revealed. Here was a panacea—a φαρμακον νηωενθες for all human woes: here was the secret of happiness, about which philosophers had disputed for so many ages, at once discovered: happiness might now be bought for a penny, and carried in the waist-coat pocket: portable ecstasies might be had corked up in a pint bottle: and peace of mind could be sent down in gallons by the mail coach. But, if I talk in this way, the reader will think I am laughing: and I can assure him, that nobody will laugh long who deals much with opium: its pleasures even are of a grave and solemn complexion; and in his happiest state, the opium-eater cannot present himself in the character of l'Allegro: even then, he speaks and

thinks as becomes Il Penseroso. Nevertheless, I have a very reprehensible way of jesting at times in the midst of my own misery: and, unless when I am checked by some more powerful feelings, I am afraid I shall be guilty of this indecent practice even in these annals of suffering or enjoyment. The reader must allow a little to my infirm nature in this respect: and with a few indulgences of that sort, I shall endeavour to be as grave, if not drowsy, as fits a theme like opium, so anti-mercurial as it really is, and so drowsy as it is falsely reputed.

And, first, one word with respect to its bodily effects: for upon all that has been hitherto written on the subject of opium, whether by travellers in Turkey (who may plead their privilege of lying as an old immemorial right), or by professors of medicine, writing ex cathedrâ— I have but one emphatic criticism to pronounce —Lies! lies! lies! I remember once, in passing a book-stall, to have caught these words from a page of some satiric author—"By this time I became convinced that the London newspapers spoke truth at least twice a week, viz. on Tuesday and Saturday, and might safely be depended upon for ———— the list of bankrupts." In like manner, I do by no means deny that some truths have been delivered to the world in regard to opium: thus it has been repeatedly affirmed by the learned, that opium is a dusky brown in colour; and this, take notice, I grant: second, that it is rather dear; which also I grant: for in my time, East-India opium has been three guineas a pound, and Turkey eight: and, third, that if you eat a good deal of it, most probably you must ———— do what is particularly disagreeable to any man of regular habits, viz. die.[2] These weighty propositions are, all and singular, true: I cannot gainsay them: and

[1] *Evanesced:* this way of going off the stage of life appears to have been well known in the seventeenth century, but at that time to have been considered a peculiar privilege of blood-royal, and by no means to be allowed to druggists. For about the year 1686, a poet of rather ominous name (and who, by the by, did ample justice to his name), viz. Mr. *Flat-man,* in speaking of the death of Charles II. expresses his surprise that any prince should commit so absurd an act as dying; because, says he,

Kings should disdain to die, and only *disappear.*

They should *abscond,* that is, into the other world.

[2] Of this, however, the learned appear latterly to have doubted: for in a pirated edition of Buchan's *Domestic Medicine,* which I once saw in the hand of a farmer's wife who was studying it for the benefit of her health, the doctor was made to say—"Be particularly careful never to take above five-and-twenty *ounces* of laudanum at once"; the true reading being probably five and twenty *drops,* which are held equal to about one grain of crude opium.

truth ever was, and will be, commendable. But in these three theorems, I believe we have exhausted the stock of knowledge as yet accumulated by man on the subject of opium. And therefore, worthy doctors, as there seems to be room for further discoveries, stand aside, and allow me to come forward and lecture on this matter.

First, then, it is not so much affirmed as taken for granted, by all who ever mention opium, formally or incidentally, that it does, or can, produce intoxication. Now, reader, assure yourself, *meo periculo*, that no quantity of opium ever did, or could intoxicate. As to the tincture of opium (commonly called laudanum) *that* might certainly intoxicate if a man could bear to take enough of it; but why? because it contains so much proof spirit, and not because it contains so much opium. But crude opium, I affirm peremptorily, is incapable of producing any state of body at all resembling that which is produced by alcohol: and not in *degree* only incapable, but even in *kind:* it is not in the quantity of its effects merely, but in the quality, that it differs altogether. The pleasure given by wine is always mounting, and tending to a crisis, after which it declines: that from opium, when once generated, is stationary for eight or ten hours: the first, to borrow a technical distinction from medicine, is a case of acute—the second, of chronic pleasure: the one is a flame, the other a steady and equable glow. But the main distinction lies in this, that whereas wine disorders the mental faculties, opium, on the contrary (if taken in a proper manner), introduces amongst them the most exquisite order, legislation, and harmony. Wine robs a man of his self-possession: opium greatly invigorates it. Wine unsettles and clouds the judgment, and gives a preternatural brightness, and a vivid exaltation to the contempts and the admirations, the loves and the hatreds, of the drinker: opium, on the contrary, communicates serenity and equipoise to all the faculties, active or passive: and with respect to the temper and moral feelings in general, it

gives simply that sort of vital warmth which is approved by the judgment, and which would probably always accompany a bodily constitution of primeval or antediluvian health. Thus, for instance, opium, like wine, gives an expansion to the heart and the benevolent affections: but then, with this remarkable difference, that in the sudden development of kind-heartedness which accompanies inebriation, there is always more or less of a maudlin character, which exposes it to the contempt of the bystander. Men shake hands, swear eternal friendship, and shed tears—no mortal knows why: and the sensual creature is clearly uppermost. But the expansion of the benigner feelings, incident to opium, is no febrile access, but a healthy restoration to that state which the mind would naturally recover upon the removal of any deep-seated irritation of pain that had disturbed and quarrelled with the impulses of a heart originally just and good. True it is, that even wine, up to a certain point, and with certain men, rather tends to exalt and to steady the intellect: I myself, who have never been a great wine-drinker, used to find that half a dozen glasses of wine advantageously affected the faculties—brightened and intensified the consciousness—and gave to the mind a feeling of being "ponderibus librata suis": and certainly it is most absurdly said, in popular language, of any man, that he is *disguised* in liquor: for, on the contrary, most men are disguised by sobriety; and it is when they are drinking (as some old gentleman says in Athenæus), that men ἑαυτοὺς ἐμφανίζουσιν οἵτινες εἰσίν—display themselves in their true complexion of character; which surely is not disguising themselves. But still, wine constantly leads a man to the brink of absurdity and extravagance; and, beyond a certain point, it is sure to volatilize and to disperse the intellectual energies: whereas opium always seems to compose what had been agitated, and to concentrate what had been distracted. In short, to sum up all in one word, a man who is inebriated, or tending to inebriation, is, and feels that he is, in a condition which calls up into supremacy the merely human, too often the brutal, part of his nature: but the opium-eater (I speak of him who is not suffering from any disease, or other remote effects of opium,) feels that the diviner part of his nature is paramount; that is, the moral affections are in a state of cloudless serenity; and over all is the great light of the majestic intellect.

This is the doctrine of the true church on the subject of opium: of which church I acknowledge myself to be the only member—the alpha and the omega: but then it is to be recollected, that I speak from the ground of a large and profound personal experience: whereas most of the unscientific[3] authors who have at all treated of opium, and even of those who have written expressly on the materia medica, make it evident, from the horror they express of it, that their experimental knowledge of its action is none at all. Some people have maintained, in my hearing, that they had been drunk upon green tea: and a medical student in London, for whose knowledge in his profession I have reason to feel great respect, assured me, the other day, that a patient, in recovering from an illness, had got drunk on a beef-steak.

[3] Amongst the great herd of travellers, &c. who show sufficiently by their stupidity that they never held any intercourse with opium, I must caution my readers specially against the brilliant author of *Anastasius*. This gentleman, whose wit would lead one to presume him an opium-eater, has made it impossible to consider him in that character from the grievous misrepresentation which he gives of its effects at p. 215–17, of Vol. 1—Upon consideration, it must appear such to the author himself: for, waiving the errors I have insisted on in the text, which (and others) are adopted in the fullest manner, he will himself admit, that an old gentleman "with a snow-white beard," who eats "ample doses of opium," and is yet able to deliver what is meant and received as very weighty counsel on the bad effects of that practice, is but an indifferent evidence that opium either kills people prematurely, or sends them into a mad-house. But, for my part, I see into this old gentleman and his motives: the fact is, he was enamoured of "the little golden receptacle of the pernicious drug" which Anastasius carried about him; and no way of obtaining it so safe and so feasible occurred, as that of frightening its owner out of his wits (which, by the by, are none of the strongest). This commentary throws a new light upon the case, and greatly improves it as a story: for the old gentleman's speech, considered as a lecture on pharmacy, is highly absurd: but, considered as a hoax on Anastasius, it reads excellently.

Having dwelt so much on this first and leading error, in respect to opium, I shall notice very briefly a second and a third; which are, that the elevation of spirits produced by opium is necessarily followed by a proportionate depression, and that the natural and even immediate consequence of opium is torpor and stagnation, animal and mental. The first of these errors I shall content myself with simply denying; assuring my reader, that for ten years, during which I took opium at intervals, the day succeeding to that on which I allowed myself this luxury was always a day of unusually good spirits.

With respect to the torpor supposed to follow, or rather (if we were to credit the numerous pictures of Turkish opium-eaters) to accompany the practice of opium-eating, I deny that also. Certainly, opium is classed under the head of narcotics; and some such effect it may produce in the end: but the primary effects of opium are always, and in the highest degree, to excite and stimulate the system: this first stage of its action always lasted with me, during my novitiate, for upwards of eight hours; so that it must be the fault of the opium-eater himself if he does not so time his exhibition of the dose (to speak medically) as that the whole weight of its narcotic influence may descend upon his sleep. Turkish opium-eaters it seems, are absurd enough to sit, like so many equestrian statues, on logs of wood as stupid as themselves. But that the reader may judge of the degree in which opium is likely to stupify the faculties of an Englishman, I shall (by way of treating the question illustratively, rather than argumentatively) describe the way in which I myself often passed an opium evening in London, during the period between 1804 and 1812. It will be seen, that at least opium did not move me to seek solitude, and much less to seek inactivity, or the torpid state of self-involution ascribed to the Turks. I give this account at the risk of being pronounced a crazy enthusiast or visionary: but I regard *that* little: I must desire my reader to bear in mind, that I was a hard student, and at severe studies for all the rest of my time: and certainly I had a right occasionally to relaxations as well as other people: these, however, I allowed myself but seldom.

The late Duke of ——— used to say, "Next Friday, by the blessing of Heaven, I purpose to be drunk": and in like manner I used to fix beforehand how often, within a given time, and when, I would commit a debauch of opium. This was seldom more than once in three weeks: for at that time I could not have ventured to call every day (as I did afterwards) for "a glass of laudanum negus, warm, and without sugar." No: as I have said, I seldom drank laudanum, at that time, more than once in three weeks: this was usually on a Tuesday or a Saturday night; my reason for which was this. In those days Grassini sang at the Opera: and her voice was delightful to me beyond all that I had ever heard. I know not what may be the state of the Opera-house now, having never been within its walls for seven or eight years, but at that time it was by much the most pleasant place of public resort in London for passing an evening. Five shillings admitted one to the gallery, which was subject to far less annoyance than the pit of the theatres: the orchestra was distinguished by its sweet and melodious grandeur from all English orchestras, the composition of which, I confess, is not acceptable to my ear, from the predominance of the clangorous instruments, and the absolute tyranny of the violin. The choruses were divine to hear: and when Grassini appeared in some interlude, as she often did, and poured forth her passionate soul as Andromache, at the tomb of Hector, &c. I question whether any Turk, of all that ever entered the paradise of opium-eaters, can have had half the pleasure I had. But, indeed, I honour the Barbarians too much by supposing them capable of any pleasures approaching to the intellectual ones of an Englishman. For music is an intellectual or a sensual pleasure, according to the temperament of him who hears it. And, by the by, with the exception of the fine extravaganza on that subject in *Twelfth Night*, I do not recollect more than one thing

said adequately on the subject of music in all literature: it is a passage in the *Religio Medici*[4] of Sir T. Brown; and, though chiefly remarkable for its sublimity, has also a philosophic value, inasmuch as it points to the true theory of musical effects. The mistake of most people is to suppose that it is by the ear, they communicate with music, and, therefore, that they are purely passive to its effects. But this is not so: it is by the reaction of the mind upon the notices of the ear, (the *matter* coming by the senses, the *form* from the mind,) that the pleasure is constructed: and therefore it is that people of equally good ear differ so much in this point from one another. Now opium, by greatly increasing the activity of the mind generally, increases, of necessity, that particular mode of its activity by which we are able to construct out of the raw material of organic sound an elaborate intellectual pleasure. But, says a friend, a succession of musical sounds is to me like a collection of Arabic characters: I can attach no ideas to them! Ideas! my good sir? there is no occasion for them: all that class of ideas, which can be available in such a case, has a language of representative feelings. But this is a subject foreign to my present purposes: it is sufficient to say, that a chorus, &c. of elaborate harmony, displayed before me, as in a piece of arras work, the whole of my past life—not as if recalled by an act of memory, but as if present and incarnated in the music: no longer painful to dwell upon: but the detail of its incidents removed, or blended in some hazy abstraction; and its passions exalted, spiritualized, and sublimed. All this was to be had for five shillings. And over and above the music of the stage and the orchestra, I had all around me, in the intervals of the performance, the music of the Italian language talked by Italian women: for the gallery was usually crowded with Italians: and I listened with a pleasure such as

[4] I have not the book at this moment to consult: but I think the passage begins—"And even that tavern music, which makes one man merry, another mad, in me strikes a deep fit of devotion," &c.

that with which Weld the traveller lay and listened, in Canada, to the sweet laughter of Indian women; for the less you understand of a language, the more sensible you are to the melody or harshness of its sounds: for such a purpose, therefore, it was an advantage to me that I was a poor Italian scholar, reading it but little, and not speaking it at all, nor understanding a tenth part of what I heard spoken.

These were my Opera pleasures: but another pleasure I had which, as it could be had only on a Saturday night, occasionally struggled with my love of the Opera; for, at that time, Tuesday and Saturday were the regular Opera nights. On this subject I am afraid I shall be rather obscure, but, I can assure the reader, not at all more so than Marinus in his life of Proclus, or many other biographers and autobiographers of fair reputation. This pleasure, I have said, was to be had only on a Saturday night. What then was Saturday night to me more than any other night? I had no labours that I rested from; no wages to receive: what needed I to care for Saturday night, more than as it was a summons to hear Grassini? True, most logical reader: what you say is unanswerable. And yet so it was and is, that, whereas different men throw their feelings into different channels, and most are apt to show their interest in the concerns of the poor, chiefly by sympathy, expressed in some shape or other, with their distresses and sorrows, I, at that time, was disposed to express my interest by sympathising with their pleasures: the pains of poverty I had lately seen too much of; more than I wished to remember: but the pleasures of the poor, their consolations of spirit, and their reposes from bodily toil, can never become oppressive to contemplate. Now Saturday night is the season for the chief, regular, and periodic return of rest to the poor: in this point the most hostile sects unite, and acknowledge a common link of brotherhood: almost all Christendom rests from its labours. It is a rest introductory to another rest: and divided by a whole day and two nights from the renewal of toil. On this account I feel always, on a Saturday

night, as though I also were released from some yoke of labour, had some wages to receive, and some luxury of repose to enjoy. For the sake, therefore, of witnessing, upon as large a scale as possible, a spectacle with which my sympathy was so entire, I used often, on Saturday nights, after I had taken opium, to wander forth, without much regarding the direction or the distance, to all the markets, and other parts of London, to which the poor resort on a Saturday night, for laying out their wages. Many a family party, consisting of a man, his wife, and sometimes one or two of his children, have I listened to, as they stood consulting on their ways and means, or the strength of their exchequer, or the price of household articles. Gradually I became familiar with their wishes, their difficulties, and their opinions. Sometimes there might be heard murmurs of discontent: but far oftener expressions on the countenance, or uttered in words, of patience, hope, and tranquillity. And taken generally, I must say, that, in this point at least, the poor are far more philosophic than the rich—that they show a more ready and cheerful submission to what they consider as irremediable evils, or irreparable losses. Whenever I saw occasion, or could do it without appearing to be intrusive, I joined their parties; and gave my opinion upon the matter in discussion, which, if not always judicious, was always received indulgently. If wages were a little higher, or expected to be so, or the quartern loaf a little lower, or it was reported that onions and butter were expected to fall, I was glad: yet, if the contrary were true, I drew from opium some means of consoling myself. For opium (like the bee, that extracts its materials indiscriminately from roses and from the soot of chimneys) can overrule all feelings into a compliance with the master key. Some of these rambles led me to great distances: for an opium-eater is too happy to observe the motion of time. And sometimes in my attempts to steer homewards, upon nautical principles, by fixing my eye on the polestar, and seeking ambitiously for a north-west passage, instead of circumnavigating all the capes and headlands I had doubled in my outward voyage, I came suddenly upon such knotty problems of alleys, such enigmatical entries, and such sphinx's riddles of streets without thoroughfares, as must, I conceive, baffle the audacity of porters, and confound the intellects of hackney-coachmen. I could almost have believed, at times, that I must be the first discoverer of some of these *terrae incognitae,* and doubted, whether they had yet been laid down in the modern charts of London. For all this, however, I paid a heavy price in distant years, when the human face tyrannized over my dreams, and the perplexities of my steps in London came back and haunted my sleep, with the feeling of perplexities moral or intellectual, that brought confusion to the reason, or anguish and remorse to the conscience.

Thus I have shown that opium does not, of necessity, produce inactivity or torpor; but that, on the contrary, it often led me into markets and theatres. Yet, in candour, I will admit that markets and theatres are not the appropriate haunts of the opium-eater, when in the divinest state incident to his enjoyment. In that state, crowds become an oppression to him; music even, too sensual and gross. He naturally seeks solitude and silence, as indispensable conditions of those trances, or profoundest reveries, which are the crown and consummation of what opium can do for human nature. I, whose disease it was to meditate too much, and to observe too little, and who, upon my first entrance at college, was nearly falling into a deep melancholy, from brooding too much on the sufferings which I had witnessed in London, was sufficiently aware of the tendencies of my own thoughts to do all I could to counteract them. I was, indeed, like a person who, according to the old legend, had entered the cave of Trophonius: and the remedies I sought were to force myself into society, and to keep my understanding in continual activity upon matters of science. But for these remedies, I should certainly have become hypochondriacally melancholy. In after years, however, when my cheerfulness was more fully re-established, I yielded to my natural inclination for a solitary life. And, at that time, I often fell into these reveries upon taking opium; and more than once it has happened to me, on a summer night when I have been at an open window, in a room from which I could overlook the sea at a mile below me, and could command a view of the great town of L——— at about the same distance, that I have sat, from sunset to sunrise, motionless, and without wishing to move.

I shall be charged with mysticism, Behmenism, quietism, &c. but *that* shall not alarm me. Sir H. Vane, the younger, was one of our wisest men; and let my readers see if he, in his philosophical works, be half as unmystical as I am. I say, then, that it has often struck me that the scene itself was somewhat typical of what took place in such a reverie. The town of L——— represented the earth, with its sorrows and its graves left behind, yet not out of sight, nor wholly forgotten. The ocean, in everlasting but gentle agitation, and brooded over by a dove-like calm, might not unfitly typify the mind and the mood which then swayed it. For it seemed to me as if then first I stood at a distance, and aloof from the uproar of life; as if the tumult, the fever, and the strife were suspended; a respite granted from the secret burthens of the heart; a sabbath of repose; a resting from human labours. Here were the hopes which blossom in the paths of life, reconciled with the peace which is in the grave; motions of the intellect as unwearied as the heavens, yet for all anxieties a halcyon calm: a tranquillity that seemed no product of inertia, but as if resulting from mighty and equal antagonisms; infinite activities, infinite repose.

Oh! just, subtle, and mighty opium! that to the hearts of poor and rich alike, for the wounds that will never heal, and for "the pangs that tempt the spirit to rebel," bringest an assuaging balm; eloquent opium! that with thy potent rhetoric stealest away the purposes of wrath; and to the guilty man, for one night givest back the hopes of his youth, and hands washed pure from blood; and to the proud man, a brief oblivion for

> Wrongs unredress'd, and insults unavenged;

that summonest to the chancery of dreams, for the triumphs of suffering innocence, false witnesses; and confoundest perjury; and dost reverse the sentences of unrighteous judges— thou buildest upon the bosom of darkness, out of the fantastic imagery of the brain, cities and temples, beyond the art of Phidias and Praxiteles —beyond the splendour of Babylon and Hekatómpylos: and "from the anarchy of dreaming sleep," callest into sunny light the faces of long-buried beauties, and the blessed household countenances, cleansed from the "dishonours of the grave." Thou only givest these gifts to man; and thou hast the keys of Paradise, oh, just, subtle, and mighty opium!

Introduction to the Pains of Opium

Courteous, and, I hope, indulgent reader (for all *my* readers must be indulgent ones, or else, I fear, I shall shock them too much to count on their courtesy), having accompanied me thus far, now let me request you to move onwards, for about eight years; that is to say, from 1804 (when I have said that my acquaintance with opium first began) to 1812. The years of academic life are now over and gone—almost forgotten—the student's cap no longer presses my temples: if my cap exist at all, it presses those of some youthful scholar, I trust, as happy as myself, and as passionate a lover of knowledge. My gown is, by this time, I dare to say, in the same condition with many thousands of excellent books in the Bodleian, viz. diligently perused by certain studious moths and worms: or departed, however (which is all that I know of its fate), to that great reservoir of *somewhere,* to which all the teacups, teacaddies, teapots, teakettles, &c. have departed (not to speak of still frailer vessels,

such as glasses, decanters, bed-makers, &c.) which occasional resemblances in the present generation of teacups, &c. remind me of having once possessed, but of whose departure and final fate I, in common with most gownsmen of either university, could give, I suspect, but an obscure and conjectural history. The persecution of the chapel-bell, sounding its unwelcome summons to six o'clock matins, interrupts my slumbers no longer: the porter who rang it, upon whose beautiful nose (bronze, inlaid with copper) I wrote, in retaliation, so many Greek epigrams, whilst I was dressing, is dead, and has ceased to disturb any body: and I, and many others, who suffered much from his tintinnabulous propensities, have now agreed to overlook his errors, and have forgiven him. Even with the bell I am now in charity: it rings, I suppose, as formerly, thrice a-day: and cruelly annoys, I doubt not, many worthy gentlemen, and disturbs their peace of mind: but as to me, in this year 1812, I regard its treacherous voice no longer (treacherous, I call it, for, by some refinement of malice, it spoke in as sweet and silvery tones as if it had been inviting one to a party): its tones have no longer, indeed, power to reach me, let the wind sit as favourable as the malice of the bell itself could wish: for I am 250 miles away from it, and buried in the depth of mountains. And what am I doing amongst the mountains? Taking opium. Yes, but what else? Why, reader, in 1812, the year we are now arrived at, as well as for some years previous, I have been chiefly studying German metaphysics, in the writings of Kant, Fichte, Schelling, &c. And how, and in what manner, do I live? In short, what class or description of men do I belong to? I am at this period, viz. in 1812, living in a cottage; and with a single female servant (honi soit qui mal y pense), who, amongst my neighbours, passes by the name of my "housekeeper." And, as a scholar and a man of learned education, and in that sense a gentleman, I may presume to class myself as an unworthy member of that indefinite body called *gentlemen.* Partly on the ground I have assigned perhaps; partly because, from my having no visible calling or business, it is rightly judged that I must be living on my private fortune; I am so classed by my neighbours: and, by the courtesy of modern England, I am usually addressed on letters, &c. *esquire*, though having, I fear, in the rigorous construction of heralds, but slender pretensions to that distinguished honour: yes, in popular estimation, I am X. Y. Z., esquire, but not Justice of the Peace, nor Custos Rotulorum. Am I married? Not yet. And I still take opium? On Saturday nights. And, perhaps have taken it unblushingly ever since "the rainy Sunday," and "the stately Pantheon," and "the beatific druggist" of 1804—even so. And how do I find my health after all this opium-eating? In short, how do I do? Why, pretty well, I thank you, reader: in the phrase of ladies in the straw, "as well as can be expected." In fact, if I dared to say the real and simple truth, though, to satisfy the theories of medical men, I *ought* to be ill, I never was better in my life than in the spring of 1812; and I hope sincerely, that the quantity of claret, port, or "particular Madeira," which, in all probability, you, good reader, have taken, and design to take, for every term of eight years, during your natural life, may as little disorder your health as mine was disordered by the opium I had taken for the eight years, between 1804 and 1812. Hence you may see again the danger of taking any medical advice from *Anastasius;* in divinity, for aught I know, or law, he may be a safe counsellor; but not in medicine. No: it is far better to consult Dr. Buchan; as I did: for I never forgot that worthy man's excellent suggestion: and I was "particularly careful not to take above five-and-twenty ounces of laudanum." To this moderation and temperate use of the article, I may ascribe it, I suppose, that as yet, at least, (i.e. in 1812,) I am ignorant and unsuspicious of the avenging terrors which opium has in store for those who abuse its lenity. At the same time, it must not be forgotten, that hitherto I have been only a dilettante eater of opium: eight years' practice

even, with the single precaution of allowing sufficient intervals between every indulgence, has not been sufficient to make opium necessary to me as an article of daily diet. But now comes a different era. Move on, if you please, reader, to 1813. In the summer of the year we have just quitted, I had suffered much in bodily health from distress of mind connected with a very melancholy event. This event, being no ways related to the subject now before me, further than through the bodily illness which it produced, I need not more particularly notice. Whether this illness of 1812 had any share in that of 1813, I know not: but so it was, that in the latter year I was attacked by a most appalling irritation of the stomach, in all respects the same as that which had caused me so much suffering in youth, and accompanied by a revival of all the old dreams. This is the point of my narrative on which, as respects my own self-justification, the whole of what follows may be said to hinge. And here I find myself in a perplexing dilemma: either, on the one hand, I must exhaust the reader's patience, by such a detail of my malady, and of my struggles with it, as might suffice to establish the fact of my inability to wrestle any longer with irritation and constant suffering: or, on the other hand, by passing lightly over this critical part of my story, I must forego the benefit of a stronger impression left on the mind of the reader, and must lay myself open to the misconstruction of having slipped by the easy and gradual steps of self-indulging persons, from the first to the final stage of opium-eating (a misconstruction to which there will be a lurking predisposition in most readers, from my previous acknowledgments.) This is the dilemma: the first horn of which would be sufficient to toss and gore any column of patient readers, though drawn up sixteen deep and constantly relieved by fresh men: consequently *that* is not to be thought of. It remains then, that I *postulate* so much as is necessary for my purpose. And let me take as full credit for what I postulate as if I had demonstrated it, good reader, at the expense of your patience and my own. Be not so ungenerous as to let me suffer in your good opinion through my own forbearance and regard for your comfort. No: believe all that I ask of you, viz. that I could resist not longer; believe it liberally, and as an act of grace: or else in mere prudence: for, if not, then in the next edition of my Opium Confessions revised and enlarged, I will make you believe and tremble: and *à force d'ennuyer*, by mere dint of happiness—winter or summer! farewell to smiles and laughter! farewell to peace of mind! farewell to hope and to tranquil dreams, and to the blessed consolations of sleep! for more than three years and a half I am summoned away from these: I am now arrived at an Iliad of woes: for I have now to record

The Pains of Opium

————as when some great painter dips
His pencil in the gloom of earthquake and eclipse.

Shelley's Revolt of Islam.

Reader, who have thus far accompanied me, I must request your attention to a brief explanatory note on three points:

1. For several reasons, I have not been able to compose the notes for this part of my narrative into any regular and connected shape. I give the notes disjointed as I find them, or have now drawn them up from memory. Some of them point to their own date; some I have dated; and some are undated. Whenever it could answer my purpose to transplant them from the natural or chronological order, I have not scrupled to do so. Sometimes I speak in the present, sometimes in the past tense. Few of the notes, perhaps, were written exactly at the period of time to which they relate; but this can little affect their accuracy; as the impressions were such that they can never fade from my mind. Much has been omitted. I could not, without effort, constrain myself to the task of either recalling, or constructing into a regular narrative, the whole burthen of horrors which lies

upon my brain. This feeling partly I plead in excuse, and partly that I am now in London, and am a helpless sort of person, who cannot even arrange his own papers without assistance; and I am separated from the hands which are wont to perform for me the offices of an amanuensis.

2. You will think, perhaps, that I am too confidential and communicative of my own private history: It may be so. But my way of writing is rather to think aloud, and follow my own humours, than much to consider who is listening to me; and, if I stop to consider what is proper to be said to this or that person, I shall soon come to doubt whether any part at all is proper. The fact is, I place myself at a distance of fifteen or twenty years ahead of this time, and suppose myself writing to those who will be interested about me hereafter; and wishing to have some record of a time, the entire history of which no one can know but myself, I do it as fully as I am able with the efforts I am now capable of making, because I know not whether I can ever find time to do it again.

3. It will occur to you often to ask, why did I not release myself from the horrors of opium, by leaving it off, or diminishing it? To this I must answer briefly: it might be supposed that I yielded to the fascinations of opium too easily; it cannot be supposed that any man can be charmed by its terrors. The reader may be sure, therefore, that I made attempts innumerable to reduce the quantity. I add, that those who witnessed the agonies of those attempts, and not myself, were the first to beg me to desist. But could not I have reduced it a drop a day, or by adding water, have bisected or trisected a drop? A thousand drops bisected would thus have taken nearly six years to reduce; and that way would certainly not have answered. But this is a common mistake of those who know nothing of opium experimentally; I appeal to those who do, whether it is not always found that down to a certain point it can be reduced with ease and even pleasure, but that, after that point, further reduction causes intense

suffering. Yes, say many thoughtless persons, who know not what they are talking of, you will suffer a little low spirits and dejection for a few days. I answer, no; there is nothing like low spirits; on the contrary, the mere animal spirits are uncommonly raised: the pulse is improved: the health is better. It is not there that the suffering lies. It has no resemblance to the sufferings caused by renouncing wine. It is a state of unutterable irritation of stomach (which surely is not much like dejection), accompanied by intense perspirations, and feelings such as I shall not attempt to describe without more space at my command.

I shall now enter *in medias res*, and shall anticipate, from a time when my opium pains might be said to be at their *acmè*, an account of their palsying effects on the intellectual faculties.

———

My studies have now been long interrupted. I cannot read to myself with any pleasure, hardly with a moment's endurance. Yet I read aloud sometimes for the pleasure of others; because, reading is an accomplishment of mine; and, in the slang use of the word *accomplishment* as a superficial and ornamental attainment, almost the only one I possess: and formerly, if I had any vanity at all connected with any endowment or attainment of mine, it was with this; for I had observed that no accomplishment was so rare. Players are the worst readers of all: ——— reads vilely: and Mrs. ———, who is so celebrated, can read nothing well but dramatic compositions: Milton she cannot read sufferably. People in general either read poetry without any passion at all, or else overstep the modesty of nature, and read not like scholars. Of late, if I have felt moved by any thing in books, it has been by the grand lamentations of Samson Agonistes, or the great harmonies of the Satanic speeches in *Paradise Regained*, when read aloud by myself. A young lady sometimes comes and drinks tea with us: at her request and M.'s I now and then read W———'s poems to them. (W., by the by, is the only poet I ever met who could read his own verses: often indeed he reads admirably.)

For nearly two years I believe that I read no book but one: and I owe it to the author, in discharge of a great debt of gratitude, to mention what that was. The sublimer and more passionate poets I still read, as I have said, by snatches, and occasionally. But my proper vocation, as I well knew, was the exercise of the analytic understanding. Now, for the most part, analytic studies are continuous, and not to be pursued by fits and starts, or fragmentary efforts. Mathematics, for instance, intellectual philosophy, &c. were all become insupportable to me; even at this time, incapable as I was of all general exertion, I drew up my *Prolegomena to All Future Systems of Political Economy*. I hope it will not be found redolent of opium; though, indeed, to most people, the subject itself is a sufficient opiate.

This exertion, however, was but a temporary flash; as the sequel showed—for I designed to publish my work: arrangements were made at a provincial press, about eighteen miles distant, for printing it. An additional compositor was retained, for some days, on this account. The work was even twice advertised: and I was, in a manner, pledged to the fulfilment of my intention. But I had a preface to write; and a dedication, which I wished to make a splendid one, to Mr. Ricardo. I found myself quite unable to accomplish all this. The arrangements were countermanded: the compositor dismissed: and my *Prolegomena* rested peacefully by the side of its elder and more dignified brother.

I have thus described and illustrated my intellectual torpor, in terms that apply, more or less, to every part of the four years during which I was under the Circean spells of opium. But for misery and suffering, I might, indeed, be said to have existed in a dormant state. I seldom could prevail on myself to write a letter; an answer of a few words, to any that I received, was the utmost that I could accomplish; and often *that* not until the letter had lain weeks, or even months, on my writing table. Without the aid of M. all records of bills paid, or *to be* paid, must have perished: and my whole domestic economy, whatever became of *Political Economy*, must have gone into irretrievable confusion—I shall not afterwards allude to this part of the case: it is one, however, which the opium-eater will find, in the end, as oppressive and tormenting as any other, from the sense of incapacity and feebleness, from the direct embarrassments incident to the neglect or procrastination of each day's appropriate duties, and from the remorse which must often exasperate the stings of these evils to a reflective and conscientious mind. The opium-eater loses none of his moral sensibilities, or aspirations: he wishes and longs, as earnestly as ever, to realize what he believes possible, and feels to be exacted by duty; but his intellectual apprehension of what is possible infinitely outruns his power, not of execution only, but even of power to attempt. He lies under the weight of incubus and nightmare: he lies in sight of all that he would fain perform, just as a man forcibly confined to his bed by the mortal languor of a relaxing disease, who is compelled to witness injury or outrage offered to some object of his tenderest love—he curses the spells which chain him down from motion—he would lay down his life if he might but get up and walk; but he is powerless as an infant, and cannot even attempt to rise.

I now pass to what is the main subject of these latter confessions, to the history and journal of what took place in my dreams; for these were the immediate and proximate cause of my acutest suffering.

The first notice I had of any important change going on in this part of my physical economy, was from the reawakening of a state of eye generally incident to childhood, or exalted states of irritability. I know not whether my reader is aware that many children, perhaps most, have a power of painting, as it were, upon the darkness, all sorts of phantoms: on some, that power is simply a mechanic affection of the eye; others have a voluntary, or a semivoluntary power to dismiss or to summon them; or, as a

child once said to me when I questioned him on this matter, "I can tell them to go, and they go; but sometimes they come, when I don't tell them to come." Whereupon I told him that he had almost as unlimited a command over apparitions, as a Roman centurion over his soldiers. In the middle of 1817, I think it was, that this faculty became positively distressing to me: at night, when I lay awake in bed, vast processions passed along in mournful pomp; friezes of never-ending stories, that to my feelings were as sad and solemn as if they were stories drawn from times before Oedipus or Priam—before Tyre—before Memphis. And, at the same time, a corresponding change took place in my dreams; a theatre seemed suddenly opened and lighted up within my brain, which presented nightly spectacles of more than earthly splendour. And the four following facts may be mentioned, as noticeable at this time:

1. That, as the creative state of the eye increased, a sympathy seemed to arise between the waking and the dreaming states of the brain in one point—that whatsoever I happened to call up and to trace by a voluntary act upon the darkness was very apt to transfer itself to my dreams; so that I feared to exercise this faculty; for, as Midas turned all things to gold, that yet baffled his hopes and defrauded his human desires, so whatsoever things capable of being visually represented I did but think of in the darkness, immediately shaped themselves into phantoms of the eye; and, by a process apparently no less inevitable, when thus once traced in faint and visionary colours, like writings in sympathetic ink, they were drawn out by the fierce chemistry of my dreams, into insufferable splendour that fretted my heart.

2. For this, and all other changes in my dreams, were accompanied by deep-seated anxiety and gloomy melancholy, such as are wholly incommunicable by words. I seemed every night to descend, not metaphorically, but literally to descend, into chasms and sunless abysses, depths below depths, from which it seemed hopeless that I could ever reascend.

Nor did I, by waking, feel that I *had* reascended. This I do not dwell upon; because the state of gloom which attended these gorgeous spectacles, amounting at least to utter darkness, as of some suicidal despondency, cannot be approached by words.

3. The sense of space, and in the end, the sense of time, were both powerfully affected. Buildings, landscapes, &c. were exhibited in proportions so vast as the bodily eye is not fitted to receive. Space swelled, and was amplified to an extent of unutterable infinity. This, however, did not disturb me so much as the vast expansion of time; I sometimes seemed to have lived for seventy or one-hundred years in one night; nay, sometimes had feelings representative of a millennium passed in that time, or, however, of a duration far beyond the limits of any human experience.

4. The minutest incidents of childhood, or forgotten scenes of later years, were often revived: I could not be said to recollect them; for if I had been told of them when waking, I should not have been able to acknowledge them as parts of my past experience. But placed as they were before me, in dreams like intuitions, and clothed in all their evanescent circumstances and accompanying feelings, I *recognised* them instantaneously. I was once told by a near relative of mine, that having in her childhood fallen into a river, and being on the very verge of death but for the critical assistance which reached her, she saw in a moment her whole life, in its minutest incidents, arrayed before her simultaneously as in a mirror; and she had a faculty developed as suddenly for comprehending the whole and every part. This, from some opium experiences of mine, I can believe; I have, indeed, seen the same thing asserted twice in modern books and accompanied by a remark which I am convinced is true; viz. that the dread book of account, which the Scriptures speak of, is, in fact, the mind itself of each individual. Of this, at least, I feel assured, that there is no such thing as *forgetting* possible to the mind; a thousand accidents may, and will

interpose a veil between our present consciousness and the secret inscriptions on the mind; accidents of the same sort will also rend away this veil; but alike, whether veiled or unveiled, the inscription remains for ever; just as the stars seem to withdraw before the common light of day, whereas, in fact, we all know that it is the light which is drawn over them as a veil—and that they are waiting to be revealed, when the obscuring daylight shall have withdrawn.

HENRY ADAMS

Adams at Harvard

One day in June, 1854, young Adams walked for the last time down the steps of Mr. Dixwell's school in Boylston Place, and felt no sensation but one of unqualified joy that this experience was ended. Never before or afterwards in his life did he close a period so long as four years without some sensation of loss—some sentiment of habit—but school was what in after life he commonly heard his friends denounce as an intolerable bore. He was born too old for it. The same thing could be said of most New England boys. Mentally they never were boys. Their education as men should have begun at ten years old. They were fully five years more mature than the English or European boy for whom schools were made. For the purposes of future advancement, as afterwards appeared, these first six years of a possible education were wasted in doing imperfectly what might have been done perfectly in one, and in any case would have had small value. The next regular step was Harvard College. He was more than glad to go. For generation after generation,

Adams at Harvard: From *The Education of Henry Adams*, by Henry Adams. Copyright 1927 by Houghton Mifflin Company. Reprinted by permission of the publisher.

Adamses and Brookses and Boylstons and Gorhams had gone to Harvard College, and although none of them, as far as known, had ever done any good there, or thought himself the better for it, custom, social ties, convenience, and, above all, economy, kept each generation in the track. Any other education would have required a serious effort, but no one took Harvard College seriously. All went there because their friends went there, and the College was their ideal of social self-respect.

Harvard College, as far as it educated at all, was a mild and liberal school, which sent young men into the world with all they needed to make respectable citizens, and something of what they wanted to make useful ones. Leaders of men it never tried to make. Its ideals were altogether different. The Unitarian clergy had given to the College a character of moderation, balance, judgment, restraint, what the French called *mesure*; excellent traits, which the College attained with singular success, so that its graduates could commonly be recognized by the stamp, but such a type of character rarely lent itself to autobiography. In effect, the school created a type but not a will. Four years of Harvard College, if successful, resulted in an autobiographical blank, a mind on which only a water-mark had been stamped.

The stamp, as such things went, was a good one. The chief wonder of education is that it does not ruin everybody concerned in it, teachers and taught. Sometimes in after life, Adams debated whether in fact it had not ruined him and most of his companions, but, disappointment apart, Harvard College was probably less hurtful than any other university then in existence. It taught little, and that little ill, but it left the mind open, free from bias, ignorant of facts, but docile. The graduate had few strong prejudices. He knew little, but his mind remained supple, ready to receive knowledge.

What caused the boy most disappointment was the little he got from his mates. Speaking exactly, he got less than nothing, a result common enough in education. Yet the College Catalogue for the years 1854 to 1861 shows a list of names rather distinguished in their time. Alexander Agassiz and Phillips Brooks led it; H. H. Richardson and O. W. Holmes helped to close it. As a rule the most promising of all die early, and never get their names into a Dictionary of Contemporaries, which seems to be the only popular standard of success. Many died in the war. Adams knew them all, more or less; he felt as much regard, and quite as much respect for them then, as he did after they won great names and were objects of a vastly wider respect; but, as help towards education, he got nothing whatever from them or they from him until long after they had left college. Possibly the fault was his, but one would like to know how many others shared it. Accident counts for much in companionship as in marriage. Life offers perhaps only a score of possible companions, and it is mere chance whether they meet as early as school or college, but it is more than a chance that boys brought up together under like conditions have nothing to give each other. The Class of 1858, to which Henry Adams belonged, was a typical collection of young New Englanders, quietly penetrating and aggressively commonplace; free from mean-nesses, jealousies, intrigues, enthusiasms, and passions; not exceptionally quick; not con-sciously sceptical; singularly indifferent to display, artifice, florid expression, but not hostile to it when it amused them; distrustful of themselves, but little disposed to trust any one else; with not much humor of their own, but full of readiness to enjoy the humor of others; negative to a degree that in the long run became positive and triumphant. Not harsh in manners or judgment, rather liberal and open-minded, they were still as a body the most formidable critics one would care to meet, in a long life exposed to criticism. They never flattered, seldom praised; free from vanity, they were not intolerant of it; but they were objectiveness itself; their attitude was a law of nature; their judgment beyond appeal, not an act either of intellect or emotion or of will, but a sort of gravitation.

This was Harvard College incarnate, but even for Harvard College, the Class of 1858 was somewhat extreme. Of unity this band of nearly one hundred young men had no keen sense, but they had equally little energy of repulsion. They were pleasant to live with, and above the average of students—German, French, English, or what not—but chiefly because each individual appeared satisfied to stand alone. It seemed a sign of force; yet to stand alone is quite natural when one has no passions; still easier when one has no pains.

Into this unusually dissolvent medium, chance insisted on enlarging Henry Adams's education by tossing a trio of Virginians as little fitted for it as Sioux Indians to a treadmill. By some further affinity, these three outsiders fell into relation with the Bostonians among whom Adams as a schoolboy belonged, and in the end with Adams himself, although they and he knew well how thin an edge of friendship separated them in 1856 from mortal enmity. One of the Virginians was the son of Colonel Robert E. Lee, of the Second United States Cavalry; and two others who seemed instinctively to form a staff for Lee, were town-Virginians from Petersburg. A fourth outsider came from Cincinnati and was half Kentuckian, N. L. Anderson, Longworth on the mother's side. For the first time Adams's education brought him in contact with new types and taught him their values. He saw the New England type measure itself with another, and he was part of the process.

Lee, known through life as "Roony," was a Virginian of the eighteenth century, much as Henry Adams was a Bostonian of the same age. Roony Lee had changed little from the type of his grandfather, Light Horse Harry. Tall, largely built, handsome, genial, with liberal Virginian openness towards all he liked, he had also the Virginian habit of command and took leadership as his natural habit. No one cared to contest it. None of the New Englanders wanted command. For a year, at least, Lee was the most popular and prominent young man in his class, but then seemed slowly to drop into the background. The habit of command was not enough, and the Virginian had little else. He was simple beyond analysis; so simple that even the simple New England student could not realize him. No one knew enough to know how ignorant he was; how childlike; how helpless before the relative complexity of a school. As an animal, the Southerner seemed to have every advantage, but even as an animal he steadily lost ground.

The lesson in education was vital to these young men, who, within ten years, killed each other by scores in the act of testing their college conclusions. Strictly, the Southerner had no mind; he had temperament. He was not a scholar; he had no intellectual training; he could not analyze an idea, and he could not even conceive of admitting two; but in life one could get along very well without ideas, if one had only the social instinct. Dozens of eminent statesmen were men of Lee's type, and maintained themselves well enough in the legislature, but college was a sharper test. The Virginian was weak in vice itself, though the Bostonian was hardly a master of crime. The habits of neither were good; both were apt to drink hard and to live low lives; but the Bostonian suffered less than the Virginian. Commonly the Bostonian would take some care of himself even in his worst stages, while the Virginian became quarrelsome and dangerous. When a Virginian had brooded a few days over an imaginary grief and substantial whiskey, none of his Northern friends could be sure that he might not be waiting, round the corner, with a knife or pistol, to revenge insult by the day light of *delirium tremens*; and when things reached this condition, Lee had to exhaust his authority over his own staff. Lee was a gentleman of the old school, and, as every one knows, gentlemen of the old school drank almost as much as gentlemen of the new school; but this was not his trouble. He was sober even in the excessive violence of political feeling in those years; he kept his temper and his friends under control.

Adams liked the Virginians. No one was more obnoxious to them, by name and prejudice; yet their friendship was unbroken and even warm. At a moment when the immediate future posed no problem in education so vital as the relative energy and endurance of North and South, this momentary contact with Southern character was a sort of education for its own sake; but this was not all. No doubt the self-esteem of the Yankee, which tended naturally to self-distrust, was flattered by gaining the slow conviction that the Southerner, with his slave-owning limitations, was as little fit to succeed in the struggle of modern life as though he were still a maker of stone axes, living in caves, and hunting the *bos primigenius*, and that every quality in which he was strong, made him weaker; but Adams had begun to fear that even in this respect one eighteenth-century type might not differ deeply from another. Roony Lee had changed little from the Virginian of a century before; but Adams was himself a good deal nearer the type of his great-grandfather than to that of a railway superintendent. He was little more fit than the Virginians to deal with a future America which showed no fancy for the past. Already Northern society betrayed a preference for economists over diplomats or soldiers—one might even call it a jealousy—against which two eighteenth-century types had little chance to live, and which they had in common to fear.

Nothing short of this curious sympathy could have brought into close relations two young men so hostile as Roony Lee and Henry Adams, but the chief difference between them as collegians consisted only in their difference of scholarship: Lee was a total failure; Adams a partial one. Both failed, but Lee felt his failure more sensibly, so that he gladly seized the chance of escape by accepting a commission offered him by General Winfield Scott in the force then being organized against the Mormons. He asked Adams to write his letter of acceptance, which flattered Adams's vanity more than any

Northern compliment could do, because, in days of violent political bitterness, it showed a certain amount of good temper. The diplomat felt his profession.

If the student got little from his mates, he got little more from his masters. The four years passed at college were, for his purposes, wasted. Harvard College was a good school, but at bottom what the boy disliked most was any school at all. He did not want to be one in a hundred—one per cent of an education. He regarded himself as the only person for whom his education had value, and he wanted the whole of it. He got barely half of an average. Long afterwards, when the devious path of life led him back to teach in his turn what no student naturally cared or needed to know, he diverted some dreary hours of faculty meetings by looking up his record in the class-lists, and found himself graded precisely in the middle. In the one branch he most needed—mathematics—barring the few first scholars, failure was so nearly universal that no attempt at grading could have had value, and whether he stood fortieth or ninetieth must have been an accident or the personal favor of the professor. Here his education failed lamentably. At best he could never have been a mathematician; at worst he would never have cared to be one; but he needed to read mathematics, like any other universal language, and he never reached the alphabet.

Beyond two or three Greek plays, the student got nothing from the ancient languages. Beyond some incoherent theories of free-trade and protection, he got little from Political Economy. He could not afterwards remember to have heard the name of Karl Marx mentioned, or the title of "Capital." He was equally ignorant of Auguste Comte. These were the two writers of his time who most influenced its thought. The bit of practical teaching he afterwards reviewed with much curiosity was the course in Chemistry, which taught him a number of theories that befogged his mind for a lifetime. The only teaching that appealed to his imagination was a course of lectures by Louis Agassiz on the Glacial Period and Palaeontology, which had more influence on his curiosity than the rest of the college instruction altogether. The entire work of the four years could have been easily put into the work of any four months in after life.

Harvard College was a negative force, and negative forces have value. Slowly it weakened the violent political bias of childhood, not by putting interests in its place, but by mental habits which had no bias at all. It would also have weakened the literary bias, if Adams had been capable of finding other amusement, but the climate kept him steady to desultory and useless reading, till he had run through libraries of volumes which he forgot even to their title pages. Rather by instinct than by guidance, he turned to writing, and his professors or tutors occasionally gave his English composition a hesitating approval; but in that branch, as in all the rest, even when he made a long struggle for recognition, he never convinced his teachers that his abilities, at their best, warranted placing him on the rank-list, among the first third of his class. Instructors generally reach a fairly accurate gauge of their scholars's powers. Henry Adams himself held the opinion that his instructors were very nearly right, and when he became a professor in his turn, and made mortifying mistakes in ranking his scholars, he still obstinately insisted that on the whole, he was not far wrong. Student or professor, he accepted the negative standard because it was the standard of the school.

He never knew what other students thought of it, or what they thought they gained from it; nor would their opinion have much affected his. From the first, he wanted to be done with it, and stood watching vaguely for a path and a direction. The world outside seemed large, but the paths that led into it were not many and lay mostly through Boston, where he did not want to go. As it happened, by pure chance, the first door of escape that seemed to offer a hope led into Germany, and James Russell Lowell opened it.

Lowell, on succeeding Longfellow as Professor of Belles-Lettres, had duly gone to Germany, and had brought back whatever he found to bring. The literary world then agreed that truth survived in Germany alone, and Carlyle, Matthew Arnold, Renan, Emerson, with scores of popular followers, taught the German faith. The literary world had revolted against the yoke of coming capitalism—its moneylenders, its bank directors, and its railway magnates. Thackeray and Dickens followed Balzac in scratching and biting the unfortunate middle class with savage ill-temper, much as the middle class had scratched and bitten the Church and Court for a hundred years before. The middle class had the power, and held its coal and iron well in hand, but the satirists and idealists seized the press, and as they were agreed that the Second Empire was a disgrace to France and a danger to England, they turned to Germany because at that moment Germany was neither economical nor military, and a hundred years behind western Europe in the simplicity of its standard. German thought, method, honesty, and even taste, became the standards of scholarship. Goethe was raised to the rank of Shakespeare—Kant ranked as a lawgiver above Plato. All serious scholars were obliged to become German, for German thought was revolutionizing criticism. Lowell had followed the rest, not very enthusiastically, but with sufficient conviction, and invited his scholars to join him. Adams was glad to accept the invitation, rather for the sake of cultivating Lowell than Germany, but still in perfect good faith. It was the first serious attempt he had made to direct his own education, and he was sure of getting some education out of it; not perhaps anything that he expected, but at least a path.

Singularly circuitous and excessively wasteful of energy the path proved to be, but the student could never see what other was open to him. He could have done no better had he foreseen every stage of his coming life, and he would probably have done worse. The preliminary step was pure gain. James Russell Lowell had brought back from Germany the only new and valuable part of its universities, the habit of allowing students to read with him privately in his study. Adams asked the privilege, and used it to read a little, and to talk a great deal, for the personal contact pleased and flattered him, as that of older men ought to flatter and please the young even when they altogether exaggerate its value. Lowell was a new element in the boy's life. As practical a New Englander as any, he leaned towards the Concord faith rather than towards Boston where he properly belonged; for Concord, in the dark days of 1856, glowed with pure light. Adams approached it in much the same spirit as he would have entered a Gothic Cathedral, for he well knew that the priests regarded him as only a worm. To the Concord Church all Adamses were minds of dust and emptiness, devoid of feeling, poetry or imagination; little higher than the common scourings of State Street; politicians of doubtful honesty; natures of narrow scope; and already, at eighteen years old, Henry had begun to feel uncertainty about so many matters more important than Adamses that his mind rebelled against no discipline merely personal, and he was ready to admit his unworthiness if only he might penetrate the shrine. The influence of Harvard College was beginning to have its effect. He was slipping away from fixed principles; from Mount Vernon Street; from Quincy; from the eighteenth century; and his first steps led toward Concord.

He never reached Concord, and to Concord Church he, like the rest of mankind who accepted a material universe, remained always an insect, or something much lower—a man. It was surely no fault of his that the universe seemed to him real; perhaps—as Mr. Emerson justly said—it was so; in spite of the long-continued effort of a lifetime, he perpetually fell back into the heresy that if anything universal was unreal, it was himself and not the appearances; it was the poet and not the banker; it was his own thought, not the thing that moved it. He did not lack the wish to be transcendental.

Concord seemed to him, at one time, more real than Quincy; yet in truth Russell Lowell was as little transcendental as Beacon Street. From him the boy got no revolutionary thought whatever —objective or subjective as they used to call it— but he got good-humored encouragement to do what amused him, which consisted in passing two years in Europe after finishing the four years of Cambridge.

The result seemed small in proportion to the effort, but it was the only positive result he could ever trace to the influence of Harvard College, and he had grave doubts whether Harvard College influenced even that. Negative results in plenty he could trace, but he tended towards negation on his own account, as one side of the New England mind had always done, and even there he could never feel sure that Harvard College had more than reflected a weakness. In his opinion the education was not serious, but in truth hardly any Boston student took it seriously, and none of them seemed sure that President Walker himself, or President Felton after him, took it more seriously than the students. For them all, the college offered chiefly advantages vulgarly called social, rather than mental.

Unluckily for this particular boy, social advantages were his only capital in life. Of money he had not much, of mind not more, but he could be quite certain that, barring his own faults, his social position would never be questioned....

Socially or intellectually, the college was for him negative and in some ways mischievous. The most tolerant man of the world could not see good in the lower habits of the students, but the vices were less harmful than the virtues. The habit of drinking—though the mere recollection of it made him doubt his own veracity, so fantastic it seemed in later life— may have done no great or permanent harm; but the habit of looking at life as a social relation —an affair of society—did no good. It cultivated a weakness which needed no cultivation. If it had helped to make men of the world, or give the manners and instincts of any profession—such as temper, patience, courtesy, or a faculty of profiting by the social defects of opponents—it would have been education better worth having than mathematics or languages; but so far as it helped to make anything, it helped only to make the college standard permanent through life. The Bostonian educated at Harvard College remained a collegian, if he stuck only to what the college gave him. If parents went on, generation after generation, sending their children to Harvard College for the sake of its social advantages, they perpetuated an inferior social type, quite as ill-fitted as the Oxford type for success in the next generation.

Luckily the old social standard of the college, as President Walker or James Russell Lowell still showed it, was admirable, and if it had little practical value or personal influence on the mass of students, at least it preserved the tradition for those who liked it. The Harvard graduate was neither American nor European, nor even wholly Yankee; his admirers were few, and his critics many; perhaps his worst weakness was his self-criticism and self-consciousness; but his ambitions, social or intellectual, were not necessarily cheap even though they might be negative. Afraid of serious risks, and still more afraid of personal ridicule, he seldom made a great failure of life, and nearly always led a life more or less worth living. So Henry Adams, well aware that he could not succeed as a scholar, and finding his social position beyond improvement or need of effort, betook himself to the single ambition which otherwise would scarcely have seemed a true outcome of the college, though it was the last remnant of the old Unitarian supremacy. He took to the pen. He wrote.

The College Magazine printed his work, and the College Societies listened to his addresses. Lavish of praise the readers were not; the audiences, too, listened in silence; but this was all the encouragement any Harvard collegian had a reasonable hope to receive; grave silence was a form of patience that meant possible

future acceptance; and Henry Adams went on writing. No one cared enough to criticize, except himself who soon began to suffer from reaching his own limits. He found that he could not be this—or that—or the other; always precisely the things he wanted to be. He had not wit or scope or force. Judges always ranked him beneath a rival, if he had any; and he believed the judges were right. His work seemed to him thin, commonplace, feeble. At times he felt his own weakness so fatally that he could not go on; when he had nothing to say, he could not say it, and he found that he had very little to say at best. Much that he then wrote must be still in existence in print or manuscript, though he never cared to see it again, for he felt no doubt that it was in reality just what he thought it. At best it showed only a feeling for form; an instinct of exclusion. Nothing shocked—not even its weakness.

Inevitably an effort leads to an ambition—creates it—and at that time the ambition of the literary student, which almost took place of the regular prizes of scholarship, was that of being chosen as the representative of his class—the Class Orator—at the close of their course. This was political as well as literary success, and precisely the sort of eighteenth-century combination that fascinated an eighteenth-century boy. The idea lurked in his mind, at first as a dream, in no way serious or even possible, for he stood outside the number of what were known as popular men. Year by year, his position seemed to improve, or perhaps his rivals disappeared, until at last, to his own great astonishment, he found himself a candidate. The habits of the college permitted no active candidacy; he and his rivals had not a word to say for or against themselves, and he was never even consulted on the subject; he was not present at any of the proceedings, and how it happened he never could quite divine, but it did happen, that one evening on returning from Boston he received notice of his election, after a very close contest, as Class Orator over the head of the first scholar, who was undoubtedly a better orator and a more popular man. In politics the success of the poorer candidate is common enough, and Henry Adams was a fairly trained politician, but he never understood how he managed to defeat not only a more capable but a more popular rival....

Henry Adams never professed the smallest faith in universities of any kind, either as boy or man, nor had he the faintest admiration for the university graduate, either in Europe or in America; as a collegian he was only known apart from his fellows by his habit of standing outside the college; and yet the singular fact remained that this commonplace body of young men chose him repeatedly to express his and their commonplaces. Secretly, of course, the successful candidate flattered himself—and them—with the hope that they might perhaps not be so commonplace as they thought themselves; but this was only another proof that all were identical....

All the same, the choice was flattering; so flattering that it actually shocked his vanity; and would have shocked it more, if possible, had he known that it was to be the only flattery of the sort he was ever to receive. The function of Class Day was, in the eyes of nine-tenths of the students, altogether the most important of the college, and the figure of the Orator was the most conspicuous in the function. Unlike the Orators at regular Commencements, the Class Day Orator stood alone, or had only the Poet for rival. Crowded into the large church, the students, their families, friends, aunts, uncles and chaperones, attended all the girls of sixteen or twenty who wanted to show their summer dresses or fresh complexions, and there, for an hour or two, in a heat that might have melted bronze, they listened to an Orator and a Poet in clergyman's gowns, reciting such platitudes as their own experience and their mild censors permitted them to utter. What Henry Adams said in his Class Oration of 1858 he soon forgot

to the last word, nor had it the least value for education; but he naturally remembered what was said of it. He remembered especially one of his eminent uncles or relations remarking that, as the work of so young a man, the oration was singularly wanting in enthusiasm. The young man—always in search of education—asked himself whether, setting rhetoric aside, this absence of enthusiasm was a defect or a merit, since, in either case, it was all that Harvard College taught, and all that the hundred young men, whom he was trying to represent, expressed. Another comment threw more light on the effect of the college education. One of the elderly gentlemen noticed the orator's "perfect self-possession." Self-possession indeed! If Harvard College gave nothing else, it gave calm. For four years each student had been obliged to figure daily before dozens of young men who knew each other to the last fibre. One had done little but read papers to Societies, or act comedy in the Hasty Pudding, not to speak of all sorts of regular exercises, and no audience in future life would ever be so intimately and terribly intelligent as these. Three-fourths of the graduates would rather have addressed the Council of Trent or the British Parliament than have acted Sir Anthony Absolute or Dr. Ollapod before a gala audience of the Hasty Pudding. Self-possession was the strongest part of Harvard College, which certainly taught men to stand alone, so that nothing seemed stranger to its graduates than the paroxysms of terror before the public which often overcame the graduates of European universities. Whether this was, or was not, education, Henry Adams never knew. He was ready to stand up before any audience in America or Europe, with nerves rather steadier for the excitement, but whether he should ever have anything to say, remained to be proved. As yet he knew nothing. Education had not begun.

MARCEL PROUST

My Mother, My Father, and I

I never took my eyes off my mother. I knew that when they were at table I should not be permitted to stay there for the whole of dinner-time, and that Mamma, for fear of annoying my father, would not allow me to give her in public the series of kisses that she would have had in my room. And so I promised myself that in the dining room, as they began to eat and drink and as I felt the hour approach, I would put before-hand into this kiss, which was bound to be so brief and stealthy in execution, everything that my own efforts could put into it: would look out very carefully first the exact spot on her cheek where I would imprint it, and would so prepare my thoughts that I might be able, thanks to these mental preliminaries, to con-secrate the whole of the minute Mamma would allow me to the sensation of her cheek against my lips, as a painter who can have his subject for short sittings only prepares his palette, and from what he remembers and from rough notes does in advance everything which he possibly can do in the sitter's absence. But tonight, before the dinner bell had sounded, my grandfather said with unconscious cruelty: "The little man looks tired; he'd better go up to bed. Besides, we are dining late tonight."

And my father, who was less scrupulous than my grandmother or mother in observing the letter of a treaty, went on: "Yes, run along; to bed with you."

I would have kissed Mamma then and there, but at that moment the dinner bell rang.

"No, no, leave your mother alone. You've said good night quite enough. These exhibitions are absurd. Go on upstairs."

And so I must set forth without viaticum; must climb each step of the staircase "against my heart," as the saying is, climbing in opposi-tion to my heart's desire, which was to return to my mother, since she had not, by her kiss, given my heart leave to accompany me forth. That hateful staircase, up which I always passed with such dismay, gave out a smell of varnish which had to some extent absorbed, made definite and fixed the special quality of sorrow that I felt each evening, and made it perhaps even more cruel to my sensibility because, when it assumed this olfactory guise, my intellect was powerless to resist it. When we have gone to sleep with a maddening toothache and are conscious of it only as a little girl whom we attempt, time after time, to pull out of the water, or as a line of Molière which we repeat in-cessantly to ourselves, it is a great relief to wake up, so that our intelligence can disentangle the idea of toothache from any artificial semblance of heroism or rhythmic cadence. It was the precise converse of this relief which I felt when my anguish at having to go up to my room invaded my consciousness in a manner infinitely more rapid, instantaneous almost, a manner at once insidious and brutal as I breathed in—a far more poisonous thing than any moral pene-tration—the peculiar smell of the varnish upon that staircase.

Once in my room I had to stop every loophole, to close the shutters, to dig my own grave as I turned down the bed-clothes, to wrap myself in the shroud of my nightshirt. But before burying myself in the iron bed which had been placed there because, on summer nights, I was too hot among the rep curtains of the four-poster, I was stirred to revolt, and attempted the desperate stratagem of a condemned prisoner. I wrote to my mother begging her to come upstairs for an important reason which I could not put in writing. My fear was that Françoise, my aunt's cook who used to be put in charge of me when I was at Combray, might refuse to take my note. I had a suspicion that, in her eyes, to carry a message to my mother when there was a stranger in the room would appear flatly inconceivable, just as it would be for the doorkeeper of a theatre to hand a letter to an actor upon the stage. For things which might or might not be done she possessed a code at once imperious, abundant, subtle, and uncompromising on points themselves imperceptible or irrelevant, which gave it a resemblance to those ancient laws which combine such cruel ordinances as the massacre of infants at the breast with prohibitions, of exaggerated refinement, against "seething the kid in his mother's milk," or "eating of the sinew which is upon the hollow of the thigh." This code, if one could judge it by the sudden obstinacy which she would put into her refusal to carry out certain of our instructions, seemed to have foreseen such social complications and refinements of fashion as nothing in Françoise's surroundings or in her career as a servant in a village household could have put into her head; and we were obliged to assume that there was latent in her some past existence in the ancient history of France, noble and little understood, just as there is in those manufacturing towns where old mansions still testify to their former courtly days, and chemical workers toil among delicately sculptured scenes of the Miracle of Theophilus or the Quatre Fils Aymon.

In this particular instance, the article of her code which made it highly improbable that—barring an outbreak of fire—Françoise would go down and disturb Mamma when M. Swann was there for so unimportant a person as myself was one embodying the respect she shewed not only for the family (as for the dead, for the clergy, or for royalty), but also for the stranger within our gates; a respect which I should perhaps have found touching in a book, but which never failed to irritate me on her lips, because of the solemn and gentle tones in which she would utter it, and which irritated me more than usual this evening when the sacred character

in which she invested the dinner-party might have the effect of making her decline to disturb its ceremonial. But to give myself one chance of success I lied without hesitation, telling her that it was not in the least myself who had wanted to write to Mamma, but Mamma who, on saying good night to me, had begged me not to forget to send her an answer about something she had asked me to find, and that she would certainly be very angry if this note were not taken to her. I think that Françoise disbelieved me, for, like those primitive men whose senses were so much keener than our own, she could immediately detect, by signs imperceptible by the rest of us, the truth or falsehood of anything that we might wish to conceal from her. She studied the envelope for five minutes as though an examination of the paper itself and the look of my handwriting could enlighten her as to the nature of the contents, or tell her to which article of her code she ought to refer the matter. Then she went out with an air of resignation which seemed to imply: "What a dreadful thing for parents to have a child like this!"

A moment later she returned to say that they were still at the ice stage and that it was impossible for the butler to deliver the note at once, in front of everybody; but that when the finger-bowls were put round he would find a way of slipping it into Mamma's hand. At once my anxiety subsided; it was now no longer (as it has been a moment ago) until tomorrow that I had lost my mother, for my little line was going—to annoy her, no doubt, and doubly so because this contrivance would make me ridiculous in Swann's eyes—but was going all the same to admit me, invisibly and by stealth, into the same room as herself, was going to whisper from me into her ear; for that forbidden and unfriendly dining room, where but a moment ago the ice itself—with burned nuts in it—and the finger bowls seemed to me to be concealing pleasures that were mischievous and of a mortal sadness because Mamma was tasting of them and I was far away, had opened its doors to me and, like a ripe fruit which bursts through its skin, was going to pour out into my intoxicated heart the gushing sweetness of Mamma's attention while she was reading what I had written. Now I was no longer separated from her; the barriers were down; an exquisite thread was binding us. Besides, that was not all, for surely Mamma would come.

As for the agony through which I had just passed, I imagined that Swann would have laughed heartily at it if he had read my letter and had guessed its purpose; whereas, on the contrary, as I was to learn in due course, a similar anguish had been the bane of his life for many years, and no one perhaps could have understood my feelings at that moment so well as himself; to him, that anguish which lies in knowing that the creature one adores is in some place of enjoyment where oneself is not and cannot follow—to him that anguish came through Love, to which it is in a sense pre-destined, by which it must be equipped and adapted; but when, as had befallen me, such an anguish possesses one's soul before Love has yet entered into one's life, then it must drift, awaiting Love's coming, vague and free, without precise attachment, at the disposal of one sentiment today, of another tomorrow, of filial piety, of affection for a comrade. And the joy with which I first bound myself apprentice, when Françoise returned to tell me that my letter would be delivered; Swann, too, had known well that false joy which a friend can give us, or some relative of the woman we love, when on his arrival at the house or theatre where she is to be found, for some ball or party or "first-night" at which he is to meet her, he sees us wandering outside, desperately awaiting some opportunity of communicating with her. He recognises us, greets us familiarly, and asks what we are doing there. And when we invent a story of having some urgent message to give to his relative or friend, he assures us that nothing could be more simple, takes us in at the door, and promises to send her down to us in five minutes. How much we love him—as at that moment I loved Françoise—the good-

natured intermediary who by a single word has made supportable, human, almost propitious the inconceivable, infernal scene of gaiety in the thick of which we have been imagining swarms of enemies, perverse and seductive, beguiling away from us, even making laugh at us, the woman whom we love....

My mother did not appear, but with no attempt to safeguard my self-respect (which depended upon her keeping up the fiction that she had asked me to let her know the result of my search for something or other) made Françoise tell me, in so many words "There is no answer"—words I have so often, since then, heard the hall-porters in "mansions" and the flunkeys in gambling clubs and the like, repeat to some poor girl, who replies in bewilderment: "What! he's said nothing? It's not possible. You did give him my letter, didn't you? Very well, I shall wait a little longer." And just as she invariably protests that she does not need the extra gas which the porter offers to light for her, and sits on there, hearing nothing further, except an occasional remark on the weather which the porter exchanges with a messenger whom he will send off suddenly, when he notices the time, to put customer's wine on the ice; so, having declined Françoise's offer to make me some tea or to stay beside me, I let her go off again to the servants' hall, and lay down and shut my eyes, and tried not to hear the voices of my family who were drinking their coffee in the garden.

But after a few seconds I realised that, by writing that line to Mamma, by approaching—at the risk of making her angry—so near to her that I felt I could reach out and grasp the moment in which I should see her again, I had cut myself off from the possibility of going to sleep until I actually had seen her, and my heart began to beat more and more painfully as I increased my agitation by ordering myself to keep calm and to acquiesce in my ill-fortune. Then, suddenly, my anxiety subsided, a feeling of intense happiness coursed through me, as when a strong medicine begins to take effect and one's pain vanishes: I had formed a resolution to abandon all attempts to go to sleep without seeing Mamma, and had decided to kiss her at all costs, even with the certainty of being in disgrace with her for long afterwards, when she herself came up to bed. The tranquillity which followed my anguish made me extremely alert, no less than my sense of expectation, my thirst for and my fear of danger.

Noiselessly I opened the window and sat down on the foot of my bed; hardly daring to move in case they should hear me from below. Things outside seemed also fixed in mute expectation, so as not to disturb the moonlight which, duplicating each of them and throwing it back by the extension, forwards, of a shadow denser and more concrete than its substance, had made the whole landscape seem at once thinner and longer, like a map which, after being folded up, is spread out upon the ground. What had to move—a leaf of the chestnut tree, for instance—moved. But its minute shuddering, complete, finished to the least detail and with utmost delicacy of gesture, made no discord with the rest of the scene, and yet was not merged in it, remaining clearly outlined. Exposed upon this surface of silence, which absorbed nothing from them, the most distant sounds, those which must have come from gardens at the far end of the town, could be distinguished with such exact "finish" that the impression they gave of coming from a distance seemed due only to their "pianissimo" execution, like those movements on muted strings so well performed by the orchestra of the Conservatoire that, although one does not lose a single note, one thinks all the same that they are being played somewhere outside, a long way from the concert hall, so that all the old subscribers, and my grandmother's sisters too, when Swann had given them his seats, used to strain their ears as if they had caught the distant approach of an army on the march, which had not yet rounded the corner of the Rue de Trévise.

I was well aware that I had placed myself in a position than which none could be counted upon to involve me in graver consequences at my parents' hands; consequences far graver, indeed, than a stranger would have imagined, and such as (he would have thought) could follow only some really shameful fault. But in the system of education which they had given me faults were not classified in the same order as in that of other children, and I had been taught to place at the head of the list (doubtless because there was no other class of faults from which I needed to be more carefully protected) those in which I can now distinguish the common feature that one succumbs to them by yielding to a nervous impulse. But such words as these last had never been uttered in my hearing; no one had yet accounted for my temptations in a way which might have led me to believe that there was some excuse for my giving in to them, or that I was actually incapable of holding out against them. Yet I could easily recognise this class of transgressions by the anguish of mind which preceded, as well as by the rigour of the punishment which followed them; and I knew that what I had just done was in the same category as certain other sins for which I had been severely chastised, though infinitely more serious than they. When I went out to meet my mother as she herself came up to bed, and when she saw that I had remained up so as to say good night to her again in the passage, I should not be allowed to stay in the house a day longer, I should be packed off to school next morning; so much was certain. Very good: had I been obliged, the next moment, to hurl myself out of the window, I should still have preferred such a fate. For what I wanted now was Mamma, and to say good night to her. I had gone too far along the road which led to the realisation of this desire to be able to retrace my steps.

I could hear my parents' footsteps as they went with Swann; and, when the rattle of the gate assured me that he had really gone, I crept to the window. Mamma was asking my father if he had thought the lobster good, and whether M. Swann had had some of the coffee-

and-pistachio ice. "I thought it rather so-so," she was saying; "next time we shall have to try another flavour."

My father and mother were left alone and sat down for a moment; then my father said: "Well, shall we go up to bed?"

"As you wish, dear, though I don't feel in the least like sleeping. I don't know why; it can't be the coffee-ice—it wasn't strong enough to keep me awake like this. But I see a light in the servants' hall: poor Françoise has been sitting up for me, so I will get her to unhook me while you go and undress."

My mother opened the latticed door which led from the hall to the staircase. Presently I heard her coming upstairs to close her window. I went quietly into the passage; my heart was beating so violently that I could hardly move, but at least it was throbbing no longer with anxiety, but with terror and with joy. I saw in the well of the stair a light coming upwards, from Mamma's candle. Then I saw Mamma herself: I threw myself upon her. For an instant she looked at me in astonishment, not realising what could have happened. Then her face assumed an expression of anger. She said not a single word to me; and, for that matter, I used to go for days on end without being spoken to, for far less offences than this. A single word from Mamma would have been an admission that further intercourse with me was within the bounds of possibility, and that might perhaps have appeared to me more terrible still, as indicating that, with such a punishment as was in store for me, mere silence, and even anger, were relatively puerile.

A word from her then would have implied the false calm in which one converses with a servant to whom one has just decided to give notice; the kiss one bestows on a son who is being packed off to enlist, which would have been denied him if it had merely been a matter of being angry with him for a few days. But she heard my father coming from the dressing-room, where he had gone to take off his clothes, and, to avoid the "scene" which he would make

if he saw me, she said, in a voice half-stifled by her anger: "Run away at once. Don't let your father see you standing there like a crazy jane!"

But I begged her again to "Come and say good night to me!" terrified as I saw the light from my father's candle already creeping up the wall, but also making use of his approach as a means of blackmail, in the hope that my mother, not wishing him to find me there, as find me he must if she continued to hold out, would give in to me, and say: "Go back to your room. I will come."

Too late: my father was upon us. Instinctively I murmured, though no one heard me, "I am done for!"

I was not, however. My father used constantly to refuse to let me do things which were quite clearly allowed by the more liberal charters granted me by my mother and grandmother, because he paid no heed to "Principles," and because in his sight there were no such things as "Rights of Man." For some quite irrelevant reason, or for no reason at all, he would at the last moment prevent me from taking some particular walk, one so regular and so consecrated to my use that to deprive me of it was a clear breach of faith; or again, as he had done this evening, long before the appointed hour he would snap out: "Run along up to bed now; no excuses!" But then again, simply because he was devoid of principles (in my grandmother's sense), so he could not, properly speaking, be called inexorable. He looked at me for a moment with an air of annoyance and surprise, and then when Mamma had told him, not without some embarrassment, what had happened, said to her: "Go along with him, then; you said just now that you didn't feel like sleep, so stay in his room for a little. I don't need anything."

"But dear," my mother answered timidly, "whether or not I feel like sleep is not the point; we must not make the child accustomed...."

"There's no question of making him accustomed," said my father, with a shrug of the shoulders; "you can see quite well that the child is unhappy. After all, we aren't gaolers. You'll end by making him ill, and a lot of good that will do. There are two beds in his room; tell Françoise to make up the big one for you, and stay beside him for the rest of the night. I'm off to bed, anyhow; I'm not nervous like you. Good night."

It was impossible for me to thank my father; what he called my sentimentality would have exasperated him. I stood there, not daring to move; he was still confronting us, an immense figure in his white nightshirt, crowned with the pink and violet scarf of Indian cashmere in which, since he had begun to suffer from neuralgia, he used to tie up his head, standing like Abraham in the engraving after Benozzo Gozzoli which M. Swann had given me, telling Sarah that she must tear herself away from Isaac. Many years have passed since that night. The wall of the staircase, up which I had watched the light of his candle gradually climb, was long ago demolished. And in myself, too, many things have perished which, I imagined, would last for ever, and new structures have arisen, giving birth to new sorrows and new joys which in those days I could not have foreseen, just as now the old are difficult of comprehension. It is a long time, too, since my father has been able to tell Mamma to "Go with the child." Never again will such hours be possible for me. But of late I have been increasingly able to catch, if I listen attentively, the sound of the sobs which I had the strength to control in my father's presence, and which broke out only when I found myself alone with Mamma. Actually, their echo has never ceased: it is only because life is now growing more and more quiet round about me that I hear them afresh, like those convent bells which are so effectively drowned during the day by the noises of the streets that one would suppose them to have stopped for ever, until they sound out again through the silent evening air.

Mamma spent that night in my room: when I had just committed a sin so deadly that I was waiting to be banished from the household, my parents gave me a far greater concession than I should ever have won as the reward of a good action. Even at the moment when it manifested itself in this crowning mercy, my father's conduct towards me was still somewhat arbitrary, and regardless of my deserts, as was characteristic of him and due to the fact that his actions were generally dictated by chance expediencies rather than based on any formal plan. And perhaps even what I called his strictness, when he sent me off to bed, deserved that title less, really, than my mother's or grandmother's attitude, for his nature, which in some respects differed more than theirs from my own, had probably prevented him from guessing, until then, how wretched I was every evening, a thing which my mother and grandmother knew well; but they loved me enough to be unwilling to spare me that suffering, which they hoped to teach me to overcome, so as to reduce my nervous sensibility and to strengthen my will. As for my father, whose affection for me was of another kind, I doubt if he would have shewn so much courage, for as soon as he had grasped the fact that I was unhappy he said to my mother: "Go and comfort him."

JAMES BALDWIN

My Conversion

I underwent, during the summer that I became fourteen, a prolonged religious crisis. I use the word "religious" in the common, and arbitrary, sense, meaning that I then discovered God, His saints and angels, and His blazing Hell. And since I had been born in a Christian

MY CONVERSION: Reprinted from *The Fire Next Time* by James Baldwin. Copyright © 1963, 1962 by James Baldwin and used by permission of the publisher, The Dial Press, Inc.

nation, I accepted this Deity as the only one. I supposed Him to exist only within the walls of a church—in fact, of *our* church—and I also supposed that God and safety were synonymous. The word "safety" brings us to the real meaning of the word "religious" as we use it. Therefore, to state it in another, more accurate way, I became, during my fourteenth year, for the first time in my life, afraid—afraid of the evil within me and afraid of the evil without. What I saw around me that summer in Harlem was what I had always seen; nothing had changed. But now, without any warning, the whores and pimps and racketeers on the Avenue had become a personal menace. It had not before occurred to me that I could become one of them, but now I realized that we had been produced by the same circumstances. Many of my comrades were clearly headed for the Avenue, and my father said that I was headed that way, too. My friends began to drink and smoke, and embarked—at first avid, then groaning—on their sexual careers. Girls, only slightly older than I was, who sang in the choir or taught Sunday school, the children of holy parents, underwent, before my eyes, their incredible metamorphosis, of which the most bewildering aspect was not their budding breasts or their rounding behinds but something deeper and more subtle, in their eyes, their heat, their odor, and the inflection of their voices. Like the strangers on the Avenue, they became, in the twinkling of an eye, unutterably different and fantastically *present*. Owing to the way I had been raised, the abrupt discomfort that all this aroused in me and the fact that I had no idea what my voice or my mind or my body was likely to do next caused me to consider myself one of the most depraved people on earth. Matters were not helped by the fact that these holy girls seemed rather to enjoy my terrified lapses, our grim, guilty, tormented experiments, which were at once as chill and joyless as the Russian steppes and hotter, by far, than all the fires of Hell.

Yet there was something deeper than these changes, and less definable, that frightened me.

It was real in both the boys and the girls, but it was, somehow, more vivid in the boys. In the case of the girls, one watched them turning into matrons before they had become women. They began to manifest a curious and really rather terrifying single-mindedness. It is hard to say exactly how this was conveyed: something implacable in the set of the lips, something farseeing (seeing what?) in the eyes, some new and crushing determination in the walk, something peremptory in the voice. They did not tease us, the boys, any more; they reprimanded us sharply, saying, "You better be thinking about your soul!" For the girls also saw the evidence on the Avenue, knew what the price would be, for them, of one misstep, knew that they had to be protected and that we were the only protection there was. They understood that they must act as God's decoys, saving the souls of the boys for Jesus and binding the bodies of the boys in marriage. For this was the beginning of our burning time, and "It is better," said St. Paul—who elsewhere, with a most unusual and stunning exactness, described himself as a "wretched man"—"to marry than to burn." And I began to feel in the boys a curious, wary, bewildered despair, as though they were now settling in for the long, hard winter of life. I did not know then what it was that I was reacting to; I put it to myself that they were letting themselves go. In the same way that the girls were destined to gain as much weight as their mothers, the boys, it was clear, would rise no higher than their fathers. School began to reveal itself, therefore, as a child's game that one could not win, and boys dropped out of school and went to work. My father wanted me to do the same. I refused, even though I no longer had any illusions about what an education could do for me; I had already encountered too many college-graduate handymen. My friends were now "downtown," busy, as they put it, "fighting the man." They began to care less about the way they looked, the way they dressed, the things they did; presently, one found them in twos and threes and fours, in a hallway, sharing a jug of wine or a bottle of whiskey, talking, cursing, fighting, sometimes weeping: lost, and unable to say what it was that oppressed them, except that they knew it was "the man"—the white man. And there seemed to be no way whatever to remove this cloud that stood between them and the sun, between them and love and life and power, between them and whatever it was that they wanted. One did not have to be very bright to realize how little one could do to change one's situation; one did not have to be abnormally sensitive to be worn down to a cutting edge by the incessant and gratuitous humiliation and danger one encountered every working day, all day long. The humiliation did not apply merely to working days, or workers; I was thirteen and was crossing Fifth Avenue on my way to the Forty-second Street library, and the cop in the middle of the street muttered as I passed him, "Why don't you niggers stay uptown where you belong?" When I was ten, and didn't look, certainly, any older, two policemen amused themselves with me by frisking me, making comic (and terrifying) speculations concerning my ancestry and probable sexual prowess, and for good measure, leaving me flat on my back in one of Harlem's empty lots. Just before and then during the Second World War, many of my friends fled into the service, all to be changed there, and rarely for the better, many to be ruined, and many to die. Others fled to other states and cities—that is, to other ghettos. Some went on wine or whiskey or the needle, and are still on it. And others, like me, fled into the church.

For the wages of sin were visible everywhere, in every wine-stained and urine-splashed hallway, in every clanging ambulance bell, in every scar on the faces of the pimps and their whores, in every helpless, newborn baby being brought into this danger, in every knife and pistol fight on the Avenue, and in every disastrous bulletin: a cousin, mother of six, suddenly gone mad, the children parcelled out here and there; an indestructible aunt rewarded for years of hard labor by a slow, agonizing death in a terrible small room; someone's bright son blown into eternity by his own hand; another turned robber and carried off to jail. It was a summer of dreadful speculations and discoveries, of which these were not the worst. Crime became real, for example—for the first time—not as *a* possibility but as *the* possibility. One would never defeat one's circumstances by working and saving one's pennies; one would never, by working, acquire that many pennies, and, besides, the social treatment accorded even the most successful Negroes proved that one needed, in order to be free, something more than a bank account. One needed a handle, a lever, a means of inspiring fear. It was absolutely clear that the police would whip you and take you in as long as they could get away with it, and that everyone else—housewives, taxi-drivers, elevator boys, dishwashers, bartenders, lawyers, judges, doctors, and grocers—would never, by the operation of any generous human feeling, cease to use you as an outlet for his frustrations and hostilities. Neither civilized reason nor Christian love would cause any of those people to treat you as they presumably wanted to be treated; only the fear of your power to retaliate would cause them to do that, or to seem to do it, which was (and is) good enough. There appears to be a vast amount of confusion on this point, but I do not know many Negroes who are eager to be "accepted" by white people, still less to be loved by them; they, the blacks, simply don't wish to be beaten over the head by the whites every instant of our brief passage on this planet. White people in this country will have quite enough to do in learning how to accept and love themselves and each other, and when they have achieved this—which will not be tomorrow and may very well be never—the Negro problem will no longer exist, for it will no longer be needed.

People more advantageously placed than we in Harlem were, and are, will no doubt find the psychology and the view of human nature sketched above dismal and shocking in the extreme. But the Negro's experience of the white world cannot possibly create in him any respect for the standards by which the white world claims to live. His own condition is overwhelming proof that white people do not live by these standards. Negro servants have been smuggling odds and ends out of white homes for generations, and white people have been delighted to have them do it, because it has assuaged a dim guilt and testified to the intrinsic superiority of white people. Even the most doltish and servile Negro could scarcely fail to be impressed by the disparity between his situation and that of the people for whom he worked; Negroes who were neither doltish nor servile did not feel that they were doing anything wrong when they robbed white people. In spite of the Puritan-Yankee equation of virtue with well-being, Negroes had excellent reasons for doubting that money was made or kept by any very striking adherence to the Christian virtues; it certainly did not work that way for black Christians. In any case, white people, who had robbed black people of their liberty and who profited by this theft every hour that they lived, had no moral ground on which to stand. They had the judges, the juries, the shotguns, the law—in a word, power. But it was a criminal power, to be feared but not respected, and to be outwitted in any way whatever. And those virtues preached but not practiced by the white world were merely another means of holding Negroes in subjection.

It turned out, then, that summer, that the moral barriers that I had supposed to exist between me and the dangers of a criminal career were so tenuous as to be nearly non-existent. I certainly could not discover any principled reason for not becoming a criminal, and it is not my poor, God-fearing parents who are to be indicted for the lack but this society. I was icily determined—more determined, really, than I then knew—never to make my peace with the ghetto but to die and go to Hell before I would let any white man spit on me, before I would accept my "place" in this republic. I did not intend to allow the white people of this country to tell me who I was, and limit me that way, and polish me off that way. And yet, of course, at the same time, I *was* being spat on and defined and described and limited, and could have been polished off with no effort whatever. Every Negro boy—in my situation during those years, at least—who reaches this point realizes, at once, profoundly, because he wants to live, that he stands in great peril and must find, with speed, a "thing," a gimmick, to lift him out, to start him on his way. *And it does not matter what the gimmick is.* It was this last realization that terrified me and—since it revealed that the door opened on so many dangers—helped to hurl me into the church. And, by an unforeseeable paradox, it was my career in the church that turned out, precisely, to be my gimmick.

For when I tried to assess my capabilities, I realized that I had almost none. In order to achieve the life I wanted, I had been dealt, it seemed to me, the worst possible hand. I could not become a prizefighter—many of us tried but very few succeeded. I could not sing. I could not dance. I had been well conditioned by the world in which I grew up, so I did not yet dare take the idea of becoming a writer seriously. The only other possibility seemed to involve my becoming one of the sordid people on the Avenue, who were not really as sordid as I then imagined but who frightened me terribly, both because I did not want to live that life and because of what they made me feel. Everything inflamed me, and that was bad enough, but I myself had also become a source of fire and temptation. I had been far too well raised, alas, to suppose that any of the extremely explicit overtures made to me that summer, sometimes by boys and girls but also, more alarmingly, by older men and women, had anything to do with my attractiveness. On the contrary, since the Harlem idea of seduction is, to put it mildly, blunt, whatever these people saw in me merely confirmed my sense of my depravity.

It is certainly sad that the awakening of one's senses should lead to such a merciless judgment of oneself—to say nothing of the time and anguish one spends in the effort to arrive at any other—but it is also inevitable that a literal attempt to mortify the flesh should be made among black people like those with whom I grew up. Negroes in this country—and Negroes do not, strictly or legally speaking, exist in any other—are taught really to despise themselves from the moment their eyes open on the world. This world is white and they are black. White people hold the power, which means that they are superior to blacks (intrinsically, that is: God decreed it so), and the world has innumerable ways of making this difference known and felt and feared. Long before the Negro child perceives this difference, and even longer before he understands it, he has begun to react to it, he has begun to be controlled by it. Every effort made by the child's elders to prepare him for a fate from which they cannot protect him causes him secretly, in terror, to begin to await, without knowing that he is doing so, his mysterious and inexorable punishment. He must be "good" not only in order to please his parents and not only to avoid being punished by them; behind their authority stands another, nameless and impersonal, infinitely harder to please, and bottomlessly cruel. And this filters into the child's consciousness through his parent's tone of voice as he is being exhorted, punished, or loved; in the sudden, uncontrollable note of fear heard in his mother's or his father's voice when he has strayed beyond some particular boundary. He does not know what the boundary is, and he can get no explanation of it, which is frightening enough, but the fear he hears in the voices of his elders is more frightening still. The fear that I heard in my father's voice, for example, when he realized that I really *believed* I could do anything a white boy could do, and had every intention of proving it, was not at all like the fear I heard when one of us was ill or had fallen down the stairs or strayed too far from the house. It was another fear, a fear that the child, in challenging the white world's assumptions, was putting himself

in the path of destruction. A child cannot, thank Heaven, know how vast and how merciless is the nature of power, with what unbelievable cruelty people treat each other. He reacts to the fear in his parents' voices because his parents hold up the world for him and he has no protection without them. I defended myself, as I imagined, against the fear my father made me feel by remembering that he was very old-fashioned. Also, I prided myself on the fact that I already knew how to outwit him. To defend oneself against a fear is simply to insure that one will, one day, be conquered by it; fears must be faced. As for one's wits, it is just not true that one can live by them—not, that is, if one wishes really to live. That summer in any case, all the fears with which I had grown up, and which were now a part of me and controlled my vision of the world, rose up like a wall between the world and me, and drove me into the church.

As I look back, everything I did seems curiously deliberate, though it certainly did not seem deliberate then. For example, I did not join the church of which my father was a member and in which he preached. My best friend in school, who attended a different church, had already "surrendered his life to the Lord," and he was very anxious about my soul's salvation. (I wasn't, but any human attention was better than none.) One Saturday afternoon, he took me to his church. There were no services that day, and the church was empty, except for some women cleaning and some other women praying. My friend took me into the back room to meet his pastor—a woman. There she sat, in her robes, smiling, an extremely proud and handsome woman, with Africa, Europe, and the America of the American Indian blended in her face. She was perhaps forty-five or fifty at this time, and in our world she was a very celebrated woman. My friend was about to introduce me when she looked at me and smiled and said, "Whose little boy are you?" Now this, unbelievably, was precisely the phrase used by pimps and racketeers on the

Avenue when they suggested, both humorously and intensely, that I "hang out" with them. Perhaps part of the terror they had caused me to feel came from the fact that I unquestionably wanted to be *somebody's* little boy. I was so frightened, and at the mercy of so many conundrums, that inevitably, that summer, *someone* would have taken me over; one doesn't, in Harlem, long remain standing on any auction block. It was my good luck—perhaps—that I found myself in the church racket instead of some other, and surrendered to a spiritual seduction long before I came to any carnal knowledge. For when the pastor asked me, with that marvellous smile, "Whose little boy are you?" my heart replied at once, "Why, yours."

The summer wore on, and things got worse. I became more guilty and more frightened, and kept all this bottled up inside me, and naturally, inescapably, one night, when this woman had finished preaching, everything came roaring, screaming, crying out, and I fell to the ground before the altar. It was the strangest sensation I have ever had in my life—up to that time, or since. I had not known that it was going to happen, or that it could happen. One moment I was on my feet, singing and clapping and, at the same time, working out in my head the plot of a play I was working on then; the next moment, with no transition, no sensation of falling, I was on my back, with the lights beating down into my face and all the vertical saints above me. I did not know what I was doing down so low, or how I had got there. And the anguish that filled me cannot be described. It moved in me like one of those floods that devastate counties, tearing everything down, tearing children from their parents and lovers from each other, and making everything an unrecognizable waste. All I really remember is the pain, the unspeakable pain; it was as though I were yelling up to Heaven and Heaven would not hear me. And if Heaven would not hear me, if love could not descend from Heaven—to wash me, to make me clean— then utter disaster was my portion. Yes, it does

indeed mean something—something unspeakable—to be born, in a white country, an Anglo-Teutonic, antisexual country, black. You very soon, without knowing it, give up all hope of communion. Black people, mainly, look down or look up but do not look at each other, not at you, and white people, mainly, look away. And the universe is simply a sounding drum; there is no way, no way whatever, so it seemed then and has sometimes seemed since, to get through a life, to love your wife and children, or your friends, or your mother and father, or to be loved. The universe, which is not merely the stars and the moon and the planets, flowers, grass, and trees, but *other people*, has evolved no terms for your existence, has made no room for you, and if love will not swing wide the gates, no other power will or can. And if one despairs —as who has not?—of human love, God's love alone is left. But God—and I felt this even then, so long ago, on the tremendous floor, unwillingly—is white. And if His love was so great, and if He loved all His children why were we, the blacks, cast down so far? Why? In spite of all I said thereafter, I found no answer on the floor—not *that* answer, anyway—and I was on the floor all night. Over me, to bring me "through," the saints sang and rejoiced and prayed. And in the morning, when they raised me, they told me that I was "saved."

Well, indeed I was, in a way, for I was utterly drained and exhausted, and released, for the first time, from all my guilty torment. I was aware then only of my relief. For many years, I could not ask myself why human relief had to be achieved in a fashion at once so pagan and so desperate—in a fashion at once so unspeakably old and so unutterably new. And by the time I was able to ask myself this question, I was also able to see that the principles governing the rites and customs of the churches in which I grew up did not differ from the principles governing the rites and customs of other churches, white. The principles were Blindness, Loneliness, and Terror, the first principle necessarily and actively cultivated in order to deny the two others. I would love to believe that the principles were Faith, Hope, and Charity, but this is clearly not so for most Christians, or for what we call the Christian world.

Questions for Review

1. What audience does St. Augustine have in mind in making his confessions? If he is addressing God only, why does he record his confessions in writing?
2. What is the meaning of the term *confession* as Augustine uses it? What does such a confession presuppose about the confessor?
3. What is more important in Augustine's *Confessions*, the facts of his life (that is, his actions and thoughts) or his attitude toward them? Explain.
4. What attitude toward his "sins" does Augustine apparently expect God to take? What attitude do you as a reader take?
5. Would you say that the tone of these *Confessions* is detached and impersonal or not? Why?
6. In the opening chapters of his *Autobiography*, Edward Gibbon explains his undertaking as a means of filling his time after completing his famous *Decline and Fall of the Roman Empire* and giving its readers some details of how it was written. Do you see in this concluding chapter any other explanations for why Gibbon wrote an autobiography?
7. Augustine seems to have, on first reading, an intense awareness of his own individuality, his uniqueness as a human being; Gibbon, on first reading, appears to describe himself rather as a typical or perhaps archetypal man. Upon reflection, how would you describe Augustine and Gibbon in their relative characterizations of themselves as "types" or "individuals"?
8. Gibbon lived in an era when irony was a common technique. (Johnson, Boswell, and Chesterfield were among his contemporaries.) Point out instances of Gibbon's irony and show how these work to create tone, attitude, and character.
9. Do you find Gibbon more or less candid about himself than the other autobiographers given here? Does he discuss any aspects of his life that the others do not? If so, how is his choice of tone and diction an element in his treatment of these matters?
10. What would you say is the best meaning of "confession" as De Quincey illustrates it in his *Confessions of an English Opium-Eater*? Does De Quincey "confess" in the same sense that St. Augustine does?
11. Are there any contradictions between what De Quincey says in one section of his confessions and in another? Note his various statements about opium and its tendency to make the user "withdraw" into himself. What do his various assertions tell the reader about De Quincey that he does not explicitly tell himself?
12. Does De Quincey appear to have in mind any very clear notion of what kind of reader he may have? Is his tone defensive, offensive, indifferent or something else toward the reader?
13. In what ways are the *Confessions of an English Opium-Eater* like Boswell's *London Journal* or *The Diary of Anne Frank*? Do these likenesses suggest anything to you about the kinship between the diary form and the autobiography?
14. Edward Gibbon was an eighteenth century man; Henry Adams was a nineteenth-century man who continually spoke of himself as an eighteenth-century one. Do you see any similarities between Gibbon's and Adams's autobiographies? Are there any significant differences?
15. Although *The Education of Henry Adams* was written by himself, Adams always refers to himself in the third person as "he" or "Adams." How do you account for his doing this? What effect does it have on the autobiography?
16. What reasons can you surmise, from the selection given, for Henry Adams's deciding to write his autobiography? Does he want to explain or justify himself? Use his experience to condemn people and institutions? Or what?

17. Does the Character-Adams seem to differ any from the Narrator-Adams? Does Adams as Narrator dominate the Character, coexist with it, or become lost in it?

18. Marcel Proust's account of his mother and father, taken from *Remembrance of Things Past*, is a fictionalized autobiography; the events described here may not have happened in precisely this way, but Proust has heightened them to make his points. What do you think is the central purpose of this account? Does Proust write autobiographically for the same reasons as Adams or Gibbon? As St. Augustine? Explain.

19. How significant are the actual events in Proust's narrative? What is the most important thing, in your opinion?

20. Proust appears to wander away from his chief narrative at times. Is his use of apparent digressions accidental or intentional? Why?

21. What does Proust reveal about himself in this anecdote from his childhood? Is he more deeply revealing of himself than the other autobiographers? Explain.

22. In some interesting ways, James Baldwin's account of his youthful conversion and grappling with sin is like St. Augustine's account. In what vital ways are they different? How do you explain these differences?

23. Baldwin speaks of himself and "the other world" of people in recounting his desire for conversion, for losing himself in the love of others or of God. By implication, where does Baldwin's reader stand in relation to him and to the "other world"? What is Baldwin's attitude toward himself in this section? Toward his reader? Toward the "other world"?

24. Does Baldwin represent himself as typical of other Harlem young people? As untypical? How?

25. Which of the autobiographers seems to you to be the most objective toward himself? The most self-critical? The most self-indulgent? Which gives you the clearest picture of himself? The most complex? The most simplified?

Questions for Discussion and Writing

1. What are the innate virtues of the autobiographical form? What are its chief weaknesses or limitations?

2. Is the possible range of points of view more or less limited in the autobiography than in the diary or the letter? Discuss.

3. What problems in dealing with time-sequence or chronology appear to confront the autobiographer? In what ways do the selections given here meet with or solve these problems?

4. Is very formal diction in an autobiography an effective way for the writer to seem detached and objective about himself? Is slang or informal, casual diction a more convincing language for autobiography than formal diction? For instance, do Baldwin's references to pimps, whores, urine and so on make his account more "real" or more psychologically convincing to you than Adams's euphemisms?

5. Do the autobiographers shown here write more to explain than confess, to educate than to convince? What seem to be the main causes for autobiographical confession as they appear here?

6. Can more be learned about a man's "real" or "true" self from his diary, his letters, or his autobiography? Give reasons for your opinion.

7. Autobiographers perhaps supply more "facts" (i.e., dates, names, places, and verifiable events) than diarists and letter writers. Is the autobiography therefore more "factual" or "true" than the other forms?

8. What benefits, if any, can you see in reading autobiographies? Have they any use to the reader? If not, explain why. If so, suggest what uses.

9. For practical purposes, what tests could you suggest to separate Kafka's *Letter to His Father* from the category of autobiography? Or is it really an autobiography? Are letters actually a form of autobiography? Are diaries? Using your knowledge of the three forms, set up definitions by which an example of writing may be safely and usefully put into one or another of the categories.

Public Versions of the Private

Like the autobiography, the biography concerns itself with a specific human being and his experiences in life; but the biographer writes not of himself but someone else whose thought or behavior he finds significant. Superficially, the biographer would appear to be capable of a greater objectivity and accuracy than the autobiographer because he is not involved emotionally with his subject while the latter, for all his seeming detachment, is speaking of matters vital to himself. Of course, the writer who chooses another man for his subject may have some direct tie—of blood or loyalty or inclination—that prevents his being impartial. In general, biographical writing appears more objective, detached, and empirical than its autobiographical counterpart. The truly detached biographer, however, may not have a firsthand knowledge of his subject and thus have to rely on the subject's own writings (journals, letters, autobiographical pieces) for his material. Or there may be a dearth of such writing and the biographer may have to depend on other sources: the opinions of contemporaries, factual records of a public order, or even the biographer's conjectures and intuitive surmises. As a rule, the biographer is confined to three kinds of evidence in composing his verbal portrait: the subject's words, his actions, and his possessions or surroundings. The task of *characterizing* in words a human being in all his contradictions and complexities is common to both the autobiographer and the biographer; but the writer of biography is both helped and hindered by having as his subject someone about whom he cannot hope to have an inclusive knowledge.

PLUTARCH

Alcibiades,
the Scapegrace
of Athens

Those who have searched into the pedigree of Alcibiades say that Eurysaces, the son of Ajax, was founder of the family and that, by his mother's side, he was descended from Alcmaeon, for Dinomache, his mother, was the daughter of Megacles who was of that line. His father Clinias gained great honor in the sea-fight at Artemisium where he fought in a galley fitted out at his own expense, and afterwards was slain in the battle of Coronea, where the Boeotians won the day.

Pericles and Ariphron, the sons of Xanthippus and near-relations to Alcibiades, were his guardians. It is said, and not without reason, that the affection and attachment of Socrates contributed much to his fame. Nicias, Demosthenes, Lamachus, Phormion, Thrasybulus and Thermenes were illustrious persons and his contemporaries, yet we do not so much as know the name of the mother of any of them, whereas we know even the nurse of Alcibiades, that she was from Lacedaemon and that her name was Amycla, and that Zopyrus was his schoolmaster, the one being recorded by Antisthenes and the other by Plato.

As to the beauty of Alcibiades, it may be sufficient to say that it retained its charms through the several stages of childhood, youth and manhood. It is not universally true what Euripides says:

Of all fair things the autumn, too, is fair.

Yet this was the case of Alcibiades, amongst a few others, by reason of his natural vigor and happy constitution.

ALCIBIADES, THE SCAPEGRACE OF ATHENS: From Plutarch's *Lives,* translated by John and William Langhorne.

He had a lisp in his speech which became him and gave a grace and persuasive turn to his discourse. Aristophanes, in those verses where he ridicules Theorus, notices that Alcibiades lisped, for instead of calling him *Corax,* Raven, he called him *Colax,* Flatterer, whence the poet takes occasion to observe that the term in that lisping pronunciation, too, was very applicable to him. With this agrees the satirical description which Archippus gives to the son of Alcibiades:

With sauntering step, to imitate his father,
The vain youth moves; his loose robe wildly floats;
He bends the neck, he lisps.

Alcibiades's manners were far from being uniform, nor is it strange that they varied according to the many vicissitudes and wonderful turns of his fortune. He was naturally a man of strong passions, but the ruling one was an ambition to contend and overcome. This appears from anecdotes told of him as a boy. When hard pressed in wrestling, to prevent his being thrown, he bit the hands of his antagonist, who let go his hold and said: "You bite, Alcibiades, like a woman." "No," he replied, "like a lion."

One day he was playing at dice with other boys in the street and when it came to his turn to throw, a loaded wagon came up. At first he called to the driver to stop because he was to throw in the way over which the wagon was to pass. The rustic disregarded him and drove on, the other boys broke away, but Alcibiades threw himself upon his face directly before the wagon and, stretching himself out, bade the fellow to drive on if he pleased. Upon this the man was so startled that he stopped his horses, while those that saw it ran up to him with terror.

In the course of his education Alcibiades willingly took the lessons from his other masters but refused to learn to play the flute, which he looked upon as a mean art and unbecoming a gentleman. "The use of the plectrum and the lyre," he would say, "has nothing in it that disorders the features or form, but a man is hardly to be known to his most intimate friends when he plays upon the flute. Besides, the lyre does not hinder the performer from speaking or accompanying it with a song, whereas the flute so engages the mouth and breath that it leaves no possibility of speaking. Therefore, let the Theban youth pipe who knows not how to discourse, but we Athenians, according to the account of our ancestors, have Minerva for our patroness and Apollo for our protector, one of whom threw away the flute and the other stripped off the man's skin who played on it."

So, partly by raillery and partly by argument, Alcibiades kept both himself and others from learning to play the flute, for it soon became the talk among the young men of condition that Alcibiades was right in holding that art in abomination and ridiculing those who practiced it. Thus it lost its place in the number of liberal accomplishments and was generally neglected.

In the invective which Antiphon wrote against Alcibiades, one story is that when a boy he ran away from his guardians to one of his friends named Democrates, and that Ariphron would have had proclamation made for him had not Pericles diverted him from it by saying: "If he is dead, we shall only find him one day the sooner for it. If he is safe, it will be a reproach to him as long as he lives." Another story is that he killed one of his servants with a stroke of his staff in Sibyrtius's place of exercise. But perhaps we should not give entire credit to these things, which were professedly written by an enemy to defame him.

Many of rank made their court to Alcibiades, but it is evident that they were charmed and attracted by the beauty of his person. Socrates alone bore witness to the young man's virtue and ingenuity, the rays of which he could distinguish through his fine form, and, fearing lest the pride of riches and high rank and the crowd of flatterers, both Athenians and strangers, should corrupt him, he used his best endeavors to prevent it and took care that so hopeful a plant should not lose its fruit and perish in the very flower. If ever fortune so

enclosed and fortified a man with what are called her goods as to render him inaccessible to the scalpel of philosophy and the searching probe of free advice, surely it was Alcibiades. From the first he was surrounded with pleasure and a multitude of admirers, determined to say nothing but what they thought would please and keep him from all admonition and reproof; yet, by his native insight he distinguished the value of Socrates and attached himself to him, rejecting the rich and great who sued for his regard.

With Socrates he soon entered into the closest intimacy and finding that he did not, like the rest of the unmanly crew, want improper favors, but that he studied to correct the errors of his heart and to cure him of his empty and foolish arrogance, then he

Dropped like the craven cock his conquered wing.

In fact, he considered the discipline of Socrates as a provision from heaven for the preservation and benefit of youth. Thus despising himself, admiring his friend, adoring his wisdom and revering his virtue, he insensibly formed in his heart the image of love, or rather came under the influence of that power which, as Plato says, secures his votaries from vicious love. It surprised all the world to see him constantly sup with Socrates, take with him the exercise of wrestling, lodge in the same tent with him, while to his other admirers he was reserved and rough. Nay, to some he behaved with great insolence, to Anytus, the son of Anthemion, for instance. Anytus was very fond of him and, happening to make an entertainment for some strangers, he desired Alcibiades to give him his company. Alcibiades would not accept the invitation but, having drunk deep with some of his acquaintances at his own house, he went thither to play some frolic. The frolic was this: he stood at the door of the room where the guests were entertained and, seeing a great number of gold and silver cups upon the table, he ordered his servants to take half of them and carry them to his own house, and then, not vouchsafing so much as to enter into the room himself, as soon as he had done this he went away. The company resented the affront and said he had behaved very rudely and insolently to Anytus. "Not at all," said Anytus, "but rather kindly, since he has left us half when he knew it was in his power to take the whole."

Alcibiades behaved in the same manner to his other admirers, except only one stranger. This man, they tell us, was in but indifferent circumstances, for when he had sold all he owned no more than the sum of one hundred staters, which he carried to Alcibiades and begged him to accept. Alcibiades was pleased at the idea and, smiling, invited him to supper. After a kind reception and entertainment, Alcibiades returned the gold but required him to be present next day when the public revenues were to be offered to farm, and to be sure to be the highest bidder. The man endeavored to excuse himself, because the rent would be too high for his purse. Alcibiades, who had a private pique against the farmers, threatened to have him beaten if he refused.

Next morning, therefore, the stranger appeared in the marketplace and offered a talent more than the existing rent. The farmers, uneasy and angry at this, called upon him to name his security, supposing that he could not find any. The poor man was indeed much startled and was about to retire in shame when Alcibiades, who stood at some distance, cried out to the magistrates: "Set down my name—he is my friend, and I will be his security." When the old farmers of the revenue heard this they were much perplexed, for their way was with the profits of the present year to pay the rent of the preceding, so that, seeing no other way to extricate themselves from the difficulty they applied to the stranger in a humble strain and offered him money. But Alcibiades would not suffer him to take less than a talent, which accordingly was paid. Having done him this service, he told him he might relinquish his bargain.

Though Socrates had many rivals, he kept possession of Alcibiades's heart by the excellence of his genius and the pathetic turn of his conversation, which often drew tears from his young companion; and though sometimes he gave Socrates the slip and was drawn away by his flatterers who exhausted all the art of pleasure for that purpose, yet the philosopher took care to hunt out his fugitive, who feared and respected none but him, for the rest he held in great contempt. Hence that saying of Cleanthes: "Socrates holds Alcibiades by the ear and leaves to his rivals other parts of his body with which he scorns to meddle."

In fact, Alcibiades was very susceptible to being led by the allurements of pleasure and what Thucydides says concerning his excesses gives occasion to believe so. Those who endeavored to corrupt him attacked him on a still weaker side, his vanity and love of distinction, and led him into vast designs and unseasonable projects, persuading him that as soon as he should apply himself to the management of public affairs, he should not only eclipse the other generals and orators but surpass even Pericles himself in point of reputation. But as iron, when softened by the fire, is soon hardened again and brought to a proper temper by cold water, so when Alcibiades was enervated by luxury, or swollen with pride, Socrates corrected and brought him to himself by his discourses, for from them he learned his many defects and the imperfection of his virtue.

When Alcibiades was past childhood, happening to go into a grammar school he asked the master for a volume of Homer, and upon the answer that he had nothing of Homer's, he gave the master a box on the ear and so left him. Another schoolmaster told him that he himself had corrected Homer. "How?" said Alcibiades. "And do you employ your time in teaching children to read? You, who are able to correct Homer, might seem to be fit to instruct men."

While Alcibiades was but a youth he made the campaign at Potidaea, where Socrates lodged in the same tent with him and was his companion in every engagement. In the principal battle they both behaved with great gallantry, but Alcibiades at last fell wounded. Socrates advanced to defend him, which he did effectively in the sight of the whole army, saving both him and his arms. For this the prize of valor was certainly due to Socrates, yet the generals inclined to give it to Alcibiades on account of his quality, and Socrates, willing to encourage his thirst after true glory, was first to testify for him and pressed them to crown him and award him a complete suit of armor. On the other hand, at the battle of Delium, where the Athenians were routed, Socrates with a few others was retreating on foot. Alcibiades, observing this, did not desert him but covered his retreat and brought him off safely, though the enemy pressed furiously forward and killed great numbers of Athenians. But this happened a considerable time after.

To Hipponicus, the father of Callias, a man respected both for his birth and fortune, Alcibiades one day gave a box on the ear, not that he had any quarrel with him or was heated by passion, but purely because, in a wanton frolic, he had agreed with his companions to do so. The whole city was full of the story of his insolence, and everybody, as it was natural to expect, expressed some resentment. Early next morning Alcibiades went to wait on Hipponicus, knocked at the door and was admitted. As soon as he came to Hipponicus, he stripped off his garment and, presenting his naked body, desired him to beat and chastise him as he pleased. But instead of that Hipponicus pardoned him and forgot all his resentment; nay, some time after, he even gave him his daughter Hipparete in marriage. Some say it was not Hipponicus but his son Callias who gave Hipparete to Alcibiades, with ten talents as her dowry, and that, when she brought him a child, he demanded ten talents more, as if he had taken her on that condition. Though this was but a groundless pretext, yet Callias, apprehensive of some bad consequence from his artful contrivances, in a full assembly of the people, declared that if he should happen to die without children, Alcibiades should be his heir.

Hipparete made a prudent and affectionate wife, but at last, growing very uneasy at her husband's associating with such a number of courtesans, both strangers and Athenians, she left his house and went to her brother's. Alcibiades pursued his debaucheries and was not concerned with his wife, but it was necessary for her, in order to obtain a legal separation, to give in a bill of divorce to the archon and to appear personally with it, for the sending of it by another hand would not do. When she came to do this according to law, Alcibiades rushed in, caught her in his arms and carried her through the marketplace to his own house, no one presuming to oppose him or take her from him. From that time on she remained with him until her death, which happened not long after when Alcibiades was upon his voyage to Ephesus. Nor does the violence used in this case seem to be contrary to the laws either of society in general or of that republic in particular. For the law of Athens, in requiring a wife who wanted to be divorced to appear publicly in person, probably intended to give the husband an opportunity to meet with her and to recover her.

Alcibiades had a dog of an uncommon size and beauty which cost him seventy minas and yet he caused the tail, which was his principal ornament, to be cut off. Some of his acquaintances found great fault with his acting so strangely and told him that all Athens rang with the story of his foolish treatment of the dog. He laughed and said: "This is the very thing I wanted, for I would have the Athenians talk of this, lest they should find something worse to say of me."

The first thing that made him popular and introduced him into the administration was his distribution of money, not by design, but by accident. Seeing one day a great crowd of people as he was walking along, he asked what it meant, and being informed there was a donative being made to the people he passed out money too as he went in amongst them. This meeting with great applause, he was so much delighted that he forgot a quail which he had under his robe and the bird, frightened with the noise, flew away. Upon this the people set up still louder acclamations, and many of them assisted him to recover it. The man who did catch it and bring it to him was one Antiochus, a pilot, for whom he had ever after a particular regard.

Alcibiades had great advantages for introducing himself into public life—his birth, his estate, his personal valor and the number of his friends and relations, but what he chose above all the rest to recommend himself to the people was the charm of his eloquence. That he was a fine speaker the comic poets bear witness, and so does the prince of public speakers in his oration against Midias, where he says that Alcibiades was the most eloquent man of his time. And, if we believe Theophrastus, a curious searcher into antiquity and more versed in history than other philosophers, Alcibiades had a peculiar happiness of invention and readiness of ideas which eminently distinguished him. But, as his care was employed not only upon the matter of the expression, and he had not the greatest facility in the latter, he often hesitated in the midst of a speech, not hitting upon the word he wanted and stopping until it occurred to him.

He was famed for his breed of horses and number of chariots. No one besides himself, whether private person or king, ever sent seven chariots at one time to the Olympic games. The first, the second and the fourth prizes, according to Thucydides—or the third, as Euripides relates it—he bore away at once, which exceeded everything performed by the most ambitious in that way. Euripides thus celebrates his success:

> ———But my song to you,
> Son of Clinias, is due.
> Victory is noble; how much more
> To do as never Greek before;
> To obtain in the great chariot race
> The first, the second, and third place;
> With easy step advanced to fame
> To bid the herald three times claim
> The olive for one victor's name.

The emulation which several Grecian cities expressed in the presents they made him gave a still greater luster to his success. Ephesus provided a magnificent pavilion for him, Chios stood the expense of keeping his horses and beasts for sacrifice, and Lesbos sent him wine and everything necessary for the most elegant public table. Yet, amidst this success, he escaped not without censure, occasioned either by the malice of his enemies or by his own misconduct. It seems there was at Athens one Diomedes, a man of good character and a friend of Alcibiades, who was very desirous of winning a prize at the Olympic games, and being informed that there was a chariot to be sold which belonged to the city of Argos where Alcibiades had a strong interest, he persuaded him to buy it for him. Accordingly he did buy it but kept it for himself, leaving Diomedes to vent his rage and to call upon gods and men to bear witness to the injustice. For this there seems to have been a lawsuit brought against him and there is extant an oration concerning a chariot, written by Isocrates, in defense of Alcibiades, but the plaintiff is named Tisias, not Diomedes.

Alcibiades was very young when he first applied himself to the business of the republic and yet he soon showed himself superior to the other orators. The persons capable of standing in some degree of competition with him were Phaeax, the son of Erasistratus, and Nicias, the son of Niceratus. The latter was advanced in years and one of the best generals of his time. The former was but a youth like himself, just beginning to make his way, for which he had the advantage of high birth but in other respects, as well as in the art of speaking, was inferior to Alcibiades. He seemed fitter for soliciting and persuading in private than for stemming the torrent of a public debate—in short, he was one of those of whom Eupolis says:

> True, he can talk, and yet he is no speaker.

There was at Athens one Hyperbolus of Perithoedae, whom Thucydides makes mention of as a very bad man and who was a constant subject of ridicule for the comic writers. But he was unconcerned at the worst things they could say of him, and, having no regard for honor, he was also insensible to shame. This, though really impudence and folly, is by some people called fortitude and a noble daring. But, though no one liked him, the people nevertheless made use of him when they wanted to strike at persons in authority. At his instigation the Athenians were ready to proceed to the ban of ostracism by which they pulled down and expelled such of the citizens as were distinguished by their dignity and power, therein consulting their envy rather than their fear.

As it was evident that this sentence was leveled against one of the three, Phaeax, Nicias, or Alcibiades, the latter took care to unite the contending parties and, leaguing with Nicias, caused the ostracism to fall upon Hyperbolus himself. Some say it was not Nicias but Phaeax with whom Alcibiades joined interest and with whose assistance he expelled their common enemy, when he expected nothing less, for no vile or infamous person had ever undergone that punishment. So Plato, the comic poet, assures us, thus speaking of Hyperbolus:

The man deserved the fate; deny't who can?
Yes, but the fate did not deserve the man;
Not for the like of him and his slave-brands
Did Athens put the sherd into our hands.

Alcibiades was not less disturbed at the great esteem in which Nicias was held by the enemies of Athens than at the respect which the Athenians themselves paid him. The rights of hospitality had long subsisted between the family of Alcibiades and the Lacedaemonians and he had taken particular care of such of them as were made prisoners at Pylos. Yet, when they found that it was chiefly through Nicias that they obtained a peace and recovered the captives, their regards centered on him. It was a common observation among the Greeks that Pericles had engaged them in a war and Nicias had set them free from it—the peace even was called the Nician peace. Alcibiades was very uneasy at this and out of envy to Nicias determined to break the league.

As soon, then, as he perceived that the people of Argos both feared and hated the Spartans and consequently wanted to get clear of all connection with them, he privately gave them hopes of assistance from Athens. Both by his agents and in person he encouraged the principal citizens not to entertain any fear or to give up any point, but to apply to the Athenians, who were almost ready to repent of the peace they had made, and would soon seek occasion to break it.

But after the Lacedaemonians had entered into alliance with the Boeotians and had delivered Panactum to the Athenians, not with its fortifications as they should have done but quite dismantled, he took the opportunity, while the Athenians were incensed at this proceeding, to inflame them still more. At the same time he raised a clamor against Nicias, alleging things which seemed probable enough, for he reproached him with having neglected, when commander in chief, to make prisoners of those who were left by the enemy in Sphacteria and with releasing them to ingratiate himself with the Lacedaemonians. He further asserted that though Nicias had an interest with the Lacedaemonians, he would not make use of it to prevent their entering into the confederacy with the Boeotians and Corinthians but that, when an alliance was offered to the Athenians by any of the Grecian states, he took care to prevent their accepting it, if it were likely to give umbrage to the Lacedaemonians.

Nicias was greatly disconcerted but at that very juncture it happened that ambassadors from Lacedaemon arrived with moderate proposals and declared that they had full powers to treat and decide all differences in an equitable way. The senate was satisfied and next day the people were to be convened, but Alcibiades, apprehensive, found occasion to speak with the ambassadors in the meantime and thus he addressed them: "Men of Lacedaemon, what is it you are going to do? Are you not apprised that the behavior of the senate is always candid and humane to those who apply to it, whereas the people are haughty and expect great concessions? If you say that you are come with full powers, you will find them untractable and extravagant in their demands. Come, then, retract that imprudent declaration and if you desire to keep the Athenians within the bounds of reason and not to have terms extorted from you, which you cannot approve, treat with them as if you had not a discretionary commission, and I will use my best endeavors in favor of the Lacedaemonians." He confirmed his promise with an oath and thus drew them away from Nicias over to himself. In Alcibiades they now placed an entire confidence, admiring both his understanding and address in business and regarding him as a very extraordinary man.

Next day the people assembled and the ambassadors were introduced. Alcibiades asked them in an obliging manner what their commission was, and they answered that they did not come as plenipotentiaries. Then he began to rave and storm, as if he had received an injury, not *done* one—calling them faithless, prevaricating men, who had come neither to do nor to say anything honorable. The senate was incensed, the people were enraged and Nicias, who was ignorant of the deceitful maneuver of Alcibiades, was filled with astonishment and confusion at this change.

The proposals of the ambassadors thus rejected, Alcibiades was declared general and soon engaged the Argives, the Mantineans and Eleans as allies to the Athenians. Nobody commended the manner of this transaction but the effect was very great since it divided and embroiled almost all Peloponnesus and in a day lifted so many arms against the Lacedaemonians at Mantinea and removed to so great a distance from Athens the scene of war, by which the Lacedaemonians, if victorious, could gain no great advantage, whereas a miscarriage would have risked the very being of their state.

Soon after this battle at Mantinea, the principal officers of the Argive army attempted to abolish the popular government of Argos and to take the administration into their own

hands. The Lacedaemonians espoused the plot and assisted them to carry it into execution. But the people took up arms again and defeated their new masters, and Alcibiades coming to their aid made the victory more complete. At the same time he persuaded them to extend their walls down to the sea, that they might always be in a condition to receive aid from the Athenians. From Athens he sent them carpenters and masons, exerting himself greatly on this occasion, which tended to increase his personal interest and power as well as that of his country.

He advised the people of Patrae to join their city to the sea by long walls. Someone observed to the Patrians that the Athenians would one day swallow them up. "Possibly it may be so," said Alcibiades, "but they will begin with the feet and do it little by little, whereas the Lacedaemonians will begin with the head and do it all at once." He exhorted the Athenians to establish an empire of the land as well as of the sea, and was forever reminding the young warriors to show by their deeds that they remembered the oath they had taken in the temple of Agraulos. The oath was: that they would consider wheat, barley, vine, and olives as the bounds of Attica, by which it was insinuated they should endeavor to possess themselves of all lands that are cultivated and fruitful.

But all his great abilities in politics, his eloquence, the reach of his genius and keenness of perception were tarnished by his luxurious living, his drinking and debauches, his effeminacy of dress and his insolent profusion. Alcibiades wore a purple robe with a long train when he appeared in public. He caused the planks of his galley to be cut away that he might lie the softer, his bed not being placed on the boards but hanging upon girths. And in the wars he bore a shield of gold which had none of the usual ensigns of his country but instead a Cupid bearing a thunderbolt. The great men of Athens viewed his behavior with uneasiness and indignation and even dreaded the consequences. They regarded his foreign manners, his prodigality and contempt of the laws as means to make himself absolute. Aristophanes well expressed how the bulk of the people were disposed toward him:

They love, they hate, but cannot live without him.

And again he satirized him still more severely by the following allusion:

Best rear no lion in your state, 'tis true;
But treat him like a lion if you do.

The truth is, his prodigious liberality, the games he exhibited, and the other extraordinary instances of his munificence to the people, the glory of his ancestors, the beauty of his person, and the force of his eloquence, together with his heroic strength, his valor and experience in war so prevailed on the Athenians that they connived at his errors and spoke of them with all imaginable tenderness, calling them sallies of youth and good-humored frolics. For instance, there was his keeping Agatharcus the painter prisoner until he had painted his house, and then dismissing him with a handsome present. And his giving a box on the ear to Taureas, who exhibited games in opposition to him and vied with him for the preference. And his taking one of the captive Melian women for his mistress and bringing up a child he had by her. These were what they called his good-natured frolics, but surely we cannot bestow that appellation upon the slaughtering of all the males in the isle of Melos who arrived at the age of puberty, which was in consequence of a decree that he promoted.

Again, when Aristophon had painted the courtesan Nemea with Alcibiades in her arms, many of the people eagerly crowded to see it, but the older Athenians were much displeased and considered these as sights fit only for a tyrant's court, and as insults to the laws of Athens. Nor was it ill observed by Archestratus that "Greece could not bear another Alcibiades." When Timon, famed for his misanthropy, saw Alcibiades, after having gained his point, conducted home with great honor from the place of assembly he did not shun him

as he did other men but went up to him and, shaking him by the hand, thus addressed him: "Go on, my brave boy, and prosper, for your prosperity will bring on the ruin of all this crowd." This occasioned various reflections: some laughed, some scoffed and others were extremely moved—so various were the judgments of Alcibiades because of his inconsistency of character.

.   .   .

JOHN AUBREY

Sir John Denham

Sir John Denham was unpolished with the smallpox: otherwise a fine complexion. He was of the tallest, but a little incurvetting at his shoulders, not very robust. His haire was but thin and flaxen, with a moist curle. His gate was slow, and was rather a Stalking (he had long legges.) His Eie was a kind of light goose-gray, not big; but it had a strange Piercingness, not as to shining and glory, but (like a Momus) when he conversed with you he look't into your very thoughts.

He was admitted of Trinity Colledge in Oxford: I have heard Mr. Josias Howe say that he was the dreamingst young fellow; he never expected such things from him as he haz left the world. When he was there he would Game extremely; when he had played away all his money he would play away his Father's wrought rich gold Cappes. He was as good a Student as any in the House. Was not suspected to be a Witt.

SIR JOHN DENHAM: Reprinted from *Aubrey's Brief Lives*, edited by Oliver Lawson Dick, 1957. By permission of The University of Michigan Press and Martin Secker & Warburg Limited. All rights reserved. First published by Secker & Warburg, 1949. Reprinted by special arrangement.

He was much rooked by Gamesters, and fell acquainted with that unsanctified Crew, to his ruine. His father had some suspition of it, and chid him severely, whereupon his son John (only child) wrot a little Essay, *Against Gameing, and to shew the Vanities and Inconveniences of it,* which he presented to his father to let him know his detestation of it. But shortly after his Father's death (who left 2000 or 1500 pounds in ready money, 2 houses well furnished, and much plate) the money was played away first, and next the plate was sold. I remember about 1646 he lost 200 pound one night at New-cutt.

He was generally temperate as to drinking; but one time when he was a Student of Lincolne's-Inne, having been merry at the Taverne with his Camerades, late at night, a frolick came into his head, to gett a playsterer's brush and a pott of Inke, and blott out all the Signes between Temple-barre and Charing-crosse, which made a strange confusion the next day, and 'twas in Terme time. But it happened that they were discovered, and it cost him and them some moneys. This I had from R. Estcott, Esq., that carried the Inke-pott.

At last, viz. 1640, his Play of The Sophy came out, which did take extremely. Mr. Edmund Waller sayd then of him, that he *broke-out like the Irish Rebellion: three score thousand strong,* before any body was aware.

At the beginning of the Civill Warre he was made Governor of Farnham Castle for the King, but he was but a young Soldier, and did not keepe it. In 1643, after Edgehill fight, his Poeme called *Cowper's-hill* was printed at Oxford, in a sort of browne paper, for then they could gett no better.

1647 he conveyed, or stole away the two Dukes of Yorke and Glocester from St. James's (from the Tuition of the Earle of Northumberland) and conveyed them into France to the Prince of Wales and Queen-mother.

Anno 1652, he returned into England, and being in some straights was kindly entertayned by the Earle of Pembroke at Wilton, where I had the honour to contract an acquaintance with him. He was, as I remember, a yeare with my Lord of Pembroke at Wilton and London; he had then sold all the Lands his Father had left him.

The parsonage-house at Egham (vulgarly called The Place) was built by Baron Denham; a house very convenient, not great, but pretty, and pleasantly scituated, and in which his son, Sir John, (though he had better seates) did take most delight in. He sold it to John Thynne, Esq. In this parish is a place called Cammomill-hill, from the Cammomill that growes there naturally; as also west of it is Prune-well-hill (formerly part of Sir John's possessions) where was a fine Tuft of Trees, a clear Spring, and a pleasant prospect to the East, over the levell of Middlesex and Surrey. Sir John tooke great delight in this place, and was wont to say (before the troubles) that he would build there a Retiring-place to entertaine his muses; but the warres forced him to sell that as well as the rest. He sold it to Mr. Anstey. In this parish W. and by N. (above Runney-Meade) is Cowper's Hill, from whence is a noble prospect, which is incomparably well described by that Sweet Swan, Sir John Denham.

In the time of the Civill-warres, George Withers, the Poet, begged Sir John Denham's Estate at Egham of the Parliament, in whose cause he was a Captaine of Horse. It happened that G. W. was taken prisoner, and was in danger of his Life, having written severely against the King, &c. Sir John Denham went to the King, and desired his Majestie not to hang him, for that *whilest G. W. lived, he should not be the worst Poet in England.*

He was much beloved by King Charles the first, who much valued him for his ingenuity. He graunted him the reversion of the Surveyor of His Majestie's buildings, after the decease of Mr. Inigo Jones; which place, after the restauration of King Charles II he enjoyed to his death, and gott seaven thousand pounds, as Sir Christopher Wren told me of, to his owne knowledge. Sir Christopher Wren was his Deputie.

He burlesqued Virgil, and burnt it, sayeing that 'twas not fitt that the best Poet should be so abused. In the verses against *Gondibert,* most of them are Sir John's. He was satyricall when he had a mind to it.

His first wife was the daughter and heire of Mr. Cotton of Glocestershire, by whom he had 500 pounds per annum, one son, and two daughters.

He maried his 2nd wife, Margaret Brookes, a very beautifull young lady: Sir John was ancient and limping. The Duke of Yorke fell deeply in love with her (though I have been morally assured he never had any carnall knowledge of her). This occasioned Sir John's distemper of madness, which first appeared when he went from London to see the famous Freestone quarries at Portland in Dorset, and when he came within a mile of it, turned back to London again, and did not see it. He went to Hounslowe, and demanded rents of Lands he had sold many years before; went to the King, and told him he was the Holy Ghost. But it pleased God that he was cured of this distemper, and writt excellent verses (particularly on the death of Mr. Abraham Cowley) afterwards. His 2nd lady had no child: was poysoned by the hands of the Countess of Rochester, with Chocolatte.

JAMES BOSWELL

Dr. Johnson Dines Out

Friday, 5 August 1763

At supper this night he talked of good eating with uncommon satisfaction. "Some people (said he,) have a foolish way of not minding, or

DR. JOHNSON DINES OUT: From *The Life of Samuel Johnson, LL.D.,* by James Boswell. First printed in 1791.

pretending not to mind, what they eat. For my part, I mind my belly very studiously, and very carefully; for I look upon it, that he who does not mind his belly will hardly mind anything else." He now appeared to me *Jean Bull philosophe,* and he was, for the moment, not only serious but vehement. Yet I have heard him, upon other occasions, talk with great contempt of people who were anxious to gratify their palates; and the 206th number of his *Rambler* is a masterly essay against gulosity. His practice, indeed, I must acknowledge, may be considered as casting the balance of his different opinions upon this subject; for I never knew any man who relished good eating more than he did. When at table, he was totally absorbed in the business of the moment; his looks seemed rivetted to his plate; nor would he, unless when in very high company, say one word, or even pay the least attention to what was said by others, till he had satisfied his appetite, which was so fierce, and indulged with such intenseness, that while in the act of eating, the veins of his forehead swelled, and generally a strong perspiration was visible. To those whose sensations were delicate, this could not but be disgusting; and it was doubtless not very suitable to the character of a philosopher, who should be distinguished by self-command. But it must be owned, that Johnson, though he could be rigidly *abstemious*, was not a *temperate* man either in eating or drinking. He could refrain, but he could not use moderately. He told me, that he had fasted two days without inconvenience, and that he had never been hungry but once. They who beheld with wonder how much he eat upon all occasions when his dinner was to his taste, could not easily conceive what he must have meant by hunger; and not only was he remarkable for the extraordinary quantity which he eat, but he was, or affected to be, a man of very nice discernment in the science of cookery. He used to descant critically on the dishes which had been at table where he had dined or supped, and to recollect very minutely what he had liked. I remember, when he was in Scotland, his praising *Gordon's palates*, (a dish of palates at the Honourable Alexander Gordon's) with a warmth of expression which might have done honour to more important subjects. "As for Maclaurin's imitation of a *made dish*, it was a wretched attempt." He about the same time was so much displeased with the performances of a nobleman's French cook, that he exclaimed with vehemence, "I'd throw such a rascal into the river"; and he then proceeded to alarm a lady at whose house he was to sup, by the following manifesto of his skill: "I, Madam, who live at a variety of good tables, am a much better judge of cookery, than any person who has a very tolerable cook, but lives much at home; for his palate is gradually adapted to the taste of his cook; whereas, Madam, in trying by a wider range, I can more exquisitely judge." When invited to dine, even with an intimate friend, he was not pleased if something better than a plain dinner was not prepared for him. I have heard him say on such an occasion, "This was a good dinner enough, to be sure; but it was not a dinner to *ask* a man to." On the other hand, he was wont to express, with great glee, his satisfaction when he had been entertained quite to his mind. One day when he had dined with his neighbour and landlord in Bolt-court, Mr. Allen, the printer, whose old housekeeper had studied his taste in every thing, he pronounced this eulogy: "Sir, we could not have had a better dinner had there been a *Synod of Cooks*."

On the 26th of October, we dined together at the Mitre tavern. I found fault with Foote for indulging his talent of ridicule at the expense of his visitors, which I colloquially termed making fools of his company. JOHNSON. "Why, Sir, when you go to see Foote, you do not go to see a saint: you go to see a man who will be entertained at your house, and then bring you on a publick stage; who will entertain you at his house, for the very purpose of bringing you on a publick stage. Sir, he does not make fools of his company; they whom he exposes are fools already: he only brings them into action."

Talking of trade, he observed, "It is a mistaken notion that a vast deal of money is brought into a nation by trade. It is not so. Commodities come from commodities: but trade produces no capital accession of wealth. However, though there should be little profit in money, there is a considerable profit in pleasure, as it gives to one nation the productions of another; as we have wines and fruits, and many other foreign articles, brought to us." BOSWELL. "Yes, Sir, and there is a profit in pleasure, by its furnishing occupation to such numbers of mankind." JOHNSON. "Why, Sir, you cannot call that pleasure to which all are averse, and which none begin but with the hope of leaving off; a thing which men dislike before they have tried it, and when they have tried it." BOSWELL. "But, Sir, the mind must be employed, and we grow weary when idle." JOHNSON. "That is, Sir, because, others being busy, we want company; but if we were all idle, there would be no growing weary; we should all entertain one another. There is, indeed, this in trade—it gives men an opportunity of improving their situation. If there were no trade, many who are poor would always remain poor. But no man loves labour for itself." BOSWELL. "Yes, Sir, I know a person who does. He is a very laborious Judge, and he loves the labour." JOHNSON. "Sir, that is because he loves respect and distinction. Could he have them without labour, he would like it less." BOSWELL. "He tells me he likes it for itself.—Why, Sir, he fancies so, because he is not accustomed to abstract."

We went home to his house to tea. Mrs. Williams made it with sufficient dexterity, notwithstanding her blindness, though her manner of satisfying herself that the cups were full enough appeared to me a little aukward; for I fancied she put her finger down a certain way, till she felt the tea touch it. In my first elation at being allowed the privilege of attending Dr. Johnson at his late visits to this lady, which was like being *è secretioribus consiliis*, I willingly drank cup after cup, as if it had been the Heliconian spring. But as the charm of novelty went off, I grew more fastidious; and besides, I discovered that she was of a peevish temper.

There was a pretty large circle this evening. Dr. Johnson was in very good humour, lively, and ready to talk upon all subjects. Mr. Fergusson, the self-taught philosopher, told him of a new-invented machine which went without horses: a man who sat in it turned a handle, which worked a spring that drove it forward. "Then, Sir, (said Johnson,) what is gained is, the man has his choice whether he will move himself alone, or himself and the machine too." Dominicetti being mentioned, he would not allow him any merit. "There is nothing in all this boasted system. No, Sir; medicated baths can be no better than warm water: Their only effect can be that of tepid moisture." One of the company took the other side, maintaining that medicines of various sorts, and some too of most powerful effect, are introduced into the human frame by the medium of the pores; and, therefore, when warm water is impregnated with salutiferous substances, it may produce great effects as a bath. This appeared to me very satisfactory. Johnson did not answer it; but talking for victory, and determined to be master of the field, he had recourse to the device which Goldsmith imputed to him in the witty words of one of Cibber's comedies: "There is no arguing with Johnson; for when his pistol misses fire, he knocks you down with the butt end of it." He turned to the gentleman, "Well, Sir, go to Dominicetti, and get thyself fumigated; but be sure that the steam be directed to thy *head*, for *that* is the *peccant part*." This produced a triumphant roar of laughter from the motley assembly of philosophers, printers, and dependents, male and female.

I know not how so whimsical a thought came into my mind, but I asked, "If, Sir, you were shut up in a castle, and a newborn child with you, what would you do?" JOHNSON. "Why, Sir, I should not much like my company." BOSWELL. "But would you take the trouble of rearing it?" He seemed, as may well be supposed, unwilling to pursue the subject: but upon my persevering in my question, replied, "Why yes, Sir, I would; but I must have all conveniences. If I had no garden, I would make a shed on the roof, and take it there for fresh air. I should feed it, and wash it much, and with warm water to please it, not with cold water to give it pain." BOSWELL. "But, Sir, does not heat relax?" JOHNSON. "Sir, you are not to imagine the water is to be very hot. I would not *coddle* the child. No, Sir, the hardy method of treating children does no good. I'll take you five children from London, who shall cuff five Highland children. Sir, a man bred in London will carry a burthen, or run, or wrestle, as well as a man brought up in the hardiest manner in the country." BOSWELL. "Good living, I suppose, makes the Londoners strong." JOHNSON. "Why, Sir, I don't know that it does. Our chairmen from Ireland, who are as strong men as any, have been brought up upon potatoes. Quantity makes up for quality." BOSWELL. "Would you teach this child that I have furnished you with, any thing?" JOHNSON. "No, I should not be apt to teach it." BOSWELL. "Would not you have a pleasure in teaching it?" JOHNSON. "No, Sir, I should *not* have a pleasure in teaching it." BOSWELL. "Have you not a pleasure in teaching men?—*There* I have you. You have the same pleasure in teaching men, that I should have in teaching children." JOHNSON. "Why, something about that."

BOSWELL. "Do you think, Sir, that what is called natural affection is born with us? It seems to me to be the effect of habit, or of gratitude for kindness. No child has it for a parent whom it has not seen." JOHNSON. "Why, Sir, I think there is an instinctive natural affection in parents towards their children."

Russia being mentioned as likely to become a great empire, by the rapid increase of population—JOHNSON. "Why, Sir, I see no prospect of their propagating more. They can have no more children than they can get. I know of no way to make them breed more than they do. It is not from reason and prudence that people marry, but from inclination. A man is poor; he thinks, "I cannot be worse, and so I'll e'en take Peggy." BOSWELL. "But have not nations been more populous at one period than another?" JOHNSON. "Yes, Sir; but that has been owing to the people being less thinned at one period than another, whether by emigrations, war, or pestilence, not by their being more or less prolifick. Births at all times bear the same proportion to the same number of people." BOSWELL. "But, to consider the state of our own country—does not throwing a number of farms into one hand hurt population?" JOHNSON. "Why no, Sir; the same quantity of food being produced, will be consumed by the same number of mouths, though the people may be disposed of in different ways. We see, if corn be dear, and butchers' meat cheap, the farmers all apply themselves to the raising of corn, till it becomes plentiful and cheap, and then butchers' meat becomes dear; so that an equality is always preserved. No, Sir, let fanciful men do as they will, depend upon it, it is difficult to disturb the system of life." BOSWELL. "But, Sir, is it not a very bad thing for landlords to oppress their tenants, by raising their rents?" JOHNSON. "Very bad. But, Sir, it never can have any general influence; it may distress some individuals. For, consider this: landlords cannot do without tenants. Now tenants will not give more for land, than land is worth. If they can make more of their money by keeping a shop, or any other way, they'll do it, and so oblige landlords to let land come back to a reasonable rent, in order that they may get tenants. Land, in England, is an article of commerce. A tenant who pays his landlord his rent, thinks himself no more obliged to him than you think yourself obliged to a man in whose shop you buy a piece of goods. He knows the landlord does not let him have his land for less than he can get from others, in the same manner as the shop-keeper sells his goods. No shopkeeper sells a

yard of ribband for sixpence when seven-pence is the current price." BOSWELL. "But, Sir, is it not better that tenants should be dependant on landlords?" JOHNSON. "Why, Sir, as there are many more tenants than landlords, perhaps, strictly speaking, we should wish not. But if you please you may let your lands cheap, and so get the value, part in money and part in homage. I should agree with you in that." BOSWELL. "So, Sir, you laugh at schemes of political improvement." JOHNSON. "Why, Sir, most schemes of political improvement are very laughable things."

He observed, "Providence has wisely ordered that the more numerous men are, the more difficult it is for them to agree in any thing, and so they are governed. There is no doubt, that if the poor should reason, 'We'll be the poor no longer, we'll make the rich take their turn,' they could easily do it, were it not that they can't agree. So the common soldiers, though so much more numerous than their officers, are governed by them for the same reason."

He said, "Mankind have a strong attachment to the habitations to which they have been accustomed. You see the inhabitants of Norway do not with one consent quit it, and go to some part of America, where there is a mild climate, and where they may have the same produce from land, with the tenth part of the labour. No, Sir; their affection for their old dwellings, and the terrour of a general change, keep them at home. Thus, we see many of the finest spots in the world thinly inhabited, and many rugged spots well inhabited."

The London Chronicle, which was the only news-paper he constantly took in, being brought, the office of reading it aloud was assigned to me. I was diverted by his impatience. He made me pass over so many parts of it, that my task was very easy. He would not suffer one of the petitions to the King about the Middlesex election to be read.

I had hired a Bohemian as my servant while I remained in London, and being much pleased with him, I asked Dr. Johnson whether his being a Roman Catholick should prevent my taking him with me to Scotland. JOHNSON. "Why no, Sir, if *he* has no objection, you can have none." BOSWELL. "So, Sir, you are no great enemy to the Roman Catholick religion." JOHNSON. "No more, Sir, than to the Presbyterian religion." BOSWELL. "You are joking." JOHNSON. "No, Sir, I really think so. Nay, Sir, of the two, I prefer the Popish." BOSWELL. "How so, Sir?" JOHNSON. "Why, Sir, the Presbyterians have no church, no apostolical ordination." BOSWELL. "And do you think that absolutely essential, Sir?" JOHNSON. "Why, Sir as it was an apostolical institution, I think it is dangerous to be without it. And, Sir, the Presbyterians have no public worship: they have no form of prayer in which they know they are to join. They go to hear a man pray, and are to judge whether they will join with him." BOSWELL. "But, Sir, their doctrine is the same with that of the Church of England. Their confession of faith, and the thirty-nine articles, contain the same points, even the doctrine of predestination." JOHNSON. "Why yes, Sir, predestination was a part of the clamour of the times, so it is mentioned in our articles, but with as little positiveness as could be." BOSWELL. "Is it necessary, Sir, to believe all the thirty-nine articles?" JOHNSON. "Why, Sir, that is a question which has been much agitated. Some have thought it necessary that they should all be believed; others have considered them to be only articles of peace, that is to say, you are not to preach against them." BOSWELL. "It appears to me, Sir, that predestination, or what is equivalent to it, cannot be avoided, if we hold an universal prescience in the Deity." JOHNSON. "Why, Sir, does not GOD every day see things going on without preventing them?" BOSWELL. "True, Sir; but if a thing be *certainly* foreseen, it must be fixed, and cannot happen otherwise; and if we apply this consideration to the human mind, there is no free will, nor do I see how prayer can be of any avail." He mentioned Dr. Clarke, and Bishop Bramhall on *Liberty and Necessity*, and bid me read South's *Sermons on Prayer*; but avoided the question which has excruciated philosophers and divines, beyond any other. I did not press it further, when I perceived that he was displeased, and shrunk from any abridgement of an attribute usually ascribed to the Divinity, however irreconcileable in its full extent with the grand system of moral government. His supposed orthodoxy here cramped the vigorous powers of his understanding. He was confined by a chain which early imagination and long habit made him think massy and strong, but which, had he ventured to try, he could at once have snapt asunder.

I proceeded: "What do you think, Sir, of Purgatory, as believed by the Roman Catholicks?" JOHNSON. "Why, Sir, it is a very harmless doctrine. They are of opinion that the generality of mankind are neither so obstinately wicked as to deserve everlasting punishment, nor so good as to merit being admitted into the society of blessed spirits; and therefore that God is graciously pleased to allow of a middle state, where they may be purified by certain degrees of suffering. You see, Sir, there is nothing unreasonable in this." BOSWELL. "But then, Sir, their masses for the dead?" JOHNSON. "Why, Sir, if it be once established that there are souls in purgatory, it is as proper to pray for *them*, as for our brethren of mankind who are yet in this life." BOSWELL. "The idolatry of the Mass?" JOHNSON. "Sir, there is no idolatry in the Mass. They believe GOD to be there, and they adore him." BOSWELL. "The worship of Saints?" JOHNSON. "Sir, they do not worship saints; they invoke them; they only ask their prayers. I am talking all this time of the *doctrines* of the Church of Rome. I grant you that in *practice*, Purgatory is made a lucrative imposition, and that the people do become idolatrous as they recommend themselves to the tutelary protection of particular saints. I think their giving the sacrament only in one kind is criminal, because it is contrary to the express institution of CHRIST, and I wonder how the Council of Trent admitted it." BOSWELL. "Confession?" JOHNSON. "Why, I don't know but that is a good thing. The scripture says, 'Confess your faults one to another,' and the priests confess as well as the laity. Then it must be considered that their absolution is only upon repentance, and often upon penance also. You think your sins may be forgiven without penance, upon repentance alone."

I thus ventured to mention all the common objections against the Roman Catholick Church, that I might hear so great a man upon them. What he said is here accurately recorded. But it is not improbable that if one had taken the other side he might have reasoned differently.

I must however mention, that he had a respect for *"the old religion,"* as the mild Melancthon called that of the Roman Catholick Church, even while he was exerting himself for its reformation in some particulars. Sir William Scott informs me, that he heard Johnson say, "A man who is converted from Protestantism to Popery may be sincere: he parts with nothing: he is only superadding to what he already had. But a convert from Popery to Protestantism gives up so much of what he has held as sacred as any thing that he retains; there is so much *laceration of mind* in such a conversion, that it can hardly be sincere and lasting." The truth of this reflection may be confirmed by many and eminent instances, some of which will occur to most of my readers.

When we were alone, I introduced the subject of death, and endeavoured to maintain that the fear of it might be got over. I told him that David Hume said to me, he was no more uneasy to think he should *not be* after this life, than that he *had not been* before he began to exist. JOHNSON. "Sir, if he really thinks so, his perceptions are disturbed; he is mad: If he does not think so, he lies. He may tell you, he holds his finger in the flame of a candle, without feeling pain; would you believe him? When he dies, he at least gives up all he has." BOSWELL. "Foote,

Sir, told me, that when he was very ill he was not afraid to die." JOHNSON. "It is not true, Sir. Hold a pistol to Foote's breast, or to Hume's breast, and threaten to kill them, and you'll see how they behave." BOSWELL. "But may we not fortify our minds for the approach of death?" Here I am sensible I was in the wrong, to bring before his view what he ever looked upon with horrour; for although when in a celestial frame, in his "Vanity of Human Wishes," he has supposed death to be "kind Nature's signal for retreat," from this state of being to "a happier seat," his thoughts upon this aweful change were in general full of dismal apprehensions. His mind resembled the vast amphitheatre, the Colisaeum at Rome. In the center stood his judgement, which, like a mighty gladiator, combated those apprehensions that, like the wild beasts of the *Arena*, were all around in cells, ready to be let out upon him. After a conflict, he drove them back into their dens; but not killing them, they were still assailing him. To my question, whether we might not fortify our minds for the approach of death, he answered, in a passion, "No, Sir, let it alone. It matters not how a man dies, but how he lives. The act of dying is not of importance, it lasts so short a time." He added, (with an earnest look,) "A man knows it must be so, and submits. It will do him no good to whine."

I attempted to continue the conversation. He was so provoked, that he said, "Give us no more of this"; and was thrown into such a state of agitation, that he expressed himself in a way that alarmed and distressed me; shewed an impatience that I should leave him, and when I was going away, called to me sternly, "Don't let us meet to-morrow."

I went home exceedingly uneasy. All the harsh observations which I had ever heard made upon his character, crowded into my mind; and I seemed to myself like the man who had put his head into the lion's mouth a great many times with perfect safety, but at last had it bit off.

F. L. LUCAS

Young Boswell

The tragicomedy called James Boswell began on October 29, 1740. He was the son of Alexander Boswell (1706–82), who in 1754 became Lord Auchinleck.[1] Their ancestor Thomas Boswell had received from James IV, with whom he was to fall at Flodden Field, the lands of Auchinleck, some thirteen miles east of Ayr, and some twenty-seven south of Glasgow.

On his mother's side Boswell could claim descent still more dignified—from Robert Bruce, and from that Earl of Lennox who was grandfather of Darnley, and so grandfather-in-law of Mary Stuart.

Hence Boswell's "feudal notions", and that family pride which made him regard himself, with constant satisfaction, as an "old Scotch Baron."

In 1753, at thirteen, he went to Edinburgh University. In 1757 that streak of mental instability in the Boswell blood which should always be borne in mind (his brother John went mad, and his daughter Euphemia became queer) showed itself in a temporary nervous collapse.[2] In 1758, at eighteen, travelling the northern circuit with his father, he already kept an exact journal. Equally early began another of Boswell's lifelong pursuits—he fell in love with an actress at Edinburgh, Mrs. Cowper, whom he wished to marry.

In 1760, having gone the previous year to Glasgow to study civil law, he became temporarily a Roman Catholic—just like the young

Gibbon at Oxford. Much to the agitation of his parents he rode off headlong to London, covering the distance from Carlisle in two days and a half. But in London he shed his papistry, with far more ease than the young Gibbon exiled to Lausanne. Both young men were perhaps seeking escape from the dryness of the eighteenth-century atmosphere, and also from dominating fathers. But Gibbon was to find his real sanctuary, not in the Roman Church, but in the Roman Empire; Boswell was to find his, less calmly, in Johnson.

In London, Boswell was taken up by Lord Eglinton, seventeen years his senior, who is said to have rescued him from bad company, but did not perhaps bring him into company much better. At Newmarket the young Scot got introduced to the Duke of York; and wrote an asinine poem, *The Cub at Newmarket,* published in 1762 with a dedicatory epistle to the Duke, and well describing himself, at least, as a "curious cub" from Scotland.

At this period he also added to the list of his famous acquaintances Laurence Sterne, to whom he composed a verse-epistle. One can imagine certain bonds of sympathy between the two—both were children of an age of reason and decorum, who went out of their way to lack either quality. Both were sons of whimsy. "I took a whim," writes Boswell later in London (December 12, 1762), "of dining at home every day last week, which I kept exactly to. The pleasure of gratifying whim is very great. It is known only by those who are whimsical."

None the less Sterne figures little in Boswell; this might be because upon "the man Sterne" lay the implacable anathema of Johnson. And yet, when it was a question of hunting lions, or ladies, Boswell was apt to go his own way. Johnson's disapproval did not keep him from Wilkes, or Rousseau, or Voltaire. The slightness of contact with Sterne may have been mainly due to lack of opportunity. For the ailing Yorick was mainly abroad from 1761 till 1766, and died in 1768.

However, Boswell's lion-hunting had begun

---

[1] Pronounced "Affléck"

[2] Sir Walter Scott suspected in Boswell "some slight touch of insanity." Euphemia, it appears, apart from other eccentricities, inserted in her will a wish to be buried in Westminster Abbey near Johnson.

well. It was to go on all his life. He was a Nimrod among lion-hunters. On the other hand, it is curious that Boswell, who has added so much to literature, seems not to have felt much for it. Unlike many, he greatly preferred authors to books. His lions must be alive and roaring; not stuffed in libraries.

After three months, in June 1760, he had to return from the fleshpots of London to the dry biscuit of law at Edinburgh. But there he at least met Lord Kames, Hume, Robertson, and others; and in 1761 he added to his list Thomas Sheridan, father of the dramatist, whom Boswell was soon invoking in typical terms of rapture—"My Mentor! My Socrates! Direct my heedless steps." "Socrates" and "Mentor" ring in rather incongruous contrast to Johnson's verdict on Thomas Sheridan—"Why, Sir, Sherry is dull, naturally dull; but it must have taken him a great deal of pains to become what we now see him. Such an excess of stupidity,[3] Sir, is not in Nature."

The young Boswell, however, was an eternal disciple, in constant search of a prophet whose mantle should cover him—of guides, philosophers, and friends—in short, of father-substitutes. Indeed to the goodly family of skeletons in the cupboards of psychoanalysis one might add, in Boswell's honour, the term "Telemachus-complex," after that son of Odysseus who found fame in seeking his lost father. Boswell would have liked to like his own father, Lord Auchinleck. Unfortunately father and son turned out to have opposite likings about almost every conceivable subject—about the right career for Boswell, and the right marriage for Boswell, and the right succession for the Boswell estates, and about politics, and about Samuel Johnson. Hence, just as Chesterfield looked persistently for young men to play father to, poor Boswell

---

[3] This charge of stupidity seems not wholly unjustified when one considers, for example, the accentuation which Thomas Sheridan enjoined for Dryden's *Alexander's Feast*:

None but the brave,
None but the *brave*,
None *but* the brave deserve the fair.

Here, at least, brays a perfect ass.

---

was driven to behave like an eternal orphan in search of a spiritual foster-parent.[4]

Towards the end of 1760 he published "Observations" on Foote's *The Minor*, "By a Genius" (price three pence). Boswell was already Boswell. In 1761 followed an *Ode to Tragedy*; anonymous ("By a Gentleman of Scotland"), but dedicated to—James Boswell. In 1762 he contributed thirty-one pieces to Volume II of *Original Poems, By Scotch Gentlemen*, including a little song on the Soaping Club, a body of that name which he had founded, with the slogan that every man should "soap his own beard"—in other words, follow his own whim.

> Boswell, of Soapers the king,
> On Tuesdays at Tom's does appear,
> And when he does talk or does sing
> To him ne'er a one can come near;
> For he talks with such ease and such grace,
> That all charm'd to attention we sit,
> And he sings with so comic a face,
> That our sides are just ready to split.
>
> Boswell does women adore,
> And never once means to deceive;
> He's in love with at least half a score;
> If they're serious he smiles in his sleeve.
> He has all the bright fancies of youth
> With the judgment of forty and five.
> In short, to declare the plain truth,
> There is no better fellow alive.

Such is the writer whom modern criticism has likened to Shakespeare. "Bright fancies of youth"—that was true enough; but "the judgment of forty and five!"

This curious effusion, still more curiously, he thought worth publishing again a generation later, at fifty-one, only four years before he died. Boswell never grew up.

But this doggerel seems worth quoting for its picture of what one side of Boswell, the gay side, wanted to be; his life-long trouble was, however,

---

[4] Cf. his comment after one of Lord Auchinleck's rare moments of geniality—"After breakfast, when I took leave of him, he embraced me with a cordiality which I valued more than the fond embrace of the finest Woman." (March 24, 1777).

that his gay side was matched, like Johnson's, with another alternating personality of immeasurable gloom. Boswell, like Johnson, seems an obvious manic-depressive.

In July 1762 he passed his trials in civil law. And that September he took a little excursion, recorded in the *Journal of my Jaunt,* which is already typical of so many of his journals to come—absolutely Boswellian.

> SEPTEMBER 14, 1762. (With his cousins, the Misses Macadam at Lagwine.) I was here perfectly happy. As a Cousin I had their Affection; as being very clever, their Admiration; as Mr. Boswell of Auchinleck, their Respect. A noble Complication.

> SEPTEMBER 19, 1762. At night Mrs. Heron[5] read the Evening Service to us, and I beheld with delight so fine a Creature employed in adoring her Creator.

> SEPTEMBER 21, 1762. (He disagrees with Lord Kames, Mr. Smith, Dr. Blair and others about the author of *The Rambler.*) They will allow him nothing but Heaviness, weakness and affected Pedantry. Whereas in my Opinion Mr. Johnson is a man of much Philosophy, extensive reading, and real knowledge of human life.

In November 1762 Boswell was even allowed to return to his beloved London. Lord Auchinleck might growl a great deal; he might even, on occasion, threaten disinheritance; but in practice he appears a far from unindulgent parent towards a son who was a completely incompatible antithesis of himself.

In returning to London, Boswell's avowed object was to get a commission in the Guards, by the favour of some great personage like the Duke of Queensberry, or the Countess of Northumberland. He could, indeed (like his brother John, who afterwards went mad), have got a commission in a line regiment. But Boswell was not at all set on death or glory; to smell powder on the plains of Germany, or be scalped in the backwoods of Canada, was by

no means his desire; his dream was to become for life a dashing guardsman about town. His father's comment (November 27, 1762) is curtly uncomplimentary, but hardly untrue— "A man of your age to enter into the Guards on a peace and live all his days and die an ensign, is a poor prospect, which no man would be sorry to lose. The entry is shabby and the exit the same."

However, Lord Auchinleck was less grim than his words; and James was allowed to try his luck, with an allowance, for the present, of £200 a year—two-thirds of the pension granted to Johnson after a lifetime of toil.

From this point, November 1762, till August 1763, when he left for Holland, we have Boswell's priceless *London Journal.*

Here the young Boswell reveals himself *in puris naturalibus;* though the Journal was composed, not (as its reader might well imagine) to be kept under triple lock and key, but to be posted in weekly instalments for perusal by his Scots friend, Johnston.

> NOVEMBER 15, 1762. (He leaves Edinburgh.) I made the chaise stop at the foot of the Canongate; asked pardon of Mr. Stewart for a minute; walked to the Abbey of Holyroodhouse, went round the Piazzas, bowed thrice: once to the Palace itself, once to the crown of Scotland above the gate in front, and once to the venerable old Chapel. I next stood in the court before the Palace, and bowed thrice to Arthur Seat, that lofty romantic mountain on which I have so often strayed in my days of youth, indulged meditation and felt the raptures of a soul filled with ideas of the magnificence of God and his creation. Having thus gratified my agreeable whim and superstitious humour, I felt a warm glow of satisfaction. Indeed, I have a strong turn to what the cool part of mankind have named superstition. But this proceeds from my genius for poetry, which ascribes many fanciful properties to everything.

A spectator would have thought the man mad. The interest lies in Boswell's constant self-dramatization, and the enormous admiration felt by Boswell the audience for Boswell the actor. He is the extreme antithesis to a Stoic like

[5] Daughter of Lord Kames. Now, or soon after, Boswell seems to have become her lover. In 1772 her husband divorced her for adultery.

Marcus Aurelius with his stress on behaving ἀτραγῴδως—"*not* like a tragic actor." Nor was Boswell particularly stoical between Stilton and Biggleswade—"I was a good deal afraid of robbers. A great many horrid ideas filled my mind." But next day, November 19, at sight of London from Highgate, Boswell became once more Boswellissimus.

> I was all life and joy. I repeated Cato's soliloquy on the immortality of the soul, and my soul bounded forth to a certain prospect of happy futurity. I sung all manner of songs, and began to make one about an amorous meeting with a pretty girl, the burthen of which was as follows:
>
> > She gave me *this*, I gave her *that*;
> > And tell me, had she not tit for tat?
>
> I gave three huzzas, and we went briskly in.

Cato, immortality, pretty girls—they had no incongruity for James Boswell. Doleful fears, lofty aspirations, grotesque dissipation—such was the trinity which would govern that farcical, pathetic life. November 25—"most miserable"; November 27—"I was all gentle felicity"; November 28—"In the midst of divine service I was laying plans for having women, and yet I had the most sincere feelings of religion"—so his disarming ingenuousness rambles on.[6] Among the tombs at Westminster, "was solemn and happy." But a meeting with some homely Scots folk in the Red Lion at Charing Cross is most mortifying—for "I felt strong dispositions to be a Mr. Addison." (Alas, Boswell's only resemblance to Addison was to lie in fondness for the bottle.)

But a few days later comes a foreshadowing of one of those gifts that were to make Boswell far more read, one day, than Addison himself—his patiently learnt skill in recording conversation. Boswell resolved to record every Saturday some snatch of talk at Child's Coffee House. For example:

---

[6] One may recall Goldsmith's Italians in *The Traveller* (1764):

> Though grave, yet trifling, zealous, yet untrue,
> And ev'n in penance planning sins anew.

Saturday, December 25, 1762:

Dialogue at Child's

> 1 CITIZEN.   Why, here is the bill of mortality. Is it right, Doctor?
> PHYSICIAN.   Why, I don't know.
> 1 CITIZEN.   I'm sure it is not. Sixteen only died of cholics! I dare say you have killed as many yourself.
> 2 CITIZEN.   Ay, and hanged but three! O Lord, ha! ha! ha!

That is all. Casual, callous, stupid! And yet what a vivid slice of life!—as if the babel of two centuries were suddenly hushed, and we actually listened in for a minute to the authentic Christmas chatter of Johnson's London. So Shakespeare might have created it; and Carlyle might have groaned and stormed over such human crassness; and Dickens have chuckled over such human humours.

A moment later Boswell approaches nearer still to his future masterpieces, with an amusing snatch of dramatic dialogue between Dodsley, Goldsmith, Davies, and himself on modern poetry—Gray, Shakespeare, Johnson. And one realizes yet again how much Boswell's biographic preeminence was to rest simply on this gift for living talk and dramatic scenes.

But quickly the fatuous side of Boswell breaks in again. There is the vivid, grotesque, pitiful amour with Louisa Lewis. There is the incredibly fatuous letter to Lord Eglinton (February 7, 1763), with its concluding climax:

> Surely I am a man of genius. I deserve to be taken notice of. O that my grandchildren might read this character to me: "James Boswell, a most amiable man. He improved and beautified his paternal estate of Auchinleck; made a distinguished figure in Parliament; had the honour to command a regiment of footguards, and was one of the brightest wits in the Court of George the Third.

One can almost hear the dry, crackling laughter of the Fates. No regiment; no Parliament; grandchildren that would blush at his very name—and yet, after all, a final blaze of glory beyond even Boswell's craziest dreams.

Then he continues:

> I was certain this epistle would please him much. I was pleased with writing it. I felt quite serene and happy, my mind unclouded and serenely gay.... All looked fine in my blest imagination.

And again, two days later:

> How easily and cleverly do I write just now! I am really pleased with myself; words come skipping to me like lambs upon Moffat Hill; and I turn my periods smoothly and imperceptibly like a skilful wheelwright turning tops in a turning-loom. There's fancy! There's simile! In short, I am at present a genius: in that does my opulence consist, and not in base metal.

That such absurdities could make Boswell think himself a genius is fantastic enough; but what remains far more fantastic is, that for quite different reasons he had not yet dreamed of, the man almost[7] *was* a genius after all.

So the months of 1763 slipped pleasantly by. Boswell ascends the Monument, is terrified half-way up, but pride drives him to the top.

> It was horrid... I durst not look round me. There is no real danger, as there is a strong rail both on the stair and the balcony. But I shuddered, and as every heavy wagon passed down Gracechurch Street, dreaded that the shaking of the earth would make the tremendous pile tumble to the foundation.

In April, 1763, may have occurred (though this is not recorded in the *London Journal*) that peculiarly Boswellian performance in the pit of Drury Lane when he won enthusiastic encores from the galleries by imitating the mooing of a cow; was rashly emboldened by success to mimic other animals "with very inferior effect"; and was anxiously admonished by his clerical companion, Dr. Hugh Blair, with "the utmost gravity and earnestness"—"My dear sir, I would confine myself to the *cow!*"

This same month saw Boswell's newly published correspondence with Erskine[8] warmly reviewed in *The London Chronicle*, as "a book of true genius"; the anonymous reviewer being—of course—James Boswell.

On May 16, 1763, Boswell, who had already made the acquaintance of Goldsmith and John Wilkes, at last met his destiny—Johnson. For several years Johnson had been on Boswell's hunting-list. Derrick had promised him an introduction, then Thomas Sheridan; in September 1762 we have already seen Boswell defending the author of *The Rambler* against Lord Kames and others who taxed him with heaviness and pedantry. Yet Boswell, giddy with his own affairs, met the sage only after seven months of amusing himself in London. He was to be far quicker with Rousseau and Voltaire. However, in May 1763, chance brought the first fateful meeting in the parlour of Tom Davies the bookseller. It was typical of many to follow; for Boswell incurred two resounding snubs. "Mr. Johnson, I do indeed come from Scotland, but I cannot help it." "That, Sir, I find, is what a great many of your countrymen cannot help." "O, Sir, I cannot think Mr. Garrick would grudge such a trifle[9] to you." "Sir, I have known David Garrick longer than you have done, and I know no right you have to talk to me on the subject." No wonder Boswell was "stunned" and "mortified". But he was to become, as Horace Walpole's old fishwife said of eels being skinned alive, "used to it."

It is most interesting to compare the parallel passages in the *London Journal* (May 16, 1763) and the *Life of Johnson*,[10] and see how the second clarifies and amplifies the first; interesting also to see in the *Journal* how unfavourable was Boswell's first impression of his future idol's exterior—"Mr. Johnson is a man of a most dreadful appearance. He is a very big man, is

---

[7] Some would delete "almost"; but, for me, if that maddeningly vague word "genius" is to be used at all, it should be kept for bigger minds than Boswell's.

[8] A laborious, whimsical book. In it Erskine seems to me the less tedious of the two.

The Hon. Andrew Erskine (1739–93), soldier, dramatist, and poet (Burns praised some of his songs), having lost heavily at whist, finally flung himself into the Forth.

[9] An order admitting Miss Williams to a play.

[10] Hill-Powell, i, 391 ff.

troubled with sore eyes, the palsy,[11] and the king's evil. He is very slovenly in his dress and speaks with a most uncouth voice."

A week later, on May 24, Boswell called on Johnson in Inner Temple Lane, and was courteously received. But intimacy did not spring up at once. Boswell had other, sometimes less reputable diversions; and after meeting twice in May, they only met twice more in the whole of June, 1763.[12] But July brought a dozen meetings, of increasing frequency; and on August 5 Johnson, most astonishingly, volunteered to go all the way to Harwich to see Boswell off to Holland. On the way, at Colchester, the sage uttered an unerring prophecy. A moth had cremated itself in the candle. "That creature," he said quietly, but solemnly, with a sly look, "was its own tormentor, and I believe its name was BOSWELL."

Next day—"as the vessel put out to sea, I kept my eyes upon him for a considerable time while he remained rolling his majestic frame in the usual manner." Thus, after only two and a half months' acquaintance, they parted for two and a half years. But the foundations were truly laid.

Boswell had now submitted to his father's will. In the same month of May as saw Boswell's first meeting with Johnson, Lord Auchinleck had written fiercely from the North. His letter begins, not "Dear James", but "James"; catalogues Boswell's low mimicries and printed indiscretions (his giggling correspondence with Andrew Erskine); and ends with a dour threat of disinheritance "from the principle that it is better to snuff a candle out than leave it to stink in the socket." However, if Boswell would turn to the law, "I would make no difficulty, when you were a little settled from your reelings, to let you go abroad for a while."

Whatever his narrowness, the old man shows far more Johnsonian vigour in his letters than

his famous son. So now at last Boswell renounced his martial dreams; he would exchange the gorgeous regimentals of the Guards for the drab robes of the bar. From August 1763 to June 1764 he endured a Dutch exile, wrestling with Roman law under Professor Trotz of Utrecht. At first he was utterly wretched.

> "I sunk," he wrote to his friend Johnston, "quite into despair. I thought that at length the time was come that I should grow mad. I actually believed myself so. I went out to the streets, and even in public could not refrain from groaning and weeping bitterly. I said always, 'Poor Boswell, is it come to this? Miserable wretch that I am! what shall I do?'"

Little wonder that Boswell in the end, like so many unfortunates seeking escape, found it in drink.

Persistently these attacks of "hyp"[13] recurred. In vain did Boswell exhort himself, like a Roman general haranguing his legions.

> Learn the usage of life. Be prudent and *retenu*. Never aim at being too brilliant. Be rather an amiable, pretty man. Have no affectation. Cure vanity. Be quite temperate and have self-command amid all the pleasures. Would Epictetus or Johnson be overturned by human beings, gay, thoughtless, corrupted? No; they would make the best of them and be superior. Have real principles. You have acquired a noble character at Utrecht. Maintain it.

In vain, too, did he indulge that curious habit, long retained in his memoranda, of adjuring himself to be somebody else—"Be Erskine"— "Be Digges"—"Be Johnson"—"Set out for Harwich, like Father, grave and comfortable"

---

[11] Untrue, of course. Boswell was misled by Johnson's nervous tics.

[12] Not counting a chance encounter at 1 a.m. near Temple Bar, when Johnson, invited by Boswell to The Mitre, replied it was too late for admission—"But I'll go with you another night with all my heart."

[13] "Hyp" = hypochondria, *lit.* "the parts of the abdomen under the ribs"—liver, gall, spleen, etc.; thence, the misery attributed to disordered gall or spleen.

In the eighteenth century this malady was especially associated with the English—indeed, it was called "the English disease." (One may suspect that over-eating, over-drinking, and too little exercise had much to do with it.) "A celebrated French novelist," writes Addison, "enters on his story thus: 'In the gloomy month of November, when the people of England hang and drown themselves.'" According to Voltaire, east winds sufficed to drive us to suicide; and Diderot describes a pond in St. James's Park as reserved for ladies so intending. See Matthew Green's charming poem *The Spleen* (1737).

—"Be Rock of Gibraltar." In vain did he fortify his soul with that "Inviolable Plan" drawn up on October 16, 1763, "to be read over frequently."

> Keep quite clear of gloomy notions which have nothing to do with the mild and elegant religion of Jesus. ... You can live quite independent and go to London every year; and you can pass some months at Auchinleck, doing good to your tenants, and living hospitably with your neighbours, beautifying your estate, rearing a family, and piously preparing for immortal felicity.... τίμα σεαυτόν: reverence thyself.

But all this could not conquer the "hyp." "You was dreadfully melancholy and had the last and most dreadful thoughts." Or again —"You got up dreary as a dromedary." Or again—"You awaked shocked, having dreamt you was condemned to be hanged...."

ELEANOR CLARK

Hadrian: The Emperor at Home

It is the saddest place in the world, gaunt as an old abandoned graveyard, only what is buried there is the Roman Empire. There was a good deal more of it after that—the "noble" Antonines and the rule of the soldiers and so on, before Constantine packed up for Byzantium, but one feels this, wandering there, as the end, the delicate ghastly moment of the turn; there was never such a fling again, thought and the arts fell fast from then on and power slowly after them. Jack and Jill had lost their pail of water.

HADRIAN: THE EMPEROR AT HOME: From "Hadrian's Villa," copyright 1950 by Eleanor Clark, from the book *Rome and a Villa* by Eleanor Clark. Reprinted by permission of Doubleday & Company, Inc.

And one wonders if at that point anyone really knew it: did Hadrian, of all people? The decay of morals, waning *virtus* were an old, old story by then and not too interesting; morals in fact were about to have a fine new heyday, glum, smug and bourgeois; nobility of that kind had not been so hard to retrieve, and the empire, just then after Trajan's death, was at its grandest. No new conquests were planned. The Jews were making trouble again, for the last time, but on the whole in his thousands of miles of travel in Roman territory Hadrian the elegant, the sophist, met with no great unpleasantness, unless he should have minded all the scraping before himself. He could indulge the building craze peacefully everywhere. Something else was at the turn; for one thing there had been no poet worth speaking of for a long time, but that was only part of the subtlety of doom, of something else—you catch your breath thinking of it, wandering through the tragic heaps of masonry that loom still so huge over the olive trees, presenting a razor's edge of history and a character more complex than any in Proust.

Complex: but perhaps not, after all, so "enigmatic." The word got stuck to him some time ago, perhaps mainly because he was not wicked, at least not in the gross way of the century before; but one knows the face only too well, statues of the emperor amounted to a plague in this case, and there is the villa; it is his memoir, no matter how wrongly its courts and rooms and gardens came to be labeled. The idea was that Hadrian had re-created there the spots that had most attracted him on his Eastern travels, and so some very unlikely names were pinned on the ruins and scholars sweated over resemblances. It is not important. The fantasy is clear enough anyway, and so are the scale and the location; and how much too familiar one is with the brainless, incredible beauty of young Antinous, dead in the Nile, the new Apollo for this time that one thinks of as a *fin-de-siécle* of giants, a tremendous mauve convulsion that afterwards was immediately hushed up and patched up as if nothing had happened. He is the other character among the ruins, poignant enough, but not heartbreaking; grandeur is missing in that story....

It took years to build, naturally, and Hadrian was not even there very much until nearly the end of his life, when his only desire was to die. He is supposed to have started it soon after the beginning of his reign in 117 and to have gone on until his death, but most of those twenty-one years he was traveling, seeking "into all curiosities" as somebody put it at the time, also looking after the empire. He was a public servant, trained under Trajan; he knew his duties; he had been a soldier and governor of a province. But something else was always driving him, not westward as people are driven in different times toward freshness and new lands, though he did his stint in Gaul and Germany, but east to the old and defeated ones, to art and symbols and the oldest mysteries; everything else was too easy, and in any case the thing was to keep moving, keep inquiring, otherwise every day would be a new boredom and life intolerable. Virtue and vice had stopped meaning anything, the oracles had gone dumb, the gods were part of the game to be played, he being one of them and for most purposes the chief one; he outdid all his predecessors in that, nobody had ever been worshipped in so many places, and he was not averse to it, which was perhaps another reason for going east: they did that sort of thing so well there. But worship does not fill up a crack in the soul.

So he came back to Rome now and then and would be off again before long, like a butterfly, really like a cargo of elephants, with all the world whispering about it every time. But it was not for him to feel weighted down by the thought of his baggage, or the thousand or ten thousand men who might be carrying it and making the arrangements. In that respect he was as free as a hobo, and could devote himself, among other things, to the serious profession of architecture. That was his passion, his true work, and it must have made up very often for the terrible absence,

though not in the beginning, of love. One imagines him working late over the plans, furious at interruption, missing his meals like someone in a garret. Unfortunately Nero only fifty years before had done the same, to practice on his lyre, and had had the same appetite for the East, especially Greece but the rest of it too, where he had been adulated just as if he had not been a monster. But the times were not so simple now. Greece was everyone's Paris, that was inevitable, but Hadrian would never steal from it; the statues he could not buy he would have copied, there were plenty of artists for that, and he would make Greece more beautiful than ever. That was the compact: He, god, and Rome his instrument would glorify the spirit, which is beyond nationality.

The spirit was a little too subtle. The truth was the water was running out of the pail, there was not much time; pretty soon nobody would know how to do anything but copy. Meantime, however, the fine new temples were being strewn over Greece and Asia Minor, many dedicated to the emperor, and cities which he had beautified were being named for him all over the place. He flitted, with a sure hand however, with all his baggage trains from one place and project to another; it was Olympus on the move, shrewd and mobile as a newspaperman, subject to fits of melancholy. His taste ran to the ornate, and his sense of scale, rather naturally, was bizarre, though not peculiar to him: bigness was in the air and was expected of him. Even so, his temple of Venus and Rome over the Forum was really overbearing, and it seems the great architect Apollodorus fell out of favor for caviling at Hadrian's designs for it, one of his objections being that if the gods stood up they would lift the roof off. Another important project was his tomb, across the Tiber from the tomb of Augustus and more splendid, to be decked with statues like a Christmas tree. But the great toy, or piece of autobiography, the true private and desperate expression of the man, was in Tivoli....

The whole sense of the place is individual,

violently so; it is the expression of a single artist, straining away from the standard so far that with the least slip of taste it could fall into freakishness or vulgarity and that achieves greatness instead: a tour de force, certainly, like a Turner or Tiepolo sky, but convincing, through sheer personal brilliance.

That is the passion in these ruins: a creative one; and the application is not so startling, not necessarily. Hadrian is one of the richest as well as brightest men in the empire, which is how he happens inevitably to be at the head of it, whatever else his cousin Trajan might really have preferred; and one of the most cultivated: he has been to the best schools, entertained the best philosophers and probably subsidized quite a stable of them. There is no need to imagine him skulking around his marble labyrinth. He is as busy as the President of the United States to begin with, the hundred-year rampage in the wake of Augustus being finally up; he has all sorts of things to see to besides architecture: codifying laws, building the first wall across barbarous Britain, like patroling the Arctic now, pulling in the empire on the east to a tenable line, pushing reforms for slaves and prisoners past a grudging if more or less power-less senate, stamping out Christians and so on; in short delivering the new golden age, and in his leisure time exemplifying it. It was never more proper to do so: for the head of the state to stroll in brilliant company through the most magnificent of country houses, concerning him-self with love, cooking and the things of the mind, while beyond the fountain at the edge of the cypress grove a favorite peacock pecks for grub. The obligations of the ruler in this age are not simple, when half Italy is studded with villas and Herodes Atticus, a private citizen, can build cities as splendid as Hadrian's. And he has other passions too, especially for hunting: he can work off his conflicts in that.

Nevertheless there is a sound in the place that leads you past the forms of art, and like a mosquito in your ear drowns out the visceral struggle of centuries that came forward for a moment in the big baths. It is a very modern sound: the scream of the *I*; the geometry of these vast courts is all a dialogue with self; they are not public at all but private as a dream and whatever company moves in them will also be a projection of the dreamer's mind. What is shared with Versailles and the palaces of the Czars, the lavishness and the arrogance of the dimensions, becomes something more insidious here, not the simple effrontery of despotism. The thrust is obsessive. The rooms high as Grand Central Station, the maze of half-lit halls and those others where slaves must have hurried with torches at high noon—containing without knowing it the end of all the emperor's culture and mystical experiments—the feminine niche in the liplike fold of a garden court, the honey-comb guardhouse and more secretive cliffside burrow of the Hundred Roomlets, the playing with planes, pure abstraction, lined as with fur with every voluptuary fantasy, the tiny tight theatrical center of it all, the impossibility of an end: all are the innermost statement of a mind, a true Folly, just the opposite of innocent Ver-sailles. And when you are this far into it it is not sad, nor even particularly ironic; it is what they call entertainment; you want to know what is hidden in the Maritime Theatre, so valuable that it has to be protected with a moat.

It is at least clear that you will not find simplicity. This is the house of a man who will always seem false, and most when he is not; whose anger is less offensive than his kindnesses; from whom the simplest goodness comes out as the worst ambiguity. Between him and shrewd, good-hearted, ambitious Trajan, his guardian and predecessor, who liked the company of honest soldiers, it must have been a more ticklish business than anyone now knows; there will have been a moat there too, and a wretched effort to cross it going on perhaps for years, until the issue could only be decided on the basis of rank power, perhaps even the rankest or almost, everything short of murder, while on both sides the heart was still crying out for confidence. The pattern will be repeated many times, when it is not broken off sooner with plain hatred. This is Hadrian's curse, and he will build it into his villa, along with the shiny, shifting dream-world in which for a moment at a time the self finds its comfort and revenge, never imagining the portrait it will have left. It is a clear one, however. No man who was loved, or who was easy in the lack of love, could have built such a house; among the gods and temples strewn about the place there is one real invisible altar, and that is to romantic sexual love, which is a version of the glorified Self.

It is in the neighborhood of the libraries that you think of Antinous, because they are the only places that look like bedrooms. There is more to the story than that, even an extraordinary perception of the future, no more perverse than most at the time. It is an age of anxiety. What will roll into the dominating force of centuries is popping up in all kinds of clownish, incongruous forms like a boxful of Punch-and-Judys whacking each other over the head, and the beautiful boy from Bithynia, Hadrian's love, has his place among them. But what his statues announce and glorify is sex, and less a fulfillment than a long languorous exacerbation, a voluptuous delay such as Tivoli had never heard of before. A new kind of experience has come in: the romantic obsession, and wrapped in a sensuality the very opposite of Roman; this sultry shepherd child could only have come from the East.

Look at him in the little Sala Rotonda, that wonderful room with its niches and cupola and the great porphyry cup, so much in Hadrian's spirit it might almost have been arranged to commemorate the love affair; you even enter it at either door between pairs of objects from the villa, the Egyptian telamones at one and herms of Tragedy and Comedy at the other. Antinous is there twice: in the bust whose gaze ironically crosses Hadrian's past the chunky primitive bronze Hercules, so strangely solid and out of place between them; and as the full-length

Bacchus by the door, with the old sexual symbol of the pine cone, turned now to what unfertile suggestion, on his head. It is a good place to see him. The beautiful mosaic floor too could as well have been Hadrian's; this was the grandeur that was left, of architecture and objects; it is in such rooms as this, and some twenty times bigger, and among such furnishings, statues, gods and all, that the boy, probably only twelve or thirteen years old in the beginning, leads his short domestic life with the most powerful man in the world.

The rest of the setting is there too, sketched in in a few strokes around the walls, the whole lurid story from five hundred years back, with its slow merciless progressions of power and belief, the whole dynamic tangle of causalities in which for a moment there occurs this particular twist; and who would dare to assign responsibility among them? The great Jove from Otricoli is there, the deep-bearded bull-like bust, five hundred years old in Hadrian's time, shown in all the raging fullness of his power as Michelangelo would have done it, with his hair like the sides of a cavern and the middle of his forehead thrust out so far with the power he has over the world it is nearly bursting; no sculptor was turning out anything like that any more; divinity has dribbled away—you can see it in the room—among the emperors, everywhere, and the emperor himself is the chief loser. Who will now be father to him? Certainly not the people; he has been turned loose among the horrors of infinite possibility, everything depends on a mere trick of disposition. And there is the terrible strength of Roman women, the good and the wicked, beginning with frigid Juno: no romance there, nothing at any rate for the anguished mind of these times to look to. It seems that this sad ponderous image of Antinous was what had to be created; it has the same dead weight of inevitability about it as Augustus; and he is undoubtedly handsome, even if the statues are not.

It is a lush Middle Eastern handsomeness, even rather gross, and more than anything, empty; you could take him for a young Armenian rug salesman, or for King David, and this is curious because the shape of the face is new, and unique; you would know it anywhere. It is rounder than any classic face though the nose and forehead line is still nearly straight, with more cheek space and the eyes farther apart, so that it is at the same time softer and more angular, more the face of a specific person, although idealized; only blank, as though the artist had not quite known what was expected of him. But this is corrected by the pose, more or less the same in all the statues, at least all that one is likely to see; there must have been thousands once. There is no confusion there. His head seems nearly too heavy to hold, not with the physical weight of the skull but the vague burden of languor, conveyed in a nuance; it is just that the old divine self-sufficiency is gone, the picture is of indeterminate sorrow and a life that has meaning only in sensual rapport. The face, crowned with the richest ringlets yet seen in art, bends just a little downwards as in the resignation of the captive, nostalgic for a happiness he is no longer fit for and can scarcely remember; playing Bacchus, he holds up his grapes, or flowers or thyrsus, in a mood that could not be farther from Bacchanalian: deadly serious. The spring and tension of the perfect body have vanished; this one would change its pose only to sink, to fall, though in build it suggests great strength, more than any Apollo; it is broad-shouldered but passive as a plum, close to fat, with untrained muscles and a succulence of flesh at the breasts and armpits; no little sleeping hermaphrodite, but a power to be shown on a scale with Hercules, a subtle and murderous triumph of the female principle.

It is the natural thing; it was to be expected, especially taken together with another of the busts in the room, his perfect antithesis: all strength and what Protestants call character, enough to have pushed the empire through a delicate moment, yet securely, even massively feminine too. This is no poor brittle Sabina. It is Plotina, Trajan's wife and Hadrian's adoptive mother, the one person who can perhaps have given him, and for many years, the sober intimate sanction he needs, and he does need it. He is not a person who can easily stand alone, though in fact he does more and more, he would wish for the security of general love if that were possible, but it is not, except from people too simple or silly to see into him at all and with them he is at his most gracious. The rest he alienates when he needs them most; he exposes himself on all sides, he who cannot stand it on any: that is not his kind of courage. This powerful woman is his natural counterpart too, and it is only after her death that he has his revenge for the lifelong devotion; it could have been told beforehand.

You could tell it even from the official face, bearded but so unfatherly and not handsome at all, which could so easily have lent itself to caricature; and in fact the whole story was probably better drawn in the back alleys of Rome than in all the solemn nudes, as Mars or Jupiter, and the portrait busts that must have had all the sculptors in the empire working like script writers. The face asks for it, aside from anything else. Everything in it is a little exaggerated, including the conflicts and irritability; the look too of having a marvelous gamut of expressions if they could only be seen, though you would never guess the great charm of the man—it must have been one of the main points, it would all have been so much simpler without that—from these features. The eyes are much too narrow set, and have something a bit weaselish about them that jars with the noble, over-protuberant nose; the hair is combed down nearly to the eyebrows across a low forehead as though in a chronic urge to concealment but perhaps really more out of vanity, not to leave too exposed the long bellying ill-proportioned cheeks, which are not cushy like the boy's but more rankly sensuous, swollen and stuffed-looking; and in his expression too there is something of the captive, but only of his own mind. His preoccupation seems real, not the kind so shrewdly wrapped around the tricky, neurotic features of Augustus; this is Hadrian himself, but the preoccupation is not quite pure, though it creates threats as chimerical and aggravations as real as if it were; and his majesty, which seems also entirely native, is more of the man of wealth than of the thinker. Yet he thinks continually; that could have been made to look very funny too.

Especially as his vice is mental, not the mere physical indulgence so easily tolerated among the Romans and by now such a worn-out theme as connected with emperors. It is the mental trappings, the lack of promiscuity in this case that will offend; the romantic agony is having its first tryout; the individual soul is asserting itself in strange and dangerous fashion, in fact in a way that seems to make even power secondary, a most un-Roman business, particularly as so entwined with the highest and rightest national aspirations....

You have come to the Maritime Theatre, the jewel-like heart of the villa and one of Hadrian's loveliest works, so drab now you could walk through without thinking about it; six columns of the colonnade around the moat are left, half of them minus their capitals, and a couple of others and three clumps of masonry on the island. Probably it was built much earlier, but it is now that you can understand it; it goes with the image of Antinous, it comes from the same need. Ordinary love does not build so tensely, it needs no protection, it can set up its cerebral center like a tent anywhere; but then the whole drive and character of the house, all the luxury and torment of it, come into their own at this time. The ego that everything combined to swell and sicken has now at one blow been nearly severed from the real world, which more and more becomes only an intrusion and a threat; true communication is with an image made flawless by death; the playboy side of the man has come into its grandest justification, among the mysteries of afterlife.

The artist keeps up with it; the wonderful private poem goes on growing, in marble and water and gold, but tight at the center of it remains this little moat-bound shrine, one of the most splendid toys in architecture, linked in all its substance to that sacrifice in the Nile. The temple of Venus and Rome above the Roman Forum could have existed without Antinous, but not this. But the colossal statue of him as an Egyptian god would not have been here, there is no room for it, and it is not necessary; perhaps it is in the apse of the structure called the Vestibule, below the baths, or more likely among the fancier trappings and richer waterfalls of Canopus, to be approached by boat down the canal: it is that kind of game, as if nobody were looking, and the little round marble island far away in the palace is part of it. Hadrian is playing Robinson Crusoe, as everyone does in childhood and longs to do forever after; the island is the oldest, most necessary image, older than the Dying God; that is the true romantic impossibile, to be separated from the rubs and nudges and impurities of society by the primordial, deathly medium of water; the perfect assertion of self and the regions of the dead are alike surrounded by water. Of course it is a game; in reality Crusoe goes crazy; but the poetry is true, and the form in this case charming.

The touch has been kept light. The whole affair is in a tub: a high circular wall and portico held up by forty columns of Ionic order; then the moat, crossed by two playful wooden bridges that swing open or shut along a semicircle—every intelligent child's desire; and within, unassailable as a foot-high fortress in the sand, the tiny elegant palace, complete, at least for the purposes of the game, with the design of some diminutive four petaled flower. It has nine more or less open roomlets, one a little bathing place, all scarcely big enough for an adult chaise longue; and an exquisite atrium, decorated with marine figures in marble, the four sides curving inward, in a graceful scalloping edged with small columns, toward the centerpiece. That is not Antinous; it seems not to have been a statue at all, though there were surely some around in the niches; it is just a fountain. The whole beautiful fantasy, set like the soul's treasure at the center of acres of methodical flamboyance, brings you to nothing but that. A real toy; just a marble gazebo.

Archaeologists a long time ago hit on the idea, and have stuck to it, that this is where Hadrian came to "be alone"; they like the thought of him swinging the bridges to behind him and welcoming the muses, that is concerning himself somehow or other with music, painting and so on, while affairs of state wait across the moat. It won't do; he is not that kind of charlatan. It is more likely that he comes there to cut himself off from women if anything, there is that feeling about it, but that too is only part of the essential poetry of the place, in which it is hard enough to imagine anyone listening to the victrola, let alone drawing up plans for a temple. It is in the middle of everything, utterly exposed, in spite of the wall, and Italians were never quiet; it could hardly give him much peace to station guards at the entrance to shoo off the guests and servants, he is far too irritable not to notice, he registers everything, and not like Julius Caesar; besides, there are the threats, more and more, to be listened for. But the place in any case is too theatrical; its seriousness is only as a poem; in real life, since he is not actually mad, far from it, the first thing he will do is what anyone else does on an island, that is to ask someone over, even if he is not very fond of them. He will have his after-dinner coffee there, an apéritif perhaps, with an acquaintance or two, among a few favorite objects; he can treat it lightly, and must if he is to be there at all; it is not adapted to anything else. For work there will be the neutral place, nothing that involves the eye or spirit, and a serious, not this fake isolation.

What is not fake is the expression; the need is real; one symbol of purity, one fountain indistinguishable to the public eye from a thousand others must be conceived of as unapproachable, beyond the touch of the commonplace. Certainly the gesture is theatrical too: to have literally built the island, actually played out the game; but what in the villa is not? This staginess is of his deepest nature, the very stuff of his genius. Everything in him, the grand and the tawdry, the terror and the boredom, requires to be turned into a visible object; if he does not express his perceptions in architecure they will grow to madness, and the deepest and most private will be the most urgent; he has to build himself a plain of philosophy, a valley of the dead guarded by a stone Cerberus; if he is not on a stage he is nothing, he will lose all belief in himself.

But on this little stage, this island, he invokes his purest part. It is the other side of the shameless public bombast that goes on around the dead Antinous, by his orders and with his inspiration. It is not enough for him to glorify his private experience to himself, the whole world has to be brought into it. The resources of the empire must be lent to the apotheosis of his love. Slaves sweat, ships scurry about the seas getting stone for it, the priests have to be dealt with, threatened if necessary, the public initiated; the shrines pop up in a dozen countries; the city of Antinopolis appears on the Nile, whose inhabitants will be scurrilously linked forever with those of the cities named for Hadrian; the statues for which gods are stripped of their symbols right and left roll out of the workshops by hundreds. You would think it would sicken him to have thrust at him from everywhere, wrapped in every atrocious hypocrisy, the face that he had known in ecstasy and sleep, to whose risky eyes he had entrusted all that is most secret and true in himself. No; he demands it. The world is his stage too, and on it through any loathsome obsequiousness, to be valued by volume, he is paying his most sacred debt, more sacred because of his guilt; such a man is always guilty toward those he loves, even if he has not killed them, it is the same; and so he calls for more and still more of the cringing adulation, refused only by Rome; he exposes himself more recklessly.

Especially after his last return; that is when the real outrage comes. But first he manages to linger on in the East for four more years, probably having one of his best creative periods as artists generally do after the tragic end of an impossible love affair; there is as much relief as grief, the dead and idealized love really suits him better than the rather embarrassing live one, and that will be part of the guilt too. He is perhaps in Athens, his true home, which he continues to beautify as though imperial hand-outs could restore the living spirit; it is Athens that he has wanted to give to the world, it will be the place for him now in his cruel detach-ment. There is the Jewish war now too, a nasty business, perhaps more than necessary; and why not: that single jealous god could never have been so repugnant to him as at this moment. But the real enemy is waiting for him at home, and is deadly; it is virtue; a horrible pedantry of virtue, always the Roman forte, is slowly closing in on the creative imagination of the world. You will see it soon in Marcus Aurelius: the fear of passion, the hatred of art, the scorn of life itself, that other, more hateful egotism of self-congratulation dressed as humility; and against that, Hadrian when he finally returns makes his last heroic, ridiculous gesture in defense of a world that is already in smithereens. There is perhaps some mysterious personal loyalty in it too, which would be like him, but it would not be only that. He appoints the worst of all the possible candidates, his friend Lucius Verus, as his successor; the perfect playboy, rich, dissipated and astonishingly beautiful it seems—almost to be deified for nothing but that —an expert in sensuality, poetaster and inventor of a certain meat pie, probably a good talker; nothing else. It is not certain he was not the emperor's illegitimate son; he was at any rate all that his bright nervous world—of joy, of wanderlust, of the mind's daring—could offer by way of an heir.

It is Hadrian's last great insult to Rome, the final alienation of all those right-minded men he has never really been able to do without; and Plotina is not by him now. That is when the madness sets in. He becomes a murderer. Not

for the first time: he had always had his suspi-cions, his spies, had been too quick to look over his shoulder, though he had sometimes exagger-ated in forgiveness too, but now it is different. He strikes out among his relatives, friends, anywhere, until nobody is safe near him, nobody is left who ever assumed a relation with him; if he refrains from poisoning his wife he will be accused of it anyway, it almost seems that she manages to die just then so that he will be. It is as though an ancient nightmare, a poetry of horror established long ago, waiting to spring forth in every scene and circumstance of his position, had finally found the crack in him to flood through and become reality, and he had no choice but to be its agent. Nero and his crazy Golden House are very close; there had perhaps not been so much difference after all. The real world is very dim....

There are ties with his further choice too, young Marcus Aurelius, intense and willowy at the time and probably with a certain adolescent leaning to the abstruse which he will outgrow shortly: his patrician mother had made part of her fortune selling bricks for the emperor's villa, and for his building in general. But this youth who also professes loyalty is a different kettle of fish from Antoninus; many hundreds of years later he turns up as the white-haired boy of a self-interested bourgeoisie very like the one that Hadrian despised, and every worthy maxim he gets off will be a crack at his imperial grandfather; that great and various nature seems to taunt him so from the grave, he cannot leave any part of it unpilloried: boys, building, art. Yet there were statues of him in the villa, the count and the others found them, and so one imagines him stopping off now and then at the crazy old place, in the triumph of his survival and the safety of an unimpeachable character: uncomfortable, out of place, jealous as a Protestant minister, and with a worm of ecstasy in his heart from the contact with what he condemns. Still, he was a good ruler as opposed to a wicked one, very good indeed; Hadrian had chosen well.

There were other posthumous items too, before the Vandals came through; the place was not quite uninhabited. There are touches of restoration from later in that century and the next, and it can happen, though this is the rarest thing, that in one of the fields near the palace you will pick up a little fragment of pottery from a still later time, left by some caretaker or squatter on the land, or perhaps the retinue of the captive Queen Zenobia. Some of the soldier-emperors will no doubt have used parts of it for a week-end camp—there was every facility for keeping fit, after all, and those who felt like it could amuse themselves in the evening knocking the noses off the statues. But really it had ceased to exist long before, and before Hadrian's death; he himself had condemned it. It had been many things, many kinds of expression noble and ignoble, but it was always, along with the rest, his private work of homage to a civilization founded, as on a rock, on the knowledge of the world's beauty and delight, and it ends, as if he had ordered its literal destruction, at that great moment of his defeat. There are no theatrics in that; he rises for once in all simplicity, and for that one last second you can see the whole villa strewn twinkling and absurd around his ankles, already old hat, the sense of it simply gone; then the nightmare closes over him again and he sinks back to wait to die.

Not patiently, he is still in character, irascible, scathing, spoiled; he longs for death with the same passionate appetite he has had for everything else, only he cannot bribe anyone to kill him and is evidently too weak or not quite willing to do it himself; there is a touch of the old game again in this, his passions have always bred their own negations. So he lingers on with his horrid disease, dropsy, in such suffering it will become a legend for generations and is thought to give him powers more miraculous than any he has as emperor; the physical pain alone is punishment enough, but the rest is worse—for him there can be no resolution— and it is just here on this last gentle hill that one imagines him then.

. . .

Questions for Review

1. Plutarch, probably the most famous of ancient biographers, lived several hundred years after the death of Alcibiades. Judging from this biography, what were Plutarch's sources for his details about Alcibiades? Where there contradictions between his sources? How did Plutarch treat these sources?

2. Much of Alcibiades's conversation is given by Plutarch. Is there any that seems improbable, inappropriate, or unlikely to have been preserved?

3. What principles of selection and arrangement of details does Plutarch follow in this life? Does he group Alcibiades's public actions in one place and his private in another? Or separate the trivial from the important? Is this technique a weakness or a strength in biography?

4. Do you have a clear idea of the character of Alcibiades from Plutarch's description? What reason did Plutarch appear to have for writing this biography?

5. John Aubrey's *Brief Lives,* including his life of Denham, were not intended as full-scale biographies but as collections of anecdotes about famous people. Aubrey considered them compilations of little-known facts or bits of true gossip about his contemporaries and near-contemporaries. Where did he get his information about Denham? How objective was it? How trustworthy?

6. Does Aubrey follow any pattern of development or principle of selection in his essay on Denham? What is the effect?

7. Is Aubrey more interested in Denham's actions, words, or possessions? Explain your answer. Compare Aubrey and Plutarch in this regard.

8. Boswell's *Life of Johnson* is probably the most highly praised biography ever written, and Boswell's technique of revealing Johnson through talk is particularly admired. What are the virtues and limitations of Boswell's dialogue techniques?

9. Boswell composed journals, diaries, and autobiography as well as biography. Compare and contrast his methods in the *Journal* and in the *Life of Johnson*. Are they like or unlike? Does a successful journal keeper necessarily make a good biographer or autobiographer?

10. Does the Johnson of Boswell's portrait seem to you to be the same man who wrote the letter on p. 93 and the poem on p. 538?

11. Boswell often asked Johnson diverse (and sometimes silly) questions to get him to talk. Point out instances of such questions in the excerpt given here. Would this practice, and the response of the subject to it, give a really accurate indication of character and intelligence?

12. F. L. Lucas's biographical sketch of Boswell is largely based on the primary materials of Boswell himself: the *Journal* and the *Life of Johnson*. What, if anything, does Lucas as biographer add to the "facts" as Boswell preserves them? In what way(s) does his purpose differ from Boswell's in presenting these facts?

13. Is Lucas's Boswell significantly different from the Boswell of the *Journal* or the *Life*? Elaborate. Is Lucas's use of Freud's theories helpful or not in delineating Boswell's character?

14. In what ways does Lucas's biography reveal the essential differences between autobiography and biography? To what extent does his interest indicate the biographer's concern with detachment, objectivity, and desire to show the subject within his milieu?

15. For what kind of reader does Lucas write? How does this affect his handling of data, diction, and tone?

16. The gap in time separating Plutarch from Alcibiades, and Lucas from Boswell is enormously widened between Eleanor Clark and the Emperor Hadrian. Historians and earlier biographers have preserved some few public "facts" about Hadrian's reign and his love affair with Antinous; but Miss Clark uses these only slightly. What parts of *Hadrian's Villa* obviously depend on research? Upon what do the other parts depend?

17. Miss Clark gives very few of Hadrian's recorded words and she glosses over his military and political actions. It is his character as it may be seen in the ruins of his villa that she is concerned with. How does she conjecture character from ruins?

18. Are there instances where Miss Clark imputes to the pagan Roman emperor ideas or feelings which he could not have had, which are really extensions of the biographer rather than insights into the subject? Explain.

19. Reread the *Meditations* of Marcus Aurelius on p. 56 above. Marcus Aurelius was second in succession to the Roman throne after Hadrian. Does the world of Rome as Marcus shows it correspond to the Rome of Miss Clark? Does her character of Marcus Aurelius correspond to the character shown in the *Meditations*?

Questions for Discussion and Writing

1. To what extent does point of view figure in biographical writing? Is the personality of the biographer a significant element in the composition itself? Ought it to be or not?

2. Of the biographers above, which is the most intimately involved with his subject? Which the least? Is the second biographer therefore a more detached and "factual" narrator than the first?

3. Is chronological sequence an important part of the biography? Discuss the role of time-sequence in the selections given here. Since human beings *do* change and develop with the passing of time, would you naturally expect the biographer to be deeply concerned with chronological problems?

4. Is the diction of the biography likely to be formal or informal? What would determine this? Can any general principles about diction in the biography be established?

5. Which of the people shown in these bio-

graphies seems the most "real" to you? Which the least? How do you account for this?

6. Compare and contrast Boswell as autobiographer (in the *Journal*) with Boswell as the subject of biography (in Lucas's essay). Or Johnson in the *Letter* with Boswell's picture of him in the *Life*. What conclusions can you draw about the differences between the demands on the biographer as contrasted with other writers?

7. Which of the approaches to character—through actions, words, and surroundings—do you find most effective? Are there other devices of characterization that you see used in these biographies? What are their strengths and weaknesses?

The Public Domain— Reportage

The kind of writing called "reportage" or "journalism" has certain resemblances to the diary on the one hand and biography on the other. The journalist is very much concerned with events in time, the recording of daily occurrences; his subject matter is essentially people and their actions. Unlike the diarist, however, the reporter must concern himself with matters that a wide reading public will find relevant or interesting and not confine himself to his personal interests. Moreover, the journalist who writes for "periodicals"—magazines and newspapers—cannot devote very much of his energy and time to gathering all the available data about the men who are his subjects. At the same time, he must have enough accurate, verifiable information to make his report worthwhile reading and protect himself from legal action against misrepresentation. Tied to the "up to the minute" concept of journalism, the reporter may limit himself to presenting the "facts" to his readers: the who, what, where, and when of current events. He "effaces" himself and his subjective feelings about his material in the name of "objectivity" or "fairness." But the theoretical ideal of "objectivity" in reportage is not held by many journalists, who maintain that it is, after all, their own intellects, their distinctly personal ways of conceptualizing events, that distinguish mere pieces of data from a meaningful "interpretation" of events. Thus, as the "reporters" below indicate, writing for a large, unknown audience demands that some kind of balance be achieved between the "immediate" and the "permanent," the "factual" and the "interpretive," the "personal" and the "impersonal" styles, and the eyewitness report and the research project. The reporter tries to attain the fusion of "understanding" what happens with the immediate impact of the experience *now*.

PLATO

Agathon Gives a Party

Characters of the Dialogue

APOLLODORUS	ARISTOPHANES
PHAEDRUS	AGATHON
PAUSANIAS	SOCRATES
ERYXIMACHUS	ALCIBIADES

A TROOP OF REVELLERS

SCENE—THE HOUSE OF AGATHON

Concerning the things about which you ask to be informed I believe that I am not ill-prepared with an answer. For the day before yesterday I was coming from my own home at Phalerum to the city, and one of my acquaintance, who had caught a sight of me from behind, calling out playfully in the distance, said: Apollodorus, O thou Phalerian man, halt! So I did as I was bid; and then he said, I was looking for you, Apollodorus, only just now, that I might ask you about the speeches in praise of love, which were delivered by Socrates, Alcibiades, and others, at Agathon's supper. Phoenix, the son of Philip, told another person who told me of them; his narrative was very indistinct, but he said that you knew, and I wish that you would give me an account of them. Who, if not you, should be the reporter of the words of your friend? And first tell me, he said, were you present at this meeting?

Your informant, Glaucon, I said, must have been very indistinct indeed if you imagine that the occasion was recent; or that I could have been of the party.

Why, yes, he replied, I thought so.

AGATHON GIVES A PARTY: From the *Symposium* by Plato, translated by Benjamin Jowett.

Impossible, I said. Are you ignorant that for many years Agathon has not resided at Athens; and not three have elapsed since I became acquainted with Socrates, and have made it my daily business to know all that he says and does. There was a time when I was running about the world, fancying myself to be well employed, but I was really a most wretched being, no better than you are now. I thought that I ought to do anything rather than be a philosopher.

Well, he said, jesting apart, tell me when the meeting occurred.

In our boyhood, I replied, when Agathon won the prize with his first tragedy, on the day after that on which he and his chorus offered the sacrifice of victory.

Then it must have been a long while ago, he said; and who told you—did Socrates?

No indeed, I replied, but the same person who told Phoenix—he was a little fellow, who never wore any shoes, Aristodemus, of the deme of Cydathenaeum. He had been at Agathon's feast; and I think that in those days there was no one who was a more devoted admirer of Socrates. Moreover, I have asked Socrates about the truth of some parts of his narrative, and he confirmed them. Then, said Glaucon, let us have the tale over again; is not the road to Athens just made for conversation? And so we walked, and talked of the discourses on love; and therefore, as I said at first, I am not ill-prepared to comply with your request, and will have another rehearsal of them if you like. For to speak or to hear others speak of philosophy always gives me the greatest pleasure, to say nothing of the profit. But when I hear another strain, especially that of you rich men and traders, such conversation displeases me; and I pity you who are my companions, because you think that you are doing something when in reality you are doing nothing. And I dare say that you pity me in return, whom you regard as an unhappy creature, and very probably you are right. But I certainly know of you what you only think of me—there is the difference.

COMPANION. I see, Apollodorus, that you are just the same—always speaking evil of yourself, and of others; and I do believe that you pity all mankind, with the exception of Socrates, yourself first of all, true in this to your old name, which, however deserved, I know not how you acquired, of Apollodorus the madman; for you are always raging against yourself and everybody but Socrates.

APOLLODORUS. Yes, friend, and the reason why I am said to be mad and out of my wits is just because I have these notions of myself and you; no other evidence is required.

COM. No more of that, Apollodorus; but let me renew my request that you would repeat the conversation.

APOLL. Well, the tale of love was on this wise—but, perhaps, I had better begin at the beginning, and endeavor to give you the exact words of Aristodemus:

He said that he met Socrates fresh from the bath and sandalled; and as the sight of the sandals was unusual, he asked him whither he was going that he had been converted into such a beau.

To a banquet at Agathon's, he replied, whose invitation to his sacrifice of victory I refused yesterday, fearing a crowd, but promising that I would come today instead; and so I have put on my finery, because he is such a fine man. What say you to going with me unasked?

I will do as you bid me, I replied.

Follow then, he said, and let us demolish the proverb:

To the feasts of inferior men the good unbidden go;

instead of which our proverb will run:

To the feasts of the good the good unbidden go—

and this alteration may be supported by the authority of Homer himself, who not only demolishes but literally outrages the proverb. For, after picturing Agamemnon as the most valiant of men, he makes Menelaus, who is but a faint-hearted warrior, come unbidden to the banquet of Agamemnon, who is feasting and offering sacrifices, not the better to the worse, but the worse to the better.

I rather fear, Socrates, said Aristodemus, lest this may still be my case; and that, like Menelaus in Homer, I shall be the inferior person, who

To the feasts of the wise unbidden goes.

But I shall say that I was bidden of you, and then you will have to make an excuse.

Two going together,

he replied, in Homeric fashion, one or other of them may invent an excuse by the way.

This was the style of their conversation as they went along. Socrates dropped behind in a fit of abstraction, and desired Aristodemus, who was waiting, to go on before him. When he reached the house of Agathon he found the doors wide open, and a comical thing happened. A servant coming out met him, and led him at once into the banqueting-hall in which the guests were reclining, for the banquet was about to begin. Welcome, Aristodemus, said Agathon, as soon as he appeared—you are just in time to sup with us; if you come on any other matter put it off and make one of us, as I was looking for you yesterday and meant to have asked you, if I could have found you. But what have you done with Socrates?

I turned round, but Socrates was nowhere to be seen; and I had to explain that he had been with me a moment before, and that I came by his invitation to the supper.

You were quite right in coming, said Agathon; but where is he himself?

He was behind me just now, as I entered, he said, and I cannot think what has become of him.

Go and look for him, boy, said Agathon, and bring him in; and do you, Aristodemus, meanwhile take the place by Eryximachus.

The servant then assisted him to wash, and he lay down, and presently another servant came in and reported that our friend Socrates had retired into the portico of the neighboring house. "There he is fixed," said he, "and when I call to him he will not stir."

How strange, said Agathon; then you must call him again, and keep calling him.

Let him alone, said my informant; he has a way of stopping anywhere and losing himself without any reason. I believe that he will soon appear; do not therefore disturb him.

Well, if you think so, I will leave him, said Agathon. And then, turning to the servants, he added, "Let us have supper without waiting for him. Serve up whatever you please, for there is no one to give you orders; hitherto I have never left you to yourselves. But on this occasion imagine that you are our hosts, and that I and the company are your guests; treat us well, and then we shall commend you." After this, supper was served, but still no Socrates; and during the meal Agathon several times expressed a wish to send for him, but Aristodemus objected; and at last when the feast was about half over—for the fit, as usual, was not of long duration— Socrates entered. Agathon, who was reclining alone at the end of the table, begged that he would take the place next to him; that "I may touch you," he said, "and have the benefit of that wise thought which came into your mind in the portico, and is now in your possession; for I am certain that you would not have come away until you had found what you sought."

How I wish, said Socrates, taking his place as he was desired, that wisdom could be infused by touch, out of the fuller into the emptier man, as water runs through wool out of a fuller cup into an emptier one; if that were so, how greatly should I value the privilege of reclining at your side! For you would have filled me full with a stream of wisdom plenteous and fair; whereas my own is of a very mean and question-able sort, no better than a dream. But yours is bright and full of promise, and was manifested forth in all the splendor of youth the day before yesterday, in the presence of more than thirty thousand Hellenes.

You are mocking, Socrates, said Agathon, and ere long you and I will have to determine who bears off the palm of wisdom—of this Dionysus shall be the judge; but at present you are better occupied with supper.

Socrates took his place on the couch and supped with the rest; and then libations were offered, and after a hymn had been sung to the god, and there had been the usual cere-monies, they were about to commence drinking, when Pausanias said, And now, my friends, how can we drink with least injury to ourselves? I can assure you that I feel severely the effect of yesterday's potations and must have time to recover; and I suspect that most of you are in the same predicament, for you were of the party yesterday. Consider then: How can the drinking be made easiest?

I entirely agree, said Aristophanes, that we should, by all means, avoid hard drinking, for I was myself one of those who were yesterday drowned in drink.

I think that you are right, said Eryximachus, the son of Acumenus; but I should still like to hear one other person speak: Is Agathon able to drink hard?

I am not equal to it, said Agathon.

Then, said Eryximachus, the weak heads like myself, Aristodemus, Phaedrus, and others who never can drink, are fortunate in finding that the stronger ones are not in a drinking mood. (I do not include Socrates, who is able either to drink or to abstain, and will not mind whichever we do.) Well, as none of the company seem disposed to drink much, I may be forgiven for saying, as a physician, that drinking deep is a bad practice, which I never follow if I can help, and certainly do not recommend to another, least of all to any one who still feels the effects of yesterday's carouse.

I always do what you advise, and especially what you prescribe as a physician, rejoined Phaedrus the Myrrhinusian, and the rest of the company, if they are wise, will do the same.

It was agreed that drinking was not to be the order of the day, but that they were all to drink only so much as they pleased.

Then, said Eryximachus, as you are all agreed

that drinking is to be voluntary and that there is to be no compulsion, I move, in the next place, that the flute-girl who has just made her appearance be told to go away and play to herself, or, if she likes to the women who are within. Today let us have conversation instead; and, if you will allow me, I will tell you what sort of conversation. This proposal having been accepted, Eryximachus proceeded as follows:

I will begin, he said, after the manner of Melanippe in Euripides,

Not mine the word

which I am about to speak, but that of Phaedrus. For often he says to me in an indignant tone: "What a strange thing it is, Eryximachus, that, whereas other gods have poems and hymns made in their honor, the great and glorious god Love has no encomiast among all the poets who are so many. There are the worthy sophists, too—the excellent Prodicus, for example—who have descanted in prose on the virtues of Heracles and other heroes; and, what is still more extraordinary, I have met with a philosophical work in which the utility of salt has been made the theme of an eloquent discourse; and many other like things have had a like honor bestowed upon them. And only to think that there should have been an eager interest created about them, and yet that to this day no one has ever dared worthily to hymn Love's praises! So entirely has this great deity been neglected." Now in this Phaedrus seems to me to be quite right, and therefore I want to offer him a contribution; also I think that at the present moment we who are here assembled cannot do better than honor the god Love. If you agree with me, there will be no lack of conversation; for I mean to propose that each of us in turn, going from left to right, shall make a speech in honor of Love. Let him give us the best which he can; and Phaedrus, because he is sitting first on the left hand, and because he is the father of the thought, shall begin.

No one will vote against you, Eryximachus, said Socrates. How can I oppose your motion, who profess to understand nothing but matters of love; nor, I presume, will Agathon and Pausanias; and there can be no doubt of Aristophanes, whose whole concern is with Dionysus and Aphrodite; nor will any one disagree of those whom I see around me. The proposal, as I am aware, may seem rather hard upon us whose place is last; but we shall be contented if we hear some good speeches first. Let Phaedrus begin the praise of Love, and good luck to him. All the company expressed their assent, and desired him to do as Socrates bade him.

Aristodemus did not recollect all that was said, nor do I recollect all that he related to me; but I will tell you what I thought most worthy of remembrance, and what the chief speakers said.

Phaedrus began by affirming that Love is a mighty god, and wonderful among gods and men, but especially wonderful in his birth. For he is the eldest of the gods, which is an honor to him; and a proof of his claim to this honor is that of his parents there is no memorial; neither poet nor prose-writer has ever affirmed that he had any. As Hesiod says:

First Chaos came, and then broad-bosomed Earth,
The everlasting seat of all that is,
And Love.

[*Phaedrus continues to praise Love in general terms until Pausanias interrupts him to describe the "manly" love of soldiers, whose bravery is increased by fighting before the eyes of their lover-companions.*]

Pausanias came to a pause—this is the balanced way in which I have been taught by the wise to speak; and Aristodemus said that the turn of Aristophanes was next, but either he had eaten too much or from some other cause, he had the hiccough, and was obliged to change turns with Eryximachus, the physician, who was reclining on the couch below him. Eryximachus, he said, you ought either to stop my hiccough, or to speak in my turn until I have left off.

I will do both, said Eryximachus: I will speak in your turn, and do you speak in mine; and while I am speaking let me recommend you to hold your breath, and if after you have done so for some time the hiccough is not better, then gargle with a little water; and if it still continues, tickle your nose with something and sneeze; and if you sneeze once or twice, even the most violent hiccough is sure to go. I will do as you prescribe, said Aristophanes, and now get on.

Eryximachus spoke as follows: Seeing that Pausanias made a fair beginning and but a lame ending, I must endeavor to supply his deficiency. I think that he has rightly distinguished two kinds of love. But my art further informs me that the double love is not merely an affection of the soul of man towards the fair, or towards anything, but is to be found in the bodies of all animals and in productions of the earth, and I may say in all that is; such is the conclusion which I seem to have gathered from my own art of medicine, whence I learn how great and wonderful and universal is the deity of love, whose empire extends over all things, divine as well as human. And from medicine I will begin that I may do honor to my art. There are in the human body these two kinds of love, which are confessedly different and unlike, and being unlike, they have loves and desires which are unlike; and the desire of the healthy is one, and the desire of the diseased is another; and as Pausanias was just now saying that to indulge good men is honorable, and bad men dishonorable—so, too, in the body the good and healthy elements are to be indulged, and the bad elements and the elements of disease are not to be indulged, but discouraged. And this is what the physician has to do, and in this the art of medicine consists; for medicine may be regarded generally as the knowledge of the loves and desires of the body, and how to satisfy them or not; and the best physician is he who is able to separate fair love from foul, or to convert one into the other; and he who knows how to eradicate and how to implant love,

whichever is required, and can reconcile the most hostile elements in the constitution and make them loving friends, is a skilful practitioner. Now the most hostile are the most opposite, such as hot and cold, bitter and sweet, moist and dry, and the like. And my ancestor, Asclepius, knowing how to implant friendship and accord in these elements, was the creator of our art, as our friends the poets here tell us, and I believe them; and not only medicine in every branch, but the arts of gymnastic and husbandry are under his dominion. Any one who pays the least attention to the subject will also perceive that in music there is the same reconciliation of opposites; and I suppose that this must have been the meaning of Heracleitus, although his words are not accurate; for he says that The One is united by disunion, like the harmony of the bow and the lyre. Now there is an absurdity in saying that harmony is discord or is composed of elements which are still in a state of discord. But what he probably meant was that harmony is composed of differing notes of higher or lower pitch which disagreed once, but are now reconciled by the art of music; for if the higher and lower notes still disagreed, there could be no harmony—clearly not. For harmony is a symphony, and symphony is an agreement; but an agreement of disagreements while they disagree there cannot be; you cannot harmonize that which disagrees. In like manner rhythm is compounded of elements short and long, once differing and now in accord; which accordance, as in the former instance medicine, so in all these other cases music, implants, making love and unison to grow up among them; and thus music, too, is concerned with the principles of love in their application to harmony and rhythm. Again, in the essential nature of harmony and rhythm there is no difficulty in discerning love which has not yet become double. But when you want to use them in actual life, either in the composition of songs or in the correct performance of airs or meters composed already, which latter is called education, then the difficulty begins, and the good artist is needed. Then the old tale has to be repeated of fair and heavenly love—the love of Urania the fair and heavenly muse, and of the duty of accepting the temperate, and those who are as yet intemperate only that they may become temperate, and of preserving their love; and, again, of the vulgar Polyhymnia, who must be used with circumspection that the pleasure be enjoyed, but may not generate licentiousness; just as in my own art it is a great matter so to regulate the desires of the epicure that he may gratify his tastes without the attendant evil of disease. Whence I infer that in music, in medicine, in all other things human as well as divine, both loves ought to be noted as far as may be, for they are both present.

The course of the seasons is also full of both these principles; and when, as I was saying, the elements of hot and cold, moist and dry, attain the harmonious love of one another and blend in temperance and harmony, they bring to men, animals, and plants health and plenty, and do them no harm; whereas the wanton love, getting the upper hand and affecting the seasons of the year, is very destructive and injurious, being the source of pestilence, and bringing many other kinds of diseases on animals and plants; for hoarfrost and hail and blight spring from the excesses and disorders of these elements of love, which to know in relation to the revolutions of the heavenly bodies and the seasons of the year is termed astronomy. Furthermore all sacrifices and the whole province of divination, which is the art of communion between gods and men— these, I say, are concerned only with the preservation of the good and the cure of the evil love. For all manner of impiety is likely to ensue if, instead of accepting and honoring and reverencing the harmonious love in all his actions, a man honors the other love, whether in his feelings towards gods or parents, towards the living or the dead. Wherefore the business of divination is to see to these loves and to heal them, and divination is the peacemaker of gods and men, working by a knowledge of the religious or irreligious tendencies which exist in human loves. Such is the great and mighty, or rather omnipotent force of love in general. And the love, more especially, which is concerned with the good, and which is perfected in company with temperance and justice, whether among gods or men, has the greatest power and is the source of all our happiness and harmony, and makes us friends with the gods who are above us, and with one another. I dare say that I too have omitted several things which might be said in praise of Love, but this was not intentional, and you, Aristophanes, may now supply the omission or take some other line of commendation; for I perceive that you are rid of the hiccough.

Yes, said Aristophanes, who followed, the hiccough is gone; not, however, until I applied the sneezing; and I wonder whether the harmony of the body has a love of such noises and ticklings, for I no sooner applied the sneezing than I was cured.

Eryximachus said: Beware, friend Aristophanes, although you are going to speak, you are making fun of me; and I shall have to watch and see whether I cannot have a laugh at your expense, when you might speak in peace.

You are quite right, said Aristophanes, laughing. I will unsay my words; but do you please not to watch me, as I fear that in the speech which I am about to make, instead of others laughing with me, which is to the manner born of our muse and would be all the better, I shall only be laughed at by them.

Do you expect to shoot your bolt and escape, Aristophanes? Well, perhaps if you are very careful and bear in mind that you will be called to account, I may be induced to let you off.

Aristophanes professed to open another vein of discourse; he had a mind to praise Love in another way, unlike that either of Pausanias or Eryximachus. Mankind, he said, judging by their neglect of him, have never, as I think, at all understood the power of Love. For if they had understood him they would surely have built noble temples and altars, and offered solemn sacrifices in his honor; but this is not done, and most certainly ought to be done: since of all the gods he is the best friend of men, the helper and the healer of the ills which are the great impediment to the happiness of the race. I will try to describe his power to you, and you shall teach the rest of the world what I am teaching you. In the first place, let me treat of the nature of man and what has happened to it; for the original human nature was not like the present, but different. The sexes were not two as they are now, but originally three in number; there was man, woman, and the union of the two, having a name corresponding to this double nature, which had once a real existence but is now lost, and the word "Androgynous" is only preserved as a term of reproach. In the second place, the primeval man was round, his back and sides forming a circle; and he had four hands and four feet, one head with two faces, looking opposite ways, set on a round neck and precisely alike; also four ears, two privy members, and the remainder to correspond. He could walk upright as men now do, backward or forward as he pleased, and he could also roll over and over at a great pace, turning on his four hands and four feet, eight in all, like tumblers going over and over with their legs in the air; this was when he wanted to run fast. Now the sexes were three, and such as I have described them; because the sun, moon, and earth are three; and the man was originally the child of the sun, the woman of the earth, and the man-woman of the moon, which is made up of sun and earth, and they were all round and moved round and round like their parents. Terrible was their might and strength, and the thoughts of their hearts were great, and they made an attack upon the gods; of them is told the tale of Otys and Ephialtes who, as Homer says, dared to scale heaven, and would have laid hands upon the gods. Doubt reigned in the celestial councils. Should they kill them and annihilate the race with thunderbolts, as they had done the giants, then there would be an end of the sacrifices and worship which men

offered to them; but, on the other hand, the gods could not suffer their insolence to be unrestrained. At last, after a good deal of reflection, Zeus discovered a way. He said: "Methinks I have a plan which will humble their pride and improve their manners; men shall continue to exist, but I will cut them in two and then they will be diminished in strength and increased in numbers; this will have the advantage of making them more profitable to us. They shall walk upright on two legs, and if they continue insolent and will not be quiet, I will split them again and they shall hop about on a single leg." He spoke and cut men in two, like a sorbapple which is halved for pickling, or as you might divide an egg with a hair; and as he cut them one after another, he bade Apollo give the face and the half of the neck a turn in order that the man might contemplate the section of himself: he would thus learn a lesson of humility. Apollo was also bidden to heal their wounds and compose their forms. So he gave a turn to the face and pulled the skin from the sides all over that which in our language is called the belly, like the purses which draw in, and he made one mouth at the centre, which he fastened in a knot (the same which is called the navel); he also molded the breast and took out most of the wrinkles, much as a shoemaker might smooth leather upon a last; he left a few, however, in the region of the belly and navel, as a memorial of the primeval state. After the division the two parts of man, each desiring his other half, came together, and throwing their arms about one another, entwined in mutual embraces, longing to grow into one, they were on the point of dying from hunger and self-neglect because they did not like to do anything apart; and when one of the halves died and the other survived, the survivor sought another mate, man or woman, as we call them—being the sections of entire men or women—and clung to that. They were being destroyed, when Zeus in pity of them invented a new plan: he turned the parts of generation round to the front, for this had not been always their position, and they sowed the seed no longer as hitherto like grasshoppers in the ground, but in one another; and after the transposition the male generated in the female in order that by the mutual embraces of man and woman they might breed, and the race might continue; or if man came to man they might be satisfied, and rest, and go their ways to the business of life: so ancient is the desire of one another which is implanted in us, reuniting our original nature, making one of two, and healing the state of man. Each of us when separated, having one side only, like a flat fish, is but the indenture of a man, and he is always looking for his other half. Men who are a section of that double nature which was once called Androgynous are lovers of women; adulterers are generally of this breed, and also adulterous women who lust after men. The women who are a section of the woman do not care for men, but have female attachments; the female companions are of this sort. But they who are a section of the male follow the male, and while they are young, being slices of the original man, they hang about men and embrace them, and they are themselves the best of boys and youths because they have the most manly nature. Some indeed assert that they are shameless, but this is not true; for they do not act thus from any want of shame, but because they are valiant and manly, and have a manly countenance, and they embrace that which is like them. And these when they grow up become our statesmen, and these only, which is a great proof of the truth of what I am saying. When they reach manhood they are lovers of youth, and are not naturally inclined to marry or beget children—if at all, they do so only in obedience to the law; but they are satisfied if they may be allowed to live with one another unwedded; and such a nature is prone to love and ready to return love, always embracing that which is akin to him. And when one of them meets with his other half, the actual half of himself, whether he be a lover of youth or a lover of another sort, the pair are lost in an amazement of love and friendship and intimacy, and will not be out of the other's sight, as I may say, even for a moment: these are the people who pass their whole lives together; yet they could not explain what they desire of one another. For the intense yearning which each of them has towards the other does not appear to be the desire of lover's intercourse, but of something else which the soul of either evidently desires and cannot tell, and of which she has only a dark and doubtful presentiment. Suppose Hephaestus, with his instruments, to come to the pair who are lying side by side and to say to them, "What do you people want of one another?" they would be unable to explain. And suppose further that when he saw their perplexity he said: "Do you desire to be wholly one; always day and night to be in one another's company? for if this is what you desire, I am ready to melt you into one and let you grow together, so that being two you shall become one, and while you live, live a common life as if you were a single man, and after your death in the world below still be one departed soul instead of two—I ask whether this is what you lovingly desire, and whether you are satisfied to attain this?"—there is not a man of them who when he heard the proposal would deny or would not acknowledge that this meeting and melting into one another, this becoming one instead of two, was the very expression of his ancient need. And the reason is that human nature was originally one and we were a whole, and the desire and pursuit of the whole is called love. There was a time, I say, when we were one, but now because of the wickedness of mankind god has dispersed us, as the Arcadians were dispersed into villages by the Lacedaemonians. And if we are not obedient to the gods, there is a danger that we shall be split up again and go about in basso-relievo, like the profile figures having only half a nose which are sculptured on monuments, and that we shall be like tallies. Wherefore let us exhort all men to piety, that we may avoid evil and obtain the good, of which Love is to us the lord and minister; and let no one oppose him—he is the enemy of the gods who oppose him. For if we are friends of the god and at peace with him we shall find our own true loves, which rarely happens in this world at present. I am serious, and therefore I must beg Eryximachus not to make fun or to find any allusion in what I am saying to Pausanias and Agathon, who, as I suspect, are both of the manly nature and belong to the class which I have been describing. But my words have a wider application—they include men and women everywhere; and I believe that if our loves were perfectly accomplished, and each one returning to his primeval nature had his original true love, then our race would be happy. And if this would be best of all, the best in the next degree and under present circumstances must be the nearest approach to such an union; and that will be the attainment of a congenial love. Wherefore, if we would praise him who has given to us the benefit, we must praise the god Love, who is our greatest benefactor, both leading us in this life back to our own nature and giving us high hopes for the future, for he promises that if we are pious he will restore us to our original state, and heal us and make us happy and blessed. This, Eryximachus, is my discourse of love, which, although different to yours, I must beg you to leave unassailed by the shafts of your ridicule, in order that each may have his turn; each, or either, for Agathon and Socrates are the only ones left.

Indeed, I am not going to attack you, said Eryximachus, for I thought your speech charming, and did I not know that Agathon and Socrates are masters in the art of love, I should be really afraid that they would have nothing to say, after the world of things which have been said already. But, for all that, I am not without hopes.

Socrates said: You played your part well, Eryximachus; but if you were as I am now, or rather as I shall be when Agathon has spoken, you would, indeed, be in a great strait.

You want to cast a spell over me, Socrates, said Agathon, in the hope that I may be dis-concerted at the expectation raised among the audience that I shall speak well.

I should be strangely forgetful, Agathon, replied Socrates, of the courage and magnanimity which you showed when your own compositions were about to be exhibited, and you came upon the stage with the actors and faced the vast theatre altogether undismayed, if I thought that your nerves could be fluttered at a small party of friends.

Do you think, Socrates, said Agathon, that my head is so full of the theatre as not to know how much more formidable to a man of sense a few good judges are than many fools?

Nay, replied Socrates, I should be very wrong in attributing to you, Agathon, that or any other want of refinement. And I am quite aware that if you happen to meet with any whom you thought wise, you would care for their opinion much more than for that of the many. But then we, having been a part of the foolish many in the theatre, cannot be regarded as the select wise; though I know that if you chanced to be in the presence, not of one of ourselves, but of some really wise man, you would be ashamed of disgracing yourself before him—would you not?

Yes, said Agathon.

But before the many you would not be ashamed if you thought that you were doing something disgraceful in their presence?

Here Phaedrus interrupted them, saying: Do not answer him, my dear Agathon; for if he can only get a partner with whom he can talk, especially a good-looking one, he will no longer care about the completion of our plan. Now I love to hear him talk; but just at present I must not forget the encomium on Love which I ought to receive from him and from every one. When you and he have paid your tribute to the god, then you may talk.

Very good, Phaedrus, said Agathon; I see no reason why I should not proceed with my speech, as I shall have many other opportunities of conversing with Socrates. Let me say first how I ought to speak, and then speak:

The previous speakers, instead of praising the god Love, or unfolding his nature, appear to have congratulated mankind on the benefits which he confers upon them. But I would rather praise the god first, and then speak of his gifts; this is always the right way of praising everything. May I say without impiety or offense that of all the blessed gods he is the most blessed because he is the fairest and best? And he is the fairest; for, in the first place, he is the youngest, and of his youth he is himself the witness, fleeing out of the way of age, who is swift enough, swifter truly than most of us like: Love hates him and will not come near him; but youth and love live and move together—like to like, as the proverb says. Many things were said by Phaedrus about Love in which I agree with him; but I cannot agree that he is older than Iapetus and Kronos—not so; I maintain him to be the youngest of the gods, and youthful ever. The ancient doings among the gods of which Hesiod and Parmenides spoke, if the tradition of them be true, were done of Necessity and not of Love; had Love been in those days, there would have been no chaining or mutilation of the gods, or other violence, but peace and sweetness, as there is now in heaven, since the rule of Love began. Love is young and also tender; he ought to have a poet like Homer to describe his tenderness, as Homer says of Ate, that she is a goddess and tender:

Her feet are tender, for she sets her steps,
Not on the ground but on the heads of men:

herein is an excellent proof of her tenderness—that she walks not upon the hard but upon the soft. Let us adduce a similar proof of the tenderness of Love; for he walks not upon the earth, nor yet upon the skulls of men, which are not so very soft, but in the hearts and souls of both gods and men, which are of all things the softest; in them he walks and dwells and makes his home. Not in every soul without exception, for where there is hardness he departs, where there is softness there he dwells; and nestling always with his feet and in all manner of ways in the

softest of soft places, how can he be other than the softest of all things? Of a truth, he is the tenderest as well as the youngest, and also he is of flexile form; for if he were hard and without flexure he could not enfold all things, or wind his way into and out of every soul of man undiscovered. And a proof of his flexibility and symmetry of form is his grace, which is universally admitted to be in an especial manner the attribute of Love; ungrace and love are always at war with one another. The fairness of his complexion is revealed by his habitation among the flowers; for he dwells not amid bloomless or fading beauties, whether of body or soul or ought else, but in the place of flowers and scents, there he sits and abides. Concerning the beauty of the god I have said enough; and yet there remains much more which I might say. Of his virtue I have now to speak: his greatest glory is that he can neither do nor suffer wrong to or from any god or any man; for he suffers not by force if he suffers; force comes not near him, neither when he acts does he act by force. For all men in all things serve him of their own free will, and where there is voluntary agreement, there, as the laws which are the lords of the city say, is justice. And not only is he just but exceedingly temperate, for Temperance is the acknowledged ruler of the pleasures and desires, and no pleasure ever masters Love; he is their master and they are his servants; and if he conquers them he must be temperate indeed. As to courage, even the God of War is no match for him; he is the captive and Love is the lord, for love, the love of Aphrodite, masters him, as the tale runs; and the master is stronger than the servant. And if he conquers the bravest of all others, he must be himself the bravest. Of his courage and justice and temperance I have spoken, but I have yet to speak of his wisdom; and according to the measure of my ability I must try to do my best. In the first place he is a poet (and here, like Eryximachus, I magnify my art), and he is also the source of poesy in others, which he could not be if he were not himself a poet. And at the touch of him every one becomes a poet, even though he had no music in him before; this also is a proof that Love is a good poet and accomplished in all the fine arts; for no one can give to another that which he has not himself, or teach that of which he has no knowledge. Who will deny that the creation of the animals is his doing? Are they not all the works of his wisdom, born and begotten of him? And as to the artists, do we not know that he only of them whom love inspires has the light of fame?—he whom Love touches not walks in darkness. The arts of medicine and archery and divination were discovered by Apollo, under the guidance of love and desire; so that he too is a disciple of Love. Also the melody of the Muses, the metallurgy of Hephaestus, the weaving of Athene, the empire of Zeus over gods and men, are all due to Love, who was the inventor of them. And so Love set in order the empire of the gods—the love of beauty, as is evident, for with deformity Love has no concern. In the days of old, as I began by saying, dreadful deeds were done among the gods, for they were ruled by Necessity; but now since the birth of Love, and from the Love of the beautiful, has sprung every good in heaven and earth. Therefore, Phaedrus, I say of Love that he is the fairest and best in himself, and the cause of what is fairest and best in all other things. And there comes into my mind a line of poetry in which he is said to be the god who—

> Gives peace on earth and calms the stormy deep,
> Who stills the winds and bids the sufferer sleep.

This is he who empties men of disaffection and fills them with affection, who makes them to meet together at banquets such as these; in sacrifices, feasts, dances, he is our lord—who sends courtesy and sends away discourtesy, who gives kindness ever and never gives unkindness; the friend of the good, the wonder of the wise, the amazement of the gods; desired by those who have no part in him, and precious to those who have the better part in him; parent of delicacy, luxury, desire, fondness, softness, grace; regard-

ful of the good, regardless of the evil; in every word, work, wish, fear—savior, pilot, comrade, helper; glory of gods and men, leader best and brightest, in whose footsteps let every man follow, sweetly singing in his honor and joining in that sweet strain with which love charms the souls of gods and men. Such is the speech, Phaedrus, half-playful, yet having a certain measure of seriousness, which, according to my ability, I dedicate to the god.

When Agathon had done speaking, Aristodemus said that there was a general cheer; the young man was thought to have spoken in a manner worthy of himself, and of the god. And Socrates, looking at Eryximachus, said: Tell me, son of Acumenus, was there not reason in my fears? and was I not a true prophet when I said that Agathon would make a wonderful oration, and that I should be in a strait?

The part of the prophecy which concerns Agathon, replied Eryximachus, appears to me to be true; but not the other part—that you will be in a strait.

Why, my dear friend, said Socrates, must not I or any one be in a strait who has to speak after he has heard such a rich and varied discourse? I am especially struck with the beauty of the concluding words—who could listen to them without amazement? When I reflected on the immeasurable inferiority of my own powers, I was ready to run away for shame if there had was a possibility of escape. For I was reminded of Gorgias, and at the end of his speech I fancied that Agathon was shaking at me the Gorginian or Gorgonian head of the great master of rhetoric, which was simply to turn me and my speech into stone, as Homer says, and strike me dumb. And then I perceived how foolish I had been in consenting to take my turn with you in praising love, and saying that I too was a master of the art, when I really had no conception how anything ought to be praised. For in my simplicity I imagined that the topics of praise should be true, and that this being presupposed, out of the true the speaker was to choose the best and set them forth in the best manner. And I felt quite proud, thinking that I knew the nature of true praise and should speak well. Whereas I now see that the intention was to attribute to Love every species of greatness and glory, whether really belonging to him or not, without regard to truth or falsehood—that was no matter; for the original proposal seems to have been not that each of you should really praise Love, but only that you should appear to praise him. And so you attribute to Love every imaginable form of praise which can be gathered anywhere; and you say that "he is all this," and "the cause of all that," making him appear the fairest and best of all to those who know him not, for you cannot impose upon those who know him. And a noble and solemn hymn of praise have you rehearsed. But as I misunderstood the nature of the praise when I said that I would take my turn, I must beg to be absolved from the promise which I made in ignorance, and which (as Euripides would say) was a promise of the lips and not of the mind. Farewell then to such a strain: for I do not praise in that way; no, indeed, I cannot. But if you like to hear the truth about love, I am ready to speak in my own manner, though I will not make myself ridiculous by entering into any rivalry with you. Say then, Phaedrus, whether you would like to have the truth about love, spoken in any words and in any order which may happen to come into my mind at the time. Will that be agreeable to you?

Aristodemus said that Phaedrus and the company bid him speak in any manner which he thought best. Then, he added, let me have your permission first to ask Agathon a few more questions, in order that I may take his admissions as the premises of my discourse.

I grant the permission, said Phaedrus: put your question. Socrates then proceeded as follows:

In the magnificent oration which you have just uttered, I think that you were right, my dear Agathon, in proposing to speak of the nature of Love first and afterwards of his works—that is a way of beginning which I very

much approve. And as you have spoken so eloquently of his nature, may I ask you further, whether love is the love of something or of nothing? And here I must explain myself: I do not want you to say that love is the love of a father or the love of a mother—that would be ridiculous; but to answer as you would, if I asked is a father a father of something? to which you would find no difficulty in replying, of a son or daughter: and the answer would be right.

Very true, said Agathon.

And you would say the same of a mother?

He assented.

Yet let me ask you one more question in order to illustrate my meaning: Is not a brother to be regarded essentially as a brother of something?

Certainly, he replied.

That is, of a brother or sister?

Yes, he said.

And now, said Socrates, I will ask about Love: Is Love of something or of nothing?

Of something, surely, he replied.

Keep in mind what this is and tell me what I want to know—whether Love desires that of which love is.

Yes, surely.

And does he possess, or does he not possess, that which he loves and desires?

Probably not, I should say.

Nay, replied Socrates, I would have you consider whether "necessarily" is not rather the word. The inference that he who desires something is in want of something, and that he who desires nothing is in want of nothing, is in my judgment, Agathon, absolutely and necessarily true. What do you think?

I agree with you, said Agathon.

Very good. Would he who is great desire to be great, or he who is strong desire to be strong?

That would be inconsistent with our previous admissions.

True. For he who is anything cannot want to be that which he is?

Very true.

And yet, added Socrates, if a man being strong desired to be strong, or being swift desired to be swift, or being healthy desired to be healthy, in that case he might be thought to desire something which he already has or is. I give the example in order that we may avoid misconception. For the possessors of these qualities, Agathon, must be supposed to have their respective advantages at the time, whether they choose or not; and who can desire that which he has? Therefore, when a person says, I am well and wish to be well, or I am rich and wish to be rich, and I desire simply to have what I have—to him we shall reply: "You, my friend, having wealth and health and strength, want to have the continuance of them; for at this moment, whether you choose or no, you have them. And when you say, I desire that which I have and nothing else, is not your meaning that you want to have what you now have in the future?" He must agree with us—must he not?

He must, replied Agathon.

Then, said Socrates, he desires that what he has at present may be preserved to him in the future, which is equivalent to saying that he desires something which is nonexistent to him, and which as yet he has not got.

Very true, he said.

Then he and every one who desires, desires that which he has not already, and which is future and not present, and which he has not, and is not, and of which he is in want—these are the sort of things which love and desire seek?

Very true, he said.

Then now, said Socrates, let us recapitulate the argument. First, is not love of something, and of something too, which is wanting to a man?

Yes, he replied.

Remember further what you said in your speech, or if you do not remember I will remind you: you said that the love of the beautiful set in order the empire of the gods, for that of deformed things there is no love—did you not say something of that kind?

Yes, said Agathon.

Yes, my friend, and the remark was a just one. And if this is true, Love is the love of beauty and not of deformity?

He assented.

And the admission has been already made that Love is of something which a man wants and has not?

True, he said.

Then Love wants and has not beauty?

Certainly, he replied.

And would you call that beautiful which wants and does not possess beauty?

Certainly not.

Then would you still say that love is beautiful?

Agathon replied: I fear that I did not understand what I was saying.

You made a very good speech, Agathon, replied Socrates; but there is yet one small question which I would fain ask: Is not the good also the beautiful?

Yes.

Then in wanting the beautiful, love wants also the good?

I cannot refute you, Socrates, said Agathon; let us assume that what you say is true.

Say rather, beloved Agathon, that you cannot refute the truth; for Socrates is easily refuted.

And now, taking my leave of you, I will rehearse a tale of love which I heard from Diotima of Mantineia, a woman wise in this and in many other kinds of knowledge, who in the days of old, when the Athenians offered sacrifice before the coming of the plague, delayed the disease ten years. She was my instructress in the art of love, and I shall repeat to you what she said to me, beginning with the admissions made by Agathon, which are nearly if not quite the same which I made to the wise woman when she questioned me: I think that this will be the easiest way, and I shall take both parts myself as well as I can. As you, Agathon, suggested, I must speak first of the being and nature of Love, and then of his works. First I said to her in nearly the same words which he used to me that Love was a mighty god, and likewise fair; and she proved to me as

I proved to him that, by my own showing, Love was neither fair nor good. "What do you mean, Diotima," I said, "is love then evil and foul?" "Hush," she cried; "must that be foul which is not fair?" "Certainly," I said. "And is that which is not wise ignorant? Do you not see that there is a mean between wisdom and ignorance?" "And what may that be?" I said. "Right opinion," she replied, "which, as you know, being incapable of giving a reason, is not knowledge (for how can knowledge be devoid of reason? nor again, ignorance, for neither can ignorance attain the truth), but is clearly something which is a mean between ignorance and wisdom." "Quite true," I replied. "Do not then insist," she said, "that what is not fair is of necessity foul, or what is not good, evil; or infer that because Love is not fair and good he is therefore foul and evil; for he is in a mean between them." "Well," I said, "Love is surely admitted by all to be a great god." "By those who know or by those who do not know?" "By all." "And how, Socrates," she said with a smile, "can Love be acknowledged to be a great god by those who say that he is not a god at all?" "And who are they?" I said. "You and I are two of them," she replied. "How can that be?" I said. "It is quite intelligible," she replied, "for you yourself would acknowledge that the gods are happy and fair—of course you would—would you dare to say that any god was not?" "Certainly not," I replied. "And you mean by the happy those who are the possessors of things good or fair?" "Yes." "And you said that Love, because he was in want, desires those good and fair things of which he is in want?" "Yes, I did." "But how can he be a god who has no portion in what is either good or fair?" "Impossible." "Then you see that you also deny the divinity of Love."

"What then is Love?" I asked; "Is he mortal?" "No." "What then?" "As in the former instance, he is neither mortal nor immortal, but in a mean between the two." "What is he, Diotima?" "He is a great spirit (*daimon*), and like all spirits he is intermediate between the divine and the mortal." "And what," I said, "is his power?" "He interprets," she replied, "between gods and men, conveying and taking across to the gods the prayers and sacrifices of men, and to men the commands and replies of the gods; he is the mediator who spans the chasm which divides them, and therefore in him all is bound together, and through him the arts of the prophet and the priest, their sacrifices and mysteries and charms, and all prophecy and incantation, find their way. For god mingles not with man; but through Love all the intercourse and converse of god with man, whether awake or asleep, is carried on. The wisdom which understands this is spiritual; all other wisdom, such as that of arts and handicrafts, is mean and vulgar. Now these spirits or intermediate powers are many and diverse, and one of them is Love." "And who," I said, "was his father, and who his mother?" "The tale," she said, "will take time; nevertheless I will tell you. On the birthday of Aphrodite there was a feast of the gods, at which the god Poros or Plenty, who is the son of Metis or Discretion, was one of the guests. When the feast was over, Penia or Poverty, as the manner is on such occasions, came about the doors to beg. Now Plenty, who was the worse for nectar (there was no wine in those days), went into the garden of Zeus and fell into a heavy sleep; and Poverty, considering her own straitened circumstances, plotted to have a child by him, and accordingly she lay down at his side and conceived Love, who partly because he is naturally a lover of the beautiful, and because Aphrodite is herself beautiful, and also because he was born on her birthday, is her follower and attendant. And as his parentage is, so also are his fortunes. In the first place, he is always poor, and anything but tender and fair, as the many imagine him; and he is rough and squalid, and has no shoes, nor a house to dwell in; on the bare earth exposed he lies under the open heaven, in the streets, or at the doors of houses, taking his rest; and like his mother he is always in distress. Like his father, too, whom he also partly resembles, he is always plotting against

the fair and good; he is bold, enterprising, strong, a mighty hunter, always weaving some intrigue or other, keen in the pursuit of wisdom, fertile in resources: a philosopher at all times, terrible as an enchanter, sorcerer, sophist. He is by nature neither mortal nor immortal, but alive and flourishing at one moment when he is in plenty, and dead at another moment, and again alive by reason of his father's nature. But that which is always flowing in is always flowing out, and so he is never in want and never in wealth; and, further, he is in a mean between ignorance and knowledge. The truth of the matter is this: no god is a philosopher or seeker after wisdom, for he is wise already; nor does any man who is wise seek after wisdom. Neither do the ignorant seek after wisdom. For herein is the evil of ignorance that he who is neither good nor wise is nevertheless satisfied with himself; he has no desire for that of which he feels no want."
"But who then, Diotima," I said, "are the lovers of wisdom, if they are neither the wise nor the foolish?" "A child may answer that question," she replied; "they are those who are in a mean between the two; Love is one of them. For wisdom is a most beautiful thing, and Love is of the beautiful; and therefore Love is also a philosopher or lover of wisdom, and being a lover of wisdom is in a mean between the wise and the ignorant. And of this, too, his birth is the cause; for his father is wealthy and wise, and his mother poor and foolish. Such, my dear Socrates, is the nature of the spirit Love. The error in your conception of him was very natural and, as I imagine from what you say, has arisen out of a confusion of love and the beloved, which made you think that love was all beautiful. For the beloved is the truly beautiful and delicate and perfect and blessed; but the principle of love is of another nature, and is such as I have described."
I said: "O thou stranger woman, thou sayest well; but, assuming Love to be such as you say, what is the use of him to men?" "That, Socrates," she replied, "I will attempt to unfold: of his nature and birth I have already spoken;

and you acknowledge that love is of the beautiful. But some one will say: Of the beautiful in what, Socrates and Diotima?—or rather let me put the question more clearly, and ask: When a man loves the beautiful, what does he desire?" I answered her "That the beautiful may be his." "Still," she said, "the answer suggests a further question: What is given by the possession of beauty?" "To what you have asked," I replied, "I have no answer ready." "Then," she said, "let me put the word 'good' in the place of the beautiful, and repeat the question once more: If he who loves loves the good, what is it then that he loves?" "The possession of the good," I said. "And what does he gain who possesses the good?" "Happiness," I replied; "there is less difficulty in answering that question." "Yes," she said, "the happy are made happy by the acquisition of good things. Nor is there any need to ask why a man desires happiness; the answer is already final." "You are right," I said. "And is this wish and this desire common to all, and do all men always desire their own good, or only some men?—what say you?" "All men," I replied; "the desire is common to all." "Why, then," she rejoined, "are not all men, Socrates, said to love, but only some of them? whereas you say that all men are always loving the same things." "I myself wonder," I said, "why this is." "There is nothing to wonder at," she replied; "the reason is that one part of love is separated off and receives the name of the whole, but the other parts have other names." "Give an illustration," I said. She answered me as follows: "There is poetry, which, as you know, is complex and manifold. All creation or passage of nonbeing into being is poetry or making, and the processes of all art are creative; and the masters of arts are all poets or makers." "Very true." "Still," she said, "you know that they are not called poets, but have other names; only that portion of the art which is separated off from the rest, and is concerned with music and metre, is termed poetry, and they who possess poetry in this sense of the word are called poets." "Very true," I said. "And the same holds of love. For you may say generally that all desire of good and happiness is only the great and subtle power of love; but they who are drawn towards him by any other path, whether the path of money-making, of gymnastics or philosophy, are not called lovers—the name of the whole is appropriated to those whose affection takes one form only—they alone are said to love, or to be lovers." "I dare say," I replied, "that you are right." "Yes," she added, "and you hear people say that lovers are seeking for their other half; but I say that they are seeking neither for the half of themselves nor for the whole unless the half or the whole be also a good. And they will cut off their own hands and feet and cast them away if they are evil; for they love not what is their own unless perchance there be some one who calls what belongs to him the good, and what belongs to another the evil. For there is nothing which men love but the good. Is there anything?" "Certainly, I should say, that there is nothing." "Then," she said, "the simple truth is that men love the good." "Yes," I said. "To which must be added that they love the possession of the good?" "Yes, that must be added." "And not only the possession, but the everlasting possession of the good?" "That must be added too." "Then love," she said, "may be described generally as the love of the everlasting possession of the good?" "That is most true."

"Then if this be the nature of love, can you tell me further," she said, "what is the manner of the pursuit? What are they doing who show all this eagerness and heat which is called love, and what is the object which they have in view? Answer me." "Nay, Diotima," I replied, "if I had known, I should not have wondered at your wisdom, neither should I have come to learn from you about this very matter." "Well," she said, "I will teach you—the object which they have in view is birth in beauty, whether of body or soul." "I do not understand you." I said; "the oracle requires an explanation." "I will make my meaning clearer," she replied. "I mean to say, that all men are bringing to the birth in their bodies and in their souls. There is a certain age at which human nature is desirous of procreation—procreation which must be in beauty and not in deformity; and this procreation is the union of man and woman, and is a divine thing; for conception and generation are an immortal principle in the mortal creature, and in the inharmonious they can never be. But the deformed is always inharmonious with the divine, and the beautiful harmonious. Beauty, then, is the destiny or goddess of parturition who presides at birth, and therefore, when approaching beauty, the conceiving power is propitious, and diffusive, and benign, and begets and bears fruit; at the sight of ugliness she frowns and contracts and has a sense of pain, and turns away, and shrivels up, and not without a pang refrains from conception. And this is the reason why, when the hour of conception arrives, and the teeming nature is full, there is such a flutter and ecstasy about beauty, whose approach is the alleviation of the pain of travail. For love, Socrates, is not, as you imagine, the love of the beautiful only." "What then?" "The love of generation and of birth in beauty." "Yes," I said. "Yes, indeed," she replied "But why of generation?" "Because to the mortal creature generation is a sort of eternity and immortality," she replied; "and if, as has been already admitted, love is of the everlasting possession of the good, all men will necessarily desire immortality together with good—wherefore love is of immortality."

All this she taught me at various times when she spoke of love. And I remember her once saying to me, "What is the cause, Socrates, of love and the attendant desire? See you not how all animals, birds as well as beasts, in their desire of procreation are in agony when they take the infection of love, which begins with the desire of union; whereto is added the care of offspring, on whose behalf the weakest are ready to battle against the strongest even to the uttermost, and to die for them, and will let themselves be tormented with hunger or suffer anything in order to maintain their young.

Man may be supposed to act thus from reason; but why should animals have these passionate feelings? Can you tell me why?" Again I replied that I did not know. She said to me: "And do you expect ever to become a master in the art of love if you do not know this?" "But I have told you already, Diotima, that my ignorance is the reason why I come to you; for I am conscious that I want a teacher; tell me then the cause of this and of the other mysteries of love." "Marvel not," she said, "if you believe that love is of the immortal, as we have several times acknowledged; for here again, and on the same principle, too, the mortal nature is seeking as far as is possible to be everlasting and immortal: and this is only to be attained by generation because generation always leaves behind a new existence in the place of the old. Nay, even in the life of the same individual there is succession and not absolute unity: a man is called the same, and yet in the short interval which elapses between youth and age, and in which every animal is said to have life and identity, he is undergoing a perpetual process of loss and reparation—hair, flesh, bones, blood, and the whole body are always changing. Which is true not only of the body but also of the soul, whose habits, tempers, opinions, desires, pleasures, pains, fears, never remain the same in any one of us, but are always coming and going; and equally true of knowledge. And what is still more surprising to us mortals, not only do the sciences in general spring up and decay, so that in respect of them we are never the same; but each of them individually experiences a like change. For what is implied in the word 'recollection' but the departure of knowledge which is ever being forgotten and is renewed and preserved by recollection, and appears to be the same although in reality new, according to that law of succession by which all mortal things are preserved, not absolutely the same, but by substitution, the old worn-out mortality leaving another new and similar existence behind—unlike the divine, which is always the same and not another? And in this way,

Socrates, the mortal body, or mortal anything, partakes of immortality; but the immortal in another way. Marvel not then at the love which all men have of their offspring; for that universal love and interest is for the sake of immortality."

I was astonished at her words and said: "Is this really true, O thou wise Diotima?" And she answered with all the authority of an accomplished sophist: "Of that, Socrates, you may be assured—think only of the ambition of men, and you wonder at the senselessness of their ways, unless you consider how they are stirred by the love of an immortality of fame. They are ready to run all risks greater far than they would have run for their children, and to spend money and undergo any sort of toil, and even to die, for the sake of leaving behind them a name which shall be eternal. Do you imagine that Alcestis would have died to save Admetus, or Achilles to avenge Patroclus, or your own Codrus in order to preserve the kingdom for his sons, if they had not imagined that the memory of their virtues, which still survives among us, would be immortal? Nay," she said, "I am persuaded that all men do all things, and the better they are the more they do them, in hope of the glorious fame of immortal virtue; for they desire the immortal.

"Those who are pregnant in the body only betake themselves to women and beget children—this is the character of their love; their offspring, as they hope, will preserve their memory and give them the blessedness and immortality which they desire in the future. But souls which are pregnant—for there certainly are men who are more creative in their souls than in their bodies—conceive that which is proper for the soul to conceive or contain. And what are these conceptions?—wisdom and virtue in general. And such creators are poets and all artists who are deserving of the name inventor. But the greatest and fairest sort of wisdom by far is that which is concerned with the ordering of states and families, and which is called temperance and justice. And he who in youth has the seed of these implanted in him and is himself inspired, when he comes to maturity, desires to beget and generate. He wanders about seeking beauty that he may beget offspring—for in deformity he will beget nothing—and naturally embraces the beautiful rather than the deformed body; above all when he finds a fair and noble and well-nurtured soul, he embraces the two in one person, and to such a one he is full of speech about virtue and the nature and pursuits of a good man; and he tries to educate him; and at the touch of the beautiful which is ever present to his memory, even when absent, he brings forth that which he had conceived long before, and in company with him tends that which he brings forth; and they are married by a far nearer tie and have a closer friendship than those who beget mortal children, for the children who are their common offspring are fairer and more immortal. Who, when he thinks of Homer and Hesiod and other great poets, would not rather have their children than ordinary human ones? Who would not emulate them in the creation of children as theirs, which have preserved their memory and given them everlasting glory? Or who would not have such children as Lycurgus left behind him to be the saviors, not only of Lacedaemon, but of Hellas, as one may say? There is Solon, too, who is the revered father of Athenian law; and many others there are in many other places, both among Hellenes and barbarians, who have given to the world many noble works and have been the parents of virtue of every kind; and many temples have been raised in their honor for the sake of children such as theirs, which were never raised in honor of any one, for the sake of his mortal children.

"These are the lesser mysteries of love into which even you, Socrates, may enter; to the greater and more hidden ones which are the crown of these, and to which, if you pursue them in a right spirit, they will lead, I know not whether you will be able to attain. But I will do my utmost to inform you, and do you follow if you can. For he who would proceed aright in this matter should begin in youth to visit beautiful forms; and, first, if he be guided by his instructor aright to love one such form only—out of that he should create fair thoughts; and soon he will of himself perceive that the beauty of one form is akin to the beauty of another; and then if beauty of form in general is his pursuit, how foolish would he be not to recognize that the beauty in every form is one and the same! And when he perceives this he will abate his violent love of the one, which he will despise and deem a small thing, and will become a lover of all beautiful form; in the next stage he will consider that the beauty of the mind is more honorable than the beauty of the outward form. So that if a virtuous soul have but a little comeliness, he will be content to love and tend him, and will search out and bring to the birth thoughts which may improve the young, until he is compelled to contemplate and see the beauty of institutions and laws, and to understand that the beauty of them all is of one family, and that personal beauty is a trifle; and after laws and institutions he will go on to the sciences, that he may see their beauty, being not like a servant in love with the beauty of one youth or man or institution, himself a slave mean and narrow-minded, but drawing towards and contemplating the vast sea of beauty, he will create many fair and noble thoughts and notions in boundless love of wisdom; until on that shore he grows and waxes strong, and at last the vision is revealed to him of a single science which is the science of beauty everywhere. To this I will proceed; please to give me your very best attention:

"He who has been instructed thus far in the things of love, and who has learned to see the beautiful in due order and succession, when he comes toward the end will suddenly perceive a nature of wondrous beauty (and this, Socrates, is the final cause of all our former toils)—a nature which in the first place is everlasting, not growing and decaying, or waxing and waning; secondly, not fair in one point of view and foul in another, or at one time or in one relation or at one place fair, at another time or in another relation or at another place foul, as if fair to some and foul to others, or in the likeness of a face or hands or any part of the bodily frame, or in any form of speech or knowledge, or existing in any other being, as for example, in an animal, or in heaven, or in earth, or in any other place; but beauty absolute, separate, simple, and everlasting, which without diminution and without increase, or any change, is imparted to the ever-growing and perishing beauties of all other things. He who from these ascending under the influence of true love begins to perceive that beauty, is not far from the end. And the true order of going, or being led by another, to the things of love is to begin from the beauties of earth and mount upwards for the sake of that other beauty, using these as steps only, and from one going on to two, and from two to all fair forms, and from fair forms to fair practices, and from fair practices to fair notions, until from fair notions he arrives at the notion of absolute beauty, and at last knows what the essence of beauty is. This, my dear Socrates," said the stranger of Mantineia, "is that life above all others which man should live, in the contemplation of beauty absolute; a beauty which if you once beheld you would see not to be after the measure of gold, and garments, and fair boys and youths, whose presence now entrances you; and you and many a one would be content to live seeing them only and conversing with them without meat or drink, if that were possible—you only want to look at them and to be with them. But what if man had eyes to see the true beauty— the divine beauty, I mean, pure and clear and unalloyed, not clogged with the pollutions of mortality and all the colors and vanities of human life—thither looking, and holding converse with the true beauty simple and divine? Remember how in that communion only, beholding beauty with the eye of the mind, he will be enabled to bring forth, not images of beauty, but realities (for he has hold not of an image but of a reality), and bringing forth and nourishing true virtue to become the friend of God and be immortal, if mortal man may. Would that be an ignoble life?"

Such, Phaedrus—and I speak not only to you, but to all of you—were the words of Diotima; and I am persuaded of their truth. And being persuaded of them, I try to persuade others that in the attainment of this end human nature will not easily find a helper better than love. And therefore also I say that every man ought to honor him as I myself honor him, and walk in his ways, and exhort others to do the same, and praise the power and spirit of love according to the measure of my ability now and ever.

The words which I have spoken, you, Phaedrus, may call an encomium of love, or anything else which you please.

When Socrates had done speaking, the company applauded, and Aristophanes was beginning to say something in answer to the allusion which Socrates had made to his own speech, when suddenly there was a great knocking at the door of the house, as of revellers, and the sound of a flute-girl was heard. Agathon told the attendants to go and see who were the intruders. "If they are friends of ours," he said, "invite them in, but if not, say that the drinking is over." A little while afterwards they heard the voice of Alcibiades resounding in the court; he was in a great state of intoxication, and kept roaring and shouting, "Where is Agathon? Lead me to Agathon," and at length, supported by the flute-girl and some of his attendants, he found his way to them. "Hail, friends," he said, appearing at the door crowned with a massive garland of ivy and violets, his head flowing with ribands. "Will you have a very drunken man as a companion of your revels? Or shall I crown Agathon, which was my intention in coming, and go away? For I was unable to come yesterday, and therefore I am here today, carrying on my head these ribands, that, taking them from my own head, I may crown the head of this fairest and wisest of men, as I may be allowed to call him. Will you laugh at me because I am drunk? Yet I know very well that I am speaking the truth, although you may laugh. But first tell me; if I come in shall we have the understanding of which I spoke? Will you drink with me or not?''

The company were vociferous in begging that he would take his place among them, and Agathon specially invited him. Thereupon he was led in by the people who were with him; and as he was being led, intending to crown Agathon, he took the ribands from his own head and held them in front of his eyes; he was thus prevented from seeing Socrates, who made way for him, and Alcibiades took the vacant place between Agathon and Socrates, and in taking the place he embraced Agathon and crowned him. Take off his sandals, said Agathon, and let him make a third on the same couch.

By all means; but who makes the third partner in our revels? said Alcibiades, turning round and starting up as he caught sight of Socrates. By Heracles, he said, what is this? Here is Socrates always lying in wait for me, and always, as his way is, coming out at all sorts of unsuspected places; and now, what have you to say for yourself, and why are you lying here, where I perceive that you have contrived to find a place, not by a joker or lover of jokes, like Aristophanes, but by the fairest of the company?

Socrates turned to Agathon and said: I must ask you to protect me, Agathon; for the passion of this man has grown quite a serious matter to me. Since I became his admirer I have never been allowed to speak to any other fair one, or so much as to look at them. If I do, he goes wild with envy and jealousy, and not only abuses me but can hardly keep his hands off me, and at this moment he may do me some harm. Please to see to this, and either reconcile me to him, or, if he attempts violence, protect me, as I am in bodily fear of his mad and passionate attempts.

There can never be reconciliation between you and me, said Alcibiades; but for the present I will defer your chastisement. And I must beg you, Agathon, to give me back some of the ribands that I may crown the marvellous head of this universal despot—I would not have

him complain of me for crowning you, and neglecting him who, in conversation, is the conqueror of all mankind; and this not only once, as you were the day before yesterday, but always. Whereupon, taking some of the ribands, he crowned Socrates, and again reclined.

Then he said: You seem, my friends, to be sober, which is a thing not to be endured; you must drink—for that was the agreement under which I was admitted—and I elect myself master of the feast until you are well drunk. Let us have a large goblet, Agathon, or rather, he said, addressing the attendant, bring me that wine-cooler. The wine-cooler which had caught his eye was a vessel holding more than two quarts—this he filled and emptied, and bade the attendant to fill it again for Socrates. Observe, my friends, said Alcibiades, that this ingenious trick of mine will have no effect on Socrates, for he can drink any quantity of wine and not be at all nearer being drunk. Socrates drank the cup which the attendant filled for him.

Eryximachus said: What is this, Alcibiades? Are we to have neither conversation nor singing over our cups; but simply to drink as if we were thirsty?

Alcibiades replied: Hail, worthy son of a most wise and worthy sire!

The same to you, said Eryximachus; but what shall we do?

That I leave to you, said Alcibiades.

The wise physician skilled our wounds to heal

shall prescribe and we will obey. What do you want?

Well, said Eryximachus, before you appeared we had passed a resolution that each one of us in turn should make a speech in praise of love, and as good a one as he could: the turn was passed round from left to right; and as all of us have spoken, and you have not spoken but have well drunken, you ought to speak, and then impose upon Socrates any task which you please, and he on his right hand neighbor, and so on.

That is good, Eryximachus, said Alcibiades; and yet the comparison of a drunken man's speech with those of sober men is hardly fair; and I should like to know, sweet friend, whether you really believe what Socrates was just now saying; for I can assure you that the very reverse is the fact, and that if I praise any one but himself in his presence, whether God or man, he will hardly keep his hands off me.

For shame, said Socrates.

Hold your tongue, said Alcibiades, for by Poseidon, there is no one else whom I will praise when you are of the company.

Well then, said Eryximachus, if you like, praise Socrates.

What do you think, Eryximachus? said Alcibiades, shall I attack him and inflict the punishment before you all?

What are you about? said Socrates, are you going to raise a laugh at my expense? Is that the meaning of your praise?

I am going to speak the truth if you will permit me.

I not only permit but exhort you to speak the truth.

Then I will begin at once, said Alcibiades, and if I say anything which is not true, you may interrupt me if you will and say "That is a lie," though my intention is to speak the truth. But you must not wonder if I speak anyhow as things come into my mind; for the fluent and orderly enumeration of all your singularities is not a task which is easy to a man in my condition.

And now, my boys, I shall praise Socrates in a figure which will appear to him to be a caricature, and yet I speak, not to make fun of him, but only for the truth's sake. I say that he is exactly like the busts of Silenus which are set up in the statuaries' shops, holding pipes and flutes in their mouths; and they are made to open in the middle, and have images of gods inside them. I say also that he is like Marsyas the satyr. You yourself will not deny, Socrates, that your face is like that of a satyr. Aye, and there is a resemblance in other points, too. For example, you are a bully, as I can prove by witnesses, if you will not confess. And are you not a flute-player? That you are, and a performer far more wonderful than Marsyas. He indeed with instruments used to charm the souls of men by the powers of his breath, and the players of his music do so still; for the melodies of Olympus are derived from Marsyas who taught them, and these, whether they are played by a great master or by a miserable flute-girl, have a power which no others have; they alone possess the soul and reveal the wants of those who have need of gods and mysteries, because they are divine. But you produce the same effect with your words only, and do not require the flute; that is the difference between you and him. When we hear any other speaker, even a very good one, he produces absolutely no effect upon us, or not much, whereas the mere fragments of you and your words, even at second-hand, and however imperfectly repeated, amaze and possess the souls of every man, woman, and child, who comes within hearing of them. And if I were not afraid that you would think me hopelessly drunk, I would have sworn as well as spoken to the influence which they have always had and still have over me. For my heart leaps within me more than that of any Corybantian reveller, and my eyes rain tears when I hear them. And I observe that many others are affected in the same manner. I have heard Pericles and other great orators, and I thought that they spoke well, but I never had any similar feeling; my soul was not stirred by them, nor was I angry at the thought of my own slavish state. But this Marsyas has often brought me to such a pass that I have felt as if I could hardly endure the life which I am leading (this, Socrates, you will admit); and I am conscious that if I did not shut my ears against him, and fly as from the voice of the siren, my fate would be like that of others—he would transfix me, and I should grow old sitting at his feet. For he makes me confess that I ought not to live as I do, neglecting the wants of my own soul and busying myself with the concerns of the Athenians; therefore, I hold my ears and tear myself away from him. And he is the only person who ever made me ashamed, which you might think not to be in my nature, and there is no one else who does the same. For I know that I cannot answer him or say that I ought not to do as he bids, but when I leave his presence the love of popularity gets the better of me. And therefore I run away and fly from him, and when I see him I am ashamed of what I have confessed to him. Many a time have I wished that he were dead, and yet I know that I should be much more sorry than glad if he were to die: so that I am at my wit's end.

And this is what I and many others have suffered from the flute-playing of this satyr. Yet hear me once more while I show you how exact the image is, and how marvellous his power. For let me tell you, none of you know him; but I will reveal him to you; having begun, I must go on. See you how fond he is of the fair? He is always with them and is always being smitten by them, and then again he knows nothing and is ignorant of all things—such is the appearance which he puts on. Is he not like a Silenus in this? To be sure he is; his outer mask is the carved head of the Silenus; but, O my companions in drink, when he is opened, what temperance there is residing within! Know you that beauty and wealth and honor, at which the many wonder, are of no account with him, and are utterly despised by him: he regards not at all the persons who are gifted with them; mankind are nothing to him; all his life is spent in mocking and flouting at them. But when I opened him, and looked within at his serious purpose, I saw in him divine and golden images of such fascinating beauty that I was ready to do in a moment whatever Socrates commanded—they may have escaped the observation of others, but I saw them. Now I fancied that he was seriously enamoured of my beauty, and I thought that I should therefore have a grand opportunity of hearing him tell what he knew, for I had a wonderful opinion of the attractions of my youth. In the prosecution of this design, when I next went to him, I sent away the attendant who usually accompanied me (I will confess the whole truth, and beg you to listen; and if I speak falsely, do you, Socrates, expose the falsehood). Well, he and I were alone together, and I thought that when there was nobody with us, I should hear him speak the language which lovers use to their loves when they are by themselves, and I was delighted. Nothing of the sort; he conversed as usual, and spent the day with me and then went away. Afterwards I challenged him to the palaestra; and he wrestled and closed with me several times when there was no one present; I fancied that I might succeed in this manner. Not a bit; I made no way with him. Lastly, as I had failed hitherto, I thought that I must take stronger measures and attack him boldly, and, as I had begun, not give him up but see how matters stood between him and me. So I invited him to sup with me, just as if he were a fair youth and I a designing lover. He was not easily persuaded to come; he did, however, after a while accept the invitation, and when he came the first time, he wanted to go away at once as soon as supper was over, and I had not the face to detain him. The second time, still in pursuance of my design, after we had supped, I went on conversing far into the night, and when he wanted to go away, I pretended that the hour was late and that he had much better remain. So he lay down on the couch next to me, the same on which he had supped, and there was no one but ourselves sleeping in the apartment. All this may be told without shame to any one. But what follows I could hardly tell you if I were sober. Yet as the proverb says, "*In vino veritas*,"...and therefore I must speak. Nor, again, should I be justified in concealing the lofty actions of Socrates when I come to praise him. Moreover I have felt the serpent's sting; and he who has suffered, as they say, is willing to tell his fellow sufferers only, as they alone will be likely to understand him, and will not be extreme in judging of the sayings or doings which have been wrung from his agony. For I have been bitten by a more than viper's tooth; I have known in my soul, or in my heart, or in some other part, that worst of pangs, more violent in ingenuous youth than any serpent's tooth, the pang of philosophy, which will make a man say or do anything. And you whom I see around me, Phaedrus and Agathon and Eryximachus and Pausanias and Aristodemus and Aristophanes, all of you, and I need not say Socrates himself, have had experience of the same madness and passion in your longing after wisdom. Therefore listen and excuse my doings then and my sayings now. But let the attendants and other profane and unmannered persons close up the doors of their ears.

When the lamp was put out and the servants had gone away, I thought that I must be plain with him and have no more ambiguity. So I gave him a shake, and I said: "Socrates, are you asleep?" "No," he said. "Do you know what I am meditating?" "What are you meditating?" he said. "I think," I replied, "that of all the lovers whom I have ever had you are the only one who is worthy of me, and you appear to be too modest to speak. Now I feel that I should be a fool to refuse you this or any other favor, and therefore I come to lay at your feet all that I have and all that my friends have, in the hope that you will assist me in the way of virtue, which I desire above all things, and in which I believe that you can help me better than any one else. And I should certainly have more reason to be ashamed of what wise men would say if I were to refuse a favor to such as you, than of what the world, who are mostly fools, would say of me if I granted it." To these words he replied in the ironical manner which is so characteristic of him: "Alcibiades, my friend, you have indeed an elevated aim if what you say is true, and if there really is in me any power by which you may become better; truly you must see in me some rare beauty of a kind infinitely higher than any which I see in you. And therefore, if you mean to share with me and to exchange beauty for beauty, you will have greatly the advantage of me; you will gain true beauty in return for appearance—like Diomede, gold in exchange for brass. But look again, sweet friend, and see whether you are not deceived in me. The mind begins to grow critical when the bodily eye fails,

and it will be a long time before you get old." Hearing this, I said: "I have told you my purpose, which is quite serious, and do you consider what you think best for you and me." "That is good," he said; "at some other time then we will consider and act as seems best about this and about other matters." Whereupon I fancied that he was smitten, and that the words which I had uttered like arrows had wounded him, and so without waiting to hear more I got up, and throwing my coat about him crept under his threadbare cloak, as the time of year was winter, and there I lay during the whole night having this wonderful monster in my arms. This again, Socrates, will not be denied by you. And yet, notwithstanding all, he was so superior to my solicitations, so contemptuous and derisive and disdainful of my beauty—which really, as I fancied, had some attractions—hear, O judges; for judges you shall be of the haughty virtue of Socrates—nothing more happened, but in the morning when I awoke (let all the gods and goddesses be my witnesses) I arose as from the couch of a father or an elder brother.

What do you suppose must have been my feelings after this rejection, at the thought of my own dishonor? And yet I could not help wondering at his natural temperance and self-restraint and manliness. I never imagined that I could have met with a man such as he is in wisdom and endurance. And therefore I could not be angry with him or renounce his company any more than I could hope to win him. For I well knew that if Ajax could not be wounded by steel, much less he by money; and my only chance of captivating him by my personal attractions had failed. So I was at my wit's end; no one was ever more hopelessly enslaved by another. All this happened before he and I went on the expedition to Potidaea; there we messed together, and I had the opportunity of observing his extraordinary power of sustaining fatigue. His endurance was simply marvellous when, being cut off from our supplies, we were compelled to go without food—on such occasions, which often happen in time of war, he was superior not only to me but to everybody; there was no one to be compared to him. Yet at a festival he was the only person who had any real powers of enjoyment; though not willing to drink, he could if compelled beat us all at that —wonderful to relate! no human being had ever seen Socrates drunk; and his powers, if I am not mistaken, will be tested before long. His fortitude in enduring cold was also surprising. There was a severe frost, for the winter in that region is really tremendous, and everybody else either remained indoors, or if they went out had on an amazing quantity of clothes and were well shod, and had their feet swathed in felt and fleeces: in the midst of this, Socrates with his bare feet on the ice and in his ordinary dress marched better than the other soldiers who had shoes, and they looked daggers at him because he seemed to despise them.

I have told you one tale, and now I must tell you another which is worth hearing,

Of the doings and sufferings of the enduring man

while he was on the expedition. One morning he was thinking about something which he could not resolve; he would not give it up, but continued thinking from early dawn until noon—there he stood fixed in thought; and at noon attention was drawn to him, and the rumor ran through the wondering crowd that Socrates had been standing and thinking about something ever since the break of day. At last, in the evening after supper, some Ionians out of curiosity (I should explain that this was not in winter but in summer) brought out their mats and slept in the open air that they might watch him and see whether he would stand all night. There he stood until the following morning; and with the return of light he offered up a prayer to the sun and went his way. I will also tell, if you please—and indeed I am bound to tell—of his courage in battle; for who but he saved my life? Now this was the engagement in which I received the prize of valor; for I was wounded and he would not leave me, but he

rescued me and my arms; and he ought to have received the prize of valor which the generals wanted to confer on me partly on account of my rank, and I told them so (this, again, Socrates will not impeach or deny), but he was more eager than the generals that I and not he should have the prize. There was another occasion on which his behavior was very remarkable—in the flight of the army after the battle of Delium, where he served among the heavy-armed—I had a better opportunity of seeing him than at Potidaea, for I was myself on horseback, and therefore comparatively out of danger. He and Laches were retreating, for the troops were in flight, and I met them and told them not to be discouraged, and promised to remain with them; and there you might see him, Aristophanes, as you describe, just as he is in the streets of Athens, stalking like a pelican and, rolling his eyes, calmly contemplating enemies as well as friends, and making very intelligible to anybody, even from a distance, that whoever attacked him would be likely to meet with a stout resistance; and in this way he and his companion escaped—for this is the sort of man who is never touched in war; those only are pursued who are running away headlong. I particularly observed how superior he was to Laches in presence of mind. Many are the marvels which I might narrate in praise of Socrates; most of his ways might perhaps be paralleled in another man, but his absolute unlikeness to any human being that is or ever has been is perfectly astonishing. You may imagine Brasidas and others to have been like Achilles; or you may imagine Nestor and Antenor to have been like Pericles; and the same may be said of other famous men, but of this strange being you will never be able to find any likeness, however remote, either among men who now are or who ever have been—other than that which I have already suggested of Silenus and the satyrs; and they represent in a figure not only himself, but his words. For, although I forgot to mention this to you before, his words are like the images of Silenus which open; they are ridiculous when you first hear them; he clothes himself in language that is like the skin of the wanton satyr—for his talk is of pack-asses and smiths and cobblers and curriers, and he is always repeating the same things in the same words, so that any ignorant or inexperienced person might feel disposed to laugh at him; but he who opens the bust and sees what is within will find that they are the only words which have a meaning in them, and also of the most divine, abounding in fair images of virtue, and of the widest comprehension or rather extending to the whole duty of a good and honorable man.

This, friends, is my praise of Socrates. I have added my blame of him for his ill-treatment of me; and he has ill-treated not only me, but Charmides the son of Glaucon, and Euthydemus the son of Diocles, and many others in the same way—beginning as their lover he has ended by making them pay their addresses to him. Wherefore I say to you, Agathon, "Be not deceived by him; learn from me and take warning, and do not be a fool and learn by experience, as the proverb says."

When Alcibiades had finished, there was a laugh at his outspokenness; for he seemed to be still in love with Socrates. You are sober, Alcibiades, said Socrates, or you would never have gone so far about to hide the purpose of your satyr's praises, for all this long story is only an ingenious circumlocution, of which the point comes in by the way at the end; you want to get up a quarrel between me and Agathon, and your notion is that I ought to love you and nobody else, and that you and you only ought to love Agathon. But the plot of this Satyric or Silenic drama has been detected, and you must not allow him, Agathon, to set us at variance.

I believe you are right, said Agathon, and I am disposed to think that his intention in placing himself between you and me was only to divide us; but he shall gain nothing by that move; for I will go and lie on the couch next to you.

Yes, yes, replied Socrates, by all means come here and lie on the couch below me.

Alas, said Alcibiades, how I am fooled by this man; he is determined to get the better of me at every turn. I do beseech you, allow Agathon to lie between us.

Certainly not, said Socrates, as you praised me, and I in turn ought to praise my neighbor on the right, he will be out of order in praising me again when he ought rather to be praised by me; and I must entreat you to consent to this and not be jealous, for I have a great desire to praise the youth.

Hurrah! cried Agathon, I will rise instantly, that I may be praised by Socrates.

The usual way, said Alcibiades; where Socrates is, no one else has any chance with the fair; and now how readily has he invented a specious reason for attracting Agathon to himself.

Agathon arose in order that he might take his place on the couch by Socrates, when suddenly a band of revellers entered and spoiled the order of the banquet. Some one who was going out having left the door open, they had found their way in and made themselves at home; great confusion ensued, and every one was compelled to drink large quantities of wine. Aristodemus said that Eryximachus, Phaedrus, and others went away—he himself fell asleep and, as the nights were long, took a good rest. He was awakened towards daybreak by a crowing of cocks, and when he awoke, the others were either asleep or had gone away; there remained only Socrates, Aristophanes, and Agathon, who were drinking out of a large goblet which they passed round, and Socrates was discoursing to them. Aristodemus was only half awake, and he did not hear the beginning of the discourse; the chief thing which he remembered was Socrates compelling the other two to acknowledge that the genius of comedy was the same with that of tragedy, and that the true artist in tragedy was an artist in comedy also. To this they were constrained to assent, being drowsy and not quite following the argument. And first of all, Aristophanes dropped off; then, when the day was already dawning, Agathon. Socrates, having laid them to sleep, rose to depart, Aristodemus, as his manner was, following him. At the Lyceum he took a bath and passed the day as usual. In the evening he retired to rest at his own home.

PLINY THE YOUNGER

The Eruption of Vesuvius

TO TACITUS

Your request that I would send you an account of my uncle's end, so that you may transmit a more exact relation of it to posterity, deserves my acknowledgements; for if his death shall be celebrated by your pen, the glory of it, I am aware, will be rendered for ever deathless. For notwithstanding he perished, as did whole peoples and cities, in the destruction of a most beautiful region, and by a misfortune memorable enough to promise him a kind of immortality; nothwithstanding he has himself composed many and lasting works; yet I am persuaded, the mentioning of him in your immortal writings, will greatly contribute to eternize his name. Happy I esteem those, whom Providence has gifted with the ability either to do things worthy of being written, or to write in a manner worthy of being read; but most happy they, who are blessed with both talents: in which latter class my uncle will be placed both by his own writings and by yours. The more willingly do I undertake, nay, solicit, the task you set me.

He was at that time with the fleet under his command at Misenum. On the 24th of August,

THE ERUPTION OF VESUVIUS: Reprinted by permission of the publishers from William Melmoth, translator, *Pliny, Letters.* Cambridge, Mass.: Harvard University Press.

about one in the afternoon, my mother desired him to observe a cloud of very unusual size and appearance. He had sunned himself, then taken a cold bath, and after a leisurely luncheon was engaged in study. He immediately called for his shoes and went up an eminence from whence he might best view this very uncommon appearance. It was not at that distance discernible from what mountain this cloud issued, but it was found afterwards to be Vesuvius. I cannot give you a more exact description of its figure, than by resembling it to that of a pinetree, for it shot up a great height in the form of a trunk, which extended itself at the top into several branches; because I imagine, a momentary gust of air blew it aloft, and then failing, forsook it; thus causing the cloud to expand laterally as it dissolved, or possibly the downward pressure of its own weight produced this effect. It was at one moment white, at another dark and spotted, as if it had carried up earth or cinders.

My uncle, true savant that he was, deemed the phenomenon important and worth a nearer view. He ordered a light vessel to be got ready, and gave me the liberty, if I thought proper, to attend him. I replied I would rather study; and, as it happened, he had himself given me a theme for composition. As he was coming out of the house he received a note from Rectina, the wife of Bassus, who was in the utmost alarm at the imminent danger (his villa stood just below us, and there was no way to escape but by sea); she earnestly entreated him to save her from such deadly peril. He changed his first design and what he began with a philosophical, he pursued with an heroical turn of mind. He ordered large galleys to be launched, and went himself on board one, with the intention of assisting not only Rectina, but many others; for the villas stand extremely thick upon that beautiful coast. Hastening to the place from whence others were flying, he steered his direct course to the point of danger, and with such freedom from fear, as to be able to make and dictate his observations upon the successive motions and figures of that terrific object.

And now cinders, which grew thicker and hotter the nearer he approached, fell into the ships, then pumice-stones too, with stones blackened, scorched, and cracked by fire, then the sea ebbed suddenly from under them, while the shore was blocked up by landslips from the mountains. After considering a moment whether he should retreat, he said to the captain who was urging that course, "Fortune befriends the brave; carry me to Pomponianus." Pomponianus was then at Stabiae, distant by half the width of the bay (for, as you know, the shore, insensibly curving in its sweep, forms here a receptacle for the sea). He had already embarked his baggage; for though at Stabiae the danger was not yet near, it was full in view, and certain to be extremely near, as soon as it spread; and he resolved to fly as soon as the contrary wind should cease. It was full favourable, however, for carrying my uncle to Pomponianus. He embraces, comforts, and encourages his alarmed friend, and in order to soothe the other's fears by his own unconcern, desires to be conducted to a bathroom; and after having bathed, he sat down to supper with great cheerfulness, or at least (what is equally heroic) with all the appearance of it.

In the meanwhile Mount Vesuvius was blazing in several places with spreading and towering flames, whose refulgent brightness the darkness of the night set in high relief. But my uncle, in order to soothe apprehensions, kept saying that some fires had been left alight by the terrified country people, and what they saw were only deserted villas on fire in the abandoned district. After this he retired to rest, and it is most certain that his rest was a most genuine slumber; for his breathing, which, as he was pretty fat, was somewhat heavy and sonorous, was heard by those who attended at his chamber door. But the court which led to his apartment now lay so deep under a mixture of pumice stones and ashes, that if he had continued longer in his bedroom, egress would have been impossible. On being aroused, he came out, and returned to Pomponianus and the others, who

had sat up all night. They consulted together as to whether they should hold out in the house, or wander about in the open. For the house now tottered under repeated and violent concussions, and seemed to rock to and fro as if torn from its foundations. In the open air, on the other hand, they dreaded the falling pumice stones, light and porous though they were; yet this, by comparison, seemed the lesser danger of the two; a conclusion which my uncle arrived at by balancing reasons, and the others by balancing fears. They tied pillows upon their heads with napkins; and this was their whole defense against the showers that fell round them.

It was now day everywhere else, but there a deeper darkness prevailed than in the most obscure night; relieved, however, by many torches and divers illuminations. They thought proper to go down upon the shore to observe from close at hand if they could possibly put out to sea, but they found the waves still run extremely high and contrary. There my uncle having thrown himself down upon a disused sail, repeatedly called for, and drank, a draught of cold water; soon after, flames, and a strong smell of sulphur, which was the forerunner of them, dispersed the rest of the company in flight; him they only aroused. He raised himself up with the assistance of two of his slaves, but instantly fell; some unusually gross vapour, as I conjecture, having obstructed his breathing and blocked his windpipe, which was not only naturally weak and constricted, but chronically inflamed. When day dawned again (the third from that he last beheld) his body was found entire and uninjured, and still fully clothed as in life; its posture was that of a sleeping, rather than a dead man.

Meanwhile my mother and I were at Misenum. But this has no connection with history, and your inquiry went no farther than concerning my uncle's death. I will therefore put an end to my letter. Suffer me only to add, that I have faithfully related to you what I was either an eyewitness of myself, or heard at the time, when report speaks most truly. You will select what is most suitable to your purpose; for there is a great difference between a letter, and an history; between writing to a friend, and writing for the public. Farewell.

DANIEL DEFOE

A Journal of the Plague Year

It was about the beginning of September 1664, that I, among the rest of my neighbors, heard, in ordinary discourse, that the plague was returned again in Holland; for it had been very violent there, and particularly at Amsterdam and Rotterdam, in the year 1663, whither, they say, it was brought, some said from Italy, others from the Levant, among some goods, which were brought home by their Turkey fleet; others said it was brought from Candia; others from Cyprus. It mattered not from whence it came; but all agreed it was come into Holland again.

We had no such thing as printed newspapers in those days to spread rumors and reports of things, and to improve them by the invention of men, as I have lived to see practiced since. But such things as those were gathered from the letters of merchants and others who corresponded abroad, and from them was handed about by word of mouth only; so that things did not spread instantly over the whole nation, as they do now. But is seems that the Government had a true account of it, and several councils were held about ways to prevent its coming over, but all was kept very private. Hence it was that this rumor died off again, and people began to forget it, as a thing we were very little

A JOURNAL OF THE PLAGUE YEAR: From *A Journal of the Plague Year*, first printed in 1722.

concerned in, and that we hoped was not true; till the latter end of November or the beginning of December, 1664, when two men, said to be Frenchmen, died of the plague in Long Acre, or rather at the upper end of Drury Lane. The family they were in endeavored to conceal it as much as possible, but as it had gotten some vent in the discourse of the neighborhood, the Secretaries of State got knowledge of it. And concerning themselves to inquire about it, in order to be certain of the truth, two physicians and a surgeon were ordered to go to the house and make inspection. This they did; and finding evident tokens of the sickness upon both the bodies that were dead, they gave their opinions publicly that they died of the plague. Whereupon it was given in to the parish clerk, and he also returned them to the Hall; and it was printed in the weekly bill of mortality in the usual manner, thus—

Plague, 2. Parishes infected, 1.

The people showed a great concern at this, and began to be alarmed all over the town, and more, because in the last week in December, 1664, another man died in the same house, and of the same distemper. And then we were easy again for about six weeks, when none having died with any marks of infection, it was said the distemper was gone; but after that, I think it was about the 12th of February, another died in another house, but in the same parish and in the same manner.

This turned the people's eyes pretty much towards that end of the town, and the weekly bills showing an increase of burials in St. Giles's parish more than usual, it began to be suspected that the plague was among the people at that end of the town, and that many had died of it, though they had taken care to keep it as much from the knowledge of the public as possible. This possessed the heads of the people very much, and few cared to go through Drury Lane, or the other streets suspected, unless they had extraordinary business that obliged them to it.

This increase of the bills stood thus: the usual

number of burials in a week, in the parishes of St. Giles-in-the-Fields and St. Andrew, Holborn, were from twelve to seventeen or nineteen each, few more or less; but from the time that the plague first began in St. Giles's parish, it was observed that the ordinary burials increased in number considerably. For example:

From December 27 to January 3	...	St. Giles's	...	16
		St. Andrew's	...	17
„ January 3 to January 10	...	St. Giles's	...	12
		St. Andrew's	...	25
„ January 10 to January 17	...	St. Giles's	...	18
		St. Andrew's	...	18
„ January 17 to January 24	...	St. Giles's	...	23
		St. Andrew's	...	16
„ January 24 to January 31	...	St. Giles's	...	24
		St. Andrew's	...	15
„ January 31 to February 7	...	St. Giles's	...	21
		St. Andrew's	...	23
„ February 7 to February 14	...	St. Giles's	...	24

Whereof one of the Plague.

The like increase of the bills was observed in the parishes of St. Bride's, adjoining on one side of Holborn parish, and in the parish of St. James's, Clerkenwell, adjoining on the other side of Holborn; in both which parishes the usual numbers that died weekly were from four to six or eight, whereas at that time they were increased as follows:

From December 20 to December 27	...	St. Bride's	...	0
		St. James's	...	8
„ December 27 to January 3	...	St. Bride's	...	6
		St. James's	...	9
„ January 3 to January 10	...	St. Bride's	...	11
		St. James's	...	7
„ January 10 to January 17	...	St. Bride's	...	12
		St. James's	...	9
„ January 17 to January 24	...	St. Bride's	...	9
		St. James's	...	15
„ January 24 to January 31	...	St. Bride's	...	8
		St. James's	...	12
„ January 31 to February 7	...	St. Bride's	...	13
		St. James's	...	5
„ February 7 to February 14	...	St. Bride's	...	12
		St. James's	...	6

Besides this, it was observed with great uneasiness by the people that the weekly bills in general increased very much during these weeks, although it was at a time of the year when usually the bills are very moderate.

The usual number of burials within the bills of mortality for a week was from about 240 or thereabouts to 300. The last was esteemed a pretty high bill; but after this we found the bills successively increasing, as follows:

		Buried		Increased
December 20 to the 27th	...	291	...	..
„ 27 „ 3rd January	...	349	...	58
January 3 „ 10th	...	394	...	45
„ 10 „ 17th	...	415	...	21
„ 17 „ 24th	...	474	...	59

This last bill was really frightful, being a higher number than had been known to have been buried in one week since the preceding visitation of 1656.

However, all this went off again, and the weather proving cold, and the frost, which began in December, still continuing very severe, even till near the end of February, attended with sharp though moderate winds, the bills decreased again, and the city grew healthy, and everybody began to look upon the danger as good as over; only that still the burials in St. Giles's continued high. From the beginning of April especially they stood at twenty-five each week, till the week from the 18th to the 25th, when there was buried in St. Giles's parish thirty, whereof two of the plague and eight of the spotted fever, which was looked upon as the same thing; likewise the number that died of the spotted fever in the whole increased, being eight the week before, and twelve the week above named.

This alarmed us all again, and terrible apprehensions were among the people, especially the weather being now changed and growing warm, and the summer being at hand. However, the next week there seemed to be some hopes again; the bills were low, the number of the dead in all was but 388; there was none of the plague, and but four of the spotted fever.

But the following week it returned again, and the distemper was spread into two or three other parishes, viz., St. Andrew's, Holborn; St. Clement Danes; and, to the great affliction of the City, one died within the walls, in the parish of St. Mary Woolchurch, that is to say, in Bearbinder Lane, near Stocks Market; in all there were nine of the plague and six of the spotted fever. It was, however, upon inquiry found that this Frenchman who died in Bearbinder Lane was one who, having lived in Long Acre, near the infected houses, had removed for fear of the distemper, not knowing that he was already infected.

This was the beginning of May, yet the weather was temperate, variable, cool enough, and people had still some hopes. That which encouraged them was that the City was healthy, the whole ninety-seven parishes buried but fifty-four, and we began to hope that as it was chiefly among the people at that end of the town, it might go no farther; and the rather because the next week, which was from the 9th of May to the 16th, there died but three, of which not one within the whole City or liberties; and St. Andrew's buried but fifteen, which was very low. 'Tis true St. Giles's buried two-and-thirty, but still, as there was but one of the plague, people began to be easy. The whole bill also was very low, for the week before the bill was but 347, and the week above mentioned but 343. We continued in these hopes for a few days, but it was but for a few, for the people were no more to be deceived thus; they searched the houses, and found that the plague was really spread every way, and that many died of it every day. So that now all our extenuations abated, and it was no more to be concealed; nay, it quickly appeared that the infection had spread itself beyond all hopes of abatement; that in the parish of St. Giles's it was gotten into several streets, and several families lay all sick together; and accordingly, in the weekly bill for the next week the thing began to show itself. There was indeed but fourteen set down of the plague, but this was all knavery and collusion, for in St.

Giles's parish they buried forty in all, whereof it was certain most of them died of the plague, though they were set down of other distempers; and though the number of all the burials were not increased above thirty-two, and the whole bill being but 385, yet there was fourteen of the spotted fever, as well as fourteen of the plague; and we took it for granted upon the whole that there were fifty died that week of the plague.

The next bill was from the 23rd of May to the 30th, when the number of the plague was seventeen. But the burials in St. Giles's were fifty-three—a frightful number—of whom they set down but nine of the plague; but on an examination more strictly by the justices of the peace, and at the Lord Mayor's request, it was found there were twenty more who were really dead of the plague in that parish, but had been set down of the spotted fever or other distempers, besides others concealed.

But those were trifling things to what followed immediately after; for now the weather set in hot, and from the first week in June the infection spread in a dreadful manner, and the bills rose high; the articles of the fever, spotted fever, and teeth began to swell: for all that could conceal their distempers did it, to prevent their neighbors shunning and refusing to converse with them, and also to prevent authority shutting up their houses, which though it was not yet practiced, yet was threatened, and people were extremely terrified at the thoughts of it.

The second week in June, the parish of St. Giles's, where still the weight of the infection lay, buried 120, whereof, though the bills said but sixty-eight of the plague, everybody said there had been 100 at least, calculating it from the usual number of funerals in that parish, as above.

Till this week the City continued free, there having never any died, except that one Frenchman whom I mentioned before, within the whole ninety-seven parishes. Now there died four within the City, one in Wood Street, one in Fenchurch Street, and two in Crooked Lane. Southwark was entirely free, having not one yet died on that side of the water.

I lived without Aldgate, about midway between Aldgate Church and Whitechapel Bars, on the left hand or north side of the street; and as the distemper had not reached to that side of the City, our neighborhood continued very easy. But at the other end of the town their consternation was very great; and the richer sort of people, especially the nobility and gentry from the west part of the City, thronged out of town with their families and servants in an unusual manner; and this was more particularly seen in Whitechapel; that is to say, the Broad Street, where I lived; indeed, nothing was to be seen but wagons and carts, with goods, women, servants, children, &c.; coaches filled with people of the better sort, and horsemen attending them, and all hurrying away; then empty wagons and carts appeared, and spare horses with servants, who, it was apparent, were returning or sent from the country to fetch more people; besides innumerable numbers of men on horseback, some alone, others with servants, and, generally speaking, all loaded with baggage and fitted out for traveling, as anyone might perceive by their appearance.

This was a very terrible and melancholy thing to see, and as it was a sight which I could not but look on from morning to night, for indeed there was nothing else of moment to be seen, it filled me with very serious thoughts of the misery that was coming upon the City, and the unhappy condition of those that would be left in it.

This hurry of the people was such for some weeks that there was no getting at the Lord Mayor's door without exceeding difficulty; there was such pressing and crowding there to get passes and certificates of health for such as traveled abroad, for without these there was no being admitted to pass through the towns upon the road, or to lodge in any inn. Now as there had none died in the City for all this time, my Lord Mayor gave certificates of health without any difficulty to all those who lived in the ninety-seven parishes, and to those within the liberties too for a while.

This hurry, I say, continued some weeks, that is to say, all the month of May and June, and the more because it was rumored that an order of the Government was to be issued out to place turnpikes and barriers on the road to prevent people traveling, and that the towns on the road would not suffer people from London to pass for fear of bringing the infection along with them, though neither of these rumors had any foundation but in the imagination, especially at first.

I now began to consider seriously with myself concerning my own case, and how I should dispose of myself; that is to say, whether I should resolve to stay in London or shut up my house and flee, as many of my neighbors did. I have set this particular down so fully, because I know not but it may be of moment to those who come after me, if they come to be brought to the same distress, and to the same manner of making their choice; and therefore I desire this account may pass with them rather for a direction to themselves to act by than a history of my actings, seeing it may not be of one farthing value to them to note what became of me.

I had two important things before me: the one was the carrying of my business and shop, which was considerable, and in which was embarked all my effects in the world; and the other was the preservation of my life in so dismal a calamity as I saw apparently was coming upon the whole City, and which, however great it was, my fears perhaps, as well as other people's, represented to be much greater than it could be.

The first consideration was of great moment to me. My trade was a saddler, and as my dealings were chiefly not by a shop or chance trade, but among the merchants trading to the English colonies in America, so my effects lay very much in the hands of such. I was a single man, 'tis true, but I had a family of servants whom I kept at my business; had a house, shop, and warehouses filled with goods; and, in short, to leave them all as things in such a case must be left, that is to say, without any overseer or person fit to be trusted with them, had been to hazard the loss not only of my trade, but of my goods, and indeed of all I had in the world.

I had an elder brother at the same time in London, and not many years before come over from Portugal; and advising with him, his answer was in three words, the same that was given in another case quite different, viz., "Master, save thyself." In a word, he was for my retiring into the country, as he resolved to do himself with his family; telling me what he had, it seems, heard abroad, that the best preparation for the plague was to run away from it. As to my argument of losing my trade, my goods, or debts, he quite confuted me. He told me the same thing which I argued for my staying, viz., that I would trust God with my safety and health, was the strongest repulse to my pretensions of losing my trade and my goods. "For," says he, "is it not as reasonable that you should trust God with the chance or risk of losing your trade, as that you should stay in so eminent a point of danger, and trust Him with your life?"

I could not argue that I was in any strait as to a place where to go, having several friends and relations in Northamptonshire, whence our family first came from; and particularly, I had an only sister in Lincolnshire, very willing to receive and entertain me.

My brother, who had already sent his wife and two children into Bedfordshire, and resolved to follow them, pressed my going very earnestly; and I had once resolved to comply with his desires, but at that time could get no horse; for though it is true all the people did not go out of the City of London, yet I may venture to say that in a manner all the horses did; for there was hardly a horse to be bought or hired in the whole City for some weeks. Once I resolved to travel on foot with one servant, and, as many did, lie at no inn, but carry a soldier's tent with us, and so lie in the fields, the weather being very warm, and no danger from taking cold. I say, as many did, because several did so at last, especially those who had been in the armies in the war which had not been many years past;

and I must needs say that, speaking of second causes, had most of the people that traveled done so, the plague had not been carried into so many country towns and houses as it was, to the great damage, and indeed to the ruin, of abundance of people.

But then my servant, whom I had intended to take down with me, deceived me; and being frightened at the increase of the distemper, and not knowing when I should go, he took other measures, and left me, so I was put off for that time; and one way or other, I always found that to appoint to go away was always crossed by some accident or other, so as to disappoint and put it off again....

I went all the first part of the time freely about the streets, though not so freely as to run myself into apparent danger, except when they dug the great pit in the churchyard of our parish of Aldgate. A terrible pit it was, and I could not resist my curiosity to go and see it. As near as I may judge, it was about forty feet in length, and about fifteen or sixteen feet broad, and, at the time I first looked at it, about nine feet deep; but it was said they dug it near twenty feet deep afterwards in one part of it, till they could go no deeper for the water; for they had, it seems, dug several large pits before this. For though the plague was long a-coming to our parish, yet, when it did come, there was no parish in or about London where it raged with such violence as in the two parishes of Aldgate and Whitechapel.

I say they had dug several pits in another ground, when the distemper began to spread in our parish, and especially when the dead-carts began to go about, which was not, in our parish, till the beginning of August. Into these pits they had put perhaps fifty or sixty bodies each; then they made larger holes, wherein they buried all that the cart brought in a week, which, by the middle to the end of August, came to from 200 to 400 a week; and they could not well dig them larger, because of the order of the magistrates confining them to leave no bodies within six feet of the surface; and the water coming on at about seventeen or eighteen feet, they could not well, I say, put more in one pit. But now, at the beginning of September, the plague raging in a dreadful manner, and the number of burials in our parish increasing to more than was ever buried in any parish about London of no larger extent, they ordered this dreadful gulf to be dug, for such it was, rather than a pit.

They had supposed this pit would have supplied them for a month or more when they dug it, and some blamed the church-wardens for suffering such a frightful thing, telling them they were making preparations to bury the whole parish, and the like; but time made it appear the churchwardens knew the condition of the parish better than they did, for the pit being finished the 4th of September, I think, they began to bury in it the 6th, and by the 20th, which was just two weeks, they had thrown into it 1114 bodies, when they were obliged to fill it up, the bodies being then come to lie within six feet of the surface. I doubt not but there may be some ancient persons alive in the parish who can justify the fact of this, and are able to show even in what place of the churchyard the pit lay better than I can. The mark of it also was many years to be seen in the churchyard on the surface, lying in length parallel with the passage which goes by the west wall of the churchyard out of Houndsditch, and turns east again into White-chapel, coming out near the Three Nuns' Inn.

It was about the 10th of September that my curiosity led, or rather drove, me to go and see this pit again, when there had been near 400 people buried in it; and I was not content to see it in the daytime, as I had done before, for then there would have been nothing to have been seen but the loose earth; for all the bodies that were thrown in were immediately covered with earth by those they called the buriers, which at other times were called bearers; but I resolved to go in the night and see some of them thrown in.

There was a strict order to prevent people coming to those pits, and that was only to prevent infection; but after some time that order was more necessary, for people that were infected and near their end, and delirious also, would run to those pits, wrapped in blankets or rugs, and throw themselves in, and, as they said, bury themselves. I cannot say that the officers suffered any willingly to lie there; but I have heard that in a great pit in Finsbury, in the parish of Cripplegate, it lying open then to the fields, for it was not then walled about, they came and threw themselves in, and expired there, before they threw any earth upon them; and that when they came to bury others, and found them there, they were quite dead, though not cold.

This may serve a little to describe the dreadful condition of that day, though it is impossible to say anything that is able to give a true idea of it to those who did not see it, other than this, that it was indeed very, very, very dreadful, and such as no tongue can express.

I got admittance into the churchyard by being acquainted with the sexton who attended, who, though he did not refuse me at all, yet earnestly persuaded me not to go, telling me very seriously, for he was a good, religious, and sensible man, that it was indeed their business and duty to venture, and to run all hazards, and that in it they might hope to be preserved; but that I had no apparent call to it but my own curiosity, which, he said, he believed I would not pretend was sufficient to justify my running that hazard. I told him I had been pressed in my mind to go, and that perhaps it might be an instructing sight, that might not be without its uses. "Nay," says the good man, "if you will venture upon that score, 'Name of God go in; for, depend upon it, 'twill be a sermon to you, it may be, the best that ever you heard in your life. 'Tis a speaking sight," says he, "and has a voice with it, and a loud one, to call us all to repentance"; and with that he opened the door and said, "Go, if you will."

His discourse had shocked my resolution a little, and I stood wavering for a good while, but just at that interval I saw two links come over from the end of the Minories, and heard the bellman, and then appeared a dead-cart, as they called it, coming over the streets; so I could no longer resist my desire of seeing it, and went in. There was nobody, as I could perceive at first, in the churchyard, or going into it, but the buriers and the fellow that drove the cart, or rather led the horse and cart; but when they came up to the pit they saw a man go to and again, muffled up in a brown cloak, and making motions with his hands under his cloak, as if he was in a great agony; and the buriers immediately gathered about him, supposing he was one of those poor delirious or desperate creatures that used to pretend, as I have said, to bury themselves. He said nothing as he walked about, but two or three times groaned very deeply and loud, and sighed as he would break his heart.

When the buriers came up to him they soon found he was neither a person infected and desperate, as I have observed above, or a person distempered in mind, but one oppressed with a dreadful weight of grief indeed, having his wife and several of his children all in the cart that was just come in with him, and he followed in an agony and excess of sorrow. He mourned heartily, as it was easy to see, but with a kind of masculine grief that could not give itself vent by tears; and calmly defying the buriers to let him alone, said he would only see the bodies thrown in and go away; so they left importuning him. But no sooner was the cart turned round and the bodies shot into the pit promiscuously, which was a surprise to him, for he at least expected they would have been decently laid in, though indeed he was afterwards convinced that was impracticable; I say, no sooner did he see the sight but he cried out aloud, unable to contain himself. I could not hear what he said, but he went backward two or three steps and fell down in a swoon. The buriers ran to him and took him up, and in a little while he came to himself, and they led him away to the Pie Tavern over against the end of Houndsditch, where, it seems,

the man was known, and where they took care of him. He looked into the pit again as he went away, but the buriers had covered the bodies so immediately with throwing in earth, that though there was light enough, for there were lanterns, and candles in them, placed all night round the sides of the pit, upon the heaps of earth, seven or eight, or perhaps more, yet nothing could be seen.

This was a mournful scene indeed, and affected me almost as much as the rest; but the other was awful and full of terror. The cart had in it sixteen or seventeen bodies; some were wrapped up in linen sheets, some in rags, some little other than naked, or so loose that what covering they had fell from them in the shooting out of the cart, and they fell quite naked among the rest; but the matter was not much to them, or the indecency much to anyone else, seeing they were all dead, and were to be huddled together into the common grave of mankind, as we may call it, for here was no difference made, but poor and rich went together; there was no other way of burials, neither was it possible there should, for coffins were not to be had for the prodigious numbers that fell in such a calamity as this.

It was reported, by way of scandal upon the buriers, that if any corpse was delivered to them decently wound up, as we called it then, in a winding sheet tied over the head and feet, which some did, and which was generally of good linen; I say, it was reported that the buriers were so wicked as to strip them in the cart and carry them quite naked to the ground. But as I cannot easily credit anything so vile among Christians, and at a time so filled with terrors as that was, I can only relate it and leave it undetermined.

Innumerable stories also went about of the cruel behaviors and practices of nurses who tended the sick, and of their hastening on the fate of those they tended in their sickness. But I shall say more of this in its place.

I was indeed shocked with this sight; it almost overwhelmed me, and I went away with my heart most afflicted, and full of afflicting thoughts, such as I cannot describe. Just at my going out of the church, and turning up the street towards my own house, I saw another cart with links, and a bellman going before, coming out of Harrow Alley in the Butcher Row, on the other side of the way, and being, as I perceived, very full of dead bodies, it went directly over the street also toward the church. I stood awhile, but I had no stomach to go back again to see the same dismal scene over again, so I went directly home, where I could not but consider with thankfulness the risk I had run, believing I had gotten no injury; as indeed I had not.

Here the poor unhappy gentleman's grief came into my head again, and indeed I could not but shed tears in the reflection upon it, perhaps more than he did himself; but his case lay so heavy upon my mind that I could not prevail with myself but that I must go out again into the street, and go to the Pie Tavern, resolving to inquire what became of him.

It was by this time one o'clock in the morning, and yet the poor gentleman was there. The truth was, the people of the house, knowing him, had entertained him, and kept him there all the night, notwithstanding the danger of being infected by him, though it appeared the man was perfectly sound himself.

It is with regret that I take notice of this tavern. The people were civil, mannerly, and an obliging sort of folks enough, and had till this time kept their house open and their trade going on, though not so very publicly as formerly; but there was a dreadful set of fellows that used their house, and who, in the middle of all this horror, met there every night, behaved with all the reveling and roaring extravagances as is usual for such people to do at other times, and indeed to such an offensive degree that the very master and mistress of the house grew first ashamed, and then terrified, at them.

They sat generally in a room next the street; and as they always kept late hours, so when the dead-cart came across the street end to go into Houndsditch, which was in view of the tavern windows, they would frequently open the windows as soon as they heard the bell and look out at them; and as they might often hear sad lamentations of people in the streets or at their windows as the carts went along, they would make their impudent mocks and jeers at them, especially if they heard the poor people call upon God to have mercy upon them, as many would do at those times in their ordinary passing along the streets.

These gentlemen being something disturbed with the clutter of bringing the poor gentleman into the house, as above, were first angry and very high with the master of the house for suffering such a fellow, as they called him, to be brought out of the grave into their house; but being answered that the man was a neighbor, and that he was sound, but overwhelmed with the calamity of his family, and the like, they turned their anger into ridiculing the man and his sorrow for his wife and children, taunted him with want of courage to leap into the great pit and go to heaven, as they jeeringly expressed it, along with them, adding some very profane and even blasphemous expressions....

I acknowledge I was one of those thoughtless ones that had made so little provision that my servants were obliged to go out of doors to buy every trifle by penny and halfpenny, just as before it begun, even till my experience showing me the folly, I began to be wiser so late that I had scarce time to store myself sufficient for our common subsistence for a month.

I had in family only an ancient woman that managed the house, a maidservant, two apprentices, and myself; and the plague beginning to increase about us, I had many sad thoughts about what course I should take, and how I should act. The many dismal objects, which happened everywhere as I went about the streets, had filled my mind with a great deal of horror, for fear of the distemper itself, which was indeed, very horrible in itself, and in some more than in others. The swellings, which were generally in the neck or groin, when they grew hard and would not break, grew so painful that it was equal to the most exquisite torture; and some, not able to bear the torment, threw themselves out at windows or shot themselves, or otherwise made themselves away, and I saw several dismal objects of that kind. Others, unable to contain themselves, vented their pain by incessant roarings, and such loud and lamentable cries were to be heard as we walked along the streets that would pierce the very heart to think of, especially when it was to be considered that the same dreadful scourge might be expected every moment to seize upon ourselves.

I cannot say but that now I began to faint in my resolutions; my heart failed me very much, and sorely I repented of my rashness. When I had been out, and met with such terrible things as these I have talked of; I say I repented my rashness in venturing to abide in town, and I wished often that I had not taken upon me to stay, but had gone away with my brother and his family.

Terrified by those frightful objects, I would retire home sometimes and resolve to go out no more; and perhaps I would keep those resolutions for three or four days, which time I spent in the most serious thankfulness for my preservation and the preservation of my family, and the constant confession of my sins, giving myself up to God every day, and applying to Him with fasting, humiliation, and meditation. Such intervals as I had I employed in reading books and in writing down my memorandums of what occurred to me every day, and out of which, afterwards, I took most of this work, as it relates to my observations without doors. What I wrote of my private meditations I reserve for private use, and desire it may not be made public on any account whatever.

I also wrote other meditations upon divine subjects, such as occurred to me at that time and were profitable to myself, but not fit for any other view, and therefore I say no more of that.

I had a very good friend, a physician, whose name was Heath, whom I frequently visited during this dismal time, and to whose advice I was very much obliged for many things which he directed me to take, by way of preventing the infection when I went out, as he found I frequently did, and to hold in my mouth when I was in the streets. He also came very often to see me, and as he was a good Christian as well as a good physician, his agreeable conversation was a very great support to me in the worst of this terrible time.

It was now the beginning of August, and the plague grew very violent and terrible in the place where I lived, and Dr. Heath coming to visit me, and finding that I ventured so often out in the streets, earnestly persuaded me to lock myself up, and my family, and not to suffer any of us to go out of doors; to keep all our windows fast, shutters and curtains close, and never to open them; but first, to make a very strong smoke in the room where the window or door was to be opened, with rosin and pitch, brimstone or gunpowder, and the like; and we did this for some time; but as I had not laid in a store of provision for such a retreat, it was impossible that we could keep within doors entirely. However, I attempted, though it was so very late, to do something towards it; and first, as I had convenience both for brewing and baking, I went and bought two sacks of meal, and for several weeks, having an oven, we baked all our own bread; also I bought malt, and brewed as much beer as all the casks I had would hold, and which seemed enough to serve my house for five or six weeks; also I laid in a quantity of salt butter and Cheshire cheese; but I had no flesh meat, and the plague raged so violently among the butchers and slaughterhouses on the other side of our street, where they are known to dwell in great numbers, that it was not advisable so much as to go over the street among them.

And here I must observe again that this necessity of going out of our houses to buy provisions was in a great measure the ruin of the whole City, for the people caught the distemper on these occasions one of another, and even the provisions themselves were often tainted; at least I have great reason to believe so; and therefore I cannot say with satisfaction what I know is repeated with great assurance, that the market people and such as brought provisions to town were never infected. I am certain the butchers of Whitechapel, where the greatest part of the flesh meat was killed, were dreadfully visited, and that at last to such a degree that few of their shops were kept open, and those that remained of them killed their meat at Mile End and that way, and brought it to market upon horses.

However, the poor people could not lay up provisions, and there was a necessity that they must go to market to buy, and others to send servants or their children; and as this was a necessity which renewed itself daily, it brought abundance of unsound people to the markets, and a great many that went thither sound brought death home with them.

It is true people used all possible precaution; when anyone bought a joint of meat in the market they would not take it off the butcher's hand, but took it off the hooks themselves. On the other hand, the butcher would not touch the money, but have it put into a pot full of vinegar, which he kept for that purpose. The buyer carried always small money to make up any odd sum, that they might take no change. They carried bottles of scents and perfumes in their hands, and all the means that could be used were used; but then the poor could not do even these things, and they went at all hazards.

Innumerable dismal stories we heard every day on this very account. Sometimes a man or woman dropped down dead in the very markets, for many people that had the plague upon them knew nothing of it till the inward gangrene had affected their vitals, and they died in a few moments. This caused that many died frequently in that manner in the streets suddenly, without any warning; others perhaps had time to go to the next bulk or stall, or to any door or porch, and just sit down and die, as I have said before.

These objects were so frequent in the streets that when the plague came to be very raging on one side, there was scarce any passing by the streets but that several dead bodies would be lying here and there upon the ground. On the other hand, it is observable that though at first the people would stop as they went along and call to the neighbors to come out on such an occasion, yet afterward no notice was taken of them; but that, if at any time we found a corpse lying, go across the way and not come near it; or, if in a narrow lane or passage, go back again and seek some other way to go on the business we were upon; and in those cases the corpse was always left till the officers had notice to come and take them away, or till night, when the bearers attending the dead-cart would take them up and carry them away. Nor did those undaunted creatures who performed these offices fail to search their pockets, and sometimes strip off their clothes if they were well dressed, as sometimes they were, and carry off what they could get.

But to return to the markets. The butchers took that care that if any person died in the market they had the officers always at hand to take them up upon handbarrows and carry them to the next churchyard; and this was so frequent that such were not entered in the weekly bill, "Found dead in the streets or fields," as is the case now, but they went into the general articles of the great distemper....

As for my little family, having thus, as I have said, laid in a store of bread, butter, cheese, and beer, I took my friend and physician's advice, and locked myself up, and my family, and resolved to suffer the hardship of living a few months without flesh meat, rather than to purchase it at the hazard of our lives.

But though I confined my family, I could not prevail upon my unsatisfied curiosity to stay within entirely myself; and though I generally came frighted and terrified home, yet I could not restrain; only that indeed I did not do it so frequently as at first.

I had some little obligations, indeed, upon me to go to my brother's house, which was in

Coleman Street parish, and which he had left to my care, and I went at first every day, but afterwards only once or twice a week.

In these walks I had many dismal scenes before my eyes, as particularly of persons falling dead in the streets, terrible shrieks and screechings of women, who, in their agonies, would throw open their chamber windows and cry out in a dismal, surprising manner. It is impossible to describe the variety of postures in which the passions of the poor people would express themselves.

Passing through Tokenhouse Yard, in Lothbury, of a sudden a casement violently opened just over my head, and a woman gave three frightful screeches, and then cried, "Oh! death, death, death!" in a most inimitable tone, and which struck me with horror and a chillness in my very blood. There was nobody to be seen in the whole street, neither did any other window open, for people had no curiosity now in any case, nor could anybody help one another, so I went on to pass into Bell Alley.

Just in Bell Alley, on the right hand of the passage, there was a more terrible cry than that, though it was not so directed out at the window; but the whole family was in a terrible fright, and I could hear women and children run screaming about the rooms like distracted, when a garret window opened, and somebody from a window on the other side the alley called and asked, "What is the matter?" upon which, from the first window it was answered, "O Lord, my old master has hanged himself!" The other asked again, "Is he quite dead?" and the first answered, "Ay, ay, quite dead; quite dead and cold!" This person was a merchant and a deputy alderman, and very rich. I care not to mention his name, though I knew his name too; but that would be an hardship to the family, which is now flourishing again.

But this is but one; it is scarce credible what dreadful cases happened in particular families every day. People in the rage of the distemper, or in the torment of their swellings, which was indeed intolerable, running out of their own government, raving and distracted, and oftentimes laying violent hands upon themselves, throwing themselves out at their windows, shooting themselves, &c.; mothers murdering their own children in their lunacy; some dying of mere grief as a passion, some of mere fright and surprise without any infection at all; others frighted into idiotism and foolish distractions, some into despair and lunacy, others into melancholy madness.

The pain of the swelling was in particular very violent, and to some intolerable; the physicians and surgeons may be said to have tortured many poor creatures even to death. The swellings in some grew hard, and they applied violent drawing plasters or poultices to break them; and if these did not do, they cut and scarified them in a terrible manner. In some those swellings were made hard partly by the force of the distemper and partly by their being too violently drawn, and were so hard that no instrument could cut them, and then they burnt them with caustics, so that many died raving mad with the torment, and some in the very operation. In these distresses, some, for want of help to hold them down in their beds, or to look to them, laid hands upon themselves, as above. Some broke out into the streets, perhaps naked, and would run directly down to the river, if they were not stopped by the watchmen or other officers, and plunge themselves into the water wherever they found it.

It often pierced my very soul to hear the groans and cries of those who were thus tormented, but of the two this was counted the most promising particular in the whole infection, for, if these swellings could be brought to a head, and to break and run, or, as the surgeons call it, to digest, the patient generally recovered; whereas those who ... were struck with death at the beginning, and had the tokens come out upon them, often went about indifferent easy till a little before they died, and some till the moment they dropped down, as in apoplexies and epilepsies is often the case. Such would be taken suddenly very sick, and would run to a bench or bulk, or any convenient place that offered itself, or to their own houses if possible, as I mentioned before, and there sit down, grow faint, and die. This kind of dying was much the same as it was with those who die of common mortifications, who die swooning, and, as it were, go away in a dream. Such as died thus had very little notice of their being infected at all till the gangrene was spread through their whole body; nor could physicians themselves know certainly how it was with them, till they opened their breasts or other parts of their body, and saw the tokens....

But to return to my particular observations during this dreadful part of the visitation. I am now come, as I have said, to the month of September, which was the most dreadful of its kind, I believe, that ever London saw; for, by all the accounts which I have seen of the preceding visitations which have been in London, nothing has been like it, the number in the weekly bill amounting to almost 40,000 from the 22nd of August to the 26th of September, being but five weeks. The particulars of the bills are as follows, viz.:

From August the 22nd to the 29th	7496
To the 5th of September	8252
To the 12th	7690
To the 19th	8297
To the 26th	6460
	38,195

This was a prodigious number of itself, but if I should add the reasons which I have to believe that this account was deficient, and how deficient it was, you would, with me, make no scruple to believe that there died above ten thousand a week for all those weeks, one week with another, and a proportion for several weeks both before and after. The confusion among the people, especially within the City at that time, was inexpressible. The terror was so great at last that the courage of the people appointed to carry away the dead began to fail them; nay, several of them died, although they

had the distemper before and were recovered, and some of them dropped down when they have been carrying the bodies even at the pit side, and just ready to throw them in; and this confusion was greater in the City, because they had flattered themselves with hopes of escaping, and thought the bitterness of death was past. One cart, they told us, going up Shoreditch was forsaken of the drivers, or being left to one man to drive, he died in the street, and the horses going on, overthrew the cart, and left the bodies, some thrown here, some there, in a dismal manner. Another cart was, it seems, found in the great pit in Finsbury Fields, the driver being dead, or having been gone and abandoned it, and the horses running too near it, the cart fell in and drew the horses in also. It was suggested that the driver was thrown in with it, and that the cart fell upon him, by reason his whip was seen to be in the pit among the bodies; but that, I suppose, could not be certain.

In our parish of Aldgate the dead-carts were several times, as I have heard, found standing at the churchyard gate full of dead bodies, but neither bellman or driver or anyone else with it; neither in these or many other cases did they know what bodies they had in their cart, for sometimes they were let down with ropes out of balconies and out of windows, and sometimes the bearers brought them to the cart, sometimes other people; nor, as the men themselves said, did they trouble themselves to keep any account of the numbers....

I would be glad if I could close the account of this melancholy year with some particular examples historically; I mean of the thankfulness to God, our preserver, for our being delivered from this dreadful calamity. Certainly the circumstances of the deliverance, as well as the terrible enemy we were delivered from, called upon the whole nation for it. The circumstances of the deliverance were indeed very remarkable, as I have in part mentioned already, and particularly the dreadful condition which we were all in, when we were, to the surprise of the whole town, made joyful with the hope of a stop of the infection.

Nothing but the immediate finger of God, nothing but omnipotent power, could have done it. The contagion despised all medicine; death raged in every corner; and had it gone on as it did then, a few weeks more would have cleared the town of all and everything that had a soul. Men everywhere began to despair; every heart failed them for fear; people were made desperate through the anguish of their souls, and the terrors of death sat in the very faces and countenances of the people.

In that very moment, when we might very well say, "Vain was the help of man"—I say, in that very moment it pleased God, with a most agreeable surprise, to cause the fury of it to abate, even of itself; and the malignity declining, as I have said, though infinite numbers were sick, yet fewer died, and the very first week's bill decreased 1843; a vast number indeed!

It is impossible to express the change that appeared in the very countenances of the people that Thursday morning when the weekly bill came out. It might have been perceived in their countenances that a secret surprise and smile of joy sat on everybody's face. They shook one another by the hands in the streets, who would hardly go on the same side of the way with one another before. Where the streets were not too broad, they would open their windows and call from one house to another, and ask how they did, and if they had heard the good news that the plague was abated. Some would return, when they said good news, and ask, "What good news?" and when they answered that the plague was abated and the bills decreased almost 2000, they would cry out, "God be praised," and would weep aloud for joy, telling them they had heard nothing of it; and such was the joy of the people that it was, as it were, life to them from the grave. I could almost set down as many extravagant things done in the excess of their joy as of their grief; but that would be to lessen the value of it.

I must confess myself to have been very much dejected just before this happened; for the prodigious number that were taken sick the week or two before, besides those that died, was such, and the lamentations were so great everywhere, that a man must have seemed to have acted even against his reason if he had so much as expected to escape; and as there was hardly a house but mine in all my neighborhood but what was infected, so had it gone on it would not have been long that there would have been any more neighbors to be infected. Indeed it is hardly credible what dreadful havoc the last three weeks had made, for if I might believe the person whose calculations I always found very well grounded, there were not less than 30,000 people dead and near 100,000 fallen sick in the three weeks I speak of; for the number that sickened was surprising; indeed it was astonishing, and those whose courage upheld them all the time before, sank under it now.

In the middle of their distress, when the condition of the City of London was so truly calamitous, just then it pleased God, as it were, by His immediate hand to disarm this enemy; the poison was taken out of the sting. It was wonderful; even the physicians themselves were surprised at it. Wherever they visited they found their patients better; either they had sweated kindly, or the tumors were broke, or the carbuncles went down, and the inflammations round them changed color, or the fever was gone, or the violent headache was assuaged, or some good symptom was in the case; so that in a few days everybody was recovering, whole families that were infected and down, that had ministers praying with them, and expected death every hour, were revived and healed, and none died at all out of them.

Nor was this by any new medicine found out, or new method of cure discovered, or by any experience in the operation which the physicians or surgeons attained to; but it was evidently from the secret invisible hand of Him that had at first sent this disease as a judgment upon us;

and let the atheistic part of mankind call my saying what they please, it is no enthusiasm. It was acknowledged at that time by all mankind. The disease was enervated and its malignity spent; and let it proceed from whencesoever it will, let the philosophers search for reasons in nature to account for it by, and labor as much as they will to lessen the debt they owe to their Maker, those physicians who had the least share of religion in them were obliged to acknowledge that it was all supernatural, that it was extraordinary, and that no account could be given of it.

If I should say that this is a visible summons to us all to thankfulness, especially we that were under the terror of its increase, perhaps it may be thought by some, after the sense of the thing was over, an officious canting of religious things, preaching a sermon instead of writing a history, making myself a teacher instead of giving my observations of things; and this restrains me very much from going on here, as I might otherwise do. But if ten lepers were healed, and but one returned to give thanks, I desire to be as that one, and to be thankful for myself.

Nor will I deny but there were abundance of people who, to all appearance, were very thankful at that time; for their mouths were stopped, even the mouths of those whose hearts were not extraordinary long affected with it. But the impression was so strong at that time that it could not be resisted, no, not by the worst of the people.

It was a common thing to meet people in the street that were strangers, and that we knew nothing at all of, expressing their surprise. Going one day through Aldgate, and a pretty many people being passing and repassing, there comes a man out of the end of the Minories, and looking a little up the street and down, he throws his hands abroad, "Lord, what an alteration is here! Why, last week I came along here, and hardly anybody was to be seen." Another man, I heard him, adds to his words, "'Tis all wonderful; 'tis all a dream." "Blessed

be God," says a third man, "and let us give thanks to Him, for 'tis all His own doing. Human help and human skill was at an end." These were all strangers to one another. But such salutations as these were frequent in the street every day; and in spite of a loose behavior, the very common people went along the streets giving God thanks for their deliverance.

It was now, as I said before, the people had cast off all apprehensions, and that too fast; indeed we were no more afraid now to pass by a man with a white cap upon his head, or with a cloth wrapped round his neck, or with his leg limping, occasioned by the sores in his groin, all which were frightful to the last degree but the week before. But now the street was full of them, and these poor recovering creatures, give them their due, appeared very sensible of their unexpected deliverance; and I should wrong them very much if I should not acknowledge that I believe many of them were really thankful. But I must own, that for the generality of the people, it might too justly be said of them as was said of the children of Israel, after their being delivered from the host of Pharaoh, when they passed the Red Sea, and looked back, and saw the Egyptians overwhelmed in the water, viz., that they sang His praise, but they soon forgot His works.

I can go no further here. I should be counted censorious, and perhaps unjust, if I should enter into the unpleasing work of reflecting, whatever cause there was for it, upon the unthankfulness and return of all manner of wickedness among us, which I was so much an eyewitness of myself. I shall conclude the account of this calamitous year therefore with a coarse but sincere stanza of my own, which I placed at the end of my ordinary memorandums the same year they were written:

A dreadful plague in London was
   In the year sixty-five,
Which swept an hundred thousand souls
   Away; yet I alive!

HANSON W. BALDWIN

R.M.S. *Titanic*

The White Star liner *Titanic*, largest ship the world had ever known, sailed from Southampton on her maiden voyage to New York on April 10, 1912. The paint on her strakes was fair and bright; she was fresh from Harland and Wolff's Belfast yards, strong in the strength of her forty-six thousand tons of steel, bent, hammered, shaped and riveted through the three years of her slow birth.

There was little fuss and fanfare at her sailing; her sister ship, the *Olympic*—slightly smaller than the *Titanic*—had been in service for some months and to her had gone the thunder of the cheers.

But the *Titanic* needed no whistling steamers or shouting crowds to call attention to her superlative qualities. Her bulk dwarfed the ships near her as longshoremen singled up her mooring lines and cast off the turns of heavy rope from the dock bollards. She was not only the largest ship afloat, but was believed to be the safest. Carlisle, her builder, had given her double bottoms and had divided her hull into sixteen watertight compartments, which made her, men thought, unsinkable. She had been built to be and had been described as a gigantic lifeboat. Her designers' dreams of a triple-screw giant, a luxurious, floating hotel, which could speed to New York at twenty-three knots, had been carefully translated from blue prints and mold-loft lines at the Belfast yards into a living reality.

The *Titanic*'s sailing from Southampton, though quiet, was not wholly uneventful. As the liner moved slowly toward the end of her

R.M.S. TITANIC: From *R.M.S. Titanic* by Hanson W. Baldwin, first published in *Harper's Magazine* (January 1934). Reprinted by permission of Collins-Knowlton-Wing, Inc. Copyright © 1933, by Harper and Row, Publishers, Incorporated; renewed 1961.

dock that April day, the surge of her passing sucked away from the quay the steamer *New York*, moored just to seaward of the *Titanic*'s berth. There were sharp cracks as the manila mooring lines of the *New York* parted under the strain. The frayed ropes writhed and whistled through the air and snapped down among the waving crowd on the pier; the *New York* swung towards the *Titanic*'s bow, was checked and dragged back to the dock barely in time to avert a collision. Seamen muttered, thought it an ominous start.

Past Spithead and the Isle of Wight the *Titanic* steamed. She called at Cherbourg at dusk and then laid her course for Queenstown. At 1:30 P.M. on Thursday, April 11, she stood out of Queenstown harbor, screaming gulls soaring in her wake, with 2,201 persons—men, women, and children—aboard.

Occupying the Empire bedrooms and Georgian suites of the first-class accommodations were many well-known men and women—Colonel John Jacob Astor and his young bride; Major Archibald Butt, military aide to President Taft, and his friend, Frank D. Millet, the painter; John B. Thayer, vice-president of the Pennsylvania Railroad, and Charles M. Hays, president of the Grand Trunk Railway of Canada; W. T. Stead, the English journalist; Jacques Futrelle, French novelist; H. B. Harris, theatrical manager, and Mrs. Harris; Mr. and Mrs. Isidor Straus; and J. Bruce Ismay, chairman and managing director of the White Star line.

Down in the plain wooden cabins of the steerage class were 706 immigrants to the land of promise, and trimly stowed in the great holds was a cargo valued at $420,000: oak beams, sponges, wine, calabashes, and an odd miscellany of the common and the rare.

The *Titanic* took her departure on Fastnet Light and, heading into the night, laid her course for New York. She was due at Quarantine the following Wednesday morning.

Sunday dawned fair and clear. The *Titanic* steamed smoothly towards the west, faint streamers of brownish smoke trailing from her funnels. The purser held services in the saloon in the morning; on the steerage deck aft the immigrants were playing games and a Scotsman was puffing "The Campbells Are Coming" on his bagpipes in the midst of the uproar.

At 9 A.M. a message from the steamer *Caronia* sputtered into the wireless shack:

CAPTAIN, TITANIC—WESTBOUND STEAMERS REPORT BERGS GROWLERS AND FIELD ICE IN 42 DEGREES N. FROM 49 DEGREES TO 51 DEGREES W. 12TH APRIL.

COMPLIMENTS—

BARR.

It was cold in the afternoon; the sun was brilliant, but the *Titanic*, her screws turning over at 75 revolutions per minute, was approaching the Banks.

In the Marconi cabin Second Operator Harold Bride, earphones clamped on his head, was figuring accounts; he did not stop to answer when he heard MWL, Continental Morse for the nearby Leyland liner, *Californian,* calling the *Titanic*. The *Californian* had some message about three icebergs; he didn't bother then to take it down. About 1:42 P.M. the rasping spark of those days spoke again across the water. It was the *Baltic*, calling the *Titanic*, warning her of ice on the steamer track. Bride took the message down and sent it up to the bridge. The officer-of-the-deck glanced at it; sent it to the bearded master of the *Titanic*, Captain E. C. Smith, a veteran of the White Star service. It was lunch time then; the Captain, walking along the promenade deck, saw Mr. Ismay, stopped, and handed him the message without comment. Ismay read it, stuffed it in his pocket, told two ladies about the icebergs, and resumed his walk. Later, about 7:15 P.M., the Captain requested the return of the message in order to post it in the chart room for the information of officers.

Dinner that night in the Jacobean dining room was gay. It was bitter on deck, but the night was calm and fine; the sky was moonless but studded with stars twinkling coldly in the clear air.

After dinner some of the second-class passengers gathered in the saloon, where the Reverend Mr. Carter conducted a "hymn singsong." It was almost ten o'clock and the stewards were waiting with biscuits and coffee as the group sang:

> O, hear us when we cry to Thee
> For those in peril on the sea.

On the bridge Second Officer Lightoller—short, stocky, efficient—was relieved at ten o'clock by First Officer Murdock. Lightoller had talked with other officers about the proximity of ice; at least five wireless ice warnings had reached the ship; lookouts had been cautioned to be alert; captains and officers expected to reach the field at any time after 9:30 P.M. At twenty-two knots, its speed unslackened, the *Titanic* plowed on through the night.

Lightoller left the darkened bridge to his relief and turned in. Captain Smith went to his cabin. The steerage was long since quiet; in the first and second cabins lights were going out; voices were growing still, people were asleep. Murdock paced back and forth on the bridge, peering out over the dark water, glancing now and then at the compass in front of Quartermaster Hichens at the wheel.

In the crow's nest, Lookout Frederick Fleet and his partner, Leigh, gazed down at the water, still and unruffled in the dim, starlit darkness. Behind and below them the ship, a white shadow with here and there a last winking light; ahead of them a dark and silent and cold ocean.

There was a sudden clang. "Dong-dong. Dong-dong. Dong-dong. Dong!" The metal clapper of the great ship's bell struck out 11:30. Mindful of the warnings, Fleet strained his eyes, searching the darkness for the dreaded ice. But there were only the stars and the sea.

In the wireless room, where Phillips, first operator, had relieved Bride, the buzz of the *Californian*'s set again crackled into the earphones:

CALIFORNIAN. Say, old man, we are stuck here, surrounded by ice.

TITANIC. Shut up, shut up; keep out. I am talking to Cape Race; you are jamming my signals.

Then, a few minutes later—about 11:40...

Out of the dark she came, a vast, dim, white, monstrous shape, directly in the *Titanic*'s path. For a moment Fleet doubted his eyes. But she was a deadly reality, this ghastly *thing*. Frantically, Fleet struck three bells—*something dead ahead*. He snatched the telephone and called the bridge:

"Iceberg! Right ahead!"

The First Officer heard but did not stop to acknowledge the message.

"Hard astarboard!"

Hichens strained at the wheel; the bow swung slowly to port. The monster was almost upon them now.

Murdock leaped to the engine-room telegraph. Bells clanged. Far below in the engine room those bells struck the first warning. Danger! The indicators on the dial faces swung round to "Stop!" Then "Full speed astern!" Frantically the engineers turned great valve wheels; answered the bridge bells....

There was a slight shock, a brief scraping, a small list to port. Shell ice—slabs and chunks of it—fell on the foredeck. Slowly the *Titanic* stopped.

Captain Smith hurried out of his cabin.

"What has the ship struck?"

Murdock answered, "An iceberg, sir. I hard-astarboarded and reversed the engines, and I was going to hard-aport around it, but she was too close. I could not do any more. I have closed the watertight doors."

Fourth Officer Boxhall, other officers, the carpenter, came to the bridge. The Captain sent Boxhall and the carpenter below to ascertain the damage.

A few lights switched on in the first and second cabins; sleepy passengers peered through port-hole glass; some casually asked the stewards:

"Why have we stopped?"

"I don't know, sir, but I don't suppose it is anything much."

In the smoking room a quorum of gamblers and their prey were still sitting round a poker table; the usual crowd of kibitzers looked on. They had felt the slight jar of the collision and had seen an eighty-foot ice mountain glide by the smoking-room windows, but the night was calm and clear, the *Titanic* was "unsinkable"; they hadn't bothered to go on deck.

But far below, in the warren of passages on the starboard side forward, in the forward holds and boiler rooms, men could see that the *Titanic*'s hurt was mortal. In No. 6 boiler room, where the red glow from the furnaces lighted up the naked, sweaty chests of coal-blackened firemen, water was pouring through a great gash about two feet above the floor plates. This was no slow leak; the ship was open to the sea; in ten minutes there were eight feet of water in No. 6. Long before then the stokers had raked the flaming fires out of the furnaces and had scrambled through the watertight doors into No. 5 or had climbed up the long steel ladders to safety. When Boxhall looked at the mail room in No. 3 hold, twenty-four feet above the keel, the mail-bags were already floating about in the slushing water. In No. 5 boiler room a stream of water spurted into an empty bunker. All six compartments forward of No. 4 were open to the sea; in ten seconds the iceberg's jagged claw had ripped a three-hundred-foot slash in the bottom of the great *Titanic*.

Reports came to the bridge; Ismay in dressing gown ran out on deck in the cold, still, starlit night, climbed up the bridge ladder.

"What has happened?"

Captain Smith: "We have struck ice."

"Do you think she is seriously damaged?"

Captain: "I'm afraid she is."

Ismay went below and passed Chief Engineer William Bell fresh from an inspection of the damaged compartments. Bell corroborated the Captain's statement; hurried back down the glistening steel ladders to his duty. Man after man followed him—Thomas Andrews, one of the ship's designers, Archie Frost, the builder's chief engineer, and his twenty assistants—men who had no posts of duty in the engine room but whose traditions called them there.

On deck, in corridor and stateroom, life flowed again. Men, women, and children awoke and questioned; orders were given to uncover the lifeboats; water rose into the firemen's quarters; half-dressed stokers streamed up on deck. But the passengers—most of them—did not know that the *Titanic* was sinking. The shock of the collision had been so slight that some were not awakened by it; the *Titanic* was so huge that she must be unsinkable; the night was too calm, too beautiful, to think of death at sea.

Captain Smith half ran to the door of the radio shack. Bride, partly dressed, eyes dulled with sleep, was standing behind Phillips, waiting.

"Send the call for assistance."

The blue spark danced: "CQD—CQD—CQD—CQ—"

Miles away Marconi men heard. Cape Race heard it, and the steamships *La Provence* and *Mt. Temple.*

The sea was surging into the *Titanic*'s hold. At 12:20 the water burst into the seamen's quarters through a collapsed fore-and-aft wooden bulkhead. Pumps strained in the engine rooms—men and machinery making a futile fight against the sea. Steadily the water rose.

The boats were swung out—slowly; for the deckhands were late in reaching their stations, there had been no boat drill, and many of the crew did not know to what boats they were assigned. Orders were shouted; the safety valves had lifted, and steam was blowing off in a great rushing roar. In the chart house Fourth Officer Boxhall bent above a chart, working rapidly with pencil and dividers.

12:15 A.M.   Boxhall's position is sent out to a fleet of vessels: "Come at once; we have struck a berg."

To the Cunarder *Carpathia* (Arthur Henry Rostron, Master, New York to Liverpool, fifty-eight miles away): "It's a CQD, old man. Position 41-46 N.; 50-14 W."

The blue spark dancing: "Sinking; cannot hear for noise of steam."

12:30 A.M.   The word is passed: "Women and children in the boats." Stewards finish waking their passengers below; life preservers are tied on; some men smile at the precaution. "The *Titanic* is unsinkable." The *Mt. Temple* starts for the *Titanic*; the *Carpathia*, with a double watch in her stokeholds, radios, "Coming hard." The CQD changes the course of many ships—but not of one; the operator of the *Californian*, near by, has just put down his earphones and turned in.

The CQD flashes over land and sea from Cape Race to New York; newspaper city rooms leap to life and presses whir.

On the *Titanic*, water creeps over the bulkhead between Nos. 5 and 6 firerooms. She is going down by the head; the engineers—fighting a losing battle—are forced back foot by foot by the rising water. Down the promenade deck, Happy Jock Hume, the bandsman, runs with his instrument.

12:45 A.M.   Murdock, in charge on the starboard side, eyes tragic, but calm and cool, orders boat No. 7 lowered. The women hang back; they want no boat ride on an ice-strewn sea; the *Titanic* is unsinkable. The men encourage them, explain that this is just a precautionary measure: "We'll see you again at breakfast." There is little confusion; passengers stream slowly to the boat deck. In the steerage the immigrants chatter excitedly.

A sudden sharp hiss—a streaked flare against the night; Boxhall sends a rocket toward the sky. It explodes, and a parachute of white stars lights up the icy sea. "God! Rockets!" The band plays ragtime.

No. 8 is lowered, and No. 5. Ismay, still in dressing gown, calls for women and children, handles lines, stumbles in the way of an officer, is told to "get the hell out of here." Third Officer Pitman takes charge of No. 5; as he swings into the boat Murdock grasps his hand. "Good-by and good luck, old man."

No. 6 goes over the side. There are only twenty-eight people in a lifeboat with a capacity of sixty-five.

A light stabs from the bridge; Boxhall is calling in Morse flashes, again and again, to a strange ship stopped in the ice jam five to ten miles away. Another rocket drops its shower of sparks above the ice-strewn sea and the dying ship.

1:00 A.M. Slowly the water creeps higher; the fore ports of the *Titanic* are dipping into the sea. Rope squeaks through blocks; lifeboats drop jerkily seaward. Through the shouting on the decks comes the sound of the band playing ragtime.

The "Millionaires' Special" leaves the ship— boat No. 1, with a capacity of forty people, carries only Sir Cosmo and Lady Duff Gordon and ten others. Aft, the frightened immigrants mill and jostle and rush for a boat. An officer's fist flies out; three shots are fired into the air, and the panic is quelled.... Four Chinese sneak unseen into a boat and hide in its bottom.

1:20 A.M. Water is coming into No. 4 boiler room. Stokers slice and shovel as water laps about their ankles—steam for the dynamos, steam for the dancing spark! As the water rises, great ash hoes rake the flaming coals from the furnaces. Safety valves pop; the stokers retreat aft, and the watertight doors clang shut behind them.

The rockets fling their splendor toward the stars. The boats are more heavily loaded now, for the passengers know the *Titanic* is sinking. Women cling and sob. The great screws aft are rising clear of the sea. Half-filled boats are ordered to come alongside the cargo ports and take on more passengers, but the ports are never opened—and the boats are never filled. Others pull for the steamer's light miles away but never reach it; the light disappears, the unknown ship steams off.

The water rises and the band plays ragtime.

1:30 A.M. Lightoller is getting the port boats off; Murdock the starboard. As one boat is lowered into the sea a boat officer fires his gun along the ship's side to stop a rush from the lower decks. A woman tries to take her great Dane into a boat with her; she is refused and steps out of the boat to die with her dog. Millet's "little smile which played on his lips all through the voyage" plays no more; his lips are grim, but he waves good-by and brings wraps for the women.

Benjamin Guggenheim, in evening clothes, smiles and says, "We've dressed up in our best and are prepared to go down like gentlemen."

1:40 A.M. Boat 14 is clear, and then 13, 16, 15, and C. The lights still shine, but the *Baltic* hears the blue spark say, "Engine room getting flooded."

The *Olympic* signals, "Am lighting up all possible boilers as fast as can."

Major Butt helps women into the last boats and waves good-by to them. Mrs Straus puts her foot on the gunwale of a lifeboat, then she draws back and goes to her husband: "We have been together many years; where you go I will go." Colonel John Jacob Astor puts his young wife in a lifeboat, steps back, taps cigarette on fingernail: "Good-by, dearie; I'll join you later."

1:45 A.M. The foredeck is under water, the fo'c'sle head almost awash; the great stern is lifted high toward the bright stars; and still the band plays. Mr. and Mrs. Harris approach a lifeboat arm in arm.

Officer: "Ladies first, please."

Harris bows, smiles, steps back: "Of course, certainly; ladies first."

Boxhall fires the last rocket, then leaves in charge of boat No. 2.

2:00 A.M. She is dying now; her bow goes deeper, her stern higher. But there must be steam. Below in the stokeholds the sweaty firemen keep steam up for the flaring lights and the dancing spark. The glowing coals slide and tumble over the slanted grate bars; the sea pounds behind that yielding bulkhead. But the spark dances on.

The *Asian* hears Phillips try the new signal—SOS.

Boat No. 4 has left now; boat D leaves ten minutes later. Jacques Futrelle clasps his wife: "For God's sake, go! It's your last chance; go!" Madame Futrelle is half forced into the boat. It clears the side.

There are about 660 people in the boats, and 1,500 still on the sinking *Titanic*.

On top of the officers' quarters, men work frantically to get the two collapsibles stowed there over the side. Water is over the forward part of A deck now; it surges up the companionways toward the boat deck. In the radio shack, Bride has slipped a coat and lifejacket about Phillips as the first operator sits hunched over his key, sending—still sending—"41-46 N.; 50-14 W. CQD—CQD—SOS—SOS—"

The Captain's tired white face appears at the radio-room door: "Men, you have done your duty. You can do no more. Now, it's every man for himself." The Captain disappears—back to his sinking bridge, where Painter, his personal steward, stands quietly waiting for orders. The spark dances on. Bride turns his back and goes into the inner cabin. As he does so, a stoker, grimed with coal, mad with fear, steals into the shack and reaches for the lifejacket on Phillips' back. Bride wheels about and brains him with a wrench.

2:10 A.M.   Below decks the steam is still holding, though the pressure is falling—rapidly. In the gymnasium on the boat deck the athletic instructor watches quietly as two gentlemen ride the bicycles and another swings casually at the punching bag. Mail clerks stagger up the boat-deck stairways, dragging soaked mail sacks. The spark still dances. The band still plays—but not ragtime:

> Nearer my God to Thee,
> Nearer to Thee...

A few men take up the refrain; others kneel on the slanting decks to pray. Many run and scramble aft, where hundreds are clinging above the silent screws on the great uptilted stern. The spark still dances and the lights still flare; the engineers are on the job. The hymn comes to its close. Bandmaster Hartley, Yorkshireman violinist, taps his bow against a bulkhead, calls for "Autumn" as the water curls about his feet, and eight musicians brace themselves against the ship's slant. People are leaping from the decks into the nearby water—the icy water. A woman cries, "Oh, save me, save me!" A man answers, "Good lady, save yourself. Only God can save you now." The band plays "Autumn":

> God of Mercy and Compassion!
> Look with pity on my pain...

The water creeps over the bridge where the *Titanic*'s master stands; heavily he steps out to meet it.

2:17 A.M.   "CQ—" The *Virginian* hears a ragged, blurred CQ, then an abrupt stop. The blue spark dances no more. The lights flicker out; the engineers have lost their battle.

2:18 A.M.   Men run about blackened decks; leap into the night; are swept into the sea by the curling wave which licks up the *Titanic*'s length. Lightoller does not leave the ship; the ship leaves him; there are hundreds like him, but only a few who live to tell of it. The funnels still swim above the water, but the ship is climbing to the perpendicular; the bridge is under and most of the foremast; the great stern rises like a squat leviathan. Men swim away from the sinking ship; others drop from the stern.

The band plays in the darkness, the water lapping upwards:

> Hold me up in mighty waters,
> Keep my eyes on things above,
> Righteousness, divine atonement,
> Peace and everlas...

The forward funnel snaps and crashes into the sea; its steel tons hammer out of existence swimmers struggling in the freezing water. Streams of sparks, of smoke and steam, burst from the after funnels. The ship upends to fifty—to sixty degrees.

Down in the black abyss of the stokeholds, of the engine rooms, where the dynamos have whirred at long last to a stop, the stokers and the engineers are reeling against hot metal, the rising water clutching at their knees. The boilers, the engine cylinders, rip from their bed plates; crash through bulkheads; rumble—steel against steel.

The *Titanic* stands on end, poised briefly for the plunge. Slowly she slides to her grave— slowly at first, and then more quickly— quickly—quickly.

2:20 A.M.   The greatest ship in the world has sunk. From the calm, dark waters, where the floating lifeboats move, there goes up, in the white wake of her passing, "one long continuous moan."

The boats that the *Titanic* had launched pulled safely away from the slight suction of the sinking ship, pulled away from the screams that came from the lips of freezing men and women in the water. The boats were poorly manned and badly equipped, and they had been unevenly loaded. Some carried so few seamen that women bent to the oars. Mrs. Astor tugged at an oar handle; the Countess of Rothes took a tiller. Shivering stokers in sweaty, coal-blackened singlets and light trousers steered in some boats; stewards in white coats rowed in others. Ismay was in the last boat that left the ship from the starboard side; with Mr. Carter of Philadelphia and two seamen he tugged at the oars. In one of the lifeboats an Italian with a broken wrist— disguised in a woman's shawl and hat—huddled on the floor boards, ashamed now that fear had left him. In another rode the only baggage saved from the *Titanic*—the carry-all of Samuel L. Goldenberg, one of the rescued passengers.

There were only a few boats that were heavily loaded; most of those that were half empty made but perfunctory efforts to pick up the moaning swimmers, their officers and crew fearing that they would endanger the living if they pulled back into the midst of the dying. Some boats

beat off the freezing victims; fear-crazed men and women struck with oars at the heads of swimmers. One woman drove her fist into the face of a half-dead man as he tried feebly to climb over the gunwale. Two other women helped him in and stanched the flow of blood from the ring cuts on his face.

One of the collapsible boats, which had floated off the top of the officers' quarters when the *Titanic* sank, was an icy haven for thirty or forty men. The boat had capsized as the ship sank; men swam to it, clung to it, climbed upon its slippery bottom, stood knee-deep in water in the freezing air. Chunks of ice swirled about their legs; their soaked clothing clutched their bodies in icy folds. Colonel Archibald Gracie was cast up there, Gracie who had leaped from the stern as the *Titanic* sank; young Thayer who had seen his father die; Lightoller who had twice been sucked down with the ship and twice blown to the surface by a belch of air; Bride, the second operator, and Phillips, the first. There were many stokers, half-naked; it was a shivering company. They stood there in the icy sea, under the far stars, and sang and prayed—the Lord's Prayer. After a while a lifeboat came and picked them off, but Phillips was dead then or died soon afterward in the boat.

Only a few of the boats had lights; only one —No. 2—had a light that was of any use to the *Carpathia*, twisting through the ice field to the rescue. Other ships were "coming hard" too; one, the *Californian*, was still dead to opportunity.

The blue sparks still danced, but not the *Titanic*'s. *Le Provence* to *Celtic*: "Nobody has heard the *Titanic* for about two hours."

It was 2:40 when the *Carpathia* first sighted the green light from No. 2 boat; it was 4:10 when she picked up the first boat and learned that the *Titanic* had foundered. The last of the moaning cries had just died away then.

Captain Rostron took the survivors aboard, boatload by boatload. He was ready for them, but only a small minority of them required much medical attention. Bride's feet were twisted and frozen; others were suffering from exposure;

one died, and seven were dead when taken from the boats, and were buried at sea.

It was then that the fleet of racing ships learned they were too late; the *Parisian* heard the weak signals of MPA, the *Carpathia*, report the death of the *Titanic*. It was then—or soon afterward, when her radio operator put on his earphones—that the *Californian*, the ship that had been within sight as the *Titanic* was sinking, first learned of the disaster.

And it was then, in all its white-green majesty, that the *Titanic*'s survivors saw the iceberg, tinted with the sunrise, floating idly, pack ice jammed about its base, other bergs heaving slowly near by on the blue breast of the sea.

JOHN HERSEY

A Noiseless Flash

At exactly fifteen minutes past eight in the morning, on August 6, 1945, Japanese time, at the moment when the atomic bomb flashed above Hiroshima, Miss Toshiko Sasaki, a clerk in the personnel department of the East Asia Tin Works, had just sat down at her place in the plant office and was turning her head to speak to the girl at the next desk. At that same moment, Dr. Masakazu Fujii was settling down cross-legged to read the Osaka *Asahi* on the porch of his private hospital, overhanging one of the seven deltaic rivers which divide Hiroshima; Mrs. Hatsuyo Nakamura, a tailor's widow, stood by the window of her kitchen, watching a neighbor tearing down his house because it lay in the path of an air-raid-defense fire lane; Father Wilhelm Kleinsorge, a German

priest of the Society of Jesus, reclined in his underwear on a cot on the top floor of his order's three-story mission house, reading a Jesuit magazine, *Stimmen der Zeit*; Dr. Terufumi Sasaki, a young member of the surgical staff of the city's large, modern Red Cross Hospital, walked along one of the hospital corridors with a blood specimen for a Wassermann test in his hand; and the Reverend Mr. Kiyoshi Tanimoto, pastor of the Hiroshima Methodist Church, paused at the door of a rich man's house in Koi, the city's western suburb, and prepared to unload a handcart full of things he had evacuated from town in fear of the massive B-29 raid which everyone expected Hiroshima to suffer. A hundred thousand people were killed by the atomic bomb, and these six were among the survivors. They still wonder why they lived when so many others died. Each of them counts many small items of chance or volition—a step taken in time, a decision to go indoors, catching one streetcar instead of the next—that spared him. And now each knows that in the act of survival he lived a dozen lives and saw more death than he ever thought he would see. At the time, none of them knew anything.

The Reverend Mr. Tanimoto got up at five o'clock that morning. He was alone in the parsonage, because for some time his wife had been commuting with their year-old baby to spend nights with a friend in Ushida, a suburb to the north. Of all the important cities of Japan, only two, Kyoto and Hiroshima, had not been visited in strength by *B-san*, or Mr. *B*, as the Japanese, with a mixture of respect and unhappy familiarity, called the *B*-29; and Mr. Tanimoto, like all his neighbors and friends, was almost sick with anxiety. He had heard uncomfortably detailed accounts of mass raids on Kure, Iwakuni, Tokuyama, and other nearby towns; he was sure Hiroshima's turn would come soon. He had slept badly the night before, because there had been several air-raid warnings. Hiroshima had been getting such warnings almost every night for weeks, for at that time the *B-29*'s were using Lake Biwa, northeast of Hiroshima, as a rendezvous point, and no matter what city the Americans planned to hit, the Superfortresses streamed in over the coast near Hiroshima. The frequency of the warnings and the continued abstinence of Mr. *B* with respect to Hiroshima had made its citizens jittery; a rumor was going around that the Americans were saving something special for the city.

Mr. Tanimoto is a small man, quick to talk, laugh, and cry. He wears his black hair parted in the middle and rather long; the prominence of the frontal bones just above his eyebrows and the smallness of his mustache, mouth, and chin give him a strange, old-young look, boyish and yet wise, weak and yet fiery. He moves nervously and fast, but with a restraint which suggests that he is a cautious, thoughtful man. He showed, indeed, just those qualities in the uneasy days before the bomb fell. Besides having his wife spend the nights in Ushida, Mr. Tanimoto had been carrying all the portable things from his church, in the closepacked residential district called Nagaragawa, to a house that belonged to a rayon manufacturer in Koi, two miles from the center of town. The rayon man, a Mr. Matsui, had opened his then unoccupied estate to a large number of his friends and acquaintances, so that they might evacuate whatever they wished to a safe distance from the probable target area. Mr. Tanimoto had had no difficulty in moving chairs, hymnals, Bibles, altar gear, and church records by pushcart himself, but the organ console and an upright piano required some aid. A friend of his named Matsuo had, the day before, helped him get the piano out to Koi; in return, he had promised this day to assist Mr. Matsuo in hauling out a daughter's belongings. That is why he had risen so early.

Mr. Tanimoto cooked his own breakfast. He felt awfully tired. The effort of moving the piano the day before, a sleepless night, weeks of worry and unbalanced diet, the cares of his parish— all combined to make him feel hardly adequate to the new day's work. There was another thing too: Mr. Tanimoto had studied theology at Emory College, in Atlanta, Georgia; he had graduated in 1940; he spoke excellent English; he dressed in American clothes; he had corresponded with many American friends right up to the time the war began; and among a people obsessed with a fear of being spied upon— perhaps almost obsessed himself—he found himself growing increasingly uneasy. The police had questioned him several times, and just a few days before, he had heard that an influential acquaintance, a Mr. Tanaka, a retired officer of the Toyo Kisen Kaisha steamship line, an anti-Christian, a man famous in Hiroshima for his showy philanthropies and notorious for his personal tyrannies, had been telling people that Tanimoto should not be trusted. In compensation, to show himself publicly a good Japanese, Mr. Tanimoto had taken on the chairmanship of his local *tonari-gumi*, or Neighborhood Association, and to his other duties and concerns this position had added the business of organizing air-raid defense for about twenty families.

Before six o'clock that morning, Mr. Tanimoto started for Mr. Matsuo's house. There he found that their burden was to be a *tansu*, a large Japanese cabinet, full of clothing and household goods. The two men set out. The morning was perfectly clear and so warm that the day promised to be uncomfortable. A few minutes after they started, the air-raid siren went off—a minute-long blast that warned of approaching planes but indicated to the people of Hiroshima only a slight degree of danger, since it sounded every morning at this time, when an American weather plane came over. The two men pulled and pushed the handcart through the city streets. Hiroshima was a fan-shaped city, lying mostly on the six islands formed by the seven estuarial rivers that branch out from the Ota River; its main commercial and residential districts, covering about four square miles in the center of the city, contained three-quarters of its population, which had been reduced by several evacuation programs from a wartime peak of 380,000 to about 245,000. Factories and other residential districts, or suburbs, lay compactly around the edges of the city. To the south were the docks, an airport, and the island-studded Inland Sea. A rim of mountains runs around the other three sides of the delta. Mr. Tanimoto and Mr. Matsuo took their way through the shopping center, already full of people, and across two of the rivers to the sloping streets of Koi, and up them to the outskirts and foothills. As they started up a valley away from the tight-ranked houses, the all clear sounded. (The Japanese radar operators, detecting only three planes, supposed that they comprised a reconnaissance.) Pushing the handcart up to the rayon man's house was tiring, and the men, after they had maneuvered their load into the driveway and to the front steps, paused to rest awhile. They stood with a wing of the house between them and the city. Like most homes in this part of Japan, the house consisted of a wooden frame and wooden walls supporting a heavy tile roof. Its front hall, packed with rolls of bedding and clothing, looked like a cool cave full of fat cushions. Opposite the house, to the right of the front door, there was a large, finicky rock garden. There was no sound of planes. The morning was still; the place was cool and pleasant.

Then a tremendous flash of light cut across the sky. Mr. Tanimoto has a distinct recollection that it travelled from east to west, from the city toward the hills. It seemed a sheet of sun. Both he and Mr. Matsuo reacted in terror—and both had time to react (for they were 3,500 yards, or two miles, from the center of the explosion). Mr. Matsuo dashed up the front steps into the house and dived among the bedrolls and buried himself there. Mr. Tanimoto took four or five steps and threw himself between two big rocks in the garden. He bellied up very hard against one of them. As his face was against the stone, he did not see what happened. He felt a sudden pressure, and then splinters and pieces of board and fragments of tile fell on him.

He heard no roar. (Almost no one in Hiroshima recalls hearing any noise of the bomb. But a fisherman in his sampan on the Inland Sea near Tsuzu, the man with whom Mr. Tanimoto's mother-in-law and sister-in-law were living, saw the flash and heard a tremendous explosion; he was nearly twenty miles from Hiroshima, but the thunder was greater than when the B-29's hit Iwakuni, only five miles away.)

When he dared, Mr. Tanimoto raised his head and saw that the rayon man's house had collapsed. He thought a bomb had fallen directly on it. Such clouds of dust had risen that there was a sort of twilight around. In panic, not thinking for the moment of Mr. Matsuo under the ruins, he dashed out into the street. He noticed as he ran that the concrete wall of the estate had fallen over—toward the house rather than away from it. In the street, the first thing he saw was a squad of soldiers who had been burrowing into the hillside opposite, making one of the thousands of dugouts in which the Japanese apparently intended to resist invasion, hill by hill, life for life; the soldiers were coming out of the hole, where they should have been safe, and blood was running from their heads, chests, and backs. They were silent and dazed.

Under what seemed to be a local dust cloud, the day grew darker and darker.

At nearly midnight, the night before the bomb was dropped, an announcer on the city's radio station said that about two hundred B-29's were approaching southern Honshu and advised the population of Hiroshima to evacuate to their designated "safe areas." Mrs. Hatsuyo Naka-mura, the tailor's widow, who lived in the section called Noboricho and who had long had a habit of doing as she was told, got her three children—a ten-year-old boy, Toshio, an eight-year-old girl, Yaeko, and a five-year-old girl, Myeko—out of bed and dressed them and walked with them to the military area known as the East Parade Ground, on the northeast edge of the city. There she unrolled some mats and the children lay down on them. They slept until about two, when they were awakened by the roar of the planes going over Hiroshima.

As soon as the planes had passed, Mrs. Nakamura started back with her children. They reached home a little after two-thirty and she immediately turned on the radio, which, to her distress, was just then broadcasting a fresh warning. When she looked at the children and saw how tired they were, and when she thought of the number of trips they had made in past weeks, all to no purpose, to the East Parade Ground, she decided that in spite of the instructions on the radio, she simply could not face starting out all over again. She put the children in their bedrolls on the floor, lay down herself at three o'clock, and fell asleep at once, so soundly that when planes passed over later, she did not waken to their sound.

The siren jarred her awake at about seven. She arose, dressed quickly, and hurried to the house of Mr. Nakamoto, the head of her Neighborhood Association, and asked him what she should do. He said that she should remain at home unless an urgent warning—a series of intermittent blasts of the siren—was sounded. She returned home, lit the stove in the kitchen, set some rice to cook, and sat down to read the morning's Hiroshima *Chugoku*. To her relief, the all-clear sounded at eight o'clock. She heard the children stirring, so she went and gave each of them a handful of peanuts and told them to stay on their bedrolls, because they were tired from the night's walk. She had hoped that they would go back to sleep, but the man in the house directly to the south began to make a terrible hullabaloo of hammering, wedging, ripping, and splitting. The prefectural government, convinced, as everyone in Hiroshima was, that the city would be attacked soon, had begun to press with threats and warnings for the completion of wide fire lanes, which, it was hoped, might act in conjunction with the rivers to localize any fires started by an incendiary raid; and the neighbor was reluctantly sacrificing his home to the city's safety. Just the day before, the prefecture had ordered all able-bodied girls from the secondary schools to spend a few days helping to clear these lanes, and they started work soon after the all-clear sounded.

Mrs. Nakamura went back to the kitchen, looked at the rice, and began watching the man next door. At first, she was annoyed with him for making so much noise, but then she was moved almost to tears by pity. Her emotion was specifically directed towards her neighbor, tearing down his home, board by board, at a time when there was so much unavoidable destruction, but undoubtedly she also felt a generalized, community pity, to say nothing of self-pity. She had not had an easy time. Her husband, Isawa, had gone into the Army just after Myeko was born, and she had heard nothing from or of him for a long time, until, on March 5, 1942, she received a seven-word telegram: "Isawa died an honorable death at Singapore." She learned later that he had died on February 15th, the day Singapore fell, and that he had been a corporal. Isawa had been a not particularly prosperous tailor, and his only capital was a Sankoku sewing machine. After his death, when his allotments stopped coming, Mrs. Nakamura got out the machine and began to take in piecework herself, and since then had supported the children, but poorly, by sewing.

As Mrs. Nakamura stood watching her neighbor, everything flashed whiter than any white she had ever seen. She did not notice what happened to the man next door; the reflex of a mother set her in motion toward her children. She had taken a single step (the house was 1,350 yards, or three-quarters of a mile, from the center of the explosion) when something picked her up and she seemed to fly into the next room over the raised sleeping platform, pursued by parts of her house.

Timbers fell around her as she landed, and a shower of tiles pommelled her; everything became dark, for she was buried. The debris did not cover her deeply. She rose up and freed herself. She heard a child cry, "Mother, help me!" and saw her youngest—Myeko, the five-year-old—buried up to her breast and unable to move. As Mrs. Nakamura started frantically to claw her way toward the baby, she could see or hear nothing of her other children.

In the days right before the bombing, Dr. Masakazu Fujii, being prosperous, hedonistic, and at the time not too busy, had been allowing himself the luxury of sleeping until nine or nine-thirty, but fortunately he had to get up early the morning the bomb was dropped to see a house guest off on a train. He rose at six, and half an hour later walked with his friend to the station, not far away, across two of the rivers. He was back home by seven, just as the siren sounded its sustained warning. He ate breakfast and then, because the morning was already hot, undressed down to his underwear and went out on the porch to read the paper. This porch—in fact, the whole building—was curiously constructed. Dr. Fujii was the proprietor of a peculiarly Japanese institution: a private, single-doctor hospital. This building, perched beside and over the water of the Kyo River, and next to the bridge of the same name, contained thirty rooms for thirty patients and their kinfolk—for, according to Japanese custom, when a person falls sick and goes to a hospital, one or more members of his family go and live there with him, to cook for him, bathe, massage, and read to him, and to offer incessant familial sympathy, without which a Japanese patient would be miserable indeed. Dr. Fujii had no beds—only straw mats—for his patients. He did, however, have all sorts of modern equipment: an X-ray machine, diathermy apparatus, and a fine tiled laboratory. The structure rested two-thirds on the land, one-third on piles over the tidal waters of the Kyo. This overhang, the part of the building where Dr. Fujii lived, was queer-looking, but it was cool in summer and from the porch, which faced away from the center of the city, the prospect of the river, with pleasure boats drifting up and down it, was always refreshing. Dr. Fujii had occasionally had anxious moments when the Ota and its mouth branches rose to flood, but the piling was apparently firm enough and the house had always held.

Dr. Fujii had been relatively idle for about a month because in July, as the number of untouched cities in Japan dwindled and as Hiroshima seemed more and more inevitably a target, he began turning patients away, on the ground that in case of a fire raid he would not be able to evacuate them. Now he had only two patients left—a woman from Yano, injured in the shoulder, and a young man of twenty-five recovering from burns he had suffered when the steel factory near Hiroshima in which he worked had been hit. Dr. Fujii had six nurses to tend his patients. His wife and children were safe; his wife and one son were living outside Osaka, and another son and two daughters were in the country on Kyushu. A niece was living with him, and a maid and a manservant. He had little to do and did not mind, for he had saved some money. At fifty, he was healthy, convivial, and calm, and he was pleased to pass the evenings drinking whiskey with friends, always sensibly and for the sake of conversation. Before the war, he had affected brands imported from Scotland and America; now he was perfectly satisfied with the best Japanese brand, Suntory.

Dr. Fujii sat down cross-legged in his underwear on the spotless matting of the porch, put on his glasses, and started reading the Osaka *Asahi*. He liked to read the Osaka news because his wife was there. He saw the flash. To him—faced away from the center and looking at his paper—it seemed a brilliant yellow. Startled, he began to rise to his feet. In that moment (he was 1,550 yards from the center), the hospital leaned behind him rising and, with a terrible ripping noise, toppled into the river. The Doctor, still in the act of getting to his feet, was thrown forward and around and over; he was buffeted and gripped; he lost track of everything, because things were so speeded up; he felt the water.

Dr. Fujii hardly had time to think that he was dying before he realized that he was alive, squeezed tightly by two long timbers in a V across his chest, like a morsel suspended between two huge chopsticks—held upright, so that he could not move, with his head miraculously above water and his torso and legs in it. The remains of his hospital were all around him in a mad assortment of splintered lumber and materials for the relief of pain. His left shoulder hurt terribly. His glasses were gone.

Father Wilhelm Kleinsorge, of the Society of Jesus, was, on the morning of the explosion, in rather frail condition. The Japanese wartime diet had not sustained him, and he felt the strain of being a foreigner in an increasingly xenophobic Japan; even a German, since the defeat of the Fatherland, was unpopular. Father Kleinsorge had, at thirty-eight, the look of a boy growing too fast—thin in the face, with a prominent Adam's apple, a hollow chest, dangling hands, big feet. He walked clumsily, leaning forward a little. He was tired all the time. To make matters worse, he had suffered for two days, along with Father Cieslik, a fellow-priest, from a rather painful and urgent diarrhea, which they blamed on the beans and black ration bread they were obliged to eat. Two other priests then living in the mission compound, which was in the Nobori-cho section—Father Superior LaSalle and Father Schiffer—had happily escaped this affliction.

Father Kleinsorge woke up about six the morning the bomb was dropped, and half an hour later—he was a bit tardy because of his sickness—he began to read Mass in the mission chapel, a small Japanese-style wooden building which was without pews, since its worshippers knelt on the usual Japanese matted floor, facing an altar graced with splendid silks, brass, silver, and heavy embroideries. This morning, a Monday, the only worshippers were Mr. Takemoto, a theological student living in the mission house; Mr. Fukai, the secretary of the diocese; Mrs. Murata, the mission's devoutly Christian housekeeper; and his fellow-priests. After Mass, while Father Kleinsorge was reading the Prayers of Thanksgiving, the siren sounded. He stopped the service and the missionaries retired across the compound to the bigger building. There, in his room on the ground floor, to the right of the front door, Father Kleinsorge changed into a military uniform which he had acquired when he was teaching at the Rokko Middle School in Kobe and which he wore during air-raid alerts.

After an alarm, Father Kleinsorge always went out and scanned the sky, and in this instance, when he stepped outside, he was glad to see only the single weather plane that flew over Hiroshima each day about this time. Satisfied that nothing would happen, he went in and breakfasted with the other Fathers on substitute coffee and ration bread, which, under the circumstances, was especially repugnant to him. The Fathers sat and talked awhile, until, at eight, they heard the all clear. They went then to various parts of the building. Father Schiffer retired to his room to do some writing. Father Cieslik sat in his room in a straight chair with a pillow over his stomach to ease his pain, and read. Father Superior LaSalle stood at the window of his room, thinking. Father Kleinsorge went up to a room on the third floor, took off all his clothes except his underwear, and stretched out on his right side on a cot and began reading his *Stimmen der Zeit.*

After the terrible flash—which, Father Kleinsorge later realized, reminded him of something he had read as a boy about a large meteor colliding with the earth—he had time (since he was 1,400 yards from the center) for one thought: A bomb has fallen directly on us. Then, for a few seconds or minutes, he went out of his mind.

Father Kleinsorge never knew how he got out of the house. The next things he was conscious of were that he was wandering around in the mission's vegetable garden in his underwear, bleeding slightly from small cuts along his left flank; that all the buildings round about had fallen down except the Jesuits' mission house, which had long before been braced and double-braced by a priest named Gropper, who was terrified of earthquakes; that the day had turned dark; and that Murata-*san*, the housekeeper, was nearby, crying over and over, "*Shu Jesusu, awaremi tamai!* Our Lord Jesus, have pity on us!"

On the train on the way into Hiroshima from the country, where he lived with his mother, Dr. Terufumi Sasaki, the Red Cross Hospital surgeon, thought over an unpleasant nightmare he had had the night before. His mother's home was in Mukaihara, thirty miles from the city, and it took him two hours by train and tram to reach the hospital. He had slept uneasily all night and had wakened an hour earlier than usual, and, feeling sluggish and slightly feverish, had debated whether to go to the hospital at all; his sense of duty finally forced him to go, and he had started out on an earlier train than he took most mornings. The dream had particularly frightened him because it was so closely associated, on the surface at least, with a disturbing actuality. He was only twenty-five years old and had just completed his training at the Eastern Medical University, in Tsingtao, China. He was something of an idealist and was much distressed by the inadequacy of medical facilities in the country town where his mother lived. Quite on his own, and without a permit, he had begun visiting a few sick people out there in the evenings, after his eight hours at the hospital and four hours' commuting. He had recently learned that the penalty for practicing without a permit was severe; a fellow-doctor whom he had asked about it had given him a serious scolding. Nevertheless, he had continued to practice. In his dream, he had been at the bedside of a country patient when the police and the doctor he had consulted burst into the room, seized him, dragged him outside, and beat him up cruelly. On the train, he just about decided to give up the work in Mukaihara, since he felt it would be impossible to get a permit, because the authorities would hold that it would conflict with his duties at the Red Cross Hospital.

At the terminus, he caught a streetcar at once. (He later calculated that if he had taken his customary train that morning, and if he had had to wait a few minutes for the streetcar, as often happened, he would have been close

to the center at the time of the explosion and would surely have perished.) He arrived at the hospital at seven-forty and reported to the chief surgeon. A few minutes later, he went to a room on the first floor and drew blood from the arm of a man in order to perform a Wassermann test. The laboratory containing the incubators for the test was on the third floor. With the blood specimen in his left hand, walking in a kind of distraction he had felt all morning, probably because of the dream and his restless night, he started along the main corridor on his way toward the stairs. He was one step beyond an open window when the light of the bomb was reflected, like a gigantic photographic flash, in the corridor. He ducked down on one knee and said to himself, as only a Japanese would, "Sasaki, *gambare!* Be brave!" Just then (the building was 1,650 yards from the center), the blast ripped through the hospital. The glasses he was wearing flew off his face; the bottle of blood crashed against one wall; his Japanese slippers zipped out from under his feet—but otherwise, thanks to where he stood, he was untouched.

Dr. Sasaki shouted the name of the chief surgeon and rushed around to the man's office and found him terribly cut by glass. The hospital was in horrible confusion: heavy partitions and ceilings had fallen on patients, beds had overturned, windows had blown in and cut people, blood was spattered on the walls and floors, instruments were everywhere, many of the patients were running about screaming, many more lay dead. (A colleague working in the laboratory to which Dr. Sasaki had been walking was dead; Dr. Sasaki's patient, whom he had just left and who a few moments before had been dreadfully afraid of syphilis, was also dead.) Dr. Sasaki found himself the only doctor in the hospital who was unhurt.

Dr. Sasaki, who believed that the enemy had hit only the building he was in, got bandages and began to bind the wounds of those inside the hospital; while outside, all over Hiroshima, maimed and dying citizens turned their unsteady steps toward the Red Cross Hospital to begin an invasion that was to make Dr. Sasaki forget his private nightmare for a long, long time.

Miss Toshiko Sasaki, the East Asia Tin Works clerk, who is not related to Dr. Sasaki, got up at three o'clock in the morning on the day the bomb fell. There was extra housework to do. Her eleven-month-old brother, Akio, had come down the day before with a serious stomach upset; her mother had taken him to the Tamura Pediatric Hospital and was staying there with him. Miss Sasaki, who was about twenty, had to cook breakfast for her father, a brother, a sister, and herself, and—since the hospital, because of the war, was unable to provide food—to prepare a whole day's meals for her mother and the baby, in time for her father, who worked in a factory making rubber earplugs for artillery crews, to take the food by on his way to the plant. When she had finished and had cleaned and put away the cooking things, it was nearly seven. The family lived in Koi, and she had a forty-five-minute trip to the tin works, in the section of town called Kannonmachi. She was in charge of the personnel records in the factory. She left Koi at seven, and as soon as she reached the plant, she went with some of the other girls from the personnel department to the factory auditorium. A prominent local Navy man, a former employee, had committed suicide the day before by throwing himself under a train—a death considered honorable enough to warrant a memorial service, which was to be held at the tin works at ten o'clock that morning. In the large hall, Miss Sasaki and the others made suitable preparations for the meeting. This work took about twenty minutes.

Miss Sasaki went back to her office and sat down at her desk. She was quite far from the windows, which were off to her left, and behind her were a couple of tall bookcases containing all the books of the factory library, which the personnel department had organized. She settled herself at her desk, put some things in a drawer, and shifted papers. She thought that before she began to make entries in her lists of new employees, discharges, and departures for the Army, she would chat for a moment with the girl at her right. Just as she turned her head away from the windows, the room was filled with a blinding light. She was paralyzed by fear, fixed still in her chair for a long moment (the plant was 1,600 yards from the center).

Everything fell, and Miss Sasaki lost consciousness. The ceiling dropped suddenly and the wooden floor above collapsed in splinters and the people up there came down and the roof above them gave way; but principally and first of all, the bookcases right behind her swooped forward and the contents threw her down, with her left leg horribly twisted and breaking underneath her. There, in the tin factory, in the first moment of the atomic age, a human being was crushed by books.

Questions for Review

1. Plato's *Symposium* is one of the most famous of the philosopher's dialogues which show the great Socrates expounding his thought and which purport to be factual reports of things done and said. Is this true reportage or not? How would you test this dialogue as reportage?

2. What authorities does Plato establish as the source of his account? Are they reliable? How does Plato reconcile differences between his sources?

3. Is there anything in the account of Agathon's dinner that could not have happened as this report presents it? If Plato was chiefly interested in presenting philosophical speculations, why did he use the techniques of the reporter?

4. The *Symposium*, as a structured dialogue in a physical setting, is very much like Boswell's account of Dr. Johnson at dinner

with his friends. Is Plato, like Boswell, interested in depicting a man's character, or do his interests lie elsewhere?

5. In many ways, Plato's dialogues resemble plays or dramas. Could the *Symposium* be acted successfully? (Compare it with other dramatic and fictional dinners by Chekov, Wilder, and Hawthorne in later sections.)

6. Why does Plato include such trivial details as Aristophanes's hiccups in his account? How important are specific details in reportage?

7. Alcibiades, whose biography by Plutarch is given on p. 157 above, is shown in action in the *Symposium* by Plato, who knew him personally. Are his actions and words consistent with those described by Plutarch or not? In which version—the biography or the report—is Alcibiades most realistically (and convincingly) shown? How does the biography differ from the report?

8. Pliny's account of the death of his uncle, Pliny the Elder, during the famous eruption of Vesuvius that destroyed Pompeii, is in the form of a letter, as Pliny himself emphasized. Does this format affect the nature of the report?

9. How does Pliny establish the authority of his sources for the information contained in his report? Is this information likely to have been full and accurate or impartial, considering Pliny's informants?

10. Pliny says that reports at the moment of an event "speak most truly." Is he correct? Does his account prove the accuracy of this assertion?

11. Reread the last sentence in Pliny's letter. Is he right or not in his assertions about a letter and a history, writing to a friend and writing for the public? What does he mean?

12. Daniel Defoe was only a child during the great Plague in London in 1665, but his *Journal* is written as an eyewitness account by an adult. (It is believed that Defoe may have gotten many details from an uncle who was a saddler during the period described.) What advantages are there in using an "eye-witness" as a narrator for a report of this kind? Compare Defoe's nar-

rative technique with that of Plato and Pliny.

13. There are no famous figures in Defoe's report—no philosophers or writers or generals. How do Defoe's interests as a reporter substitute other emphases for those on "names" and "personalities"? What *is* Defoe mainly interested in?

14. In what ways does Defoe use details to carry his narrative along? Notice especially his use of statistics. What is the effect of these?

15. Why does Defoe call his report a "journal"? Is it like or unlike the journals given above on pp. 56–84?

16. The sinking of the *R.M.S. Titanic*, the subject of Hanson Baldwin's research reportage, was one of the most written about and moving stories of the early twentieth century. (See Thomas Hardy's "The Convergence of the Twain" on p. 532 below). Is this account one that you find emotionally moving? Does Baldwin emphasize the significance ("meaning") of the events he relates?

17. What parts of Baldwin's report are clearly "factual" and which are "interpretive" or "attitudes"? Identify the words and phrases the writer uses to impart his own reactions and values to the events he relates.

18. Is Baldwin's tone different in any way from that of the other reports in this selection? Does his tone have a decisive part in determining the effect of the report?

19. What were Baldwin's sources of information for this article? Point out evidence in the report itself for your answer.

20. One of the chief purposes of the reporter is to present detailed information: dates, names, figures, geographical details, human relationships, etc. Much of this sort of information is necessary for the reader to understand the context of the reported events; but the central event can be lost in too numerous or superfluous details. How does John Hersey present details in "A Noiseless Flash" without distracting the reader from the central event of his report?

21. Is Hersey's report merely a recounting of factual information? If not, what is it?

22. Does Hersey have any purpose in writing this report beyond conveying information? Is he arguing for anything or suggesting or accusing? Is this account any more biased or lacking in detachment than those by the other reporters given here?

23. Which of the other reports would you say is most similar to Hersey's in subject matter? In tone? In style? In point of view? In purpose? In effect?

24. The atom-bombing of Hiroshima is probably the greatest single news event of the present century, beginning as it did, the atomic age. Does Hersey suggest that he is writing about a great historical event? Why does he choose to concentrate on the personal experiences of six Hiroshimans? As an historian could he have done this? Is he actually writing six biographies?

25. How did Hersey get the information reported in this account? Explain your reasoning.

Questions for Discussion and Writing

1. Reportage, or journalism, is basically a day-to-day account. Is the reporter's use of time-sequence therefore a simplified one? What kinds of chronological techniques are used in the reports in this section? Can one generalize about the chronological method of the reporter?

2. Is it possible to write a report without including anything but facts? To eliminate entirely the personality of the reporter and narrate events from a totally impersonal point of view? Is it desirable?

3. Journalists differ in their use of the personal pronoun "I" and the consequent part they play in the accounts they give. Compare and contrast the "I" narrators of Plato, Pliny, and Defoe.

4. Neither Baldwin nor Hersey was an eyewitness to the events he tells about, so the first person is not used. What would their reports have gained by their being eyewitnesses? What would they have lost?

5. Compare the treatment of his subject by the reporter with the treatment of the same, or a similar, subject by writers of other literary types and list some principles of form or technique that distinguish "reportage" from other literary genres. (Compare the description of a plague by Defoe with that of Thucydides the historian on pp. 259–261, Zinsser the sociological and medical historian on pp. 350–357, and Poe the storyteller and allegorist on pp. 450–453. Or compare Pliny's interest in volcanoes with that of Williams' on pp. 322–327. Or Baldwin's report of shipwreck with Hardy's poem on p. 532 and Shakespeare's "song" on p. 522.)

SECTION TWO

The Public Domain—Historiography

The writer of "history" is something of a reporter on a grand scale: he writes about the *res gestae* ("things done") by groups of men or the single man which are believed to have had wide cultural or political or intellectual significance through a long span of time. The term "history' itself means an account of events in time; it is etymologically related to "story," which is generally used to refer to fictional events, whereas "history" refers to the "factual" or empirically provable narrative. Yet, if he is basically concerned with factual data, the writer of history, or the "historiographer," is not a mere chronicler or recorder. In his selection of subject matter, he imposes his own standards of relevance and importance; through the arrangement of his data he conceptualizes events in such a manner as to convey the "meaning" or "value" that he himself perceives in events—or the values that he imputes to events. At the present time, there is much consideration being given by historiographical theorists to the nature of historiography and the function of the historian. "History" was once thought to be a "record" of "true" events; at other times it was believed to be a revelation of God's guidance of mankind or a "science" of political and personal behavior based on demonstrable "truth." In the following group of essays, one of the most influential of twentieth century historians suggests the underlying assumptions of current theory, while the selections demonstrate the range and variety of historical literature from ancient Greece to modern America.

CARL L. BECKER

Everyman His Own Historian

One upon a time, long long ago, I learned how to reduce a fraction to its lowest terms. Whether I could still perform that operation is uncertain; but the discipline involved in early training had its uses, since it taught me that in order to understand the essential nature of anything it is well to strip it of all superficial and irrelevant accretions—in short, to reduce it to its lowest terms. That operation I now venture, with some apprehension and all due apologies, to perform on the subject of history.

I ought first of all to explain that when I use the term *history* I mean knowledge of history. No doubt throughout all past time there actually occurred a series of events which, whether we know what it was or not, constitutes history in some ultimate sense. Nevertheless, much the greater part of these events we can know nothing about, not even that they occurred; many of them we can know only imperfectly; and even the few events that we think we know for sure we can never be absolutely certain of, since we can never revive them, never observe or test them directly. The event itself once occurred, but as an actual event it has disappeared; so that in dealing with it the only objective reality we can observe or test is some material trace which the event has left—usually a written document. With these traces of vanished events, these documents, we must be content since they are all we have; from them we infer what the event was, we affirm that it is a fact that the event was so and so. We do not say "Lincoln is assassinated"; we say "it is a fact that Lincoln

From EVERYMAN HIS OWN HISTORIAN by Carl L. Becker, originally printed in *American Historical Review* (January 1932). Reprinted by permission of the American Historical Association.

was assassinated." The event *was*, but is no longer; it is only the affirmed fact about the event that *is*, that persists, and will persist until we discover that our affirmation is wrong or inadequate. Let us then admit that there are two histories: the actual series of events that once occurred; and the ideal series that we affirm and hold in memory. The first is absolute and unchanged—it was what it was whatever we do or say about it; the second is relative, always changing in response to the increase or refinement of knowledge. The two series correspond more or less; it is our aim to make the correspondence as exact as possible; but the actual series of events exists for us only in terms of the ideal series which we affirm and hold in memory. This is why I am forced to identify history with knowledge of history. For all practical purposes history is, for us and for the time being, what we know it to be.

It is history in this sense that I wish to reduce to its lowest terms. In order to do that I need a very simple definition. I once read that "History is the knowledge of events that have occurred in the past." That is a simple definition, but not simple enough. It contains three words that require examination. The first is knowledge. Knowledge is a formidable word. I always think of knowledge as something that is stored up in the *Encyclopaedia Britannica* or the *Summa Theologica*; something difficult to acquire, something at all events that I have not. Resenting a definition that denies me the title of historian, I therefore ask what is most essential to knowledge. Well, memory, I should think (and I mean memory in the broad sense, the memory of events inferred as well as the memory of events observed); other things are necessary too, but memory is fundamental: without memory no knowledge. So our definition becomes, "History is the memory of events that have occurred in the past." But events—the word carries an implication of something grand, like the taking of the Bastille or the Spanish-American War. An occurrence need not be spectacular to be an event. If I drive a motor car down the crooked streets of Ithaca, that is an event—something done; if the traffic cop bawls me out, that is an event—something said; if I have evil thoughts of him for so doing, that is an event—something thought. In truth anything done, said, or thought is an event, important or not as may turn out. But since we do not ordinarily speak without thinking, at least in some rudimentary way, and since the psychologists tell us that we cannot think without speaking, or at least not without having anticipatory vibrations in the larynx, we may well combine thought events and speech events under one term; and so our definition becomes, "History is the memory of things said and done in the past." But the past—the word is both misleading and unnecessary: misleading, because the past, used in connection with history, seems to imply the distant past, as if history ceased before we were born; unnecessary, because after all everything said or done is already in the past as soon as it is said or done. Therefore I will omit that word, and our definition becomes, "History is the memory of things said and done." This is a definition that reduces history to its lowest terms, and yet includes everything that is essential to understanding what it really is.

If the essence of history is the memory of things said and done, then it is obvious that every normal person, Mr. Everyman, knows some history. Of course we do what we can to conceal this invidious truth. Assuming a professional manner, we say that so and so knows no history, when we mean no more than that he failed to pass the examinations set for a higher degree; and simpleminded persons, undergraduates and others, taken in by academic classifications of knowledge, think they know no history because they have never taken a course in history in college, or have never read Gibbons' *Decline and Fall of the Roman Empire*. No doubt the academic convention has its uses, but it is one of the superficial accretions that must be stripped off it if we would understand history reduced to its lowest terms. Mr. Everyman, as well as you and I, remembers things

said and done, and must do so at every waking moment. Suppose Mr. Everyman to have awakened this morning unable to remember anything said or done. He would be a lost soul indeed. This has happened, this sudden loss of all historical knowledge. But normally it does not happen. Normally the memory of Mr. Everyman, when he awakens in the morning, reaches out into the country of the past and of distant places and instantaneously recreates his little world of endeavor, pulls together as it were things said and done in his yesterdays, and coordinates them with his present perceptions and with things to be said and done in his tomorrows. Without this historical knowledge, this memory of things said and done, his today would be aimless and his tomorrow without significance.

Since we are concerned with history in its lowest terms, we will suppose that Mr. Everyman is not a professor of history, but just an ordinary citizen without excess knowledge. Not having a lecture to prepare, his memory of things said and done, when he awakened this morning, presumably did not drag into consciousness any events connected with the Liman von Sanders mission or the Pseudo-Isidorian Decretals; it presumably dragged into consciousness an image of things said and done yesterday in the office, the highly significant fact that General Motors has dropped three points, a conference arranged for ten o'clock in the morning, a promise to play nine holes at four-thirty in the afternoon, and other historical events of similar import. Mr. Everyman knows more history than this, but at the moment of awakening this is sufficient: memory of things said and done, history functioning, at seven-thirty in the morning, in its very lowest terms, has effectively oriented Mr. Everyman in his little world of endeavor.

Yet not quite effectively after all perhaps; for unaided memory is notoriously fickle; and it may happen that Mr. Everyman, as he drinks his coffee, is uneasily aware of something said or done that he fails now to recall. A common enough occurrence, as we all know to our sorrow—this remembering, not the historical event, but only that there was an event which we ought to remember but can not. This is Mr. Everyman's difficulty, a bit of history lies dead and inert in the sources, unable to do any work for Mr. Everyman because his memory refuses to bring it alive in consciousness. What then does Mr. Everyman do? He does what any historian would do: he does a bit of historical research in the sources. From his little Private Record Office (I mean his vest pocket) he takes a book in MS., Volume XXXV, it may be, and turns to page 23, and there he reads: "December 29, pay Smith's coal bill, 20 tons, $1017.20." Instantaneously a series of historical events comes to life in Mr. Everyman's mind. He has an image of himself ordering twenty tons of coal from Smith last summer, of Smith's wagons driving up to his house, and of the precious coal sliding dustily through the cellar window. Historical events, these are, not so important as the forging of the Isidorian Decretals, but still important to Mr. Everyman: historical events which he was not present to observe, but which, by an artificial extension of memory, he can form a clear picture of, because he has done a little original research in the manuscripts preserved in his Private Record Office.

The picture Mr. Everyman forms of Smith's wagons delivering the coal at his house is a picture of things said and done in the past. But it does not stand alone, it is not a pure antiquarian image to be enjoyed for its own sake; on the contrary, it is associated with a picture of things to be said and done in the future; so that throughout the day Mr. Everyman intermittently holds in mind, together with a picture of Smith's coal wagons, a picture of himself going at four o'clock in the afternoon to Smith's office in order to pay his bill. At four o'clock Mr. Everyman is accordingly at Smith's office. "I wish to pay that coal bill," he says. Smith looks dubious and disappointed, takes down a ledger (or a filing case), does a bit of

original research in his Private Record Office, and announces: "You don't owe me any money, Mr. Everyman. You ordered the coal here all right, but I didn't have the kind you wanted, and so turned the order over to Brown. It was Brown delivered your coal: he's the man you owe." Whereupon Mr. Everyman goes to Brown's office; and Brown takes down a ledger, does a bit of original research in his Private Record Office, which happily confirms the researches of Smith; and Mr. Everyman pays his bill, and in the evening, after returning from the Country Club, makes a further search in another collection of documents, where, sure enough, he finds a bill from Brown, properly drawn, for twenty tons of stove coal, $1017.20 The research is now completed. Since his mind rests satisfied, Mr. Everyman has found the explanation of the series of events that concerned him.

Mr. Everyman would be astonished to learn that he is an historian, yet it is obvious, isn't it, that he has performed all the essential operations involved in historical research. Needing or wanting to do something (which happened to be, not to deliver a lecture or write a book, but to pay a bill; and this is what misleads him and us as to what he is really doing), the first step was to recall things said and done. Unaided memory proving inadequate, a further step was essential—the examination of certain documents in order to discover the necessary but as yet unknown facts. Unhappily the documents were found to give conflicting reports, so that a critical comparison of the texts had to be instituted in order to eliminate error. All this having been satisfactorily accomplished, Mr. Everyman is ready for the final operation— the formation in his mind, by an artificial extension of memory, of a picture, a definitive picture let us hope, of a selected series of historical events—of himself ordering coal from Smith, of Smith turning the order over to Brown, and of Brown delivering the coal at his house. In the light of this picture Mr. Everyman could, and did, pay his bill. If Mr. Everyman had undertaken these researches in order to write a book instead of to pay a bill, no one would think of denying that he was an historian.

I have tried to reduce history to its lowest terms, first by defining it as the memory of things said and done, second by showing concretely how the memory of things said and done is essential to the performance of the simplest acts of daily life. I wish now to note the more general implications of Mr. Everyman's activities. In the realm of affairs Mr. Everyman has been paying his coal bill; in the realm of consciousness he has been doing that fundamental thing which enables man alone to have, properly speaking, a history: he has been reinforcing and enriching his immediate perceptions to the end that he may live in a world of semblance more spacious and satisfying than is to be found within the narrow confines of the fleeting present moment.

We are apt to think of the past as dead, the future as nonexistent, the present alone as real; and prematurely wise or disillusioned counselors have urged us to burn always with "a hard, gemlike flame" in order to give "the highest quality to the moments as they pass, and simply for those moments' sake." This no doubt is what the glowworm does; but I think that man, who alone is properly aware that the present moment passes, can for that very reason make no good use of the present moment simply for its own sake. Strictly speaking, the present doesn't exist for us, or is at best no more than an infinitesimal point in time, gone before we can note it as present. Nevertheless, we must have a present; and so we create one by robbing the past, by holding on to the most recent events and pretending that they all belong to our immediate perceptions. If, for example, I raise my arm, the total event is a series of occurrences of which the first are past before the last have taken place; and yet you perceive it as a single movement executed in one present instant. This telescoping of successive events into a single instant philosophers call the "specious present." Doubtless they would assign rather narrow limits to the specious present; but I will willfully make a free use of it, and say that we can extend the specious present as much as we like. In common speech we do so: we speak of the "present hour," the "present year," the "present generation." Perhaps all living creatures have a specious present; but man has this superiority, as Pascal says, that he is aware of himself and the universe, can as it were hold himself at arm's length and with some measure of objectivity watch himself and his fellows functioning in the world during a brief span of allotted years. Of all the creatures, man alone has a specious present that may be deliberately and purposefully enlarged and diversified and enriched.

The extent to which the specious present may thus be enlarged and enriched will depend upon knowledge, the artificial extension of memory, the memory of things said and done in the past and distant places. But not upon knowledge alone; rather upon knowledge directed by purpose. The specious present is an unstable pattern of thought, incessantly changing in response to our immediate perceptions and the purposes that arise therefrom. At any given moment each one of us (professional historian no less than Mr. Everyman) weaves into this unstable pattern such actual or artificial memories as may be necessary to orient us in our little world of endeavor. But to be oriented in our little world of endeavor we must be prepared for what is coming to us (the payment of a coal bill, the delivery of a presidential address, the establishment of a League of Nations, or whatever); and to be prepared for what is coming to us it is necessary, not only to recall certain past events, but to anticipate (note I do not say predict) the future. Thus from the specious present, which always includes more or less of the past, the future refuses to be excluded; and the more of the past we drag into the specious present, the more a hypothetical, patterned future is likely to crowd into it also. Which comes first, which is cause and which effect, whether our memories construct a pattern of past events at the behest of our desires and hopes, or whether our desires and hopes spring from a pattern of past events imposed upon us by experience and knowledge, I shall not attempt to say. What I suspect is that memory of past and anticipation of future events work together, go hand in hand as it were in a friendly way, without disputing over priority and leadership.

At all events they go together, so that in a very real sense it is impossible to divorce history from life: Mr. Everyman cannot do what he needs or desires to do without recalling past events; he cannot recall past events without in some subtle fashion relating them to needs or desires to do. This is the natural function of history, of history reduced to its lowest terms, of history conceived as the memory of things said and done: memory of things said and done (whether in our immediate yesterdays or in the long past of mankind), running hand in hand with the anticipation of things to be said and done, enables us, each to the extent of his knowledge and imagination, to be intelligent, to push back the narrow confines of the fleeting present moment so that what we are doing may be judged in the light of what we have done and what we hope to do. In this sense all *living* history, as Croce says, is contemporaneous: in so far as we think the past (and otherwise the past, however fully related in documents, is nothing to us) it becomes an integral and living part of our present world of semblance.

It must then be obvious that living history, the ideal series of events that we affirm and hold in memory, since it is so intimately associated with what we are doing and with what we hope to do, cannot be precisely the same for all at any given time, or the same for one generation as for another. History in this sense cannot be reduced to a verifiable set of statistics or formulated in terms of universally valid mathematical formulas. It is rather an imaginative creation, a personal possession which each one of us, Mr. Everyman, fashions out of his individual experience, adapts to his practical or emotional needs, and adorns

as well as may be to suit his esthetic tastes. In thus creating his own history, there are, nevertheless, limits which Mr. Everyman may not overstep without incurring penalties. The limits are set by his fellows. If Mr. Everyman lived quite alone in an unconditioned world, he would be free to affirm and hold in memory any ideal series of events that struck his fancy, and thus create a world of semblance quite in accord with the heart's desire. Unfortunately, Mr. Everyman has to live in a world of Browns and Smiths; a sad experience, which has taught him the expediency of recalling certain events with much exactness. In all the immediately practical affairs of life Mr. Everyman is a good historian, as expert, in conducting the researches necessary for paying his coal bill, as need be. His expertness comes partly from long practice, but chiefly from the circumstance that his researches are prescribed and guided by very definite and practical objects which concern him intimately. The problem of what documents to consult, what facts to select, troubles Mr. Everyman not at all. Since he is not writing a book on "Some Aspects of the Coal Industry Objectively Considered," it does not occur to him to collect all the facts and let them speak for themselves. Wishing merely to pay his coal bill, he selects only such facts as may be relevant; and not wishing to pay it twice, he is sufficiently aware, without ever having read Bernheim's *Lehrbuch*, that the relevant facts must be clearly established by the testimony of independent witnesses not self-deceived. He does not know, or need to know, that his personal interest in the performance is a disturbing bias which will prevent him from learning the whole truth or arriving at ultimate causes. Mr. Everyman does not wish to learn the whole truth or to arrive at ultimate causes. He wishes to pay his coal bill. That is to say, he wishes to adjust himself to a practical situation, and on that low pragmatic level he is a good historian precisely because he is not disinterested: he will solve his problems, if he does solve them, by virtue of his intelligence, and not by virtue of his indifference.

Nevertheless, Mr. Everyman does not live by bread alone; and on all proper occasions his memory of things said and done, easily enlarging his spacious present beyond the narrow circle of daily affairs, will, must inevitably, in mere compensation for the intolerable dullness and vexation of the fleeting present moment, fashion for him a more spacious world than that of the immediately practical. He can readily recall the days of his youth, the places he has lived in, the ventures he has made, the adventures he has had—all the crowded events of a lifetime; and beyond and around this central pattern of personally experienced events, there will be embroidered a more dimly seen pattern of artificial memories, memories of things reputed to have been said and done in past times which he has not known, in distant places which he has not seen. This outer pattern of remembered events that encloses and completes the central pattern of his personal experience, Mr. Everyman has woven, he could not tell you how, out of the most diverse threads of information, picked up in the most casual way, from the most unrelated sources—from things learned at home and in school, from knowledge gained in business or profession, from newspapers glanced at, from books (yes, even history books) read or heard of, from remembered scraps of newsreels or educational films of *ex cathedra* utterances of presidents and kings, from fifteen-minute discourses on the history of civilization broadcast by the courtesy (it may be) of Pepsodent, the Bulova Watch Company, or the Shepard Stores in Boston. Daily and hourly, from a thousand unnoted sources, there is lodged in Mr. Everyman's mind a mass of unrelated and related information and misinformation, of impressions and images, out of which he somehow manages, undeliberately for the most part, to fashion a history, a patterned picture of remembered things said and done in past times and distant places. It is not possible, it is not essential, that this picture should be complete or completely true: it is essential that it should be useful to Mr. Everyman; and that it

may be useful to him he will hold in memory, of all the things he might hold in memory, those things only which can be related with some reasonable degree of relevance and harmony to his idea of himself and of what he is doing in the world and what he hopes to do.

In constructing this more remote and far-flung pattern of remembered things, Mr. Everyman works with something of the freedom of a creative artist; the history which he imaginatively recreates as an artificial extension of his personal experience will inevitably be an engaging blend of fact and fancy, a mythical adaptation of that which actually happened. In part it will be true, in part false; as a whole perhaps neither true nor false, but only the most convenient form of error. Not that Mr. Everyman wishes or intends to deceive himself or others. Mr. Everyman has a wholesome respect for cold, hard facts, never suspecting how malleable they are, how easy it is to coax and cajole them; but he necessarily takes the facts as they come to him, and is enamored of those that seem best suited to his interests or promise most in the way of emotional satisfaction. The exact truth of remembered events he has in any case no time, and no need, to curiously question or meticulously verify. No doubt he can, if he be an American, call up an image of the signing of the Declaration of Independence in 1776 as readily as he can call up an image of Smith's coal wagons creaking up the hill last summer. He suspects the one image no more than the other; but the signing of the Declaration, touching not his practical interests, calls for no careful historical research on his part. He may perhaps, without knowing why, affirm and hold in memory that the Declaration was signed by the members of the Continental Congress on the fourth of July. It is a vivid and sufficient image which Mr. Everyman may hold to the end of his days without incurring penalties. Neither Brown nor Smith has any interest in setting him right; nor will any court ever send him a summons for failing to recall that the Declaration, "being engrossed and compared at the table, was signed by the members" on the second of August. As an actual event, the signing of the Declaration was what it was; as a remembered event it will be, for Mr. Everyman, what Mr. Everyman contrives to make it: will have for him significance and magic, much or little or none at all, as it fits well or ill into his little world of interests and aspirations and emotional comforts.

What then of us, historians by profession? What have we to do with Mr. Everyman, or he with us? More, I venture to believe, than we are apt to think. For each of us is Mr. Everyman too. Each of us is subject to the limitations of time and place; and for each of us, no less than for the Browns and Smiths of the world, the pattern of remembered things said and done will be woven, safeguard the process how we may, at the behest of circumstance and purpose.

True it is that although each of us is Mr. Everyman, each is something more than his own historian. Mr. Everyman, being but an informal historian, is under no bond to remember what is irrelevant to his personal affairs. But we are historians by profession. Our profession, less intimately bound up with the practical activities, is to be directly concerned with the ideal series of events that is only of casual or occasional import to others; it is our business in life to be ever preoccupied with that far-flung pattern of artificial memories that encloses and completes the central pattern of individual experience. We are Mr. Everyman's historian as well as our own, since our histories serve the double purpose, which written histories have always served, of keeping alive the recollection of memorable men and events. We are thus of that ancient and honorable company of wise men of the tribe, of bards and story-tellers and minstrels, of soothsayers and priests, to whom in successive ages has been entrusted the keeping of the useful myths. Let not the harmless, necessary word "myth" put us out of countenance. In the history of history a myth is a once valid but now discarded version of the human story, as our now valid versions will in due course be relegated to the category of discarded myths.

With our predecessors, the bards and story-tellers and priests, we have therefore this in common: that it is our function, as it was theirs, not to create, but to preserve and perpetuate the social tradition; to harmonize, as well as ignorance and prejudice permit, the actual and the remembered series of events; to enlarge and enrich the specious present common to us all to the end that "society" (the tribe, the nation, or all mankind) may judge of what it is doing in the light of what it has done and what it hopes to do.

History as the artificial extension of the social memory (and I willingly concede that there are other appropriate ways of apprehending human experience) is an art of long standing, necessarily so since it springs instinctively from the impulse to enlarge the range of immediate experience; and however camouflaged by the disfiguring jargon of science, it is still in essence what it has always been. History in this sense is story, in aim always a true story; a story that employs all the devices of literary art (statement and generalization, narration and description, comparison and comment and analogy) to present the succession of events in the life of man, and from the succession of events thus presented to derive a satisfactory meaning. The history written by historians, like the history informally fashioned by Mr. Everyman, is thus a convenient blend of truth and fancy, of what we commonly distinguish as "fact" and "interpretation." In primitive times, when tradition is orally transmitted, bards and storytellers frankly embroider or improvise the facts to heighten the dramatic import of the story. With the use of written records, history, gradually differentiated from fiction, is understood as the story of events that actually occurred; and with the increase and refinement of knowledge the historian recognizes that his first duty is to be sure of his facts, let their meaning be what it may. Nevertheless, in every age history is taken to be a story of actual events from which a significant meaning may be derived; and in every age the illusion is that the present version is valid because the related facts are true, whereas former versions are invalid because based upon inaccurate or inadequate facts.

Never was this conviction more impressively displayed than in our own time—that age of erudition in which we live, or from which we are perhaps just emerging. Finding the course of history littered with the *débris* of exploded philosophies, the historians of the last century, unwilling to be forever duped, turned away (as they fondly hoped) from "interpretation" to the rigorous examination of the factual event, just as it occurred. Perfecting the technique of investigation, they laboriously collected and edited the sources of information, and with incredible persistence and ingenuity ran illusive error to earth, letting the significance of the Middle Ages wait until it was certainly known "whether Charles the Fat was at Ingelheim or Lustnau on July 1, 887," shedding their "life-blood," in many a hard fought battle, "for the sublime truths of Sac and Soc." I have no quarrel with this so great concern with *hoti*'s business. One of the first duties of man is not to be duped, to be aware of his world; and to derive the significance of human experience from events that never occurred is surely an enterprise of doubtful value. To establish the facts is always in order, and is indeed the first duty of the historian; but to suppose that the facts, once established in all their fullness, will "speak for themselves" is an illusion. It was perhaps peculiarly the illusion of those historians of the last century who found some special magic in the word "scientific." The scientific historian, it seems, was one who set forth the facts without injecting any extraneous meaning into them. He was the objective man whom Nietzsche described—"a mirror: accustomed to prostration before something that wants to be known, ... he waits until something comes, and then expands himself sensitively, so that even the light footsteps and gliding past of spiritual things may not be lost in his surface and film." "It is not I who speak, but history which speaks through me," was Fustel's reproof to applauding students. "If a certain philosophy emerges from this scientific history, it must be permitted to emerge naturally, of its own accord, all but independently of the will of the historian." Thus the scientific historian deliberately renounced philosophy only to submit to it without being aware. His philosophy was just this, that by not taking thought a cubit would be added to his stature. With no other preconception than the will to know, the historian would reflect in his surface and film the "order of events throughout past times in all places"; so that, in the fullness of time, when innumerable patient expert scholars by "exhausting the sources," should have reflected without refracting the truth of all the facts, the definitive and impregnable meaning of human experience would emerge of its own accord to enlighten and emancipate mankind. Hoping to find something without looking for it, expecting to obtain final answers to life's riddle by resolutely refusing to ask questions—it was surely the most romantic species of realism yet invented, the oddest attempt ever made to get something for nothing!

That mood is passing. The fullness of time is not yet, overmuch learning proves a weariness to the flesh, and a younger generation that knows not Von Ranke is eager to believe that Fustel's counsel, if one of perfection, is equally one of futility. Even the most disinterested historian has at least one preconception, which is the fixed idea that he has none. The facts of history are already set forth, implicitly, in the sources; and the historian who could restate without reshaping them would, by submerging and suffocating the mind in diffuse existence, accomplish the superfluous task of depriving human experience of all significance. Left to themselves, the facts do not speak; left to themselves they do not exist, not really, since for all practical purposes there is no fact until someone affirms it. The least the historian can do with any historical fact is to select and affirm it. To select and affirm even the simplest complex of facts is to give them a certain place in a certain pattern of ideas, and this alone is sufficient to give them a special meaning. However "hard" or "cold" they may be, historical facts are after all not material substances which, like bricks or scantlings, possess definite shape and clear, persistent outline. To set forth historical facts is not comparable to dumping a barrow of bricks. A brick retains its form and pressure wherever placed; but the form and substance of historical facts, having a negotiable existence only in literary discourse, vary with the words employed to convey them. Since history is not part of the external material world, but an imaginative reconstruction of vanished events, its form and substance are inseparable: in the realm of literary discourse substance, being an idea, *is* form; and form, conveying the idea, *is* substance. It is thus not the undiscriminated fact, but the perceiving mind of the historian that speaks: the special meaning which the facts are made to convey emerges from the substance-form which the historian employs to re-create imaginatively a series of events not present to perception.

In constructing this substance-form of vanished events, the historian, like Mr. Everyman, like the bards and the storytellers of an earlier time, will be conditioned by the specious present in which alone he can be aware of his world. Being neither omniscient nor omnipresent, the historian is not the same person always and everywhere; and for him, as for Mr. Everyman, the form and significance of remembered events, like the extension and velocity of physical objects, will vary with the time and place of the observer. After fifty years we can clearly see that it was not history which spoke through Fustel, but Fustel who spoke through history. We see less clearly perhaps that the voice of Fustel was the voice, amplified and freed from static as one may say, of Mr. Everyman; what the admiring students applauded on that famous occasion was neither history nor Fustel, but a deftly colored pattern of selected events which Fustel fashioned, all the more skillfully for not being aware of doing so, in the service of Mr. Everyman's emotional needs—the emotional satisfaction, so essential to Frenchmen at that time, of perceiving that French institutions were not of German origin. And so it must always be. Played upon by all the diverse, unnoted influences of his own time, the historian will elicit history out of documents by the same principle, however more consciously and expertly applied, that Mr. Everyman employs to breed legends out of remembered episodes and oral tradition.

Berate him as we will for not reading our books, Mr. Everyman is stronger than we are, and sooner or later we must adapt our knowledge to his necessities. Otherwise he will leave us to our own devices, leave us it may be to cultivate a species of dry professional arrogance growing out of the thin soil of antiquarian research. Such research, valuable not in itself but for some ulterior purpose, will be of little import except in so far as it is transmuted into common knowledge. The history that lies inert in unread books does no work in the world. The history that does work in the world, the history that influences the course of history, is living history, that pattern of remembered events, whether true or false, that enlarges and enriches the collective specious present, the specious present of Mr. Everyman. It is for this reason that the history of history is a record of the "new history" that in every age rises to confound and supplant the old. It should be a relief to us to renounce omniscience, to recognize that every generation, our own included, will, must inevitably, understand the past and anticipate the future in the light of its own restricted experience, must inevitably play on the dead whatever tricks it finds necessary for its own peace of mind. The appropriate trick for any age is not a malicious invention designed to take anyone in, but an unconscious and necessary effort on the part of "society" to understand what it is doing in the light of what it has done and what it hopes to do. We, historians by profession, share in this necessary effort. But we do not impose our version of the human story on Mr. Everyman; in the end it is rather Mr. Everyman who imposes his version on us—compelling us, in an age of political revolution, to see that history is past politics, in an age of social stress and conflict to search for the economic interpretation. If we remain too long recalcitrant Mr. Everyman will ignore us, shelving our recondite works behind glass doors rarely opened. Our proper function is not to repeat the past but to make use of it, to correct and rationalize for common use Mr. Everyman's mythological adaptation of what actually happened. We are surely under bond to be as honest and as intelligent as human frailty permits; but the secret of our success in the long run is in conforming to the temper of Mr. Everyman, which we seem to guide only because we are so sure, eventually, to follow it.

Neither the value nor the dignity of history need suffer by regarding it as a foreshortened and incomplete representation of the reality that once was, an unstable pattern of re-membered things redesigned and newly colored to suit the convenience of those who make use of it. Nor need our labors be the less highly prized because our task is limited, our contribu-tions of incidental and temporary significance. History is an indispensable even though not the highest form of intellectual endeavor, since it makes, as Santayana says, a gift of "great interests...to the heart. A barbarian is not less subject to the past than is the civic man who knows what the past is and means to be loyal to it; but the barbarian, for want of a trans-personal memory, crawls among superstitions which he cannot understand or revoke and among people whom he may hate or love, but whom he can never think of raising to a higher plane, to the level of a purer happiness. The whole dignity of human endeavor is thus bound up with historic issues, and as conscience needs to be controlled by experience if it is to become rational, so personal experience itself needs to

be enlarged ideally if the failures and successes it reports are to touch impersonal interests."

I do not present this view of history as one that is stable and must prevail. Whatever validity it may claim, it is certain, on its own premises, to be supplanted; for its premises, imposed upon us by the climate of opinion in which we live and think, predispose us to regard all things, and all principles of things, as no more than "inconstant modes or fashions," as but the "concurrence, renewed from moment to moment, of forces parting sooner or later on their way." It is the limitation of the genetic approach to human experience that it must be content to transform problems since it can never solve them. However accurately we may deter-mine the "facts" of history, the facts themselves and our interpretations of them, and our interpretation of our own interpretations, will be seen in a different perspective or a less vivid light as mankind moves into the unknown future. Regarded historically, as a process of becoming, man and his world can obviously be understood only tentatively, since it is by definition some-thing still in the making, something as yet unfinished. Unfortunately for the "permanent contribution" and the universally valid philo-sophy, time passes; time, the enemy of man as the Greeks thought; tomorrow and tomorrow and tomorrow creeps in this petty pace, and all our yesterdays diminish and grow dim: so that, in the lengthening perspective of the centuries, even the most striking events (the Declaration of Independence, the French Revolution, the Great War itself; like the Diet of Worms before them, like the signing of the Magna Carta and the coronation of Charle-magne and the crossing of the Rubicon and the battle of Marathon) must inevitably, for posterity, fade away into pale replicas of the original picture, for each succeeding generation losing, as they recede into a more distant past, some significance that once was noted in them, some quality of enchantment that once was theirs.

THUCYDIDES

The Plague in Athens

Such was the order of the funeral celebrated in this winter, with the end of which ended the first year of the Peloponnesian War. As soon as summer returned, the Peloponnesian army, comprising as before two-thirds of the force of each confederate state, under the command of the Lacedaemonian king Archidamus, the son of Zeuxidamus, invaded Attica, where they established themselves and ravaged the country. They had not been there many days when the plague broke out at Athens for the first time. A similar disorder is said to have previously smitten many places, particularly Lemnos, but there is no record of such a pestilence occurring elsewhere, or of so great a destruction of human life. For a while physicans, in ignorance of the nature of the disease, sought to apply remedies; but it was in vain, and they themselves were among the first victims, because they oftenest came into contact with it. No human art was of any avail, and as to supplications in temples, enquiries of oracles, and the like, they were utterly useless, and at last men were overpowered by the calamity and gave them all up.

The disease is said to have begun south of Egypt in Aethiopia; thence it descended into Egypt and Libya, and after spreading over the greater part of the Persian empire, suddenly fell upon Athens. It first attacked the inhabitants of the Piraeus, and it was supposed that the Peloponnesians had poisoned the cisterns, no conduits having as yet been made there. It afterwards reached the upper city, and then the mortality became far greater. As to its probable origin or the causes which might or could have

THE PLAGUE IN ATHENS: From *A History of the Peloponnesian Wars* by Thucydides. Translated by Thomas Hobbes.

produced such a disturbance of nature, every man, whether a physician or not, will give his own opinion. But I shall describe its actual course, and the symptoms by which any one who knows them beforehand may recognise the disorder should it ever reappear. For I was myself attacked, and witnessed the sufferings of others.

The season was admitted to have been remarkably free from ordinary sickness; and if anybody was already ill of any other disease, it was absorbed in this. Many who were in perfect health, all in a moment, and without any apparent reason, were seized with violent heats in the head and with redness and inflammation of the eyes. Internally the throat and the tongue were quickly suffused with blood, and the breath became unnatural and fetid. There followed sneezing and hoarseness; in a short time the disorder, accompanied by a violent cough, reached the chest; then fastening lower down, it would move the stomach and bring on all the vomits of bile to which physicians have ever given names; and they were very distressing. An ineffectual retching producing violent convulsions attacked most of the sufferers; some as soon as the previous symptoms had abated, others not until long afterwards. The body externally was not so very hot to the touch, nor yet pale; it was of a livid colour inclining to red, and breaking out in pustules and ulcers. But the internal fever was intense; the sufferers could not bear to have on them even the finest linen garment; they insisted on being naked, and there was nothing which they longed for more eagerly than to throw themselves into cold water. And many of those who had no one to look after them actually plunged into the cisterns, for they were tormented by unceasing thirst, which was not in the least assuaged whether they drank little or much. They could not sleep; a restlessness which was intolerable never left them. While the disease was at its height the body, instead of wasting away, held out amid these sufferings in a marvellous manner, and either they died on the seventh or ninth day, not of weakness, for their strength was not exhausted, but of internal fever, which was the end of most; or, if they survived, then the disease descended into the bowels and there produced violent ulceration; severe diarrhoea at the same time set in, and at a later stage caused exhaustion, which finally with few exceptions carried them off. For the disorder which had originally settled in the head passed gradually through the whole body, and, if a person got over the worst, would often seize the extremities and leave its mark, attacking the privy parts and the fingers and the toes; and some escaped with the loss of these, some with the loss of their eyes. Some again had no sooner recovered than they were seized with a forgetfulness of all things and knew neither themselves nor their friends.

The malady took a form not to be described, and the fury with which it fastened upon each sufferer was too much for human nature to endure. There was one circumstance in particular which distinguished it from ordinary diseases. The birds and animals which feed on human flesh, although so many bodies were lying unburied, either never came near them, or died if they touched them. This was proved by a remarkable disappearance of the birds of prey, who were not to be seen either about the bodies or anywhere else; while in the case of the dogs the fact was even more obvious, because they live with man.

Such was the general nature of the disease: I omit many strange peculiarities which characterised individual cases. None of the ordinary sicknesses attacked any one while it lasted, or, if they did, they ended in the plague. Some of the sufferers died from want of care, others equally who were receiving the greatest attention. No single remedy could be deemed a specific; for that which did good to one did harm to another. No constitution was of itself strong enough to resist or weak enough to escape the attacks; the disease carried off all alike and defied every mode of treatment. Most appalling was the despondency which seized upon any one who felt himself sickening; for he instantly

abandoned his mind to despair and, instead of holding out, absolutely threw away his chance of life. Appalling too was the rapidity with which men caught the infection; dying like sheep if they attended on one another; and this was the principal cause of mortality. When they were afraid to visit one another, the sufferers died in their solitude, so that many houses were empty because there had been no one left to take care of the sick; or if they ventured they perished, especially those who aspired to heroism. For they went to see their friends without thought of themselves and were ashamed to leave them, even at a time when the very relations of the dying were at last growing weary and ceased to make lamentations, overwhelmed by the vastness of the calamity. But whatever instances there may have been of such devotion, more often the sick and the dying were tended by the pitying care of those who had recovered, because they knew the course of the disease and were themselves free from apprehension. For no one was ever attacked a second time, or not with a fatal result. All men congratulated them, and they themselves, in the excess of their joy at the moment, had an innocent fancy that they could not die of any other sickness.

The crowding of the people out of the country into the city aggravated the misery; and the newly-arrived suffered most. For, having no houses of their own, but inhabiting in the height of summer stifling huts, the mortality among them was dreadful, and they perished in wild disorder. The dead lay as they had died one upon another, while others hardly alive wallowed in the streets and crawled about every fountain craving for water. The temples in which they lodged were full of the corpses of those who died in them; for the violence of the calamity was such that men, not knowing where to turn, grew reckless of all law, human and divine. The customs which had hitherto been observed at funerals were universally violated, and they buried their dead each one as best he could. Many, having no proper appliances, because the deaths in their household had been so frequent, made no scruple of using the burial-place of others. When one man had raised a funeral pile, others would come, and throwing on their dead first, set fire to it; or when some other corpse was already burning, before they could be stopped would throw their own dead upon it and depart.

There were other and worse forms of lawlessness which the plague introduced at Athens. Men who had hitherto concealed their indulgence in pleasure now grew bolder. For, seeing the sudden change—how the rich died in a moment, and those who had nothing immediately inherited their property—they reflected that life and riches were alike transitory, and they resolved to enjoy themselves while they could, and to think only of pleasure. Who would be willing to sacrifice himself to the law of honour when he knew not whether he would ever live to be held in honour? The pleasure of the moment and any sort of thing which conduced to it took the place both of honour and of expediency. No fear of God or law of man deterred a criminal. Those who saw all perishing alike, thought that the worship or neglect of the Gods made no difference. For offenses against human law no punishment was to be feared; no one would live long enough to be called to account. Already a far heavier sentence had been passed and was hanging over a man's head; before that fell, why should he not take a little pleasure?

Such was the grievous calamity which now afflicted the Athenians; within the walls their people were dying, and without, their country was being ravaged. In their troubles they naturally called to mind a verse which the elder men among them declared to have been current long ago:—

A Dorian war will come and a plague with it.

There was a dispute about the precise expression; some saying that *limos*, a famine, and not *loimos*, a plague, was the original word. Nevertheless, as might have been expected, for men's memories reflected their sufferings, the argument in favour of *loimos* prevailed at the time. But if ever in future years another Dorian war arises which happens to be accompanied by a famine, they will probably repeat the verse in the other form. The answer of the oracle to the Lacedaemonians when the God was asked "whether they should go to war or not," and he replied "that if they fought with all their might, they would conquer, and that he himself would take their part," was not forgotten by those who had heard of it, and they quite imagined that they were witnessing the fulfilment of his words. The disease certainly did set in immediately after the invasion of the Peloponnesians, and did not spread into Peloponnesus in any degree worth speaking of, while Athens felt its ravages most severely, and next to Athens the places which were most populous. Such was the history of the plague.

EDWARD GIBBON

The Fall of Constantinople

During the siege of Constantinople the words of peace and capitulation had been sometimes pronounced; and several embassies had passed between the camp and the city. The Greek emperor was humbled by adversity; and would have yielded to any terms compatible with religion and royalty. The Turkish sultan was desirous of sparing the blood of his soldiers; still more desirous of securing for his own use the Byzantine treasures; and he accomplished a sacred duty in presenting to the *Gabours* the

THE FALL OF CONSTANTINOPLE: From *The History of the Decline and Fall of the Roman Empire* by Edward Gibbon. First printed in 1788.

choice of circumcision, of tribute, or of death. The avarice of Mohammed might have been satisfied with an annual sum of one hundred thousand ducats; but his ambition grasped the capital of the East: to the prince he offered a rich equivalent, to the people a free toleration, or a safe departure: but after some fruitless treaty, he declared his resolution of finding either a throne or a grave under the walls of Constantinople. A sense of honour, and the fear of universal reproach, forbade Palaeologus to resign the city into the hands of the Ottomans; and he determined to abide the last extremities of war. Several days were employed by the sultan in the preparations of the assault; and a respite was granted by his favourite science of astrology, which had fixed on the twenty-ninth of May as the fortunate and fatal hour. On the evening of the twenty-seventh he issued his final orders; assembled in his presence the military chiefs; and dispersed his heralds through the camp to proclaim the duty and the motives of the perilous enterprise. Fear is the first principle of a despotic government; and his menaces were expressed in the Oriental style, that the fugitives and deserters, had they the wings of a bird, should not escape from his inexorable justice. The greatest part of his bashaws and Janizaries were the offspring of Christian parents: but the glories of the Turkish name were perpetuated by successive adoption; and in the gradual change of individuals, the spirit of a legion, a regiment, or an *oda*, is kept alive by imitation and discipline. In this holy warfare the Moslems were exhorted to purify their minds with prayer, their bodies with seven ablutions; and to abstain from food till the close of the ensuing day. A crowd of dervishes visited the tents, to instil the desire of martyrdom, and the assurance of spending an immortal youth amidst the rivers and gardens of paradise, and in the embraces of the black-eyed virgins. Yet Mohammed principally trusted to the efficacy of temporal and visible rewards. A double pay was promised to the victorious troops; "The city and the buildings," said Mohammed, "are

mine; but I resign to your valour the captives and the spoil, the treasures of gold and beauty; be rich and be happy. Many are the provinces of my empire: the intrepid soldier who first ascends the walls of Constantinople shall be rewarded with the government of the fairest and most wealthy; and my gratitude shall accumulate his honours and fortunes above the measure of his own hopes." Such various and potent motives diffused among the Turks a general ardour, regardless of life and impatient for action: the camp re-echoed with the Moslem shouts of "God is God: There is but one God, and Mohammed is the apostle of God"; and the sea and land, from Galata to the seven towers, were illuminated by the blaze of their nocturnal fires.

Far different was the state of the Christians; who, with loud and impotent complaints, deplored the guilt, or the punishment, of their sins. The celestial image of the Virgin had been exposed in solemn procession; but their divine patroness was deaf to their entreaties: they accused the obstinacy of the emperor for refusing a timely surrender; anticipated the horrors of their fate; and sighed for the repose and security of Turkish servitude. The noblest of the Greeks, and the bravest of the allies, were summoned to the palace, to prepare them, on the evening of the twenty-eighth, for the duties and dangers of the general assault. The last speech of Palaeologus was the funeral oration of the Roman empire: he promised, he conjured, and he vainly attempted to infuse the hope which was extinguished in his own mind. In this world all was comfortless and gloomy; and neither the Gospel nor the church have proposed any conspicuous recompense to the heroes who fall in the service of their country. But the example of their prince, and the confinement of a siege, had armed these warriors with the courage of despair; and the pathetic scene is described by the feelings of the historian Phranza, who was himself present at this mournful assembly. They wept, they embraced: regardless of their families and fortunes, they devoted their lives; and each commander, departing to his station, maintained all night a vigilant and anxious watch on the rampart. The emperor, and some faithful companions, entered the dome of St. Sophia, which in a few hours was to be converted into a mosque; and devoutly received, with tears and prayers, the sacrament of the holy communion. He reposed some moments in the palace, which resounded with cries and lamentations; solicited the pardon of all whom he might have injured; and mounted on horseback to visit the guards, and explore the motions of the enemy. The distress and fall of the last Constantine are more glorious than the long prosperity of the Byzantine Caesars.

In the confusion of darkness an assailant may sometimes succeed; but in this great and general attack, the military judgment and astrological knowledge of Mohammed advised him to expect the morning, the memorable twenty-ninth of May, in the fourteen hundred and fifty-third year of the Christian era. The preceding night had been strenuously employed: the troops, the cannon, and the fascines were advanced to the edge of the ditch, which in many parts presented a smooth and level passage to the breach; and his fourscore galleys almost touched, with the prows and their scaling ladders, the less defensible walls of the harbour. Under pain of death, silence was enjoined; but the physical laws of motion and sound are not obedient to discipline or fear: each individual might suppress his voice and measure his footsteps; but the march and labour of thousands must inevitably produce a strange confusion of dissonant clamours, which reached the ears of the watchmen of the towers. At daybreak, without the customary signal of the morning gun, the Turks assaulted the city by sea and land; and the similitude of a twined or twisted thread has been applied to the closeness and continuity of their line of attack. The foremost ranks consisted of the refuse of the host, a voluntary crowd who fought without order or command; of the feebleness of age or childhood, of peasants and vagrants, and of all who had joined the camp in the blind hope of plunder and martyrdom. The common impulse drove them onwards to the wall; the most audacious to climb were instantly precipitated; and not a dart, not a bullet, of the Christians, was idly wasted on the accumulated throng. But their strength and ammunition were exhausted in this laborious defense: the ditch was filled with the bodies of the slain; they supported the footsteps of their companions; and of this devoted vanguard the death was more serviceable than the life. Under their respective bashaws and sanjaks, the troops of Anatolia and Romania were successively led to the charge: their progress was various and doubtful; but, after a conflict of two hours, the Greeks still maintained and improved their advantage; and the voice of the emperor was heard, encouraging his soldiers to achieve, by a last effort, the deliverance of their country. In that fatal moment the Janizaries arose, fresh, vigorous, and invincible. The sultan himself on horseback, with an iron mace in his hand, was the spectator and judge of their valour; he was surrounded by ten thousand of his domestic troops, whom he reserved for the decisive occasion; and the tide of battle was directed and impelled by his voice and eye. His numerous ministers of justice were posted behind the line, to urge, to restrain, and to punish; and if danger was in the front, shame and inevitable death were in the rear, of the fugitives. The cries of fear and of pain were drowned in the martial music of drums, trumpets, and attaballs; and experience has proved that the mechanical operation of sounds, by quickening the circulation of the blood and spirits, will act on the human machine more forcibly than the eloquence of reason and honour. From the lines, the galleys, and the bridge, the Ottoman artillery thundered on all sides; and the camp and city, the Greeks and the Turks, were involved in a cloud of smoke, which could only be dispelled by the final deliverance or destruction of the Roman empire. The single combats of the heroes of history or fable amuse our fancy and engage our affections: the skilful evolutions of war may inform the mind, and improve a necessary, though pernicious, science. But in the uniform and odious pictures of a general assault, all is blood, and horror, and confusion; nor shall I strive, at the distance of three centuries and a thousand miles, to delineate a scene of which there could be no spectators, and of which the actors themselves were incapable of forming any just or adequate idea.

The immediate loss of Constantinople may be ascribed to the bullet, or arrow, which pierced the gauntlet of John Justiniani. The sight of his blood, and the exquisite pain, appalled the courage of the chief, whose arms and counsels were the firmest rampart of the city. As he withdrew from his station in quest of a surgeon, his flight was perceived and stopped by the indefatigable emperor. "Your wound," exclaimed Palaeologus, "is slight; the danger is pressing: your presence is necessary; and whither will you retire?"—"I will retire," said the trembling Genoese, "by the same road which God has opened to the Turks"; and at these words he hastily passed through one of the breaches of the inner wall. By this pusillanimous act he stained the honours of a military life; and the few days which he survived in Galata, or the isle of Chios, were embittered by his own and the public reproach. His example was imitated by the greatest part of the Latin auxiliaries, and the defense began to slacken when the attack was pressed with redoubled vigour. The number of the Ottomans was fifty, perhaps a hundred, times superior to that of the Christians; the double walls were reduced by the cannon to a heap of ruins: in a circuit of several miles some places must be found more easy of access, or more feebly guarded; and if the besiegers could penetrate in a single point, the whole city was irrecoverably lost. The first who deserved the sultan's reward was Hassan the Janizary, of gigantic stature and strength. With his scimitar in one hand and his buckler in the other, he ascended the outward fortification: of the thirty Janizaries who were emulous of his valour, eighteen perished in the bold adventure.

Hassan and his twelve companions had reached the summit: the giant was precipitated from the rampart: he rose on one knee, and was again oppressed by a shower of darts and stones. But his success had proved that the achievement was possible: the walls and towers were instantly covered with a swarm of Turks; and the Greeks, now driven from the vantage ground, were overwhelmed by increasing multitudes. Amidst these multitudes, the emperor, who accomplished all the duties of a general and a soldier, was long seen and finally lost. The nobles, who fought round his person, sustained, till their last breath, the honourable names of Palaeologus and Cantacuzene: his mournful exclamation was heard, "Cannot there be found a Christian to cut off my head?" and his last fear was that of falling alive into the hands of the infidels. The prudent despair of Constantine cast away the purple: amidst the tumult he fell by an unknown hand, and his body was buried under a mountain of the slain. After his death resistance and order were no more: the Greeks fled towards the city; and many were pressed and stifled in the narrow pass of the gate of St. Romanus. The victorious Turks rushed through the breaches of the inner wall; and as they advanced into the streets, they were soon joined by their brethren, who had forced the gate Phenar on the side of the harbour. In the first heat of the pursuit about two thousand Christians were put to the sword; but avarice soon prevailed over cruelty; and the victors acknowledged that they should immediately have given quarter, if the valour of the emperor and his chosen bands had not prepared them for a similar opposition in every part of the capital. It was thus, after a siege of fifty-three days, that Constantinople, which had defied the power of Chosroes, the Chagan, and the caliphs, was irretrievably subdued by the arms of Mohammed the Second. Her empire only had been subverted by the Latins: her religion was trampled in the dust by the Moslem conquerors.

The tidings of misfortune fly with a rapid

wing; yet such was the extent of Constantinople, that the more distant quarters might prolong, some moments, the happy ignorance of their ruin. But in the general consternation, in the feelings of selfish or social anxiety, in the tumult and thunder of the assault, a *sleepless* night and morning must have elapsed; nor can I believe that many Grecian ladies were awakened by the Janizaries from a sound and tranquil slumber. On the assurance of the public calamity, the houses and convents were instantly deserted; and the trembling inhabitants flocked together in the streets, like a herd of timid animals, as if accumulated weakness could be productive of strength, or in the vain hope that amid the crowd each individual might be safe and invisible. From every part of the capital they flowed into the church of St. Sophia: in the space of an hour, the sanctuary, the choir, the nave, the upper and lower galleries, were filled with the multitudes of fathers and husbands, of women and children, of priests, monks, and religious virgins: the doors were barred on the inside, and they sought protection from the sacred dome which they had so lately abhorred as a profane and polluted edifice. Their confidence was founded on the prophecy of an enthusiast or impostor, that one day the Turks would enter Constantinople, and pursue the Romans as far as the column of Constantine in the square before St. Sophia: but that this would be the term of their calamities; that an angel would descend from heaven with a sword in his hand, and would deliver the empire, with that celestial weapon, to a poor man seated at the foot of the column. "Take this sword," would he say, "and avenge the people of the Lord." At these animating words the Turks would instantly fly, and the victorious Romans would drive them from the West, and from all Anatolia, as far as the frontiers of Persia. It is on this occasion that Ducas, with some fancy and much truth, upbraids the discord and obstinacy of the Greeks. "Had that angel appeared," exclaims the historian, "had he offered to exterminate your foes if you would consent to

the union of the church, even then, in that fatal moment, you would have rejected your safety, or have deceived your God."

While they expected the descent of the tardy angel, the doors were broken with axes; and as the Turks encountered no resistance, their bloodless hands were employed in selecting and securing the multitude of their prisoners. Youth, beauty, and the appearance of wealth, attracted their choice; and the right of property was decided among themselves by a prior seizure, by personal strength, and by the authority of command. In the space of an hour the male captives were bound with cords, the females with their veils and girdles. The senators were linked with their slaves; the prelates with the porters of the church; and young men of a plebeian class with noble maids whose faces had been invisible to the sun and their nearest kindred. In this common captivity the ranks of society were confounded; the ties of nature were cut asunder; and the inexorable soldier was careless of the father's groans, the tears of the mother, and the lamentations of the children. The loudest in their wailings were the nuns, who were torn from the altar with naked bosoms, outstretched hands, and dishevelled hair; and we should piously believe that few could be tempted to prefer the vigils of the harem to those of the monastery. Of these unfortunate Greeks, of these domestic animals, whole strings were rudely driven through the streets; and as the conquerors were eager to return for more prey, their trembling pace was quickened with menaces and blows. At the same hour a similar rapine was exercised in all the churches and monasteries, in all the palaces and habitations, of the capital; nor could any place, however sacred or sequestered, protect the persons or the property of the Greeks. Above sixty thousand of this devoted people were transported from the city to the camp and fleet; exchanged or sold according to the caprice or interest of their masters, and dispersed in remote servitude through the provinces of the Ottoman empire. Among these we may notice some remarkable characters. The historian Phranza, first chamberlain and principal secretary, was involved with his family in the common lot. After suffering four months the hardships of slavery, he recovered his freedom: in the ensuing winter he ventured to Adrianople, and ransomed his wife from the *mir bashi*, or master of the horse; but his two children, in the flower of youth and beauty, had been seized for the use of Mohammed himself. The daughter of Phranza died in the seraglio, perhaps a virgin: his son, in the fifteenth year of his age, preferred death to infamy, and was stabbed by the hand of the royal lover. A deed thus inhuman cannot surely be expiated by the taste and liberality with which he released a Grecian matron and her two daughters, on receiving a Latin ode from Philelphus, who had chosen a wife in that noble family. The pride or cruelty of Mohammed would have been most sensibly gratified by the capture of a Roman legate; but the dexterity of Cardinal Isidore eluded the search, and he escaped from Galata in a plebeian habit. The chain and entrance of the outward harbour was still occupied by the Italian ships of merchandise and war. They had signalised their valour in the siege: they embraced the moment of retreat, while the Turkish mariners were dissipated in the pillage of the city. When they hoisted sail, the beach was covered with a suppliant and lamentable crowd; but the means of transportation were scanty; the Venetians and Genoese selected their countrymen; and, notwithstanding the fairest promises of the sultan, the inhabitants of Galata evacuated their houses, and embarked with their most precious effects.

In the fall and the sack of great cities an historian is condemned to repeat the tale of uniform calamity: the same effects must be produced by the same passions; and when those passions may be indulged without control, small, alas! is the difference between civilised and savage man. Amidst the vague exclamations of bigotry and hatred, the Turks are not accused of a wanton or immoderate effusion of Christian blood: but according to

their maxims (the maxims of antiquity), the lives of the vanquished were forfeited; and the legitimate reward of the conqueror was derived from the service, the sale, or the ransom of his captives of both sexes. The wealth of Constantinople had been granted by the sultan to his victorious troops; and the rapine of an hour is more productive than the industry of years. But as no regular division was attempted of the spoil, the respective shares were not determined by merit; and the rewards of valour were stolen away by the followers of the camp, who had declined the toil and danger of the battle. The narrative of their depredations could not afford either amusement or instruction: the total amount, in the last poverty of the empire, has been valued at four millions of ducats; and of this sum a small part was the property of the Venetians, the Genoese, the Florentines, and the merchants of Ancona. Of these foreigners the stock was improved in quick and perpetual circulation: but the riches of the Greeks were displayed in the idle ostentation of palaces and wardrobes, or deeply buried in treasures of ingots and old coin, lest it should be demanded at their hands for the defense of their country. The profanation and plunder of the monasteries and churches excited the most tragic complaints. The dome of St. Sophia itself, the earthly heaven, the second firmament, the vehicle of the cherubim, the throne of the glory of God, was despoiled of the oblations of ages; and the gold and silver, the pearls and jewels, the vases and sacerdotal ornaments, were most wickedly converted to the service of mankind. After the divine images had been stripped of all that could be valuable to a profane eye, the canvas, or the wood, was torn, or broken, or burnt, or trod under foot, or applied, in the stables or the kitchen, to the vilest uses. The example of sacrilege was imitated, however, from the Latin conquerors of Constantinople; and the treatment which Christ, the Virgin, and the saints had sustained from the guilty Catholic, might be inflicted by the zealous Musulman on the monuments of idolatry. Perhaps, instead of joining the public clamour, a philosopher will observe that in the decline of the arts the workmanship could not be more valuable than the work, and that a fresh supply of visions and miracles would speedily be renewed by the craft of the priest and the credulity of the people. He will more seriously deplore the loss of the Byzantine libraries, which were destroyed or scattered in the general confusion: one hundred and twenty thousand manuscripts are said to have disappeared; ten volumes might be purchased for a single ducat; and the same ignominious price, too high perhaps for a shelf of theology, included the whole works of Aristotle and Homer, the noblest productions of the science and literature of ancient Greece. We may reflect with pleasure that an inestimable portion of our classic treasures was safely deposited in Italy; and that the mechanics of a German town had invented an art which derides the havoc of time and barbarism.

From the first hour of the memorable twenty-ninth of May, disorder and rapine prevailed in Constantinople till the eighth hour of the same day, when the sultan himself passed in triumph through the gate of St. Romanus. He was attended by his vizirs, bashaws, and guards, each of whom (says a Byzantine historian) was robust as Hercules, dexterous as Apollo, and equal in battle to any ten of the race of ordinary mortals. The conqueror gazed with satisfaction and wonder on the strange though splendid appearance of the domes and palaces, so dissimilar from the style of Oriental architecture. In the hippodrome, or *atmeidan*, his eye was attracted by the twisted column of the three serpents; and, as a trial of his strength, he shattered with his iron mace or battle-axe the under jaw of one of these monsters, which in the eyes of the Turks were the idols or talismans of the city. At the principal door of St. Sophia he alighted from his horse and entered the dome; and such was his jealous regard for that monument of his glory, that, on observing a zealous Musulman in the act of breaking the marble pavement, he admonished him with his scimitar that, if the

spoil and captives were granted to the soldiers, the public and private buildings had been reserved for the prince. By his command the metropolis of the Eastern church was transformed into a mosque: the rich and portable instruments of superstition had been removed; the crosses were thrown down; and the walls, which were covered with images and mosaics, were washed and purified, and restored to a state of naked simplicity. On the same day, or on the ensuing Friday, the *muezin*, or crier, ascended the most lofty turret, and proclaimed the *ezan*, or public invitation, in the name of God and his prophet; the imam preached; and Mohammed the Second performed the *namaz* of prayer and thanksgiving on the great altar, where the Christian mysteries had so lately been celebrated before the last of the Caesars. From St. Sophia he proceeded to the august but desolate mansion of a hundred successors of the great Constantine, but which in a few hours had been stripped of the pomp of royalty. A melancholy reflection on the vicissitudes of human greatness forced itself on his mind, and he repeated an elegant distich of Persian poetry: "The spider has wove his web in the Imperial palace, and the owl hath sung her watch-song on the towers of Afrasiab."

THOMAS CARLYLE

The Taking of the Bastille

But, to the living and the struggling, a new, Fourteenth morning dawns. Under all roofs of this distracted City is the nodus of a drama, not untragical, crowding towards solution. The bustlings and preparings, the tremors and menaces; the tears that fell from old eyes! This day, my sons, ye shall quit you like men. By the memory

---

THE TAKING OF THE BASTILLE: From *The French Revolution* by Thomas Carlyle. First printed in 1837.

of your fathers' wrongs, by the hope of your children's rights! Tyranny impends in red wrath; help for you is none, if not in your own right hands. This day ye must do or die.

From earliest light, a sleepless Permanent Committee has heard the old cry, now waxing almost frantic, mutinous: Arms! Arms! Provost Flesselles, or what traitors there are among you, may think of those Charleville Boxes. A hundred-and-fifty-thousand of us, and but the third man furnished with so much as a pike! Arms are the one thing needful; with arms we are an unconquerable man-defying National Guard; without arms, a rabble to be whiffed with grape-shot.

Happily the word has arisen—for no secret can be kept—that there lie muskets at the Hôtel des Invalides. Thither will we; King's Procureur M. Ethys de Corny, and whatsoever of authority a Permanent Committee can lend, shall go with us. Besenval's Camp is there; perhaps he will not fire on us; if he kill us, we shall but die.

Alas! poor Besenval, with his troops melting away in that manner, has not the smallest humor to fire! At five o'clock this morning, as he lay dreaming, oblivious in the École Militaire, a "figure" stood suddenly at his bedside; "with face rather handsome, eyes inflamed, speech rapid and curt, air audacious"—such a figure drew Priam's curtains! The message and monition of the figure was that resistance would be hopeless; that if blood flowed, woe to him who shed it. Thus spoke the figure, and vanished. "Withal there was a kind of eloquence that struck one." Besenval admits that he should have arrested him, but did not. Who this figure with inflamed eyes, with speech rapid and curt, might be? Besenval knows, but mentions not. Camille Desmoulins? Pythagorean Marquis Valadi, inflamed with "violent motions all night at the Palais Royal"? Fame names him "Young M. Meillar"; then shuts her lips about him forever.

In any case, behold, about nine in the morning, our National Volunteers rolling in long wide flood, south-westward to the Hôtel des Invalides, in search of the one thing needful. King's Procureur M. Ethys de Corny and officials are there; the Curé of Saint-Étienne du Mont marches unpacific at the head of his militant Parish; the Clerks of the Basoche in red coats we see marching, now Volunteers of the Basoche; the Volunteers of the Palais Royal— National Volunteers, numerable by tens of thousands; of one heart and mind. The King's muskets are the Nation's; think old M. de Sombreuil, how, in this extremity, thou wilt refuse them! Old M. de Sombreuil would fain hold parley, send couriers; but it skills not—the walls are scaled, no Invalide firing a shot; the gates must be flung open. Patriotism rushes in, tumultuous, from grunsel up to ridge-tile, through all rooms and passages; rummaging distractedly for arms. What cellar, or what cranny can escape it? The arms are found, all safe there; lying packed in straw—apparently with a view to being burned! More ravenous than famishing lions over dead prey, the multitude, with clangor and vociferation, pounces on them; struggling, dashing, clutching —to the jamming-up, to the pressure, fracture, and probable extinction of the weaker Patriot. And so, with such protracted crash of deafening, most discordant Orchestra music, the Scene is changed; and eight-and-twenty thousand sufficient firelocks are on the shoulders of as many National Guards, lifted thereby out of darkness into fiery light.

Let Besenval look at the glitter of these muskets, as they flash by! Gardes Françaises, it is said, have cannon leveled on him; ready to open, if need were, from the other side of the River. Motionless sits he, "astonished," one may flatter oneself, "at the proud bearing (*fière contenance*) of the Parisians."—And now, to the Bastille, ye intrepid Parisians! There grapeshot still threatens; thither all men's thoughts and steps are now tending.

Old De Launay, as we hinted, withdrew "into his interior" soon after midnight of Sunday. He remains there ever since, hampered, as all military gentlemen now are, in the saddest conflict of uncertainties. The Hôtel-de-Ville "invites" him to admit National Soldiers, which is a soft name for surrendering. On the other hand, His Majesty's orders were precise. His garrison is but eighty-two old Invalides, reinforced by thirty-two young Swiss; his walls, indeed, are nine feet thick; he has cannon and powder, but, alas! only one day's provision of victuals. The city, too, is French, the poor garrison mostly French. Rigorous old De Launay, think what thou wilt do!

All morning, since nine, there has been a cry everywhere: To the Bastille! Repeated "deputations of citizens" have been here, passionate for arms; whom De Launay has got dismissed by soft speeches through portholes. Towards noon, Elector Thuriot de la Rosière gains admittance; finds De Launay indisposed for surrender; nay, disposed for blowing up the place, rather. Thuriot mounts with him to the battlements; heaps of paving-stones, old iron, and missiles lie piled; cannon all duly leveled; in every embrasure a cannon—only drawn back a little! But outwards, behold, O Thuriot, how the multitude flows on, welling through every street—tocsin furiously pealing, all drums beating the *générale*; the Suburb Saint-Antoine rolling hitherward wholly as one man! Such vision (spectral, yet real) thou, O Thuriot, as from thy Mount of Vision, beholdest in this moment—prophetic of what other Phantasmagories, and loud-gibbering Spectral Realities, which thou yet beholdest not, but shalt! "*Que voulez-vous?*" said De Launay, turning pale at the sight, with an air of reproach, almost of menace. "Monsieur," said Thuriot, rising into the moral-sublime, "what mean *you?* Consider if I could not precipitate *both* of us from this height"—say only a hundred feet, exclusive of the walled ditch! Whereupon De Launay fell silent. Thuriot shows himself from some pinnacle, to comfort the multitude becoming suspicious, fremescent; then descends; departs with protest; with warning addressed also to the Invalides—on whom, however, it produces but a mixed, indistinct impression. The old heads are none of the clearest; besides, it is said, De Launay has been profuse of beverages (*prodigue des boissons*). They think they will not fire—if not fired on—if they can help it; but must, on the whole, be ruled considerably by circumstances.

Woe to thee, De Launay, in such an hour, if thou canst not, taking some one firm decision, *rule* circumstances! Soft speeches will not serve; hard grapeshot is questionable; but hovering between the two is *un*questionable. Ever wilder swells the tide of men; their infinite hum waxing ever louder, into imprecations, perhaps into crackle of stray musketry—which latter, on walls nine feet thick, cannot do execution. The Outer Drawbridge has been lowered for Thuriot; new *deputation of citizens* (it is the third, and noisiest of all) penetrates that way into the Outer Court; soft speeches producing no clearance of these, De Launay gives fire; pulls up his Drawbridge. A slight sputter—which has *kindled* the too combustible chaos; made it a roaring fire-chaos! Bursts forth Insurrection, at sight of its own blood (for there were deaths by that sputter of fire), into endless, rolling explosion of musketry, distraction, execration—and overhead, from the Fortress, let one great gun, with its grapeshot, go booming, to show what we *could* do. The Bastille is besieged!

On, then, all Frenchmen that have hearts in your bodies! Roar with all your throats of cartilage and metal, ye Sons of Liberty; stir spasmodically whatsoever of utmost faculty is in you, soul, body, or spirit; for it is the hour! Smite, thou, Louis Tournay, cartwright of the Marais, old soldier of the Regiment Dauphiné; smite at that Outer Drawbridge chain, though the fiery hail whistles round thee! Never, over nave or felloe, did thy ax strike such a stroke. Down with it, man; down with it to Orcus; let the whole accursed Edifice sink thither, and Tyranny be swallowed up forever! Mounted, some say, on the roof of the guardroom, some "on bayonets stuck into joints of the wall," Louis Tournay smites, brave Aubin Bonnemère (also an old soldier) seconding him—the chain yields, breaks; the huge Drawbridge slams down, thundering (*avec fracas*). Glorious! and yet, alas! it is still but the outworks. The Eight grim Towers, with their Invalide musketry, their paving-stones and cannon-mouths, still soar aloft intact—Ditch yawning impassable, stone-faced; the inner Drawbridge with its *back* towards us; the Bastille is still to take!

To describe this Siege of the Bastille (thought to be one of the most important in History) perhaps transcends the talent of mortals. Could one but, after infinite reading, get to understand so much as the plan of the building! But there is open Esplanade, at the end of the Rue Saint-Antoine; there are such Forecourts, *Cour Avancé*, *Cour de l'Orme*, arched Gateway (where Louis Tournay now fights); then new drawbridges, dormant-bridges, rampart-bastions, and the grim Eight Towers—a labyrinthic Mass, high-frowning there, of all ages from twenty years to four hundred and twenty—beleaguered, in this its last hour, as we said, by mere Chaos come again! Ordnance of all calibers; throats of all capacities; men of all plans, every man his own engineer; seldom since the war of Pygmies and Cranes was there seen so anomalous a thing. Half-pay Elie is home for a suit of regimentals; no one would heed him in colored clothes; half-pay Hulin is haranguing Gardes Françaises in the Place de Grève. Frantic Patriots pick up the grapeshots; bear them, still hot (or seemingly so), to the Hôtel-de-Ville—Paris, you perceive, is to be burned! Flesselles is "pale to the very lips"; for the roar of the multitude grows deep. Paris wholly has got to the acme of its frenzy; whirled, all ways, by panic madness. At every street-barricade, there whirls simmering a minor whirlpool, strengthening the barricade, since God knows what is coming; and all minor whirlpools play distractedly into that grand Fire-Maelstrom which is lashing round the Bastille.

And so it lashes and it roars. Cholat the wine-merchant has become an impromptu cannoneer. See Georget, of the Marine Service, fresh from Brest, ply the King of Siam's cannon. Singular (if we were not used to the like); Georget lay, last night, taking his ease at his inn; the King of Siam's cannon also lay, knowing nothing of *him*, for a hundred years. Yet now, at the right instant, they have got together, and discourse eloquent music. For, hearing what was toward, Georget sprang from the Brest Diligence, and ran. Gardes Françaises, also, will be here, with real artillery—were not the walls so thick!—Upwards from the Esplanade, horizontally from all neighboring roofs and windows, flashes one irregular deluge of musketry, without effect. The Invalides lie flat, firing comparatively at their ease from behind stone; hardly through portholes show the tip of a nose. We fall, shot; and make no impression!

Let conflagration rage; of whatsoever is combustible! Guardrooms are burned, Invalides messrooms. A distracted "Peruke-maker with two fiery torches" is for burning "the saltpeters of the Arsenal"—had not a woman run screaming; had not a Patriot, with some tincture of Natural Philosophy, instantly struck the wind out of him (butt of musket on pit of stomach), overturned barrels, and stayed the devouring element. A young beautiful lady, seized, escaping, in these Outer Courts, and thought falsely to be De Launay's daughter, shall be burned in De Launay's sight; she lies swooned on a paillasse; but again a Patriot—it is brave Aubin Bonnemère the old soldier—dashes in, and rescues her. Straw is burned; three cartloads of it, hauled thither, go up in white smoke—almost to the choking of Patriotism itself; so that Elie had, with singed brows, to drag back one cart; and Réole the "gigantic haberdasher" another. Smoke as of Tophet; confusion as of Babel; noise as of the Crack of Doom!

Blood flows; the aliment of new madness. The wounded are carried into houses of the Rue Cerisaie; the dying leave their last mandate not to yield till the accursed Stronghold fall. And yet, alas, how fall? The walls are so thick! Deputations, three in number, arrive from the Hôtel-de-Ville; Abbé Fauchet (who was of one) can say, with what almost superhuman courage of benevolence. These wave their Town-flag in the arched Gateway; and stand, rolling their drum; but to no purpose. In such Crack of Doom, De Launay cannot hear them, dare not believe them; they return, with justified rage, the whew of lead still singing in their ears. What to do? The Firemen are here, squirting with their fire-pumps on the Invalides cannon, to wet the touchholes; they unfortunately cannot squirt so high; but produce only clouds of spray. Individuals of classical knowledge propose *catapults*. Santerre, the sonorous Brewer of the Suburb Saint-Antoine, advises rather that the place be fired, by a "mixture of phosphorus and oil-of-turpentine spouted up through forcing pumps." O Spinola-Santerre, hast thou the mixture *ready*? Every man his own engineer! And still the fire-deluge abates not; even women are firing, and Turks; at least one woman (with her sweetheart), and one Turk. Gardes Françaises have come; real cannon, real cannoneers. Usher Maillard is busy; half-pay Elie, half-pay Hulin, rage in the midst of thousands.

How the great Bastille Clock ticks (inaudible) in its Inner Court there, at its ease, hour after hour; as if nothing special, for it or the world, were passing! It tolled One when the firing began; and is now pointing towards Five, and still the firing slakes not.—Far down, in their vaults, the seven Prisoners hear muffled din as of earthquakes; their Turnkeys answer vaguely.

Woe to thee, De Launay, with thy poor hundred Invalides! Broglie is distant, and his ears heavy; Besenval hears, but can send no help. One poor troop of Hussars has crept, reconnoitering, cautiously along the Quais, as far as the Pont Neuf. "We are come to join you," said the Captain; for the crowd seems shoreless. A large-headed dwarfish individual, of smoke-bleared aspect, shambles forward, opening his blue lips, for there is sense in him; and croaks: "Alight then, and give up your arms!" The Hussar-Captain is too happy to be escorted to the Barriers, and dismissed on parole. Who the squat individual was? Men answer, It is M.

Marat, author of the excellent pacific *Avis au Peuple*! Great, truly, O thou remarkable Dog-leech, is this thy day of emergence and new-birth; and yet this same day come four years!—But let the curtains of the Future hang.

What shall De Launay do? One thing only De Launay could have done: what he said he would do. Fancy him sitting, from the first, with lighted taper, within arm's length of the Powder-Magazine; motionless, like old Roman Senator, or Bronze Lamp-holder; coldly apprising Thuriot, and all men, by a slight motion of his eye, what his resolution was.—Harmless he sat there, while unharmed; but the King's Fortress, meanwhile, could, might, would, or should in no wise be surrendered, save to the King's Messenger; one old man's life is worthless, so it be lost with honor; but think, ye brawling *canaille*, how will it be when a whole Bastille springs skyward!—In such statuesque, taper-holding attitude, one fancies De Launay might have left Thuriot, the red Clerks of the Basoche, Curé of Saint-Stephen, and all the tagrag-and-bobtail of the world, to work their will.

And yet, withal, he could not do it. Hast thou considered how each man's heart is so tremulously responsive to the hearts of all men? Hast thou noted how omnipotent is the very sound of many men? How their shriek of indignation palsies the strong soul; their howl of contumely withers with unfelt pangs? The Ritter Gluck confessed that the ground-tone of the noblest passage in one of his noblest Operas was the voice of the Populace he had heard at Vienna, crying to their Kaiser: Bread! Bread! Great is the combined voice of men; the utterance of their *instincts*, which are truer than their *thoughts*; it is the greatest a man encounters, among the sounds and shadows which make up this World of Time. He who can resist that, has his footing somewhere *beyond* Time. De Launay could not do it. Distracted, he hovers between two; hopes in the middle of despair; surrenders not his Fortress; declares that he will blow it up, seizes torches to blow it up, and does not blow it. Unhappy old De

Launay, it is the death-agony of thy Bastille and thee! Jail, Jailoring, and Jailor, all three, such as they may have been, must finish.

For four hours now has the World-Bedlam roared; call it the World-Chimera, blowing fire! The poor Invalides have sunk under their battlements, or rise only with reversed muskets; they have made a white flag of napkins; go beating the *chamade*, or seeming to beat, for one can hear nothing. The very Swiss at the Port-cullis look weary of firing, disheartened in the fire-deluge; a porthole at the drawbridge is opened, as by one that would speak. See Huissier Maillard, the shifty man! On his plank, swinging over the abyss of that stone Ditch; plank resting on parapet, balanced by weight of Patriots—he hovers perilous; such a Dove towards such an Ark! Deftly, thou shifty Usher; one man already fell; and lies smashed, far down there, against the masonry! Usher Maillard falls not; deftly, unerring, he walks, with outspread palm. The Swiss holds a paper through his porthole; the shifty Usher snatches it, and returns. Terms of surrender: Pardon, immunity to all! Are they accepted?—"*Foi d'officier*, On the word of an officer," answers half-pay Hulin—or half-pay Elie, for men do not agree on it—"they are!" Sinks the draw-bridge—Usher Maillard bolting it when down; rushes-in the living deluge; the Bastille is fallen! *Victoire! La Bastille est prise!*

BARBARA TUCHMAN

A Funeral

So gorgeous was the spectacle on the May morning of 1910 when nine kings rode in the funeral of Edward VII of England that the

A FUNERAL: Reprinted with permission of The Macmillan Company from *The Guns of August* by Barbara Tuchman. © Barbara Tuchman 1962.

crowd, waiting in hushed and black-clad awe, could not keep back gasps of admiration. In scarlet and blue and green and purple, three by three the sovereigns rode through the palace gates, with plumed helmets, gold braid, crimson sashes, and jeweled orders flashing in the sun. After them came five heirs apparent, forty more imperial or royal highnesses, seven queens—four dowager and three regnant—and a scatter-ing of special ambassadors from uncrowned countries. Together they represented seventy nations in the greatest assemblage of royalty and rank ever gathered in one place and, of its kind, the last. The muffled tongue of Big Ben tolled nine by the clock as the cortege left the palace, but on history's clock it was sunset, and the sun of the old world was setting in a dying blaze of splendor never to be seen again.

In the center of the front row rode the new king, George V, flanked on his left by the Duke of Connaught, the late king's only surviving brother, and on his right by a personage to whom, acknowledged *The Times*, "belongs the first place among all the foreign mourners," who "even when relations are most strained has never lost his popularity amongst us"— William II, Emperor of Germany. Mounted on a gray horse, wearing the scarlet uniform of a British Field Marshal, carrying the baton of that rank, the Kaiser had composed his features behind the famous upturned mustache in an expression "grave even to severity." Of the several emotions churning his susceptible breast, some hints exist in his letters. "I am proud to call this place my home and to be a member of this royal family," he wrote home after spending the night in Windsor Castle in the former apart-ments of his mother. Sentiment and nostalgia induced by these melancholy occasions with his English relatives jostled with pride in his supremacy among the assembled potentates and with a fierce relish in the disappearance of his uncle from the European scene. He had come to bury Edward his bane; Edward the arch plotter, as William conceived it, of Germany's encirclement; Edward his mother's brother whom he could neither bully nor impress, whose fat figure cast a shadow between Germany and the sun. "He is Satan. You cannot imagine what a Satan he is!"

This verdict, announced by the Kaiser before a dinner of three hundred guests in Berlin in 1907, was occasioned by one of Edward's continental tours undertaken with clearly diabolical designs at encirclement. He had spent a provocative week in Paris, visited for no good reason the King of Spain (who had just married his niece), and finished with a visit to the King of Italy with obvious intent to seduce him from his Triple Alliance with Germany and Austria. The Kaiser, possessor of the least inhibited tongue in Europe, had worked himself into a frenzy ending in another of those comments that had periodically over the past twenty years of his reign shattered the nerves of diplomats.

Happily the Encircler was now dead and replaced by George who, the Kaiser told Theodore Roosevelt a few days before the funeral, was "a very nice boy" (of forty-five, six years younger than the Kaiser). "He is a thorough Englishman and hates all foreigners but I do not mind that as long as he does not hate Germans more than other foreigners." Alongside George, William now rode confidently, saluting as he passed the regimental colors of the 1st Royal Dragoons of which he was honorary colonel. Once he had distributed photographs of himself wearing their uniform with the Delphic inscription written above his signature, "I bide my time." Today his time had come; he was supreme in Europe.

Behind him rode the widowed Queen Alexandra's two brothers, King Frederick of Denmark and King George of the Hellenes; her nephew, King Haakon of Norway; and three kings who were to lose their thrones: Alfonso of Spain, Manuel of Portugal and, wearing a silk turban, King Ferdinand of Bulgaria who annoyed his fellow sovereigns by calling himself Czar and kept in a chest a Byzantine Emperor's full regalia, acquired from a theatrical costumer, against the day when he should reassemble the Byzantine dominions beneath his scepter.

Dazzled by these "splendidly mounted princes," as *The Times* called them, few observers had eyes for the ninth king, the only one among them who was to achieve greatness as a man. Despite his great height and perfect horsemanship, Albert, King of the Belgians, who disliked the pomp of royal ceremony, contrived in that company to look both embarrassed and absent-minded. He was then thirty-five and had been on the throne barely a year. In later years when his face became known to the world as a symbol of heroism and tragedy, it still always wore that abstracted look, as if his mind were on something else.

The future source of tragedy, tall, corpulent, and corseted, with green plumes waving from his helmet, Archduke Franz Ferdinand of Austria, heir of the old Emperor Franz Josef, rode on Albert's right, and on his left another scion who would never reach his throne, Prince Yussuf, heir of the Sultan of Turkey. After the kings came the royal highnesses: Prince Fushimi, brother of the Emperor of Japan; Grand Duke Michael, brother of the Czar of Russia; the Duke of Aosta in bright blue with green plumes, brother of the King of Italy; Prince Carl, brother of the King of Sweden; Prince Henry, consort of the Queen of Holland; and the Crown Princes of Serbia, Rumania, and Montenegro. The last named, Prince Danilo, "an amiable, extremely handsome young man of delightful manners," resembled the Merry Widow's lover in more than name, for, to the consternation of British functionaries, he had arrived the night before accompanied by a "charming young lady of great personal attractions" whom he introduced as a lady in waiting of his wife's, come to London to do some shopping.

A regiment of minor German royalty followed: grand dukes of Mecklenburg-Schwerin, Mecklenburg-Strelitz, Schleswig-Holstein, Waldeck-Pyrmont, of Coburg, Saxe-Coburg, and Saxe-Coburg-Gotha, of Saxony, Hesse, Württemberg, Baden, and Bavaria, of whom the last, Crown

Prince Ruprecht, was soon to lead a German army in battle. There were a Prince of Siam, a Prince of Persia, five princes of the former French royal house of Orléans, a brother of the Khedive of Egypt wearing a gold-tasseled fez, Prince Tsia-tao of China in an embroidered light-blue gown whose ancient dynasty had two more years to run, and the Kaiser's brother, Prince Henry of Prussia, representing the German Navy, of which he was Commander in Chief. Amid all this magnificence were three civilian-coated gentlemen, M. Gaston-Carlin of Switzerland, M. Pichon, Foreign Minister of France, and former President Theodore Roosevelt, special envoy of the United States.

Edward, the object of this unprecedented gathering of nations, was often called the "uncle of Europe," a title which, insofar as Europe's ruling houses were meant, could be taken literally. He was the uncle not only of Kaiser Wilhelm but also, through his wife's sister, the Dowager Empress Marie of Russia, of Czar Nicolas II. His own niece Alix was the Czarina; his daughter Maud was Queen of Norway; another niece, Ena, was Queen of Spain; a third niece, Marie, was soon to be Queen of Rumania. The Danish family of his wife, besides occupying the throne of Denmark, had mothered the Czar of Russia and supplied kings to Greece and Norway. Other relatives, the progeny at various removes of Queen Victoria's nine sons and daughters, were scattered in abundance throughout the courts of Europe.

Yet not family feeling alone nor even the suddenness and shock of Edward's death—for to public knowledge he had been ill one day and dead the next—accounted for the unexpected flood of condolences at his passing. It was in fact a tribute to Edward's great gifts as a sociable king which had proved invaluable to his country. In the nine short years of his reign England's splendid isolation had given way, under pressure, to a series of "understandings" or attachments, but not quite alliances—for England dislikes the definitive—with two old enemies, France and Russia, and one promising new power, Japan. The resulting shift in balance registered itself around the world and affected every state's relations with every other. Though Edward neither initiated nor influenced his country's policy, his personal diplomacy helped to make the change possible.

Taken as a child to visit France, he had said to Napoleon III: "You have a nice country. I would like to be your son." This preference for things French, in contrast to or perhaps in protest against his mother's for the Germanic, lasted, and after her death was put to use. When England, growing edgy over the challenge implicit in Germany's Naval Program of 1900, decided to patch up old quarrels with France, Edward's talents as *Roi Charmeur* smoothed the way. In 1903 he went to Paris, disregarding advice that an official state visit would find a cold welcome. On his arrival the crowds were sullen and silent except for a few taunting cries of *"Vivent les Boers!"* and *"Vive Fashoda!"* which the King ignored. To a worried aide who muttered, "The French don't like us," he replied, "Why should they?" and continued bowing and smiling from his carriage.

For four days he made appearances, reviewed troops at Vincennes, attended the races at Longchamps, a gala at the Opéra, a state banquet at the Elysée, a luncheon at the Quai d'Orsay and, at the theater, transformed a chill into smiles by mingling with the audience in the entr'acte and paying gallant compliments in French to a famous actress in the lobby. Everywhere he made gracious and tactful speeches about his friendship and admiration for the French, their "glorious traditions," their "beautiful city," for which he confessed an attachment "fortified by many happy memories," his "sincere pleasure" in the visit, his belief that old misunderstandings are "happily over and forgotten," that the mutual prosperity of France and England was interdependent and their friendship his "constant preoccupation." When he left, the crowds now shouted, *"Vive notre roi!"* "Seldom has such a complete change of attitude been seen as that which has taken place in this country. He has won the hearts of all the French," a Belgian diplomat reported. The German ambassador thought the King's visit was "a most odd affair," and supposed that an Ango-French *rapprochement* was the result of a "general aversion to Germany." Within a year, after hard work by ministers settling disputes, the *rapprochement* became the Anglo-French Entente, signed in April, 1904.

Germany might have had an English entente for herself had not her leaders, suspecting English motives, rebuffed the overtures of the Colonial Secretary, Joseph Chamberlain, in 1899 and again in 1901. Neither the shadowy Holstein who conducted Germany's foreign affairs from behind the scenes nor the elegant and erudite Chancellor, Prince Bülow, nor the Kaiser himself was quite sure what they suspected England of but they were certain it was something perfidious. The Kaiser always wanted an agreement with England if he could get one without seeming to want it. Once, affected by English surroundings and family sentiment at the funeral of Queen Victoria, he allowed himself to confess the wish to Edward. "Not a mouse could stir in Europe without our permission," was the way he visualized an Anglo-German alliance. But as soon as the English showed signs of willingness, he and his ministers veered off, suspecting some trick. Fearing to be taken advantage of at the conference table, they preferred to stay away altogether and depend upon an ever-growing navy to frighten the English into coming to terms.

Bismarck had warned Germany to be content with land power, but his successors were neither separately nor collectively Bismarcks. He had pursued clearly seen goals unswervingly; they groped for larger horizons with no clear idea of what they wanted. Holstein was a Machiavelli without a policy who operated on only one principle: Suspect everyone. Bülow had no principles; he was so slippery, lamented his colleague Admiral Tirpitz, that compared to him an eel was a leech. The flashing, inconstant, always freshly inspired Kaiser had a different goal every hour, and practiced diplomacy as an exercise in perpetual motion.

None of them believed England would ever come to terms with France, and all warnings of that event Holstein dismissed as "naïve," even a most explicit one from his envoy in London, Baron Eckhardstein. At a dinner at Marlborough House in 1902, Eckhardstein had watched Paul Cambon, the French ambassador, disappear into the billiard room with Joseph Chamberlain, where they engaged in "animated conversation" lasting twenty-eight minutes of which the only words he could overhear (the baron's memoirs do not say whether the door was open or he was listening at the keyhole) were "Egypt" and "Morocco." Later he was summoned to the King's study where Edward offered him an 1888 Uppmann cigar and told him that England was going to reach a settlement with France over all disputed colonial questions.

When the Entente became a fact, William's wrath was tremendous. Beneath it, and even more galling, rankled Edward's triumph in Paris. The *reise-Kaiser*, as he was known from the frequency of his travels, derived balm from ceremonial entries into foreign capitals, and the one above all he wished to visit was Paris, the unattainable. He had been everywhere, even to Jerusalem, where the Jaffa Gate had to be cut to permit his entry on horseback; but Paris, the center of all that was beautiful, all that was desirable, all that Berlin was not, remained closed to him. He wanted to receive the acclaim of Parisians and be awarded the Grand Cordon of the Legion of Honor, and twice let the imperial wish be known to the French. No invitation ever came. He could enter Alsace and make speeches glorifying the victory of 1870; he could lead parades through Metz in Lorraine; but it is perhaps the saddest story of the fate of kings that the Kaiser lived to be eighty-two and died without seeing Paris.

Envy of the older nations gnawed at him. He complained to Theodore Roosevelt that the

English nobility on continental tours never visited Berlin but always went to Prais. He felt unappreciated. "All the long years of my reign," he told the King of Italy, "my colleagues, the Monarchs of Europe, have paid no attention to what I have to say. Soon, with my great Navy to endorse my words, they will be more respectful." The same sentiments ran through his whole nation, which suffered, like their emperor, from a terrible need for recognition. Pulsing with energy and ambition, conscious of strength, fed upon Nietzsche and Treitschke, they felt entitled to rule, and cheated that the world did not acknowledge their title. "We must," wrote Friedrich von Bernhardi, the spokesman of militarism, "secure to German nationality and German spirit throughout the globe that high esteem which is due them ... and has hitherto been withheld from them." He frankly allowed only one method of attaining the goal; lesser Bernhardis from the Kaiser down sought to secure the esteem they craved by threats and show of power. They shook the "mailed fist," demanded their "place in the sun," and proclaimed the virtues of the sword in paeans to "blood and iron" and "shining armor." In German practice Mr. Roosevelt's current precept for getting on with your neighbors was Teutonized to, "Speak loudly and brandish a big gun." When they brandished it, when the Kaiser told his troops departing for China and the Boxer Rebellion to bear themselves as the Huns of Attila (the choice of Huns as German prototypes was his own), when Pan-German Societies and Navy Leagues multiplied and met in congresses to demand that other nations recognize their "legitimate aims" toward expansion, the other nations answered with alliances, and when they did, Germany screamed *Einkreisung!*—Encirclement! The refrain *Deutschland ganzlich einzukreisen* grated over the decade.

Edward's foreign visits continued—Rome, Vienna, Lisbon, Madrid—and not to royalty only. Every year he took the cure at Marienbad where he would exchange views with the Tiger of France, born in the same year as himself, who was premier for four of the years that Edward was king. Edward, whose two passions in life were correct clothes and unorthodox company, overlooked the former, and admired M. Clemenceau. The Tiger shared Napoleon's opinion that Prussia "was hatched from a cannon ball," and saw the cannon ball coming in his direction. He worked, he planned, he maneuvered in the shadow of one dominant idea: "the German lust for power ... has fixed as its policy the extermination of France." He told Edward that when the time came when France needed help, England's sea power would not be enough, and reminded him that Napoleon was beaten at Waterloo, not Trafalgar.

In 1908, to the distaste of his subjects, Edward paid a state visit to the Czar aboard the imperial yacht at Reval. English imperialists regarded Russia as the ancient foe of the Crimea and more recently as the menace looming over India, while to the Liberals and Laborites Russia was the land of the knout, the pogrom, and the massacred revolutionaries of 1905, and the Czar, according to Mr. Ramsay MacDonald, "a common murderer." The distaste was reciprocated. Russia detested England's alliance with Japan and resented her as the power that frustrated Russia's historic yearning for Constantinople and the Straits. Nicholas II once combined two favorite prejudices in the simple statement, "An Englishman is a *zhid* (Jew)."

But old antagonisms were not so strong as new pressures, and under the urging of the French, who were anxious to have their two allies come to terms, an Anglo-Russian Convention was signed in 1907. A personal touch of royal friendliness was felt to be required to clear away any lingering mistrust, and Edward embarked for Reval. He had long talks with the Russian Foreign Minister, Isvolsky, and danced the Merry Widow waltz with the Czarina with such effect as to make her laugh, the first man to accomplish this feat since the unhappy woman put on the crown of the Romanovs. Nor was it such a frivolous achievement as might appear, for though it could hardly be said that the Czar governed Russia in a working sense, he ruled as an autocrat and was in turn ruled by his strong-willed if weak-witted wife. Beautiful, hysterical, and morbidly suspicious, she hated everyone but her immediate family and a series of fanatic or lunatic charlatans who offered comfort to her desperate soul. The Czar, neither well endowed mentally nor very well educated, was, in the Kaiser's opinion, "only fit to live in a country house and grow turnips."

The Kaiser regarded the Czar as his own sphere of influence and tried by clever schemes to woo him out of his French alliance which had been the consequence of William's own folly. Bismarck's maxim "Keep friends with Russia" and the Reinsurance Treaty that implemented it, William had dropped, along with Bismarck, in the first, and worst, blunder of his reign. Alexander III, the tall, stern Czar of that day, had promptly turned around in 1892 and entered into alliance with republican France, even at the cost of standing at attention to "The Marseillaise." Besides, he snubbed William, whom he considered "*un garçon mal élevé*," and would only talk to him over his shoulder. Ever since Nicholas acceded to the throne, William had been trying to repair his blunder by writing the young Czar long letters (in English) of advice, gossip, and political harangue addressed to "Dearest Nicky" and signed "Your affectionate friend, Willy." An irreligious republic stained by the blood of monarchs was no fit company for him, he told the Czar. "Nicky, take my word for it, the curse of God has stricken that people forever." Nicky's true interests, Willy told him, were with a *Drei-Kaiser Bund*, a league of the three emperors of Russia, Austria, and Germany. Yet, remembering the old Czar's snubs, he could not help patronizing his son. He would tap Nicholas on the shoulder, and say, "My advice to you is more speeches and more parades, more speeches, more parades," and he offered to send German troops to protect Nicholas from his rebellious subjects, a suggestion

which infuriated the Czarina, who hated William more after every exchange of visits.

When he failed, under the circumstances, to wean Russia away from France, the Kaiser drew up an ingenious treaty engaging Russia and Germany to aid each other in case of attack, which the Czar, after signing, was to communicate to the French and invite them to join. After Russia's disasters in her war with Japan (which the Kaiser had strenuously urged her into) and the revolutionary risings that followed, when the regime was at its lowest ebb, he invited the Czar to a secret rendezvous, without attendant ministers, at Björkö in the Gulf of Finland. William knew well enough that Russia could not accede to his treaty without breaking faith with the French, but he thought that sovereigns' signatures were all that was needed to erase the difficulty. Nicholas signed.

William was in ecstasy. He had made good the fatal lapse, secured Germany's back door, and broken the encirclement. "Bright tears stood in my eyes," he wrote to Bülow, and he was sure Grandpapa (William I, who had died muttering about a war on two fronts) was looking down on him. He felt his treaty to be the master coup of German diplomacy, as indeed it was, or would have been, but for a flaw in the title. When the Czar brought the treaty home, his ministers, after one horrified look, pointed out that by engaging to join Germany in a possible war he had repudiated his alliance with France, a detail which "no doubt escaped His Majesty in the flood of the Emperor William's eloquence." The Treaty of Björkö lived its brief shimmering day, and expired.

Now came Edward hobnobbing with the Czar at Reval. Reading the German ambassador's report of the meeting which suggested that Edward really desired peace, the Kaiser scribbled furiously in the margin, "Lies. He wants war. But I have to start it so he does not have the odium."

The year closed with the most explosive *faux pas* of the Kaiser's career, an interview given to the *Daily Telegraph* expressing his ideas of the day on who should fight whom, which this time unnerved not only his neighbors but his countrymen. Public disapproval was so outspoken that the Kaiser took to his bed, was ill for three weeks, and remained comparatively reticent for some time thereafter.

Since then no new excitements had erupted. The last two years of the decade while Europe enjoyed a rich fat afternoon, were the quietest. Nineteen-ten was peaceful and prosperous, with the second round of Moroccan crises and Balkan wars still to come. A new book, *The Great Illusion* by Norman Angell, had just been published, which proved that war was impossible. By impressive examples and incontrovertible argument Angell showed that in the present financial and economic interdependence of nations, the victor would suffer equally with the vanquished; therefore war had become unprofitable; therefore no nation would be so foolish as to start one. Already translated into eleven languages, *The Great Illusion* had become a cult. At the universities, in Manchester, Glasgow, and other industrial cities, more than forty study groups of true believers had formed, devoted to propagating its dogma. Angell's most earnest disciple was a man of great influence on military policy, the King's friend and adviser, Viscount Esher, chairman of the War Committee assigned to remaking the British Army after the shock of its performance in the Boer War. Lord Esher delivered lectures on the lesson of *The Great Illusion* at Cambridge and the Sorbonne wherein he showed how "new economic factors clearly prove the inanity of aggressive wars." A twentieth-century war would be on such a scale, he said, that its inevitable consequences of "commercial disaster, financial ruin and individual suffering" would be "so pregnant with restraining influences" as to make war unthinkable. He told an audience of officers at the United Service Club, with the Chief of General Staff, Sir John French, in the chair, that because of the interlacing of nations war "becomes every day more difficult and improbable."

Germany, Lord Esher felt sure, "is as receptive as Great Britain to the doctrine of Norman Angell." How receptive were the Kaiser and the Crown Prince to whom he gave, or caused to be given, copies of *The Great Illusion* is not reported. There is no evidence that he gave one to General von Bernhardi, who was engaged in 1910 in writing a book called *Germany and the Next War*, published in the following year, which was to be as influential as Angell's but from the opposite point of view. Three of its chapter titles, "The Right to Make War," "The Duty to Make War," and "World Power or Downfall" sum up its thesis.

As a twenty-one-year-old cavalry officer in 1870, Bernhardi had been the first German to ride through the Arc de Triomphe when the Germans entered Paris. Since then flags and glory interested him less than the theory, philosophy, and science of war as applied to "Germany's Historic Mission," another of his chapter titles. He had served as chief of the Military History section of the General Staff, was one of the intellectual elite of that hard-thinking, hard-working body, and author of a classic on cavalry before he assembled a lifetime's studies of Clausewitz, Treitschke, and Darwin, and poured them into the book that was to make his name a synonym for Mars.

War, he stated, "is a biological necessity"; it is the carrying out among humankind of "the natural law, upon which all the laws of Nature rest, the law of the struggle for existence." Nations, he said, must progress or decay; "there can be no standing still," and Germany must choose "world power or downfall." Among the nations Germany "is in social-political respects at the head of all progress in culture" but is "compressed into narrow, unnatural limits." She cannot attain her "great moral ends" without increased political power, an enlarged sphere of influence, and new territory. This increase in power, "befitting our importance," and "which we are entitled to claim," is a "political necessity" and "the first and foremost duty of the State." In his own italics Bernhardi announced, "What we now wish to attain must be *fought for*," and from here he galloped home to the finish line: "Conquest thus becomes a law of necessity."

Having proved the "necessity" (the favorite word of German military thinkers), Bernhardi proceeded to method. Once the duty to make war is recognized, the secondary duty, to make it successfully, follows. To be successful a state must begin war at the "most favorable moment" of its own choosing; it has "the acknowledged right...to secure the proud privilege of such initiative." Offensive war thus becomes another "necessity" and a second conclusion inescapable: "It is incumbent on us...to act on the offensive and strike the first blow." Bernhardi did not share the Kaiser's concern about the "odium" that attached to an aggressor. Nor was he reluctant to tell where the blow would fall. It was "unthinkable," he wrote, that Germany and France could ever negotiate their problems. "France must be so completely crushed that she can never cross our path again"; she "must be annihilated once and for all as a great power."

King Edward did not live to read Bernhardi. In January, 1910, he sent the Kaiser his annual birthday greetings and the gift of a walking stick before departing for Marienbad and Biarritz. A few months later he was dead.

"We have lost the mainstay of our foreign policy," said Isvolsky when he heard the news. This was hyperbole, for Edward was merely the instrument, not the architect, of the new alignments. In France the king's death created "profound emotion" and "real consternation," according to *Le Figaro*. Paris, it said, felt the loss of its "great friend" as deeply as London. Lampposts and shop windows in the Rue de la Paix wore the same black as Piccadilly; cab drivers tied crepe bows on their whips; black-draped portraits of the late king appeared even in the provincial towns as at the death of a great French citizen. In Tokyo, in tribute to the Anglo-Japanese alliance, houses bore the crossed flags of England and Japan with the staves draped in black. In Germany, whatever the feelings, correct procedures were observed. All officers of the army and navy were ordered to wear mourning for eight days, and the fleet in home waters fired a salute and flew its flags at half-mast. The Reichstag rose to its feet to hear a message of sympathy read by its President, and the Kaiser called in person upon the British ambassador in a visit that lasted an hour and a half.

In London the following week the royal family was kept busy meeting royal arrivals at Victoria Station. The Kaiser came over on his yacht the *Hohenzollern*, escorted by four British destroyers. He anchored in the Thames Estuary and came the rest of the way to London by train, arriving at Victoria Station like the common royalty. A purple carpet was rolled out on the platform, and purple-covered steps placed where his carriage would stop. As his train drew in on the stroke of noon, the familiar figure of the German emperor stepped down to be greeted by his cousin, King George, whom he kissed on both cheeks. After lunch they went together to Westminster Hall where the body of Edward lay in state. A thunderstorm the night before and drenching rains all morning had not deterred the quiet, patient line of Edward's subjects waiting to pass through the hall. On this day, Thursday, May 19, the line stretched back for five miles. It was the day the earth was due to pass through the tail of Halley's comet, whose appearance called forth reminders that it was traditionally the prophet of disaster— had it not heralded the Norman Conquest?— and inspired journals with literary editors to print the lines from *Julius Caesar*:

> When beggars die there are no comets seen;
> The heavens themselves blaze forth the death
> of princes.

Inside the vast hall the bier lay in somber majesty, surmounted by crown, orb, and scepter and guarded at its four corners by four officers, each from different regiments of the empire, who stood in the traditional attitude of mourning with bowed heads and white gloved hands crossed over sword hilts. The Kaiser eyed all the customs of an imperial Lying-in-State with professional interest. He was deeply impressed, and years later could recall every detail of the scene in its "marvelous medieval setting." He saw the sun's rays filtered through the narrow Gothic windows lighting up the jewels of the crown; he watched the changing of the guards at the bier as the four new guards marched forward with swords at the carry-up and turned them point down as they reached their places, while the guards they relieved glided away in slow motion to disappear through some unseen exit in the shadows. Laying his wreath of purple and white flowers on the coffin, he knelt with King George in silent prayer and on rising grasped his cousin's hand in a manly and sympathetic handshake. The gesture, widely reported, caused much favorable comment.

Publicly his performance was perfect; privately he could not resist the opportunity for fresh scheming. At a dinner given by the King that night at Buckingham Palace for the seventy royal mourners and special ambassadors, he buttonholed M. Pichon of France and proposed to him that in the event Germany should find herself opposed to England in a conflict, France should side with Germany. In view of the occasion and the place, this latest imperial brainstorm caused the same fuss, that had once moved Sir Edward Grey, England's harassed Foreign Secretary, to remark wistfully, "The other sovereigns are so much *quieter*." The Kaiser later denied he had ever said anything of the kind; he had merely discussed Morocco and "some other political matters." M. Pichon could only be got to say discreetly that the Kaiser's language had been "amiable and pacific."

Next morning, in the procession, where for once he could not talk, William's behavior was exemplary. He kept his horse reined in, a head behind King George's, and, to Conan Doyle, special correspondent for the occasion, looked so "noble that England has lost something of her old kindliness if she does not take him back into her heart today." When the procession reached

Westminster Hall he was the first to dismount and, as Queen Alexandra's carriage drew up, "he ran to the door with such alacrity that he reached it before the royal servants," only to find that the Queen was about to descend on the other side. William scampered nimbly around, still ahead of the servants, reached the door first, handed out the widow, and kissed her with the affection of a bereaved nephew. Fortunately, King George came up at this moment to rescue his mother and escort her himself, for she loathed the Kaiser, both personally and for the sake of Schleswig-Holstein. Though he had been but eight years old when Germany seized the duchies from Denmark, she had never forgiven him or his country. When her son on a visit to Berlin in 1890 was made honorary colonel of a Prussian regiment, she wrote to him: "And so my Georgie boy has become a real live filthy blue-coated Pickelhaube German soldier!!! Well, I never thought to have lived to see that! But never mind, ...it was your misfortune and not your fault."

A roll of muffled drums and the wail of bagpipes sounded as the coffin wrapped in the Royal Standard was borne from the Hall by a score of bluejackets in straw hats. A sudden shiver of sabers glittered in the sun as the cavalry came to attention. At a signal of four sharp whistles the sailors hoisted the coffin on to the gun carriage draped in purple, red, and white. The cortege moved on between motionless lines of grenadiers like red walls that hemmed in the packed black masses of perfectly silent people. London was never so crowded, never so still. Alongside and behind the gun carriage, drawn by the Royal Horse Artillery, walked His late Majesty's sixty-three aides-de-camp, all colonels or naval captains and all peers, among them five dukes, four marquises, and thirteen earls. England's three Field Marshals, Lord Kitchener, Lord Roberts, and Sir Evelyn Wood, rode together. Six Admirals of the Fleet followed, and after them, walking all alone, Edward's great friend, Sir John Fisher, the stormy, eccentric former First Sea Lord with his queer un-English mandarin's face. Detachments from all the famous regiments, the Coldstreams, the Gordon Highlanders, the household cavalry and cavalry of the line, the Horse Guards and Lancers and Royal Fusiliers, brilliant Hussars and Dragoons of the German, Russian, Austrian, and other foreign cavalry units of which Edward had been honorary officer, admirals of the German Navy—almost, it seemed to some disapproving observers, too great a military show in the funeral of a man called the "Peacemaker."

His horse with empty saddle and boots reversed in the stirrups led by two grooms and, trotting along behind, his wire-haired terrier, Caesar, added a pang of personal sentiment. On came the pomp of England: Poursuivants of Arms in emblazoned medieval tabards, Silver Stick in Waiting, White Staves, equerries, archers of Scotland, judges in wigs and black robes, and the Lord Chief Justice in scarlet, bishops in ecclesiastical purple, Yeomen of the Guard in black velvet hats and frilled Elizabethan collars, an escort of trumpeters, and then the parade of kings, followed by a glass coach bearing the widowed Queen and her sister, the Dowager Empress of Russia, and twelve other coaches of queens, ladies, and Oriental potentates.

Along Whitehall, the Mall, Piccadilly, and the Park to Paddington Station, where the body was to go by train to Windsor for burial, the long procession moved. The Royal Horse Guards' band played the "Dead March" from *Saul*. People felt a finality in the slow tread of the marchers and in the solemn music. Lord Esher wrote in his diary after the funeral: "There never was such a break-up. All the old buoys which have marked the channel of our lives seem to have been swept away."

Questions for Review

1. In "Everyman His Own Historian," Carl Becker describes the thought processes used by everyone and especially formulated by the historian. Compare Becker's ideas of how the historian thinks with William James's essay on thinking (p. 6ff. above). Are Becker and James basically in agreement about the thought process? Would Becker's historian be more like James's "analytical" or "intuitive" thinker? Would James agree with Becker's ideas about the relationship between the historian and the average man?

2. Becker speaks of history as myth-making. Does he use "myth" in the sense that Carl Jung does (p. 29f. above)? If not, how does his meaning differ? Does Becker appear to be indebted to Freud's theories of thought and neurosis in any way?

3. Does Becker think the historian any more detached or objective in his thinking than the common man? How are they significantly unlike?

4. How does Becker implicitly define "fact"? What part does "fact" play in historical writing? Does Becker think "facts" the sole content of historical literature?

5. By Becker's standards would Hanson Baldwin (p. 231f. above), and John Hersey be authentic historians? Would Becker consider Mr. Tanimoto and Mrs. Nakamura historians?

6. Thucydides's famous account of the plague in Athens in 431–430 B.C. is a part of his history of the Peloponnesian Wars between Athens and Sparta and their allies. Is this long account really related to the military and political events of the war? Why does Thucydides include it?

7. What authorities does Thucydides use for his description of the plague? What effect does this use have upon the objective character of the description? (Compare Pliny's account of the eruption of Vesuvius.)

8. Would Becker consider Thucydides's account that of a professional historian or something else? Are there any mythic elements in it? What human needs would Thucydides's history fulfill for his own age? For ours?

9. Thucydides does not show the suffering of individuals but of unnamed persons; Hersey describes individuals. Which ac-

count is more effective? Which conveys the greater sense of significance in terms of human experience?

10. Gibbon is greatly admired for his *History of the Decline and Fall of the Roman Empire,* from which "The Fall of Constantinople" comes. Is his style or tone as historian different from his style and tone as auto-biographer (see p. 117f. above)?

11. Gibbon was a scholar who knew the ancient languages and consulted hundreds of sources before writing his *History.* Does this research make his account demonstrably "factual" and "authoritative"? Does it make the account detached and objective?

12. Gibbon is describing the end of an age and an empire in this section. Does his *History* make these events seem realistic in human terms? Or is his description largely the flourishes of rhetoric? Compare and contrast his technique and effect with those of John Hersey and Thomas Carlyle.

13. To what extent does the personality of Gibbon the man intrude upon the historical scenes he describes? By Becker's standards, is this a weakness or a strength?

14. Like other writers, the historiographer must decide from what point of view (physical as well as intellectual) he will describe his event. Compare and contrast the use of point of view by Gibbon and Carlyle. Which do you find more suitable to the event?

15. Is Carlyle's personality—i.e., bias and feeling—more obvious in his writing than that of Thucydides or Gibbon? Is he more emotionally involved with his subject?

16. Carlyle's style is unique. What are the outstanding characteristics of his diction? His tone? Are they appropriate to the writing of history, in your opinion?

17. Is Carlyle less scholarly a historian than Gibbon? What sources has he consulted before writing his account? Are these adequate to the demands of fact or not? How interested in giving facts does Carlyle seem to be?

18. Barbara Tuchman's description of the funeral of King Edward VII begins her

book, *The Guns of August,* a full scale history of World War I. Why does she begin with this event? Is the funeral itself a cause of the War? What relationship between this event and later ones is implied by Mrs. Tuchman?

19. To what extent is Mrs. Tuchman interested in the personalities of historical figures? What relationship does she assume to exist between individual personality and historic action? Do the other historians given here share her beliefs?

20. *The Guns of August* has been awarded prizes and praise for its thorough research and scholarship. Point out instances of Mrs. Tuchman's use of diaries, journals, letters, and newspaper reports as sources of information.

21. Is Mrs. Tuchman interested only in giving facts? Defend your answer by specific references to her style, diction, and use of details.

Questions for Discussion and Writing

1. What major differences are there between reportage and history? Which of the historians in this selection seem nearest to reporting events? In what ways do they differ from Baldwin and Hersey in the Reportage section?

2. The introduction to this section suggested that historiography is concerned with public actions, yet all of the historians given here show some concern with private sources and details and several show an extensive concern. How can the "private" and the "public" be distinguished by the historian? Do they need to be?

3. Becker says that the historian shapes the materials of the past in order to fill the needs of his contemporaries. Is this true of the historians included above? Does Gibbon or Carlyle fill less or more of our needs as twentieth-century Americans than Mrs. Tuchman does?

4. The Peloponnesian Wars, the fall of Con-

stantinople, the taking of the Bastille, the death of Edward VII—all are considered by their respective historian to be major turning points in history, decisive events in the sequence of human actions. Are these events really major in themselves or are they arbitrary choices by historians who want to see a cause and effect relationship between essentially unrelated events? Does the historian automatically choose the most spectacular and violent incidents for his "causes" because they strike his attention or because they are true causes? Is it possible that quiet, unheeded, "insignificant" events may well be the real causes of historic development? Is it possible, that the historian, like the reporter, seizes on violence and color largely because of their interest rather than their real importance?

5. Is historiography (or reportage) really more "factual" than diaries and autobiographies? In what way? (Make clear the definition of "factual" you are using.)

6. Is historiography more properly concerned with the political and military than it is with, say, the literary, the social, and the spiritual? Justify your opinion. To what extent do literary, social, and spiritual concerns interest Thucydides? Gibbon? Carlyle? Mrs. Tuchman? What *are* they interested in?

7. Which of these historians do you find most able to convey a sense of common human destiny? Of personal emotions? Can you see any relationship between these feelings?

8. N. O. Brown (see p. 17 above) argues that human history is really a working out of personal neuroses and mass (collective) neuroses. Do the accounts of Gibbon, Carlyle, and Tuchman support this theory?

9. The historiographer has peculiar problems of chronology and point of view because he must give background information, convey the sequence of events, and indicate a pattern of cause and effect all at once. Choose one of the historians here and show how these problems operate for him and how he treats them.

III
EMPIRICAL REALITIES

The "Scientific" Perspective

As we have seen in Sections I and II, the writer's motives for forming word-compositions may be of several different kinds; the processes by which he transforms conceptions into literature are complex, being a combination of creative and literal thinking; and the particular point of view which he adopts—whether the highly private and subjective or the ostensibly impersonal and public—is effected by many considerations: the nature of the experience itself, the emotional and intellectual significance of the experience to the writer, his attitude(s) toward it, the audience that he wants to communicate with, and the ends of that communication as the writer envisions them and the reader is led to accept them.

Of the kinds of literature that adopt the perspectives and literary techniques called "public" and "impersonal" that which deals with "scientific" matters conventionally de-emphasizes the individuality of the writer. Certainly in the kinds of scientific writing that is comprised largely of statistics, measurements, and formulae, the emotions and personality of the writer-scientist are not apparent. But in much of the other literature dealing with the kinds of experiences termed empirical, the writer, even though a scientist, must deal with many of the same matters as all other writers, even though he is concerned with testable "data" or "facts." Scientists themselves confess that if their concerns are with the material substances—rock formations, algae, meteors, radium—nevertheless the scientist's ways of dealing with these involves a large amount of "intuition" as well as observation in formulating (conceiving) the operative "principles" that "explain" the phenomena they observe.

Furthermore, scientific writers readily declare their human limitations in striving for total "impersonality" and "objectivity." They are men, first and last, and not data processing computers; inevitably the data they observe will have emotional as well as intellectual significance for them to some degree. The scientist who writes down his theories or observations—or "discoveries"— seems to be akin to the historian or biographer or critic in his attitudes toward communication with others and the satisfactions such communication brings to the writer.

In the present section, therefore, first appears a collection of essays on how the scientist thinks and writes. This is followed by a group of essays on subjects that are natural phenomena, the observable objects and processes of the physical world. Finally, there is a group of works applying the methods of the scientist to human beings. From the theory of the "scientific method" in the first essays, through the writings of the physical and social scientists (or critics) following, the similarity between scientific thinking and writing and other kinds of conceptualization and verbalization may be seen together with the qualities peculiar to the scientist.

JAMES BRYANT CONANT

Concerning the Alleged Scientific Method

From attempts to define science we now turn to a no less controversial subject—the methods of science. Those who favor the use of the word science to embrace all the activities of the learned world are inclined to belief in the existence of *a* scientific method. Indeed, a few go further and not only claim the existence of *a* method but believe in its applicability to a wide variety of practical affairs as well. For example, a distinguished American biologist declared not long ago that "Men and women effectively

CONCERNING THE ALLEGED SCIENTIFIC METHOD: From *Science and Common Sense* by James Bryant Conant, 1951. Reprinted by permission of Yale University Press.

trained in science *and in the scientific method,* usually ask for the evidence, almost automatically." He was referring not to scientific matters but to the vexing problems which confront us in everyday life—in factories, offices, and political gatherings.

One cannot help wondering where the author of such a categorical statement obtained his evidence. But this is perhaps making a debater's point. The significance of the statement is that it reflects a persistent belief in the correctness of the analysis of science presented by Pearson in *The Grammar of Science.* Throughout the volume Karl Pearson refers to science as the classification of facts, and in his summary of the first chapter he writes as follows: "The scientific method is marked by the following features: (a) careful and accurate classification of facts and observation of their correlation and sequence; (b) the discovery of scientific laws by aid of the creative imagination; (c) self-criticism and the final touchstone of equal validity for all normally constituted minds." With (b) and (c) one can have little quarrel since all condensed statements of this type are by necessity incomplete, but from (a) I dissent entirely. And it is the point of view expressed in this sentence that dominates Pearson's whole discussion. It seems to me, indeed, that one who had little or no direct experience with scientific investigations might be completely misled as to the nature of the methods of science by studying this famous book.

If science were as simple as this very readable account would have us believe, why did it take so long a period of fumbling before scientists were clear on some very familiar matters? Newton's famous work was complete by the close of the seventeenth century. The cultured gentlemen of France and England in the first decade of the eighteenth century talked in terms of a solar system almost identical with that taught in school today. The laws of motion and their application to mechanics were widely understood. This being the case it might be imagined that the common phenomenon of combustion would have been formulated in terms of comparable clarity once people put their minds on scientific problems. Yet it was not until the late 1770's that the role of oxygen in combustion was discovered. Another hotly debated problem, the spontaneous generation of life, was an open question as late as the 1870's. Darwin convinced himself and later the scientific world and later still the educated public of the correctness of the general idea of evolution because of his theory as to the mechanism by which evolution might have occurred. Today the basic idea of the evolutionary development of higher plants and animals stands almost without question, but Darwin's mechanism has been so greatly altered that we may say a modern theory has evolved. And we are no nearer a solution of the problem of how life originated on this planet than we were in Darwin's day.

The stumbling way in which even the ablest of the scientists in every generation have had to fight through thickets of erroneous observations, misleading generalizations, inadequate formulations, and unconscious prejudice is rarely appreciated by those who obtain their scientific knowledge from textbooks. It is largely neglected by those expounders of the alleged scientific method who are fascinated by the logical rather than the psychological aspects of experimental investigations. Science as I have defined the term represents one segment of the much larger field of accumulative knowledge. The common characteristic of all the theoretical and practical investigations which fall within this framework —a sense of progress—gives no clue as to the *activities* of those who have advanced our knowledge. To attempt to formulate in one set of logical rules the way in which mathematicians, historians, archaeologists, philologists, biologists, and physical scientists have made progress would be to ignore all the vitality in these varied undertakings. Even within the narrow field of the development of "concepts and conceptual schemes from experiment" (experimental science) it is all too easy to be fascinated by oversimplified accounts of the methods used by the pioneers.

To be sure, it is relatively easy to deride any definition of scientific activity as being oversimplified, and it is relatively hard to find a better substitute. But on one point I believe almost all modern historians of the natural sciences would agree and be in opposition to Karl Pearson. There is no such thing as *the* scientific method. If there were, surely an examination of the history of physics, chemistry, and biology would reveal it. For as I have already pointed out, few would deny that it is the progress in physics, chemistry, and experimental biology which gives everyone confidence in the procedures of the scientist. Yet, a careful examination of these subjects fails to reveal any *one* method by means of which the masters in these fields broke new ground.

The Birth of Experimental Science in the Seventeenth Century

As I interpret the history of science, the sudden burst of activity in the seventeenth century which contemporaries called the "new philosophy" or the "experimental philosophy" was the result of the union of three streams of thought and action. These may be designated as 1. speculative thinking 2. deductive reasoning 3. cut-and-try or empirical experimentation. The first two are well illustrated by the writings of the learned men of the Middle Ages. The professor of law and theology as well as the teacher of mathematics and logic from the eleventh to the seventeenth century was concerned with a rational ordering of general ideas and the development of logical processes. In so doing, they extended to some degree the philosophical and mathematical ideas of the ancient Greeks and laid the foundations for the science of mechanics, the first of the branches of physics to take on modern dress.

A simple illustration of deductive reasoning is to be found in recalling one's experience in school with plane geometry. A set of postulates or axioms is given; then by logical processes of deduction many conclusions follow. Similarly, less formal and rigid general ideas—speculative ideas—can be manipulated by logical procedures which, however, frequently lack the rigor of mathematical reasoning. The discussion of general speculative ideas and the more detailed handling of mathematics, it should be noted, involve processes of thought which are believed to be sufficient unto themselves. No one feels impelled to appeal to observation in building a purely rational system of ideas.

The sudden burst of interest in the seventeenth century in the new experimental philosophy was to a considerable extent the result of a new curiosity on the part of thoughtful men. Practical matters ranging from agriculture and medicine to the art of pumping, the working of metals, and the ballistics of cannon balls began to attract the attention of learned professors or inquiring men of leisure. The early history of science is full of examples where the observation of a practical art by a scientist suggested a problem. *But the solution of a scientific problem is something quite different from the advances which had hitherto been made by the empirical experimentation of the agriculturist or the workman.* The new element which was introduced was the use of deductive reasoning. This was coupled with one or more generalizations often derived from speculative ideas of an earlier time. The focus of attention was shifted from an immediate task of improving a machine or a process to a curiosity about the phenomena in question. New ideas or concepts began to be as important as new inventions. The experimentation of the skilled artisans or the ingenious contriver of machines and processes became joined to the mathematical mode of reasoning of the learned profession. But it took many generations before deductive reasoning and experimentation could be successfully combined and applied to many areas of inquiry.

Speculative Ideas, Working Hypotheses, and Conceptual Schemes

Science we defined in the last chapter as "an interconnected series of concepts and conceptual schemes that have developed as a result of experimentation and observation and are fruitful of further experimentation and observations." A conceptual scheme when first formulated may be considered *a working hypothesis on a grand scale.* From it one can deduce, however, *many* consequences, each of which can be the basis of chains of reasoning yielding deductions that can be tested by experiment. *If these tests confirm the deductions in a number of instances, evidence accumulates tending to confirm the working hypothesis on a grand scale, which soon becomes accepted as a new conceptual scheme.* Its subsequent life may be short or long, for from it new deductions are constantly being made which can be verified or not by careful experimentation.

In planning the experiments to test the deductions it became necessary, as science advanced, to make more precise and accurate many vague common-sense ideas, notably those connected with measurement. Old ideas were clarified or new ones introduced. These are the new concepts which are often quite as important as the broad conceptual schemes. It is often much more difficult than at first sight appears to get a clear-cut yes or no answer to a simple experimental question. And the broader hypotheses must remain only speculative ideas until one can relate them to experiment.

An understanding of the relationship between broad speculative ideas and a wide conceptual scheme is of the utmost importance to an understanding of science. A good example is furnished by the history of the atomic theory. The notion that there were fundamental units—ultimate particles—of which matter was composed goes back to ancient times. But expressed merely in general terms this is a speculative idea and can hardly be considered an integral part of the fabric of science until it becomes the basis of a working hypothesis on a grand scale from which deductions capable of experimental test can be made. This particular speculative idea or working hypothesis on a grand scale became a new conceptual scheme only after Dalton had shown, about 1800, how fruitful it was in connection with the quantitative chemical experimentation that had been initiated by the chemical revolution. Here is an instance where we can see in some detail the origins of a working hypothesis, while in other instances we are uncertain how the idea came to the proponent's mind.

The great working hypotheses in the past have often originated in the minds of the pioneers as a result of mental processes which can best be described by such words as "inspired guess," "intuitive hunch," or "brilliant flash of imagination." Rarely if ever do they seem to have been the product of a careful examination of all the facts and a logical analysis of various ways of formulating a new principle. Pearson and other

nineteenth-century writers about the methods of science largely overlooked this phenomenon. They were so impressed by the classification of facts and the drawing of generalizations from facts that they tended to regard this activity as all there was to science. Nowadays the pendulum has swung to the other extreme and some writers seem to concentrate attention on the development of new ideas and their manipulation, that is on theoretical science. Both points of view minimize the significance of the experiment. To my mind this distorts the history of science and, what is worse, confuses the layman who is interested in the scientific activity which is going on all about him. For these reasons and because of the author's own predilection, the present discussion of science and common sense emphasizes and re-emphasizes the interrelation of experiments and theory.

Experimentation

The three elements in modern science already mentioned are: 1. speculative general ideas, 2. deductive reasoning, and 3. experimentation. We have discussed in a general way the manner in which new working hypotheses on a grand scale arise and how from them one may deduce certain consequences that can be tested by experiment. It has been implied that the art of experimentation long antedates the rise of science in the seventeenth century. If so, this is one way in which science and common sense are connected. A rather detailed analysis of experimentation in everyday life may serve a useful purpose at this point. For, as I hope to show, there is a continuous gradation between the simplest rational acts of an individual and the most refined scientific experiment. Not that the two extremes of this spectrum are identical. Quite the contrary: to understand science one must have an appreciation of just how common-sense trials differ from experiments in science.

Since the reader may well have been exposed at some time in his or her life to various statements about the alleged scientific method, it may be permissible to set up a few straw men and knock them down. I have read statements about the scientific method which describe fairly accurately the activity of an experimental scientist on many occasions (but not all). They run about as follows:

1. a problem is recognized and an objective formulated; 2. all the relevant information is collected (many a hidden pitfall lies in the word "relevant"!); 3. a working hypothesis is formulated; 4. deductions from the hypothesis are drawn; 5. the deductions are tested by actual trial; 6. depending on the outcome, the working hypothesis is accepted, modified, or discarded.

If this were all there was to science, one might say, in the words of a contemporary believer in *the* scientific method, that science as a method "consists of asking clear, answerable questions in order to direct one's observations which are made in a calm, unprejudiced manner, reported as accurately as possible and in such a way as to answer the questions that were asked to begin with; any assumptions that were held before the observations are now revised in the light of what has happened." But if one examines his own behavior whenever faced with a practical emergency (such as the failure of his car to start) he will recognize in the preceding quotation a description of what he himself has often done. Indeed, if one attempts to present the alleged scientific method in any such way to a group of discerning young people they may well come back with the statement that they have been scientists all their lives! The layman confronted with some such description of science is in a similar situation to that of the famous character in Molière's comedy who had been speaking prose all his life without knowing it.

Testing Deductions by Experiment

Is there then no difference between science and common sense as far as method is concerned? Let us look at this question by con-

sidering in some detail first an everyday example of experimentation and then a scientific investigation. The type of activity by which the practical arts have developed over the ages is in essence a trial and error procedure. The same sort of activity is familiar in everyday life; we may call it experimentation. Let us take a very restricted and perhaps trivial example. Faced with a locked door and a bunch of keys lying on the floor, a curious man may wish to experiment with the purpose of opening the door in question. He tries first one key and then the other, each time essentially saying to himself, "If I place this key in the lock and turn it, then the result will either confirm or negate my hypothesis that this key fits the lock." This "if... then" type of statement is a recurring pattern in rational activity in everyday life. The hypothesis that is involved in such a specific trial is limited to the case at hand, the particular key in question. We may call it therefore a *limited working hypothesis*.

Let me turn now from an example of common-place experimentation to a consideration of a scientific experiment. Let us examine the role of the limited working hypothesis in the testing of some scientific idea in the laboratory. For if you brought all the writers on scientific method with the most varied views together, I imagine that every one of them would agree that the testing of a deduction from a broad working hypothesis (some would say a theory) was at least a part of science. In the next chapter we are going to consider in some detail several instances of such procedures. Let us anticipate the story about atmospheric pressure only to the extent of fixing our minds on one actual experiment. It makes little difference which one we choose, for we wish to center attention on the last step, the actual experimental manipulation.

We will imagine that someone has related the broad hypothesis that we live in a sea of air that exerts pressure to a particular experiment with a particular piece of apparatus. Just before turning a certain stopcock, which we may assume to be the final step in the experiment, the investigator may formulate his ideas in some such statement as, "If all my reasoning and plans are right, when I turn the stopcock, such and such will happen." He turns the stopcock and makes the observation; he can then say he has confirmed or failed to confirm his hypothesis. But strictly speaking, let it be noted, it is only a highly limited hypothesis that has been tested by turning the stopcock and making the observation; this hypothesis may be thrown into some such form as "If I turn the stopcock, then such and such will happen." The confirmation or not of this extremely limited hypothesis is regarded as an experimental fact if repetition yields the same result. The outcome of the experiment is usually connected with the main question by a highly complex process of thought and action which brings in many other concepts and conceptual schemes. The examination of such processes is involved in a study of the examples of "science in the making" in the following chapters. The point to be emphasized here is the existence of a complicated chain of reasoning connecting the consequence deduced from a broad hypothesis and the actual experimental manipulation; furthermore, we shall repeatedly see how many assumptions, some conscious and some unconscious, are almost always involved in this chain of reasoning.

Now perhaps I may be permitted to jump from the scientist to the everyday experiments of a householder in his garage or a housewife in her kitchen or an amateur with his radio set. If a car won't start, we certainly have a problem; we think over the various possibilities based on our knowledge of automobiles in general and the particular car in question; we construct at least one working hypothesis (the gas tank is empty!); we proceed to carry out a trial or test (an experiment) which should prove the correctness of this particular working hypothesis; if we are right then we believe we have found the trouble and proceed accordingly. (But how often have we been misled; perhaps there is more than one trouble; perhaps the tank is empty and the battery run down too!) Let us assume the simple

hypothesis has led to a trial which consists of turning a particular switch or making a certain connection of wires after various other manipulations have been performed. Then one says to oneself, "Now at last if I turn the switch (or make the connection) the engine will turn over." The test is made and what is confirmed (or not) is a very limited working hypothesis hardly to be distinguished from the extremely limited working hypothesis of the scientists we have just been considering. Here science and common sense certainly seem to have come together. But notice carefully, they are joined only in the statement of the final operation. As we trace back the line of argument the differences become apparent. These are differences as to aims, as to auxiliary hypotheses and as to assumptions.

Aims and Assumptions in Scientific Experimentation

First, as regards aims, you want the car to start (or the radio set to work, to mention another example); you wish to reach a practical objective. The scientific experimenter on the other hand wants to test a deduction from a conceptual scheme (a theory), a very different matter. But we cannot leave the distinction between science and common sense resting on that point, important as it is. The conceptual scheme is not only being tested by the experimenter but it has given rise to the experiment. And that takes us back to our definition of science and our emphasis on the significance of the fruitfulness of a new conceptual scheme. The artisans who improved the practical arts over the centuries proceeded much as you or I do today when we are confronted with a practical problem. The aim of the artisan or the agriculturist was practical, the motivation was practical, though the objective was more general than just starting a given automobile. The workmen of the Middle Ages experimented and sometimes their results left a permanent residue because their contemporaries incorporated a new procedure into an evolving art. But the artisan rarely, if ever, bothered about the testing of the consequences of any general ideas. General ideas, logical thought, were the province of learned men. Drawing deductions from conceptual schemes was the type of activity known to the mathematicians and philosophers of the Middle Ages, not to the workmen. And with rare exceptions those who understood these recondite matters paid no attention to the workmen. In the next two chapters we shall consider examples of how the two activities—those of the logicians and the artisans—came together in the sixteenth and seventeenth centuries.

There is another important difference between the artisan and the scientist. The typical procedure of the artisan is very much like that of the housewife in the kitchen. Not only are the trials of new procedures for very practical and immediate ends, but the relevant information is largely unconnected with general ideas or theories. Until as late as the nineteenth century the practical man paid very little attention to the growing body of science. By and large the practical arts and science went their own ways during the seventeenth and eighteenth centuries. We may say that experimentation in the practical arts or in the kitchen is almost wholly empirical, meaning thereby to indicate the absence of a theoretical component. However, since the transition from common sense to science is gradual and continuous, one may well question if there is ever a total absence of a theoretical background. It can be argued that the concepts and conceptual schemes we take for granted in everyday life and share in common with our ancestors are not different in principle from the "well-established" ideas of science. This I believe to be true in the sense that infrared light is not different in principle from X rays; both forms of radiant energy are parts of a spectrum, but the two forms of light are certainly not interchangeable for most practical purposes. Quite the contrary. So too, commonsense ideas are distinct in many respects from the more abstract part of the scientific fabric.

During the last two hundred years more and more of the material of science has become incorporated into our common-sense assumptions. But every age and cultural group has its own way of looking at the world. The pictures of the total universe which can be collected by anthropologists and students of cultural history, while having many assumptions in common, likewise show great divergences. Therefore, if the modern man in his garage "takes for granted" many things his grandfather would have believed impossible, this in no way invalidates the differentiation between common-sense ideas and scientific theories. (Though there is a wide, fuzzy, intermediary zone.)

The Degree of Empiricism in a Science or a Practical Art

In analyzing the present relation of science to technology and medicine I have found it useful to use the term "degree of empiricism" to indicate the extent to which our knowledge can be expressed in terms of broad conceptual schemes. The same phrase is likewise useful, I am inclined to think, in connection with the history of both the sciences and the practical arts in the last three hundred years. The importance of the notion which lies back of the term, however, is that it may be of real help to the layman who is confused about the relation of "pure" and "applied" science. In the last one hundred years science and technology have become so intertwined that even the practitioners in the field may be uncertain when they attempt to analyze the role of scientific theories. Yet anyone familiar with the physical sciences and modern industry would at once grant that there were wide differences in the extent to which scientists in different industries can apply scientific knowledge to the work at hand.

To illustrate what to me is a highly important point, let me contrast the business of making optical instruments with that of manufacturing rubber tires. The design of lenses and mirrors for telescopes, microscopes, and cameras is based on a theory of light which was developed 150 years ago and which can be expressed in simple mathematical terms. With the aid of this theory and a few measurements of the properties of the glasses used, it is possible to calculate with great accuracy the performance of optical equipment. Since theoretical knowledge is so complete in the field of optics, we may say that the degree of empiricism is low in this branch of physics. Because theory is so effective in the optical industry, the degree of empiricism is low. The manufacture of rubber tires is a totally different story. There is nothing comparable to the theory of light to provide a mathematical basis for calculation of what ingredients should be mixed with the rubber. The chemical change which is basic to the whole process is known as vulcanization but no one is very clear even today how to formulate it in theoretical terms. The action of the sulfur which was long thought to be an essential ingredient and of certain other chemicals known as "accelerators" is but little understood. The whole process has been built up by trial and error, by a procedure in which a vast number of experiments finally yielded knowledge in every way comparable to the knowledge of a first-rate chef. In this industry the degree of empiricism is high, and this reflects in turn the small extent to which the chemistry of rubber has been formulated in wide theoretical terms.

As in all comparative statements we must have some fixed points for standards. Therefore, without entering further into the philosophic analysis of common-sense knowledge (including the knowledge of an "art" such as cooking, or glass blowing, or metal making in the Middle Ages), we may take as an example of essentially empirical procedures those of the artisan before the advent of modern science and of the cook in a modern kitchen. Here one may arbitrarily say the degree of empiricism is practically 100 per cent. To find a case where the degree is so low that we can take it as zero

on our scale, I call your attention to the work of the surveyor. The theoretical framework is here largely one branch of mathematics—geometry—and, except to a very slight extent in the building of the instruments and the efficiency of their handling, empirical procedures are conspicuous by their absence. Therefore if the reader of this book whose acquaintance with science or technology is slight will envisage from time to time the surveyor with his transit and his measuring instruments on the one hand and the chef in the Grand Hotel on the other, he will have in mind a range of activities from zero to 100 as regards the degree of empiricism involved.

We shall return from time to time to the relation of scientific knowledge to the practical activities of the artisan, the agriculturist, and the medical man. We shall see that for an amazingly long time advances in science and progress in the practical arts ran parallel with few interconnecting ties. Thus if we take the birth of modern science as somewhere around 1600 (neglecting the long prenatal period which goes back to antiquity), one can say that it was two hundred years or more before the practical arts benefited much from science. Indeed, it would be my contention that it was not until the electrical and dyestuff industries were well started, about 1870, that science became of real significance to industry.

Let me conclude this discussion by pointing out that the degree of empiricism in a practical field today largely depends on the extent to which the corresponding scientific area can be formulated in terms of broad conceptual schemes. Therefore one may consider science as an attempt either to lower the degree of empiricism or to extend the range of theory. When scientific work is undertaken without regard for any practical application of the knowledge, it is convenient to speak of the activity as part of "pure" science. But there are certain overtones in the adjective which are unpleasant and seem to imply a hierarchy of values as between the scientists interested in theories and those interested in the practical arts. Therefore the phrase "basic science" is frequently employed. Almost all significant work of scientists today, I believe, comes under the heading of attempts to reduce the degree of empiricism; the distinction between one group and another is in the motivation. Those who are interested in the fabric of science as such are ready to follow any lead that gives promise of being fruitful in terms of extending theoretical knowledge. Others are primarily concerned with one of the ancient practical arts in modern dress; if it is some branch of industry, say metallurgy, they will be just as interested in widening the theoretical knowledge *in this field* as their colleagues in a university; they will be endeavoring to lower the degree of empiricism too, but in a limited area for a practical objective. The medical scientist is like the metallurgist except that his goal is not better metals but healthier people; both are working in applied science.

In the 1950's, therefore, we find a complex state of affairs. About three centuries ago the trial-and-error experimentation of the artisan was wedded to the deductive method of reasoning of the mathematician; the progeny of this union have returned after many generations to assist the "sooty empiric" in his labors. In so doing the applied scientist finds himself face to face with one of his distant ancestors, so to speak. For as he works in an industrial laboratory he will often find himself called on to carry out experiments for a practical purpose on nearly as empirical a basis as the artisan of the distant past. Particularly in those practical arts where the degree of empiricism is still high, men with the most advanced scientific training and using the latest equipment will often have to resort to wholly empirical procedures. On the one hand they will labor to reduce the degree of empiricism as best they can; on the other they must improve the art by using the knowledge and methods then at hand. In short, advances in science and progress in the practical arts today go hand in hand.

STEPHEN E. TOULMIN

The Scientist and the Layman

Not everyone can be an expert physicist, but everybody likes to have a general grasp of physical ideas. The learned journals and treatises which record the progress of the physical sciences are open only to trained readers—the *Proceedings of the Royal Society* are less readable nowadays than they were in the Royal Society's early days, when Pepys, Dryden and Evelyn were Fellows. In consequence, there have grown up two classes of writings, less needed in those days, on which the nonscientific reader has to rely for his understanding of the physical sciences. For the ordinary man, there are works of popular science, in which the theoretical advances in physics are explained in a way designed to avoid technicalities; and for students of philosophy there are, in addition, books and articles on logic, in which the nature and problems of the physical sciences are discussed under the heading "Induction and Scientific Method."

There are, however, certain important questions which both these classes of work leave undiscussed; and, as a result, the defenseless reader tends to get from them a distorted picture of the aims, methods and achievements of the physical sciences. These are questions for which the phrase "the philosophy of science" has come to be used; it is the task of this book to draw attention to them, to show in part at least how they are to be answered, and to indicate the kinds of misconception which have been generated in the past by leaving them unconsidered.

THE SCIENTIST AND THE LAYMAN: From *The Philosophy of Science* by Stephen E. Toulmin, 1953. Reprinted by permission of the author and Hutchinson Publishing Group Ltd.

1.1. Logic and the Physical Sciences

Notice first the topics one finds discussed in books of logic. Induction, Causality, whether the results of the sciences are true or only highly probable, the Uniformity of Nature, the accumulation of confirming instances, Mill's Methods and the probability-calculus: such things form the staple of most expositions. But to anyone with practical experience of the physical sciences there is a curious air of unreality about the results. Lucid, erudite and carefully argued they may be; yet somehow they seem to miss the mark. It is not that the things that are said are untrue or fallacious, but rather that they are irrelevant: the questions which are so impeccably discussed have no bearing on physics. Meanwhile the actual methods of argument physical scientists employ are only rarely examined. French writers on the philosophy of science, Poincaré for instance, at any rate recognize that in this field one must not take too much for granted. English and American writers on the subject tend nowadays, by contrast, to set off on their work assuming that we are all familiar with the things that scientists say and do, and can therefore get on to the really interesting philosophical points that follow.

This attitude exposes one to serious dangers. For if one has too simple an idea of what scientific arguments are like, one may regard as serious philosophical problems questions having no application to the practice of physicists at all. If one takes it for granted, for instance, that laws of nature can be classed for logical purposes with generalizations like "Women are bad drivers" and "Ravens are black," one may conclude that all appeal to such laws must rest on some presupposition about the reliability of generalizations. But unless one sees in some detail what the status of laws of nature in practice is, one cannot decide whether this is a proper conclusion or no. In fact, laws of nature will not easily fit into the traditional array of logical categories, and their discussion calls for a more refined logical classification. Similarly, one can continue to write about "Causation and its Place in Modern Science" indefinitely, if one fails to notice how rarely the word "cause" appears in the writings of professional scientists. Yet there are good reasons for this rarity, and to ignore them is again to divorce the philosophical discussion of scientific arguments from the reality.

The student of philosophy therefore needs an introductory guide to the types of argument and method scientists in actual practice employ: in particular, he needs to know how far these arguments and methods are like those which logicians have traditionally considered. How far do the problems the logic books discuss have any bearing on the things working scientists do? Do we want to attack these problems in the customary fashion, and attempt to propound some novel solution; or should we rather see the problems themselves as arising from an over-naïve conception of what the sciences are like? How do physicists in fact decide that an explanation is acceptable? What sort of job must an expression perform to qualify for the title of "law of nature"; and how do laws of nature differ from hypotheses? Is the difference a matter of our degrees of confidence in the two classes of propositions, or is the distinction drawn on other grounds? Again, how does mathematics come to play so large a part in the physical sciences? And as for those new entities scientists talk so much about—genes, electrons, meson fields and so on—how far are they thought of as really existing, and how far as mere explanatory devices? These are all questions about whose answers it is easy to be mistaken, unless one pays sufficient attention to the actual practice of scientists: one aim of what follows will be to present these features of the physical sciences which must be understood before we can settle such questions.

1.2 Popular Physics and the Layman

The difficulties that arise over books on popular science are rather different. Here there is no doubt that authentic science is being discussed; but the terms in which it is presented are not as explanatory as they at first seem. There is a tendency for a writer in this field to tell us only about the models and conceptions employed in a novel theory, instead of first giving us a firm anchor in the facts which the theory explains, and afterwards showing us in what manner the theory fits these facts. The best the layman can then hope for is a misleadingly unbalanced picture of the theory; while, at worst, he is liable to put the book down more mystified than when he began it.

Recall, for instance, the way in which Sir James Jeans and Sir Arthur Eddington set about popularizing the theories of modern physics. Too often they did what was comparatively inessential, that is, introduced us to the particular conceptions and models used in the theories, while failing to do what is essential, namely, explain in detail the function of these models, theoretical conceptions and the rest. Eddington's well-known account of "the two tables" is a case in point: to be told that there is not only a commonsense, solid table, but also a scientific one, mostly consisting of empty space, does not particularly help one to understand the atomic theory of matter. The whole reason for accepting the atomic model is that it helps us to explain things we could not explain before. Cut off from these phenomena, the model can only mislead, raising unreal and needless fears about what will happen when we put the tea tray down. The same also goes, regrettably, for many of those pretty pictures which captured our imaginations: the picture of the electrons in an atom as like bees in a cathedral, the picture of the brain as a telephone exchange, and the rest. Regrettably, it can be said, because as literary devices they certainly have a value and, if they were not left to stand on their own feet, might genuinely help us to understand. As things are, however, they act like a searchlight in the darkness, which picks up here a pinnacle, here a chimney, and there an attic window: the detail it catches is lit up dazzlingly, but

everything around is thrown into even greater obscurity and we lose all sense of the proportions of the building.

But this is not the worst that happens. At times the attempt to popularize a physical theory may even end by unpopularizing it. Jeans, for instance, relied on finding a happy analogy which would by itself bring home to his readers the chief features of the General Theory of Relativity. And how did he invite them to think of the Universe? As the three-dimensional surface of a four-dimensional balloon. The poor layman, who had been brought up to use the word "surface" for two-dimensional things alone, now found himself instructed to visualize what for him was a self-contradiction, so it was no wonder if he agreed to Jeans's calling the Universe a mysterious one. This mystification was also unnecessary. There is no reason why the principles of the Theory of Relativity should not be explained in terms the ordinary reader can make something of— Einstein himself does this very well. But Jeans's method defeated its own end: by trying to make the subject too easy and to do with a simile what no simile alone can do, he led many readers to conclude that the whole thing was utterly incomprehensible, and so must be put aside as not for them.

This might suggest that Jeans was just careless, but there is more to it than that. For the fact that he picked on a mode of expression which to the outsider is self-contradictory points to something which the layman needs to be told about the language of physical theories. When a theory is developed, all kinds of phrases which in ordinary life are devoid of meaning are given a use, many familiar terms acquire fresh meanings, and a variety of new terms is introduced to serve the purposes of the theory. A scientist, who learns his physics the hard way, gradually becomes accustomed to using the novel technical terms and the everyday-sounding phrases in the way required; but he may only be half-aware of what is happening—as Professor Born remarks, the building of the language of the sciences is not entirely a conscious process. This has its consequences when the scientist comes to explain some new theory to the layman. For then he may unwittingly use in his exposition terms and turns of phrase which can be understood properly only by someone already familiar with the theory. To a man trained in the use of sophisticated kinds of geometry the phrase "three-dimensional surface" may no longer be a self-contradiction, but for him to use it in talking to a non-mathematician is to invite incomprehension. And what applies to "three-dimensional surfaces" applies equally to "invisible light" and the like: when scientific notions are being popularized, it is necessary to explain the point of such phrases, instead of making an unexplained use of them.

To introduce a distinction we shall find important later: the adoption of a new theory involves a *language-shift*, and one can distinguish between an account of the theory in the new terminology—in "participant's language"—and an account in which the new terminology is not used but described—an account in "onlooker's language." "Suppose," as Wittgenstein once said, "that a physicist tells you that he has at last discovered how to see what people look like in the dark, which no one had ever before known. Then you should not be surprised. If he goes on to explain to you that he has discovered how to photograph by infrared rays, then you have a right to be surprised if you feel like it. But then it is a different kind of surprise, not just a mental whirl. Before he reveals to you the discovery of infrared photography, you should not just gape at him; you should say, 'I do not know what you mean.' "

An analogy will help to explain how misconceptions may follow if we attempt to popularize the physical sciences in this way. When we tell children stories at bedtime, we talk to them about all kinds of people—by which is meant not just rich and poor, white and black, beggars and kings, but logically different kinds of people. Some nights we tell them stories from history, other nights ancient myths; sometimes legends,

sometimes fables, sometimes accounts of things that we ourselves have done, sometimes stories by contemporary authors. So in bedtime stories Julius Caesar, Hercules, Achilles, the Boy who cried "Wolf!", Uncle George and Winnie-the-Pooh all appear, at first sight, on the same footing. A clever child, no doubt, soon learns to spot from internal evidence what kind of story tonight's story is; and what sort of people its characters are—fabulous, legendary, or historical. But to begin with we have to explain, in asides, what the logical status of each character and story is, saying, "No, there aren't really any talking bears: this is just a made-up story," or "Yes, this really did happen, when my father's father was a boy." Unless the child is told these things in addition to the stories themselves, he may not know how to take them; and thus he may get quite false ideas about the world into which he has been born, about its history, its inhabitants, and the kinds of thing he might encounter one day as he turned the corner of the street. If entertainment alone were needed, the story alone might do. But the risks of misunderstanding are serious, and for real understanding more is needed.

So also in popular science: the layman is not just ignorant of the theories of science, but also unequipped to understand the terms in which a scientist will naturally begin to explain them. To explain the sciences to him by giving him only potted theories and vivid analogies, without a good number of logical asides, is accordingly like telling a child all the sorts of stories we do tell children and not warning him how very different they are: he will not know how much weight to put on the various things that are said, which of the statements about physics are to be taken at their face value, and which of the characters in the stories he could ever hope to meet.

Perhaps the nub of the difficulty is this, that the popularizer has a double aim. For the layman wants to be told about the theories of the sciences in language he can understand; and he also wants to be told about them briefly, "in a nutshell." These two demands are bound in practice to conflict. For a major virtue of the language of the sciences is its conciseness. It is always *possible* to say what a scientific theory amounts to without using the technical terms which scientists introduce to serve the purposes of the theory, but one can do so only by talking at very much greater length. If the popularizer is to explain a theory in everyday terms, and at the same time put it in a nutshell, something must be sacrificed: usually the logical asides are the first things to go, and drastic cuts follow in the account of the phenomena the theory is employed to explain. Once this has happened, the layman is given no real entrance to the subject; for unless he is told a good deal about the phenomena a theory is introduced to explain, and what is even more important, just how much further on we are when this "explanation" has been given, he might as well have been left quite in the dark. Even a real key is of little use if we do not know what rooms it will let us into. And there is no point at all in being told that Einstein has discovered the metaphorical Key to the Universe if we are not also told what sort of thing counts as opening a door with this Key.

Something can be done, however, to remedy this state of affairs. With the help of a few elementary examples, it should be possible to show the common reader some of the more important things he needs to know about the logic of the physical sciences. There is no reason why he need rest content with the idea that physics is a conglomeration of self-contradictions, like "invisible light" and "three-dimensional surfaces," and mysteries like "the curvature of space": armed with the right questions, he can penetrate behind this screen of words to the living subject. For the words of scientists are not always what they seem, and may be misleading taken out of their original context. The vital thing to know is, what sorts of questions need to be asked, if one is to get a satisfactory account of a theory; and this, fortunately, is something which can be shown as well with simple as with sophisticated examples. To show, with illustra-

tions, what these questions are is the principal aim of this book; and it will require us, not so much to quote the things that scientists say, as to see what sort of things they do with the words they employ. As Einstein has said, "If you want to find out anything from the theoretical physicists about the methods they use, I advise you to stick closely to one principle: Don't listen to their words, fix your attention on their deeds."

STEPHEN LEACOCK

Common Sense and the Universe

1

Speaking last December at the annual convention of the American Association for the Advancement of Science, and speaking, as it were, in the name of the great 100-inch telescope under his control, Professor Edwin Hubble, of the Mount Wilson Observatory, California, made the glad announcement that the universe is not expanding. This was good news indeed, if not to the general public who had no reason to suspect that it was expanding, at least to those of us who humbly attempt to "follow science." For some twenty-five years past, indeed ever since the promulgation of this terrific idea in a paper published by Professor W. de Sitter in 1917, we had lived as best we could in an expanding universe, one in which everything, at terrific speed, kept getting farther away from everything else. It suggested to us the disappointed lover in the romance who leaped on his horse and rode madly off in all directions. The idea was majestic in its sheer size, but it somehow gave an uncomfortable sensation.

Yet we had to believe it. Thus, for example, we had it on the authority of Dr. Spencer Jones, the British Astronomer Royal, in his new and fascinating book of 1940, *Life on Other Worlds*, that "a distant universe in the constellation of Boötes has been found to be receding with a velocity of 24,300 miles a second. We can infer that this nebula is at a distance of 230,000,000 light-years." I may perhaps remind my fellow followers of science that a light-year means the distance travelled in one year by light, moving at 186,000 miles a second. In other words, this "distant universe" is now 1,049,970,980,000,000, 000,000 miles away!

"Some distance!" as Mr. Churchill would say.

But now it appears that that distant universe has *not* been receding at all; in fact, it isn't way out there. Heaven knows where it is. Bring it back. Yet not only did the astronomers assert the expansion, but they proved it from the behaviour of the red band in the spectrum, which blushed a deeper red at the revelation of it, like the conscious water that "saw its God and blushed" at Cana in Galilee long ago. One of the most distinguished and intelligible of our astronomers, Sir Arthur Eddington, had written a book about it, *The Expanding Universe*, to bring it down to our level. Astronomers at large accepted this universal explosion in all directions as calmly as they once accepted the universal fall of gravitation, or the universal death in the cold under Carnot's Second Law of Thermodynamics.

But the relief brought by Professor Hubble is tempered, on reflection, by certain doubts and afterthoughts. It is not that I venture any disbelief or disrespect toward science, for that is atrocious in our day as disbelief in the Trinity was in the days of Isaac Newton. But we begin to doubt whether science can quite keep on believing in and respecting itself. If we expand today and contract tomorrow; if we undergo all the doubled-up agonies of the curvature of space, only to have the link called off, as it has been; if we get reconciled to dying a martyr's death at one general, distributed temperature of 459 degrees below zero, the same for all, only to find that the world is perhaps unexpectedly warming up again—then we ask, where are we? To which, of course, Einstein answers, "Nowhere," since there is no place to be. So we must pick up our little book again, follow science, and wait for the next astronomical convention.

Let us take this case of the famous Second Law of Thermodynamics, that inexorable scroll of fate which condemned the universe—or at least all life in it—to die of cold. I look back now with regret to the needless tears I have wasted over that, the generous sympathy for the last little band of survivors, dying at 459 degrees below our zero ($-273°$ centigrade); the absolute zero of cold when the molecules cease to move and heat ends. No stove will light at that, for the wood is as cold as the stove, and the match is as cold as both, and the dead fingers motionless.

I remember meeting this inexorable law for the first time in reading, as a little boy, a piece of "popular science" entitled *Our Great Timepiece Running Down*. It was by Richard Proctor, whose science-bogeys were as terrifying as Mrs. Crow's *Night Thoughts*, only slower in action. The sun, it appeared, was cooling; soon it would be all over. Lord Kelvin presently ratified this. Being Scotch, he didn't mind damnation and he gave the sun and the whole solar system only ninety million years more to live.

This famous law was first clearly enunciated in 1824 by the great French physicist, Nicolas Carnot. It showed that all bodies in the universe kept exchanging their temperature—hot things heated cold, and cold things chilled hot. Thus they pooled their temperature. Like the division of a rich estate among a flock of poor relations, it meant poverty for all. We must all share ultimately the cold of absolute space.

It is true that a gleam of hope came when Ernest Rutherford and others, working on radioactivity, discovered that there might be a contrary process of "stocking up." Atoms exploding into radioactivity would keep the home fires burning in the sun for a long time. This glad news meant that the sun was both much older and much younger than Lord Kelvin had ever thought it was. But even at that it was only a respite. The best they could offer was 1,500,000,000 years. After that we freeze.

And now what do you think! Here comes the new physics of the Quantum Theory and shatters the Second Law of Thermodynamics into gas— a word that is Dutch for chaos. The world may go on forever. All of this because of the final promulgation of the Law of the *Quantum*—or, shall we say, the Law of Just So Much—of which we shall presently speak. These physical people do not handle their Latin with the neat touch of those of us who knew our declensions as they know their dimensions. Of course they mean *Tantum*—but let it go at that. *Quantum* is drugstore Latin, *quantum sufficit*. *Tantum* is the real thing—*Virgilium vidi tantum* ("I saw something of Virgil").

At this point I may perhaps pause to explain that the purpose of this article is not to make fun of science, nor to express disbelief in it, but only to suggest its limits. What I want to say is that when the scientist steps out from recording phenomena and offers a general statement of the nature of what is called "reality," the ultimate nature of space, of time, of the beginning of things, of life, of a universe, then he stands exactly where you and I do, and the three of us stand where Plato did—and long before him Rodin's primitive thinker.

Consider this. Professor Hubble, like Joshua, has called upon the universe to be still. All is quiet. The universe rests, motionless, in the night sky. The mad rush is over. Every star in every galaxy, every island universe, is at least right where it is. But the old difficulty remains: Does it go forever, this world in the sky, or does it stop? Such an alternative has posed itself as a problem for every one of us, somewhere about the age of twelve. We cannot imagine that the stars go on forever. It's unthinkable. But we equally cannot imagine that they come to a stop and that beyond them is nothing, and then more nothing. Unending nothing is as incomprehensible as unending something. This alternative I cannot fathom, nor can Professor Hubble, nor can any one ever hope to.

Let me turn back in order to make my point of view a little clearer. I propose to traverse again the path along which modern science has dragged those who have tried to follow it for about a century past. It was, at first, a path singularly easy to tread, provided that one could throw aside the inherited burden of superstition, false belief, and prejudice. For the direction seemed verified and assured all along by the corroboration of science by actual physical results. Who could doubt electricity after the telegraph? Or doubt the theory of light after photography? Or the theory of electricity after reading under electric light? At every turn, each new advance of science unveiled new power, new mechanism of life—and of death. To "doubt science" was to be like the farmer at the circus who doubted the giraffe. Science, of course, had somehow to tuck into the same bed as Theology, but it was the theologian who protested. Science just said, "Lie over."

Let us follow then this path.

2

When the mediaeval superstition was replaced by the new learning, mathematics, astronomy, and physics were the first sciences to get organized and definite. By the opening of the nineteenth century they were well set; the solar system was humming away so drowsily that Laplace was able to assure Napoleon that he didn't need God to watch over it. Gravitation worked like clockwork, and clockwork worked like gravitation. Chemistry, which, like electricity, was nothing but a set of experiments in Benjamin Franklin's time, turned into a science after Lavoisier had discovered that fire was not a thing but a process, something happening to things—an idea so far above the common thought that they guillotined him for it in 1794. Dalton followed and showed that all things could be broken up into a set of very, very small atoms, grouped into molecules all acting according to plan. With Faraday and Maxwell, electricity, which turned out to be the same as magnetism, or interchangeable with it, fell into its place in the new order of science.

By about 1880 it seemed as if the world of science was fairly well explained. Metaphysics still talked in its sleep. Theology still preached sermons. It took issue with much of the new science, especially with geology and the new evolutionary science of life that went with the new physical world. But science paid little attention.

For the whole thing was so amazingly simple. There you had your space and time, two things too obvious to explain. Here you had your matter, made up of solid little atoms, infinitely small but really just like birdseed. All this was set going by and with the Law of Gravitation. Once started, the nebulous world condensed into suns, the suns threw off planets, the planets cooled, life resulted and presently became conscious, conscious life got higher up and higher up till you had apes, then Bishop Wilberforce, and then Professor Huxley.

A few little mysteries remained, such as the question of what space and matter and time and life and consciousness really were. But all this was conveniently called by Herbert Spencer the *Unknowable,* and then locked in a cupboard and left there.

Everything was thus reduced to a sort of Dead Certainty. Just one awkward skeleton remained in the cupboard. And that was the peculiar, mysterious aspect of electricity, which was not exactly a thing and yet was more than an idea. There was also, and electricity only helped to make it worse, the old puzzle about "action at a distance." How does gravitation pull all the way from here to the sun? And if there is *nothing* in space, how does light get across from the sun in eight minutes, and even all the way from Sirius in eight years?

Even the invention of "ether" as a sort of universal jelly that could have ripples shaken across it proved a little unconvincing.

Then, just at the turn of the century, the whole structure began to crumble.

The first note of warning that something was going wrong came with the discovery of X rays. Sir William Crookes, accidentally leaving around tubes of rarefied gas, stumbled on "radiant matter," or "matter in the fourth state," as accidentally as Columbus discovered America. The British Government knighted him at once (1897), but it was too late. The thing had started. Then came Guglielmo Marconi with the revelation of more waves, and universal at that. Light, the world had learned to accept, because we can see it, but this was fun in the dark.

There followed the researches of the radio-activity school and, above all, those of Ernest Rutherford which revolutionized the theory of matter. I knew Rutherford well as we were colleagues at McGill for seven years. I am quite sure that he had no original intention of upsetting the foundations of the universe. Yet that is what he did, and he was in due course very properly raised to the peerage for it.

When Rutherford was done with the atom, all the solidity was pretty well knocked out of it.

Till these researches began, people commonly thought of atoms as something like birdseed— little round, solid particles, ever so little, billions to an inch. They were small. But they were there. You could weigh them. You could apply to them all the laws of Isaac Newton about weight and velocity and mass and gravitation—in other words, the whole of first-year physics.

Let us try to show what Rutherford did to the atom. Imagine to yourself an Irishman whirling a shillelagh around his head with the rapidity and dexterity known only in Tipperary or Donegal. If you come anywhere near, you'll get hit with the shillelagh. Now make it go faster; faster still; get it going so fast that you can't tell which is Irishman and which is shillelagh. The whole combination has turned into a green blur. If you shoot a bullet at it, it will probably go through, as there is mostly nothing there. Yet if you go up against it, it won't hit you now, because the shillelagh is going so fast that you will seem to come against a solid surface. Now make the Irishman smaller and the shillelagh longer. In fact, you don't need the Irishman at all; just his force, his Irish determination, so to speak. Just keep that, the *disturbance*. And you don't need the shillelagh either, just the *field of force* that it sweeps. There! Now put in two Irishmen and two shillelaghs and reduce them in the same way to one solid body— at least it seems solid but you can shoot bullets through it anywhere now. What you have now is a hydrogen atom—one proton and one electron flying around as a *disturbance* in space. Put in more Irishmen and more shillelaghs—or, rather, more protons and electrons—and you get other kinds of atoms. Put in a whole lot— eleven protons, eleven electrons; that is a sodium atom. Bunch the atoms together into combinations called molecules, themselves flying round—and there you are! That's solid matter, and nothing in it at all except disturbance. You're standing on it right now: the molecules are beating against your feet. But there is nothing there, and nothing in your feet. This may help you to understand how "waves," ripples of disturbance—for instance, the disturbance you call radio—go right through all matter, indeed right through *you*, as if you weren't there. You see, you aren't.

The peculiar thing about this atomic theory was that whatever the atoms were, birdseed or disturbance, it made no difference in the way they acted. They followed all the laws of mechanics and motion, or they seemed to. There was no need to change any idea of space or time because of them. Matter was their forte, like wax figures with Artemus Ward.

One must not confuse Rutherford's work on atoms with Einstein's theories of space and time. Rutherford worked all his life without reference to Einstein. Even in his later days at the Cavendish Laboratory at Cambridge when he began, ungratefully, to smash up the atom that had made him, he needed nothing from Einstein. I once asked Rutherford—it was at the height of the popular interest in Einstein in 1923—what he thought of Einstein's relativity. "Oh, that stuff!" he said. "We never bother with that in our work!" His admirable biographer, Professor A. S. Eve, tells us that when the German physicist, Wien, told Rutherford that no Anglo-Saxon could understand relativity, Rutherford answered, "No, they have too much sense."

But it was Einstein who made the real trouble. He announced in 1905 that there was no such thing as absolute rest. After that there never was. But it was not till just after the Great War that the reading public caught on to Einstein and that little books on "Relativity" covered the bookstalls.

Einstein knocked out space and time, as Rutherford knocked out matter. The general viewpoint of relativity toward space is very simple. Einstein explains that there is no such place as *here*. "But," you answer, "I'm here; here is where I am right now." But you're moving, you're spinning around as the earth spins; and you and the earth are both spinning around the sun, and the sun is rushing through space toward a distant galaxy, and the galaxy itself is beating it away at 26,000 miles a second. Now, where is that spot that is here! How did you mark it? You remember the story of the two idiots who were out fishing, and one said, "We should have marked that place where we got all the fish," and the other said, "I did; I marked it on the boat." Well, that's it. That's *here*.

You can see it better still if you imagine the universe swept absolutely empty: nothing in it, not even *you*. Now put a *point* in it, just one point. Where is it? Why, obviously it's nowhere. If you say it's right there, where do you mean by there? In which direction is there? In *that* direction? Oh! Hold on, you're sticking yourself in to make a direction. It's in *no* direction; there aren't any directions. Now put in another point. Which is which? You can't tell. They *both* are. One is on the right, you say, and one on the left. You keep out of that space! There's no right and no left. Join the points with a line. Now you think you've got something, and I admit this is the nearest you have come to it. But is the line long or short? How long is it? Length soon vanishes into a purely relative term. One thing is longer than another: That's all.

There's no harm in all this, so far. To many people it's as obvious as it is harmless. But that's only the beginning. Leave space alone for a moment and take on time and then things begin to thicken. If there is no such place as here, a similar line of thought will show that there's no such time as now—not absolutely now. Empty the universe again as you did before, with not a speck in it, and now ask, What time is it? God bless me, how peculiar! It isn't any time. It can't be; there's nothing to tell the time by. You say you can feel it go; oh, but you're not there. There will be no *time* until you put something into space with dimensions to it— and then there'll be time, but only as connected somehow—no knowing how—with things in space. But just as there is no such thing as absolute top or bottom in space, so there is a similar difficulty as to time backward and time forward.

The relativity theory undertakes to explain both space and time by putting them together, since they are meaningless without one another, into a compound called "space-time continuum." Time thus becomes, they say, the fourth dimension of space. Until just recently it was claimed further that to fit these relationships together, to harmonize space and time, space must have a curve, or curvature. This was put over to the common mind by comparing what happens in space with what happens to a fly walking on a sphere (a globe). The fly walks and walks and never gets to the end. It's curved. The joke is on the fly. So was the joke long ago on the mediaeval people who thought the world was flat. "What happened to the theory of the earth," writes Eddington, "has happened also to the world of space and time."

The idea was made plainer for us by comparing space-time to an onion skin, or rather to an infinite number of onion skins. If you have enough, you can fill all space. The universe is your onion, as it was Shakespeare's oyster.

The discovery by Einstein of this curvature of space was greeted by the physicists with the burst of applause that greets a winning home run at baseball. That brilliant writer just mentioned, Sir Arthur Eddington, who can handle space and time with the imagery of a poet, and even infiltrate humour into gravitation—as when he says that a man in an elevator falling twenty stories has an ideal opportunity to study gravitation—is loud in his acclaim. Without this curve, it appears, things won't fit into their place. The fly on the globe, as long as he thinks it flat (like Mercator's map), finds things shifted, as by some unaccountable demon, to all sorts of wrong distances. Once he gets the idea of a sphere, everything comes straight. So with our space. The mystery of gravitation puzzles us, except those who have the luck to fall in an elevator, and even for them knowledge comes too late. They weren't falling at all: just curving. "Admit a curvature of the world," wrote Eddington in his Gifford Lectures of 1927, "and the mysterious agency disappears. Einstein has exorcised this demon."

But it appears now, fourteen years later, that Einstein doesn't care if space is curved or not. He can take it either way. A prominent physicist of today, head of the department in one of the greatest universities of the world, wrote me on this point: "Einstein had stronger hopes that a general theory which involved the assumption of a property of space, akin to what is ordinarily called curvature, would be more useful than he now believes to be the case." Plain talk for a professor. Most people just say Einstein has given up curved space. It's as if Sir Isaac Newton years after had said, with a yawn, "Oh, about that apple—perhaps it wasn't falling."

Now with the curve knocked out of it, the space-time continuum, with these so-called four dimensions, becomes really a very simple matter;

in fact, only a very pretentious name for a very obvious fact. It just means that information about an occurrence is not complete unless we know both where it happened and when it happened. It is no use telling me that Diogenes is dead if I didn't know that he was alive.

Obviously "time-when" or "place-where" are bound together and coexist with one another. If there were no space—just emptiness —there could be no time. It wouldn't count itself. And if there were no time, there could be no space. Start it and it would flicker out again in no time—like an electric bulb on a wobble-plug. Space-time continuum is just a pretentious name for this consequence of consciousness. We can't get behind it. We begin life with it, as the chicken out of the egg begins with its cell memory. All the mathematics based on "space-time continu-um" get no further, as far as concerns the search for reality. It gets no further than the child's arithmetic book that says, "If John walks two miles every day for ten days," etc., etc. The child hooks space and time with a continuum as easily as the chicken picks up gravel.

3

But, unhappily, we can't get away from the new physics quite as simply as that. Even if we beat them out on space and time, there is far worse to come. That's only the start of it, for now, as the fat boy in *Pickwick* said, "I'm going to make your flesh creep." The next thing to go is cause and effect. You may think that one thing causes another. It appears that it doesn't. And, of course, when cause and effect go, the bottom is out of the universe, since you can't tell, literally can't, what's going to happen next. This is the consequence of the famous Quantum Theory, first hinted at by Professor Max Planck about forty years ago and since then scrambled for by the physicists like dogs after a bone. It changes so fast that when Sir Arthur Eddington gave the Gifford Lectures referred to, he said to his students that it might not be the same when they met next autumn.

But we cannot understand the full impact of the Quantum Theory in shattering the world we lived in, without turning back again to discuss time in a new relation, namely, the forward-and-backwardness of it, and to connect it up again with the Second Law of Thermodynamics —the law, it will be recalled, that condemns us to die of cold. Only we will now call it by its true name—which we had avoided before—as the Law of Entropy. All physicists sooner or later say, "Let us call it Entropy," just as a man says when you get to know him, "Call me Charlie."

So we make a new start.

I recall, as some other people still may, a thrilling melodrama called *The Silver King*. In this the hero, who thinks he has committed a murder (of course, he hasn't really), falls on his knees and cries, "Oh, God, turn back the universe and give me yesterday." The supposed reaction of the audience was, "Alas, you *can't* turn back the universe!"

But nowadays it would be very different. At the call, the Spirit of Time would appear—not Father Time, who is all wrong, being made old —but a young, radiant spirit in a silver frock made the same back and front. "Look," says the Spirit, "I'm going to turn back the universe. You see this wheel turning around? Presto! It's going the other way. You see this elastic ball falling to the floor? Presto! It's bouncing back. You see out of the window that star moving west? Presto! It's going east. Hence accordingly," continues the Spirit, now speaking like a professor, so that the Silver King looks up in apprehension, "time, as evidenced by any primary motion, is entirely reversible so that we cannot distinguish between future time and past time: indeed, if they move in a circle both are one."

The Silver King leaps up, shouts, "Innocent! Innocent!" and dashes off, thus anticipating Act V and spoiling the whole play. The musing Spirit, musing of course backwards, says, "Poor fellow, I hadn't the heart to tell him that this only applies to primary motion and not to

Entropy. And murder, of course, is a plain case of Entropy."

And now let us try to explain. Entropy means the introduction into things that happen of a random element, as opposed to things that happen and "unhappen," like a turning wheel, good either way, or a ball falling and bouncing as high as it falls, or the earth going around the sun. These primary motions are "reversible." As far as they are concerned, time could just as well go backwards as forward. But now introduce the element of random chance. You remember how Humpty Dumpty fell off the wall? All the king's horses and all the king's men couldn't put Humpty together again. Of course not. It was a straight case of Entropy. But now consider a pack of cards fresh from the maker. Are they all in suits, all in order again? They might so arrange themselves, but they won't. Entropy. Take this case. You show a motion picture of a wheel spinning. You run it backwards; it spins the other way. That's time, the time of primary motion, both ways alike. Now show a motion picture of a waiter with a tray of teacups. He drops them; they roll in a hundred fragments. Now run it backwards; you see all the little fragments leap up in the air, join neatly into cups, and rest on the tray. Don't think that the waiter smiles with relief. He doesn't: he can't smile backwards: he just relaxes from horror to calm.

Here then is Entropy, the smashing down of our world by random forces that don't reverse. The heat and cold of Carnot's Second Law are just one case of it. This is the only way by which we can distinguish which of two events came first. It's our only clue as to which way time is going. If procrastination is the thief of time, Entropy is the detective.

The Quantum Theory begins with the idea that the quantities of disturbance in the atom, of which we spoke, are done up, at least they act that way, in little fixed quantities (each a Quantum—no more, no less), as if sugar only existed by the pound. The smallness of the Quantum is beyond comprehension. A Quan-

tum is also peculiar. A Quantum in an atom flies around in an orbit. This orbit may be a smaller ring or a bigger ring. But when the Quantum shifts from orbit to orbit, it does not pass or drift or move *from one to the other*. No, sir. First, it's here and then it's there. Believe it or not, it has just shifted. Its change of place is random, and *not because of anything*. Now the things that we think of as matter and movements and events (things happening) are all based, infinitely far down, on this random dance of Quantums. Hence, since you can't ever tell what a Quantum will do, you can't ever say what will happen next. Cause and effect are all gone.

But as usual in this bright, new world of the new physics, the statement is no sooner made than it is taken back again. There are such a lot of Quantums that we can feel sure that one at least will turn up in the right place—by chance, not by cause.

The only difficulty about the Quantum Theory has been that to make the atomic "orbits" operate properly, and to put the Quantum *into two places at once*, it is necessary to have "more dimensions" in space. If they are not in one, they are in another. You ask next door. What this means I have no idea.

Nor does it tell us any ultimate truth about the real nature of things to keep on making equations about them. Suppose I wish to take a holiday trip and am selecting a place to go. I ask, "How far is it? How long does it take to get there? What does it cost?" These things all come into it. If I like I can call them "dimensions." It does no harm. If I like I can add other dimensions—how hot it is, how much gold it has, and what sort of women. I can say, if I wish, that the women are therefore found out to be the seventh dimension of locality. But I doubt if I can find anything sillier to say than the physicists' talk of ten and twelve dimensions added to space.

Let it be realized, I say, that making equations and functions about a thing does not tell us anything about its real nature. Suppose that I sometimes wonder just what sort of man

Chipman, my fellow club member, is. While I am wondering, another fellow member, a mathematician, comes in. "Wondering about Chipman, were you?" he says. "Well, I can tell you all about him as I have computed his dimensions. I have here the statistics of the number of times he comes (t), the number of steps he takes before he sits down (s), his orbit in moving round (o), aberrations as affected by other bodies (ab), velocity (v), specific gravity (sp), and his saturation (S)." He is therefore a function of these things, or shall we say quite simply:

$$F\int \frac{s.v.o.sp.S}{t.ab}$$

Now this would be mathematically useful. With it I can calculate the likelihood of my friend's being at the Club at any particular time, and whether available for billiards. In other words, I've got him in what is called a "frame" in space-time. But just as all this tells me nothing of ultimate reality, neither do the super-dimensions of the new physics.

People who know nothing about the subject, or just less than I do, will tell you that science and philosophy and theology have nowadays all come together. So they have, in a sense. But the statement, like those above, is just a "statistical" one. They have come together as three people may come together in a picture theater, or three people happen to take apartments in the same building, or, to apply the simile that really fits, as three people come together at a funeral. The funeral is that of Dead Certainty. The interment is over, and the three turn away together.

"Incomprehensible," murmurs Theology reverently.

"What was that word?" asks Science.

"Incomprehensible; I often use it in my litanies."

"Ah, yes," murmurs Science, with almost equal reverence, "incomprehensible!"

"The comprehensibility of comprehension," begins Philosophy, staring straight in front of him.

"Poor fellow," says Theology, "he's wandering again; better lead him home."

"I haven't the least idea where he lives," says Science.

"Just below me," says Theology. "We're both above you."

TOBIAS DANZIG

Fingerprints

Ten cycles of the moon the Roman year comprised:
This number then was held in high esteem,
Because, perhaps, on fingers we are wont to count,
Or that a woman in twice five months brings forth,
Or else that numbers wax till ten they reach
And then from one begin their rhythm anew.

OVID, Fasti, III

1

Man, even in the lower stages of development, possesses a faculty which, for want of a better name, I shall call *Number Sense*. This faculty permits him to recognize that something has changed in a small collection when, without his direct knowledge, an object has been removed from or added to the collection.

Number sense should not be confused with counting, which is probably of a much later vintage, and involves, as we shall see, a rather intricate mental process. Counting, so far as we know, is an attribute exclusively human, whereas some brute species seem to possess a rudimentary number sense akin to our own. At least, such is the opinion of competent observers of animal behavior, and the theory is supported by a weighty mass of evidence.

Many birds, for instance, possess such a number sense. If a nest contains four eggs one can safely be taken, but when two are removed the bird generally deserts. In some unaccountable way the bird can distinguish two from three. But this faculty is by no means confined to birds. In fact the most striking instance we know is that of the insect called the "solitary wasp." The mother wasp lays her eggs in individual cells and provides each egg with a number of live caterpillars on which the young feed when hatched. Now, the number of victims is remarkably constant for a given species of wasp: some species provide five, others twelve, others again as high as twenty-four caterpillars per cell. But most remarkable is the case of the *Genus Eumenus*, a variety in which the male is much smaller than the female. In some mysterious way the mother knows whether the egg will produce a male or a female grub and apportions the quantity of food accordingly; she does not change the species or size of the prey, but if the egg is male she supplies it with five victims, if female with ten.

The regularity in the action of the wasp and the fact that this action is connected with a fundamental function in the life of the insect make this last case less convincing than the one which follows. Here the action of the bird seems to border on the conscious:

A squire was determined to shoot a crow which made its nest in the watchtower of his estate. Repeatedly he had tried to surprise the bird, but in vain: at the approach of man the crow would leave its nest. From a distant tree it would watchfully wait until the man had left the tower and then return to its nest. One day the squire hit upon a ruse: two men entered the tower, one remained within, the other came out and went on. But the bird was not deceived: it kept away until the man within came out. The experiment was repeated on the succeeding days with two, three, then four men, yet without success. Finally, five men were sent: as before, all entered the tower, and one remained while the other four came out and went away. Here

the crow lost count. Unable to distinguish between four and five it promptly returned to its nest.

2

Two arguments may be raised against such evidence. The first is that the species possessing such a number sense are exceedingly few, that no such faculty has been found among mammals, and that even the monkeys seem to lack it. The second argument is that in all known cases the number sense of animals is so limited in scope as to be ignored.

Now the first point is well taken. It is indeed a remarkable fact that the faculty of perceiving number, in one form or another, seems to be confined to some insects and birds and to men. Observation and experiments on dogs, horses and other domestic animals have failed to reveal any number sense.

As to the second argument, it is of little value, because the scope of the human number sense is also quite limited. In every practical case where civilized man is called upon to discern number, he is consciously or unconsciously aiding his direct number sense with such artifices as symmetric pattern reading, mental grouping or counting. *Counting* especially has become such an integral part of our mental equipment that psychological tests on our number perception are fraught with great difficulties. Nevertheless some progress has been made; carefully conducted experiments lead to the inevitable conclusion that the direct *visual* number sense of the average civilized man rarely extends beyond four, and that the *tactile* sense is still more limited in scope.

Anthropological studies on primitive peoples corroborate these results to a remarkable degree. They reveal that those savages *who have not reached the stage of finger counting* are almost completely deprived of all perception of number. Such is the case among numerous tribes in Australia, the South Sea Islands, South

America, and Africa. Curr, who has made an extensive study of primitive Australia, holds that but few of the natives are able to discern four, and that no Australian in his wild state can perceive seven. The Bushmen of South Africa have no number-words beyond *one, two* and *many*, and these words are so inarticulate that it may be doubted whether the natives attach a clear meaning to them.

We have no reasons to believe and many reasons to doubt that our own remote ancestors were better equipped, since practically all European languages bear traces of such early limitations. The English *thrice*, just like the Latin *ter*, has the double meaning: three times, and many. There is a plausible connection between the Latin *tres*, three, and *trans*, beyond; the same can be said regarding the French *très*, very, and *trois*, three.

The genesis of number is hidden behind the impenetrable veil of countless prehistoric ages. Has the concept been born of experience, or has experience merely served to render explicit what was already latent in the primitive mind? Here is a fascinating subject for metaphysical speculation, but for this very reason beyond the scope of this study.

If we are to judge of the development of our own remote ancestors by the mental state of contemporary tribes we cannot escape the conclusion that the beginnings were extremely modest. A rudimentary number sense, not greater in scope than that possessed by birds, was the nucleus from which the number concept grew. And there is little doubt that, left to this direct number perception, man would have advanced no further in the art of reckoning than the birds did. But through a series of remarkable circumstances man has learned to aid his exceedingly limited perception of number by an artifice which was destined to exert a tremendous influence on his future life. This artifice is counting, and it is to *counting* that we owe the extraordinary progress which we have made in expressing our universe in terms of number.

3

There are primitive languages which have words for every color of the rainbow but have no word for color; there are others which have all number words but no word for number. The same is true of other conceptions. The English language is very rich in native expressions for particular types of collections: *flock, herd, set, lot* and *bunch* apply to special cases; yet the words *collection* and *aggregate* are of foreign extraction.

The concrete preceded the abstract. "It must have required many ages to discover," says Bertrand Russell, "that a brace of pheasants and a couple of days were both instances of the number two." To this day we have quite a few ways of expressing the idea *two*: pair, couple, set, team, twin, brace, etc., etc.

A striking example of this extreme concreteness of the early number concept is the Thimshian language of a British Columbia tribe. There we find seven distinct sets of number words: one for flat objects and animals; one for round objects and time; one for counting men; one for long objects and trees; one for canoes; one for measures; one for counting when no definite object is referred to. The last is probably a later development; the others must be relics of the earliest days when the tribesmen had not yet learned to count.

It is counting that consolidated the concrete and therefore heterogeneous notion of plurality, so characteristic of primitive man, into the *homogeneous abstract number concept*, which made mathematics possible.

4

Yet, strange though it may seem, it is possible to arrive at a logical, clear-cut number concept without bringing in the artifices of counting.

We enter a hall. Before us are two collections: the seats of the auditorium, and the audience. *Without counting* we can ascertain whether the two collections are equal and, if not equal, which is the greater. For if every seat is taken and no man is standing, *we know without counting* that the two collections are equal. If every seat is taken and some in the audience are standing, *we know without counting* that there are more people than seats.

We derive this knowledge through a process which dominates all mathematics and which has received the name of *one-to-one correspondence*. It consists in assigning to every object of one collection an object of the other, the process being continued until one of the collections, or both, are exhausted.

The number technique of many primitive peoples is confined to just such a matching or tallying. They keep the record of their herds and armies by means of notches cut in a tree or pebbles gathered in a pile. That our own ancestors were adept in such methods is evidenced by the etymology of the words *tally* and *calculate*, of which the first comes from the Latin *talea*, cutting, and the second from the Latin *calculus*, pebble.

It would seem at first that the process of correspondence gives only a means for comparing two collections, but is incapable of creating number in the absolute sense of the word. Yet the transition from relative number to absolute is not difficult. It is necessary only to create *model collections*, each typifying a possible collection. Estimating any given collection is then reduced to the selection among the available models of one which can be matched with the given collection member by member.

Primitive man finds such models in his immediate environment: the wings of a bird may symbolize the number two, clover-leaves three, the legs of an animal four, the fingers on his own hand five. Evidence of this origin of number words can be found in many a primitive language. Of course, once the *number-word* has been created and adopted, it becomes as good a model as the object it originally represented. The necessity of discriminating between the name of the borrowed object and the number symbol itself would naturally tend to bring about a change in sound, until in the course of time the very connection between the two is lost to memory. As man learns to rely more and more on his language, the sounds supersede the images for which they stood, and the originally concrete models take the abstract form of number-words. Memory and habit lend concreteness to these abstract forms, and so mere words become measures of plurality.

5

The concept I just described is called *cardinal number*. The cardinal number rests on the principle of correspondence: it implies *no counting*. To create a counting process it is not enough to have a motley array of models, comprehensive though this latter may be. We must devise a number *system*: our set of models must be arranged in an ordered sequence, a sequence which progresses in the sense of growing magnitude, the *natural sequence*: one, two, three.... Once this system is created, *counting a collection* means assigning to every member a term in the natural sequence in *ordered succession* until the collection is exhausted. The term of the natural sequence assigned to the *last* member of the collection is called the *ordinal number* of the collection.

The ordinal system may take the concrete form of a rosary, but this, of course, is not essential. The *ordinal* system acquires existence when the first few number-words have been committed to memory in their *ordered succession*, and a phonetic scheme has been devised to pass from any larger number to its *successor*.

6, 7

. . .

Artifices of the same nature have been observed in widely separated places, such as Bessarabia, Serbia and Syria. Their striking similarity and the fact that these countries were all at one time parts of the great Roman

Empire lead one to suspect the Roman origin of these devices. Yet, it may be maintained with equal plausibility that these methods evolved independently, similar conditions bringing about similar results.

Even today the greater portion of humanity is counting on fingers: to primitive man, we must remember, this is the only means of performing the simple calculations of his daily life.

8

How old is our number language? It is impossible to indicate the exact period in which number words originated, yet there is unmistakable evidence that it preceded written history by many thousands of years. One fact we have mentioned already: all traces of the original meaning of the number words in European languages, with the possible exception of *five*, are lost. And this is the more remarkable, since, as a rule, number words possess an extraordinary stability. While time has wrought radical changes in all other aspects we find that the number vocabulary has been practically unaffected. In fact this stability is utilized by philologists to trace kinships between apparently remote language groups....

Why is it then that in spite of this stability no trace of the original meaning is found? A plausible conjecture is that while number words have remained unchanged since the days when they originated, the names of the concrete objects from which the number words were borrowed have undergone a complete metamorphosis.

9

As to the structure of the number language, philological researches disclose an almost universal uniformity. Everywhere the ten fingers of man have left their permanent imprint.

Indeed, there is no mistaking the influence of our ten fingers on the "selection" of the base of our number system. In all Indo-European languages, as well as Semitic, Mongolian, and most primitive languages, the base of numeration is ten, i.e., there are independent number words up to ten, beyond which some compounding principle is used until 100 is reached. All these languages have independent words for 100 and 1000, and some languages for even higher decimal units. There are apparent exceptions, such as the English *eleven* and *twelve*, or the German *elf* and *zwölf*, but these have been traced to *ein-lif* and *zwo-lif*; *lif* being old German for *ten*.

It is true that in addition to the decimal system, two other bases are reasonably widespread, but their character confirms to a remarkable degree the *anthropomorphic* nature of our counting scheme. These two other systems are the quinary, base 5, and the vigesimal, base 20.

In the *quinary* system there are independent number words up to *five*, and the compounding begins thereafter. It evidently originated among people who had the habit of counting on one hand. But why should man confine himself to one hand? A plausible explanation is that primitive man rarely goes about unarmed. If he wants to count, he tucks his weapon under his arm, the left arm as a rule, and counts on his left hand, using his right hand as check-off. This may explain why the left hand is almost universally used by right-handed people for counting.

Many languages still bear the traces of a quinary system, and it is reasonable to believe that some decimal systems passed through the quinary stage. Some philologists claim that even the Indo-European number languages are of a quinary origin. They point to the Greek word *pempazein*, to count by fives, and also to the unquestionably quinary character of the Roman numerals. However, there is no other evidence of this sort, and it is much more probable that our group of languages passed through a preliminary *vigesimal stage*.

This latter probably originated among the primitive tribes who counted on their toes as well as on their fingers. A most striking example of such a system is that used by the Maya Indians of Central America. Of the same general character was the system of the ancient Aztecs. The day of the Aztecs was divided into 20 hours; a division of the army contained 8000 soldiers $(8000 = 20 \times 20 \times 20)$.

While pure vigesimal systems are rare, there are numerous languages where the decimal and the vigesimal systems have merged. We have the English *score, two-score,* and *three-score*; the French *vingt* (20) and *quatre-vingt* (4×20). The old French used this form still more frequently; a hospital in Paris originally built for 300 blind veterans bears the quaint name of *Quinze-Vingt* (Fifteen-score); the name *Onze-Vingt* (Eleven-score) was given to a corps of police-sergeants comprising 220 men.

10

There exists among the most primitive tribes of Australia and Africa a system of numeration which has neither 5, 10, nor 20 for base. It is a *binary* system, i.e., of base two. These savages have not yet reached finger counting. They have independent numbers for one and two, and composite numbers up to six. Beyond six everything is denoted by "heap."

Curr, whom we have already quoted in connection with the Australian tribes, claims that most of these count by pairs. So strong, indeed, is this habit of the native that he will rarely notice that two pins have been removed from a row of seven; he will, however, become immediately aware if one pin is missing. His sense of *parity* is stronger than his number sense.

Curiously enough, this most primitive of bases had an eminent advocate in relatively recent times in no less a person than Leibnitz. A binary numeration requires but two symbols, 0 and 1, by means of which all other numbers are expressed, as shown in the following table:

Decimal	1	2	3	4	5	6	7	8
Binary	1	10	11	100	101	110	111	1000

Decimal	9	10	11	12	13	14
Binary	1001	1010	1011	1100	1101	1110

Decimal	15	16
Binary	1111	10000

The advantages of the *base two* are economy of symbols and tremendous simplicity in operations. It must be remembered that every system requires that tables of addition and multiplication be committed to memory. For the binary system these reduce to $1+1=10$ and $1 \times 1 = 1$; whereas for the decimal, each table has 100 entries. Yet this advantage is more than offset by lack of compactness: thus the decimal number $4096 = 2^{12}$ would be expressed in the binary system by 1,000,000,000,000.

It is the mystic elegance of the binary system that made Leibnitz exclaim: *Omnibus ex nihil ducendis sufficit unum.* (One suffices to derive all out of nothing.) Says Laplace:

> Leibnitz saw in his binary arithmetic the image of Creation.... He imagined that Unity represented God, and Zero the void; that the Supreme Being drew all beings from the void, just as unity and zero express all numbers in his system of numeration. This conception was so pleasing to Leibnitz that he communicated it to the Jesuit, Grimaldi, president of the Chinese tribunal for mathematics, in the hope that this emblem of creation would convert the Emperor of China, who was very fond of the sciences. I mention this merely to show how the prejudices of childhood may cloud the vision even of the greatest men!

11

It is interesting to speculate what turn the history of culture would have taken if instead of flexible fingers man had had just two "inarticulate" stumps. If any system of numeration could at all have developed under such circumstances, it would have probably been of the binary type.

That mankind adopted the decimal system is a *physiological accident*. Those who see the hand of Providence in everything will have to admit that Providence is a poor mathematician. For outside its physiological merit the decimal base has little to commend itself. Almost any other base, with the possible exception of *nine*, would have done as well and probably better.

Indeed, if the choice of a base were left to a group of experts, we should probably witness a conflict between the practical man, who would insist on a base with the greatest number of divisors, such as *twelve*, and the mathematician, who would want a prime number, such as *seven* or *eleven*, for a base. As a matter of fact, late in the eighteenth century the great naturalist Buffon proposed that the duodecimal system (base 12) be universally adopted. He pointed to the fact that 12 has 4 divisors, while 10 has only two, and maintained that throughout the ages this inadequacy of our decimal system had been so keenly felt that, in spite of ten being the universal base, most measures had 12 secondary units.

On the other hand the great mathematician Lagrange claimed that a prime base is far more advantageous. He pointed to the fact that with a prime base every systematic fraction would be irreducible and would therefore represent the number in a unique way. In our present numeration, for instance, the decimal fraction .36 stands really for many fractions: 36/100, 18/50, and 9/25... Such an ambiguity would be considerably lessened if a prime base, such as eleven, were adopted.

But whether the enlightened group to whom we would entrust the selection of the base decided on a prime or a composite base, we may rest assured that the number *ten* would not even be considered, for it is neither prime nor has it a sufficient number of divisors.

In our own age, when calculating devices have largely supplanted mental arithmetic, nobody would take either proposal seriously. The advantages gained are so slight, and the tradition of counting by tens so firm, that the challenge seems ridiculous.

From the standpoint of the history of culture a change of base, even if practicable, would be highly undesirable. As long as man counts by tens, his ten fingers will remind him of the human origin of this most important phase of his mental life. So may the decimal system stand as a living monument to the proposition:

Man is the measure of all things.

Questions for Review

1. Lionel Trilling (pp. 22-23 above) suggests that scientists, as well as creative writers, are "neurotic" as Freud defines the term. Do any of the writers in the above section subscribe to this view of the neurotic scientist? What are the implications of this view?

2. Do any of the writers in this section agree with William James's theories of how we think? Compare and contrast the ideas of J. B. Conant and James on the matter of how "scientific" thought differs from other kinds of conceptualization.

3. J. B. Conant, the author of "Concerning the Alleged Scientific Method," is a former president of Harvard University and an expert on education as well as a scientist. Does he believe that students can be educated to be scientists, or are scientists men of a particular mental bent? Are scientists made or born, according to this essay?

4. Summarize Conant's argument concerning the so-called scientific method and its fallacies. Is scientific thinking more "factual" than other kinds of thought? Are "facts" the result of using the "empirical" method?

5. What does Conant mean by "empirical"? Is he saying that the difference between science and technology is that the first is theoretical and conceptual and the second is empirical and practical? According to him, can the principles of science be put into practice or not? Explain.

6. What are the chief similarities between the scientific method and common sense? The chief differences?

7. Carl Becker has asserted (p. 249f. above) that the method of the historian is a refinement of the method of common sense; Conant says the scientific method is close to common sense. Do they both use "common sense" to mean the same thing? Is the historian's method similar to the scientist's?

8. Stephen Toulmin's introduction to his book, *The Philosophy of Science*, is included here because it raises some problems of how the scientist and the layman are separated by language. Would Toulmin maintain that good scientific writing is like good creative writing? Explain.

9. Does Toulmin believe that scientists think in a different way from the average man? What relationship has language to their thought? Why is it difficult for laymen to understand scientific language? Why is it difficult for the scientist to put his ideas into language understandable to the layman?

10. Toulmin criticizes certain scientific writers for using similes (figures of speech that compare two things). The simile is often used by poets and other writers of fictional literature. Would Toulmin deny the use of some rhetorical devices to the scientist and reserve them for poets and philosophers?

11. Stephen Leacock's humorous essay on science and common sense is basically quite serious. What is Leacock really attacking: science? scientists? the scientific method?

12. Compare Leacock's use of "common sense" with Conant's. Can the scientific method both *be* common sense and be *destroyed by* common sense? Does the term mean different things to Conant and Leacock? Or is "common sense" really the basis of the scientific method? Does Leacock think it is?

13. Toulmin criticizes scientists for not explaining their ideas in clear language to the layman, and Leacock characterizes himself as a layman. Is Leacock actually picking flaws in the theories of physics or is he criticizing the similes used by physicists?

14. Is Leacock completely dispassionate and objective in his treatment of science? Does he misrepresent scientific thinking in any way? How do you interpret the dialogue between Science, Philosophy, and Theology at the end of the essay?

15. Mathematics is the language and chief device of many of the sciences. Tobias Danzig's *Fingerprints* examines the basis of mathematics—the number system. Does his essay indicate that mathematics is a firm "factual" basis for science?

16. How significant to number systems and mathematics in general is the fact that man possesses ten fingers? Is the importance of the number ten to mathematics a logical and essential one or is it irrational and emotional? What does this do to theories of the absolute nature of mathematics and the sciences dependent on it?

17. What proof does Danzig offer for his statements about the origin and nature of numbers? Is this proof demonstrable or not? Is Danzig's argument dependent to any extent on guessing and intuition?

Questions for Discussion and Writing

1. What is a scientific "hypothesis"? How does it differ from a guess or hunch or "brilliant flash"? Does the scientific hypothesis differ from an artistic "inspiration"?

2. Is the scientist's method of dealing with his hypotheses like or unlike the artist's way of using his inspirations? Can hypotheses be "proved" and inspirations not be "proved"?

3. How do scientists define the term "fact"? Is science "factual" or not?

4. Do the theories advanced in this group of essays differ to any extent from those in the group in section I above? How?

5. Would Conant and Danzig agree with Trilling's theory about the emotional basis of scientific investigation? Are the essays of Conant and Danzig entirely unemotional? Are their essays devoid of the writers' personal viewpoints?

6. To what degree is tone important in essays of this kind? Diction? Point of view?

7. Which of these essays is most like historiographical writing? Like reportage? In what ways?

8. Is chronology or time-sequence at all important as an element in scientific literature? What use does Leacock make of chronological order? How does his use reflect on the scientist's attitudes toward time?

9. To what extent does Tobias Danzig rely on chronological sequence in presenting his information to the reader? Is Danzig adopting the historian's techniques to his own uses?

10. The distance intellectually between the scientist and the layman, discussed by Toulmin, has led to several "popular" but differing views of the scientist: as a prophet, a "good" magician, a "wicked" magician, the "mad" scientist, and so on. Arthur Koestler discusses some of these in his book, *The Act of Creation*. On the basis of the essays in this section, can you account for the widespread nature of these attitudes toward scientists?

11. In "The Imagination of Disaster" (pp. 361–370 below), Susan Sontag surveys attitudes toward science and the science fiction movie. Read her essay, compare her views with the views of the theorists above, and suggest the ways that the "scientific" method encourages such development of "science fiction." What is implied in science fiction about the relationship of "facts" to the "imagination"?

SECTION THREE

The Natural World

Man's natural environment, the universe he inhabits, is a constant challenge to him: it presents him with the objects and the forces that he either learns to control or remains subject to, but at the same time, it defies most of his efforts to discover the basic or final sources and causes of the natural phenomena that are obvious to his senses. Natural scientists are men who set out to observe systematically the patterns of phenomena in the physical world in order to comprehend their nature or origins or ends; they believe that by amassing as much relevant data as possible and formulating it into coherent or logical order, they will gain a control of some sort over natural forces. Whether they gather data about volcanoes, corn, or the common cold, the natural scientists are seeking the "why" of the observable; and the various procedures and methods that they establish are followed out of some preconceived idea of meaning (working hypothesis) or in order to extrapolate from "evidence" some "theory" that will account for what they observe. The essays here, though written for the layman, suggest some of the difficulties that natural scientists experience in trying to arrange sense data into a coherent structure; and the verbal compositions in which they embody their experiments and research show how scientists must reconceive their conceptualizations in order to instruct the reader who is a nonspecialist.

317

GEORGE GAMOW

Galaxies in Flight

In the year 1929 the Mount Wilson astronomer Edwin P. Hubble made a very remarkable discovery. He found that the giant accumulations of stars known as galaxies, which are scattered in great multitude through the vast expanses of the universe as far as the best telescopes can see, seem to be running away from one another at fabulously high speeds. From this observed fact originated the famous theory of the expanding universe. Although the theory is still not finally proved, it seeded a whole generation of fruitful study, not only in astronomy but also in geology, physics and chemistry. It gave us a new start for investigating the age of the universe and the creation of the stuff of which it is made.

The idea of stellar galaxies is a comparatively recent discovery in astronomy. The celestial shapes that we now recognize as galaxies had been observed for a long time as faint nebulosities of various regular forms, but they were generally believed to be simply luminous clouds of gas floating in the spaces between the stars of the Milky Way. Observations with more powerful telescopes, however, resolved these "nebulosities" and showed that they were not clouds but huge collections of extremely faint stars. These giant stellar aggregates were far beyond the outer limits of our own stellar system, the Milky Way; in fact, it soon became clear that they formed systems very similar in shape and structure to the Milky Way galaxy itself.

The nearest and most familiar external galaxy is the great nebula in Andromeda, which can be seen with the naked eye as a faint, spindle-shaped speck of light in the upper part (from the Northern Hemisphere) of the constellation of Andromeda. Photographs made with large

telescopes show that this galaxy has a rather complicated structure consisting of an elliptical center, or "galactic nucleus," and "spiral arms" flung into the surrounding space from the central body. The photographs also show two nearly spherical nebulosities close by, probably satellites of the central system.

Among the myriads of stars in the arms of the Andromeda Nebula are many pulsating ones, of the type called Cepheid variables. They brighten and fade in a regular rhythm, and their pulsation period provides a method of determining their absolute brightness. By comparing their apparent brightness (which depends on their distance from us) with their calculated absolute brightness, Hubble was able to prove that the Andromeda Nebula is some 680,000 light-years from the Milky Way. To a hypothetical observer in the Andromeda galaxy, the Milky Way would look much the same as the Andromeda system looks to us, except that the spiral arms of the Milky Way are somewhat more open. Our sun, with its family of planets, would be seen through a telescope within the Andromeda Nebula as a rather faint star near the end of one of the spiral arms, some 30,000 light-years from the Milky Way center.

The galaxies generally are shaped like a discus. The Andromeda system looks like an elongated spindle to us because it is tilted to our line of sight, but there are many other galaxies that we see from the top or straight on edge. All large galaxies have the same sort of spiral arms as the Milky Way and Andromeda, but smaller ones are usually armless. The galaxies are scattered more or less uniformly through space as far as our telescopes can probe. The average distance between neighboring nebulae is about two million light-years. The limit of our vision with the 100-inch telescope is about 500 million light-years. Hence in the observable region of space there are some 100 million galaxies.

The 200-inch telescope on Mount Palomar, which doubles the distance we can see into space, will reveal about one billion galaxies. Most galaxies are isolationist, dwelling in remote and solitary splendor, but we find a number that group themselves together to form more or less compact clusters. In the constellation of Corona Borealis, for example, there is a cluster containing some 400 galaxies. Our Milky Way is a member of a small cluster which embraces, among others, the Andromeda Nebula and the two galaxies known as the Magellanic Clouds, which are of a relatively rare type that has no well-defined shape.

The distances of all but the nearest galaxies are so great that even the most powerful telescopes fail to resolve them into individual stars. Astronomers' calculations of their distances depend entirely on their apparent brightness. Hubble, studying a group of about 100 well-known neighboring galaxies, established the fact that on the average they were of about the same size and the same intrinsic luminosity. Using this standard, we can estimate the distances of remote groups of galaxies by comparing their mean apparent brightness with that of nearby galaxies whose distances are known. Such measurements give the value of 7·5 million light-years for the distance of one of the nearest groups of galaxies in Virgo. Similar galactic groups in the constellations of Coma Berenices, Corona Borealis and Boötes are respectively 30 million, 100 million and 180 million light-years away.

Now what was it that gave Hubble the notion that the galaxies are running away from one another and that the universe is expanding? His basic discovery was made with that indispensable tool of the astronomer, the spectrograph, which analyzes the color components of the light coming from stars. Studying the spectra of distant galaxies, he noticed a curious fact: all the lines in their spectra, regardless of the wavelength or color of the line, were displaced toward the red end of the spectrum. Furthermore, the amount of this "red shift" was always directly proportional to the distance of the galaxy from us. The most natural explanation of this shift was that the source of the light was moving away. This is the so-called Doppler effect, of which the classic and most familiar example is the change in pitch of a locomotive whistle as the train approaches us and then speeds away. A light wave, like a sound wave, appears to shift to a longer wavelength when it reaches us from a receding source. And the speed with which the source is moving away is directly proportional to the shift in wavelength. Since the red shift of the galaxies also varied as their distance from us, Hubble concluded that the speed of the receding stars was proportional to their distance; the farther away they moved from one another, the faster they traveled. The red shift of the most distant galaxies that have thus far been observed is 13 per cent, which suggests that they are receding from us at the terrific velocity of 25,000 miles per second.

You must not conclude from this that we stand at the center of the universe and that all the rest of it is running away from us. Picture a slowly inflated rubber balloon with a large number of dots painted on its surface. An observer on one of the spots would be under the impression that the other dots were racing away from him in all directions, and so indeed they would be, but the same thing would be true no matter which dot he was on. In the case of the galaxies, we are dealing with the effect of a uniform expansion throughout all of space.

If you pick an arbitrary point in space, say the Milky Way, and divide the distance of a given galaxy by its recession velocity, you get a figure which represents the length of time that the galaxy has been receding from that point. The strange and wonderful consequence of Hubble's observations is that the figure will be the same no matter what pair of galaxies you pick. Thus it works out that at a fixed, calculable time in the past all the galaxies now so widely scattered were packed tightly together. And the time figure you arrive at is the age of the universe, measured from that instant when the originally highly condensed universal matter was torn apart by the primordial "explosion" that started its headlong expansion.

To get this figure, we must know the exact values for the distances and the recession velocities of distant galaxies. This is less simple than it sounds. The velocities, as we have seen, can be computed from the observed red shift, and the distances, presumably, from the galaxies' apparent brightness. But there is a catch: the apparent brightness of the stars is affected not only by their distance but also by the fact that the light coming from them is redder, and therefore carries less energy, than if the light source were stationary. To illustrate this, suppose for a moment that you are shot at by a gangster operating a submachine gun from the back window of a speeding car. Since the vehicle is receding, the bullets move more slowly toward you than they would from a stationary gun, and they strike your bulletproof jacket with less energy. A receding light source produces exactly the same effect; its emitted light quanta strike the eye with less energy and therefore look redder than they should. An astronomer must make the same correction for the weakening of light intensity as a ballistics expert would make in estimating the muzzle speed of the bullets.

There is a further complication. If the submachine gun shoots, say, one bullet per second, its bullets will strike you at longer and longer intervals as the gun recedes, for each successive bullet will have farther to travel. Similarly, light quanta from receding galaxies enter the observer's eye with less frequency, and this fact calls for another correction of the observed brightness.

Applying both corrections, and taking the most accurate possible observations, Hubble calculated that the universe began to expand less than one billion years ago. This result stands in contradiction to geological evidence, which indicates that the age of the solid earth crust, estimated quite reliably from radioactive decay in the rocks, must be at least two billion years. Since numerous pieces of evidence in various sciences support the two billion-year estimate, Hubble was forced to reconsider the

expansion theory and consider the possibility that the red shift was due not to the normal Doppler effect but to some unknown physical factor which caused light to lose part of its energy during its long trip through intergalactic space.

Such a conclusion would ruin many beautiful scientific developments that have flowed from the hypothesis of the expanding universe. It would confront physicists with the difficult task of explaining the red shift in non-Dopplerian terms—which would seem to contradict everything we know at present about light. Fortunately, there is a simple way out of the dilemma which is usually overlooked by the proponents of the "stop-the-expansion" point of view. The point is that Hubble's method of estimating the distances of faraway galaxies assumes that at the moment when they emitted their light they were just as bright as the galaxies we see closer at hand. It must be remembered, however, that the light we see from the distant galaxies was emitted at a fantastically distant time in the past; the light now coming to us from the Coma Berenices cluster, for example, started on its way some 40 million years ago, and the most distant galaxies used by Hubble are seen as they were almost half a billion years ago!

Do we have the right to assume that the galaxies, which are evolving like everything else in the universe, have kept their luminosity constant over such long periods of time? In view of the known facts about the evolutionary life of individual stars, which maintain their luminosity by the expenditure of nuclear energy, such an assumption would be very strange indeed. Actually, we can remove the entire difficulty in Hubble's time scale by remembering that the nuclear processes that fuel the stars are not endlessly self-perpetuating but are accompanied by a gradual dissipation of the originally available energy. The assumption that an average galaxy loses a mere five per cent of its luminosity in the course of 500 million years would bring the age of the universe to the two billion-year figure demanded by other astronomical, geological and physical evidence.[1]

This conclusion finds strong confirmation in recent work by Joel Stebbins and A. E. Whitford at the Mount Wilson Observatory, who have studied the apparent luminosities of distant galaxies on special plates sensitive to red light. To everyone's surprise, they found these galaxies much brighter in the red part of the spectrum than they had previously appeared to be on ordinary photographic plates, which are sensitive mostly to the blue rays. It looked at first as if this phenomenon was due to the same kind of optical scattering which makes the sun look red during dust storms; light from the galaxies, it was thought, was reddened by the clouds of fine intergalactic dust through which it passed. Calculations showed, however, that to account for the observed reddening would take a fantastic quantity of dust—100 times as much as the total amount of matter in the galaxies themselves. Such an assumption would come into serious conflict with many facts and theories about the structure of the universe. It therefore seems more reasonable to suppose that the distant galaxies look redder simply because they actually were redder when they emitted the light which is now reaching our telescopes. This could be explained if we assumed that young galaxies contain more red stars than more mature ones.[2]

Having made this fiery defense of the right of our universe to expand, let us consider the physical consequence of the expansion theory suggested at the beginning of this article. What physical process was responsible for the present relative quantities of the various chemical elements that make up the universe? Why, for example, are oxygen, iron and silicon so abundant; and gold, silver and mercury so rare?

[1] Because of new evidence obtained in 1952, all the time and distance figures for galaxies given in this article must be doubled.
[2] More detailed study of the Stebbins-Whitford effect shows that it is confined to the armless galaxies; no excess reddening is found in spirals. This disproves the hypothesis that the reddening might be due to dust and provides direct evidence that the galaxies do evolve in time.

We know that, except for the lightest elements (such as hydrogen, helium, nitrogen and carbon, involved in the sun's nuclear cycle), transformation of one atomic nucleus into another requires tremendous temperatures such as do not exist at the present time even in the hot interiors of the stars. Consequently there can not have been any revolutionary change in the relative abundance of the various elements since the expansion of the universe began. On the other hand, there has been some change, for a number of atoms are radioactive and have gradually decayed into more stable elements.

Considering the latter case first, we note, for example, that the lighter isotope of uranium, U-235 (atomic bomb stuff), constitutes only .7 per cent of a given amount of uranium found in nature; the rest is the heavier isotope U-238. The half-life of U-235 is only .7 billion years, while that of U-238 is 4.5 billion years. If we make the reasonable assumption that at the original formation of the universe both isotopes were produced in about equal amounts, the age of the universe figures up to about four billion years. Similar calculations based on the naturally radioactive isotope of potassium (relative abundance—.01 per cent; half-life—.4 billion years) yields the figure of 1.6 billion years. While these figures are only very approximate, they agree roughly in order of magnitude with the age of the universe as estimated from the red shift and other evidence. Thus we have fairly good reason to suppose that the radioactive elements were formed at the beginning of the universe.

Actually, the picture presented by the expanding universe theory, which assumes that in its original state all matter was squeezed together and possessed extremely high density and temperature, gives us exactly the right conditions for building up all the known elements in the periodic system. Recently, Alpher, Bethe and Gamow have attempted to reconstruct in some detail the processes by which the various elements may have been created during the early evolutionary stages of the expanding universe.

Our studies indicate that, under the tremendous temperatures and densities prevailing in the universe during the stage of its maximum contraction, primordial matter must have consisted entirely of free neutrons and protons moving much too fast to stick together and form stable nuclei. As the universe started to expand, this primordial gas began to cool. When its temperature dropped to about one billion degrees, particle condensation began. The growth of heavier nuclei was achieved by adding free neutrons to already existing lighter nuclei. It is known that neutron aggregates are intrinsically unstable unless about half of their particles carry a positive electric charge. Hence they must have emitted electrons until they achieved a state of electrical equilibrium. The electrons fell into orbits around the nuclei and formed electronic envelopes around them; thus atoms were created.

According to our calculations, the formation of elements must have started five minutes after the maximum compression of the universe. It was fully accomplished, in all essentials, about 30 minutes later. By that time the density of matter had dropped below the minimum necessary for nuclear-building processes. All the elements were created in that critical 30 minutes, and their relative abundance in the universe has remained essentially constant throughout the three billion years of subsequent expansion.

HOWEL WILLIAMS

Volcanoes

During the past 400 years some 500 volcanoes have erupted from the depths of our planet. They have killed 190,000 people; the most

VOLCANOES: Originally published in *Scientific American* (November 1951). Reprinted with permission. Copyright © 1951 by Scientific American, Inc. All rights reserved.

destructive eruption, that of Tamboro in the East Indies in 1815, wiped out 56,000 in one gigantic explosion. Volcanoes have always terrified mankind. Yet it should not be forgotten that they also play a constructive role. It is not merely that volcanic eruptions have provided some of the world's richest soils—and some of our most magnificent scenery. Throughout geologic time volcanoes and their attendant hot springs and gas vents have been supplying the oceans with water and the atmosphere with carbon dioxide. But for these emanations there would be no plant life on earth, and therefore no animal life. In very truth, but for them we would not be here!

What exactly are volcanoes, and how are they formed? Obviously they are symptoms of some kind of internal disorder in the earth. The eruptions we see at the surface are only small manifestations of great events going on below, events about which we can only speculate. We do, however, have some clues to what may be happening—a few tantalizing points of light that make volcanoes a most fascinating field of study.

The first clue lies in the location of the volcanic regions on the world map. We know that active volcanoes are concentrated in parts of the world where earthquakes are most common, particularly where earthquakes have a tendency to originate at a level about 60 miles down in the earth's crust. This suggests that volcanoes are connected with disturbances in the earth at that depth. Secondly, we know that most of the world's volcanoes are in young mountain belts, that is, where the face of the earth has recently been wrinkled and cracked.

Tens of miles below the surface of the earth there is an extremely hot shell of glassy or crystalline material. This solid material becomes liquefied if the pressure on it is reduced or the temperature rises. The pressure may be reduced by the bending or cracking of the rocks lying about it; the temperature may be increased by radio-active heating. In either case, the liquefied material forms a fluid mass, called magma, that is lighter than the overlying rocks, and so tends to rise wherever it finds an opening.

Disturbances of the earth in regions of mountain-building produce conditions favorable to formation of molten magma and its escape to the surface. To be sure, not all young mountains have volcanoes; there is none in the Alps or the Himalayas. These mountains were formed by low-angle thrusting and overfolding of the earth's skin; one layer is piled on another, making a thick cover of rock through which magma does not escape. In mountain belts where volcanoes do occur there is less overlapping of the rock layers; these mountains have steep fractures that go deep into the earth.

A volcano is usually pictured as a cone with a crater at the top which from time to time blasts forth streams and glowing bombs of lava and shattered rock. Actually there are almost as many types of volcanoes as there are landscapes. They range from the explosive kind to the sluggish and gentle, and they come in a great variety of shapes and sizes. The form a volcano takes depends not only on the structure of the earth below it but also on the physical nature of the erupted magma, or lava. One of the most important factors determining the shape and activity of a volcano is the magma's viscosity. This varies greatly; some lavas are so fluid that they flow over the ground at more than 20 miles an hour; others are so viscous that they move at little more than a snail's pace, and even the strong blow of a pick scarcely dents their incandescent surfaces.

Usually the more fluid the magma, the more extensive is the flow of lava, the flatter the resultant edifice and the fewer and weaker the explosive eruptions. A volcano formed mainly by quiet effusions of liquid lava generally has the shape of an inverted saucer. The volcanoes of Hawaii are of this kind, and they illustrate various stages in its growth. During the early stages of formation of such a volcano copious streams of extremely hot and fluid basalt are discharged from two or three intersecting rifts in the rock at the earth's surface. Where the

rifts intersect a small summit-crater forms. As the volcano grows to maturity, the summit-crater is much enlarged by gradual collapse of its surrounding walls, and lines of pit-craters develop along the rift-zones cutting the flanks of the volcano. The Hawaiian volcanoes Kilauea and Mauna Loa are now in this stage of evolution. Later, in the volcano's old age, new lava flows fill up and obliterates the summit- and pit-craters. Eruptions take place at longer intervals; the lavas become more varied in composition, and, because most of them are more viscous than the earlier flows and therefore stick on the sides of the mountain near the top, the upper part of the volcano becomes increasingly steep. At the same time, because the longer intervals of rest permit development of greater gas-pressure in the viscous magma, explosive activity becomes more frequent and violent. Cones of ash grow in clusters on the higher flanks of the mountain. Mauna Kea and Kohala on Hawaii are now in this stage of old age, and Hualalai has lately entered it.

At the opposite extreme there are volcanoes formed by lava squeezed out of the earth in an exceedingly viscous condition, somewhat like toothpaste from a tube. This produces very steep-sided mountains. Indeed, lava may be so nearly solid when it is thrust up through its "feeding pipe" that it rises as a slender obelisk, like the one pushed to a height of 1,000 feet on top of the dome of the celebrated Mount Pelée in the West Indies in 1902. Lassen Peak in California is another good example of a viscous protrusion.

Other volcanoes, such as Mount Shasta and Mount Rainier in this country, Mount Mayon in the Philippines, Orizaba and Popocatepetl in Mexico and Fujiyama in Japan, are built in part by outpouring of lava and in part by the explosive discharge of fragments of rock. These so-called composite volcanoes have concave slopes that steepen to the summit. Their graceful profiles rise from a wide base to a tall, slender peak. Still other volcanoes are composed wholly of explosion debris. This type of volcano is likely to grow very rapidly, and usually builds a cone with even slopes.

It may take a million years or more to build a giant volcano of the Hawaiian type or one of the composite variety such as Mount Shasta. The viscous kind grows much faster; the steep dome at the top of Mount Pelée, for instance, mushroomed to a height of 1,300 feet within 18 months. But the speed of growth of explosive volcanoes is even more spectacular. The young Mexican volcano of Paricutín was 1,200 feet high on its first anniversary. Monte Nuovo, which grew on the edge of the Bay of Naples in 1538, rose to a height of 440 feet in one day. The record goes to a volcano that sprang suddenly from Blanche Bay on the island of New Britain in 1937. It attained a height of no less than 600 feet within the first twenty-four hours; when it stopped growing several days later, it was 742 feet high.

Volcanoes of the kinds we have been considering so far are all made by discharge of material through a more or less cylindrical conduit in the earth's crust. Such discharge generally produces a cone, a dome or a sharp, slender spine. But there are also volcanoes in which the magma issues from long fissures in the crust. In that case the flood of lava or ash usually produces a plateau, the nature of which depends on the composition of the escaping magma. There are two general kinds of magma. One is represented by basalt—a dark, heavy material, poor in silica and rich in lime, iron and magnesia. The other is a lighter material, rich in silica and alkalies; its most typical variety is rhyolite. A basaltic magma is usually hotter and less viscous than a rhyolitic one.

Between 10 and 20 million years ago colossal eruptions of basaltic lava poured out of a region of fissures in the Pacific Northwest. There was a series of eruptions, sometimes separated by long quiet intervals, so that soils and even forests grew on one flow before being buried by the next. All together some 100,000 cubic miles of fluid lava erupted from the earth and spread over the surface; flow piled on flow until what

had been a mountainous terrain was completely buried by a plateau of lava more than 5,000 feet thick and about 200,000 square miles in extent.

The rhyolitic type of fissure eruption, on the other hand, is exemplified by one that took place in 1912 in the Valley of Ten Thousand Smokes in Alaska. In that year swarms of cracks suddenly opened on the valley floor, and a gas-charged, effervescent magma foamed to the surface. It was loaded with droplets and clots of incandescent liquid, which cooled to fragments of cellular glass and lumps of white pumice. So mobile was the mixture that it poured for long distances down the valley in the form of glowing avalanches. Since then many other examples of such deposits have been discovered in this country, notably in Nevada and Utah, on the Yellowstone Plateau, in the Globe district of Arizona, and in the Sierra Nevada and Owens Valley of California. Fissure eruptions of this kind often cause a sinking and downbending of the earth's crust; they account for some of the largest volcanic basins in the world, including those that hold the beautiful lakes of Taupo in New Zealand, of Toba in Sumatra and of Ilopango in El Salvador.

One of the most impressive volcanic structures is the type known as a caldera. Calderas are huge pits, shaped like craters but much larger, usually several miles across. They are also made in a very different way. A crater is the opening through which a volcano discharges its products; it is built during the construction of the cone. A caldera, on the other hand, is a product not of construction but of collapse, for it is created by the cave-in of a crater's sides. In other words, few large volcanoes blow their heads off; usually they are decapitated by engulfment of their tops.

What brings about such a collapse? In composite volcanoes—those built partly of flows and partly of exploded fragments—tremendous explosions of pumice and ash may disembowel the cone and remove support for the volcano's top. The walls of the crater at the summit then founder into the depths. The majestic Crater Lake of Oregon was formed in this way. A 12,000-foot peak which we now call Mount Mazama once stood there. Some 6,500 years ago volcanic eruptions blew 10 cubic miles of pumice out of its subterranean feeding chamber, leaving a caldera six miles wide and 4,000 feet deep. In the gigantic explosion of Krakatoa in 1883, which expelled some four and a half cubic miles of pumice, the tops of the old volcanoes foundered into the ocean. This produced a caldera five miles wide and propelled a catastrophic tidal wave that drowned 36,000 people on the adjacent coasts of Java and Sumatra.

On the present site of Vesuvius there once stood a much higher volcano. It had lain dormant for so long that vineyards extended to the summit. During this long interval of rest gas pressure accumulated in the underlying magma-chamber. In A.D. 79 it suddenly found release in a succession of terrific explosions. First the lighter, gas-rich head of the magma-column was expelled as showers of white pumice. These buried the town of Pompeii. Then came the debris of a heavier and darker magma from lower levels of the feeding chamber. This clinkerlike material, water-soaked from heavy rains, swept down the mountainsides as mud-flows and demolished the town of Herculaneum. During these violent but short-lived eruptions so much magma was emptied from the volcano's reservoir that the top of the mountain collapsed, leaving a huge, semicircular amphitheatre. Today the wrecked volcano is called Monte Somma; Vesuvius is the younger cone that has risen from the floor of its caldera.

In many volcanic eruptions ground water plays an important part, for its sudden contact with rising magma produces steam and violent explosions. This was the cause of a series of strong blasts from the Kilauea volcano in Hawaii in May, 1924. Lava drained from the feed pipes through fissures that opened far down on the sides of the volcano. Many avalanches then tumbled into the pit from the walls and ground water rushed into the empty conduits. The conversion of the water to steam generated

enough pressure to blow out the plug of avalanche debris in a series of violent blasts. In 1888 the Japanese volcano of Bandai, which had long been quiescent, erupted with alarming violence. Almost half of the mountain was destroyed and 27 square miles of land were devastated by avalanches resulting from steam blasts that lasted only a few minutes. Presumably ground water had found sudden entry to the hot interior of the dormant volcano.

We have noted that the nature of an eruption depends largely on the viscosity of the magma. The viscosity in turn depends on the magma's composition, its temperature and the amount of gas it holds. The most important factor in producing eruptions probably is the gas. Without gas a magma becomes inert; it can neither flow nor explode. Once the magma, impelled by its relative lightness, has risen from the depths, it reaches a level not far below the surface where the major role in its further advance is played by the effervescence and expansion of bubbles of gas.

What is this gas, this "eruptive element *par excellence*"? In order of importance the gases originally present in the magma seem to be hydrogen, carbon monoxide and nitrogen, with lesser amounts of sulfur, fluorine, chlorine and other vapors. But in the cloud of gas that emerges from a volcano well over 90 per cent is water vapor, with carbon dioxide next in abundance. How much of this water vapor is due to oxidation of hydrogen in the magma, how much is ground water and how much is derived from water-bearing rocks surrounding the magma reservoirs at depth is unknown. Some idea of the prodigious quantities of gas given off from some volcanoes may be gained from the fact that long after the glowing avalanches covered the Valley of Ten Thousand Smokes in 1912, the deposits of pumice continued to give off steam at the rate of six million gallons per second and discharged into the atmosphere some one and a quarter million tons of hydrochloric acid and 200,000 tons of hydrofluoric acid per year.

Apparently gases are important in maintaining high temperatures in magma, in keeping volcanoes alive and in awakening those that are dormant. But this is a speculative matter on which we have little information. The volcano-furnace may be kept hot by the burning of combustible gases; it may also be fueled by other heat-yielding reactions.

At all events, it is the sudden release of gas that accounts for the violent eruptions of long-dormant volcanoes. The gas may be held in solution in viscous magma until heat-yielding reactions near the surface make it boil at an accelerating and finally at a cataclysmic rate; this was the way Mount Pelée discharged the glowing avalanches that destroyed the town of St. Pierre and its 30,000 inhabitants in 1902. Sometimes gases may rise slowly to the top of a magma-column during long intervals of quiet until they either melt or blast an opening to the surface. The spectacular fountains of lava that gush for hundreds of feet into the air during the opening phases of most eruptions of Mauna Loa bear vivid testimony to this upward concentration of gas in a magma-column.

The activity of Vesuvius alternates between periods of relative quiet, when it erupts sluggish flows of lava or rhythmically tosses out glowing bombs, and explosions that burst forth with tremendous strength. Vesuvius produced catastrophic eruptions in 1872, 1906, and 1944. During the intervals between these explosions minor eruptions gradually increased the height of the central conelet and therewith the height of the central column of magma. Then the sudden opening of fissures far down the sides of the mountain allowed lava to escape quickly from the lower part of the column. The draining of the column greatly reduced the pressure on the underlying magma, allowed a large amount of dissolved gas to escape suddenly from solution and thereby produced colossal explosions.

One object of any science, perhaps the chief, is to improve our powers of prediction. Is it possible to say when volcanoes may erupt? To some extent, yes. We can get some warning from the seismograph. An increase in the number and intensity of local quakes in a volcanic region is fairly sure to herald an eruption. For 16 years prior to the great eruption of Vesuvius in A.D. 79 the neighboring region was repeatedly shaken. For 20 days before Paricutín was born in Mexico in 1943 the surrounding country trembled from increasingly numerous and vigorous shocks. T. A. Jaggar and R. H. Finch of the Hawaiian Volcano Observatory have foretold when Kilauea and Mauna Loa would erupt, by study of the distribution of quakes caused by fissuring of the ground as magma surged toward the surface. In many volcanic regions such preliminary quakes are accompanied by subterranean rumblings and by avalanches from the walls of craters.

Next to seismic evidence, tilting of the ground around dormant volcanoes is perhaps the most reliable clue to impending activity. The underground movement of magma often causes rapidly changing tilts on the surface. Indeed, active volcanoes almost seem to breathe; they are forever swelling and subsiding as the subterranean magma fluctuates in level. By combining strategically placed tiltmeters and seismographs, it has been found possible to say approximately where, as well as when, an eruption of Mauna Loa would take place. Accurate measurement of the cracks along the rim of the Kilauea crater also serves as a guide, for these cracks are not just superficial openings caused by slippage but mark fundamental planes of weakness that go deep, and when they widen rapidly it usually means that magma is rising beneath the crater floor.

Another hint of imminent eruption may be given by strong local disturbances of the earth's magnetism. These are produced by the rise of hot, nonmagnetic magma in the volcanic pipes and by heating of the adjacent wall-rocks. Along with the magnetic changes there are commonly changes in electrical currents in the earth; these are detected, for instance, several hours before every violent explosion of the Japanese volcano Asama.

Some volcanoes behave in a roughly cyclic fashion, so that the likely sequence of events may be foretold. For instance, when the central conduit of Vesuvius has grown to unusual height, the danger of a flank outburst of lava followed by catastrophic explosions from the summit is at a maximum. And once an eruption has begun, it may be possible to predict fairly well what is likely to follow. Thus the late Frank Perret of the Carnegie Institution of Washington, by a careful analysis of the early phases of an eruption of Mount Pelée in 1928, was able to reassure the frightened inhabitants of St. Pierre that there would be no repetition of the awful calamity of 1902.

Given sufficient warning, it is sometimes possible to minimize the damage caused by a volcano's eruption. The first recorded effort of this kind was undertaken during an eruption of Mount Etna in Sicily in 1669. The inhabitants of Catania, a town in the path of the lava pouring down the mountain, made a brave attempt to save their city by digging a channel to divert some of the lava. Unfortunately the new stream moved toward a neighboring town, the angry citizens of which soon put a stop to the efforts of the Catanians. In recent years the U.S. Air Force has tried the experiment of bombing Mauna Loa during eruptions. These tests were directed both at diverting the main lava flow and at breaking down the cinder cone itself in order to dissipate the energy of the eruption into many minor flows.

Naturally a good deal of thought has been given to how the immense energy of volcanoes might be harnessed for man's use. It has been done on a relatively minor scale in several countries, notably Italy and Iceland. In Iceland many buildings are heated by volcanic steam, and by warming fields with steam pipes the country is able to raise crops that normally grow only in more temperate climates. In Italy natural steam has been used to generate electricity since 1904. There is a region in Tuscany where steam from a deeply buried body of magma comes out of the ground through rifts and is also tapped artificially by means of wells. A typical well develops a pressure of about 63 pounds per square inch, and it yields 485,000 pounds of steam per hour at a temperature of about 400 degrees Fahrenheit. In 1941 Tuscany's harnessed volcanic steam generated 100,000 kilowatts of electric power. In addition, a large amount of boric acid, borax, ammonium carbonate, carbon dioxide and other chemicals was recovered from the vapors.

The energy available from the gas vents and hot spring waters of volcanic regions is of fantastic proportions. The hot springs and geysers of Yellowstone National Park, for instance, are calculated to give off 220,000 kilogram-calories of heat—enough to melt three tons of ice—every second. A well drilled to 264 feet in the Norris Basin there developed a steam pressure of more than 300 pounds per square inch. At "The Geysers," 35 miles north of San Fransisco, there are wells which, it is estimated, could provide an average of more than 1,300 horsepower each.

Thus far little use has been made of this available energy. There are many technical difficulties, of course, in the way of large-scale utilization of volcanic power, not least among them being the acidity of many of the vapors. But one can expect with confidence that these difficulties will be largely overcome, and that more widespread use will be made of the stores of energy now running to waste.

PAUL C. MANGELSDORF

The Mystery of Corn

The most important plant in America is corn. It is grown in every state and on three-fourths of all the farms of the U.S. Corn is the backbone of our agriculture. It is the most efficient plant that we Americans have for trapping the energy of the sun and converting it into food. True, we consume only small amounts of corn directly, but transformed into meat, milk, eggs and other animal products, it is the basic food plant of our civilization.

Yet corn is also a mystery—a botanical mystery as baffling and intriguing as any in the pages of fiction. The plant has become so highly domesticated that it is no longer capable of reproducing itself without man's intervention. A grass, it differs from all other grasses, wild or cultivated, in the nature of its seed-bearing organ: the ear. This is a highly specialized inflorescence, or flower cluster, enclosed in husks, which when mature bears several hundred or more naked seeds upon a rigid cob. The pollen-bearing inflorescence, the tassel, occurs separately on the same plant. The ear of corn has no counterpart anywhere else in the plant kingdom, either in nature or among other cultivated plants. It is superbly constructed for producing grain under man's protection, but it has a low survival value in nature, for it lacks a mechanism of seed dispersal. When an ear of corn drops to the ground, scores of seedlings emerge, creating such fierce competition among themselves for moisture and soil nutrients that usually all die and none reaches the reproductive stage.

What could have been the nature of the wild or primitive corn from which this pampered cereal has developed? Where, when and how was a species, once so hardy that it could survive in the wild, converted to a cultivated plant so specialized and so dependent upon man's ministrations that it would soon become extinct if deprived of man's help? These are questions that have puzzled botanists and anthropologists for more than a century. Now, as a result of research in botany, genetics, archaeology and history, the answers are a little nearer. The mystery has not been solved, but the web of circumstantial evidence is drawing tighter and the final solution is almost in sight.

The first reference to corn in recorded history occurs on November 5, 1492. On that day two Spaniards, whom Christopher Columbus had delegated to explore the interior of Cuba, returned with a report of "a sort of grain they call maiz which was well tasted, bak'd, dry'd and made into flour." Later explorers to the New World found corn being grown by Indians in all parts of America, from Canada to Chile. Corn proved to be as ubiquitous in the New World as it was unknown in the Old. There was a great diversity of corn varieties; all of the principal types we recognize today—dent corn, flint corn, flour corn, sweet corn and pop corn— were already in existence when America was discovered.

The evidence that corn originated in America is so overwhelming that it seems sensible to concentrate, if not to confine, our search for its wild ancestor to the Western Hemisphere. In America corn has obviously had an ancient history. The seminomadic hunting and fishing Indians in both North and South America augmented their diet of fish and game with corn from cultivated fields. The more advanced Mound Builders of the Mississippi Valley and the Cliff Dwellers of the Southwest were corn-growing and corn-eating peoples. The highly civilized Mayas of Central America, the warlike and energetic Aztecs of Mexico and the fabulous Incas of Peru and Bolivia all looked to corn for their daily bread.

This universal reliance of the pre-Columbian cultures on corn as the basic food plant, and its great diversity of varieties, greater than that of any other cereal, bespeak a long period of domestication. How old is corn as a cultivated plant? Fortunately this investigation is no longer wholly a matter of guesswork. Radio-carbon dating of corncobs and kernels found in various ancient sites bears out previous archaeological and geological estimates that the oldest corn yet found in South America goes back to about 1000 B.C., and the oldest in North America to not earlier than 2000 B.C. The oldest prehistoric ears in both North and South America are small and primitive; they differ decidedly in several characteristics from the modern varieties of the Corn Belt. Yet almost any American farm boy would recognize them instantly as corn. So some 4,000 years ago corn was already well on the road to becoming the unique cereal it is now.

In what part of America did corn originate? And what kind of wild grass was it that gave rise to the multitude of present-day varieties of corn?

One theory has corn originating from a plant called by the Aztecs *teocintle* (now Anglicized to teosinte). Teosinte is undoubtedly the closest wild relative of cultivated corn. Like corn, it has tassels and ears borne separately, although its "ears" contain only five or six seeds, each enclosed in a hard, bony shell—characteristics that make teosinte a most unpromising food plant. Also like corn, it has 10 chromosomes, indicating that it is a closely related species. Teosinte can readily be crossed with corn to produce hybrids that are completely fertile or almost so. If corn came from teosinte, as many botanists have supposed, it must have originated in Guatemala or Mexico, for teosinte is found only in these two areas.

The second principal theory is that corn originated in South America from a peculiar primitive plant called "pod" corn. Primitive pod corn today has virtually vanished; it is no longer found in pure form but as an admixture in modern varieties. As described in early references, and as obtained by inbreeding from present-day mixtures, pod corn has its kernels enclosed in a pod or chaffy shell similar to that found in all other cereals—a condition which almost certainly was characteristic of wild corn.

Which, if either, of these two theories is more likely to be correct? Botanists, in attempting to determine the place of origin of a cultivated plant, place considerable reliance upon two criteria. One is the occurrence of wild relatives of the plant in question; the other is diversity in the cultivated species itself. It is assumed that other things being equal, the region of maximum

diversity should coincide with the center of origin, since diversification has progressed longer at the center than at the periphery of the plant's present range. In the case of corn the two clues point in opposite directions: the wild-relative clue points to Guatemala and Mexico, where teosinte, corn's closest relative, grows; the diversity clue points to South America, where, on the eastern slopes of the Andes, occurs the greatest diversity of corn varieties found anywhere in America in a region of comparable size.

Some twenty years ago my colleague Robert G. Reeves and I began working at the Agricultural Experiment Station of Texas A. & M. College on a series of genetic and cytological studies of corn and its relatives to test these two conflicting theories. We hybridized corn with teosinte to determine how the genes that differentiate the two species are inherited and how they are distributed on the chromosomes. We also hybridized corn with tripsacum, a more distant wild relative of corn, which occurs in both North and South America. Our hybrids of corn and teosinte revealed that corn differs from teosinte not by a relatively few genes, as might be expected if the one had been derived from the other as a result of domestication, but by a large number of genes inherited in blocks. Our hybrids of corn and tripsacum, the first such hybrids ever to be made, showed that the chromosomes of tripsacum, eighteen in number, differed greatly from those of corn. Microscopic studies of the reproductive cells of the tripsacum-corn hybrids showed little pairing (a criterion of relationship) between the chromosomes of the two species. Nevertheless, there was some chromosome association and consequently some opportunity for exchange of genes. Especially important was the discovery that some of the plants that occurred in later generations of the tripsacum-corn hybrid resembled teosinte in some of their characteristics. This discovery led to the conclusion that teosinte might well be not the ancestor but a descendant of corn—the product of the natural hybridization of corn and tripsacum. Such a possibility had been suggested years earlier by Edgar Anderson of the Missouri Botanical Garden.

Since 1937, when we arrived at this working hypothesis, much additional research has been done on corn, pod corn, teosinte and tripsacum, and upon their hybrids. There is abundant circumstantial evidence, but still no conclusive proof, that teosinte is the product of the hybridization of corn and tripsacum. There is even more evidence to show that teosinte could scarcely have been corn's ancestor. Reeves, who has made an intensive study of the botanical characteristics of corn, teosinte and tripsacum, has found that teosinte is intermediate between corn and tripsacum or is identical with one or the other of these two species in the fifty or more features in which they differ. John S. Rogers, also working at the Texas Experiment Station, has found that numerous genes, many more than previously supposed, are involved in differentiating teosinte from corn. The possibility that these considerable genetic differences could have originated during a few thousand years of domestication seems remote indeed.

So the teosinte theory has become increasingly untenable. Meanwhile the theory that corn originated from pod corn has become more and more plausible. When a modern hybrid form of pod corn is inbred (a process that usually intensifies inherent traits) the result is a plant quite different from ordinary cultivated corn. The ear disappears and the kernels, now borne on the branches of the tassel, are enclosed in glumes, or chaff, as in other cereals. This pure pod corn possesses a means of dispersal, since its seeds are not on a heavy ear but on fragile branches. In the proper environment it could undoubtedly survive in the wild and reproduce itself. It has characteristics like those of many wild grasses; indeed, in its principal botanical features it is quite similar to its wild relative tripsacum. Pure pod corn has virtually all of the characteristics we would expect to find in the ancestral form of corn. Furthermore, it is more than a relative of corn; it *is* corn—a form of corn that differs from cultivated corn in exactly the way a wild species ought to differ from its cultivated counterpart. Finally, all the hereditary differences between pod corn and cultivated corn are traceable to just one gene on one chromosome. Thus a single mutation can change pod corn to the non-podded form, and it has actually done so in many cultures.

The aboriginal wild corn that man began to cultivate undoubtedly had other primitive characteristics in addition to those of the ancestral pod corn. Its kernels, for example, were probably small, hard and pointed. Kernels of this kind are found today in varieties of pop corn. Indeed, the U.S. botanist E. Lewis Sturtevant, one of corn's most astute investigators, concluded more than half a century ago that primitive corn must have been both a pod corn and a pop corn. Evidence is now accumulating to show that Sturtevant was right.

In the remains of prehistoric civilizations unearthed in South America, pop corn predominates over other types. Pottery utensils for popping corn, as well as actual specimens of the popped grains, have been found in prehistoric Peruvian graves. Certainly there is nothing new about the pop corn which modern Americans consume so lavishly as part of the movie-going ritual. Pop corn is an ancient food, and it is quite possible that primitive man first discovered the usefulness of corn as a food plant when a wild corn was accidentally exposed to heat. This would have exploded the small, vitreous, glume-covered kernels, and transformed what to people with no grinding tools other than their own teeth was a very unpromising food into tender, tasty, nutritious morsels.

There is an interesting historical reference which lends support to Sturtevant's conclusion that primitive corn was both a pod corn and a pop corn. A century and a half ago Félix de Azara, the Spanish Commissioner to Paraguay, wrote of a peculiar variety of corn in Paraguay in which small seeds enclosed in "envelopes" were borne in the tassel. When the tassels were heated in hot oil, the kernels exploded to produce "a superb bouquet capable of adorning at night the head of a lady."

By a very simple experiment in our breeding plots, we have succeeded in duplicating exactly the corn Azara described. Pod corn was hybridized with pop corn and was then inbred to produce an earless plant bearing in the branches of the tassel small hard seeds enclosed in glumes. When a tassel of this pod-pop corn was heated in hot oil, it behaved exactly like the corn of Azara. The kernels exploded but remained attached to the tassel to produce the "bouquet" he described.

These recent findings have quite naturally given new impetus to the search for wild corn in South America, since the most convincing and conclusive proof of the pod-corn theory would be the discovery of a primitive pod corn still existing in the wild state. The search for a wild corn has not so far been successful in its primary objective, but it has been quite fruitful in turning up new types of corn, especially less extreme forms of pod corn whose kernels are only partially enclosed in glumes. Perhaps wild corn will still be discovered in some remote protected spot in a region not yet thoroughly explored. The odds are at least even, however, that it no longer exists. Corn in the wild may well have been a plant with low survival value, restricted in its range, and already well on the road to eventual extinction when first used by man.

In the meantime a wholly unexpected discovery, made within the past two years, has furnished direct evidence for the theory that primitive corn was both a pod corn and a pop corn. During the summer of 1948 an expedition sponsored by the Peabody Museum of Harvard University and led by Herbert W. Dick, a graduate student in anthropology, uncovered many cobs and other parts of corn from the accumulated refuse in an abandoned rock shelter in New Mexico known as Bat Cave.

This shelter was occupied from about 2000 B.C. to 1000 A.D. Uninhibited by modern concepts of sanitation, its successive generations of occupants allowed refuse and trash to accumulate in the cave to a depth of about six feet. Carefully removed and sifted by the archaeologists, the refuse yielded 766 specimens of shelled cobs, 125 loose kernels and various fragments of husks, leaf sheaths and tassels. The cobs are of particular interest, since they reveal a distinct evolutionary sequence. The oldest, at the bottom of the refuse heap, are the smallest and most primitive. These cobs and loose kernels from the same level prove that the earliest Bat Cave people grew a primitive variety of corn which was both a pop corn and a form of pod corn. The pod corn, however, was not as extreme as the earless synthetic "wild" corn described above. It probably represents a type already partly modified by domestication, more nearly like the weak forms of pod corn still found in South American varieties.

The Bat Cave corn has answered another of our questions: What is the relationship of corn to teosinte? The oldest and most primitive of the Bat Cave corn shows no evidence whatever of having stemmed from teosinte. But beginning about midway in the sequence there is strong evidence of the introduction of a corn that had become contaminated with teosinte. Thus the Bat Cave cobs suggest that early botanical investigators were not completely wrong in believing that teosinte played a role in the evolution of corn. Although teosinte clearly was not the progenitor of corn, it contributed its genes to corn's progress toward its present form.

The Bat Cave remains still leave unanswered the question: Where in America did corn originate? It seems improbable that corn could have been a native of the region where these remains were found, since corn is a moisture-loving plant and the region is now and was then quite dry. Probably it was brought into the Bat Cave region as a cultivated plant from Mexico.

Whether corn was native to Mexico or had been introduced there still earlier from South America is an open question.

How did the primitive pod-pop corn that the Bat Cave people grew 4,000 years ago evolve in so short a period, as evolutionary time is measured, into the modern ear of the Corn Belt? Some botanists are inclined to endow the American Indian with unusual abilities as a plant breeder. If the great changes that have occurred in corn in this relatively brief period are the product of his skill, he was indeed remarkably adroit. The corn from Bat Cave does not, however, support this view. On the contrary, there is no evidence that the Bat Cave people were any more concerned with plant improvement than they were with sanitation. If selection was practiced at all, it was probably an unplanned "negative" selection—the good ears were consumed and the leftover nubbins were used for seed. Nevertheless, thanks probably to accidental hybridization with teosinte and with other races of corn, there was a gradual increase in the average size of ears and kernels and an enormous increase in total variation during the 3,000 years of the Bat Cave's history.

The evolutionary sequence in the Bat Cave indicates that four principal factors operated in the evolution of corn during this period: 1. the pressure of natural selection, one of the most important suppressive factors in evolution, was greatly reduced; 2. mutations from the more to the less extreme forms of pod corn occurred; 3. corn was modified by contamination with teosinte; 4. crossing of varieties and races produced new combinations of characters and a high degree of hybridity.

All of these factors contributed to a tremendous increase in variation, so that when man finally did begin to practice selection in corn, he had a rich diversity at his disposal. From this, by accident or design, he chose a combination of characteristics that makes corn the most efficient of all cereals as a producer of foodstuffs.

ALEXANDER PETRUNKEVITCH

The Spider and the Wasp

In the feeding and safeguarding of their progeny insects and spiders exhibit some interesting analogies to reasoning and some crass examples of blind instinct. The case I propose to describe here is that of the tarantula spiders and their arch-enemy, the digger wasps of the genus Pepsis. It is a classic example of what looks like intelligence pitted against instinct—a strange situation in which the victim, though fully able to defend itself, submits unwittingly to its destruction.

Most tarantulas live in the tropics, but several species occur in the temperate zone and a few are common in the southern U.S. Some varieties are large and have powerful fangs with which they can inflict a deep wound. These formidable looking spiders do not, however, attack man; you can hold one in your hand, if you are gentle, without being bitten. Their bite is dangerous only to insects and small mammals such as mice; for a man it is no worse than a hornet's sting.

Tarantulas customarily live in deep cylindrical burrows, from which they emerge at dusk and into which they retire at dawn. Mature males wander about after dark in search of females and occasionally stray into houses. After mating, the male dies in a few weeks, but a female lives much longer and can mate several years in succession. In a Paris museum is a tropical specimen which is said to have been living in captivity for twenty-five years.

A fertilized female tarantula lays from 200 to 400 eggs at a time; thus it is possible for a single tarantula to produce several thousand young. She takes no care of them beyond weaving a

THE SPIDER AND THE WASP: Originally published in *Scientific American* (August 1952). Reprinted with permission. Copyright © 1952 by Scientific American, Inc. All rights reserved.

cocoon of silk to enclose the eggs. After they hatch, the young walk away, find convenient places in which to dig their burrows and spend the rest of their lives in solitude. The eyesight of tarantulas is poor, being limited to a sensing of change in the intensity of light and to the perception of moving objects. They apparently have little or no sense of hearing, for a hungry tarantula will pay no attention to a loudly chirping cricket placed in its cage unless the insect happens to touch one of its legs.

But all spiders, and especially hairy ones, have an extremely delicate sense of touch. Laboratory experiments prove that tarantulas can distinguish three types of touch: pressure against the body wall, stroking of the body hair and riffling of certain very fine hairs on the legs called trichobothria. Pressure against the body, by a finger or the end of a pencil, causes the tarantula to move off slowly for a short distance. The touch excites no defensive response unless the approach is from above where the spider can see the motion, in which case it rises on its hind legs, lifts its front legs, opens its fangs and holds this threatening posture as long as the object continues to move.

The entire body of a tarantula, especially its legs, is thickly clothed with hair. Some of it is short and woolly, some long and stiff. Touching this body hair produces one of two distinct reactions. When the spider is hungry, it responds with an immediate and swift attack. At the touch of a cricket's antennae the tarantula seizes the insect so swiftly that a motion picture taken at the rate of sixty-four frames per second shows only the result and not the process of capture. But when the spider is not hungry, the stimulation of its hairs merely causes it to shake the touched limb. An insect can walk under its hairy belly unharmed.

The trichobothria, very fine hairs growing from disklike membranes on the legs, are sensitive only to air movement. A light breeze makes them vibrate slowly without disturbing the common hair. When one blows gently on the trichobothria, the tarantula reacts with a quick jerk of its four front legs. If the front and hind legs are stimulated at the same time, the spider makes a sudden jump. This reaction is quite independent of the state of its appetite.

These three tactile responses—to pressure on the body wall, to moving of the common hair and to flexing of the trichobothria—are so different from one another that there is no possibility of confusing them. They serve the tarantula adequately for most of its needs and enable it to avoid most annoyances and dangers. But they fail the spider completely when it meets its deadly enemy, the digger wasp Pepsis.

These solitary wasps are beautiful and formidable creatures. Most species are either a deep shiny blue all over, or deep blue with rusty wings. The largest have a wing span of about four inches. They live on nectar. When excited, they give off a pungent odor—a warning that they are ready to attack. The sting is much worse than that of a bee or common wasp, and the pain and swelling last longer. In the adult stage the wasp lives only a few months. The female produces but a few eggs, one at a time at intervals of two or three days. For each egg the mother must provide one adult tarantula, alive but paralyzed. The mother wasp attaches the egg to the paralyzed spider's abdomen. Upon hatching from the egg, the larva is many hundreds of times smaller than its living but helpless victim. It eats no other food and drinks no water. By the time it has finished its single gargantuan meal and become ready for wasphood, nothing remains of the tarantula but its indigestible chitinous skeleton.

The mother wasp goes tarantula-hunting when the egg in her ovary is almost ready to be laid. Flying low over the ground late on a sunny afternoon, the wasp looks for its victim or for the mouth of a tarantula burrow, a round hole edged by a bit of silk. The sex of the spider makes no difference, but the mother is highly discriminating as to species. Each species of Pepsis requires a certain species of tarantula, and the wasp will not attack the wrong species. In a cage with a tarantula which is not its normal prey the wasp avoids the spider, and is usually killed by it in the night.

Yet when a wasp finds the correct species, it is the other way about. To identify the species the wasp apparently must explore the spider with her antennae. The tarantula shows an amazing tolerance to this exploration. The wasp crawls under it and walks over it without evoking any hostile response. The molestation is so great and so persistent that the tarantula often rises on all eight legs, as if it were on stilts. It may stand this way for several minutes. Meanwhile the wasp, having satisfied itself that the victim is of the right species, moves off a few inches to dig the spider's grave. Working vigorously with legs and jaws, it excavates a hole eight to ten inches deep with a diameter slightly larger than the spider's girth. Now and again the wasp pops out of the hole to make sure that the spider is still there.

When the grave is finished, the wasp returns to the tarantula to complete her ghastly enterprise. First she feels it all over once more with her antennae. Then her behavior becomes more aggressive. She bends her abdomen, protruding her sting, and searches for the soft membrane at the point where the spider's leg joins its body—the only spot where she can penetrate the horny skeleton. From time to time, as the exasperated spider slowly shifts ground, the wasp turns on her back and slides along with the aid of her wings, trying to get under the tarantula for a shot at the vital spot. During all this maneuvering, which can last for several minutes, the tarantula makes no move to save itself. Finally the wasp corners it against some obstruction and grasps one of its legs in her powerful jaws. Now at last the harassed spider tries a desperate but vain defense. The two contestants roll over and over on the ground. It is a terrifying sight and the outcome is always the same. The wasp finally manages to thrust her sting into the soft spot and holds it there for a few seconds while she pumps in the poison. Almost immediately the tarantula falls paralyzed on its back. Its legs stop twitching; its heart stops beating. Yet it is not dead,

as is shown by the fact that if taken from the wasp it can be restored to some sensitivity by being kept in a moist chamber for several months.

After paralyzing the tarantula, the wasp cleans herself by dragging her body along the ground and rubbing her feet, sucks the drop of blood oozing from the wound in the spider's abdomen, then grabs a leg of the flabby, helpless animal in her jaws and drags it down to the bottom of the grave. She stays there for many minutes, sometimes for several hours, and what she does all that time in the dark we do not know. Eventually she lays her egg and attaches it to the side of the spider's abdomen with a sticky secretion. Then she emerges, fills the grave with soil carried bit by bit in her jaws, and finally tramples the ground all around to hide any trace of the grave from prowlers. Then she flies away, leaving her descendant safely started in life.

In all this the behavior of the wasp evidently is qualitatively different from that of the spider. The wasp acts like an intelligent animal. This is not to say that instinct plays no part or that she reasons as man does. But her actions are to the point; they are not automatic and can be modified to fit the situation. We do not know for certain how she identifies the tarantula—probably it is by some olfactory or chemo-tactile sense—but she does it purposefully and does not blindly tackle a wrong species.

On the other hand, the tarantula's behavior shows only confusion. Evidently the wasp's pawing gives it no pleasure, for it tries to move away. That the wasp is not simulating sexual stimulation is certain, because male and female tarantulas react in the same way to its advances. That the spider is not anesthetized by some odorless secretion is easily shown by blowing lightly at the tarantula and making it jump suddenly. What, then, makes the tarantula behave as stupidly as it does?

No clear, simple answer is available. Possibly the stimulation by the wasp's antennae is masked by a heavier pressure on the spider's body, so that it reacts as when prodded by a pencil. But the explanation may be much more complex. Initiative in attack is not in the nature of tarantulas; most species fight only when cornered so that escape is impossible. Their inherited patterns of behavior apparently prompt them to avoid problems rather than attack them. For example, spiders always weave their webs in three dimensions, and when a spider finds that there is insufficient space to attach certain threads in the third dimension, it leaves the place and seeks another, instead of finishing the web in a single plane. This urge to escape seems to arise under all circumstances, in all phases of life and to take the place of reasoning. For a spider to change the pattern of its web is as impossible as for an inexperienced man to build a bridge across a chasm obstructing his way.

In a way the instinctive urge to escape is not only easier but often more efficient than reasoning. The tarantula does exactly what is most efficient in all cases except in an encounter with a ruthless and determined attacker dependent for the existence of her own species on killing as many tarantulas as she can lay eggs. Perhaps in this case the spider follows its usual pattern of trying to escape, instead of seizing and killing the wasp, because it is not aware of its danger. In any case, the survival of the tarantula species as a whole is protected by the fact that the spider is much more fertile than the wasp.

CHRISTOPHER HOWARD ANDREWES

The Common Cold

Why has the solution of the common cold problem so long eluded us? Perhaps the fact that it is not a dangerous disease has detracted from

THE COMMON COLD: Originally published in *Scientific American* (February 1951). Reprinted with permission. Copyright © 1951 by Scientific American, Inc. All rights reserved.

the pressure to solve the problem. There are, however, more important reasons. Virus diseases are studied mainly by observing the effects produced in experimental animals or plants, for viruses cannot be grown on artificial culture media. Unfortunately there is no convenient experimental animal for investigating the cold virus. Neither the mouse, the guinea pig nor any other readily available species can be infected with colds. The only animal, besides man, that will catch a true cold is the chimpanzee, and chimpanzees are so hard to come by and to handle and so expensive as to be almost useless.

Furthermore, the whole subject of colds is overlaid by stratum upon stratum of folklore, superstition and pseudo-science. Colds touch each of us personally, and it is a human failing that where our own afflictions are concerned our scientific judgment becomes faulty. We are apt, when we unexpectedly catch a cold—or avoid catching one—to attribute this to some unwise or wise act on our part. He who would solve the cold problem would do well to consider only scientifically checked facts and to keep a very critical attitude toward the folklore and toward what his friends tell him about how they catch or avoid colds.

What do we know about colds? There is ample evidence that colds are "catching": we know that an infected person can pass on infection to another person, and that chimpanzees can catch colds from human beings. Yet it is also true that often an individual intimately associated with a cold-sufferer fails to catch a cold at all. Another very well attested fact is that among a group of people isolated on a remote island, particularly if the community is small, colds tend to die out. But when such a cold-free community re-establishes contact with civilization, as by the visit of a ship from outside, its inhabitants are found to be abnormally susceptible and are pretty sure to catch a real "snorter."

In the ordinary way, the immunity acquired after a cold apparently is of brief duration. It is fairly clear that the freedom from colds of isolated groups is dependent not on increased resistance but on disappearance of the cold germ during their isolation. Their fate when they do meet cold germs shows that their resistance has waned with their freedom from attack. The temporary resistance developed by people in ordinary communities seemingly is maintained by frequent and repeated contact with cold virus.

Attempts to transmit colds artificially from one person to another are successful in about 50 per cent of the trials: a number of people at any one time prove resistant. The technique used has been to wash the noses of people who have colds with a salt solution and to drop some of this mucus-containing solution in the noses of normal people. Careful study of these solutions by the standard bacteriological methods has failed to show that any of the cultivable bacteria can be incriminated as the cause of colds. Indeed, during the early stages of colds the nasal secretions often have a subnormal content of bacteria. Several investigators have shown that after nasal secretions from people with colds have been passed through filters so fine that they hold back ordinary bacteria, the filtered material is still infective; it can pass in series from one person to another and continue to produce colds. This indicates that the infective agent is something which can multiply and is smaller than bacteria: i.e., a virus.

I propose to describe here the attack on the cold problem that has been carried out since 1946 in the Common Cold Research Unit of the Medical Research Council at Salisbury, England. Naturally the first objective of a study of this kind is to find a reliable, simple test, if possible, for the presence or absence of the virus. With such a test we could determine whether the virus is present in nasal secretions at various stages of the disease, whether it can be killed by various disinfectants, and so on. The only test we have at present, a very expensive and rather unreliable one, is to drop material in people's noses and see if it produces a cold. As a first step toward attaining our

objective of finding a simpler and better test, we had, perforce, to resort to this method, and to set up a very complicated organization to carry it out.

Our "laboratory" is the Harvard Hospital at Salisbury, consisting of a number of pre-fabricated huts which during the war were used as an American hospital with a staff from the Harvard Medical School and at the end of the war were generously handed over to the British Ministry of Health. As now set up, the unit has six rather luxurious huts, each divided into two separate flats. The 12 flats house 12 pairs of volunteers. We decided to take the subjects in pairs because it seemed obvious that people would be more likely to volunteer if they could have a friend with them. Each pair is kept in isolation and studied for 10 days; a fresh lot of about 24 volunteers comes along every fortnight. During university vacations we have no difficulty in getting students to come; at other times we have managed to keep pretty full with other people coming along in response to appeals on the radio or in the press. Since we started, four years ago, more than 2,000 volunteers have passed through our hands.

What have been the over-all results of our tests with the 2,000 volunteers? The first thing to be said is that those who received harmless control inoculations remained satisfactorily free from colds during their 10-day stay. This is an indication that our quarantine and other precautionary measures are adequate. Of those who received the active secretions taken from people with colds, some 50 per cent, as I have mentioned, caught colds. An interesting point is that many of those who were inoculated with active material seemed to be starting a cold on the second or third day after inoculation but next day had lost all their symptoms: the cold had aborted. Possibly most colds abort naturally. If this is true, it is easy to see why remedies purporting to cure the common cold so often gain a wholly unmerited reputation.

Women, according to our observations, are definitely more susceptible to colds than men;

the comparative scores were 55 per cent to 43 per cent. Age has very little effect on vulnerability, within the age group of 18 to 40 from which our volunteers come. The incubation period of a cold is usually two to three days. On the whole the colds have been milder than we expected. Perhaps in ordinary life it is only the severe colds that attract one's attention; we remember the virus' offensive triumphs rather than our own defensive successes. The colds of our volunteers have usually cleared up by the time they go home, several days after the cold's onset. Those departing are given post cards to send back a fortnight later with news of any nasal happenings in the meantime. Not a few relate that the colds, which had cleared up in our sheltered environment, got worse again in the hard outside world.

All this is very interesting, but what about the primary objective, the development of a better technique for studying colds? We cannot yet, unfortunately, report success. Much effort has been devoted to cultivation of the cold virus in fertile hens' eggs, by each of several different techniques that have proved useful with other viruses. No unequivocal success has been attained. Nor have we succeeded in inducing colds in experimental animals. We have tried rabbits, rats, mice, guinea pigs, hamsters, voles, cotton rats, gray squirrels, flying squirrels, hedgehogs, pigs, chickens, kittens, ferrets, baboons, green monkeys, capuchin monkeys, red patas monkeys and a sooty mangabey. People have told us that they have observed that such-and-such an animal develops colds in captivity when in contact with human colds. Such clues we have followed up, but in vain. The "colds" in these animals have either not been reproducible or have seemed to be due to bacteria rather than to a true cold virus.

Efforts have been made to determine the properties of the cold virus, for knowledge of these should help us toward our objective of the simple laboratory test. We have, for instance, learned something about the size of the virus. Virus-containing fluids can be filtered through a special type of collodion filter having pores of very uniform and accurately graded diameter. We find that the cold virus passes with but little loss in potency through membranes with pores as small as 120 millimicrons, or 120 millionths of a millimeter. In one experiment patients took colds from material passed through a filter with pores of only 57 millimicrons. If we can believe this single positive result, we can deduce that the cold germ is one of the smaller viruses— about as big as that of yellow fever, which has a diameter of some 25 millimicrons. At most the cold virus seems to be no more than about 60 millimicrons across; that is, decidedly smaller than the influenza virus.

Cold virus is very stable when kept frozen at 76 degrees below zero centigrade; some of it has retained its potency for as long as two years at this temperature. This knowledge is very useful to us. At any point we can bottle our "pedigree" strains of virus, put it away in dry ice and forget about it till it is next needed.

We have also established several negative facts about the virus: it is not affected by penicillin or streptomycin, nor is it adsorbed, as is influenza virus, on human or fowl red blood cells.

We need to know not only these rather abstract properties but also something of how the virus behaves in man—the relation of the parasite to its host. We have no way of telling how many virus particles our infectious dose of material contains; it may take thousands of particles to overcome a person's normal resistance and produce a good cold. We have found, however, that nasal secretions are infectious even when diluted up to 1,000 times with salt solution. Apparently the saliva secretions in the front of the mouth also contain much virus. This is important in relation to the means of spread, for most of the liquid expelled when you sneeze comes from the front of the mouth.

Nasal secretions contain plenty of virus during the incubation period of a cold, even before symptoms develop. We found this out by washing out the noses of infected subjects 12, 24, 48 and 72 hours after inoculation and testing the washings for infectivity. The 12-hour specimen was negative, all the rest positive. The subject who provided the washings developed symptoms 48 hours after inoculation. Our impression is that secretions from the early stages of a cold are the most potent, but we have had "takes" with washings taken seven days after inoculation. We have occasionally produced mild colds with secretions from normal, symptom-free people; this suggests that some people may be carriers of cold infection without showing symptoms themselves, as in diphtheria, typhoid fever and many other diseases. There is some evidence that children are especially "efficient" in spreading cold infection.

We have tried many dodges to increase the rate of successful transmission of colds from 50 per cent to 100 per cent. Obviously if we could produce a cold every time we tried, we could work faster and more certainly, and we might find some clues to the reasons for people's varying susceptibility and resistance. But so far we have not been able to increase or decrease the rate of cold "takes" very much.

For instance, we put to the test the practically universal idea that chilling induces colds, or at least increases one's chances of catching a cold. Three groups of six volunteers each were used in this experiment. One lot received a dose of dilute virus, calculated not to produce many colds. The next lot were given no virus but were put through a severe chilling treatment: that is, they had a hot bath and were then made to stand about in a draughty passage in wet bathing suits for half an hour, by which time they felt pretty chilly and miserable. They were further made to wear wet socks for the rest of the morning. A third group received the dilute virus plus the chilling treatment. On one occasion, in a variation of the experiment, the chilling consisted in a walk in the rain, following which the subjects were not allowed to dry themselves for half an hour and were made to stay in unheated flats.

Now this experiment was performed three times. In not one instance did chilling alone produce a cold. And in two out of the three tests chilling plus inoculation with the virus actually produced fewer colds than inoculation alone; in the other the chilled people who also got virus did have more colds than the "virus only" group. So we failed to convince ourselves that chilling either induces or favors colds.

One of the great puzzles about colds is that even repeated attacks do not confer any lasting immunity. We have found some evidence in the blood that the body produces antibodies to cold virus. But in contrast to the antibodies called forth by the virus of a disease such as measles, which guard the body against future attacks, the antibodies that respond to a cold seem almost powerless to help. A person may develop two successive colds within a matter of months. Why are the antibodies so effective against the one disease and so ineffective against the other?

The answer may possibly be that in the latter case the antibodies are not in the right place. In the case of measles the virus always appears in the bloodstream at one stage of the attack, and this is where the antibodies are, ready to intercept and destroy it. On the other hand, the virus of the common cold (and of influenza, in which the antibodies are also relatively ineffectual) attacks the superficial membranes lining the nose and other respiratory passages, without having to pass through the bloodstream and encounter the antibodies. True, some influenzal antibodies apparently can pass from the blood into the mucus covering these membranes, and this doubtless helps to keep infection under control. But there is usually much less antibody there than in the blood.

Consequently a promising approach to the prevention of colds is to try to determine what conditions control the amount of antibody in the mucus. Perhaps frequently repeated contacts with small doses of virus, doses insufficient to produce a manifest cold, stimulate the body to provide the mucus with enough antibody to protect it. Very probably it is the lack of such stimuli that renders small isolated communities so susceptible to colds. It may be that in the future colds may be kept at bay by repeated doses of an attenuated virus taken as a snuff, rather than by vaccines given in the orthodox ways used in other diseases.

As explained earlier, it is not always easy to decide just when a person has or has not got a cold; often this can be determined only by carefully designed techniques. It is still more difficult to decide when a cold has been prevented or cured. A cold's natural duration is extremely variable, and it is likely that at least as many colds abort in their early stages as go on to be full-blown. Hence people often draw rash conclusions about "cures" on slender evidence, as testified by the correspondence sent to us by over 200 persons with the most helpful intentions. Not only can we place little or no faith in conclusions based on individual experience, but we can be readily deceived by trials carried out on a fairly extensive basis.

Unfortunately for the poor public, a "cold-cure" is news and is well publicized. Pricking of a bubble is not news and word of it gets around slowly. Antihistamines, for example, are worthless for curing colds, but they are still sold in quantity for that purpose. Claims to prevent colds by means of oral or other vaccines rest on just as shaky foundations as those of the antihistamines: adequately controlled trials have failed to demonstrate their value.

There are things that can be done to relieve the unpleasantness of colds, but up to the present it still remains true that the untreated cold will last about seven days, while with careful treatment it can be cured in a week!

Questions for Review

1. George Gamow's *Galaxies in Flight* deals with the theory of the Expanding Universe that Stephen Leacock has treated humorously in the previous section. Does Gamow make the theory comprehensible? Do Leacock's criticisms apply to this essay or not?

2. To what extent does mathematics supply the "facts" given by Gamow here? Are these facts convincing? Are they accurate? What effect on the credibility of the essay as a whole has the footnote on p. 321?

3. Does Gamow explain to your satisfaction the meaning of all the technical terms he uses? Are any uncertain or vague in meaning?

4. How would you describe Gamow's tone in this essay? His point of view? Does the essay capture the interest of someone not already knowledgeable about Gamow's subject?

5. Howel Williams's *Volcanoes* on p. 322 discusses the famous eruption of Vesuvius in 79 A.D. that Pliny also describes on p. 215. Compare and contrast the purpose, selection of details, emphasis, and effect of Williams's account with Pliny's. Is Williams's discussion indebted to Pliny's in any way? If so, how?

6. Gamow's essay depends largely upon statistics. What does William's essay depend on: statistics, classification, description of a process, collecting authorities, analysis, or what?

7. Obviously, Williams could not have personally observed all of the volcanic eruptions mentioned here. Where did he get his information? How authoritative is it and how reputable are his experts?

8. Which do you find more "human" in emphasis: Gamow's essay or Williams's? Elaborate. Which do you find more interesting? Why?

9. Paul Mangelsdorf describes in *The Mystery of Corn* a process of scientific experiment. Outline the steps of the process. Are they like the method discussed in Conant's essay on p. 288 above or not?

10. Compare the botanist's scientific method with the astronomer's procedure as the latter appears in Gamow's essay. How are they alike? How different? Is one more "empirical" than the other or not?

11. What sort of evidence for his hypothesis does Mangelsdorf present? Is his evidence basically like or unlike the evidence of the astronomer and the geologist? Is his hypothesis more or less testable than theirs?

12. Do you find Mangelsdorf an effective writer? Does his "personality" as a man show in his essay?

13. "Anthropomorphism" may be defined as seeing nonhuman beings in human terms or imputing human thoughts and feelings to lower orders of being. Is Alexander Petrunkevitch's discussion of the tarantula and the wasp anthropomorphic in any way?

14. How was the evidence in Petrunkevitch's essay collected? Was the method "scientific" in Conant's terms? How are the procedures of the entomologist different from those of the geologist? the botanist?

15. Petrunkevitch often uses descriptive adjectives that have emotional connotations: "beautiful and formidable creatures," "an amazing tolerance," "her ghastly enterprise." What is the effect of this diction? Is it appropriate in "scientific" writing?

16. Like the other essays, C. H. Andrewes's *The Common Cold* outlines an experiment or scientific method. How does the experiment of the biologist compare with that of the entomologist? the botanist? Is it more or less empirical?

17. The cold is a peculiarly human phenomenon, as Andrewes points out. What consequence has this had on approaching the study of it "scientifically"? Is it easier to be "scientific" about galaxies than headcolds?

18. Are there any humorous details or comments in Andrewes's essay? Are they intentional? To what extent can humor be used by the scientific writer, if this collection of essays is an example? Can pathos (an appeal to sympathy or feeling) be used in scientific writing? Do any of the essayists here use it?

19. Which of these essays is the most "factual"? the most hypothetical? the most informative to you? the least interesting? Are your responses due to your previous interest in a subject, the author's style, or something else?

Questions for Discussion and Writing

1. Suggest the major problems facing the writer of an essay about a natural science. What are some ways of solving them, to judge from the sample here?

2. Do these essays support the contention that the scientist is an emotional and intuitive being or not?

3. Is the "scientific method" as Conant discusses it really the procedure used by the scientists included in this group? Can there be any such thing as *a* scientific method or *the* scientific method, or must the method be determined by the nature of the thing studied?

4. Do the writers in this selection manage to avoid the difficulties in communication suggested by Toulmin in his essay on p. 296?

5. How important is mathematics in the essays other than Gamow's? Is measurement really a basic technique for the botanist? the geologist? the entomologist? the biologist?

6. Poets and fiction writers have absorbed some of the theories of the natural scientists but have used scientific data for purposes other than simple exposition. Read Archibald MacLeish's poem on p. 527; then compare the emphasis and intention of the poet with those of Gamow the scientist. See Whitman's, Cummings's, and Auden's treatment of celestial phenomena (pp. 448, 527, and 548) and suggest the basic differences between the techniques of the scientific essayist and the poet.

7. Often scientific writing is called a "report." Do the essays here have anything in common as a form or method of exposition with the examples of reportage in Section II above? Succinctly indicate the similar or dissimilar qualities of the two kinds of "reportage."

The Nature of Man

The social scientist is a literal adherent to the maxim: The proper study of mankind is man. The subject of his observation is people, singly and collectively; and the social sciences—anthropology, ethnology, sociology, economics, history, political science—are ways of formulating certain aspects of observable human behavior. Several of the social sciences have accepted the methods of the natural sciences in attempting to compile empirical information about people and arrive at a logical system for understanding men and their actions. As subjects, however, people are much more complex than bees, rock formations, and gases, which are largely acted upon by physical forces. Men, however, have the power to alter themselves at will—and they frequently do. Just when the sociologist seems to have worked out a practicable method for dealing with juvenile delinquents or Tahitians, his subjects may display previously unrevealed aspects of their thought and behavior. Or once fixed in a scientific formula, man has a way of reappraising himself through the formulation and becoming something else. Because of the shifting, fluctuating nature of his subjects, the social scientist (who as a man himself does some fluctuating and shifting as well) is constantly having to clarify his terminology and his methodology. The literature of the social sciences is, by its very nature, somewhat tentative and topical; and within the several approaches to the same topic—the burial customs of primitive people, for instance, or the Negro's role in American society—there may be assumptions and ways of conceptualizing at odds with each other. The essays here show these and other problems affecting the literature of the social sciences.

SIR JAMES FRAZER

The Death of the
Corn Goddess

European peoples, ancient and modern, have not been singular in personifying the corn as a mother goddess. The same simple idea has suggested itself to other agricultural races in distant parts of the world, and has been applied by them to other indigenous cereals than barley and wheat. If Europe has its Wheat-mother and its Barley-mother, America has its Maize-mother and the East Indies their Rice-mother. These personifications I will now illustrate, beginning with the American personification of the maize.

We have seen that among European peoples it is a common custom to keep the plaited corn-stalks of the last sheaf, or the puppet which is formed out of them, in the farmhouse from harvest to harvest. The intention no doubt is, or rather originally was, by preserving the representative of the corn-spirit to maintain the spirit itself in life and activity throughout the year, in order that the corn may grow and the crops be good. This interpretation of the custom is at all events rendered highly probable by a similar custom observed by the ancient Peruvians, and thus describe by the old Spanish historian Acosta: "They take a certain portion of the most fruitful of the maize that grows in their farms, the which they put in a certain granary which they do call *Pirua*, with certain ceremonies, watching three nights; they put this maize in the richest garments they have, and being thus wrapped and dressed, they worship this *Pirua*, and hold it in great veneration, saying it is the

mother of the maize of their inheritances, and that by this means the maize augments and is preserved. In this month [the sixth month, answering to May] they make a particular sacrifice, and the witches demand of this *Pirua* if it hath strength sufficient to continue until the next year; and if it answers no, then they carry this maize to the farm to burn, whence they brought it, according to every man's power; then they make another *Pirua*, with the same ceremonies, saying that they renew it, to the end the seed of maize may not perish, and if it answers that it hath force sufficient to last longer, they leave it until the next year. This foolish vanity continueth to this day, and it is very common amongst the Indians to have these *Piruas*."

In this description of the custom there seems to be some error. Probably it was the dressed-up bunch of maize, not the granary (*Pirua*), which was worshipped by the Peruvians and regarded as the Mother of the Maize. This is confirmed by what we know of the Peruvian custom from another source. The Peruvians, we are told, believed all useful plants to be animated by a divine being who causes their growth. According to the particular plant, these divine beings were called the Maize-mother (*Zara-mama*), the Quinoa-mother (*Quinoa-mama*), the Coca-mother (*Coca-mama*), and the Potato-mother (*Axo-mama*). Figures of these divine mothers were made respectively of ears of maize and leaves of the quinoa and coca plants; they were dressed in women's clothes and worshipped. Thus the Maize-mother was represented by a puppet made of stalks of maize dressed in full female attire; and the Indians believed that "as mother, it had the power of producing and giving birth to much maize." Probably, therefore, Acosta misunderstood his informant, and the Mother of the Maize which he describes was not the granary (*Pirua*), but the bunch of maize dressed in rich vestments. The Peruvian Mother of the Maize, like the harvest-Maiden at Balquhidder, was kept for a year in order that by her means the corn might grow and multiply. But lest her strength might not suffice to last till the next harvest, she was asked in the course of the year how she felt, and if she answered that she felt weak, she was burned and a fresh Mother of the Maize made, "to the end the seed of maize may not perish." Here, it may be observed, we have a strong confirmation of the explanation already given of the custom of killing the god, both periodically and occasionally. The Mother of the Maize was allowed, as a rule, to live through a year, that being the period during which her strength might reasonably be supposed to last un-impaired; but on any symptom of her strength failing she was put to death, and a fresh and vigorous Mother of the Maize took her place, lest the maize which depended on her for its existence should languish and decay....

By no people does the custom of sacrificing the human representative of a god appear to have been observed so commonly and with so much solemnity as by the Aztecs of ancient Mexico. With the ritual of these remarkable sacrifices we are well acquainted, for it has been fully described by the Spaniards who conquered Mexico in the sixteenth century, and whose curiosity was naturally excited by the discovery in this distant region of a barbarous and cruel religion which presented many curious points of analogy to the doctrine and ritual of their own church. "They took a captive," says the Jesuit Acosta, "such as they thought good; and afore they did sacrifice him unto their idols, they gave him the name of the idol, to whom he should be sacrificed, and apparelled him with the same ornaments like their idol, saying, that he did represent the same idol. And during the time that this representation lasted, which was for a year in some feasts, in others six months, and in others less, they reverenced and wor-shipped him in the same manner as the proper idol; and in the meantime he did eat, drink, and was merry. When he went through the streets, the people came forth to worship him, and every one brought him an alms, with children and

sick folks, that he might cure them, and bless them, suffering him to do all things at his pleasure, only he was accompanied with ten or twelve men lest he should fly. And he (to the end he might be reverenced as he passed) sometimes sounded upon a small flute, that the people might prepare to worship him. The feast being come, and he grown fat, they killed him, opened him, and ate him, making a solemn sacrifice of him."

This general description of the custom may now be illustrated by particular examples. Thus at the festival called Toxcatl, the greatest festival of the Mexican year, a young man was annually sacrificed in the character of Tezcatli-poca, "the god of gods," after having been maintained and worshipped as that great deity in person for a whole year. According to the old Franciscan monk Sahagun, our best authority on the Aztec religion, the sacrifice of the human god fell at Easter or a few days later, so that, if he is right, it would correspond in date as well as in character to the Christian festival of the death and resurrection of the Redeemer. More exactly he tells us that the sacrifice took place on the first day of the fifth Aztec month, which according to him began on the twenty-third or twenty-seventh day of April.

At this festival the great god died in the person of one human representative and came to life again in the person of another, who was destined to enjoy the fatal honour of divinity for a year and to perish, like all his predecessors, at the end of it. The young man singled out for this high dignity was carefully chosen from among the captives on the ground of his personal beauty. He had to be of unblemished body, slim as a reed and straight as a pillar, neither too tall nor too short. If through high living he grew too fat, he was obliged to reduce himself by drinking salt water. And in order that he might behave in his lofty station with becoming grace and dignity he was carefully trained to comport himself like a gentleman of the first quality, to speak correctly and elegantly, to play the flute, to smoke cigars and to snuff at flowers with a dandified air. He was honourably lodged in the temple, where the nobles waited on him and paid him homage, bringing him meat and serving him like a prince. The king himself saw to it that he was apparelled in gorgeous attire, "for already he esteemed him as a god." Eagle down was gummed to his head and white cock's feathers were stuck in his hair, which drooped to his girdle. A wreath of flowers like roasted maize crowned his brows, and a garland of the same flowers passed over his shoulders and under his armpits. Golden ornaments hung from his nose, golden armlets adorned his arms, golden bells jingled on his legs at every step he took; earrings of turquoise dangled from his ears, bracelets of turquoise bedecked his wrists; necklaces of shells encircled his neck and depended on his breast; he wore a mantle of network, and round his middle a rich waistcloth. When this bejewelled exquisite lounged through the streets playing on his flute, puffing at a cigar, and smelling at a nosegay, the people whom he met threw themselves on the earth before him and prayed to him with sighs and tears, taking up the dust in their hands and putting it in their mouths in token of the deepest humiliation and subjection. Women came forth with children in their arms and presented them to him, saluting him as a god. For "he passed for our Lord God; the people acknowledged him as the Lord." All who thus worshipped him on his passage he saluted gravely and courteously. Lest he should flee, he was everywhere attended by a guard of eight pages in the royal livery, four of them with shaven crowns like the palace-slaves, and four of them with the flowing locks of warriors; and if he contrived to escape, the captain of the guard had to take his place as the representative of the god and to die in his stead. Twenty days before he was to die, his costume was changed, and four damsels delicately nurtured and bearing the names of four goddesses—the Goddess of Flowers, the Goddess of the Young Maize, the Goddess "Our Mother among the Water," and the Goddess of Salt—were given him to be his

brides, and with them he consorted. During the the last five days divine honours were showered on the destined victim. The king remained in his palace while the whole court went after the human god. Solemn banquets and dances followed each other in regular succession and at appointed places. On the last day the young man, attended by his wives and pages, embarked in a canoe covered with a royal canopy and was ferried across the lake to a spot where a little hill rose from the edge of the water. It was called the Mountain of Parting, because there his wives bade him a last farewell. Then, accompanied only by his pages, he repaired to a small and lonely temple by the wayside. Like the Mexican temples in general, it was built in the form of a pyramid; and as the young man ascended the stairs he broke at every step one of the flutes on which he had played in the days of his glory. On reaching the summit he was seized and held down by the priests on his back upon a block of stone, while one of them cut open his breast, thrust his hand into the wound, and wrenching out his heart held it up in sacrifice to the sun. The body of the dead god was not, like the bodies of common victims, sent rolling down the steps of the temple, but was carried down to the foot, where the head was cut off and spitted on a pike. Such was the regular end of the man who personated the greatest god of the Mexican pantheon.

The honour of living for a short time in the character of a god and dying a violent death in the same capacity was not restricted to men in Mexico; women were allowed, or rather compelled, to enjoy the glory and to share the doom as representatives of goddesses. Thus at a great festival in September, which was preceded by a strict fast of seven days, they sanctified a young slave girl of twelve or thirteen years, the prettiest they could find, to represent the Maize Goddess Chicomecohuatl. They invested her with the ornaments of the goddess, putting a mitre on her head and maize-cobs round her neck and in her hands, and fastening a green feather upright on the crown of her head to imitate an ear of maize.

This they did, we are told, in order to signify that the maize was almost ripe at the time of the festival, but because it was still tender they chose a girl of tender years to play the part of the Maize Goddess. The whole long day they led the poor child in all her finery, with the green plume nodding on her head, from house to house dancing merrily to cheer people after the dullness and privations of the fast.

In the evening all the people assembled at the temple, the courts of which they lit up by a multitude of lanterns and candles. There they passed the night without sleeping, and at midnight, while the trumpets, flutes, and horns discoursed solemn music, a portable framework or Palanquin was brought forth, bedecked with festoons of maize-cobs and peppers and filled with seeds of all sorts. This the bearers set down at the door of the chamber in which the wooden image of the goddess stood. Now the chamber was adorned and wreathed, both outside and inside, with wreaths of maize-cobs, peppers, pumpkins, roses, and seeds of every kind, a wonder to behold; the whole floor was covered deep with these verdant offerings of the pious. When the music ceased, a solemn procession came forth of priests and dignitaries, with flaring lights and smoking censers, leading in their midst the girl who played the part of the goddess. Then they made her mount the framework, where she stood upright on the maize and peppers and pumpkins with which it was strewed, her hands resting on two bannisters to keep her from falling. Then the priest swung the smoking censers round her; the music struck up again, and while it played, a great dignitary of the temple suddenly stepped up to her with a razor in his hand and adroitly shore off the green feather she wore on her head, together with the hair in which it was fastened, snipping the lock off by the root. The feather and the hair he then presented to the wooden image of the goddess with great solemnity and elaborate ceremonies, weeping and giving her thanks for the fruits of the earth and the abundant crops which she had bestowed on the

people that year; and as he wept and prayed, all the people, standing in the courts of the temple, wept and prayed with him. When that ceremony was over, the girl descended from the framework and was escorted to the place where she was to spend the rest of the night. But all the people kept watch in the courts of the temple by the light of torches till break of day.

The morning being come, and the courts of the temple being still crowded by the multitude, who would have deemed it sacrilege to quit the precincts, the priests again brought forth the damsel attired in the costume of the goddess, with the mitre on her head and the cobs of maize about her neck. Again she mounted the portable framework or Palanquin and stood on it, supporting herself by her hands on the bannisters. Then the elders of the temple lifted it on their shoulders, and while some swung burning censers and others played on instruments or sang, they carried it in procession through the great courtyard to the hall of the god Huitzilopochtli and then back to the chamber, where stood the wooden image of the Maize Goddess, whom the girl personated. There they caused the damsel to descend from the palanquin and to stand on the heaps of corn and vegetables that had been spread in profusion on the floor of the sacred chamber. While she stood there all the elders and nobles came in a line, one behind the other, carrying saucers full of dry and clotted blood which they had drawn from their ears by way of penance during the seven days' fast. One by one they squatted on their haunches before her, which was the equivalent of falling on their knees with us, and scraping the crust of blood from the saucer cast it down before her as an offering in return for the benefits which she, as the embodiment of the Maize Goddess, had conferred upon them. When the men had thus humbly offered their blood to the human representative of the goddess, the women, forming a long line, did so likewise, each of them dropping on her hams before the girl and scraping her blood from the saucer. The ceremony lasted a long time, for great and small, young and old, all without exception had to pass before the incarnate deity and make their offering. When it was over, the people returned home with glad hearts to feast on flesh and viands of every sort as merrily, we are told, as good Christians at Easter partake of meat and other carnal mercies after the long abstinence of Lent. And when they had eaten and drunk their fill and rested after the night watch, they returned quite refreshed to the temple to see the end of the festival. And the end of the festival was this. The multitude being assembled, the priests solemnly incensed the girl who personated the goddess; then they threw her on her back on the heap of corn and seeds, cut off her head, caught the gushing blood in a tub, and sprinkled the blood on the wooden image of the goddess, the walls of the chamber, and the offerings of corn, peppers, pumpkins, seeds, and vegetables which cumbered the floor. After that they flayed the headless trunk, and one of the priests made shift to squeeze himself into the bloody skin. Having done so they clad him in all the robes which the girl had worn; they put the mitre on his head, the necklace of golden maize-cobs about his neck, the maize-cobs of feathers and gold in his hands; and thus arrayed they led him forth in public, all of them dancing to the tuck of drum, while he acted as fugleman, skipping and posturing at the head of the procession as briskly as he could be expected to do, incommoded as he was by the tight and clammy skin of the girl and by her clothes, which must have been much too small for a grown man.

In the foregoing custom the identification of the young girl with the Maize Goddess appears to be complete. The golden maize-cobs which she wore round her neck, the artificial maize-cobs which she carried in her hands, the green feather which was stuck in her hair in imitation (we are told) of a green ear of maize, all set her forth as a personification of the corn-spirit; and we are expressly informed that she was specially chosen as a young girl to represent the young maize, which at the time of the festival had not

yet fully ripened. Further, her identification with the corn and the corn-goddess was clearly announced by making her stand on the heaps of maize and there receive the homage and blood-offerings of the whole people, who thereby returned her thanks for the benefits which in her character of a divinity she was supposed to have conferred upon them. Once more, the practice of beheading her on a heap of corn and seeds and sprinkling her blood, not only on the image of the Maize Goddess, but on the piles of maize, peppers, pumpkins, seeds, and vegetables, can seemingly have had no other object but to quicken and strengthen the crops of corn and the fruits of the earth in general by infusing into their representatives the blood of the Corn Goddess herself. The analogy of this Mexican sacrifice, the meaning of which appears to be indisputable, may be allowed to strengthen the interpretation which I have given of other human sacrifices offered for the crops. If the Mexican girl, whose blood was sprinkled on the maize, indeed personated the Maize Goddess, it becomes more than ever probable that the girl whose blood the Pawnees similarly sprinkled on the seed corn personated in like manner the female Spirit of the Corn; and so with the other human beings whom other races have slaughtered for the sake of promoting the growth of the crops.

Lastly, the concluding act of the sacred drama, in which the body of the dead Maize Goddess was flayed and her skin worn, together with all her sacred insignia, by a man who danced before the people in this grim attire, seems to be best explained on the hypothesis that it was intended to ensure that the divine death should be immediately followed by the divine resurrection. If that was so, we may infer with some degree of probability that the practice of killing a human representative of a deity has commonly, perhaps always, been regarded merely as a means of perpetuating the divine energies in the fulness of youthful vigour, untainted by the weakness and frailty of age, from which they must have suffered if the deity had been allowed to die a natural death.

These Mexican rites suffice to prove that human sacrifices of the sort I suppose to have prevailed at Aricia were, as a matter of fact, regularly offered by a people whose level of culture was probably not inferior, if indeed it was not distinctly superior, to that occupied by the Italian races at the early period to which the origin of the Arician priesthood must be referred. The positive and indubitable evidence of the prevalence of such sacrifices in one part of the world may reasonably be allowed to strengthen the probability of their prevalence in places for which the evidence is less full and trustworthy. Taken all together, the facts which we have passed in review seem to show that the custom of killing men whom their worshippers regard as divine has prevailed in many parts of the world.

GILBERT KEITH CHESTERTON

Science and the Savages

A permanent disadvantage of the study of folklore and kindred subjects is that the man of science can hardly be in the nature of things very frequently a man of the world. He is a student of nature; he is scarcely ever a student of human nature. And even where this difficulty is overcome, and he is in some sense a student of human nature, this is only a very faint beginning of the painful progress towards being human. For the study of primitive race and religion stands apart in one important respect from all, or nearly all, the ordinary scientific studies. A

SCIENCE AND THE SAVAGES: Reprinted by permission of Dodd, Mead & Company, Inc. from *Heretics* by G. K. Chesterton, 1905. Also printed by permission of The Bodley Head.

man can understand astronomy only by being an astronomer; he can understand entomology only by being an entomologist (or, perhaps, an insect); but he can understand a great deal of anthropology merely by being a man. He is himself the animal which he studies. Hence arises the fact which strikes the eye everywhere in the records of ethnology and folklore—the fact that the same frigid and detached spirit which leads to success in the study of astronomy or botany leads to disaster in the study of mythology or human origins. It is necessary to cease to be a man in order to do justice to a microbe; it is not necessary to cease to be a man in order to do justice to men. That same suppression of sympathies, that same waving away of intuitions or guesswork which make a man preternaturally clever in dealing with the stomach of a spider, will make him preternaturally stupid in dealing with the heart of man. He is making himself inhuman in order to understand humanity. An ignorance of the other world is boasted by many men of science; but in this matter their defect arises, not from ignorance of the other world, but from ignorance of this world. For the secrets about which anthropologists concern themselves can be best learnt not from books or voyages, but from the ordinary commerce of man with man. The secret of why some savage tribe worships monkeys or the moon is not to be found even by travelling among those savages and taking down their answers in a notebook, although the cleverest man may pursue this course. The answer to the riddle is in England; it is in London; nay, it is in his own heart. When a man has discovered why men in Bond Street wear black hats he will at the same moment have discovered why men in Timbuctoo wear red feathers. The mystery in the heart of some savage war-dance should not be studied in books of scientific travel; it should be studied at a subscription ball. If a man desires to find out the origins of religions, let him not go to the Sandwich Islands; let him go to church. If a man wishes to know the origin of human society, to know what society, philosophically speaking, really is, let him not go into the British Museum; let him go into society.

This total misunderstanding of the real nature of ceremonial gives rise to the most awkward and dehumanized versions of the conduct of men in rude lands or ages. The man of science, not realizing that ceremonial is essentially a thing which is done without a reason, has to find a reason for every sort of ceremonial, and, as might be supposed, the reason is generally a very absurd one—absurd because it originates not in the simple mind of the barbarian, but in the sophisticated mind of the professor. The learned man will say, for instance, "The natives of Mumbojumbo Land believe that the dead man can eat, and will require food upon his journey to the other world. This is attested by the fact that they place food in the grave, and that any family not complying with this rite is the object of the anger of the priests and the tribe." To anyone acquainted with humanity this way of talking is topsy-turvy. It is like saying, "The English in the twentieth century believed that a dead man could smell. This is attested by the fact that they always covered his grave with lilies, violets, or other flowers. Some priestly and tribal terrors were evidently attached to the neglect of this action, as we have records of several old ladies who were very much disturbed in mind because their wreaths had not arrived in time for the funeral." It may be of course that savages put food with a dead man because they think that a dead man can eat, or weapons with a dead man because they think that a dead man can fight. But personally I do not believe that they think anything of the kind. I believe they put food or weapons on the dead for the same reason that we put flowers, because it is an exceedingly natural and obvious thing to do. We do not understand, it is true, the emotion which makes us think it obvious and natural; but that is because, like all the important emotions of human existence, it is essentially irrational. We do not understand the savage for the same reason that the savage does

not understand himself. And the savage does not understand himself for the same reason that we do not understand ourselves either.

The obvious truth is that the moment any matter has passed through the human mind it is finally and for ever spoilt for all purposes of science. It has become a thing incurably mysterious and infinite; his mortality has put on immortality. Even what we call our material desires are spiritual, because they are human. Science can analyse a pork-chop, and say how much of it is phosphorus and how much is protein; but science cannot analyse any man's wish for a pork-chop, and say how much of it is hunger, how much custom, how much nervous fancy, how much a haunting love of the beautiful. The man's desire for the pork-chop remains literally as mystical and ethereal as his desire for heaven. All attempts, therefore, at a science of any human things, at a science of history, a science of folklore, a science of sociology, are by their nature not merely hopeless, but crazy. You can no more be certain in economic history that a man's desire for money was merely a desire for money than you can be certain in hagiology that a saint's desire for God was merely a desire for God. And this kind of vagueness in the primary phenomena of the study is an absolutely final blow to anything in the nature of a science. Men can construct a science with very few instruments, or with very plain instruments; but no one on earth could construct a science with unreliable instruments. A man might work out the whole of mathematics with a handful of pebbles, but not with a handful of clay which was always falling apart into new fragments, and falling together into new combinations. A man might measure heaven and earth with a reed, but not with a growing reed.

As one of the enormous follies of folklore, let us take the case of the transmigration of stories, and the alleged unity of their source. Story after story the scientific mythologists have cut out of its place in history, and pinned side by side with similar stories in their museum of fables. The process is industrious, it is fascinating, and the whole of it rests on one of the plainest fallacies in the world. That a story has been told all over the place at some time or other not only does not prove that it really never happened; it does not even faintly indicate or make slightly more probable that it never happened. That a large number of fishermen have falsely asserted that they have caught a pike two feet long does not in the least affect the question of whether anyone ever really did so. That numberless journalists announce a Franco-German war merely for money is no evidence one way or the other upon the dark question of whether such a war ever occurred. Doubtless in a few hundred years the innumerable Franco-German wars that did not happen will have cleared the scientific mind of any belief in the legendary war of '70 which did. But that will be because, if folklore students remain at all, their nature will be unchanged; and their services to folklore will be still as they are at present, greater than they know. For in truth these men do something far more godlike than studying legends; they create them.

There are two kinds of stories which the scientists say cannot be true, because everybody tells them. The first class consists of the stories which are told everywhere, because they are somewhat odd or clever; there is nothing in the world to prevent their having happened to somebody as an adventure any more than there is anything to prevent their having occurred, as they certainly did occur, to somebody as an idea. But they are not likely to have happened to many people. The second class of their "myths" consist of the stories that are told everywhere for the simple reason that they happen everywhere. Of the first class, for instance, we might take such an example as the story of William Tell, now generally ranked among legends upon the sole ground that it is found in the tales of other peoples. Now, it is obvious that this was told everywhere because whether true or fictitious it is what is called "a good story"; it is odd, exciting, and it has a climax. But to suggest that some such eccentric incident can never have

happened in the whole history of archery, or that it did not happen to any particular person of whom it is told, is stark impudence. The idea of shooting at a mark attached to some valuable or beloved person is an idea doubtless that might easily have occurred to any inventive poet. But it is also an idea that might easily occur to any boastful archer. It might be one of the fantastic caprices of some story-teller. It might equally well be one of the fantastic caprices of some tyrant. It might occur first in real life and afterwards occur in legends. Or it might just as well occur first in legends and afterwards occur in real life. If no apple has ever been shot off a boy's head from the beginning of the world, it may be done to-morrow morning, and by somebody who had never heard of William Tell.

This type of tale, indeed, may be pretty fairly paralleled with the ordinary anecdote terminating in a repartee or an Irish bull. Such a retort as the famous "*Je ne vois pas la nécessité*"[1] we have all seen attributed to Talleyrand, to Voltaire, to Henri Quatre, to an anonymous judge, and so on. But this variety does not in any way make it more likely that the thing was never said at all. It is highly likely that it was really said by somebody unknown. It is highly likely that it was really said by Talleyrand. In any case, it is not any more difficult to believe that the *mot* might have occurred to a man in conversation than to a man writing memoirs. It might have occurred to any of the men I have mentioned. But there is this point of distinction about it, that it is not likely to have occurred to all of them. And this is where the first class of so-called myth differs from the second to which I have previously referred. For there is a second class of incident found to be common to the stories of five or six heroes, say to Sigurd, to Hercules, to Rustem, to the Cid, and so on. And the peculiarity of this myth is that not only is it highly reasonable to imagine that it

---

[1] "I do not see the necessity"—the reputed answer given to one who said by way of defense that he had to live somehow.

really happened to one hero, but it is highly reasonable to imagine that it really happened to all of them. Such a story, for instance, is that of a great man having his strength swayed or thwarted by the mysterious weakness of a woman. The anecdotal story, the story of William Tell, is, as I have said, popular because it is peculiar. But this kind of story, the story of Samson and Delilah, of Arthur and Guinevere, is obviously popular because it is not peculiar. It is popular as good, quiet fiction is popular, because it tells the truth about people. If the ruin of Samson by a woman, and the ruin of Hercules by a woman, have a common legendary origin, it is gratifying to know that we can also explain, as a fable, the ruin of Nelson by a woman and the ruin of Parnell by a woman. And, indeed, I have no doubt whatever that, some centuries hence, the students of folklore will refuse altogether to believe that Elizabeth Barrett eloped with Robert Browning, and will prove their point up to the hilt by the unquestionable fact that the whole fiction of the period was full of such elopements from end to end.

Possibly the most pathetic of all the delusions of the modern students of primitive belief is the notion they have about the thing they call anthropomorphism. They believe that primitive men attributed phenomena to a god in human form in order to explain them, because his mind in its sullen limitation could not reach any further than his own clownish existence. The thunder was called the voice of a man, the lightning the eyes of a man, because by this explanation they were made more reasonable and comfortable. The final cure for all this kind of philosophy is to walk down a lane at night. Anyone who does so will discover very quickly that men pictured something semi-human at the back of all things, not because such a thought was natural, but because it was supernatural; not because it made things more comprehensible, but because it made them a hundred times more incomprehensible and mysterious. For a man walking down a lane at night can see the conspicuous fact that as long as nature keeps to her own course, she has no power with us at all. As long as a tree is a tree, it is a top-heavy monster with a hundred arms, a thousand tongues, and only one leg. But so long as a tree is a tree, it does not frighten us at all. It begins to be something alien, to be something strange, only when it looks like ourselves. When a tree really looks like a man our knees knock under us. And when the whole universe looks like a man we fall on our faces.

HANS K. ZINSSER

Rats, Men, and History

The oldest recorded epidemic often regarded as an outbreak of typhus is the Athenian plague of the Peloponnesian Wars, which is described in the Second Book of the *History* of Thucydides.

In trying to make the diagnosis of epidemics from ancient descriptions, when the differentiation of simultaneously occurring diseases was impossible, it is important to remember that in any great outbreak, while the large majority of cases may represent a single type of infection, there is usually a coincident increase of other forms of contagious diseases; for the circumstances which favor the spread of one infectious agent often create opportunities for the transmission of others. Very rarely is there a pure epidemic of a single malady. It is not unlikely that the description of Thucydides is confused by the fact that a number of diseases were epidemic in Athens at the time of the great plague. The conditions were ripe for it. Early in the summer of 430 B.C. large armies were

RATS, MEN, AND HISTORY: From *Rats, Lice and History* by Hans Zinsser, permission of Atlantic-Little, Brown and Co. Copyright, 1934, 1935, 1963 by Hans Zinsser.

camped in Attica. The country population swarmed into Athens, which became very much overcrowded. The disease seems to have started in Ethiopia, thence traveled through Egypt and Libya, and at length reached the seaport of Piraeus. It spread rapidly. Patients were seized suddenly, out of a clear sky. The first symptoms were severe headache and redness of the eyes. These were followed by inflammation of the tongue and pharynx, accompanied by sneezing, hoarseness, and cough. Soon after this, there was acute intestinal involvement, with vomiting, diarrhoea, and excessive thirst. Delirium was common. The patients that perished usually died between the seventh and ninth days. Many of those who survived the acute stage suffered from extreme weakness and a continued diarrhoea that yielded to no treatment. At the height of the fever, the body became covered with reddish spots, some of which ulcerated. When one of the very severe cases recovered, convalescence was often accompanied by necrosis of the fingers, the toes, and the genitals. Some lost their eyesight. In many there was complete loss of memory. Those who recovered were immune, so that they could nurse the sick without further danger. None of those who, not thoroughly immunized, had it for the second time died of it. Thucydides himself had the disease. After subsiding for a while, when the winter began, the disease reappeared and seriously diminished the strength of the Athenian state.

The plague of Athens, whatever it may have been, had a profound effect upon historical events. It was one of the main reasons why the Athenian armies, on the advice of Pericles, did not attempt to expel the Lacedaemonians, who were ravaging Attica. Athenian life was completely demoralized, and a spirit of extreme lawlessness resulted. Men no longer took trouble about what was estimated honor. As Thucydides expresses it: "They saw how sudden was the change of fortune in the case both of those who were prosperous and suddenly died, and of those who before had nothing but, in a moment,

were in possession of the property of others." There was no fear of the laws of God or man. Piety and impiety came to the same thing, and no one expected that he would live to be called to account. Finally, the Peloponnesians left Attica in a hurry, not for fear of the Athenians, who were locked up in their cities, but because they were afraid of the disease. At the same time, the pestilence followed the Athenian fleet, which was attacking the Peloponnesian coast, and prevented the carrying out of the objectives for which their expeditions had been organized. Thus it is likely that the struggle between the two contending powers was influenced in its duration and in the swinging back and forth of the fortunes of war as much by the epidemic as by any generalship or force of arms.

The plague of Thucydides can be identified with no single known epidemic disease of our day. Haeser believes it to be more like typhus fever than any of the conditions familiar to us, and Hecker takes the view that it was typhus in a form from which it has been altered in the centuries that followed. The eruption was certainly not like that of typhus at the present time, but corresponds more nearly to that of smallpox. When all is said, we must conclude that the nature of the Athenian epidemic cannot be determined with certainty. The rapidity of spread in a crowded town of 10,000 relatively small buildings, with a tremendous influx of population, is consistent with many forms of epidemic disease. The onset, the immediate respiratory symptoms, the nature of the eruption, and the sequelae might reasonably be interpreted as smallpox.

In trying to make a diagnosis of the Athenian plague, we must take seriously the suggestion made by Hecker that epidemic diseases may have been modified considerably in the course of centuries of alternating widespread prevalence and quiescence. One of the greatest achievements in the war which the medical sciences have waged against epidemic diseases is the discovery that, during times of quiescence in interepidemic periods, the potential agents of disease may smoulder in human carriers, in domestic animals—especially rodents—and in insects. And modern bacteriology has made considerable progress in revealing changes that take place in the characteristics of bacteria and virus agents in the course of their adaptation to different environments. In the typhus-fever group, these circumstances have been most particularly studied, and we already have knowledge of a number of varieties of typhus and typhus-like fevers which have developed within historic times, probably because of the passage of the virus through different varieties of rodents and of insects and through man. These are matters which we have discussed more precisely in another place.

Thus, in endeavoring to classify the plague of Athens in the fifth century B.C., we have to choose between typhus, bubonic and pneumonic plague, and smallpox....

The effects of a succession of epidemics upon a state are not measurable in mortalities alone. Whenever pestilences have attained particularly terrifying proportions, their secondary consequences have been much more far-reaching and disorganizing than anything that could have resulted from the mere numerical reduction of the population. In modern times, these secondary effects have been—to some extent—mitigated by knowledge which has removed much of the terror that always accompanies the feeling of complete helplessness in the face of mysterious perils.

In this respect, modern bacteriology has brought about a state of affairs which may exert profound influence upon the future economic and political history of the world. Some epidemic diseases it has converted from uncontrolled savagery into states of relatively mild domestication. Others it can confine to limited territories or reservations. Others again, though still at large, can be prevented from developing a velocity which—once in full swing—is irresistible. But even in cases where no effective means of defense have as yet been discovered—as, for instance, in influenza, infantile paralysis, and encephalitis—the enemy can be faced in an orderly manner, with determination and with some knowledge of his probable tactics; still, no doubt, with terror, but at least without the panic and disorganization which have been as destructive to ancient and mediaeval society as the actual mortalities sustained.

In earlier ages, pestilences were mysterious visitations, expressions of the wrath of higher powers which came out of a dark nowhere, pitiless, dreadful, and inescapable. In their terror and ignorance, men did the very things which increased death rates and aggravated calamity. They fled from towns and villages, but death mysteriously traveled along with them. Panic bred social and moral disorganization; farms were abandoned, and there was shortage of food; famine led to displacement of populations, to revolution, to civil war, and, in some instances, to fanatical religious movements which contributed to profound spiritual and political transformations.

The disintegration of the Roman power was a gradual process brought about by complex causes. Although, at the death of Honorius, in 423 A.D., Britain alone had broken away from formal Roman control, the cracks along which the eventual cleavages were to come had already been well started. The edict of Caracalla, long before this, had raised the inhabitants of the provinces to the dignity of Roman citizenship, but in actuality the knights of Rome had no more in common with the burghers of Nicomedia or Augusta Trevirorum than a banker Republican of Boston or New York to-day has in common with a farmer Democrat of Oklahoma. Gigantic bureaucracies were eating up the government, budgets were almost modernly unbalanced, and the barbarians—already settled in the Empire—immigrants in the modern sense, were expressing their aspirations for political power by marching on the capital whenever farming ceased to pay.

The Visigoths, settled by Theodosius south of the Danube, started a farmer's strike in 396 under Alaric, and were stopped from occupying Rome only by the payment of a large farm loan, then spoken of as a ransom. The Vandals and Suebi, in 405, took possession of Spain, crossed into Africa, and established a sort of Middle West, which could enforce its desires by controlling the grain supply.

The problem has been dealt with from every conceivable angle, for there is no greater historic puzzle than that of the disappearance of the ancient civilization—a disappearance so complete that not a spark from its embers shone through the barbaric darkness of several hundred years. Historians have analyzed the causes according to the prejudices of their own varieties of erudition. Mommsen, Gibbon, Ferrero, deduce the disintegration of the state, with variations of emphasis, from a combination of political, religious (moral), and sociological causes. Ferrero lays fundamental stress upon the "interminable civil wars which resulted from the efforts of later Rome to reconcile the two essentially different principles of monarchy and republican organizations." Some have attempted to explain the breakdown on a basis of agricultural failure (Simkhovitch, *Hay and History*); a few associated with this the influence of a formidable increase of malaria, which accelerated the desertion of the farm lands (Ross). Pareto (*Traité de Sociologie Générale*, Vol. II, Chap. XIII—"L'Equilibre Social dans l'Histoire") seems to us to have given the most reasonable analysis, in which, in an extraordinarily brief treatment, he correlates the many complex factors that were coöperatively active. But even he has failed to include any consideration of the calamitous epidemics which—sweeping the Roman world again and again during its most turbulent political periods—must have exerted a material, if not a decisive influence upon the final outcome.

We are far from wishing to make the error against which Pareto warns, "*d'envisager comme simples des faits extrêmement compliqués*"; and we do not mean to add to other one-sided views an epidemic theory of the Roman decline. But we believe that a simple survey of the frequency, extent, and violence of the pestilences to which Roman Europe and Asia were subjected, from the year one to the final barbarian triumph, will convince the unprejudiced that these calamities must be interpolated in any appraisal of the causes that wore down the power of the greatest state the world has known. Indeed, we are inclined to believe, from a consideration of the circumstances prevailing at that time, that it would be impossible to maintain permanently a political and social organization of the type and magnitude of Rome in the face of complete lack of modern sanitary knowledge. A concentration of large populations in cities, free communication with all other parts of the world—especially Africa and the East—constant and extensive military activity involving the mobilization of armies in camps, and the movement of large forces back and forth from all corners of the world—these alone are conditions which inevitably determine the outbreak of epidemic disease.[2] And against such outbreaks there was absolutely no defense available at the time. Pestilences encountered no obstacles. They were free to sweep across the entire world, like flames through dry grass, finding fuel wherever men lived, following trade routes on land, and

[2] This is still entirely applicable to modern times. Experience in the cantonments of 1917 and in the sanitation of active troops convincingly showed that war is today, as much as ever, seventy-five per cent an engineering and sanitary problem and a little less than twenty-five per cent a military one. Other things being approximately equal, that army will win which has the best engineering and sanitary services. The wise general will do what the engineers and the sanitary officers let him. The only reason why this is not entirely apparent in wars is because the military minds on both sides are too superb to notice that both armies are simultaneously immobilized by the same diseases.

Incidentally, medicine has another indirect influence on war which is not negligible. There seems little doubt that some of the reckless courage of the American troops in the late war was stimulated by the knowledge that in front of them were only the Germans, but behind them there were the assembled surgeons of America, with sleeves rolled up.

carried over the sea in ships. They slowed down only when they had burned themselves out—and even then, when they had traveled as slowly as did the plagues of Cyprian and Justinian, they often doubled on their own paths, finding, in a new generation or in a community with fading immunity, materials on which they could flame up again for another period of terror. As soon as a state ceases to be mainly agricultural, sanitary knowledge becomes indispensable for its maintenance.

Justinian died in 565. Charlemagne was crowned in 800. Between 600 and 800, Italy was the battleground of barbarian immigrants who were fighting for the spoils. Rome, in the ancient sense, had ceased to exist. The final collapse of its defensive energy corresponds, in time, with the calamity of the great pestilence which bears Justinian's name. And while it would not be sensible to hold this plague alone responsible, it can hardly be questioned that it was one of the factors—perhaps the most potent single influence—which gave the *coupe de grâce* to the ancient empire.

Moreover, the history of the preceding six hundred years furnishes any number of examples to show that, again and again, the forward march of Roman power and world organization was interrupted by the only force against which political genius and military valor were utterly helpless—epidemic disease. There is no parallel in recent history by which the conditions then prevailing can be judged, unless it is the state of Russia between 1917 and 1923. There, too, the unfettered violence of typhus, cholera, dysentery, tuberculosis, malaria, and their brothers exerted a profound influence upon political events. But of this we shall have more to say presently. It was only the highly developed system of sanitary defense on the Polish and the southern fronts that prevented, during those years, an invasion—first of disease, misery, and famine; then of political disruption—from spreading across Europe. This statement may, perhaps, be debatable. But it is, at least, a reasonable probability.

At any rate, during the first centuries after Christ, disease was unopposed by any barriers. And when it came, as though carried on storm clouds, all other things gave way, and men crouched in terror, abandoning all their quarrels, undertakings, and ambitions, until the tempest had blown over.

.   .   .

It is a curious fact that long before there could have been any knowledge concerning the dangerous character of rodents as carriers of disease, mankind dreaded and pursued these animals. Sticker has collected a great many references to this subject from ancient and mediaeval literature, and has found much evidence in the folklore of mediaeval Europe which points to the vague recognition of some connection between plague and rats. In ancient Palestine, the Jews considered all seven mouse varieties (akbar) unclean, and as unsuited for human nourishment as were pigs. The worshipers of Zoroaster hated water rats, and believed that the killing of rats was a service to God. It is also significant that Apollo Smintheus, the god who was supposed to protect against disease, was also spoken of as the killer of mice, and Saint Gertrude was besought by the bishops of the early Catholic Church to protect against plague and mice. The year 1498, Sticker tells us, was a severe plague year in Germany, and there were so many rats in Frankfurt that an attendant was stationed for several hours each day on a bridge in the town and directed to pay a pfennig for every rat brought in. The attendant cut off the tail of the rat—probably as a primitive method of accounting—and threw the bodies into the river. Heine, according to Sticker, speaks of a tax levied on the Jews of Frankfurt in the fifteenth century, which consisted of the annual delivery of five thousand rat tails. Folklore originating in a number of different parts of Europe during the great plague epidemics mentions cats and dogs, the hereditary enemies of rats and mice, as guardians against the plague.

Most scholars agree that there is no reliable mention of rats—as such—in classical literature. The Greeks had the word μῦς. Herodotus mentions the field mouse—μῦς ἀρουραῖος. The expression μῦς ἐν πίττῃ (mouse in a pickle jar) meant "to be in a bad hole or scrape." The Greeks also knew ὕραξ—the later Roman "Sorex"—which, though not a rodent at all (the shrewmouse), looked enough like one to get into the literature with the mouse. Our learned friend Professor Rand tells us of a story quoted by Keller (*Die Antike Thierwelt*) about Heliogabalus, who "staged a fight between ten thousand mice, one thousand shrewmice and one thousand weasels." Needless to relate, the shrewmice "polished off" the mice, and the weasels got both of them.

The Romans knew the mouse well. It was recognized as a pest, and *musculus* (little mouse) was even used as a term of endearment by Martial. The word root (*muishi*, Persian; *musa, musi*, Hindu; *musiko*, Pali) indicates the world-wide ancient knowledge of mice.

There is, however, no specific early differentiation between mice and rats, and authorities seem to agree quite generally that nothing in the references to mice, at least among the Greeks and Romans, justifies the assumption that rats may have been referred to. Yet, in view of the probable ancient prevalence of rats in Eastern countries, and the close communications by sea between the Greeks and the Mediterranean coastal cities, as well as the regular grain traffic between Egypt and Rome, it is difficult to credit the complete absence of rats from the European littoral throughout antiquity.

In regard to mice and rats in the Near East, Herodotus tells us of Libya that "in this country there are three kinds of mice. One is called the 'two-legged' mouse; another the 'Zegeris' [a word that means a hill—possibly a sort of prairie dog]; a third, the 'prickly' mouse." Also he recounts that when Sanachrib, King of Arabia and Assyria, marched a great host against Egypt, on the night before the battle "there swarmed upon them mice of the fields,

and ate up their quivers and their bows and the handles of their shields" so that, on the next day, they fled. This sounds much more like rats than like the timid field mouse. However, these things are hardly evidence.

It is quite impossible to make a case for the presence of true rats in Europe proper during classical times, much as this would clarify the epidemiological situation. It is conceivable that the manner of transmission of plague and typhus may have undergone modification since the Peloponnesian Wars by changed adaptations to hosts, both insect and rodent. But it would seem much more likely that the zoölogical differentiations between rodents so similar and closely related as mice and rats were inaccurate in ancient records, and that rats may have existed—though undomesticated. This would give us a wider latitude for speculation regarding the nature of epidemics, which, to be sure, were rarely, under the circumstances of ancient life, as widespread or deadly as they became with the later concentrations of population and of urban habits. At any rate, if rats had been present in those times in anything like the numbers in which they are found today, we should probably have reliable records. It may well be that the frugality of well-run households, like that of Penelope, gave little encouragement to house rats to become parasitic on man to the extent to which they have since.

All this is conjecture. According to the wisest students of the subject, there is no certain knowledge of rats in Europe, within historic periods, until shortly after the Crusades. In prehistoric days they certainly existed there—but later disappeared. Fossil remains of rats have been found in the Pliocene period of Lombardy (the Mastodon period of Europe) and in the later Pleistocene of Crete. They were present during the glacial period with the lake dwellers, whom they pestered in Mecklenburg and Western Germany. From that time on, there were either few or no rats until thousands of years later.

In regard to the reappearance of rats in

Europe, our industrious colleagues, the zoölogists, have gathered an immense amount of information, much of which has been interestingly summarized by Barrett-Hamilton and Hinton in their *History of British Mammals*, and by Donaldson in his *Memoir on the Rat*. Before we proceed to this subject, however, it will be profitable to consider the striking analogy between rats and men. More than any other species of animal, the rat and mouse have become dependent on man, and in so doing they have developed characteristics which are amazingly human.

In the first place, like man, the rat has become practically omnivorous. It eats anything that lets it and—like man—devours its own kind, under stress. It breeds at all seasons and—again like man—it is most amorous in the springtime. It hybridizes easily and, judging by the strained relationship between the black and the brown rat, develops social or racial prejudices against this practice. The sex proportions are like those among us. Inbreeding takes place readily. The males are larger, the females fatter. It adapts itself to all kinds of climates. It makes ferocious war upon its own kind, but has not, as yet, become nationalized. So far, it has still stuck to tribal wars—like man before nations were invented. If it continues to ape man as heretofore, we may, in a few centuries, have French rats eating German ones, or Nazi rats attacking Communist or Jewish rats; however, such a degree of civilization is probably not within the capacities of any mere animal. Also—like man—the rat is individualistic until it needs help. That is, it fights bravely alone against weaker rivals, for food or for love; but it knows how to organize armies and fight in hordes when necessary.

Donaldson, basing his calculations mainly on stages in the development of the nervous system, reckons three years of a rat life as ninety years for man. By this scale, the rat reaches puberty at about sixteen, and arrives at the menopause at the equivalent of forty-five. In following man about all over the earth, the rat

has—more than any other living creature except man—been able to adapt itself to any conditions of seasonal changes or climate....

As we have indicated in a preceding paragraph, the natural history of the rat is tragically similar to that of man. Offspring of widely divergent evolutionary directions, men and rats reached present stages of physical development within a few hundred thousand years of each other—since remnants of both are found in the fossils of the glacial period.

Some of the more obvious qualities in which rats resemble men—ferocity, omnivorousness, and adaptability to all climates—have been mentioned above. We have also alluded to the irresponsible fecundity with which both species breed at all seasons of the year with a heedlessness of consequences which subjects them to wholesale disaster on the inevitable, occasional failure of the food supply. In this regard, it is only fair to state—in justice to man—that, as far as we can tell, the rat does this of its own free and stupid gluttony, while man has tradition, piety, and the duty of furnishing cannon fodder to contend with, in addition to his lower instincts. But these are, after all, phenomena of human biology, and man cannot be absolved of responsibility for his stupidities because they are the results of wrong-headedness rather than the consequences of pure instinct—certainly not if they result in identical disasters.

Neither rat nor man has achieved social, commercial, or economic stability. This has been, either perfectly or to some extent, achieved by ants and by bees, by some birds, and by some of the fishes in the sea. Man and the rat are merely, so far, the most successful animals of prey. They are utterly destructive of other forms of life. Neither of them is of the slightest earthly use to any other species of living things. Bacteria nourish plants; plants nourish man and beast. Insects, in their well-organized societies, are destructive of one form of living creature, but helpful to another. Most other animals are content to lead peaceful and adjusted lives, rejoicing in vigor, grateful for this gift of living, and doing the minimum of injury to obtain the things they require. Man and the rat are utterly destructive. All that nature offers is taken for their own purposes, plant or beast.

Gradually these two have spread across the earth, keeping pace with each other and unable to destroy each other, though continually hostile. They have wandered from East to West, driven by their physical needs, and—unlike any other species of living things—have made war upon their own kind. The gradual, relentless, progressive extermination of the black rat by the brown has no parallel in nature so close as that of the similar extermination of one race of man by another. Did the Danes conquer England; or the Normans the Saxon-Danes; or the Normans the Sicilian-Mohammedans; or the Moors the Latin-Iberians; or the Franks the Moors; or the Spanish the Aztecs and the Incas; or the Europeans in general the simple aborigines of the world by qualities other than those by which *Mus decumanus* has driven out *Mus rattus?* In both species, the battle has been pitilessly to the strong. And the strong have been pitiless. The physically weak have been driven before the strong—annihilated, or constrained to the slavery of doing without the bounties which were provided for all equally. Isolated colonies of black rats survive, as weaker nations survive until the stronger ones desire the little they still possess.

The rat has an excuse. As far as we know, it does not appear to have developed a soul, or that intangible quality of justice, mercy, and reason that psychic evolution has bestowed upon man. We must not expect too much. It takes a hundred thousand years to alter the protuberances on a bone, the direction of a muscle; much longer than this to develop a lung from a gill, or to atrophy a tail. It is only about twenty-five hundred years since Plato, Buddha, and Confucius; only two thousand years since Christ. In the meantime, we have had Homer and Saint Francis, Copernicus and Galileo; Shakespeare, Pascal, Newton, Goethe, Bach, and Beethoven, and a great number of lesser

men and women of genius who have demonstrated the evolutionary possibilities of the human spirit. If such minds have been rare, and spread thinly over three thousand years, after all, they still represent the sorts that indicate the high possibilities of fortunate genetic combinations. And these must inevitably increase if the environment remains at all favorable. If no upward progress in spirit or intelligence seems apparent let us say, between the best modern minds and that of Aristotle, we must remember that, in terms of evolutionary change, three thousand years are negligible. If, as in the last war and its subsequent imbecilities, mankind returns completely to the rat stage of civilization, this surely shows how very rudimentary an emergence from the Neanderthal our present civilization represents—how easily the thin, spiritual veneer is cracked under any strain that awakens the neolithic beast within. Nevertheless, for perhaps three or five thousand years, the beast has begun to ponder and grope. Isolated achievements have demonstrated of what the mind and spirit are capable when a happy combination of genes occurs under circumstances that permit the favored individual to mature. And the most incomprehensible but hopeful aspect of the matter is the fact that successive generations have always bred an adequate number of individuals sufficiently superior to the brutal mass to keep alive a reverence for these supreme achievements and make them a cumulative heritage. It is more than likely—biologically considered—that by reason of this progressive accumulation of the best that superior specimens of our species have produced, the evolution toward higher things may gain velocity with time, and that in another hundred thousand years the comparison of the race of men with that of rats may be less humiliatingly obvious.

Man and the rat will always be pitted against each other as implacable enemies. And the rat's most potent weapons against mankind have been its perpetual maintenance of the infectious agents of plague and of typhus fever.

ERIC BERNE

Why People Play Games

1   *Social Intercourse*

The theory of social intercourse, which has been outlined at some length in *Transactional Analysis* may be summarized as follows.

Spitz has found that infants deprived of handling over a long period will tend at length to sink into an irreversible decline and are prone to succumb eventually to intercurrent disease. In effect, this means that what he calls emotional deprivation can have a fatal outcome. These observations give rise to the idea of *stimulus-hunger*, and indicate that the most favored forms of stimuli are those provided by physical intimacy, a conclusion not hard to accept on the basis of everyday experience.

An allied phenomenon is seen in grown-ups subjected to sensory deprivation. Experimentally, such deprivation may call forth a transient psychosis, or at least give rise to temporary mental disturbances. In the past, social and sensory deprivation is noted to have had similar effects in individuals condemned to long periods of solitary imprisonment. Indeed, solitary confinement is one of the punishments most dreaded even by prisoners hardened to physical brutality, and is now a notorious procedure for inducing political compliance. (Conversely, the best of the known weapons against political compliance is social organization.)

On the biological side, it is probable that emotional and sensory deprivations tend to bring about or encourage organic changes. If the reticular activating system of the brain stem is not sufficiently stimulated, degenerative changes in the nerve cells may follow, at least

indirectly. This may be a secondary effect due to poor nutrition, but the poor nutrition itself may be a product of apathy, as in infants suffering from marasmus. Hence a biological chain may be postulated leading from emotional and sensory deprivation through apathy to degenerative changes and death. In this sense, stimulus-hunger has the same relationship to survival of the human organism as food-hunger.

Indeed, not only biologically but also psychologically and socially, stimulus-hunger in many ways parallels the hunger for food. Such terms as malnutrition, satiation, gourmet, gourmand, faddist, ascetic, culinary arts, and good cook are easily transferred from the field of nutrition to the field of sensation. Overstuffing has its parallel in overstimulation. In both spheres, under ordinary conditions where ample supplies are available and a diversified menu is possible, choices will be heavily influenced by an individual's idiosyncrasies. It is possible that some or many of these idiosyncrasies are constitutionally determined, but this is irrelevant to the problems at issue here.

The social psychiatrist's concern in the matter is with what happens after the infant is separated from his mother in the normal course of growth. What has been said so far may be summarized by the "colloquialism": "If you are not stroked, your spinal cord will shrivel up." Hence, after the period of close intimacy with the mother is over, the individual for the rest of his life is confronted with a dilemma upon whose horns his destiny and survival are continually being tossed. One horn is the social, psychological and biological forces which stand in the way of continued physical intimacy in the infant style; the other is his perpetual striving for its attainment. Under most conditions he will compromise. He learns to do with more subtle, even symbolic, forms of handling, until the merest nod of recognition may serve the purpose to some extent, although his original craving for physical contact may remain unabated.

This process of compromise may be called by various terms, such as sublimation; but whatever it is called, the result is a partial transformation of the infantile stimulus-hunger into something which may be termed *recognition-hunger*. As the complexities of compromise increase, each person becomes more and more individual in his quest for recognition, and it is these differentia which lend variety to social intercourse and which determine the individual's destiny. A movie actor may require hundreds of strokes each week from anonymous and undifferentiated admirers to keep his spinal cord from shriveling, while a scientist may keep physically and mentally healthy on one stroke a year from a respected master.

"Stroking" may be used as a general term for intimate physical contact; in practice it may take various forms. Some people literally stroke an infant; others hug or pat it, while some people pinch it playfully or flip it with a fingertip. These all have their analogues in conversation, so that it seems one might predict how an individual would handle a baby by listening to him talk. By an extension of meaning, "stroking" may be employed colloquially to denote any act implying recognition of another's presence. Hence a *stroke* may be used as the fundamental unit of social action. An exchange of strokes constitutes a *transaction*, which is the unit of social intercourse.

As far as the theory of games is concerned, the principle which emerges here is that any social intercourse whatever has a biological advantage over no intercourse at all. This has been experimentally demonstrated in the case of rats through some remarkable experiments by S. Levine in which not only physical, mental and emotional development but also the bio-chemistry of the brain and even resistance to leukemia were favorably affected by handling. The significant feature of these experiments was that gentle handling and painful electric shocks were equally effective in promoting the health of the animals.

This validation of what has been said above encourages us to proceed with increased confidence to the next section.

2   *The Structuring of Time*

Granted that handling of infants, and its symbolic equivalent in grown-ups, recognition, have a survival value. The question is, What next? In everyday terms, what can people do after they have exchanged greetings, whether the greeting consists of a collegiate "Hi!" or an Oriental ritual lasting several hours? After stimulus-hunger and recognition-hunger comes *structure-hunger*. The perennial problem of adolescents is: "What do you say to her (him) then?" And to many people besides adolescents, nothing is more uncomfortable than a social hiatus, a period of silent, unstructured time when no one present can think of anything more interesting to say than: "Don't you think the walls are perpendicular tonight?" The eternal problem of the human being is how to structure his waking hours. In this existential sense, the function of all social living is to lend mutual assistance for this project.

The operational aspect of time-structuring may be called programing. It has three aspects: material, social and individual. The most common, convenient, comfortable, and utilitarian method of structuring time is by a project designed to deal with the material of external reality: what is commonly known as work. Such a project is technically called an *activity*; the term "work" is unsuitable because a general theory of social psychiatry must recognize that social intercourse is also a form of work.

Material programing arises from the vicissitudes encountered in dealing with external reality; it is of interest here only insofar as activities offer a matrix for "stroking," recognition, and other more complex forms of social intercourse. Material programing is not primarily a social problem; in essence it is based on data processing. The activity of building a boat relies on a long series of measurements and probability estimates, and any social exchange which occurs must be subordinated to these in order for the building to proceed.

Social programing results in traditional ritualistic or semi-ritualistic interchanges. The chief criterion for it is local acceptability, popularly called "good manners." Parents in all parts of the world teach their children manners, which means that they know the proper greeting, eating, emunctory, courting and mourning rituals, and also how to carry on topical conversations with appropriate strictures and reinforcements. The strictures and reinforcements constitute tact or diplomacy, some of which is universal and some local. Belching at meals or asking after another man's wife are each encouraged or forbidden by local ancestral tradition, and indeed there is a high degree of inverse correlation between these particular transactions. Usually in localities where people belch at meals, it is unwise to ask after the womenfolk; and in localities where people are asking after the womenfolk, it is unwise to belch at meals. Usually formal rituals precede semi-ritualistic topical conversations, and the latter may be distinguished by calling them *pastimes*.

As people become better acquainted, more and more *individual programing* creeps in, so that "incidents" begin to occur. These incidents superficially appear to be adventitious, and may be so described by the parties concerned, but careful scrutiny reveals that they tend to follow definite patterns which are amenable to sorting and classification, and that the sequence is circumscribed by unspoken rules and regulations. These regulations remain latent as long as the amities or hostilities proceed according to Hoyle, but they become manifest if an illegal move is made, giving rise to a symbolic, verbal or legal cry of "Foul!" Such sequences, which in contrast to pastimes are based more on individual than on social programing, may be called *games*. Family life and married life, as well as life in organizations of various kinds, may year after year be based on variations of the same game.

To say that the bulk of social activity consists of playing games does not necessarily mean that it is mostly "fun" or that the parties are not seriously engaged in the relationship. On the one hand, "playing" football and other athletic "games" may not be fun at all, and the players may be intensely grim; and such games share with gambling and other forms of "play" the potentiality for being very serious indeed, sometimes fatal. On the other hand, some authors, for instance Huizinga, include under "play" such serious things as cannibal feasts. Hence calling such tragic behavior as suicide, alcohol and drug addiction, criminality or schizophrenia "playing games" is not irresponsible, facetious or barbaric. The essential characteristic of human play is not that the emotions are spurious, but that they are regulated. This is revealed when sanctions are imposed on an illegitimate emotional display. Play may be grimly serious, or even fatally serious, but the social sanctions are serious only if the rules are broken.

Pastimes and games are substitutes for the real living of real intimacy. Because of this they may be regarded as preliminary engagements rather than as unions, which is why they are characterized as poignant forms of play. Intimacy begins when individual (usually instinctual) programing becomes more intense, and both social patterning and ulterior restrictions and motives begin to give way. It is the only completely satisfying answer to stimulus-hunger, recognition-hunger and structure-hunger. Its prototype is the act of loving impregnation.

Structure-hunger has the same survival value as stimulus-hunger. Stimulus-hunger and recognition-hunger express the need to avoid sensory and emotional starvation, both of which lead to biological deterioration. Structure-hunger expresses the need to avoid boredom, and Kierkegaard has pointed out the evils which result from unstructured time. If it persists for any length of time, boredom becomes synonymous with emotional starvation and can have the same consequences.

The solitary individual can structure time in two ways: activity and fantasy. An individual can remain solitary even in the presence of others, as every schoolteacher knows. When one is a member of a social aggregation of two or more people, there are several options for structuring time. In order of complexity, these are: 1. Rituals, 2. Pastimes, 3. Games, 4. Intimacy and 5. Activity, which may form a matrix for any of the others. The goal of each member of the aggregation is to obtain as many satisfactions as possible from his transactions with other members. The more accessible he is, the more satisfactions he can obtain. Most of the programing of his social operations is automatic. Since some of the "satisfactions" obtained under this programing, such as self-destructive ones, are difficult to recognize in the usual sense of the word "satisfactions," it would be better to substitute some more non-committal term, such as "gains" or "advantages."

The advantages of social contact revolve around somatic and psychic equilibrium. They are related to the following factors: 1. the relief of tension, 2. the avoidance of noxious situations, 3. the procurement of stroking and, 4. the maintenance of an established equilibrium. All these items have been investigated and discussed in great detail by physiologists, psychologists, and psychoanalysts. Translated into terms of social psychiatry, they may be stated as 1. the primary internal advantages, 2. the primary external advantages, 3. the secondary advantages and 4. the existential advantages. The first three parallel the "gains from illness" described by Freud: the internal paranosic gain, the external paranosic gain, and the epinosic gain, respectively. Experience has shown that it is more useful and enlightening to investigate social transactions from the point of view of the advantages gained than to treat them as defensive operations. In the first place, the best defense is to engage in no transactions at all; in the second place, the concept of "defenses" covers only part of the first two classes of advantages, and the rest of them, together with the third and fourth classes, are lost to this point of view.

The most gratifying forms of social contact, whether or not they are embedded in a matrix of activity, are games and intimacy. Prolonged intimacy is rare, and even then it is primarily a private matter; significant social intercourse most commonly takes the form of games, and that is the subject which principally concerns us here. For further information about time-structuring, the author's book on group dynamics should be consulted.

SUSAN SONTAG

The Imagination of Disaster

The typical science fiction film has a form as predictable as a Western, and is made up of elements which, to a practiced eye, are as classic as the saloon brawl, the blonde schoolteacher from the East, and the gun duel on the deserted main street.

One model scenario proceeds through five phases.

1. The arrival of the thing. (Emergence of the monsters, landing of the alien spaceship, etc.) This is usually witnessed or suspected by just one person, a young scientist on a field trip. Nobody, neither his neighbors nor his colleagues, will believe him for some time. The hero is not married, but has a sympathetic though also incredulous girl friend.

2. Confirmation of the hero's report by a host of witnesses to a great act of destruction. (If the invaders are beings from another planet, a fruitless attempt to parley with them and get them to leave peacefully.) The local police are summoned to deal with the situation and massacred.

3. In the capital of the country, conferences between scientists and the military take place, with the hero lecturing before a chart, map, or blackboard. A national emergency is declared. Reports of further destruction. Authorities from other countries arrive in black limousines. All international tensions are suspended in view of the planetary emergency. This stage often includes a rapid montage of news broadcasts in various languages, a meeting at the UN, and more conferences between the military and the scientists. Plans are made for destroying the enemy.

4. Further atrocities. At some point the hero's girl friend is in grave danger. Massive counterattacks by international forces, with brilliant displays of rocketry, rays, and other advanced weapons, are all unsuccessful. Enormous military casualties, usually by incineration. Cities are destroyed and/or evacuated. There is an obligatory scene here of panicked crowds stampeding along a highway or a big bridge, being waved on by numerous policemen who, if the film is Japanese, are immaculately white-gloved, preternaturally calm, and call out in dubbed English, "Keep moving. There is no need to be alarmed."

5. More conferences, whose motif is: "They must be vulnerable to something." Throughout the hero has been working in his lab to this end. The final strategy, upon which all hopes depend, is drawn up; the ultimate weapon—often a super-powerful, as yet untested, nuclear device—is mounted. Countdown. Final repulse of the monster or invaders. Mutual congratulations, while the hero and girl friend embrace cheek to cheek and scan the skies sturdily. "But have we seen the last of them?"

The film I have just described should be in color and on a wide screen. Another typical scenario, which follows, is simpler and suited to black-and-white films with a lower budget. It has four phases.

1. The hero (usually, but not always, a scientist) and his girl friend, or his wife and two children, are disporting themselves in some innocent ultra-normal middle-class surroundings—their house in a small town, or on vacation (camping, boating). Suddenly, someone starts behaving strangely; or some innocent form of vegetation becomes monstrously enlarged and ambulatory. If a character is pictured driving an automobile, something gruesome looms up in the middle of the road. If it is night, strange lights hurtle across the sky.

2. After following the thing's tracks, or determining that It is radioactive, or poking around a huge crater —in short, conducting some sort of crude investigation —the hero tries to warn the local authorities, without effect; nobody believes anything is amiss. The hero knows better. If the thing is tangible, the house is elaborately barricaded. If the invading alien is an invisible parasite, a doctor or friend is called in, who is himself rather quickly killed or "taken possession of" by the thing.

3. The advice of whoever further is consulted proves useless. Meanwhile, It continues to claim other victims in the town, which remains implausibly isolated from the rest of the world. General helplessness.

4. One of two possibilities. Either the hero prepares to do battle alone, accidentally discovers the thing's one vulnerable point, and destroys it. Or, he somehow manages to get out of town and succeeds in laying his case before competent authorities. They, along the lines of the first script but abridged, deploy a complex technology which (after initial setbacks) finally prevails against the invaders.

Another version of the second script opens with the scientist-hero in his laboratory, which is located in the basement or on the grounds of his tasteful, prosperous house. Through his experiments, he unwittingly causes a frightful metamorphosis in some class of plants or animals which turn carnivorous and go on a rampage. Or else, his experiments have caused him to be injured (sometimes irrevocably) or "invaded" himself. Perhaps he has been experimenting with radiation, or has built a machine to communicate with beings from other planets or transport him to other places or times.

Another version of the first script involves the discovery of some fundamental alteration in the conditions of existence of our planet, brought about by nuclear testing, which will lead to the extinction in a few months of all human life. For example: the temperature of the earth is becoming too high or too low to support life, or the earth is cracking in two, or it is gradually being blanketed by lethal fallout.

A third script, somewhat but not altogether different from the first two, concerns a journey through space—to the moon, or some other planet. What the space-voyagers discover commonly is that the alien terrain is in a state of dire emergency, itself threatened by extra-planetary invaders or nearing extinction through the practice of nuclear warfare. The terminal dramas of the first and second scripts are played out there, to which is added the problem of getting away from the doomed and/or hostile planet and back to Earth.

I am aware, of course, that there are thousands of science fiction novels (their heyday was the late 1940's), not to mention the transcriptions of science fiction themes which, more and more, provide the principal subject-matter of comic books. But I propose to discuss science fiction films (the present period began in 1950 and continues, considerably abated, to this day) as an independent subgenre, without reference to other media—and, most particularly, without reference to the novels from which, in many cases, they were adapted. For, while novel and film may share the same plot, the fundamental difference between the resources of the novel and the film makes them quite dissimilar.

Certainly, compared with the science fiction novels, their film counterparts have unique strengths, one of which is the immediate representation of the extraordinary: physical deformity and mutation, missile and rocket combat, toppling skyscrapers. The movies are, naturally, weak just where the science fiction novels (some of them) are strong—on science. But in place of an intellectual workout, they can supply something the novels can never provide—sensuous elaboration. In the films it is by means of images and sounds, not words that have to be translated by the imagination, that one can participate in the fantasy of living through one's own death and more, the death of cities, the destruction of humanity itself.

Science fiction films are not about science. They are about disaster, which is one of the oldest subjects of art. In science fiction films disaster is rarely viewed intensively; it is always

extensive. It is a matter of quantity and ingenuity. If you will, it is a question of scale. But the scale, particularly in the wide-screen color films (of which the ones by the Japanese director Inoshiro Honda and the American director George Pal are technically the most convincing and visually the most exciting), does raise the matter to another level.

Thus, the science fiction film (like that of a very different contemporary genre, the Happening) is concerned with the aesthetics of destruction, with the peculiar beauties to be found in wreaking havoc, making a mess. And it is in the imagery of destruction that the core of a good science fiction film lies. Hence, the disadvantage of the cheap film—in which the monster appears or the rocket lands in a small dull-looking town. (Hollywood budget needs usually dictate that the town be in the Arizona or California desert. In *The Thing From Another World* [1951] the rather sleazy and confined set is supposed to be an encampment near the North Pole.) Still, good black-and-white science fiction films have been made. But a bigger budget, which usually means color, allows a much greater play back and forth among several model environments. There is the populous city. There is the lavish but ascetic interior of the spaceship—either the invaders' or ours—replete with streamlined chromium fixtures and dials and machines whose complexity is indicated by the number of colored lights they flash and strange noises they emit. There is the laboratory crowded with formidable boxes and scientific apparatus. There is a comparatively old-fashioned-looking conference room, where the scientists unfurl charts to explain the desperate state of things to the military. And each of these standard locales or backgrounds is subject to two modalities—intact and destroyed. We may, if we are lucky be treated to a panorama of melting tanks, flying bodies, crashing walls, awesome craters and fissures in the earth, plummeting spacecraft, colorful deadly rays; and to a symphony of screams, weird electronic signals, the noisiest military hardware going, and the leaden tones of the laconic denizens of alien planets and their subjugated earthlings.

Certain of the primitive gratifications of science fiction films—for instance, the depiction of urban disaster on a colossally magnified scale—are shared with other types of films. Visually there is little difference between mass havoc as represented in the old horror and monster films and what we find in science fiction films, except (again) scale. In the old monster films, the monster always headed for the great city, where he had to do a fair bit of rampaging, hurling busses off bridges, crumpling trains in his bare hands, toppling buildings, and so forth. The archetype is King Kong, in Schoedsack and Cooper's great film of 1933, running amok, first in the native village (trampling babies, a bit of footage excised from most prints), then in New York. This is really no different in spirit from the scene in Inoshiro Honda's *Rodan* (1957) in which two giant reptiles—with a wingspan of 500 feet and supersonic speeds— by flapping their wings whip up a cyclone that blows most of Tokyo to smithereens. Or the destruction of half of Japan by the gigantic robot with the great incinerating ray that shoots forth from his eyes, at the beginning of Honda's *The Mysterians* (1959). Or, the devastation by the rays from a fleet of flying saucers of New York, Paris, and Tokyo, in *Battle in Outer Space* (1960). Or, the inundation of New York in *When Worlds Collide* (1951). Or, the end of London in 1966 depicted in George Pal's *The Time Machine* (1960). Neither do these sequences differ in aesthetic intention from the destruction scenes in the big sword, sandal, and orgy color spectaculars set in Biblical and Roman times— the end of Sodom in Aldrich's *Sodom and Gomorrah*, of Gaza in De Mille's *Samson and Delilah*, of Rhodes in *The Colossus of Rhodes*, and of Rome in a dozen Nero movies. Griffith began it with the Babylon sequence in *Intolerance*, and to this day there is nothing like the thrill of watching all those expensive sets come tumbling down.

In other respects as well, the science fiction films of the 1950's take up familiar themes. The famous 1930's movie serials and comics of the adventures of Flash Gordon and Buck Rogers, as well as the more recent spate of comic book super-heroes with extraterrestrial origins (the most famous is Superman, a foundling from the planet Krypton, currently described as having been exploded by a nuclear blast), share motifs with more recent science fiction movies. But there is an important difference. The old science fiction films, and most of the comics, still have an essentially innocent relation to disaster. Mainly they offer new versions of the oldest romance of all—of the strong invulnerable hero with a mysterious lineage come to do battle on behalf of good and against evil. Recent science fiction films have a decided grimness, bolstered by their much greater degree of visual credibility, which contrasts strongly with the older films. Modern historical reality has greatly enlarged the imagination of disaster, and the protagonists— perhaps by the very nature of what is visited upon them—no longer seem wholly innocent.

The lure of such generalized disaster as a fantasy is that it releases one from normal obligations. The trump card of the end-of-the-world movies—like *The Day the Earth Caught Fire* (1962)—is that great scene with New York or London or Tokyo discovered empty, its entire population annihilated. Or, as in *The World, The Flesh, and The Devil* (1957), the whole movie can be devoted to the fantasy of occupying the deserted metropolis and starting all over again, a world Robinson Crusoe.

Another kind of satisfaction these films supply is extreme moral simplification—that is to say, a morally acceptable fantasy where one can give outlet to cruel or at least amoral feelings. In this respect, science fiction films partly overlap with horror films. This is the undeniable pleasure we derive from looking at freaks, beings excluded from the category of the human. The sense of superiority over the freak conjoined in varying proportions with the titillation of fear and aversion makes it possible for moral scruples to be lifted, for cruelty to be enjoyed. The same thing happens in science fiction films. In the figure of the monster from outer space, the freakish, the ugly, and the predatory all converge—and provide a fantasy target for righteous bellicosity to discharge itself, and for the aesthetic enjoyment of suffering and disaster. Science fiction films are one of the purest forms of spectacle; that is, we are rarely inside anyone's feelings. (An exception is Jack Arnold's *The Incredible Shrinking Man* [1957].) We are merely spectators; we watch.

But in science fiction films, unlike horror films, there is not much horror. Suspense, shocks, surprises are mostly abjured in favor of a steady, inexorable plot. Science fiction films invite a dispassionate, aesthetic view of destruction and violence—a *technological* view. Things, objects, machinery play a major role in these films. A greater range of ethical values is embodied in the décor of these films than in the people. Things, rather than the helpless humans, are the locus of values because we experience them, rather than people, as the sources of power. According to science fiction films, man is naked without his artifacts. *They* stand for different values, they are potent, they are what get destroyed, and they are the indispensable tools for the repulse of the alien invaders or the repair of the damaged environment.

The science fiction films are strongly moralistic. The standard message is the one about the proper, or humane, use of science, versus the mad, obsessional use of science. This message the science fiction films share in common with the classic horror films of the 1930's, like *Frankenstein, The Mummy, Island of Lost Souls, Dr. Jekyll and Mr. Hyde.* (Georges Franju's brilliant *Les Yeux Sans Visage* [1959], called here *The Horror Chamber of Doctor Faustus*, is a more recent example.) In the horror films, we have the mad or obsessed or misguided scientist who pursues his experiments against good advice to the contrary, creates a monster or monsters, and is himself destroyed—often recognizing his folly

himself, and dying in the successful effort to destroy his own creation. One science fiction equivalent of this is the scientist, usually a member of a team, who defects to the planetary invaders because "their" science is more advanced than "ours."

This is the case in *The Mysterians*, and, true to form, the renegade sees his error in the end, and from within the Mysterian space ship destroys it and himself. In *This Island Earth* (1955), the inhabitants of the beleaguered planet Metaluna propose to conquer earth, but their project is foiled by a Metalunan scientist named Exeter who, having lived on earth a while and learned to love Mozart, cannot abide such viciousness. Exeter plunges his spaceship into the ocean after returning a glamorous pair (male and female) of American physicists to earth. Metaluna dies. In *The Fly* (1958), the hero, engrossed in his basement-laboratory experiments on a matter-transmitting machine, uses himself as a subject, exchanges head and one arm with a housefly which had accidentally gotten into the machine, becomes a monster, and with his last shred of human will destroys his laboratory and orders his wife to kill him. His discovery, for the good of mankind, is lost.

Being a clearly labeled species of intellectual, scientists in science fiction films are always liable to crack up or go off the deep end. In *Conquest of Space* (1955), the scientist-commander of an international expedition to Mars suddenly acquires scruples about the blasphemy involved in the undertaking, and begins reading the Bible mid-journey instead of attending to his duties. The commander's son, who is his junior officer and always addresses his father as "General," is forced to kill the old man when he tries to prevent the ship from landing on Mars. In this film, both sides of the ambivalence towards scientists are given voice. Generally, for a scientific enterprise to be treated entirely sympathetically in these films, it needs the certificate of utility. Science, viewed without ambivalence, means an efficacious response to danger. Disinterested intellectual curiosity rarely appears in any form other than caricature, as a maniacal dementia that cuts one off from normal human relations. But this suspicion is usually directed at the scientist rather than his work. The creative scientist may become a martyr to his own discovery, through an accident or by pushing things too far. But the implication remains that other men, less imaginative—in short, technicians—could have administered the same discovery better and more safely. The most ingrained contemporary mistrust of the intellect is visited, in these movies, upon the scientist-as-intellectual.

The message that the scientist is one who releases forces which, if not controlled for good, could destroy man himself seems innocuous enough. One of the oldest images of the scientist is Shakespeare's Prospero, the overdetached scholar forcibly retired from society to a desert island, only partly in control of the magic forces in which he dabbles. Equally classic is the figure of the scientist as satanist (*Doctor Faustus*, and stories of Poe and Hawthorne). Science is magic, and man has always known that there is black magic as well as white. But it is not enough to remark that contemporary attitudes—as reflected in science fiction films—remain ambivalent, that the scientist is treated as both satanist and savior. The proportions have changed, because of the new context in which the old admiration and fear of the scientist are located. For his sphere of influence is no longer local, himself or his immediate community. It is planetary, cosmic.

One gets the feeling, particularly in the Japanese films but not only there, that a mass trauma exists over the use of nuclear weapons and the possibility of future nuclear wars. Most of the science fiction films bear witness to this trauma, and, in a way, attempt to exorcise it.

The accidental awakening of the superdestructive monster who has slept in the earth since prehistory is, often, an obvious metaphor for the Bomb. But there are many explicit references as well. In *The Mysterians*, a probe ship from the planet Mysteroid has landed on earth, near Tokyo. Nuclear warfare having been practiced on Mysteroid for centuries (their civilization is "more advanced than ours"), ninety percent of those now born on the planet have to be destroyed at birth, because of defects caused by the huge amounts of Strontium 90 in their diet. The Mysterians have come to earth to marry earth women, and possibly to take over our relatively uncontaminated planet. …In *The Incredible Shrinking Man*, the John Doe hero is the victim of a gust of radiation which blows over the water, while he is out boating with his wife; the radiation causes him to grow smaller and smaller, until at the end of the movie he steps through the fine mesh of a window screen to become "the infinitely small." …In *Rodan*, a horde of monstrous carnivorous prehistoric insects, and finally a pair of giant flying reptiles (the prehistoric Archeopteryx), are hatched from dormant eggs in the depths of a mine shaft by the impact of nuclear test explosions, and go on to destroy a good part of the world before they are felled by the molten lava of a volcanic eruption…. In the English film, *The Day the Earth Caught Fire*, two simultaneous hydrogen bomb tests by the United States and Russia change by eleven degrees the tilt of the earth on its axis and alter the earth's orbit so that it begins to approach the sun.

Radiation casualties—ultimately, the conception of the whole world as a casualty of nuclear testing and nuclear warfare—is the most ominous of all the notions with which science fiction films deal. Universes become expendable. Worlds become contaminated, burnt out, exhausted, obsolete. In *Rocketship X-M* (1950) explorers from the earth land on Mars, where they learn that atomic warfare has destroyed Martian civilization. In George Pal's *The War of the Worlds* (1953), reddish spindly alligator-skinned creatures from Mars invade the earth because their planet is becoming too cold to be inhabitable. In *This Island Earth*, also American, the planet Metaluna, whose population has long ago been driven underground by warfare, is dying under the missile attacks of an enemy planet. Stocks of uranium, which power the force field shielding Metaluna, have been used up; and an unsuccessful expedition is sent to earth to enlist earth scientists to devise new sources for nuclear power. In Joseph Losey's *The Damned* (1961), nine icy-cold radioactive children are being reared by a fanatical scientist in a dark cave on the English coast to be the only survivors of the inevitable nuclear Armageddon.

There is a vast amount of wishful thinking in science fiction films, some of it touching, some of it depressing. Again and again, one detects the hunger for a "good war," which poses no moral problems, admits of no moral qualifications. The imagery of science fiction films will satisfy the most bellicose addict of war films, for a lot of the satisfactions of war films pass, untransformed, into science fiction films. Examples: the dogfights between earth "fighter rockets" and alien spacecraft in the *Battle in Outer Space* (1960); the escalating firepower in the successive assaults upon the invaders in *The Mysterians*, which Dan Talbot correctly described as a non-stop holocaust; the spectacular bombardment of the underground fortress of Metaluna in *This Island Earth*.

Yet at the same time the bellicosity of science fiction films is neatly channeled into the yearning for peace, or for at least peaceful coexistence. Some scientist generally takes sentи́tious note of the fact that it took the planetary invasion to make the warring nations of the earth come to their senses and suspend their own conflicts. One of the main themes of many science fiction films—the color ones usually, because they have the budget and resources to develop the military spectacle—is this UN fantasy, a fantasy of united warfare. (The same wishful UN theme cropped up in a recent spectacular which is not science fiction, *Fifty-Five Days in Peking* [1963]. There, topically enough, the Chinese, the Boxers, play the role of Martian invaders who unite the earthmen, in this case the United States,

England, Russia, France, Germany, Italy, and Japan.) A great enough disaster cancels all enmities and calls upon the utmost concentration of earth resources.

Science—technology—is conceived of as the great unifier. Thus the science fiction films also project a Utopian fantasy. In the classic models of Utopian thinking—Plato's *Republic*, Campanella's *City of the Sun*, More's *Utopia*, Swift's land of the Houyhnhnms, Voltaire's Eldorado—society had worked out a perfect consensus. In these societies reasonableness had achieved an unbreakable supremacy over the emotions. Since no disagreement or social conflict was intellectually plausible, none was possible. As in Melville's *Typee*, "they all think the same." The universal rule of reason meant universal agreement. It is interesting, too, that societies in which reason was pictured as totally ascendant were also traditionally pictured as having an ascetic or materially frugal and economically simple mode of life. But in the Utopian world community projected by science fiction films, totally pacified and ruled by scientific consensus, the demand for simplicity of material existence would be absurd.

Yet alongside the hopeful fantasy of moral simplification and international unity embodied in the science fiction films lurk the deepest anxieties about contemporary existence. I don't mean only the very real trauma of the Bomb—that it has been used, that there are enough now to kill everyone on earth many times over, that those new bombs may very well be used. Besides these new anxieties about physical disaster, the prospect of universal mutilation and even annihilation, the science fiction films reflect powerful anxieties about the condition of the individual psyche.

For science fiction films may also be described as a popular mythology for the contemporary *negative* imagination about the impersonal. The other-world creatures that seek to take "us" over are an "it," not a "they." The planetary invaders are usually zombielike. Their movements are either cool, mechanical, or lumbering, blobby. But it amounts to the same thing. If they are non-human in form, they proceed with an absolutely regular, unalterable movement (unalterable save by destruction). If they are human in form—dressed in space suits, etc.— then they obey the most rigid military discipline, and display no personal characteristics whatsoever. And it is this regime of emotionlessness, of impersonality, of regimentation, which they will impose on the earth if they are successful. "No more love, no more beauty, no more pain," boasts a converted earthling in *The Invasion of the Body Snatchers* (1956). The half-earthling, half-alien children in *The Children of the Damned* (1960) are absolutely emotionless, move as a group and understand each other's thoughts, and are all prodigious intellects. They are the wave of the future, man in his next stage of development.

These alien invaders practice a crime which is worse than murder. They do not simply kill the person. They obliterate him. In *The War of the Worlds*, the ray which issues from the rocket ship disintegrates all persons and objects in its path, leaving no trace of them but a light ash. In Honda's *The H-Man* (1959), the creeping blob melts all flesh with which it comes in contact. If the blob, which looks like a huge hunk of red Jello and can crawl across floors and up and down walls, so much as touches your bare foot, all that is left of you is a heap of clothes on the floor. (A more articulated, size-multiplying blob is the villain in the English film *The Creeping Unknown* [1956].) In another version of this fantasy, the body is preserved but the person is entirely reconstituted as the automatized servant or agent of the alien powers. This is, of course, the vampire fantasy in new dress. The person is really dead, but he doesn't know it. He is "undead," he has become an "unperson." It happens to a whole California town in *The Invasion of the Body Snatchers*, to several earth scientists in *This Island Earth*, and to assorted innocents in *It Came From Outer Space, Attack of the Puppet People* (1958), and *The Brain Eaters*

(1958). As the victim always backs away from the vampire's horrifying embrace, so in science fiction films the person always fights being "taken over"; he wants to retain his humanity. But once the deed has been done, the victim is eminently satisfied with his condition. He has not been converted from human amiability to monstrous "animal" bloodlust (a metaphoric exaggeration of sexual desire), as in the old vampire fantasy. No, he has simply become far more efficient—the very model of technocratic man, purged of emotions, volitionless, tranquil, obedient to all orders. (The dark secret behind human nature used to be the upsurge of the animal—as in *King Kong*. The threat to man, his availability to dehumanization, lay in his own animality. Now the danger is understood as residing in man's ability to be turned into a machine.)

The rule, of course, is that this horrible and irremediable form of murder can strike anyone in the film except the hero. The hero and his family, while greatly threatened, always escape this fate and by the end of the film the invaders have been repulsed or destroyed. I know of only one exception, *The Day That Mars Invaded Earth* (1963), in which after all the standard struggles the scientist-hero, his wife, and their two children are "taken over" by the alien invaders —and that's that. (The last minutes of the film show them being incinerated by the Martians' rays and their ash silhouettes flushed down their empty swimming pool, while their simulacra drive off in the family car.) Another variant but upbeat switch on the rule occurs in *The Creation of the Humanoids* (1964), where the hero discovers at the end of the film that he, too, has been turned into a metal robot, complete with highly efficient and virtually indestructible mechanical insides, although he didn't know it and detected no difference in himself. He learns, however, that he will shortly be upgraded into a "humanoid" having all the properties of a real man.

Of all the standard motifs of science fiction films, this theme of dehumanization is perhaps the most fascinating. For, as I have indicated, it is scarcely a black-and-white situation, as in the old vampire films. The attitude of the science fiction films toward depersonalization is mixed. On the one hand, they deplore it as the ultimate horror. On the other hand, certain characteristics of the dehumanized invaders, modulated and disguised—such as the ascendancy of reason over feelings, the idealization of teamwork and the consensus-creating activities of science, a marked degree of moral simplification—are precisely traits of the savior-scientist. It is interesting that when the scientist in these films is treated negatively, it is usually done through the portrayal of an individual scientist who holes up in his laboratory and neglects his fiancée or his loving wife and children, obsessed by his daring and dangerous experiments. The scientist as a loyal member of a team, and therefore considerably less individualized, is treated quite respectfully.

There is absolutely no social criticism, of even the most implicit kind, in science fiction films. No criticism, for example, of the conditions of our society which create the impersonality and dehumanization which science fiction fantasies displace onto the influence of an alien It. Also, the notion of science as a social activity, interlocking with social and political interests, is unacknowledged. Science is simply either adventure (for good or evil) or a technical response to danger. And, typically, when the fear of science is paramount—when science is conceived of as black magic rather than white—the evil has no attribution beyond that of the perverse will of an individual scientist. In science fiction films the antithesis of black magic and white is drawn as a split between technology, which is beneficent, and the errant individual will of a lone intellectual.

Thus, science fiction films can be looked at as thematically central allegory, replete with standard modern attitudes. The theme of depersonalization (being "taken over") which I have been talking about is a new allegory reflecting the age-old awareness of man that, sane, he is always perilously close to insanity and

unreason. But there is something more here than just a recent, popular image which expresses man's perennial, but largely unconscious, anxiety about his sanity. The image derives most of its power from a supplementary and historical anxiety, also not experienced *consciously* by most people, about the depersonalizing conditions of modern urban life. Similarly, it is not enough to note that science fiction allegories are one of the new myths about— that is, one of the ways of accommodating to and negating—the perennial human anxiety about death. (Myths of heaven and hell, and of ghosts, had the same function.) For, again, there is a historically specifiable twist which intensifies the anxiety. I mean, the trauma suffered by everyone in the middle of the twentieth century when it became clear that, from now on to the end of human history, every person would spend his individual life under the threat not only of individual death, which is certain, but of something almost insupportable psychologically—collective incineration and extinction which could come at any time, virtually without warning.

From a psychological point of view, the imagination of disaster does not greatly differ from one period in history to another. But from a political and moral point of view, it does. The expectation of the apocalypse may be the occasion for a radical disaffiliation from society, as when thousands of Eastern European Jews in the seventeenth century, hearing that Sabbatai Zevi had been proclaimed the Messiah and that the end of the world was imminent, gave up their homes and businesses and began the trek to Palestine. But people take the news of their doom in diverse ways. It is reported that in 1945 the populace of Berlin received without great agitation the news that Hitler had decided to kill them all, before the Allies arrived, because they had not been worthy enough to win the war. We are, alas, more in the position of the Berliners of 1945 than of the Jews of seventeenth-century Eastern Europe; and our response is closer to theirs, too. What I am suggesting is that the imagery of disaster in science fiction is above all the emblem of an *inadequate response*. I don't mean to bear down on the films for this. They themselves are only a sampling, stripped of sophistication, of the inadequacy of most people's response to the unassimilable terrors that infect their consciousness. The interest of the films, aside from their considerable amount of cinematic charm, consists in this intersection between a naive and largely debased commercial art product and the most profound dilemmas of the contemporary situation.

Ours is indeed an age of extremity. For we live under continual threat of two equally fearful, but seemingly opposed, destinies: unremitting banality and inconceivable terror. It is fantasy, served out in large rations by the popular arts, which allows most people to cope with these twin specters. For one job that fantasy can do is to lift us out of the unbearably humdrum and to distract us from terrors—real or anticipated—by an escape into exotic, dangerous situations which have last-minute happy endings. But another of the things that fantasy can do is normalize what is psychologically unbearable, thereby inuring us to it. In one case, fantasy beautifies the world. In the other, it neutralizes it.

The fantasy in science fiction films does both jobs. The films reflect world-wide anxieties, and they serve to allay them. They inculcate a strange apathy concerning the processes of radiation, contamination, and destruction which I for one find haunting and depressing. The naïve level of the films neatly tempers the sense of otherness, of alien-ness, with the grossly familiar. In particular, the dialogue of most science fiction films, which is of a monumental but often touching banality, makes them wonderfully, unintentionally funny. Lines like "Come quickly, there's a monster in my bathtub," "We must do something about this," "Wait, Professor. There's someone on the telephone," "But that's incredible," and the old American stand-by, "I hope it works!" are

hilarious in the context of picturesque and deafening holocaust. Yet the films also contain something that is painful and in deadly earnest.

There is a sense in which all these movies are in complicity with the abhorrent. They neutralize it, as I have said. It is no more, perhaps, than the way all art draws its audience into a circle of complicity with the thing represented. But in these films we have to do with things which are (quite literally) unthinkable. Here, "thinking about the unthinkable"—not in the way of Herman Kahn, as a subject for calculation, but as a subject for fantasy—becomes, however inadvertently, itself a somewhat questionable act from a moral point of view. The films perpetuate clichés about identity, volition, power, knowledge, happiness, social consensus, guilt, responsibility which are, to say the least, not serviceable in our present extremity. But collective nightmares cannot be banished by demonstrating that they are, intellectually and morally, fallacious. This nightmare—the one reflected, in various registers, in the science fiction films—is too close to our reality.

ROBERT PENN WARREN

The Negro Now

Somewhere back in the minds of many people, is an image of *the* Negro leader—a glare-eyed robot propelled by a merciless mechanism, stalking forward over the smiling landscape, where good, clean American citizens (including well-adjusted Negroes) go happily about their constructive business. Many of us who are

THE NEGRO NOW: © 1965 by Robert Penn Warren. An expanded version of this article appears in *Who Speaks for the Negro*, by Robert Penn Warren. Reprinted by permission of Random House, Inc. Originally printed in *Look* (March 23, 1965).

white—in our moments of stereotype and cartoon thinking—share that vision. In those moments, we do not realize that there is, in one sense, no Negro leader. There are, merely, a number of Negroes who happen to occupy positions of leadership.

And a number of those Negroes, some of the best advertised, did not seek such positions. Neither their training nor temperament nor aspirations had seemed to point in that direction. James Forman of the Student Nonviolent Coordinating Committee (Snick), who wanted to be a novelist, said to me he wished he could be talking about something other than the Negro Revolution—he wished the whole thing were over. The young Martin Luther King, Jr., with the beribboned sheepskin, proclaiming his new doctorate, to hang on the wall of his study in his first parsonage, could not have foreseen the Montgomery Improvement Association, *Time's* cover and the Nobel Peace Prize. The whirl of history created a vacuum, and they were sucked in.

Some of them have, indeed, found in leadership a natural fulfillment. Here, the unsuspected talent and the unsuspected self have blossomed, and it is no crime for a man to feel at home with, and take pleasure in, what he can do well. Nor is it necessarily a crime to seek leadership. The will to power, grisly as it appears in certain lights, can mate, if uneasily, with love of justice and dedicated selflessness. Even in the bloody infighting among Negro leaders, more may be at stake than organizational aggrandizement or personal vanity; principles and policies may be involved too.

One should not be more appalled by complications among Negroes than by those among white people. Regardless of complexion, social movements are always powerful magnets for self-anointed prophets, spiritual DP's and deviants, sufferers from footless ambition, masochists, bloodlusters and common pilferers from the poor box; and it should be no wonder that the Negro Revolution has attracted some. What is remarkable is that it has attracted so few—or that so few have risen to the threshold of public mention.

In general, the Negro leadership has given the public little reason to be appalled, for in a situation as complicated as this, it would not be easy to imagine a higher level of idealism, dedication and realistic intelligence. If leadership of that quality is supplanted by other, less savory types that are already lurking in the wings, and that certainly do not have any vision of a reconciled society, the white man has only himself to blame. Mayor Robert F. Wagner had only himself to blame if his European vacation, in the summer of 1964, was cut short by riots in Harlem and Bedford-Stuyvesant; everybody knew there would be riots (except perhaps the Mayor), and everything he did afterwards by way of appeasement or amelioration could have been done beforehand and as part of a program that would have inspired the Negro community to some hope and confidence. Then, if there had been disorders, the issues would have been looters and not liberty-looters.

If now in Mississippi—with no convictions for the Neshoba County killings of the three civil-rights workers—terrorist organizations, like the Russian nihilists or the Stern Gang of Palestine, emerge among Negroes, then white people must, at one level, assume themselves responsible. Romantic, ruinous and desperate gestures are implicit in the situation. In reference to such a gang of "dedicated retaliators," the Rev. Milton Galamison, leader of the New York school boycott, says: "I refuse to advocate violence as a principle, but almost all oppressed people have had such a group that will retaliate in kind, and this might serve some kind of purpose in bringing about a swifter resolution of a problem that exists." How delicately Galamison balances the matter!

Whitney Young, Jr., of the National Urban League is right when he says that the leaders need victories in order to contain the danger of over-reach and to forestall violence; they need something solid and negotiable in the Negro power market. If, in the summer of 1964, they had had something a little more solid and negotiable, James Farmer of CORE and John Lewis of Snick perhaps could have strung along with Roy Wilkins of NAACP and the others in proclaiming a preelection moratorium on demonstrations. It seems that Farmer, in the spring of 1964, following a policy of sweet reason, had put himself on the defensive in repudiating the World's Fair stall-ins; so, at the time of the summer riots and after, he had to insist on a stance of militancy or feel the jerk as the wild boys snatched the rug out from under his feet. If Farmer found himself forced to adopt the new stance, the white people helped force him. They had given little reason for the Negro to believe that they would surrender anything except under pressure. As Galamison put it, there was the fear that LBJ would go Right if he thought he had "the Negro people in his vest pocket."

Negro leaders have, we can be quite certain, a sense of power, and they are willing to apply it when and where it pinches. For power is the key. What the Negro hasn't the power to get, he won't get. But power—as both Negroes and whites need to remember—may operate in more than one dimension. A number of Negroes, feeling the new headiness of power and not bothering to reflect deeply on the dimensions in which it may operate, think of a physical showdown in the streets as their big threat. According to the survey in *The Negro Revolution in America*, by William Brink and Louis Harris, some fifty-two per cent of all Negroes think that if things came to gut-fighting, the Negro would win, and in the Northern slums, the percentage is higher. But among the leaders, the survey can discover only twenty-nine per cent who feel that, in a showdown, the Negroes would win; and I am certain that almost all of that twenty-nine per cent would be leaders in very low echelons. The leadership, aside from any theological or moral convictions about non-violence, is realistic. As the Rev. Ralph Abernathy of SCLC summed it up, "The white folks have more guns." And he might have added that they have more votes, more money and more education.

Power in the absolute sense—even in the showdown short of gunpoint—is out for the Negro. Negro leadership is concerned with *relative* power, and the art of picking the spot where a little pinch will hurt a lot. For instance, in 1948, the Negro vote was significant, but in 1960, it elected a President. A Negro boycott might not do decisive damage to a Cadillac agency in Atlanta (and then, again, it might), but would certainly bring howling to his knees a distributor of malt beverages in that city. The art is in locating the vulnerable point, and there are many kinds of vulnerability.

There is another aspect to the art of applying relative power. A man may say that he is a hardcore segregationist. But how hard is that core? Is it as hard as his love for, or need of, money? As his desire to have his children educated? As his preference for social order? As his wish to be considered respectable? As his simple inclination to stay out of jail? The only real hard-core segrationist is one whose feeling about Negroes takes precedence over all other feelings mobilized in a given situation. For instance, the feeling for segregation among the parents of Prince Edward County, Va., took precedence over their desire for education for their children. But when parents in some other Southern communities—such as Jackson, Miss. —band together to keep the schools open despite integration, though it is probable that those same parents would prefer to have the schools segregated, their desire to have a school takes precedence over the desire for segregation. In all sorts of subtle and shifting combinations, the Negro leadership is committed to playing a most complicated tune on the strings of white desires and convictions.

And the string the harpist touches most often, sometimes lightly, sometimes with an authoritative *whang*, is the white man's desire to be a just man. For few men are willing to say: "I am unjust."

To state it differently: by and large, the Negro

leadership is concerned with relative power. There is one kind of power Negro leaders feel they have that is not relative. It is moral power. For by the white man's own professed standards, the Negro is in the right.

It is clear to the Negro leaders that drift would doom the Revolution to a dwindling failure or a bloodbath. The floundering consequent upon such a lack of philosophy would deflate one of the proudest boasts of the New Negro—that he, for once, can set the terms on which the question of his fate will be treated. Furthermore, the floundering of the Negro leadership would invite, in the white reaction, similar floundering, similarly disastrous. And, perhaps worst of all, the lack of a philosophy would invite the adventurer to try his hand. But what is to prevent drift or confusion?

We must recognize that the option does not lie between drift and confusion on one hand and an ironbound, brass-studded orthodoxy on the other. Fortunately, a number of Negroes in key, or influential, positions are men of intellectual power and depth of purpose, and these men have put their minds on these problems. This is not to say that one man puts his mind on all the problems, but the thinking of one man supplements that of another. What is important in this *communal* effort is not the quick whipping up of an orthodoxy, but the envisagement of a number of possibilities, options, relations and consequences to be intellectually analyzed and imaginatively explored.

There may be, and sometimes obviously are, violent disagreements on general policy or on particular programs of action. In fact, there is always the possibility of a fundamental split in leadership, with the resultant danger of violence as some fragment of the movement spins out of control, as in the murder of Black Nationalist Malcolm X. But as long as even the characteristically uneasy cooperation prevails, centripetal force will probably continue to balance the centrifugal, and the communal effort will continue to mean that choices of action do not have to be made blind. Whatever choices may be made, the purpose is presumably to bring the Negro into full and responsible participation in American society—that is, to achieve integration. But what is integration? For some, integration is rhetoric; for some, it is lines on a school map; for some, it is a quota in a Federally subsidized housing project; for some, it is FEPC. It is, in one sense, all of these things, but at the same time, it is none. It is, ideally considered, the state of mind, the condition of the soul, in which human recognition and appreciation would be mutually possible for us all, black and white.

In speaking of a state of mind and a condition of the soul, I am not complacently repeating President Dwight D. Eisenhower's notion that "you cannot change people's hearts by law." To say that a certain condition of heart must generally and ideally prevail before a social change can occur is to say that no social change can ever come except in the sweet by-and-by. We know from history that you do not achieve an ideal spiritual condition, and then set up a society to express it. Ideals grow out of the act of living, out of the logic of life; and in a long dialectic, even as they grow, they modify living. And so, for all practical purposes, we may think of integration as that process by which we exercise our will to realize and explore, individually and institutionally, that ideal of mutual human recognition and appreciation. If we take this approach, we render irrelevant all the debate about race—whether it is "real" or merely a "superstition." And in doing so, we even undercut the argument, so dear to so many liberals, that the Negro is only, as the historian Kenneth Stampp argues, a white man with a black face. For we are assuming that *if* he is more than that, he may even be more interesting. For if there is a human community to be "recognized," there are also human differences to be "appreciated" —and sometimes, we may add, criticized.

Negro leadership is inevitably concerned with trying to define the crucial points and predict and control institutional development in that process of integration. But since the process of integration is part of the process by which a free society evolves, it is very hard to predict particular arrangements. By its very definition, a free society is one in which there is a maximum range for all people in the expression of taste and preference, and it is very hard to predetermine what, under shifting circumstances, people will want.

Let us assume a time when all desirable legal, economic and social reforms have been accomplished, and there is a reasonable sincerity in white acceptance of them. Now, in that free society of civil rights, fair employment, welcoming suburbs, general prosperity and brotherly love, who has the slightest notion how many Negroes might perversely choose to live in their own communities—James Farmer and Ruth Turner of CORE predict many would—and how many would bleed off into the prevailing white society? There may be, of course, some doctrinaire bureaucrat skulking in the bushes who thinks he can plan it all out and, at benign gunpoint, make Negroes eat cake—i.e., move to Scarsdale, N.Y. But it is doubtful that, in that happy time to come, he could swing it if the Negroes didn't really want that kind of cake.

Some Negro leaders do, no doubt, want to make Negroes eat cake, but it would seem that the great majority of them merely defend the right of a Negro to eat whatever he wants, or will, under new circumstances, want—even turnip greens and hog jowl. Ruth Turner, and others, have observed that once the barriers are down, the human need to "prove" certain things tends to disappear. With freedom, a man doesn't have to think he wants to live in a certain place merely because he is not permitted to. As the novelist Ralph Ellison says: "When the political structure changes and desegregation is achieved, it will be easily seen where Negroes were stopped by law and where they would have stopped anyway, because of income and their own preference—a matter of taste."

If Negroes can't predict as simple a thing as where they might want to live, think of the difficulty in imagining what integration in its deeper aspects might mean.

The word "integration" refers to a shifting, shadowy mass of interfusing possibilities. It refers, in short, to the future. Here, not only the unpredictability of the future is involved, but the fact that among Negroes—among Negro leaders—there is no commonly held vision of what they want the future to be.

Whatever integration may come to mean, it will mean a great change; and change, however deeply willed, is always shocking; old stances and accommodations, like the twinge of an old wound, are part of the self, and even as we desire new life and more life, we must realize that a part of us—of each individual person, black or white—has to *die* into that new life. And there is, of course, the unappeasable resentment that many Negroes must carry, and the suspicion of anything white—sometimes compounded because there is a chic of anger and an imperative of suspicion. I remember a pretty young woman who would not eat with her white guests. Her husband said to me later, "It's funny about my wife. The way she is. She just doesn't like to be around white people."

Many Negro leaders—more and more of them—are becoming aware of the fundamental need for an act of imagination to deal as systematically as possible with that fog of contingency that is the future. For many know that if you do not try to feel into, predict and examine the possibilities of the future, you will become the victim of the future.

Judge William Hastie of the U.S. Circuit Court of Appeals points out that the leader of any movement must play a double game: "One of the great problems of leadership is that, though ideas be oversimplified in the minds of people, the leadership with more sophisticated thinking attempts to adjust itself to the total need, viewed in a sophisticated way." In other words, the leader must be able to shout the slogan—but he must know its meaning at a level very different from that at which it starts the squirt of adrenalin in the bloodstream of the good foot soldier.

While moving through the hot dust or black

mire of a backcountry road in Mississippi, Robert Moses of Snick tries "to see ahead to what the shape of this country will look like in ten years." He gets lost, he says, but he tries to see.

There is another question of means and ends that is acutely important for Negro leadership. A free society, one in which there is a range of choice for the individual, is the minimal aim of the Revolution. But it is clear that a certain amount of force is required to create the context for this freedom.

It is all too easy to call for force; it is sometime hard to know how to pick up the pieces afterwards. Some years ago, in the course of a conversation about the 1954 Supreme Court school-desegregation decision, Carl Rowan, the journalist who became head of the United States Information Agency, said to me that "bayonets are very educational." They are. They were used with marked educational effect in Little Rock and Oxford, and I cannot see that Presidents Eisenhower and Kennedy had any choice, for the duty of the Government is to govern. But I should doubt that Rowan, after his prolonged sojourn in the shifting lights and shadows of the political jungle, would now be as gaily prompted to pick up that particular hickory stick to beat out the tune for education.

In matters outside of education, it is easily understood why the Negro, suspicious or contemptuous of local and state government, turns to Washington for protection and redress. Without Federal intervention, he may not get the vote—or even live out the day; and if it had not been for the FBI, the three bodies would have lain forever under the dam near Philadelphia, Miss., and no arrests would ever have been made. I hazard, in an unlawyerly way, that the Negro Revolution will work some shift in the relation of Washington to state and local authorities, and that may be all to the good. But the appeal to Washington may raise real problems, not merely legalistic ones, about the centralization of power.

The doctrine of states' rights has frequently been used, and is being used, as an alibi and a screen for some very unworthy proceedings—often quite cynically used and only for some special ad hoc advantage, with total contempt for the principle as principle. But the doctrine of states' rights, as it now anachronistically appears, is a very different thing from responsible localism, and we must ask ourselves if we are prepared to inaugurate a system in which such localisms are encouraged to wither—or to have roots cut. One thing is certain: in the concentration of power, there is no guarantee of the virtuous exercise thereof.

There is a need for double vision: force of any kind used for immediate tactical purposes, however worthy, has to be regarded in relation to the freedom being striven for, and the human context in which that freedom is to be exercised. What is now sauce for the goose might someday turn out to be sauce for any number of outraged ganders.

Although on many important questions there is no consensus among Negro leaders, this lack of consensus, of an orthodoxy, should be of cold comfort to the hard-shelled segregationist, for there *are* matters on which Negro leaders *are* in agreement. And these are bedrock matters.

Negro leaders have the will and the strength to demand that they be recognized and respected. As Judge Hastie emphasizes, nothing that the white man can give the Negro is as important as the respect he withholds. And he goes on to say: "As the Negro wins the white man's respect, regardless of fondness or affection, it becomes easier for the two to deal with each other. That respect can no longer be denied."

The Negro leaders are in agreement in their will to face the white man across the table, or across the gun muzzle or hose muzzle, eyeball to eyeball. Behind him, each leader feels the weight of the mass of Negroes who may walk straighter because of what he does. As Dr. King has put it, in *Why We Can't Wait:* "The Revolution of the Negro not only attacked the external cause of his misery, but revealed him to himself. He was *somebody*. He had a sense of *somebodiness*." Dr. King has also written: "The upsurge of power in the civil-rights movement has given it greater maneuverability...to form alliances, to make commitments in exchange for pledges, and if the pledges are not redeemed, it remains powerful enough to walk out...." The Negro leaders are determined that whatever change now comes in the status of the Negro will not come, as in the past, as merely a by-blow of the white man's history.

Some people say that the present success of the Negro's drive for recognition as a citizen of the United States is, again, only a by-blow of the white man's history—that as the war between the North and the South made emancipation possible, so the Cold War, in conjunction with the rise of Africa, makes success possible in the Negro's present endeavor. In one very broad sense, this is true: nothing happens without context. But in another and more significant sense, it is false. History does provide the context in which the Negro's power—a relative power—may be used, but the will to use that power, the method of assembling it and the strategy of its deployment are the work of the Negro himself. It is clear now that the Negro intends to be a maker, not a victim, or, to use Howard Zinn's term, a mere "hitchhiker" of history.

Even those leaders who recognize that the Negro cannot go it alone are agreed on this. They even feel independent of the white money that has, in considerable part, financed the Negro Revolution. And though, as is generally agreed, it would be healthier if there were more Negro money in the pot, it still seems highly improbable that the white hand that holds the purse strings can control policy. It would require a higher-than-usual quotient of paranoia to see here a white plot to control Negro policy. For another thing, the number and variety of Negro organizations and leaders would scarcely permit white control of policy. The logic of the moment prescribes Negro leadership.

The most bedrock of all matters on which

Negro leaders agree is simple: they mean business. They have been to jail, they have been beaten, they have been shot, and they are still in business. And they are in business for the long pull. However loudly in the schizophrenia of leadership they may shout "Freedom Now!" they know that the pull will be long.

Months before the college students began to pour into Mississippi in 1964 to work in the voter-registration drive, Robert Moses told me it would be ten years before the Negroes could elect a single legislator. And Ronnie Moore, a Louisiana civil-rights worker, had counted each change of heart a victory, and such victories add up slowly.

How far has the Negro come in the past decade? The major victories can be listed in a few sentences. A record six million Negroes registered to vote in November, 1964, hundreds of thousands send their children to unsegregated schools, thousands live in unsegregated houses, thousands at least feel that it is worthwhile to apply for jobs once considered automatically closed to them.

But Whitney Young, Jr., reminded me how far the Negro, and the United States, still have to go. According to his statistics, 20 per cent of all Negro workers are unemployed. Family income for Negroes is 53 per cent of white income, and the gap is widening. Of 1,000,000 young people (under 21) who are out of school and out of work, 50 per cent are Negroes. Negroes get three and one-half year's less school than whites. The Negro adult life span is seven years shorter than the white. Negro infant mortality is actually increasing. Unless the situation of the Negro can be relieved, unless he can be drawn productively into the economic mainstream of American life, civil rights become a travesty.

It will be a long pull, and the leaders are willing to face the hard fact. Many of them are even willing to face the harder fact that the iniquity of the white man is not the only reason it will be a long pull. But they can face the long pull because they know they will win. They are riding the tide of history, and they know it.

And part of that tide is their own conviction of strength.

What reaction has the white man had to the Negro Revolution? And on what terms can mere reaction be converted into action?

We cannot discuss this question about the white man in a lump. For the white man is not a lump. To make the simplest relevant division, there is the Southern white man, and the Northern (or non-Southern) white man. They are different from one another, and the difference is a little more than what James Baldwin suggests when he says that the South and the North merely have different ways of castrating you.

As a basis for indicating this difference, we may set up a little formula:

In the South, the Negro is recognized, but his rights are not.
In the North, the rights of the Negro are recognized, but he is not.

But the formula needs a little footnote. If, in the South, as white Southerns like to claim, the Negro is recognized as human, this occurs only when the Negro is in certain roles. If, in the North, the Negro's rights are recognized, they are recognized only in the legal sense; the shadow of a "human right" rarely clouds the picture.

What is the white Southerner ready to concede? He has had a shock. All at once, with little or no preparation, he has been confronted with the fact that what his cook or yard boy or tenant farmer had told him is not true. It is not true that the colored folks invariably just love the white folks. It is not true that the colored folks invariably like it the way it is. It is not true that just a few "bad niggers" are making all the trouble. It is not true that just some "Jew Communists" are making the trouble. A lot of things are not necessarily true. And maybe, even, never were.

If the white Southerner is a book-reading man, he is in for another shock when he finds out that certain things he had been taught in school

as gospel aren't true either. These things include some very important bits of anthropology, psychology and history—even Southern history, particularly of the Reconstruction. It is a shock, too, to discover that a high percentage of the faculties of Southern colleges (including, even after massive diaspora, a number at Oxford, Miss.) don't believe in segregation, that one professor of unimpeachably Southern origin, C. Vann Woodward, is the author of a book called *The Strange Career of Jim Crow*, and that a professor of "Ole Miss," a past president of the Southern Historical Association and, incidentally, a friend of Dr. Aaron Henry of NAACP, wrote a book called *Mississippi: The Closed Society*. It is a shock to discover that eleven members of the faculty of the Divinity School of Vanderbilt University resigned when a Negro student organizing the Nashville sit-ins was expelled, or that Ralph (better known in the States' Rights party and Citizens Council as "Rastus") McGill of the Atlanta *Constitution* got a Medal of Freedom from the hands of Lyndon Johnson (another Southerner of dubious inclinations).

It is a shock to realize that in Marietta, Ga., the biggest single airplane factory in the world employs high-placed Negro engineers, mathematicians and technicians, and, more horrendously, Negro foremen bossing white workers; that an Arkansas bank president is willing to hire Negro tellers because, as he puts it, "It's coming." It is a shock to realize that the Memphis *Press-Scimitar* strongly supported the civil-rights bill. Or to read an editorial in the student paper of Vanderbilt University rebuking the dean of women for trying to ease out a co-ed who had allowed herself to be kissed good-night by a Negro student (not a Vandy man) at the dormitory door:

"In dating the Negro, the co-ed was violating no rule of this University. Any rule forbidding such conduct would be incompatible with the tenets of the institution, which prides itself as being a center of tolerance for diverging behavior, so long as the behavior violates no valid, legal or moral rule. That is why we see Dean ———'s behind-the-scenes enforcement of a regional social norm as placing the University in a somewhat hypocritical stance. If there are any man-made institutions that still can afford to respect integrity of principle, it seems that a university should make the greatest effort."

Such items are even more shocking to many white Southerners than the discovery that Michael Schwerner, Andrew Goodman and James E. Chaney had really been butchered and buried under the dam, and had not run off and hidden just to get publicity, as Neshoba County Sheriff L. A. Rainey had chosen to believe. The discovery of the corpses under the dam is not as shocking because, deep down and unacknowledged in his guts, the Southerner knows that that event, evil as it is, is implicit in the structure of the society in which he lives.

The other discoveries are not, he had thought, implicit in his society. Therefore, he is shocked. It is not evil that shocks, it is the unexpected.

Long before these recent shocks, the white Southerner, in one dimension of his being, had harbored the scarcely specified memory of a gallantly defeated nationalism, and had felt himself part of a culture waning sadly before the dominant American ethos. Now, when the world, which even in its decay had seemed stable, begins to crack, he is shaken to the core. He is then inclined to strike back blindly.

With the white Southerner, the striking back has a special desperation, for, in a way, he strikes at the part of himself that has sold out, that is the household traitor, that lusts after the gauds and gewgaws of high-powered Yankee-dom. He is killing his bad self, and suddenly stands clean in the good self, guilt washed away—by somebody else's blood. The mystical, compulsive thing comes out over and over: I have had a dozen Southerners involved in the "resistance" tell me they didn't expect to win, they "just somehow had to do it."

So, if the Negro is experiencing a "crisis of identity," the white Southerner is too. And now

and then, we get hints of some sort of mutual recognition of the fact. The jailer in Jackson, Miss., comes down to tell Stokeley Carmichael of Snick good-bye, and clasps the steel bar and weeps and tries to explain what is happening to him. He wants to be understood. And in some sort of recognition springing from his own plight, he knows that the Negroes are "sincere," that they have to do what they have to do. And the same thing appears with the sheriff of Canton, who, as Robert Moses reports, said to several Negro Snick workers: "Well, you are fighting for what you believe is right, and you're going to fight. And we are fighting for what we believe is right, and we're going to fight also." Here and elsewhere, we find the sense of both the Southern white man and the Negro being caught in the same unspecified thing—acting out a role.

It is easy to say to the Southerner that he should give up his Southern-ness and just be a good American. It is easy to say to the Negro that he should give up his Negro-ness and just be a good American—in incidental black face. Negroes and white Southerners do, in fact, want to be Americans, but by and large, they want to be themselves too; and the fact that both belong to minorities means that both may cling defensively to what they are, or what they take themselves to be. They may refuse to be totally devalued, gutted and scraped before being flung into the melting pot. But that is one solution, and some Negroes and white Southerners, in self-hatred or in self-seeking, accept it; they "pass."

It is not the only solution. For the Southerner, a much more significant and healthy solution is to inspect what his Southern-ness really means. If he chose to dip into the history of his South, he would find that it is a very complicated thing; that the orthodoxy of slavery (for which, in later times, read "segregation" as the emotional equivalent) was a very late growth, and did not number among its adherents many a man who gallantly wore the sacred gray, among them Robert E. Lee; that Charleston, S.C.—in fact, the whole Confederacy—between

1861 and 1865 was more tolerant of the dissident than is Mississippi today; that segregation was a latter-day artificial phenomenon that many a Confederate veteran, in his self-certainty, would have found absurd, or perhaps an insult to his own personal liberties.

The modern white Southerner, if he looks a little deeper than the rhetoric of the United Daughters of the Confederacy and the hustings, might decide that being against segregation would not necessarily mean that he is spitting on Grandpa's grave, or is lacking in piety for those who held ranks up Cemetery Ridge on July 3, 1863, or for those who rode with Nathan Bedford Forrest. The white Southerner might realize that human history is a story of the constant revision of values, and that the mastodon frozen in the glacier is not necessarily the creature most worthy of emulation. He might realize that a revision of values was implicit in the very past that commands his piety. He might find many ancestors, spiritual or biological, who would not see eye to eye with Faubus, Wallace, Paul Johnson or Bull Connor. Yes, the white Southerner might find some ancestors who, were they alive, would not agree with the current heroes of Klan or Council, and would not be afraid to say so. That fact might even give the present-day Southerner the courage to say that he, too, disagrees.

Discovering his past, the Southerner might find himself, and the courage to be himself. He might free himself from a stereotype that does violence to some of his own deeply cherished values and to the complexity of his history. He might realize that the obscene caricatures of humanity who have made Philadelphia, Miss., newsworthy are scarcely the finest flower of Southern chivalry or the most judicious arbiters of the Southern tradition. He might rediscover the strong and cantankerous brand of democratic temper that is part of his heritage—and then reapply it. He might begin the reapplication by insisting on his right to reject the ready-made attitudes of the local press or the local politico or the local bully boys, and to seek facts and make judgments for himself.

The Yankee, like the white Southerner, has been in for a shock. He has lived in his dream world too. I have heard many a Yankee say of Negroes, "Who do they think they are?" Or: "They've got every chance anybody has if they'd just get off relief." Or: "Look at the way they're acting, after all we've done for them up here." However little he likes the fact, the white man on the commuter train to Westchester has had to lift his eyes from the *Wall Street Journal*, to paraphrase Whitney Young, Jr., and look up the streets of Harlem. Or Harlem has come busting into his living room to dominate the TV screen. The Yankee white man, at last, has had to recognize the Negro as a human being, sometimes a rather appalling human being. And he has had to realize that the legal rights he had so complacently regarded all these years as his largess to the Negro hadn't, in themselves, amounted to a hill of beans.

If the Yankee is a liberal—even if he is what is called a "fighting liberal" and has signed statements and sponsored dinners and rung doorbells and made speeches and gone to biracial parties and has a life membership in the NAACP—he is apt to discover that nobody is very grateful to him. Nobody is going to be grateful to him just because he gives a "freedom dance" (discreetly integrated) in Westchester or a "freedom garden party" on Long Island, tickets $100 a couple, and sends the take to help liberate Mississippi. In fact, in regard to Mississippi, he might find it a penitential exercise to ponder a remark by James Farmer, who says that, among Northern supporters, he has observed a slightly greater willingness to give to a project earmarked for Mississippi than for one next door, "for it is always easier to slay cobras in Borneo."

Not only may the Yankee liberal find that gratitude is in short supply; he may find that even the most charitable Negro is apt to regard him as a quaint figure of fun, a curious relic in the body politic like the spleen, without function. The only way he can be sure to regain function, and even then not in all circles, is to go to jail or get his head cracked by the "rosewood"— which is what the cop's stick is called in Harlem. Even then, his function is to play third fiddle and take orders. He is declassed; and this is the worst shock of all.

No, the worst shock for the Yankee is to discover what he, himself, really feels. He has to find out if he really wants a Negro family next door. If he really wants to take orders from a Negro department head. If he really wants to be arrested by a Negro cop. If he really wants to have his children bused into a school in a Negro neighborhood. If he really wants a tax boost for a crash program for the "disadvantaged"—i.e., Negroes. If he really wants his daughter on mixed dates. If he really wants for himself this, that and the other thing that he used to think was just fine for somebody else —usually some degrees of latitude down the social or geographic scale. He is, in fact, not only going to find out what he really wants. He is going to find out what he himself really is.

And if he is a book-reading man, he may find out, too, what his grandfather was. Even if his grandfather was a dyed-in-the-wool, card-carrying Abolitionist who regarded Abraham Lincoln as a minion of slaveocracy and, to quote Wendell Phillips, "the hell-hound of Illinois," he is apt to find out that the old boy— his grandfather—was also a dyed-in-the-wool racist. He is apt to find out that most Northern states then denied Negroes the franchise, and, even after the Civil War, Connecticut, Ohio, Michigan, Minnesota and Kansas voted down proposals for Negro suffrage, and that it wasn't until 1870 that the Fifteenth Amendment was passed; and that in New York City, a Negro couldn't ride the streetcar or attend an unsegregated ward school. He is apt to find out that Reconstruction was a time replete with shame, brutal grabs, ignoble deals on the back stairs and defaulting on high pledges, and that all

this was not south of the Ohio River. He will find out that the noise he heard in his dream was somebody knocking the molasses jug off a very high shelf, and now he has to pick up the pieces, and they are sticky. He has to leave his dream and put reality back together again—the reality of America and himself.

Out of the two different kinds of shock that the Southerner and the Yankee have had, they may now be able to extract recognition of the desperate gravity of the situation. Out of the shock, they both may extract, too, self-discovery. Face to face with the Negro, and recognizing his human reality and the basic justice of his demands, they may now be able to substitute reasoned action for automatic reaction: to the Negro and to each other.

There is one kind of sentimentality that the white man cannot afford: a sentimentality about himself. He cannot afford to feel that he is going to redeem the Negro. For the age of philanthropy is over, and it would be a vicious illusion to think that, if he acts now to resolve the problem, he is giving something away, is being "liberal," or is performing an act of charity, Christian or any other kind. The safest, soberest, most humble and perhaps not the most ignoble way for him to think of grounding his action is, not on generosity, but on a proper awareness of self-interest.

It is self-interest to want to live in a society operating by the love of justice and the concept of law. We have not been living in such a society. It is self-interest to want all members of society to contribute as fully as possible to the enrichment of that society. The structure of our society has prevented that. It is self-interest to seek friends and companions among those whose experience and capacities are congenial with and extend our own. Our society has restricted such a quest. It is self-interest to want to escape from the pressure to conform to values that we feel immoral or antiquated. Our society has maintained such pressures. It is self-interest to want to escape from the burden of vanity into the hard and happy realization that in the diminishment of others, there is a deep diminishment of the self.

It would be sentimentality to think that our society can be changed easily and without pain. It would be worse sentimentality to think that it can be changed without some pain to our particular selves—black and white. It would be realism to think that that pain would be a reasonable price to pay for what we all, selfishly, might get out of it: our own freedom.

Questions for Review

1. Sir James Frazer, author of *The Golden Bough,* from which the essay on the sacrificial slaying of the Corn Goddess is taken, was one of the first "cultural anthropologists" to study the customs of primitive peoples. His "scientific" findings were much admired in their time but are now criticized by some as unscientific folklore or biased hypotheses. Do you find any obvious faults in the data or methods of the essay here? Is Frazer "scientific" as Conant has described the scientific method? Is this essay proven "fact" or an imaginative hypothesis? How can you decide?

2. What is the nature of Frazer's evidence for the reconstruction of the rituals involving the sacrifice of the Corn Goddess? How credible is it? Does Frazer use evidence objectively or does he manipulate it? For what purposes might he wish to manipulate it?

3. How objective (or impersonal) is Frazer in this essay? Is he more or less so than Gamow, Williams, Mangelsdorf, or Petrunkevitch?

4. How would you characterize Frazer's style, diction, and tone? Point out instances of word choice that create his tone and style.

5. Compare and contrast Frazer's interest in corn (or maize) in the Americas with Mangelsdorf's. Is the difference in interest between the two men properly described as "objective' and "subjective"? "Impersonal" and "personal"? "Factual" and "imaginative"?

6. G. K. Chesterton's *Science and the Savages*

makes the point that knowledge about human beings can never be "scientific." How does he prove his point? Does he think the social scientist would be better off by abandoning his "scientific" techniques and relying on "intuition"? By involving himself emotionally with the people he studies? By examining himself instead of other people? Or by forgetting entirely the idea that human beings can be the subjects of systematic study?

7. Chesterton's attack on social science was partially stimulated by Frazer's studies. What in Frazer's essay here would Chesterton appear to be criticizing? Is the criticism justified? Is it just?

8. How objective is Chesterton in his attack on social science? Is he like or unlike Leacock (who attacks physical science) in his motives, attitudes, and method?

9. Is Chesterton, in attacking social "science," really defending some other system of attitudes or methodology? Some personal belief of his own? Would he agree with Leacock that theology and philosophy rank higher than science?

10. History has often been called one of the "social sciences." Are the historical writings on pp. 259–281 above "scientific" in any way or not?

11. Is Hans Zinsser's essay on rats and history a piece of "scientific" investigation and writing (an essay on epidemiology), a specimen of "historiography" (the plague in Athens; the fall of Rome), or neither? Is it more or less scientific than the essay by Gamow and others? How does it compare with the historical writing by Thucydides, Gibbon, and Mrs. Tuchman?

12. What is the most important thing about Zinsser's essay: its "facts" (that is, data); the interpretation of these data; or something else?

13. Compare Zinsser's treatment of the plague with those of Thucydides and Defoe. Compare his view of the decline of Rome with Gibbon's. How do they differ? What is Zinsser really concerned with?

14. Does Zinsser's essay provide greater insight into the nature of rats, of men, or of history?

15. Like William James, Eric Berne is greatly interested in how people think and feel; like Freud and Carl Jung, he is a psychiatrist, concerned with helping people understand human motivation and behavior. How does the focus of Berne's interests differ from that of James, Freud, and Jung? How does this difference affect the nature of his writing?

16. What are the bases for Berne's generalizations about human beings: his personal experiences; his observations; his readings; or his teachers? Could Berne "prove" any of the assertions he makes here? How? Does he need proof to convince you that what he says is valid?

17. Many of the terms which Berne uses sound highly technical or specialized. Are they really? Can you, as a layman and student, understand what he is talking about without going to a medical dictionary? What audience has Berne in mind in writing this psychological analysis?

18. The diction in *Games People Play*, the book from which this essay is taken, is a mixture of medical terms, slang, and ordinary speech. Point out examples of each of these in the essay here. What is the purpose of mixing diction this way? What is the result?

19. Susan Sontag's analysis of science fiction movies in *The Imagination of Disaster* throws some interesting additional light on "scientific" attitudes in modern culture. Do her views agree with those of such scientific "apologists" as Conant? With the psychiatric opinions of Freud or Berne?

20. Discuss the implications of Miss Sontag's depiction of the "scientist" as a "normal, average family man" on the one hand and a "mad destroyer" on the other. What relation have these stereotypes to the idea of the scientist as neurotic?

21. Miss Sontag is ostensibly talking about movies. What is she really concerned with in this essay? What does she assume about the relationship of motion pictures to the people who go to see them? Is her assumption justified?

22. Compare Miss Sontag's description of the plot of a science fiction film with Conant's description of the scientific method. Does the film illustrate flaws in the scientific method or accept the method as absolute and factual?

23. Compare the initial stages of the science fiction movie ("The hero and…his wife and children are disporting themselves in some innocent ultra-normal middle-class surroundings….") with John Hersey's opening chapter of *Hiroshima* above (p. 238). Are there similarities? Are *Hiroshima* and *The Day the Earth Caught Fire* (or some other science film) concerned with the same experience? How are they different? Does Miss Sontag's essay help you to see the emotions common to both?

24. To what extent is the Sontag essay "scientific"? Is it scientific in its aims, interests, methods, techniques, or not?

25. Both Robert Penn Warren and James Baldwin (in *The Fire Next Time*) are concerned with race relations in America in the 1960's. Compare and contrast their points of view, interests, and techniques. Is one more "objective" than the other? More "factual"? More "true" or "right"?

26. Warren takes the role of reporter and student of society in his essay, *The Negro Now*. How does he resemble the reporter? The sociologist (such as Frazer or Margaret Mead)? the psychologist?

27. Are race relations, as Warren discusses them, explainable in the terms of such psychiatrists as Freud and Berne? Does Berne's game theory help to explain race riots?

28. What authorities does Warren use in his essay? How has he collected his data or "facts"? Has he been "scientific"? Is the essay subjective or "personal" in any way?

29. Frazer, Berne, Sontag, and Warren are all concerned with describing the collective behavior of groups of people. Compare and evaluate the relative merits (and limitations) of their several approaches.

Questions for Discussion and Writing

1. From the theories and specimens of its writing in Section III above, how would you define "science"? What are its chosen subjects of examination? How does it approach these subjects?
2. Which of the sciences illustrated here is the most "factual" (empirically demonstrable)? Which the least? Reasoning from your answer, how are the proper limits of "scientific" materials and methods set up to include these two extremes?
3. Which of the examples of the scientific writing above—physical and social—is the most subjectively approached by the author? The most objectively? Is the more objective approach necessarily the one producing the more "factual" conclusions or insights?
4. If "imagination" is defined as "the ability to perceive new and original relationships" or "to conceive of new combinations of data," may imagination be considered an important part of scientific thinking? Is scientific knowledge "imaginative"?
5. Becker insists that history must be rewritten to suit the needs of every generation. Does science similarly have to be revised for every new generation? Is "science" thus arbitrary and subjective or does it possess some absolute and unchanging qualities?
6. Which of the sciences—physical or social—depends most on the formation of hypotheses? on measurement? on direct observation? on authority? on intuition by the scientist?
7. Since most scientific "findings" are partial and soon to be modified, is there really any need for laymen to be kept informed of these changes? Must scientific writing for the layman, then, appear more tentative and hypothetical than scientific knowledge actually is?
8. Is reportage scientific or not? Is historiography? Is biography?
9. Do you as reader find the essays in this section more or less interesting in subject matter than those in Section II? How do you account for your preference? Which kind of writing do you find the most readable (i.e., clear, comprehensible, organized, and intellectually stimulating)?

IV
AESTHETIC REALITIES

SECTION FOUR

The "Creative" Mind

Up until now, you have been reading "records" of one kind or another—transcriptions of experiences that, by and large, are empirically testable. Because it lends itself to objective verification, such literature is considered "factual," even though intuitive elements are involved in composing a sociological survey or a galactic hypothesis just as surely as they are an epistle or autobiography. The "factual" is closely connected with the criteria of "proof," "authenticity," and "usefulness" (or practicability) in the minds of many people, particularly those who rely on empirical knowledge as the only form of "truth" and "reality."

Despite the range of experiences covered by it, however, empirical—or "logical"—writing is limited in what it can achieve. There are experiences in life that cannot be subjected to "scientific" observation, much less testing; and for most people, it is these experiences that have the deepest impact and significance. They are also among the most difficult to comprehend and objectify in language. The basic emotions of hate, love, fear, desire; the thought processes that William James called "reveries"; the "feelings" (both physical and emotional) that the physiologist and psychiatrist can name but not really clarify in words; the vivid experiences of dreams—these and other experiences that make up much of human consciousness have not yet been successfully formulated by empirical methods of conceptualization.

It is the "imaginative" writer, therefore, who undertakes to illuminate for his reader these kinds of "truth." "Imagination" is another name for "intuition" of an especially keen nature: the capacity for envisioning that not previously formulated or the ability to conceptualize experiences that cannot yet be systematized because they are intangible or lack sense data that can be objectified. The kinds of writing that embody these "truths" of feeling are those whose methods are aesthetic rather than empirical; they are "creative" literature, not because they make a word composition out of nothing, but because they use words as the material by which immaterial experiences take on a structure. They make language do something that it is not basically designed to do: convey nonverbal experiences. "Consciousness is not a verbal process," Marshall McLuhan has said. "Many a page of prose and many a narrative has been devoted to expressing what was, in effect, a sob, a moan, a laugh, or a piercing scream." It is in their use of language, then, that both the writer of fiction and the poet "create." (Both "fiction" and "poetry" mean "creation.")

To be sure, the mental processes of the intuitive thinker would appear much the same, whether the thinker is forming a mathematical theorem or a sonnet. A comparison between a scientist's explanation of how he thinks and the explanations of an historian and a poet reveal similar modes of conceiving experience. But there are some striking differences between the way a "creative" writer selects and transforms his conceptions into words and the methods used by the natural or social scientist. The poets are their own best spokesmen, however; in the selections here, they speak eloquently for their way of perceiving the vital reality of being.

MARIANNE MOORE

The Mind Is an Enchanting Thing

is an enchanted thing
  like the glaze on a
katydid-wing
    subdivided by sun
    till the nettings are legion.   5
Like Gieseking playing Scarlatti;

like the apteryx-awl
  as a beak, or the
kiwi's rain-shawl
    of haired feathers, the mind   10
    feeling its way as though blind,
walks along with its eyes on the ground.

It has memory's ear
  that can hear without
having to hear.   15
    Like the gyroscope's fall,
    truly unequivocal
because trued by regnant certainty,

it is a power of
  strong enchantment. It   20
is like the dove-
    neck animated by
    sun; it is memory's eye;
it's conscientious inconsistency.

It tears off the veil; tears   25
  the temptation, the
mist the heart wears,
    from its eyes,—if the heart
    has a face; it takes apart
dejection. It's fire in the dove-neck's   30

iridescence; in the
  inconsistencies
of Scarlatti.
    Unconfusion submits
    its confusion to proof; it's   35
not a Herod's oath that cannot change.

Questions

1. Is this poem indebted for its ideas on how the mind works to any of the psychological or scientific theorists you read earlier? Are its statements hypotheses, statements of fact, data? Are they true?
2. Does Miss Moore use any scientific knowledge in developing her depiction of how the mind works?
3. From what areas of knowledge does she take her particulars of comparison; e.g., "katydid-wing," "subdivided by the sun," "apteryx-awl," "gyroscope's fall"? Is her factual knowledge of ornithology, engineering, etc., accurate or not? Why does she use the data of the natural sciences in her poem?
4. Gieseking was a brilliant German pianist of the period between 1930 and 1950. Scarlatti was a composer of the seventeenth century whose baroque and convoluted music is a challenge to modern performers. Does Miss Moore have the right to expect you as a reader to know these facts in order to understand what she is saying? Is the poet less entitled to demand specialized knowledge from the reader than the scientist, the historiographer, or the journalist?
5. In lines 2–3, 7–8, 13 and 23, what is being compared and for what characteristics are the similarities pointed out?
6. Are there logical contradictions in such phrases as "conscientious inconsistency" and "blind…with its eyes on the ground"? Look up the meaning of the word *paradox* and discuss its application to these statements.
7. Does this poem *explain* how the mind operates? What does the poem do?
8. If the poem were printed in the format of prose, would you notice anything unusual about its diction and effect? Why does the poet break up the parts of her long sentences into line divisions like these?

Poetry

I, too, dislike it: there are things that are important beyond all this fiddle.
  Reading it, however, with a perfect contempt for it, one discovers in
      it, after all, a place for the genuine.
    Hands that can grasp, eyes
    that can dilate, hair that can rise   5
      if it must, these things are important not because a

high-sounding interpretation can be put upon them but because they are
  useful. When they become so derivative as to become unintelligible,
    the same things may be said for all of us, that we
      do not admire what   10
      we cannot understand: the bat
        holding on upside down or in quest of something to

eat, elephants pushing, a wild horse taking a roll, a tireless wolf under
  a tree, the immovable critic twitching his skin like a horse that feels a flea, the
    base-
  ball fan, the statistician—
    nor is it valid
      to discriminate against 'business documents and

school-books'; all these phenomena are important. One must make a distinction
  however: when dragged into prominence by half poets, the result is not poetry,
  nor till the poets among us can be
    'literalists of
    the imagination'—above
      insolence and triviality and can present

for inspection, imaginary gardens with real toads in them, shall we have
  it. In the meantime, if you demand on the one hand,
    the raw material of poetry in
      all its rawness and
      that which is on the other hand
        genuine, then you are interested in poetry.

15
20
25
30

Questions

1. Why does Miss Moore say she dislikes poetry? How genuine is her dislike? Is it possible to write poetry and still dislike it?
2. What is poetry, according to this poem? How does it differ from "business documents and school-books"? Why is this phrase in half quotes?
3. What does Miss Moore mean by "genuine"? Is the "genuine" what she calls "useful" in line 8? What is the relationship of human emotion ("eyes that can dilate," "hair that can rise") to the genuine, in her opinion?
4. Miss Moore's definition of poems as "imaginary gardens with real toads in them" is often quoted. What elements in a poem would be the "garden" and what would be the "toads"? Why does she use "toads" rather than "bees" or "butterflies"? Is this a way of saying the genuine is ugly?
5. How regular are the rhyme and meter of this poem? Are meter and rhyme used or is this a specimen of "free verse" (verse without rhyme or meter)? Are there many figures of speech in the poem? What reason can you advance for this?
6. Are Miss Moore's poems more obviously "personal" or "private" than the essays by the natural and social scientists above? Are her interests more narrow than theirs or not? Is her diction more or less concrete than theirs? Are her references more or less abstruse and uncommon?

WILLIAM WORDSWORTH

Lines Composed
a Few Miles
Above Tintern Abbey

Five years have past; five summers, with the length
Of five long winters! and again I hear
These waters, rolling from their mountain-springs

With a soft inland murmur.—Once again
Do I behold these steep and lofty cliffs, 5
That on a wild secluded scene impress
Thoughts of more deep seclusion; and connect
The landscape with the quiet of the sky.
The day is come when I again repose
Here, under this dark sycamore, and view 10
These plots of cottage-ground, these orchard-tufts,
Which at this season, with their unripe fruits,
Are clad in one green hue, and lose themselves
'Mid groves and copses. Once again I see
These hedge-rows, hardly hedge-rows, little lines 15
Of sportive wood run wild: these pastoral farms,
Green to the very door; and wreaths of smoke
Sent up, in silence, from among the trees!
With some uncertain notice, as might seem
Of vagrant dwellers in the houseless woods, 20
Or of some Hermit's cave, where by his fire
The Hermit sits alone.
        These beauteous forms,
Through a long absence, have not been to me
As is a landscape to a blind man's eye:
But oft, in lonely rooms, and 'mid the din 25
Of towns and cities, I have owed to them
In hours of weariness, sensations sweet,
Felt in the blood, and felt along the heart;
And passing even into my purer mind,
With tranquil restoration:—feelings too 30
Of unremembered pleasure: such, perhaps,
As have no slight or trivial influence
On that best portion of a good man's life,
His little, nameless, unremembered acts
Of kindness and of love. Nor less, I trust, 35
To them I may have owed another gift,
Of aspect more sublime; that blessed mood,
In which the burthen of the mystery,
In which the heavy and the weary weight
Of all this unintelligible world, 40
Is lightened:—that serene and blessed mood,
In which the affections gently lead us on,—
Until, the breath of this corporeal frame
And even the motion of our human blood
Almost suspended, we are laid asleep 45
In body, and become a living soul:
While with an eye made quiet by the power
Of harmony, and the deep power of joy,
We see into the life of things.
        If this
Be but a vain belief, yet, oh! how oft— 50
In darkness and amid the many shapes

Of joyless daylight; when the fretful stir
Unprofitable, and the fever of the world,
Have hung upon the beatings of my heart—
How oft, in spirit, have I turned to thee, 55
O sylvan Wye! thou wanderer through the woods,
How often has my spirit turned to thee!

     And now, with gleams of half-extinguished
          thought,
With many recognitions dim and faint,
And somewhat of a sad perplexity, 60
The picture of the mind revives again:
While here I stand, not only with the sense
Of present pleasure, but with pleasing thoughts
That in this moment there is life and food
For future years. And so I dare to hope, 65
Though changed, no doubt, from what I was when
     first
I came among these hills; when like a roe
I bounded o'er the mountains, by the sides
Of the deep rivers, and the lonely streams,
Wherever nature led: more like a man 70
Flying from something that he dreads, than one
Who sought the thing he loved. For nature then
(The coarser pleasures of my boyish days,
And their glad animal movements all gone by)
To me was all in all.—I cannot paint 75
What then I was. The sounding cataract
Haunted me like a passion: the tall rock,
The mountain, and the deep and gloomy wood,
Their colors and their forms, were then to me
An appetite; a feeling and a love, 80
That had no need of a remoter charm,
By thought supplied, nor any interest
Unborrowed from the eye.—That time is past,
And all its aching joys are now no more,
And all its dizzy raptures. Not for this 85
Faint I, nor mourn nor murmur; other gifts
Have followed; for such loss, I would believe,
Abundant recompense. For I have learned
To look on nature, not as in the hour
Of thoughtless youth; but hearing oftentimes 90
The still, sad music of humanity,
Nor harsh nor grating, though of ample power
To chasten and subdue. And I have felt
A presence that disturbs me with the joy
Of elevated thoughts; a sense sublime 95
Of something far more deeply interfused,
Whose dwelling is the light of setting suns,
And the round ocean and the living air,

And the blue sky, and in the mind of man:
A motion and a spirit, that impels   100
All thinking things, all objects of all thought,
And rolls through all things. Therefore am I still
A lover of the meadows and the woods,
And mountains; and of all that we behold
From this green earth; of all the mighty world   105
Of eye, and ear,—both what they half create,
And what perceive; well pleased to recognize
In nature and the language of the sense
The anchor of my purest thoughts, the nurse,
The guide, the guardian of my heart, and soul   110
Of all my moral being.
        Nor perchance,
If I were not thus taught, should I the more
Suffer my genial spirits to decay:
For thou art with me here upon the banks
Of this fair river; thou my dearest Friend,   115
My dear, dear Friend; and in thy voice I catch
The language of my former heart, and read
My former pleasures in the shooting lights
Of thy wild eyes. Oh! yet a little while
May I behold in thee what I was once,   120
My dear, dear Sister! and this prayer I make,
Knowing that Nature never did betray
The heart that loved her; 'tis her privilege,
Through all the years of this our life, to lead
From joy to joy; for she can so inform   125
The mind that is within us, so impress
With quietness and beauty, and so feed
With lofty thoughts, that neither evil tongues,
Rash judgments, nor the sneers of selfish men,
Nor greetings where no kindness is, nor all   130
The dreary intercourse of daily life,
Shall e'er prevail against us, or disturb
Our cheerful faith, that all which we behold
Is full of blessings. Therefore let the moon
Shine on thee in thy solitary walk;   135
And let the misty mountain-winds be free
To blow against thee: and, in after years,
When these wild ecstasies shall be matured
Into a sober pleasure; when thy mind
Shall be a mansion for all lovely forms,   140
Thy memory be as a dwelling-place
For all sweet sounds and harmonies; oh! then,
If solitude, or fear, or pain, or grief,
Should be thy portion, with what healing thoughts
Of tender joy wilt thou remember me,   145
And these my exhortations! Nor, perchance—
If I should be where I no more can hear

Thy voice, nor catch from thy wild eyes these
    gleams
Of past existence—wilt thou then forget
That on the banks of this delightful stream   150
We stood together; and that I, so long
A worshipper of Nature, hither came
Unwearied in that service: rather say
With warmer love—oh! with far deeper zeal
Of holier love. Nor wilt thou then forget,   155
That after many wanderings, many years
Of absence, these steep woods and lofty cliffs,
And this green pastoral landscape, were to me
More dear, both for themselves and for thy sake!

Questions

1. Lines 22–48 express the basic assumptions of this poetic description of how the mind operates and how the writer forms his conceptions. What are Wordsworth's fundamental premises? Is his psychological theory like or unlike that of James pp. 6–13 above? Upon what is it based?

2. What does Wordsworth mean by the statement, "We see into the life of things"? How does he define "see" and "life"? (Note their use in former lines.)

3. Wordsworth describes in lines 70–111 his love of "nature," that is, the natural world. How is his interest in physical nature different from that of the botanist, the geographer, the geologist, the agronomer?

4. The "dear, dear Sister" of line 121 is Dorothy Wordsworth (see pp. 70–73). Is William's description of her and his feelings about her consistent with the depiction of their relationship in her diary? How do you account for this?

5. Wordsworth's "I Wandered Lonely As a Cloud" (see below) is startlingly close to Dorothy's *Journal* in its phrases. Do the two works say the same thing? Have they the same tone or mood? Is one more "factual" or "real" than the other?

I Wandered Lonely
as a Cloud

I wandered lonely as a cloud
That floats on high o'er vales and hills,
When all at once I saw a crowd,
A host, of golden daffodils;
Beside the lake, beneath the trees,   5
Fluttering and dancing in the breeze.

Continuous as the stars that shine
And twinkle on the milky way,
They stretched in never-ending line
Along the margin of a bay: 10
Ten thousand saw I at a glance,
Tossing their heads in sprightly dance.

The waves beside them danced; but they
Out-did the sparkling waves in glee:
A poet could not but be gay,   15
In such a jocund company:
I gazed—and gazed—but little thought
What wealth the show to me had brought:

For oft, when on my couch I lie
In vacant or in pensive mood,   20
They flash upon that inward eye
Which is the bliss of solitude;
And then my heart with pleasure fills,
And dances with the daffodils.

Questions

1. What are the rhyme scheme and meter of this poem? Are they appropriate for the subject matter or not? Explain.
2. What figures of speech does Wordsworth use in this poem? Does his language differ much from that of ordinary speech? Is this poem more or less like prose than "Tintern Abbey"? Than Marianne Moore's poems?
3. Are the psychological theories of this poem different from those in "Tintern Abbey"? Does Wordsworth aid you in understanding how the poet conceptualizes and why he writes? Why did Wordsworth compose these poems, do you suppose?

The Solitary Reaper

Behold her, single in the field,
Yon solitary Highland Lass!
Reaping and singing by herself;
Stop here, or gently pass!
Alone she cuts and binds the grain,   5
And sings a melancholy strain;
O listen! for the Vale profound
Is overflowing with the sound.

No Nightingale did ever chaunt
More welcome notes to weary bands   10
Of travellers in some shady haunt,
Among Arabian sands;
A voice so thrilling ne'er was heard
In spring-time from the Cuckoo-bird
Breaking the silence of the seas   15
Among the farthest Hebrides.

Will no one tell me what she sings?—
Perhaps the plaintive numbers flow
For old, unhappy, far-off things,
And battles long ago: 20
Or is it some more humble lay,
Familiar matter of today?
Some natural sorrow, loss, or pain,
That has been, and may be again?

Whate'er the theme, the Maiden sang   25
As if her song could have no ending;
I saw her singing at her work,
And o'er the sickle bending;—
I listened, motionless and still;
And, as I mounted up the hill,   30
The music in my heart I bore,
Long after it was heard no more.

WALLACE STEVENS

The Idea of Order
at Key West

She sang beyond the genius of the sea.
The water never formed to mind or voice,
Like a body wholly body, fluttering

Its empty sleeves; and yet its mimic motion
Made constant cry, caused constantly a cry,   5
That was not ours although we understood,
Inhuman, of the veritable ocean.

The sea was not a mask. Nor more was she.
The song and water were not medleyed sound,
Even if what she sang was what she heard,   10
Since what she sang she uttered word by word.
It may be that in all her phrases stirred
The grinding water and the gasping wind;
But it was she and not the sea we heard.

For she was the maker of the song she sang.   15
The ever-hooded, tragic-gestured sea
Was merely a place by which she walked to sing.
Whose spirit is this? we said, because we knew
It was the spirit that we sought and knew
That we should ask this often as she sang.   20

If it was only the dark voice of the sea
That rose, or even colored by many waves;
If it was only the outer voice of sky
And cloud, of the sunken coral water-walled,
However clear, it would have been deep air,   25
The heaving speech of air, a summer sound
Repeated in a summer without end
And sound alone. But it was more than that,
More even than her voice, and ours, among
The meaningless plungings of water and the wind,   30
Theatrical distances, bronze shadows heaped
On high horizons, mountainous atmospheres
Of sky and sea.
      It was her voice that made
The sky acutest at its vanishing.   35
She measured to the hour its solitude.
She was the single artificer of the world
In which she sang. And when she sang, the sea,
Whatever self it had, became the self
That was her song, for she was maker. Then we,   40
As we beheld her striding there alone,
Knew that there never was a world for her
Except the one she sang and, singing, made.

Ramon Fernandez, tell me, if you know,
Why, when the singing ended and we turned   45
Toward the town, tell why the glassy lights,
The lights in the fishing boats at anchor there,
As the night descended, tilting in the air,

Mastered the night and portioned out the sea,
Fixing emblazoned zones and fiery poles,   50
Arranging, deepening, enchanting night.

Oh! Blessed rage for order, pale Ramon,
The maker's rage to order words of the sea,
Words of the fragrant portals, dimly-starred,
And of ourselves and of our origins,   55
In ghostlier demarcations, keener sounds.

Questions

1. This poem by Stevens is amazingly similar to Wordsworth's "Solitary Reaper" in many ways: the poet hears a lone girl singing in some remote spot; he is struck by the song; he cannot identify it; he speaks reflectively to a companion about the meaning of the song, and so on. Is Stevens's attitude toward nature (the sea, in this poem) like Wordsworth's? Is Stevens more or less close to the attitude of the scientist?
2. Does order exist in nature, according to Stevens? Where does it exist?
3. Explain the significance to the poem as a whole of these phrases: "the single artificer," "maker," "glassy lights ... mastered the night and portioned out the sea," "rage for order."
4. If the singer in the poem is a symbol for the poet, what is Stevens's view of the nature and function of the poet? What is his view of language? What is the relationship of language to knowledge? To reality?
5. Identify the meter, rhyme, and tropes used by this poem. Is Stevens's diction distinctive in any way? Does he use concrete or abstract words more often? Are his ideas more abstract than those in "The Mind Is an Enchanting Thing"? Do you find Stevens's ideas of language more difficult to understand than Moore's and Wordsworth's?

ARCHIBALD MACLEISH

Ars Poetica

A poem should be palpable and mute
As a globed fruit,

Dumb
As old medallions to the thumb,

Silent as the sleeve-worn stone   5
Of casement ledges where the moss has grown—

A poem should be wordless
As the flight of birds.

    .   .   .

A poem should be motionless in time
As the moon climbs,   10

Leaving, as the moon releases
Twig by twig the night-entangled trees,

Leaving, as the moon behind the winter leaves,
Memory by memory the mind—

A poem should be motionless in time   15
As the moon climbs.

    .   .   .

A poem should be equal to:
Not true.

For all the history of grief
An empty doorway and a maple leaf.   20

For love
The leaning grasses and two lights above the sea—

A poem should not mean
But be.

Questions

1. The title of MacLeish's poem comes from Horace, an ancient Roman poet who critically wrote on "The Art of Poetry," or how to write poetry. Does MacLeish actually tell how to write a poem? What is he concerned with?

2. Examine in detail the individual similes, or poetic comparisons ("like," "as") that this poem uses. Are they logically connected in any way? How are they related to the five senses?

3. How can a poem be "wordless" (line 7)? Can you explain this paradox?

4. The metaphors in lines 19–20 and 21–22 are supposed to illustrate the way poetic figures evoke states of emotion. How can grief be contained in "an empty doorway" or "a maple leaf"? Is love really connoted by "leaning grasses and two lights above the sea"? How?

5. Explain the statement: "A poem should be equal to: not true."

6. Are the poems by Moore, Wordsworth, and Stevens "true" in MacLeish's terms? Are they "equal to" anything?

Dramatic Fictions

Of the three basic divisions of fictive literature—dramatic, narrative, and lyric—it is the dramatic which most tries to resemble the "factual" world. The drama is, first of all, the most *mimetic* kind of creative literature: it "mimes" or closely imitates (mimics) human speech and behavior in order to create the illusion that these are actual people engaged in vital actions. The fictional personalities of the characters in the drama are simulated by actors, who become for the moment the *dramatis personae,* or "imitation people" who carry on their lives as an audience watches. These characters of the drama move among surroundings (or stage "sets") that often represent specific places at particular times in historic periods; the play "setting" thus simulates an historical milieu. The costumes, stage furnishings, and paraphernalia (properties or "props") used by the actors further help to create the impression of reality in external or physical details. The chief intention of the drama is to involve the spectator in its heightened and carefully controlled events ("plot") to such an extent that he believes in the truth of what is happening before his eyes. Whether on the stage, in the motion picture, or on television, dramatic fiction pretends to show people and events as they *are* so as to give the viewer a vicarious experience.

As the creator of an illusory world, the dramatist, or playwright, uses the literary form which has the appeal of factual events, but he also has to solve certain distinct difficulties. How can he preserve the lifelike character of his events and avoid the dullness and repetitiousness of life itself, which would bore the spectator? As a creator, he must choose and select with some intention in mind, unless he wants to let the actors follow their own caprices, saying and doing what they like. The contemporary *happening* does just that; but its name—

the happenstance or chance occurrence—indicates its basic difference from the controlled artifice of the play. As an artificer, a dramatic craftsman, the writer has to use his materials expertly without letting the audience become aware of his guiding hand, just as he must let the play-people express his ideas without interrupting the action to appear on the stage and speak in his own person. How can he show the differences in personality between his characters with only their words ("dialogue"), contrived actions, and such devices as costumes to help him? Like the biographer, he must contrive to show hearts and minds through words, actions, and things; but his task is harder because these hearts and minds are all aspects of his own or he otherwise could not envision them convincingly.

There is also the problem of time-sequence or chronology. How much time is taken by the events the dramatist must show in order to develop his view of experience? To act a modern play takes about one to three hours, but all the events in a meaningful sequence in life itself are unlikely to take place in three consecutive hours. The ancient Greeks were able, in *Oedipus Tyrannus* or *Agamemnon,* to make the time of action and the time of acting the same; they almost exhausted the variations of the technique, however. Even if the actual events of the play are made to take place in two or three hours, all of the interesting and necessary *causes* leading up to these events must be conveyed to the audience somehow through expository (explanatory) dialogue that appears natural under the circumstances.

The development of the events of his plot also takes much care on the playwright's part. He must interest the audience as soon after the play begins as he can, but human attention spans being what they are, he cannot expect to begin with a high pitch of emotion and sustain it for two hours. An emotional and intellectual *climax* cannot go on and on; thus the dramatist must carefully develop his situation as he lets his characters reveal themselves in word and action, introducing *complications* as he goes, through which the dramatic *conflict* is shown and finally resolved in a *dénouement,* or outcome. There is no set pattern for this development, and the dramatist must adapt it to his specialized interests and themes. He may wish to begin his events with a violent physical action and then spend the rest of his drama in an *anti-climax,* a gradual unfolding of the causes leading up to the opening event.

Plot, characters, settings, chronology—any or all may be manipulated as he desires by the dramatist in order to create his own version of human behavior. So long as it convinces the spectator and expresses the author's conception of some aspect of life in effective terms, the drama may take any number of forms and appeal to any emotion, from comic to pathetic to tragic. Like Chekov, the playwright may present a "slice of life": a sharply realistic representation of an everyday event involving ordinary people mouthing recognizably garbled speeches. Like Tennessee Williams, he may reveal a way of life by presenting a conversation between two men in a hotel room. Or, like Thornton Wilder, the dramatist may violate the kind of time shown by clocks to say something about human life and destiny. Or Maria Irene Fornés may forcibly join bizarre events with feverishly unreal dialogue to show the underlying emotions beneath a relationship. Though the writer wants us to react emotionally to his play, he is also conveying what is for him a true perspective on life. Thus, although our primary reaction to the play may be emotional, we should not stop with that but go on to examine in detail the ways in which the writer contrives his effect. In reading drama, we must remember that plays are composed to be *enacted* and therefore use our visual imagination to supply those qualities the printed page cannot give.

There are some exceptions to the practice of composing plays to be acted rather than read: both the *closet drama* (which is read aloud without sets, costumes, and actions) and the *dramatic monologue* are primarily composed for readers instead of viewers. The closet drama is a full-length play of one to five basic divisions ("acts") which stresses language and ideas above the portrayal of character. The *dramatic monologue* is the poet's adaptation of one part of a full-scale play: it is a single, long speech by one character ("monologue" means "one speech") which reveals the basic nature or disposition of the speaker. Usually the poetic dramatic monologue implies other characters who are listening to the speech, perhaps even engaging in concurrent actions. It also reveals something of the surroundings in which the speaker is placed and suggests a situation of conflict or tension. But the dramatic monologue, as Browning or Tennyson or T. S. Eliot writes it, is essentially the revelation of a man's character through hearing him speak. It is thus an exercise in composing one of the parts of a total play. By reading critically specimens of the monologue, one begins to understand some of the compositional elements of dramatic fiction.

ALFRED, LORD TENNYSON

Ulysses

It little profits that an idle king,
By this still hearth, among these barren crags,
Matched with an aged wife, I mete and dole
Unequal laws unto a savage race,
That hoard, and sleep, and feed, and know not me. 5
I cannot rest from travel; I will drink
Life to the lees. All times I have enjoyed

Greatly, have suffered greatly, both with those
That loved me, and alone; on shore, and when
Through scudding drifts the rainy Hyades   10
Vexed the dim sea. I am become a name;
For always roaming with a hungry heart
Much have I seen and known—cities of men
And manners, climates, councils, governments,
Myself not least, but honoured of them all—   15
And drunk delight of battle with my peers,
Far on the ringing plains of windy Troy.
I am a part of all that I have met;
Yet all experience is an arch wherethrough
Gleams that untraveled world whose margin fades 20

Forever and forever when I move.
How dull it is to pause, to make an end,
To rust unburnished, not to shine in use!
As though to breathe were life! Life piled on life
Were all too little, and of one to me   25
Little remains; but every hour is saved
From that eternal silence, something more,
A bringer of new things; and vile it were
For some three suns to store and hoard myself,
And this gray spirit yearning in desire   30
To follow knowledge like a sinking star,
Beyond the utmost bound of human thought.

   This is my son, mine own Telemachus,
To whom I leave the scepter and the isle—
Well-loved of me, discerning to fulfill   35
This labor, by slow prudence to make mild
A rugged people, and through soft degrees
Subdue them to the useful and the good.
Most blameless is he, centered in the sphere
Of common duties, decent not to fail   40
In offices of tenderness, and pay
Meet adoration to my household gods,
When I am gone. He works his work, I mine.

   There lies the port; the vessel puffs her sail;
There gloom the dark, broad seas. My mariners,   45
Souls that have toiled, and wrought, and thought
      with me—
That ever with a frolic welcome took
The thunder and the sunshine, and opposed
Free hearts, free foreheads—you and I are old;
Old age hath yet his honor and his toil.   50
Death closes all; but something ere the end,
Some work of noble note, may yet be done,
Not unbecoming men that strove with gods.
The lights begin to twinkle from the rocks;
The long day wanes; the slow moon climbs; the
      deep   55
Moans round with many voices. Come, my friends.
'Tis not too late to seek a newer world.
Push off, and sitting well in order smite
The sounding furrows; for my purpose holds
To sail beyond the sunset, and the baths   60
Of all the western stars, until I die.
It may be that the gulfs will wash us down;
It may be we shall touch the Happy Isles,
And see the great Achilles, whom we knew.
Though much is taken, much abides; and though 65
We are not now that strength which in old days
Moved earth and heaven, that which we are, we
      are—

One equal temper of heroic hearts,
Made weak by time and fate, but strong in will
To strive, to seek, to find, and not to yield.   70

Questions

1. The speaker in this *dramatic monologue* is Ulysses, the hero of Homer's epic poem, the *Odyssey,* and a leading figure in other Greek legends and stories. He supposedly spent twenty years fighting in the Trojan War and in returning to his island kingdom of Ithaca. Most of the stories end with his return to Ithaca and his reunion with his faithful wife, Penelope, and his son, Telemachus, an infant when the Trojan War began. Tennyson here represents Ulysses some time after the other stories end. Is a knowledge of the facts given here necessary for understanding this poem? Are they useful? What is Tennyson concerned with in this monologue?

2. How fully is the setting of Ulysses's speech suggested in the poem? Are other characters present or not? To what extent is this poem properly called a "soliloquy"?

3. Is there any dramatic conflict created in this monologue: a clash of wills, or disagreement of personalities or opposition of choices? Explain.

4. What is the dominant element in *Ulysses*: action, setting, character, ideas, emotions, or something else?

ROBERT BROWNING

The Bishop Orders His Tomb at Saint Praxed's Church

ROME, 15—

Vanity, saith the preacher, vanity!
Draw round my bed: is Anselm keeping back?
Nephews—sons mine....ah God, I know not! Well—

She, men would have to be your mother once,
Old Gandolf envied me, so fair she was!   5
What's done is done, and she is dead beside,
Dead long ago, and I am Bishop since,
And as she died so must we die ourselves,
And thence ye may perceive the world's a dream.
Life, how and what is it? As here I lie   10
In this state-chamber, dying by degrees,
Hours and long hours in the dead night, I ask
"Do I live, am I dead?" Peace, peace seems all.
Saint Praxed's ever was the church for peace;
And so, about this tomb of mine. I fought   15
With tooth and nail to save my niche, ye know:
—Old Gandolf cozened me, despite my care;
Shrewd was that snatch from out the corner South
He graced his carrion with, God curse the same!
Yet still my niche is not so cramped but thence   20
One sees the pulpit o' the epistle-side,
And somewhat of the choir, those silent seats,
And up into the aery dome where live
The angels, and a sunbeam's sure to lurk:
And I shall fill my slab of basalt there,   25
And 'neath my tabernacle take my rest,
With those nine columns round me, two and two,
The odd one at my feet where Anselm stands:
Peach-blossom marble all, the rare, the ripe
As fresh-poured red wine of a mighty pulse.   30
—Old Gandolf with his paltry onion-stone,
Put me where I may look at him! True peach,
Rosy and flawless: how I earned the prize!
Draw close: that conflagration of my church
—What then? So much was saved if aught were
    missed!   35
My sons, ye would not be my death? Go dig
The white-grape vineyard where the oil-press stood,
Drop water gently till the surface sink,
And if ye find.... Ah God, I know not, I!....
Bedded in store of rotten fig leaves soft,   40
And corded up in a tight olive-frail,
Some lump, ah God, of *lapis lazuli,*
Big as a Jew's head cut off at the nape,
Blue as a vein o'er the Madonna's breast....
Sons, all have I bequeathed you, villas, all,   45
That brave Frascati villa with its bath,
So, let the blue lump poise between my knees,
Like God the Father's globe on both his hands
Ye worship in the Jesu Church so gay,
For Gandolf shall not choose but see and burst!   50
Swift as a weaver's shuttle fleet our years:
Man goeth to the grave, and where is he?

Did I say basalt for my slab, sons? Black—
'Twas ever antique-black I meant! How else
Shall ye contrast my frieze to come beneath?   55
The bas-relief in bronze ye promised me,
Those Pans and Nymphs ye wot of, and perchance
Some tripod, thyrsus, with a vase or so,
The Savior at his sermon on the mount,
Saint Praxed in a glory, and one Pan   60
Ready to twitch the Nymph's last garment off,
And Moses with the tables....but I know
Ye mark me not! What do they whisper thee,
Child of my bowels, Anselm? Ah, ye hope
To revel down my villas while I gasp   65
Bricked o'er with beggar's moldy travertine
Which Gandolf from his tomb-top chuckles at!
Nay, boys, ye love me—all of jasper, then!
'Tis jasper ye stand pledged to, lest I grieve
My bath must needs be left behind, alas!   70
One block, pure green as a pistachio-nut,
There's plenty jasper somewhere in the world—
And have I not Saint Praxed's ear to pray
Horses for ye, and brown Greek manuscripts,
And mistresses with great smooth marbly limbs?   75
—That's if ye carve my epitaph aright,
Choice Latin, picked phrase, Tully's every word,
No gaudy ware like Gandolf's second line—
Tully, my masters? Ulpian serves his need!
And then how I shall lie through centuries,   80
And hear the blessed mutter of the mass,
And see God made and eaten all day long,
And feel the steady candle-flame, and taste
Good strong thick stupefying incense-smoke!
For as I lie here, hours of the dead night,   85
Dying in state and by such slow degrees,
I fold my arms as if they clasped a crook,
And stretch my feet forth straight as stone can
    point,
And let the bedclothes, for a mortcloth, drop
Into great laps and folds of sculptor's-work: 90
And as yon tapers dwindle, and strange thoughts
Grow, with a certain humming in my ears,
About the life before I lived this life,
And this life too, popes, cardinals and priests,
Saint Praxed at his sermon on the mount,   95
Your tall pale mother with her talking eyes,
And new-found agate urns as fresh as day,
And marble's language, Latin pure, discreet,
—Aha, ELUCESCEBAT quoth our friend?
No Tully, said I, Ulpian at the best!   100
Evil and brief hath been my pilgrimage.

All *lapis*, all, sons! Else I give the Pope
My villas! Will ye ever eat my heart?
Ever your eyes were as a lizard's quick,
They glitter like your mother's for my soul,   105
Or ye would heighten my impoverished frieze,
Piece out its starved design, and fill my vase
With grapes, and add a visor and a term,
And to the tripod ye would tie a lynx
That in his struggle throws the thyrsus down,   110
To comfort me on my entablature
Whereon I am to lie till I must ask
"Do I live, am I dead?" There, leave me, there!
For ye have stabbed me with ingratitude
To death—ye wish it—God, ye wish it! Stone—   115
Gritstone, a-crumble! Clammy squares which
     sweat
As if the corpse they keep were oozing through—
And no more *lapis* to delight the world!
Well go! I bless ye. Fewer tapers there,
But in a row: and, going, turn your backs   120
—Ay, like departing altar-ministrants,
And leave me in my church, the church for peace,
That I may watch at leisure if he leers—
Old Gandolf—at me, from his onion-stone,
As still he envied me, so fair she was!   125

Questions

1. What is the meaning of the notation at the head of the poem? Is it necessary or not? What does it correspond to in a play script?

2. Describe the situation that is presented in this *dramatic monologue*. Is the situation more unusual than that shown in "Ulysses"? Are they alike in any way?

3. What is most interesting to Browning about the situation he shows? The Bishop's character? The conflict between the Bishop and his sons? The magnificence of the physical setting? The culture and society reflected in the situation?

4. This poem is full of contradictions, as in lines 14–16, 42–43, 56–61, 73–75, 80–82, and elsewhere. Are they contradictions for the Bishop himself or not? How is this fact related to his character? Do the contradictions of the poem appear to be paradoxical? Ironic? Logical mistakes by the poet?

5. How would you describe the overall tone or impression of this monologue? Pathetic? Funny? Shocking? Disgusting?

6. What do you consider Browning's central purpose or theme in this monologue? What does he do: dramatize history, falsify it, or comment on it?

T. S. ELIOT

The Love Song of J. Alfred Prufrock

S'io credesse che mia risposta fosse
A persona che mai tornasse al mondo,
Questa fiamma staria senza piu scosse.
Ma perciocche giammai di questo fondo
Non torno vivo alcun, s'i'odo il vero,
Senza tema d'infamia ti rispondo.[1]

[1] THE LOVE SONG. *S'io credesse, etc.:* From Dante, *Divine Comedy: Inferno,* XXVII, 61-66: "If I thought my answer were to one who ever / could return to the world, this flame should / shake no more; / But since none ever did return alive from this / depth, if what I hear be true, without fear of / infamy I answer thee."

Let us go then, you and I,
When the evening is spread out against the sky
Like a patient etherised upon a table;
Let us go, through certain half-deserted streets,
The muttering retreats   5
Of restless nights in one-night cheap hotels
And sawdust restaurants with oyster-shells:
Streets that follow like a tedious argument
Of insidious intent
To lead you to an overwhelming question...   10
Oh, do not ask, "What is it?"
Let us go and make our visit.

   In the room the women come and go
Talking of Michelangelo.

   The yellow fog that rubs its back upon the window-panes,   15
The yellow smoke that rubs its muzzle on the window-panes
Licked its tongue into the corners of the evening,
Lingered upon the pools that stand in drains,
Let fall upon its back the soot that falls from chimneys,
Slipped by the terrace, made a sudden leap,   20
And seeing that it was a soft October night,
Curled once about the house, and fell asleep.

   And indeed there will be time
For the yellow smoke that slides along the street,
Rubbing its back upon the window-panes;   25
There will be time, there will be time
To prepare a face to meet the faces that you meet;
There will be time to murder and create,
And time for all the works and days of hands
That lift and drop a question on your plate;   30
Time for you and time for me,
And time yet for a hundred indecisions,
And for a hundred visions and revisions,
Before the taking of a toast and tea.

   In the room the women come and go   35
Talking of Michelangelo.

   And indeed there will be time
To wonder, "Do I dare?" and, "Do I dare?"
Time to turn back and descend the stair,
With a bald spot in the middle of my hair—   40
[They will say: "How his hair is growing thin!"]
My morning coat, my collar mounting firmly to the chin,
My necktie rich and modest, but asserted by a simple pin—
[They will say: "But how his arms and legs are thin!"]
Do I dare   45
Disturb the universe?
In a minute there is time
For decisions and revisions which a minute will reverse.

For I have known them all already, known them all:—
Have known the evenings, mornings, afternoons,   50
I have measured out my life with coffee spoons;
I know the voices dying with a dying fall
Beneath the music from a farther room.
   So how should I presume?

And I have known the eyes already, known them all—   55
The eyes that fix you in a formulated phrase,
And when I am formulated, sprawling on a pin,
When I am pinned and wriggling on the wall,
Then how should I begin
To spit out all the butt-ends of my days and ways?   60
   And how should I presume?

And I have known the arms already, known them all—
Arms that are braceleted and white and bare
[But in the lamplight, downed with light brown hair!]
Is it perfume from a dress   65
That makes me so digress?
Arms that lie along a table, or wrap about a shawl.
   And should I then presume?
   And how should I begin?

     .   .   .   .   .

Shall I say, I have gone at dusk through narrow streets   70
And watched the smoke that rises from the pipes
Of lonely men in shirt-sleeves, leaning out of windows? ...

I should have been a pair of ragged claws
Scuttling across the floors of silent seas.

     .   .   .   .   .

And the afternoon, the evening, sleeps so peacefully!   75
Smoothed by long fingers,
Asleep ... tired ... or it malingers,
Stretched on the floor, here beside you and me.
Should I, after tea and cakes and ices,
Have the strength to force the moment to its crisis?   80
But though I have wept and fasted, wept and prayed,
Though I have seen my head [grown slightly bald] brought
     in upon a platter,
I am no prophet—and here's no great matter;
I have seen the moment of my greatness flicker,
And I have seen the eternal Footman hold my coat, and
     snicker,   85
And in short, I was afraid.

  And would it have been worth it, after all,
After the cups, the marmalade, the tea,
Among the porcelain, among some talk of you and me,

Would it have been worth while,   90
To have bitten off the matter with a smile,
To have squeezed the universe into a ball,
To roll it toward some overwhelming question,
To say: "I am Lazarus, come from the dead,
Come back to tell you all, I shall tell you all"—   95
If one, settling a pillow by her head,
    Should say: "That is not what I meant at all.
    That is not it, at all."

    And would it have been worth it, after all,
Would it have been worth while,   100
After the sunsets and the dooryards and the sprinkled streets,
After the novels, after the teacups, after the skirts that trail
        along the floor—
And this, and so much more?—
It is impossible to say just what I mean!
But as if a magic lantern threw the nerves in patterns on a screen: 105
Would it have been worth while
If one, settling a pillow or throwing off a shawl,
And turning toward the window, should say:
    "That is not it at all,
    That is not what I meant, at all."   110

                 .   .   .   .   .

No! I am not Prince Hamlet, nor was meant to be;
Am an attendant lord, one that will do
To swell a progress, start a scene or two,
Advise the prince; no doubt, an easy tool,
Deferential, glad to be of use,   115
Politic, cautious, and meticulous;
Full of high sentence, but a bit obtuse;
At times, indeed, almost ridiculous—
Almost, at times, the Fool.

    I grow old…. I grow old…   120
I shall wear the bottoms of my trousers rolled.

    Shall I part my hair behind? Do I dare to eat a peach?
I shall wear white flannel trousers, and walk upon the beach.
I have heard the mermaids singing, each to each.

    I do not think that they will sing to me.   125

    I have seen them riding seaward on the waves
Combing the white hair of the waves blown back
When the wind blows the water white and black.

    We have lingered in the chambers of the sea
By sea-girls wreathed with seaweed red and brown   130
Till human voices wake us, and we drown.

Questions

1. Whereas Browning's dramatic monologues are carefully placed in particular periods and settings, "The Love Song of J. Alfred Prufrock" is seemingly more vague about the speaker's surroundings. Read the poem carefully and answer these questions:

   A. Who is J. Alfred Prufrock? To what class of society does he belong? Does he have a regular occupation? Is he rich or poor? What does his name suggest about his character and personality?
   B. The title says this monologue is a "love song." Whom does Prufrock love? Who is the "you" to whom he is speaking here? Does the identity of "you" matter or not?
   C. In what physical setting (or settings) does this speech take place? Consider the repeated references to women moving about a room, talking of Michelangelo; tea; plates; casual conversation and questions; formal clothing.
   D. In what country does the action of the poem probably take place: France, England, the United States? At what period: after 1950; between 1900 and 1950; before 1900; before 1800? Explain your answers.

2. What is the most important element in "Prufrock"—the character of Prufrock? His society? The mood of the poem? The action? The setting?
3. What is the nature of the dramatic conflict in this monologue? Who are the opponents: Prufrock and his "love"? Prufrock and his society? Prufrock and himself?
4. Is Prufrock more significant as an individual or a type? How does he compare with Browning's Bishop in this respect?
5. Does this poem have any of the elements of a diary, or letter, or autobiography? If so, how are they altered by the poet to suit the particular demands of his subject and literary form?

ANTHONY HECHT

Behold the Lilies of the Field

And now. An attempt.
Don't tense yourself; take it easy.
Look at the flowers there in the glass bowl.
Yes, they are lovely and fresh. I remember
Giving my mother flowers once, rather like those   5
(Are they narcissus or jonquils?)
And I hoped she would show some pleasure in the them
But got that mechanical enthusiastic show
She used on the telephone once in praising some friend
For thoughtfulness or good taste or whatever it was,   10
And when she hung up, turned to us all and said,
"God, what a bore she is!"
I think she was trying to show us how honest she was,
At least with us. But the effect
Was just the opposite, and now I don't think   15
She knows what honesty is. "Your mother's a whore,"
Someone said, not meaning she slept around,
Though perhaps this was part of it, but
Meaning she had lost all sense of honor,
And I think this is true.   20

But that's not what I wanted to say.
What was it I wanted to say?
When he said that about Mother, I had to laugh,
I really did, it was so amazingly true.
Where was I?   25
Lie back. Relax.
Oh yes. I remember now what it was.
It was what I saw them do to the emperor.
They captured him, you know. Eagles and all.
They stripped him, and made an iron collar for his neck,   30
And they made a cage out of our captured spears,
And they put him inside, naked and collared,
And exposed to the view of the whole enemy camp.
And I was tied to a post and made to watch
When he was taken out and flogged by one of their generals   35
And then forced to offer his ripped back
As a mounting block for the barbarian king

To get on his horse;
And one time to get down on all fours to be the
  royal throne
When the king received our ambassadors   40
To discuss the question of ransom.
Of course, he didn't want ransom.
And I was tied to a post and made to watch.
That's enough for now. Lie back. Try to relax.
No, that's not all.   45
They kept it up for two months.
We were taken to their outmost provinces.
It was always the same, and we were always made
  to watch,
The others and I. How he stood it, I don't know.
And then suddenly   50
There were no more floggings or humiliations,
The king's personal doctor saw to his back,
He was given decent clothing, and the collar was
  taken off,
And they treated us all with a special courtesy.
By the time we reached their capital city   55
His back was completely healed.
They had taken the cage apart—
But of course they didn't give us back our spears.
Then later that month, it was a warm afternoon
  in May,
The rest of us were marched out to the central
  square.   60
The crowds were there already, and the posts were
  set up,
To which we were tied in the old watching
  positions.
And he was brought out in the old way, and
  stripped,
And then tied flat on a big rectangular table
So that only his head could move.   65
Then the king made a short speech to the crowds,
To which they responded with gasps of wild
  excitement,
And which was then translated for the rest of us.
It was the sentence. He was to be flayed alive,
As slowly as possible, to drag out the pain.   70
And we were made to watch. The king's personal
  doctor,
The one who had tended his back,
Came forward with a tray of surgical knives.
They began at the feet.
And we were not allowed to close our eyes   75
Or to look away. When they were done, hours
  later,

The skin was turned over to one of their saddle-
  makers
To be tanned and stuffed and sewn. And for
  what?
A hideous life-sized doll, filled out with straw,
In the skin of the Roman Emperor, Valerian,   80
With blanks of mother-of-pearl under the eyelids,
And painted shells that had been prepared
  beforehand
For the fingernails and toenails,
Roughly cross-stitched on the inseam of the legs
And up the back to the center of the head,   85
Swung in the wind on a rope from the palace
  flag-pole;
And young girls were brought there by their
  mothers
To be told about the male anatomy.
His death had taken hours.
They were very patient.   90
And with him passed away the honour of Rome.

In the end, I was ransomed. Mother paid for me.
You must rest now. You must. Lean back.
Look at the flowers.
Yes. I am looking. I wish I could be like them.   95

Questions

1. Anthony Hecht's "Behold the Lilies of the
    Field" is actually a dialogue rather than a
    monologue, and thus it has added dramatic
    elements. Who are the two "characters" or
    speakers in the poem? What is their rela-
    tionship? Is the tension of the situation due
    to a conflict (difference of wills or desires)
    between the two speakers or to something
    else?

2. This dialogue reveals a mental process,
    among other things. What sort of process
    is represented? Can it be identified by
    reference to the terms of William James
    (*reverie, inference, reasoning*)? To those of
    Freud, Trilling, or Berne?

3. The time-structure of Hecht's dialogue is
    one of its most interesting elements. Does
    the poem take place in the present or the
    ancient past? Are the telephone and the
    Emperor Valerian contemporary? In what
    sense?

4. Valerian was one of the last of the Roman emperors to rule before the dissolution of the Empire. The historic account of his fate is given in Chapter X of Gibbon's *Decline and Fall*. Is Hecht concerned with the factual details about Valerian? His historic importance? Or is the flaying of the emperor a symbol of something else?

5. In what ways is Roman history used quite differently in this poem from its use by Gibbon, Miss Clark, Hans Zinsser, and Byron (pp. 261, 178, 352–354, 530)? Which writer sees Roman events in the most intensely personal dimensions: Hecht or Byron?

6. What is the relationship of the phrase "Mother paid for me" to the first stanzas of the poem? To the account of Valerian's flaying? To the overall subject and attitudes in the poem? Are there similarities between the central theme and purpose of "Behold the Lilies" and Kafka's *Dear Father*?

7. Discuss the use of flowers as symbols in this poem. The title refers to Jesus's *Sermon on the Mount* (Matt. 6:28), which described the lilies of the field as not toiling or spinning but arrayed in a glory greater than Solomon's. How is the literary allusion connected with the bowl of flowers mentioned in the first lines and the wish of the speaker in the final line?

ANTON CHEKHOV

The Wedding
A Farce in One Act

Characters in the Play

YEVDOKIM ZAHAROVITCH ZHIGALOV [*retired Collegiate registry-clerk*].

NASTASYA TIMOFEYEVNA [*his wife*].

THE WEDDING, A Farce in One Act: From *Three Sisters and Other Plays*, by Anton Chekhov, translated by Constance and David Garnett. Copyright © 1923 by Chatto & Windus. Reprinted by permission of Collins-Knowlton-Wing, Inc. and Chatto & Windus.

DASHENKA [*their daughter*].

EPAMINOND MAXIMOVITCH APLOMBOV [*her bridegroom*].

FYODOR YAKOVLEVITCH REVUNOV-KARAULOV [*retired Naval Captain of the second rank*].

ANDREY ANDREYEVITCH NYUNIN [*Insurance Agent*].

ANNA MARTYNOVNA ZMEYUKIN [*a Midwife, about thirty, in a bright magenta dress*].

IVAN MIHAILOVITCH YAT [*a Telegraph Clerk*].

HARLAMPY SPIRIDONOVITCH DYMBA [*a Greek keeper of a confectioner's shop*].

DMITRY STEPANOVITCH MOZGOVOY [*a Sailor in the Volunteer fleet*].

BEST MEN, DANCING GENTLEMEN, WAITERS, *etc.*

[*The action takes place in one of the rooms of a second-class restaurant.*

[*A brilliantly lighted room. A big table laid for supper.* WAITERS *in swallow-tails are busy at the tables. Behind the scenes a band is playing the last figure of the quadrille.*

MADAME ZMEYUKIN, YAT, *and the Bridegroom's* BEST MAN *walk across the stage.*

MADAME ZMEYUKIN. No, no, no!

YAT [*following her*]. Have pity on me!

MADAME ZMEYUKIN. No, no, no!

THE BEST MAN. [*hastening after them*]. I say, you can't go on like that! Where are you off to? And the *Grand-rond? Grand-rond*, silvoo-play! [*They go out*].

[*Enter* NASTASYA TIMOFEYEVNA *and* APLOMBOV.

NASTASYA. Instead of worrying me, saying all sorts of things, you had much better go and dance.

APLOMBOV. I am not a Spinoza, to go twirling my legs like a top. I am a practical man and a man of character, and I find no entertainment in idle diversions. But dancing is not what I am talking about. Forgive me, *maman*, but there's a great deal I can't make out in your conduct. For instance, apart from objects of household utility, you promised to give me two lottery tickets with your daughter. Where are they?

NASTASYA. I've got a shocking headache….. It must be the weather….. There's going to be a thaw!

APLOMBOV. Don't try to put me off. I found out to-day that your tickets are pawned. Excuse me, *maman*, no one but an exploiter would do a thing like that. I don't say this from egoisticism—I don't want your lottery tickets—but it's a matter of principle, and I won't allow anyone to do me. I've made your daughter's happiness, and if you don't give me the tickets to-day, I'll make it hot for her! I am a man of honour!

NASTASYA. [*looking round the table and counting the places laid*]. One, two, three, four, five....

A WAITER. The cook told me to ask you how you will have the ices served: with rum, with Madeira, or with nothing.

APLOMBOV. With rum. And tell the manager there is not enough wine. Tell him to send some Haut-Sauterne as well. [*To* NASTASYA TIMOFEYEVNA] You promised, too, and it was an agreed thing, that at supper to-night there should be a general. And where is he, I should like to know?

NASTASYA. That's not my fault, my dear.

APLOMBOV. Who's then?

NASTASYA. Andrey Andreyevitch's. He was here yesterday and promised to bring a real general [*sighs*]. I suppose he could not find one anywhere, or he would have brought him. As though we were mean about it! There's nothing we'd grudge for our child's happiness. A general by all means, if you want one....

APLOMBOV. And another thing.... Everybody knows, and so do you, *manan*, that that telegraph clerk Yat was courting Dashenka before I made her an offer. Why have you invited him? Surely you must have known I should dislike it?

NASTASYA. Oh, what's your name? Epaminond Maximitch, here you have not been married one day, and already you've worn me out, and Dashenka too, with your talk. And what will it be in a year? You are a trying man, you really are!

APLOMBOV. You don't like to hear the truth? A-ha! So that's how it is. But you should behave honourably. All I want of you is to be honourable!

[*Couples dancing the Grand-rond come in at one door, cross the stage, and go out at another. The first couple are* DASHENKA *and the* BEST MAN, *the last* YAT *and* MADAME ZMEYUKIN. *The last couple drop behind and remain in the room.* ZHIGALOV *and* DYMBA *enter and go up to the table.*

THE BEST MAN [*shouts*]. Promenade! Messieurs, promenade! [*Behind the scenes*] Promenade!

[*The couples dance out.*

YAT [*to* MADAME ZMEYUKIN]. Have pity, have pity, enchanting Anna Martynovna!

MADAME ZMEYUKIN. Oh, what a man!...I have told you already that I am not in voice to-day.

YAT. I entreat you, do sing! If it's only one note! Have pity! If only one note!

MADAME ZMEYUKIN. You worry me...[*sits down and waves her fan*].

YAT. Yes, you really are pitiless! To think of such a cruel creature, if I may use the expression, having such a lovely voice! With such a voice you oughtn't to be a midwife, if you'll allow me to say so, but to sing at public concerts! How divine is your rendering of this phrase, for instance...this one...[*hums*]..."I loved you, love that was in vain"...Exquisite!

MADAME ZMEYUKIN. [*hums*]. "I loved you, and still it may be love"...Is that it?

YAT. Yes, that's it. Exquisite!

MADAME ZMEYUKIN. No, I am not in voice to-day ....There, fan me...it's hot! [*To* APLOMBOV] Epaminond Maximitch, why are you so melancholy? That's not the thing on your wedding day! You ought to be ashamed, you horrid man! Why, what are you thinking about?

APLOMBOV. Marriage is a serious step. It needs serious consideration from every point of view.

MADAME ZMEYUKIN. What hateful sceptics you all are! I cannot breathe in your society.... Give me atmosphere! Do you hear? Give me atmosphere! [*Hums*]

YAT. Exquisite! exquisite!

MADAME ZMEYUKIN. Fan me, fan me! I feel as though my heart were going to burst.... Tell me, please, why is it I feel suffocated?

YAT. It's because you are in a sweat....

MADAME ZMEYUKIN. Ough, what vulgarity! Don't dare to use such expressions!

YAT. I beg your pardon! Of course you are used to aristocratic society, if you'll excuse the expression....

MADAME ZMEYUKIN. Oh, let me alone! Give me poetry, raptures! Fan me, fan me!...

ZHIGALOV [*to* DYMBA]. Shall we repeat? [*Fills glasses.*] One can drink at any minute. The great thing is not to neglect one's business, Harlampy Spiridonitch. Drink, but keep your wits about you!... But as for drinking, why not drink? There's no harm in a drink.... To your good health! [*They drink.*] And are there tigers in Greece?

DYMBA. Dere are.

ZHIGALOV. And lions?

DYMBA. Yes, lions too. In Russia dere's noding, but in Greece dere's everyding. Dere I have fader, and uncle, and broders, and here I have noding.

ZHIGALOV. Hm.... And are there whales in Greece?

DYMBA. Dere's everyding.

NASTASYA [*to her husband*]. Why are you eating and drinking all anyhow? It's time for everyone to sit down. Don't stick your fork into the tinned lobster.... That's for the general. Perhaps he may come yet....

ZHIGALOV. And are there lobsters in Greece, too?

DYMBA. Yes...dere's everyding dere.

ZHIGALOV. Hm.... And collegiate registry clerks too?

MADAME ZMEYUKIN. I can imagine what the atmosphere is in Greece!

ZHIGALOV. And I expect there's a lot of roguery.... Greeks are much the same as Armenians or gypsies. They sell you a sponge or a goldfish, and are all agog to fleece you over it. Shall we repeat?

NASTASYA. What's the good of repeating? It's time we were all sitting down. It's past eleven....

ZHIGALOV. Well, let us sit down, then. Ladies and gentlemen, pray come to supper! [*Shouts*] Supper! Young people!

NASTASYA. Dear friends, please come! Sit down!

MADAME ZMEYUKIN [*sitting down at the table*]. Give me poetry! "His restless spirit seeks the storm as though in tempest there were peace!" Give me tempest!

YAT [*aside*]. A remarkable woman! I am in love! head over ears in love!

[*Enter* DASHENKA, MOZGOVOY, *the* BEST MAN, *gentlemen and ladies. They all sit down noisily; a moment's pause; the band plays a march.*

MOZGOVOY [*getting up*]. Ladies and gentlemen, I have something to say....We have a great many toasts to drink and speeches to make. Don't let us put them off, but begin at once. Ladies and gentlemen, I propose the toast of the bride and bridegroom!

[*The band plays a flourish. Shouts of* "Hurrah!" *and clinking of glasses.*

MOZGOVOY. It needs sweetening!

ALL. It needs sweetening!

[APLOMBOV *and* DASHENKA *kiss.*

YAT. Exquisite! exquisite! I must declare, ladies and gentlemen—and it's only paying credit where credit is due—that this room and the establishment generally is magnificent! Superb, enchanting! But, you know, there's one thing wanting to complete it: electric lighting, if you will excuse the expression! In all countries they have electric light now, and only Russia lags behind.

ZHIGALOV [*with an air of profundity*]. Electric light. ...Hm....But to my mind electric light is nothing but roguery....They stick a bit of coal in, and think they will hoax you with that! No, my good man, if you are going to give us light, don't give us a little bit of coal, but give us something substantial, something solid that you can get hold of! Give us light—you understand—light that's natural and not intellectual!

YAT. If you had seen an electric battery, and what it's made of, you'd think differently.

ZHIGALOV. I don't want to see it. It's roguery. They take simple folks in....Squeeze the last drop out of them....We know all about them....Instead of sticking up for roguery, young man, you had better have a drink and fill other people's glasses. Yes, indeed!

APLOMBOV. I quite agree with you, Pa. What's the use of trotting out these learned subjects? I am quite ready to talk of all sorts of discoveries in the scientific sense, but there's a time for everything! (*To* DASHENKA) What do you think about it, *ma chère?*

DASHENKA. He wants to show off his learning, and always talks of things no one can understand.

NASTASYA. Thank God, we have lived all our lives without learning, and this is the third daughter we are marrying to a good husband. And if you think we are so uneducated, why do you come to see us? You should go to your learned friends!

YAT. I've always had a respect for your family, Nastasya Timofeyevna, and if I did say a word about electric lighting, it doesn't mean I spoke out of conceit. I am ready enough to have a drink! I have always wished Darya Yevdokimovna a good husband with all the feelings of my heart. It's difficult to find a good husband nowadays, Nastasya Timofeyevna. Nowadays everybody is keen on marrying for money.

APLOMBOV. That's a hint at me!

YAT [*scared*]. Not the slightest hint intended....I was not speaking of present company....I meant it as a general remark....Upon my word! Everyone knows you are marrying for love.... The dowry is not worth talking about!

NASTASYA. Not worth talking about, isn't it? You mind what you are saying, sir. Besides a thousand roubles in cash, we are giving three pelisses, the bedding and all the furniture. You try and find a dowry to match that!

YAT. I didn't mean anything.... The furniture is certainly nice...and...and the pelisses, of course; I only spoke in the sense that they're offended as though I'd dropped a hint.

NASTASYA. Well, you shouldn't drop hints. It's out of regard for your parents we asked you to the wedding, and you keep saying all sorts of things. And if you knew that Epaminond Maximovitch was after her money, why didn't you speak before? [*Tearfully*] I have reared and nurtured her.... I've watched over her like a diamond or an emerald, my sweet child....

APLOMBOV. And you believe him? Much obliged, I am sure! Very much obliged. [*To* YAT] And as for you, Mr. Yat, though you are a friend, I won't allow you to behave so disgracefully in other people's houses! Kindly take yourself off!

YAT. What do you mean?

APLOMBOV. I could wish you were as much of a gentleman as I am! In fact, kindly take yourself off.

[*The band plays a flourish.*

GENTLEMEN [*to* APLOMBOV]. Oh, stop it! Leave off! It doesn't matter! Sit down! Let him alone!

YAT. I wasn't saying anything...why, I...In fact I don't understand it.... Certainly, I'll go.... But first pay me the five roubles you borrowed from me a year ago to buy yourself a piqué waistcoat; excuse the expression. I'll have another drink and I'll...I'll go, only first pay me what you owe me.

GENTLEMEN. Come, stop it, stop it! That's enough! Making such a fuss about nothing!

THE BEST MAN [*shouts*]. To the health of the bride's parents, Yevdokim Zaharitch and Nastasya Timofeyevna!

[*The band plays a flourish. Shouts of "Hurrah!"*

ZHIGALOV [*touched, bows in all directions*]. Thank you, good friends! I am very grateful to you for not forgetting us and not being too proud to come!... Don't think that I am a knave or that it's roguery. I speak merely as I feel! In the simplicity of my heart!

For my friends I grudge nothing! I thank you sincerely! [*Kisses those near him.*]

DASHENKA [*to her mother*]. Ma, why are you crying? I am so happy.

APLOMBOV. Maman is upset at the approaching separation. But I would advise her to think over our conversation.

YAT. Don't cry, Nastasya Timofeyevna! Think what human tears are! Neurotic weakness, that's all!

ZHIGALOV. And are there mushrooms in Greece?

DYMBA. Yes, dere is everyding dere.

ZHIGALOV. But, I bet, there are no brown ones, like ours.

DYMBA. Yes, dere are.

MOZGOVOY. Harlampy Spiridonitch, it's your turn to make a speech! Ladies and gentlemen, let him make a speech!

ALL. A speech! a speech! It's your turn.

DYMBA. Why? What for? I not understand what it is....

MADAME ZMEYUKIN. No, no! Don't dare to refuse! It's your turn! Get up!

DYMBA [*stands up, in confusion*]. I can say dis.... Dere's Russia and dere's Greece. Dere's people in Russia and dere's people in Greece.... And *caravies* floating on de sea, dat is in Russia, ships, and on de earth de different railways. I know very well.... We Greeks, you Russians, and not want noding. I can tell you.... dere's Russia and dere's Greece.

[*Enter* NYUNIN.

NYUNIN. Stay, ladies and gentlemen, don't eat yet! Wait a bit! Nastasya Timofeyevna, one minute; Come this way! [*Draws* NASTASYA TIMOFEYEVNA *aside, breathlessly.*] I say, the general is just coming.... At last I've got hold of him.... I am simply worn out.... A real general, so dignified, elderly, eighty I should think, or perhaps ninety....

NASTASYA. When is he coming?

NYUNIN. This minute You will be grateful to me to the end of your days. Not a general but a peach, a Boulanger! Not a common general, not an infantry man, but a naval one! In grade he is a captain of the second rank, but in their reckoning, in the fleet, it's equal to a major-general, or, in the civil service, to an actual civil councillor. It's exactly the same; higher, in fact.

NASTASYA. You are not deceiving me, Andryushenka?

NYUNIN. What next! Am I a swindler? Set your mind at rest.

NASTASYA [*with a sigh*]. I don't want to spend my money for nothing, Andryushenka....

NYUNIN. Set your mind at rest! He is a perfect picture of a general! [*Raising his voice*] I said to him: "You have quite forgotten us, your Excellency! It's too bad, your Excellency, to forget your old friends! Nastasya Timofeyevna," I said, "is quite huffy!" [*Goes to the table and sits down.*] And he said to me: "Upon my soul, my boy, how can I go when I don't know the bridegroom?" "What next, your Excellency! why stand on ceremony? The bridegroom is a splendid fellow, an open-hearted chap. He is a valuer in a pawnbroker's shop," I told him, "but don't imagine, your Excellency, that he is a paltry beggar or a cad. Even well-born ladies serve in pawn-shops nowadays." He slapped me on the shoulder, we each had a Havana cigar, and here he is coming now....Wait a minute, ladies and gentlemen, don't eat....

APLOMBOV. And when will he be here?

NYUNIN. This minute. He was putting on his goloshes when I came away.

APLOMBOV. Then we must tell them to play a march.

NYUNIN [*shouts*]. Hey, bandmaster! A march! [*The band plays a march for a minute.*]

A WAITER [*announces*]. Mr. Revunov-Karaulov!

[ZHIGALOV, NASTASYA TIMOFEYEVNA, *and* NYUNIN *hasten to meet him. Enter* REVUNOV-KARAULOV.

NASTASYA [*bowing*]. You are very welcome, your Excellency! Delighted to see you!

REVUNOV. Delighted!

ZHIGALOV. We are not distinguished or wealthy people, your Excellency, we are plain folks; but don't think there's any roguery on our part. We grudge nothing for nice people, nothing is too good for them. You are very welcome!

REVUNOV. Delighted!

NYUNIN. Allow me to introduce, your Excellency! The bridegroom Epaminond Maximitch Aplombov, with his new-born...I mean newly married bride! Ivan Mihailitch Yat, of the telegram department. Harlampy Spiridonitch Dymba, a foreigner of Greek extraction, in the confectionery line! Osip Lukitch Babelmandebsky! and so on...and so on.... The rest are not much account. Sit down, your Excellency.

REVUNOV. Delighted! Excuse me, ladies and gentlemen, I want to say a couple of words to Andryusha [*leads* NYUNIN *aside*]. I feel rather awkward, my boy....Why do you call me "your Excellency"? Why, I am not a general! A captain of the second rank; it isn't even as good as a colonel.

NYUNIN [*speaks into his ear as to a deaf man*]. I know, but, Fyodor Yakovlevitch, be so good as to let us say "your Excellency"! They are a patriarchal family here, you know; they honour their betters, and like to show respect where respect is due....

REVUNOV. Well, if that's how it is, of course... [*going to the table*]. Delighted!

NASTASYA. Sit down, your Excellency! Do us the honour! What will you take, your Excellency? Only you must excuse us, you are accustomed to dainty fare at home, while we are plain people!

REVUNOV [*not hearing*]. What? Hm....Yes....[*a pause*]. Yes....In old days people all lived plainly and were satisfied. I am a man of rank in the service, but I live plainly....Andryusha came to me to-day and invited me here to the wedding. "How can I go," said I, "when I don't know them? That would be awkward!" But, he said, "They are plain people, a patriarchal family, always glad to see a visitor." "Oh well, of course if that is how it is...Why not? I am delighted. It's dull for me at home all alone, and if my being at the wedding can give pleasure to anyone, well, by all means," I said.

ZHIGALOV. So it was in the kindness of your heart, your Excellency? I honour you! I am a plain man, with no sort of roguery about me, and I respect those that are the same. Pray take something, your Excellency.

APLOMBOV. Have you long left the service, your Excellency?

REVUNOV. Eh? Yes, yes...to be sure. That's true. Yes....But how is this? The herring is bitter and the bread is bitter, I can't eat it.

ALL. It needs sweetening!

[APLOMBOV *and* DASHENKA *kiss.*

REVUNOV. He-he-he!...Your health! [*a pause*] Yes....In old days everything was plain, and everyone was satisfied....I like plain ways....I am an old man,

Of course, I retired from the service in 1865. I am seventy-two....Yes. In old days to be sure, they liked, too, on occasion to make a show, but...[*seeing* Mozgovoy]. You...er...are a sailor, aren't you?

MOZGOVOY. Yes, sir.

REVUNOV. Aha!...To be sure....Yes....The naval service was always a hard one. You've something to think about and rack your brains over. Every trivial word has, so to say, a special meaning. For instance: Mast-hands, to the top-sail lifts and the mainsail braces! What does that mean? A sailor understands, no fear about that! Ha-ha! It's as hard as any mathematics.

NYUNIN. To the health of his Excellency, Fyodor Yakovlevitch Revunov-Karaulov!

[*Band plays a flourish.*

ALL. Hurrah!

YAT. Well, your Excellency, you've just been pleased to tell us something about the difficulties of the naval service. But is the telegraph service any easier? Nowadays, your Excellency, no one can go in for the telegraph service unless he can read and write French and German. But the hardest job for us is transmitting the telegrams! It's awfully difficult! Just listen [*taps with his fork on the table, imitating the telegraph code*].

REVUNOV. And what does that mean?

YAT. That means: I respect you, your Excellency, for your noble qualities. Do you suppose that's easy? And now listen [*taps*].

REVUNOV. A little louder....I don't hear.

YAT. That means: Madam, how happy I am to hold you in my arms.

REVUNOV. What madam are you talking about? Yes...[*to* Mozgovoy]. And now if you are sailing with a strong wind and want to hoist the top-gallant sail and the royal, then you must shout: Sail hands, on the cross-trees to the top-gallant sail and the royal sail!...and while they pay out the sails on the yards below, they are at the top-gallant and royal halyards, stays and braces....

THE BEST MAN [*getting up*]. Ladies and gentle...

REVUNOV [*interrupting*]. Yes...there are all sorts of orders to be given....Yes....Top-gallant sheets and royal sheets taut, let go the lifts! Sounds fine, doesn't it? But what does it mean? Oh, it's very simple. They pull the top-gallant and royal sheets and raise the lifts.....All at once! And at the same time as they raise them, level the royal sheets and the royal lifts, and, where necessary, slacken the braces of those sails, and when the sheets are taut and all the lifts have been raised to their places, the top-gallant braces and the royal braces are taut and the yards are turned the way of the wind....

NYUNIN [*to* REVUNOV]. Fyodor Yakovlevitch! our hostess begs to talk of something else. Our guests can't understand this, they are bored....

REVUNOV. What? Who is bored? [*To* Mozgovoy] Young man! Now, if the ship is lying with the wind on the starboard tack, under full sail, and you want to bring her round before the wind, what order must you give? Why, pipe all hands on deck, bring her round before the wind.

NYUNIN. Fyodor Yakovlevitch, that's enough, eat your supper!

REVUNOV. As soon as they have all run up, you give the command at once: Stand to your places, bring her round before the wind! Ah, what a life! You give the command and see the sailors run like lightning to their places and pull the stays and the braces, then you can't help shouting, Bravo, lads! [*Chokes and coughs.*]

THE BEST MAN [*hastening to take advantage of the ensuing pause*]. On this, so to speak, festive occasion, on which we, all gathered together here, to do honour to our beloved....

REVUNOV [*interrupting*]. Yes! And you have to remember all that! For instance: let out the fore-top-sail-sheet, top-gallant-sail sheet!...

THE BEST MAN [*offended*]. Why does he interrupt? At this rate we shan't get through a single speech!

NASTASYA. We are ignorant people, your Excellency, we don't understand a word of all this. If you would tell us something that would amuse....

REVUNOV [*not hearing*]. Thank you, I have had some. Did you say goose? Thank you....Yes. I was recalling old days. It's a jolly life, young man! You float over the sea without a care in your heart and... [*In a shaking voice*] Do you remember the excitement of tacking? What sailor isn't fired by the thought of that manœuvre! Why, as soon as the command is given: Pipe all hands on deck, it's like an electric shock running through them all. From the commanding officer to the lowest sailor they are all in a flutter....

MADAME ZMEYUKIN. I am bored, I am bored! [*A general murmur*].

REVUNOV [*not hearing*]. Thank you, I have had some. [*With enthusiasm*]. Everyone is ready and all eyes are fixed on the senior officer.... "Fore-topsail and mainsail braces to starboard, mizzen-braces to larboard, counter-braces to port," shouts the senior officer. Every order is carried out instantly. "Slacken fore-sheet and jib-stay....right to starboard!" [*Gets up.*] Then the ship rolls to the wind and the sails begin to flap. The senior officer shouts "To the braces! to the braces! look alive!" While he fixes his eyes on the topsail and when at last it begins to flap, that is, when the ship begins to turn, a terrific yell is heard: "Loose the mainsail-stays, let go the braces!" Then everything is flying and creaking—a regular tower of Babel! it's all done without a break. The ship is turned!

NASTASYA [*flaring up*]. For all you are a general, you've no manners! You should be ashamed at your age!

REVUNOV. Greengage? No, I have not had any.... Thank you.

NASTASYA [*aloud*]. I say, you ought to be ashamed at your age! You are a general, but you have no manners!

NYUNIN [*in confusion*]. Come, friends!...why make a fuss?...really.

REVUNOV. To begin with, I am not a general, but a captain of the second rank, which corresponds to a lieutenant-colonel of military rank.

NASTASYA. If you are not a general, what did you take the money for? We did not pay you money to be rude to us!

REVUNOV [*in perplexity*]. What money?

NASTASYA. You know very well what money. You got the twenty-five roubles from Andrey Andreyevitch right enough...[*to* NYUNIN]. It's too bad of you, Andryusha! I didn't ask you to engage a fellow like this.

NYUNIN. Oh, come....Drop it! Why make a fuss?

REVUNOV. Engaged...Paid...What does it mean?

APLOMBOV. Allow me....You've received twenty-five roubles from Andrey Andreyevitch, haven't you?

REVUNOV. Twenty-five roubles? [*Grasping the situation*]. So that's how it is! Now I understand it! What a dirty trick! What a dirty trick!

APLOMBOV. Well, you had the money, hadn't you?

REVUNOV. I've had no money! Get away with you! [*Gets up from the table.*] What a dirty trick! What a mean trick! To insult an old man like this—a sailor—an officer who has seen honourable service!...If these were decent people I might challenge someone to a duel, but as it is, what can I do? [*Distractedly*] Where is the door? Which way do I go? Waiter! show me out! Waiter! [*Going*] What a mean trick! What a dirty trick! [*Goes out.*]

NASTASYA. Andryusha, where is that twenty-five roubles, then?

NYUNIN. Oh, don't make a fuss about such a trifle! As though it matters! Here everyone is rejoicing, while you keep on about this silly business. [*Shouts*] To the health of the happy pair! Band, a march! [*The band plays a march.*] To the health of the happy pair!

MADAME ZMEYUKIN. I am stifling! Give me atmosphere! At your side I am suffocated!

YAT [*delighted*]. Exquisite creature!

[*Hubbub.*

THE BEST MAN [*trying to shout above the rest*]. Ladies and gentlemen! On this, so to say, festive occasion...

CURTAIN

THE END

Questions

1. What are the time and social milieu in which *The Wedding* takes place? What level of society is represented? Is this fact meaningful or not?

2. Given its setting, is there anything in the dialogue or action of this play that seems unreal or inappropriate? Is the dialogue believable? What is Chekhov attempting to effect in the spectator by having his characters utter such banal thoughts?

3. Notice the professions of the wedding guests. Have they any importance to the theme and mood of the play? Do they have any broader, symbolic significance to Chekhov's theme: a confectioner, an in-

surance man, a pawnbroker, a registry clerk, a midwife at a wedding?

4. Why do the parents of the bride want a "general" at the wedding banquet? Is there any appropriate irony about the "general" they get?

5. Does Chekhov mean the viewer to feel pity for any of his characters? To laugh at them? To despise them? What is a *farce* and why does Chekhov call his play one? What is farcical: the situation, characters, action, setting?

6. What is Chekhov saying about human beings and life in this play? Why does he make a wedding the central episode in the action?

J. M. SYNGE

Riders to the Sea

Cast of Characters

MAURYA, an old woman
BARTLEY, her son
CATHLEEN, her daughter
NORA, a younger daughter
MEN AND WOMEN
    SCENE. *An island off the West of Ireland*

[*Cottage kitchen, with nets, oilskins, spinning-wheel, some new boards standing by the wall, etc. CATHLEEN, a girl of about twenty, finishes kneading cake, and puts it down in the pot-oven by the fire; then wipes her hands, and begins to spin at the wheel.*
    NORA, a young girl, puts her head in at the door.

NORA [*In a low voice*]. Where is she?

CATHLEEN. She's lying down, God help her, and maybe sleeping, if she's able.

[*NORA comes in softly and takes a bundle from under her shawl.*

RIDERS TO THE SEA: Originally acted in 1904 and published by George Allen & Unwin Ltd.

CATHLEEN [*Spinning the wheel rapidly*]. What is it you have?

NORA. The young priest is after bringing them. It's a shirt and a plain stocking were got off a drowned man in Donegal. [*Cathleen stops her wheel with a sudden movement, and leans out to listen.*] We're to find out if it's Michael's they are, sometime herself will be down looking by the sea.

CATHLEEN. How would they be Michael's, Nora? How would he go the length of that way to the far north?

NORA. The young priest says he's known the like of it. "If it's Michael's they are," says he, "you can tell herself he's got a clean burial, by the grace of God; and if they're not his, let no one say a word about them, for she'll be getting her death," says he, "with crying and lamenting."

    [*The door which Nora half closed is blown open by a gust of wind.*

CATHLEEN [*Looking out anxiously*]. Did you ask him would he stop Bartley going this day with the horses to the Galway fair?

NORA. "I won't stop him," says he; "but let you not be afraid. Herself does be saying prayers half through the night, and the Almighty God won't leave her destitute," says he, "with no son living."

CATHLEEN. Is the sea bad by the white rocks, Nora?

NORA. Middling bad, God help us. There's a great roaring in the west, and it's worse it'll be getting when the tide's turned to the wind. [*She goes over to the table with the bundle.*] Shall I open it now?

CATHLEEN. Maybe she'd wake up on us, and come in before we'd done. [*Coming to the table.*] It's a long time we'll be, and the two of us crying.

NORA [*Goes to the inner door and listens*]. She's moving about on the bed. She'll be coming in a minute.

CATHLEEN. Give me the ladder, and I'll put them up in the turf-loft, the way she won't know of them at all, and maybe when the tide turns she'll be going down to see would he be floating from the east.

    [*They put the ladder against the gable of the chimney; CATHLEEN goes up a few steps and hides the bundle in the turf-loft. MAURYA comes from the inner room.*

MAURYA [*Looking up at CATHLEEN and speaking querulously*]. Isn't it turf enough you have for this day and evening?

CATHLEEN. There's a cake baking at the fire for a short space [*throwing down the turf*], and Bartley will want it when the tide turns if he goes to Connemara.

[NORA *picks up the turf and puts it round the pot-oven.*

MAURYA [*Sitting down on a stool at the fire*]. He won't go this day with the wind rising from the south and west. He won't go this day, for the young priest will stop him surely.

NORA. He'll not stop him, mother; and I heard Eamon Simon and Stephen Pheety and Colum Shawn saying he would go.

MAURYA. Where is he itself?

NORA. He went down to see would there be another boat sailing in the week, and I'm thinking it won't be long till he's here now, for the tide's turning at the green head, and the hooker's tacking from the east.

CATHLEEN. I hear someone passing the big stones.

NORA [*Looking out*]. He's coming now, and he in a hurry.

BARTLEY [*Comes in and looks round the room; speaking sadly and quietly*]. Where is the bit of new rope, Cathleen, was bought in Connemara?

CATHLEEN [*Coming down*]. Give it to him, Nora; it's on a nail by the white boards. I hung it up this morning, for the pig with the black feet was eating it.

NORA [*Giving him a rope*]. Is that it, Bartley?

MAURYA. You'd do right to leave that rope, Bartley, hanging by the boards. [BARTLEY *takes the rope.*] It will be wanting in this place, I'm telling you, if Michael is washed up to-morrow morning, or the next morning, or any morning in the week; for it's a deep grave we'll make him, by the grace of God.

BARTLEY [*Beginning to work with the rope*]. I've no halter the way I can ride down on the mare, and I must go now quickly. This is the one boat going for two weeks or beyond it, and the fair will be a good fair for horses, I heard them saying below.

MAURYA. It's a hard thing they'll be saying below if the body is washed up and there's no man in it to make the coffin, and I after giving a big price for the finest white boards you'd find in Connemara.

[*She looks round at the boards.*

BARTLEY. How would it be washed up, and we after looking each day for nine days, and a strong wind blowing a while back from the west and south?

MAURYA. If it isn't found itself, that wind is raising the sea, and there was a star up against the moon, and it rising in the night. If it was a hundred horses, or a thousand horses, you had itself, what is the price of a thousand horses against a son where there is one son only?

BARTLEY [*Working at the halter, to* CATHLEEN]. Let you go down each day, and see the sheep aren't jumping in on the rye, and if the jobber comes you can sell the pig with the black feet if there is a good price going.

MAURYA. How would the like of her get a good price for a pig?

BARTLEY [*To* CATHLEEN]. If the west wind holds with the last bit of the moon let you and Nora get up weed enough for another cock for the kelp. It's hard set we'll be from this day with no one in it but one man to work.

MAURYA. It's hard set we'll be surely the day you're drowned with the rest. What way will I live and the girls with me, and I an old woman looking for the grave?

[BARTLEY *lays down the halter, takes off his old coat, and puts on a newer one of the same flannel.*

BARTLEY [*To* NORA]. Is she coming to the pier?

NORA [*Looking out*]. She's passing the green head and letting fall her sails.

BARTLEY [*Getting his purse and tobacco*]. I'll have half an hour to go down, and you'll see me coming again in two days, or in three days, or maybe in four days if the wind is bad.

MAURYA [*Turning round to the fire and putting the shawl over her head*]. Isn't it a hard and cruel man won't hear a word from an old woman, and she holding him from the sea?

CATHLEEN. It's the life of a young man to be going on the sea, and who would listen to an old woman with one thing and she saying it over?

BARTLEY [*Taking the halter*]. I must go now quickly. I'll ride down on the red mare, and the grey pony 'll run behind me....The blessing of God on you.

[*He goes out.*

MAURYA [*Crying out as he is in the door*]. He's gone now, God spare us, and we'll not see him again. He's gone now, and when the black night is falling I'll have no son left me in the world.

CATHLEEN. Why wouldn't you give him your blessing and he looking round in the door? Isn't it sorrow enough is on every one in this house without your sending him out with an unlucky word behind him, and a hard word in his ear?

[MAURYA *takes up the tongs and begins raking the fire aimlessly without looking round.*

NORA [*Turning towards her*]. You're taking away the turf from the cake.

CATHLEEN [*Crying out*]. The Son of God forgive us, Nora, we're after forgetting his bit of bread.

[*She comes over to the fire.*

NORA. And it's destroyed he'll be going till dark night, and he after eating nothing since the sun went up.

CATHLEEN [*Turning the cake out of the oven*]. It's destroyed he'll be surely. There's no sense left on any person in a house where an old woman will be talking for ever.

[MAURYA *sways herself on her stool.*

CATHLEEN [*Cutting off some of the bread and rolling it in a cloth; to* MAURYA]. Let you go down now to the spring well and give him this and he passing. You'll see him then and the dark word will be broken, and you can say "God speed you," the way he'll be easy in his mind.

MAURYA [*Taking the bread*]. Will I be in it as soon as himself?

CATHLEEN. If you go now quickly.

MAURYA [*Standing up unsteadily*]. It's hard set I am to walk.

CATHLEEN [*Looking at her anxiously*]. Give her the stick, Nora, or maybe she'll slip on the big stones.

NORA. What stick?

CATHLEEN. The stick Michael brought from Connemara.

MAURYA [*Taking a stick* NORA *gives her*]. In the big world the old people do be leaving things after them for their sons and children, but in this place it is the young men do be leaving things behind for them that do be old.

[*She goes out slowly.* NORA *goes over to the ladder.*

CATHLEEN. Wait, Nora, maybe she'd turn back quickly. She's that sorry, God help her, you wouldn't know the thing she'd do.

NORA. Is she gone round by the bush?

CATHLEEN [*Looking out*]. She's gone now. Throw it down quickly, for the Lord knows when she'll be out of it again.

NORA [*Getting the bundle from the loft*]. The young priest said he'd be passing to-morrow, and we might go down and speak to him below if it's Michael's they are surely.

CATHLEEN [*Taking the bundle*]. Did he say what way they were found?

NORA [*Coming down*]. "There were two men," says he, "and they rowing round with poteen before the cocks crowed, and the oar of one of them caught the body, and they passing the black cliffs of the north."

CATHLEEN [*Trying to open the bundle*]. Give me a knife, Nora; the string's perished with the salt water, and there's a black knot on it you wouldn't loosen in a week.

NORA [*Giving her a knife*]. I've heard tell it was a long way to Donegal.

CATHLEEN [*Cutting the string*]. It is surely. There was a man in here a while ago—the man sold us that knife—and he said if you set off walking from the rocks beyond, it would be in seven days you'd be in Donegal.

NORA. And what time would a man take, and he floating?

[CATHLEEN *opens the bundle and takes out a bit of a shirt and a stocking. They look at them eagerly.*

CATHLEEN [*In a low voice*]. The Lord spare us, Nora! Isn't it a queer hard thing to say if it's his they are surely?

NORA. I'll get his shirt off the hook the way we can put the one flannel on the other. [*She looks through some clothes hanging in the corner.*] It's not with them, Cathleen, and where will it be?

CATHLEEN. I'm thinking Bartley put it on him in the morning, for his own shirt was heavy with the salt in it. [*Pointing to the corner.*] There's a bit of a sleeve was of the same stuff. Give me that and it will do. [NORA *brings it to her and they compare the flannel.*] It's the same stuff, Nora; but if it is itself aren't there great rolls of it in the shops of Galway, and isn't it many another man may have a shirt of it as well as Michael himself?

NORA [*Who has taken up the stocking and counted the stitches, crying out*]. It's Michael, Cathleen, it's Michael;

God spare his soul, and what will herself say when she hears this story, and Bartley on the sea?

CATHLEEN [*Taking the stocking*]. It's a plain stocking.

NORA. It's the second one of the third pair I knitted, and I put up three-score stitches, and I dropped four of them.

CATHLEEN [*Counts the stitches*]. It's that number is in it. [*Crying out.*] Ah, Nora, isn't it a bitter thing to think of him floating that way to the far north, and no one to keen him but the black hags that do be flying on the sea?

NORA [*Swinging herself half round, and throwing out her arms on the clothes*]. And isn't it a pitiful thing when there is nothing left of a man who was a great rower and fisher but a bit of an old shirt and a plain stocking?

CATHLEEN [*After an instant*]. Tell me is herself coming, Nora? I hear a little sound on the path.

NORA [*Looking out*]. She is, Cathleen. She's coming up to the door.

CATHLEEN. Put these things away before she'll come in. Maybe it's easier she'll be after giving her blessing to Bartley, and we won't let on we've heard anything the time he's on the sea.

NORA [*Helping* CATHLEEN *to close the bundle*]. We'll put them here in the corner.

[*They put them into a hole in the chimney-corner.* CATHLEEN *goes back to the spinning-wheel.*

NORA. Will she see it was crying I was?

CATHLEEN. Keep your back to the door the way the light'll not be on you.

[NORA *sits down at the chimney-corner, with her back to the door.* MAURYA *comes in very slowly, without looking at the girls, and goes over to her stool at the other side of the fire. The cloth with the bread is still in her hand. The girls look at each other, and* NORA *points to the bundle of bread.*

CATHLEEN [*After spinning for a moment*]. You didn't give him his bit of bread?

[MAURYA *begins to keen softly, without turning round.*

CATHLEEN. Did you see him riding down?

[MAURYA *goes on keening.*

CATHLEEN [*A little impatiently*]. God forgive you; isn't it a better thing to raise your voice and tell what you seen, than to be making lamentation for a thing that's done? Did you see Bartley, I'm saying to you?

MAURYA [*With a weak voice*]. My heart's broken from this day.

CATHLEEN [*As before*]. Did you see Bartley?

MAURYA. I seen the fearfullest thing.

CATHLEEN [*Leaves her wheel and looks out*]. God forgive you; he's riding the mare now over the green head, and the grey pony behind him.

MAURYA [*Starts, so that her shawl falls back from her head and shows her white tossed hair. With a frightened voice*]. The grey pony behind him....

CATHLEEN [*Coming to the fire*]. What is it ails you at all?

MAURYA [*Speaking very slowly*]. I've see the fearfullest thing any person has seen since the day Bride Dara seen the dead man with the child in his arms.

CATHLEEN and NORA. Uah.

[*They crouch down in front of the old woman at the fire.*

NORA. Tell us what it is you seen.

MAURYA. I went down to the spring well, and I stood there saying a prayer to myself. Then Bartley came along, and he riding on the red mare with the grey pony behind him. [*She puts up her hands as if to hide something from her eyes.*] The Son of God spare us, Nora!

CATHLEEN. What is it you seen?

MAURYA. I seen Michael himself.

CATHLEEN [*Speaking softly*]. You did not, mother. It wasn't Michael you see, for his body is after being found in the far north, and he's got a clean burial, by the grace of God.

MAURYA [*A little defiantly*]. I'm after seeing him this day, and he riding and galloping. Bartley came first on the red mare, and I tried to say "God speed you," but something choked the words in my throat. He went by quickly; and "The blessing of God on you," says he, and I could say nothing. I looked up then, and I crying, at the grey pony, and there was Michael upon it—with fine clothes on him, and new shoes on his feet.

CATHLEEN [*Begins to keen*]. It's destroyed we are from this day. It's destroyed, surely.

NORA. Didn't the young priest say the Almighty God won't leave her destitute with no son living?

MAURYA [*In a low voice, but clearly*]. It's little the like of him knows of the sea.... Bartley will be lost now, and let you call in Eamon and make me a good coffin out of the white boards, for I won't live after them. I've had a husband, and a husband's father, and six sons in this house—six fine men, though it was a hard birth I had with every one of them and they coming to the world—and some of them were found and some of them were not found, but they're gone now the lot of them.... There were Stephen and Shawn were lost in the great wind, and found after in the Bay of Gregory of the Golden Mouth, and carried up the two of them on one plank, and in by that door.

[*She pauses for a moment, the girls start as if they heard something through the door that is half open behind them.*

NORA [*In a whisper*]. Did you hear that, Cathleen? Did you hear a noise in the north-east?

CATHLEEN [*In a whisper*]. There's someone after crying out by the seashore.

MAURYA [*Continues without hearing anything*]. There was Sheamus and his father, and his own father again, were lost in a dark night, and not a stick or sign was seen of them when the sun went up. There was Patch after was drowned out of a curragh that was turned over. I was sitting here with Bartley, and he a baby lying on my two knees, and I seen two women, and three women, and four women coming in, and they crossing themselves and not saying a word. I looked out then, and there were men coming after them, and they holding a thing in the half of a red sail, and water dripping out of it—it was a dry day, Nora—and leaving a track to the door.

[*She pauses again with her hands stretched out towards the door. It opens softly and old women begin to come in, crossing themselves on the threshold, and kneeling down in front of the stage with red petticoats over their heads.*

MAURYA [*Half in a dream, to Cathleen*]. Is it Patch, or Michael, or what is it at all?

CATHLEEN. Michael is after being found in the far north, and when he is found there how could he be here in this place?

MAURYA. There does be a power of young men floating round in the sea, and what way would they know if it was Michael they had, or another man like him, for when a man is nine days in the sea, and the wind blowing, it's hard set his own mother would be to say what man was in it.

CATHLEEN. It's Michael, God spare him, for they're after sending us a bit of his clothes from the far north.

[*She reaches out and hands MAURYA the clothes that belonged to MICHAEL. MAURYA stands up slowly and takes them in her hands. NORA looks out.*

NORA. They're carrying a thing among them, and there's water dripping out of it and leaving a track by the big stones.

CATHLEEN [*In a whisper to the women who have come in*]. Is it Bartley it is?

ONE OF THE WOMEN. It is surely, God rest his soul.

[*Two younger women come in and pull out the table. Then men carry in the body of BARTLEY, laid on a plank, with a bit of sail over it, and lay it on the table.*

CATHLEEN [*To the women as they are doing so*]. What way was he drowned?

ONE OF THE WOMEN. The grey pony knocked him over into the sea, and he was washed out where there is a great surf on the white rocks.

[*MAURYA has gone over and knelt down at the head of the table. The women are keening softly and swaying themselves with a slow movement. CATHLEEN and NORA kneel at the other end of the table. The men kneel near the door.*

MAURYA [*Raising her head and speaking as if she did not see the people around her*]. They're all gone now, and there isn't anything more the sea can do to me.... I'll have no call now to be up crying and praying when the wind breaks from the south, and you can hear the surf is in the east, and the surf is in the west, making a great stir with the two noises, and they hitting one on the other. I'll have no call now to be going down and getting Holy Water in the dark nights after Samhain, and I won't care what way the sea is when the other women will be keening. [*To NORA.*] Give me the Holy Water, Nora; there's a small sup still on the dresser.

[*NORA gives it to her.*

MAURYA [*Drops MICHAEL's clothes across BARTLEY's feet, and sprinkles the Holy Water over him*]. It isn't that I haven't prayed for you, Bartley, to the Almighty God. It isn't that I haven't said prayers in the dark night till you wouldn't know what I'd be saying; but it's a great rest I'll have now, and it's time, surely. It's a great rest I'll have now, and great sleeping in the long nights after Samhain, if it's only a bit of wet flour we do have to eat, and maybe a fish that would be stinking.

[*She kneels down again, crossing herself, and saying prayers under her breath.*

CATHLEEN [*To an old man*]. Maybe yourself and Eamon would make a coffin when the sun rises. We have fine white boards herself bought, God help her, thinking Michael would be found, and I have a new cake you can eat while you'll be working.

THE OLD MAN [*Looking at the boards*]. Are there nails with them?

CATHLEEN. There are not, Colum; we didn't think of the nails.

ANOTHER MAN. It's a great wonder she wouldn't think of the nails, and all the coffins she's seen made already.

CATHLEEN. It's getting old she is, and broken.

[MAURYA *stands up again very slowly, and spreads out the pieces of* MICHAEL's *clothes beside the body, sprinkling them with the last of the Holy Water.*

NORA [*In a whisper to* CATHLEEN]. She's quiet now and easy; but the day Michael was drowned you could hear her crying out from this to the spring well. It's fonder she was of Michael, and would any one have thought that?

CATHLEEN [*Slowly and clearly*]. An old woman will be soon tired with anything she will do, and isn't it nine days herself is after crying and keening, and making great sorrow in the house?

MAURYA [*Puts the empty cup mouth downwards on the table, and lays her hands together on* BARTLEY's *feet*]. They're all together this time, and the end is come. May the Almighty God have mercy on Bartley's soul, and on Michael's soul, and on the souls of Sheamus and Patch, and Stephen and Shawn [*bending her head*]; and may He have mercy on my soul, Nora, and on the soul of every one is left living in the world.

[*She pauses, and the keen rises a little more loudly from the women, then sinks away.*

MAURYA [*Continuing*]. Michael has a clean burial in the far north, by the grace of the Almighty God. Bartley will have a fine coffin out of the white boards, and a deep grave surely. What more can we want than that? No man at all can be living for ever, and we must be satisfied.

[*She kneels down again, and the curtain falls slowly.*

Questions

1. At what time and in what place does the action of *Riders to the Sea* take place? Is the milieu of the play necessary to the characters? action? theme? Is the locale of Synge's play more important than Chekhov's?

2. What are the most significant elements in this play in attaining a dramatic, (or aesthetic, or emotional) effect?

3. The chief theme of *Riders to the Sea* depends on the impression of repetition: the recurrence of events and emotions. How does the playwright give the sense of repetition without monotony? How does he use exposition to enforce character and action in the play?

4. Does this play violate the "natural" laws of time, character, causation, or logic in any fashion? Does anything take place that could not "factually" happen in just that way? What effect has this upon the credibility of the play? In what sense can a drama remain "true" though it discards logic?

5. Chekhov's play shows a wedding and is comic; Synge's play shows a funeral and is tragic or pathetic. Is there a real correspondence between subject matter and tone—or mood—in a play? Could there be a "comic" death scene or a "tragic" wedding? What controls the emotional effect of a play?

6. *Riders to the Sea* is often called a short "tragedy." Look up some treatments of "tragedy" and the "tragic" view of life and write a critical analysis of Synge's drama as tragedy.

7. Do the characters in *Riders* change or develop in any way? Or are they simply revealed as constant by the action of the play? Is it possible to show believable changes in character in a short play like this, or does a play need three or more acts—with time lapses between—to create an evolving or reforming or otherwise "changing" character?

TENNESSEE WILLIAMS

The Last of My Solid Gold Watches

Characters

MR. CHARLIE COLTON.

A NEGRO, *a porter in the hotel.*

HARPER, *a traveling salesman.*

> SCENE: *A hotel room in a Mississippi Delta town. The room has looked the same, with some deterioration, for thirty or forty years. The walls are mustard-colored. There are two windows with dull green blinds, torn slightly, a ceiling-fan, a white iron bed with a pink counterpane, a washstand with rose-buds painted on the pitcher and bowl, and on the wall a colored lithograph of blind-folded Hope with her broken lyre.*
>
> *The door opens and* MR. CHARLIE COLTON *comes in. He is a legendary character, seventy-eight years old but still "going strong." He is lavish of flesh, superbly massive and with a kingly dignity of bearing. Once he moved with a tidal ease and power. Now he puffs and rumbles; when no one is looking he clasps his hand to his chest and cocks his head to the warning heart inside him. His huge expanse of chest and belly is criss-crossed by multiple gold chains with various little fobs and trinkets suspended from them. On the back of his head is a derby and in his mouth a cigar. This is "Mistuh Charlie"—who sadly but proudly refers to himself as "the last of the Delta drummers." He is followed into the room by a* NEGRO *porter, as old as he is—thin and toothless and grizzled. He totes the long orange leather sample cases containing the shoes which* MR. CHARLIE *is selling. He sets them down at the foot of the bed as* MR. CHARLIE *fishes in his pocket for a quarter.*

MR. CHARLIE [*handing the coin to the* NEGRO]. Hyunh!

NEGRO [*breathlessly*]. Thankyseh!

MR. CHARLIE. Huh! You're too old a darkey to tote them big heavy cases.

NEGRO [*grinning sadly*]. Don't say that, Mistuh Charlie.

MR. CHARLIE. I reckon you'll keep right at it until yuh drop some day.

NEGRO. That's right, Mistuh Charlie.

> [MR. CHARLIE *fishes in his pocket for another quarter and tosses it to the* NEGRO, *who crouches and cackles as he receives it.*

MR. CHARLIE. Hyunh!

NEGRO. Thankyseh, thankyseh!

MR. CHARLIE. Now set that fan in motion an' bring me in some ice-water by an' by!

NEGRO. De fan don' work, Mistuh Charlie.

MR. CHARLIE. Huh! Deterioration! Everything's going downhill around here lately!

NEGRO. Yes, suh, dat's de troof, Mistuh Charlie, ev'ything's goin' down-hill.

MR. CHARLIE. Who all's registered here of my acquaintance? Any ole-timers in town?

NEGRO. Naw, suh, Mistuh Charlie.

MR. CHARLIE. "Naw-suh-Mistuh-Charlie" 's all I get any more! You mean to say I won't be able to scare up a poker-game?

NEGRO [*chuckling sadly*]. Mistuh Charlie, you's de bes' judge about dat!

MR. CHARLIE. Well, it's mighty slim pickin's these days. Ev'ry time I come in a town there's less of the old and more of the new and by God, nigguh, this new stand of cotton I see around the Delta's not worth pickin' off th' ground! Go down there an' tell that young fellow, Mr. Bob Harper, to drop up here for a drink!

NEGRO [*withdrawing*]. Yes, suh.

MR. CHARLIE. It looks like otherwise I'd be playin' solitaire!

> [*The* NEGRO *closes the door.* MR. CHARLIE *crosses to the window and raises the blind. The evening is turning faintly blue. He sighs and opens his valise to remove a quart of whisky and some decks of cards which he slaps down on the table. He pauses and clasps his hand over his chest.*

MR. CHARLIE [*ominously to himself*]. Boom-boom-boom-boom-boom! Here comes th' parade! [*After some moments there comes a rap at the door.*] Come awn in!

[HARPER, *a salesman of thirty-five, enters. He has never known the "great days of the road" and there is no vestige of grandeur in his manner. He is lean and sallow and has a book of colored comics stuffed in his coat pocket.*

HARPER. How is the ole war-horse?

MR. CHARLIE [*heartily*]. Mighty fine an' dandy! How's the young squirrel?

HARPER. Okay.

MR. CHARLIE. That's the right answer! Step on in an' pour you'self a drink! Cigar?

HARPER [*accepting both*]. Thanks, Charlie.

MR. CHARLIE [*staring at his back with distaste*]. Why do you carry them comic sheets around with yuh?

HARPER. Gives me a couple of laughs ev'ry once and a while.

MR. CHARLIE. Poverty of imagination! [HARPER *laughs a little resentfully.*] You can't tell me there's any real amusement in them things. [*He pulls it out of* HARPER's *coat pocket.*] "Superman," "The Adventures of Tom Tyler!" Huh! None of it's half as fantastic as life itself! When you arrive at my age—which is seventy-eight—you have a perspective of time on earth that astounds you! Literally astounds you! Naw, you say it's not true, all of that couldn't have happened! And for what *reason?* Naw! You begin to wonder....Well...You're with Schultz and Werner?

HARPER. That's right, Charlie.

MR. CHARLIE. That concern's comparatively a new one.

HARPER. I don't know about that. They been in th' bus'ness fo' goin' on twenty-five years now, Charlie.

MR. CHARLIE. Infancy! You heard this one, Bob? A child in its infancy don't have half as much fun as adults—in their adultery!

[*He roars with laughter.* HARPER *grins.* MR. CHARLIE *falls silent abruptly. He would have appreciated a more profound response. He remembers the time when a joke of his would precipitate a tornado. He fills up* HARPER's *glass with whisky.*

HARPER. Ain't you drinkin'?

MR. CHARLIE. Naw, suh. Quit!

HARPER. How come?

MR. CHARLIE. Stomach! Perforated!

HARPER. Ulcers? [MR. CHARLIE *grunts. He bends with difficulty and heaves a sample case onto the bed.*] I had ulcers once.

MR. CHARLIE. Ev'ry drinkin' man has ulcers once. Some *twice.*

HARPER. You've fallen off some, ain't you?

MR. CHARLIE. [*opening the sample case*]. Twenty-seven pounds I lost since August. [HARPER *whistles.* MR. CHARLIE *is fishing among his samples.*] Yay-*ep!* Twenty-seven pounds I lost since August. [*He pulls out an oxford which he regards disdainfully.*] Hmmm...A waste of cow-hide! [*He throws it back in and continues fishing.*] A man of my age an' constitution, Bob—he oughtn't to carry so much of that—adipose tissue! It's— [*He straightens up, red in the face and puffing.*]—a terrible strain—on the *heart!* Hand me that other sample—over yonder. I wan' t' show you a little eyeful of queenly footwear in our new spring line! Some people say that the Cosmopolitan's not abreast of the times! That is an allegation which I deny and which I intend to disprove by the simple display of one little calf-skin slipper! [*opening up the second case*] Here we are, Son! [*fishing among the samples*] You knew ole "Marblehead" Langner in Friar's Point, Mississippi?

HARPER. Ole "Marblehead" Langner? Sure.

MR. CHARLIE. They found him dead in his bath-tub a week ago Satiddy night. *Here's* what I'm lookin' faw!

HARPER. "Marblehead"? Dead?

MR. CHARLIE. *Buried!* Had a Masonic funeral. I helped carry th' casket. Bob, I want you t' look at this Cuban-heel, shawl-tongue, perforated toe, calf-skin Misses' sport-oxford! [*He elevates it worshipfully.*] I want you to look at this shoe—and tell me what you think of it in plain language! [HARPER *whistles and bugs his eyes.*] Ain't that a piece of *real* merchandise, you squirrel? Well, suh, I want you t' know—!

HARPER. Charlie, that certainly is a piece of merchandise there!

MR. CHARLIE. Bob, that piece of merchandise is only a small indication—of what our spring line consists of! You don't have to pick up a piece of merchandise like that—with I.S.C. branded on it!—and examine it with the microscope t' find out if it's quality stuff as well as quality *looks!* This ain't a shoe that Mrs. Jones of Hattiesburg, Mississippi, is going to throw back in your face a couple or three weeks later because it come to pieces like *card*-board in th' first *rain!* No, suh—I want you to know! We got some pretty fast-movers in our spring line—I'm layin' my samples out down there in th' lobby first thing in th' mornin'—I'll pack 'em up an' be gone out of town by *noon*— But by the Almighty Jehovah I bet you I'll have to *wire* the office to mail me a bunch of *brand-new* order-books at my next stopping-*off* place, Bob! *Hot* cakes! *That's* what I'm sellin'!

[*He returns exhaustedly to the sample case and tosses the shoe back in, somewhat disheartened by* HARPER's *vaguely benevolent contemplation of the brass light-fixture. He remembers a time when people's attention could be more securely riveted by talk. He slams the case shut and glances irritably at* HARPER *who is staring very sadly at the brown carpet.*]

Well, suh— [*He pours a shot of whisky.*] It was a mighty shocking piece of news I received this afternoon.

HARPER [*blowing a smoke ring*]. What piece of news was that?

MR. CHARLIE. The news about ole Gus Hamma— one of the old war-horses from *way* back, Bob. He and me an' this boy's daddy, C. C., used t' play poker ev'ry time we hit town together in this here self-same room! Well, suh, I want you t' know—

HARPER [*screwing up his forehead*]. I think I heard about that. Didn't he have a stroke or something a few months ago?

MR. CHARLIE. He *did*. An' partly *recovered*.

HARPER. Yeah? Last I heard he had t' be fed with a spoon.

MR. CHARLIE [*quickly*]. He did an' he partly recovered! He's been goin' round, y'know, in one of them chairs with a 'lectric motor on it. Goes chug-chug-chuggin' along th' road with th' butt of a cigar in his mouth. Well, suh, yestuddy in Blue Mountain, as I go out the Elks' Club door I pass him comin' in, bein' helped by th' nigguh— "Hello! Hiyuh, Gus!" That was at six-fifteen. Just half an hour later Carter Bowman stepped inside the hotel lobby where I was packin' up my sample cases an' give me the information that ole Gus Hamma had just now burnt himself to death in the Elks' Club lounge!

HARPER [*involuntarily grinning*]. What uh yuh talkin' about?

MR. CHARLIE. Yes, suh, the ole war-horse had fallen asleep with that nickel cigar in his mouth—set his clothes on fire—and burnt himself right up like a piece of paper!

HARPER. I don't believe yuh!

MR. CHARLIE. Now, why on earth would I be lyin' to yuh about a thing like that? He burnt himself right up like a piece of paper!

HARPER. Well, ain't that a bitch of a way for a man to go?

MR. CHARLIE. *One* way—*another* way—! [*gravely*] Maybe you don't *know* it—but all of us ole-timers, Bob, are disappearin' *fast!* We all gotta quit th' road one time or another. Me, I reckon I'm pretty nearly the last of th' Delta drummers!

HARPER [*restively squirming and glancing at his watch*]. The last—of th' Delta drummers! How long you been on th' road?

MR. CHARLIE. Fawty-six yeahs in Mahch!

HARPER. I don't believe yuh.

MR. CHARLIE. Why would I tell you a lie about something like that? No, suh, I want you t' know—I want you t' know— Hmmm.... I lost a mighty good customer this week.

HARPER [*with total disinterest, adjusting the crotch of his trousers*]. How's that, Charlie?

MR. CHARLIE [*grimly*]. Ole Ben Summers—Friar's Point, Mississippi...Fell over dead like a bolt of lightning had struck him just as he went to pour himself a drink at the Cotton Planters' Cotillion!

HARPER. Ain't that terrible, though! What was the trouble?

MR. CHARLIE. Mortality, that was the trouble! Some people think that millions now living are never going to *die*. I don't think that—I think it's a mis-apprehension not borne out by the facts! We go like flies when we come to the end of the summer... And who is going to prevent it? [*He becomes depressed.*] Who—is going—to prevent it! [*He nods gravely.*] The road is changed. The shoe industry is changed. These times are—revolution! [*He rises and moves to the window.*] I don't like the way that it looks. You can take it from me—the world that I used to know—the world that this boy's father used t' know—the world we belonged to, us old time war-horses!—is slipping and sliding away from under our shoes. Who is going to prevent it? The ALL LEATHER slogan don't sell shoes any more. The stuff that a shoe's made of is not what's going to sell it any more! No! STYLE! SMARTNESS! APPEARANCE! That's what counts with the modern shoe-purchaser, Bob! But try an' tell your style department that. Why, I remember the time when all I had to do was lay out my samples down there in the lobby. Open up my order-book an' write out orders until my fingers *ached!* A *sales*-talk was not *necessary.* A store was a place where people sold merchandise and to sell merchandise the retail-dealer had to obtain it from the wholesale manufacturer, Bob! Where they get merchandise now I do not pretend to know. But it don't look like they buy it from wholesale dealers! Out of the air—I guess it materializes! Or maybe stores don't *sell* stuff any more! Maybe I'm living in a world of illusion! I recognize that possibility, too!

HARPER [*casually, removing the comic paper from his pocket*]. Yep—yep. You must have witnessed some changes.

MR. CHARLIE. Changes? A mild expression. Young man—I have witnessed—a REVOLUTION! [HARPER *has opened his comic paper but* MR. CHARLIE *doesn't notice, for now his peroration is really addressed to himself.*] Yes, a *revolution!* The atmosphere that I *breathe* is not the same! Ah, well—I'm an old war-horse. [*He opens his coat and lifts the multiple golden chains from his vest. An amazing number of watches rise into view. Softly, proudly he speaks.*] Looky here, young fellow! You ever seen a man with this many watches? How did I *acquire* this many time-pieces? [HARPER *has seen them before. He glances above the comic sheet with affected amazement.*] At every one of the annual sales conventions of the Cosmopolitan Shoe Company in St. Louis a seventeen-jewel, solid-gold, Swiss-movement Hamilton watch is presented to the ranking salesman of the year! Fifteen of those watches have been awarded to me! I think that represents something! I think that's *something* in the way of achievement!...Don't *you?*

HARPER. Yes, *siree!* You bet I *do,* Mistuh Charlie!

[*He chuckles at a remark in the comic sheet.* MR. CHARLIE *sticks out his lips with a grunt of disgust and snatches the comic sheet from the young man's hands.*

MR. CHARLIE. Young man—I'm talkin' to *you,* I'm talkin' for your *benefit.* And I expect the courtesy of your attention until I am through! I may be an old war-horse. I may have received—the last of my solid gold watches...But just the same—good manners are still a part of the road's tradition. And part of the *South's* tradition. Only a young peckerwood would look at the comics when old Charlie Colton is talking.

HARPER [*taking another drink*]. Excuse me, Charlie. I got a lot on my mind. I got some business to attend to directly.

MR. CHARLIE. And directly you shall attend to it! I just want you to know what I think of this new world of yours! I'm not one of those that go howling about a Communist being stuck in the White House now! I don't say that Washington's been took over by Reds! I don't say all of the wealth of the country is in the hands of the Jews! I like the Jews and I'm a friend to the niggers! I *do* say *this*—however....The world I knew is gone—gone—gone with the wind! My pockets are full of watches which tell me that my time's just about over! [*A look of great trouble and bewilderment appears on his massive face. The rather noble tone of his speech slackens into a senile complaint.*] All of them—pigs that was slaughtered—carcasses dumped in the river! Farmers receivin' payment *not* t' grow wheat an' corn an' *not* t' plant cotton! All of these alphabet letters that's sprung up all about me! Meaning—unknown—to men of my generation! The rudeness—the lack of respect—the newspapers full of strange items! The terrible—fast—dark—rush of events in the world! Toward what and where and why?...I don't pretend to have any knowledge of now! I only say—and I say this very humbly—I don't understand—what's happened....I'm one of them monsters you see reproduced in museums—out of the dark old ages—the giant *rep*-tiles, and the dino-whatever-you-call-ems. BUT—I *do* know *this!* And I state it without any shame! Initiative—self-reliance—independence of character! The old sterling qualities that distinguished one man from another—the clay from the potters—the potters from the clay—are— [*kneading the air with his hands*] How is it the old song goes?...Gone with the roses of *yesterday!* Yes—with the *wind!*

HARPER [*whose boredom has increased by leaps and bounds*]. You old-timers make one mistake. You only read one side of the vital statistics.

MR. CHARLIE [*stung*]. What do you mean by that?

HARPER. In the papers they print people *dead* in one corner and people *born* in the next and usually *one* just about levels *off* with the *other.*

MR. CHARLIE. Thank you for that information. I happen to be the godfather of several new infants in various points on the road. However, I think you have missed the whole point of what I was saying.

HARPER. I don't think so, Mr. Charlie.

MR. CHARLIE. Oh, yes, you have, young fellow. My point is this: the ALL-LEATHER slogan is not what sells any more—not in shoes and not in humanity, neither! The emphasis isn't on quality. Production, production, yes! But out of inferior goods! *Ersatz*—that's what they're making 'em out of!

HARPER [*getting up*]. That's your opinion because you belong to the past.

MR. CHARLIE [*furiously*]. A piece of impertinence, young man! I expect to be accorded a certain amount of respect by whipper-snappers like you!

HARPER. Hold on, Charlie.

MR. CHARLIE. I belong to—tradition. I am a *legend*. Known from one end of the Delta to the other. From the Peabody hotel in Memphis to Cat-Fish Row in Vicksburg. Mistuh Charlie—*Mistuh Charlie!* Who knows *you?* What do *you* represent? A line of goods of doubtful value, some kike concern in the East! Get out of my room! I'd rather play solitaire, than poker with men who're no more solid characters than the jacks in the deck!

[*He opens the door for the young salesman who shrugs and steps out with alacrity. Then he slams the door shut and breathes heavily. The* NEGRO *enters with a pitcher of ice water.*]

NEGRO [*grinning*]. What you shoutin' about, Mistuh Charlie?

MR. CHARLIE. I lose my patience sometimes. Nigger—

NEGRO. Yes, suh?

MR. CHARLIE. You remember the way it used to be.

NEGRO [*gently*]. Yes, suh.

MR. CHARLIE. I used to come in town like a conquering hero! Why, my God, nigger—they all but laid red carpets at my feet! Isn't that so?

NEGRO. That's so, Mistuh Charlie.

MR. CHARLIE. This room was like a *throne*-room. My samples laid out over there on green velvet cloth! The ceiling-fan *going*—now *broken!* And over here—the wash-bowl an' pitcher removed and the table-top *loaded* with *liquor!* In and out from the time I arrived till the time I left, the men of the road who knew me, to whom I stood for things commanding respect! Poker—continuous! Shouting, laughing—hilarity! Where have they all gone to?

NEGRO [*solemnly nodding*]. The graveyard is crowded

with folks we knew, Mistuh Charlie. It's mighty late in the day!

MR. CHARLIE. Huh! [*He crosses to the window.*] Nigguh, it ain't even late in the day any more— [*He throws up the blind.*] It's NIGHT! [*The space of the window is black.*]

NEGRO [*softly, with a wise old smile*]. Yes, suh ... *Night*, Mistuh Charlie!

CURTAIN

Questions

1. This play, by Tennessee Williams, is more obviously concerned with characterization than the others included here. Is the depiction of Mr. Charlie Colton sympathetic, unsympathetic, or is it simply objective? What function do the other two characters have in helping the author to develop Mr. Charlie's character?

2. Is the situation in this play true to life or not? Are the dialogue and characters?

3. In a way, Mr. Charlie is speaking his autobiography. Compare and contrast the presentation of his life with the written forms of autobiography on pp. 114f, above. What differences can you see between the factual autobiography and the fictive one?

4. Chekhov's *The Wedding* and Wilder's *Long Christmas Dinner* suggest views toward large groups of society and mankind as a whole. Does Williams's play deal with anything beyond Mr. Charlie's personality and feelings? How does Williams give the drama a dimension beyond Charlie's character?

5. Is Williams's play at all unusual or innovational in its handling of dialogue, situations, chronology, characters, or properties? Does it use symbols; if so to what effect?

6. Like Chekhov and Synge, Williams uses a specific milieu ("local color") to add emphasis and connotation to his play. Is he commenting on Mr. Charlie's society as well as on Mr. Charlie himself? Compare Williams's fictional depiction of Southern

culture with those of William Faulkner and Eudora Welty (pp. 474, 484).

7. "Mr. Charlie" is a name for white Southerners used contemptuously by many Negroes; see James Baldwin's play, *Blues for Mr. Charlie,* for example. Does Williams's play make any comment on racial relations in the South? Compare his views with those of Baldwin and Warren (pp. 148, 370). Which makes his points most convincingly: the autobiographer, the social commentator, or the dramatist?

THORNTON WILDER

The Long Christmas Dinner

[*The dining-room of the Bayard home. Close to the footlights a long dining table is handsomely spread for Christmas dinner. The carver's place with a great turkey before it is at the spectator's right. A door, left back, leads into the hall.*

At the extreme left, by the proscenium pillar, is a strange portal trimmed with garlands of fruit and flowers. Directly opposite is another edged and hung with black velvet. The portals denote birth and death.

Ninety years are to be traversed in this play which

THE LONG CHRISTMAS DINNER: from *The Long Christmas Dinner and Other Plays in One Act* by Thornton Wilder. Copyright 1931 by Yale University Press and Coward-McCann, Inc. Copyright 1959 by Thornton Wilder. Reprinted by permission of Harper & Row, Publishers.

represents in accelerated motion ninety Christmas dinners in the Bayard household. The actors are dressed in inconspicuous clothes and must indicate their gradual increase in years through their acting. Most of them carry wigs of white hair which they adjust upon their heads at the indicated moment, simply and without comment. The ladies may have shawls concealed beneath the table that they gradually draw up about their shoulders as they grow older.

Throughout the play the characters continue eating imaginary food with imaginary knives and forks.

There is no curtain. The audience arriving at the theatre sees the stage set and the table laid, though still in partial darkness. Gradually the lights in the auditorium become dim and the stage brightens until sparkling winter sunlight streams through the dining room windows.

Enter LUCIA. *She inspects the table, touching here a knife and there a fork. She talks to a servant girl who is invisible to us.*

LUCIA. I reckon we're ready now, Gertrude. We won't ring the chimes today. I'll just call them myself.

[*She goes into the hall and calls:*

Roderick. Mother Bayard. We're all ready. Come to dinner.

[*Enter* RODERICK *pushing* MOTHER BAYARD *in a wheel chair*.

MOTHER BAYARD. . . . and a new horse too, Roderick. I used to think that only the wicked owned two horses. A new horse and a new house and a new wife!

RODERICK. Well, Mother, how do you like it? Our first Christmas dinner in the new house, hey?

MOTHER BAYARD. Tz-Tz-Tz! I don't know what your dear father would say!

LUCIA. Here, Mother Bayard, you sit between us.

[RODERICK *says grace*.

MOTHER BAYARD. My dear Lucia, I can remember when there were still Indians on this very ground, and I wasn't a young girl either. I can remember when we had to cross the Mississippi on a new-made raft. I can remember when St. Louis and Kansas City were full of Indians.

LUCIA [*tying a napkin around* MOTHER BAYARD'S *neck*]. Imagine that! There!—What a wonderful day for our first Christmas dinner: a beautiful sunny morning, snow, a splendid sermon. Dr. McCarthy preaches a splendid sermon. I cried and cried.

RODERICK [*extending an imaginary carving-fork*]. Come now, what'll you have, Mother? A little sliver of white?

LUCIA. Every least twig is wrapped around with ice. You almost never see that. Can I cut it up for you, dear? [*over her shoulder*] Gertrude, I forgot the jelly. You know,—on the top shelf.—Mother Bayard, I found your mother's gravy-boat while we were moving. What was her name, dear? What were all your names? You were...a...Genevieve Wainright. Now your mother—

MOTHER BAYARD. Yes, you must write it down somewhere. I was Genevieve Wainright. My mother was Faith Morrison. She was the daughter of a farmer in New Hampshire who was something of a blacksmith too. And she married young John Wainright—

LUCIA [*memorizing on her fingers*]. Genevieve Wainright. Faith Morrison.

RODERICK. It's all down in a book somewhere upstairs. We have it all. All that kind of thing is very interesting. Come, Lucia, just a little wine. Mother, a little red wine for Christmas day. Full of iron. "Take a little wine for thy stomach's sake."

LUCIA. Really, I can't get used to wine! What would my father say? But I suppose it's all right.

[*Enter COUSIN BRANDON from the hall. He takes his place by LUCIA.*

COUSIN BRANDON [*rubbing his hands*]. Well, well, I smell turkey. My dear cousins, I can't tell you how pleasant it is to be having Christmas dinner with you all. I've lived out there in Alaska so long without relatives. Let me see, how long have you had this new house, Roderick?

RODERICK. Why, it must be...

MOTHER BAYARD. Five years. It's five years, children. You should keep a diary. This is your sixth Christmas dinner here.

LUCIA. Think of that, Roderick. We feel as though we had lived here twenty years.

COUSIN BRANDON. At all events it still looks as good as new.

RODERICK [*over his carving*]. What'll you have, Brandon, light or dark?—Frieda, fill up Cousin Brandon's glass.

LUCIA. Oh, dear, I can't get used to these wines. I don't know what my father'd say, I'm sure. What'll you have, Mother Bayard?

[*During the following speeches MOTHER BAYARD's chair, without any visible propulsion, starts to draw away from the table, turns towards the right, and slowly goes toward the dark portal.*

MOTHER BAYARD. Yes, I can remember when there were Indians on this very land.

LUCIA [*softly*]. Mother Bayard hasn't been very well lately, Roderick.

MOTHER BAYARD. My mother was a Faith Morrison. And in New Hampshire she married a young John Wainright, who was a Congregational minister. He saw her in his congregation one day...

LUCIA. Mother Bayard, hadn't you better lie down, dear?

MOTHER BAYARD. ....and right in the middle of his sermon he said to himself: "I'll marry that girl." And he did, and I'm their daughter.

LUCIA [*half rising and looking after her with anxiety*]. Just a little nap, dear?

MOTHER BAYARD. I'm all right. Just go on with your dinner. I was ten, and I said to my brother—

[*She goes out. A very slight pause.*

COUSIN BRANDON. It's too bad it's such a cold dark day today. We almost need the lamps. I spoke to Major Lewis for a moment after church. His sciatica troubles him, but he does pretty well.

LUCIA [*dabbing her eyes*]. I know Mother Bayard wouldn't want us to grieve for her on Christmas day, but I can't forget her sitting in her wheel chair right beside us, only a year ago. And she would be so glad to know our good news.

RODERICK [*patting her hand*]. Now, now. It's Christmas. [*formally*] Cousin Brandon, a glass of wine with you, sir.

COUSIN BRANDON [*half rising, lifting his glass gallantly*]. A glass of wine with you, sir.

LUCIA. Does the Major's sciatica cause him much pain?

COUSIN BRANDON. Some, perhaps. But you know his way. He says it'll be all the same in a hundred years.

LUCIA. Yes, he's a great philosopher.

RODERICK. His wife sends you a thousand thanks for her Christmas present.

LUCIA. I forget what I gave her.—Oh, yes, the workbasket!

[*Through the entrance of birth comes a nurse wheeling a perambulator trimmed with blue ribbons.* LUCIA *rushes toward it, the men following.*

O my wonderful new baby, my darling baby! Who ever saw such a child! Quick, nurse, a boy or a girl? A boy! Roderick, what shall we call him? Really, nurse, you've never seen such a child!

RODERICK. We'll call him Charles after your father and grandfather.

LUCIA. But there are no Charleses in the Bible, Roderick.

RODERICK. Of course, there are. Surely there are.

LUCIA. Roderick!—Very well, but he will always be Samuel to me.—What miraculous hands he has! Really, they are the most beautiful hands in the world. All right, nurse. Have a good nap, my darling child.

RODERICK. Don't drop him, nurse. Brandon and I need him in our firm.

[*Exit nurse and perambulator into the hall. The others return to their chairs,* LUCIA *taking the place left vacant by* MOTHER BAYARD *and* COUSIN BRANDON *moving up beside her.* COUSIN BRANDON *puts on his white hair.*

Lucia, a little white meat? Some stuffing? Cranberry sauce, anybody?

LUCIA [*over her shoulder*]. Margaret, the stuffing is very good today.—Just a little, thank you.

RODERICK. Now something to wash it down. [*half rising*] Cousin Brandon, a glass of wine with you sir. To the ladies, God bless them.

LUCIA. Thank you, kind sirs.

COUSIN BRANDON. Pity it's such an overcast day today. And no snow.

LUCIA. But the sermon was lovely. I cried and cried. Dr. Spaulding does preach such a splendid sermon.

RODERICK. I saw Major Lewis for a moment after church. He says his rheumatism comes and goes. His wife says she has something for Charles and will bring it over this afternoon.

[*Enter nurse again with perambulator. Pink ribbons. Same rush toward the left.*

LUCIA. O my lovely new baby! Really, it never occurred to me that it might be a girl. Why, nurse, she's perfect.

RODERICK. Now call her what you choose. It's your turn.

LUCIA. Looloolooloo. Aië. Aië. Yes, this time I shall have my way. She shall be called Genevieve after your mother. Have a good nap, my treasure.

[*She looks after it as the nurse wheels the perambulator into the hall.*

Imagine! Sometime she'll be grown up and say "Good morning, Mother. Good morning, Father." —Really, Cousin Brandon, you don't find a baby like that every day.

COUSIN BRANDON. *And* the new factory.

LUCIA. A new factory? Really? Roderick, I shall be very uncomfortable if we're going to turn out to be rich. I've been afraid of that for years.— However, we mustn't talk about such things on Christmas day. I'll just take a little piece of white meat, thank you. Roderick, Charles is destined for the ministry. I'm sure of it.

RODERICK. Woman, he's only twelve. Let him have a free mind. *We* want him in the firm, I don't mind saying. Anyway, no time passes as slowly as this when you're waiting for your urchins to grow up and settle down to business.

LUCIA. I don't want time to go any faster, thank you. I love the children just as they are.—Really, Roderick, you know what the doctor said: One glass a meal. [*putting her hand over his glass*] No, Margaret, that will be all.

[RODERICK *rises, glass in hand. With a look of dismay on his face he takes a few steps toward the dark portal.*

RODERICK. Now I wonder what's the matter with me.

LUCIA. Roderick, do be reasonable.

RODERICK [*tottering, but with gallant irony*]. But, my dear, statistics show that we steady, moderate drinkers…

LUCIA [*rises, gazing at him in anguish*]. Roderick! My dear! What…?

RODERICK [*returns to his seat with a frightened look of relief*]. Well, it's fine to be back at table with you again. How many good Christmas dinners have I had to miss upstairs? And to be back at a fine bright one, too.

LUCIA. O my dear, you gave us a very alarming

time! Here's your glass of milk.—Josephine, bring Mr. Bayard his medicine from the cupboard in the library.

RODERICK. At all events, now that I'm better I'm going to start doing something about the house.

LUCIA. Roderick! You're not going to change the house?

RODERICK. Only touch it up here and there. It looks a hundred years old.

[CHARLES *enters casually from the hall. He kisses his mother's hair and sits down.*

LUCIA. Charles, you carve the turkey, dear. Your father's not well.—You always said you hated carving, though you *are* so clever at it.

[*Father and son exchange places.*

CHARLES. It's a great blowy morning, mother. The wind comes over the hill like a lot of cannon.

LUCIA. And such a good sermon. I cried and cried. Mother Bayard loved a good sermon so. And she used to sing the Christmas hymns all around the year. Oh, dear, oh, dear, I've been thinking of her all morning!

RODERICK. Sh, Mother. It's Christmas day. You mustn't think of such things.—You mustn't be depressed.

LUCIA. But sad things aren't the same as depressing things. I must be getting old: I like them.

CHARLES. Uncle Brandon, you haven't anything to eat. Pass his plate, Hilda…and some cranberry sauce…

[*Enter* GENEVIEVE. *She kisses her father's temple and sits down.*

GENEVIEVE. It's glorious. Every least twig is wrapped around with ice. You almost never see that.

LUCIA. Did you have time to deliver those presents after church, Genevieve?

GENEVIEVE. Yes, Mama. Old Mrs. Lewis sends you a thousand thanks for hers. It was just what she wanted, she said. Give me lots, Charles, lots.

RODERICK [*rising and starting toward the dark portal*]. Statistics, ladies and gentlemen, show that we steady, moderate…

CHARLES. How about a little skating this afternoon, Father?

RODERICK. I'll live till I'm ninety.

LUCIA. I really don't think he ought to go skating.

RODERICK [*at the very portal, suddenly astonished*]. Yes, but…but…not yet!

[*He goes out.*

LUCIA [*dabbing her eyes*]. He was so young and so clever, Cousin Brandon. [*raising her voice for* COUSIN BRANDON'S *deafness*] I say he was so young and so clever.—Never forget your father, children. He was a good man.—Well, he wouldn't want us to grieve for him today.

CHARLES. White or dark, Genevieve? Just another sliver, Mother?

LUCIA [*putting on her white hair*]. I can remember our first Christmas dinner in this house, Genevieve. Twenty-five years ago today. Mother Bayard was sitting here in her wheel chair. She could remember when Indians lived on this very spot and when she had to cross the river on a new-made raft.

CHARLES AND GENEVIEVE. She couldn't have, Mother. That can't be true.

LUCIA. It certainly was true—even I can remember when there was only one paved street. We were very happy to walk on boards. [*louder, to* COUSIN BRANDON] We can remember when there were no sidewalks, can't we, Cousin Brandon?

COUSIN BRANDON [*delighted*]. Oh, yes! And those were the days.

CHARLES AND GENEVIEVE [*sotto voce. This is a family refrain*]. Those were the days.

LUCIA.…and the ball last night, Genevieve? Did you have a nice time? I hope you didn't *waltz*, dear. I think a girl in your position ought to set an example. Did Charles keep an eye on you?

GENEVIEVE. He had none left. They were all on Leonora Banning. He can't conceal it any longer, Mother. I think he's engaged to marry Leonora Banning.

CHARLES. I'm not engaged to marry anyone.

LUCIA. Well, she's very pretty.

GENEVIEVE. I shall never marry, Mother—I shall sit in this house beside you forever, as though life were one long, happy Christmas dinner.

LUCIA. O my child, you mustn't say such things!

GENEVIEVE [*playfully*]. You don't want me? You don't want me?

[LUCIA *bursts into tears.*

Why, Mother, how silly you are! There's nothing sad about that—what could possibly be sad about that.

LUCIA [*drying her eyes*]. Forgive me. I'm just unpredictable, that's all.

[CHARLES *go to the door and leads in* LEONORA BANNING.

LEONORA [*kissing* LUCIA's *temple*]. Good morning, Mother Bayard. Good morning, everybody. It's really a splendid Christmas day today.

CHARLES. Little white meat? Genevieve, Mother, Leonora?

LEONORA. Every least twig is encircled with ice.— You never see that.

CHARLES [*shouting*]. Uncle Brandon, another?— Rogers, fill my uncle's glass.

LUCIA [*to Charles*]. Do what your father used to do. It would please Cousin Brandon so. You know— [*pretending to raise a glass*]—"Uncle Brandon, a glass of wine—"

CHARLES [*rising*]. Uncle Brandon, a glass of wine with you, sir.

BRANDON. A glass of wine with you, sir. To the ladies, God bless them every one.

THE LADIES. Thank you, kind sirs.

GENEVIEVE. And if I go to Germany for my music I promise to be back for Christmas. I wouldn't miss that.

LUCIA. I hate to think of you over there all alone in those strange pensions.

GENEVIEVE. But, darling, the time will pass so fast that you'll hardly know I'm gone. I'll be back in the twinkling of an eye.

[*Enter Left, the nurse and perambulator. Green ribbons.*

LEONORA. Oh, what an angel! The darlingest baby in the world. Do let me hold it, nurse.

[*But the nurse resolutely wheels the perambulator across the stage and out the dark door.*

Oh, I did love it so!

[LUCIA *goes to her, puts her arm around* LEONORA's *shoulders, and they encircle the room whispering—* LUCIA *then hands her over to* CHARLES *who conducts her on the same circuit.*

GENEVIEVE [*as her mother sits down,—softly*]. Isn't there anything I can do?

LUCIA [*raises her eyebrows, ruefully*]. No, dear. Only time, only the passing of time can help in these things.

[CHARLES *and* LEONORA *return to the table.*

Don't you think we could ask Cousin Ermengarde to come and live with us here? There's plenty for everyone and there's no reason why she should go on teaching the First Grade for ever and ever. She wouldn't be in the way, would she, Charles?

CHARLES. No, I think it would be fine.—A little more potato and gravy, anybody? A little more turkey, Mother?

[BRANDON *rises and starts slowly toward the dark portal.*
[LUCIA *rises and stands for a moment with her face in her hands.*

COUSIN BRANDON [*muttering*]. It was great to be in Alaska in those days...

GENEVIEVE [*half rising, and gazing at her mother in fear*]. Mother, what is...?

LUCIA [*hurriedly*]. Hush, my dear. It will pass. —Hold fast to your music, you know. [*as* GENEVIEVE *starts toward her*] No, no. I want to be alone for a few minutes.

[*She turns and starts after* COUSIN BRANDON *toward the Right.*

CHARLES. If the Republicans collected all their votes instead of going off into cliques among themselves, they might prevent his getting a second term.

GENEVIEVE. Charles, Mother doesn't tell us, but she hasn't been very well these days.

CHARLES. Come, Mother, we'll go to Florida for a few weeks.

[*Exit* BRANDON.

LUCIA [*smiling at* GENEVIEVE *and waving her hand*]. Don't be foolish. Don't grieve.

[*She clasps her hands under her chin; her lips move, whispering; she walks serenely into the portal.* GENEVIEVE *stares after her, frozen. At the same moment the nurse and perambulator enter from the Left. Pale yellow ribbons.* LEONORA *rushes to it.*

LEONORA. O my darlings...twins...Charles, aren't they glorious! Look at them. Look at them.

GENEVIEVE [*sinks down on the table her face buried in her arms*]. But what will I do? What's left for me to do?

CHARLES [*bending over the basket*]. Which is which?

LEONORA. I feel as though I were the first mother who ever had twins.—Look at them now!—But why wasn't Mother Bayard allowed to stay and see them!

GENEVIEVE [*rising suddenly distraught, loudly*]. I don't want to go on. I can't bear it.

CHARLES [*goes to her quickly. They sit down. He whispers to her earnestly taking both her hands*]. But Genevieve, Genevieve! How frightfully Mother would feel to think that...Genevieve!

GENEVIEVE [*shaking her head wildly*]. I never told her how wonderful she was. We all treated her as though she were just a friend in the house. I thought she'd be here forever.

LEONORA [*timidly*]. Genevieve darling, do come one minute and hold my babies' hands. We shall call the girl Lucia after her grandmother,—will that please you? Do just see what adorable little hands they have.

[GENEVIEVE *collects herself and goes over to the perambulator. She smiles brokenly into the basket.*

GENEVIEVE. They are wonderful, Leonora.

LEONORA. Give him your finger, darling. Just let him hold it.

CHARLES. And we'll call the boy Samuel.—Well, now everybody come and finish your dinners. Don't drop them, nurse; at least don't drop the boy. We need him in the firm.

LEONORA [*stands looking after them as the nurse wheels them into the hall*]. Someday they'll be big. Imagine! They'll come in and say "Hello, Mother!" [*She makes clucking noises of rapturous consternation.*

CHARLES. Come, a little wine, Leonora, Genevieve? Full of iron. Eduardo, fill the ladies' glasses. It certainly is a keen, cold morning. I used to go skating with Father on mornings like this and Mother would come back from church saying—

GENEVIEVE [*dreamily*]. I know: saying "Such a splendid sermon. I cried and cried."

LEONORA. Why did she cry, dear?

GENEVIEVE. That generation all cried at sermons. It was their way.

LEONORA. Really, Genevieve?

GENEVIEVE. They had had to go since they were children and I suppose sermons reminded them of their fathers and mothers, just as Christmas dinners do us. Especially in an old house like this.

LEONORA. It really is pretty old, Charles. And so ugly, with all that ironwork filigree and that dreadful cupola.

GENEVIEVE. Charles! You aren't going to change the house!

CHARLES. No, no. I won't give up the house but great heavens! it's fifty years old. This Spring we'll remove the cupola and build a new wing toward the tennis courts.

[*From now on* GENEVIEVE *is seen to change. She sits up more straightly. The corners of her mouth become fixed. She becomes a forthright and slightly disillusioned spinster.* CHARLES *becomes the plain business man and a little pompous.*

LEONORA. And then couldn't we ask your dear old Cousin Ermengarde to come and live with us? She's really the self-effacing kind.

CHARLES. Ask her now. Take her out of the First Grade.

GENEVIEVE. We only seem to think of it on Christmas day with her Christmas card staring us in the face.

[*Enter Left, nurse and perambulator. Blue ribbons.*

LEONORA. Another boy! Another boy! Here's a Roderick for you at last.

CHARLES. Roderick Brandon Bayard. A regular little fighter.

LEONORA. Goodbye, darling. Don't grow up too fast. Yes, yes. Aïe, aïe, aïe—stay just as you are.—Thank you, nurse.

GENEVIEVE [*who has not left the table, repeats dryly*]. Stay just as you are.

[*Exit nurse and perambulator. The others return to their places.*

LEONORA. Now I have three children. One, two, three. Two boys and a girl. I'm collecting them. It's very exciting. [*over her shoulder*] What, Hilda? Oh, Cousin Ermengarde's come! Come in, Cousin.

[*She goes to the hall and welcomes* COUSIN ERMENGARDE *who already wears her white hair.*

ERMENGARDE [*shyly*]. It's such a pleasure to be with you all.

CHARLES [*pulling out her chair for her*]. The twins have taken a great fancy to you already, Cousin.

LEONORA. The baby went to her at once.

CHARLES. Exactly how are we related, Cousin Ermengarde?—There, Genevieve, that's your specialty.—First a little more turkey and stuffing, Mother? Cranberry sauce, anybody?

GENEVIEVE. I can work it out: Grandmother Bayard was your...

ERMENGARDE. Your Grandmother Bayard was a second cousin of my Grandmother Haskins through the Wainrights.

CHARLES. Well, it's all in a book somewhere upstairs. All that kind of thing is awfully interesting.

GENEVIEVE. Nonsense. There are no such books. I collect my notes off gravestones, and you have to scrape a good deal of moss—let me tell you—to find one great-grandparent.

CHARLES. There's a story that my Grandmother Bayard crossed the Mississippi on a raft before there were any bridges or ferryboats. She died before Genevieve or I were born. Time certainly goes very fast in a great new country like this. Have some more cranberry sauce, Cousin Ermengarde.

ERMENGARDE [*timidly*]. Well, time must be passing very slowly in Europe with this dreadful, dreadful war going on.

CHARLES. Perhaps an occasional war isn't so bad after all. It clears up a lot of poisons that collect in nations. It's like a boil.

ERMENGARDE. Oh, dear, oh, dear!

CHARLES [*with relish*]. Yes, it's like a boil.—Ho! ho! Here are your twins.

[*The twins appear at the door into the hall. SAM is wearing the uniform of an ensign. LUCIA is fussing over some detail on it.*

LUCIA. Isn't he wonderful in it, Mother?

CHARLES. Let's get a look at you.

SAM. Mother, don't let Roderick fool with my stamp album while I'm gone.

LEONORA. Now, Sam, do write a letter once in a while. Do be a good boy about that, mind.

SAM. You might send some of those cakes of yours once in a while, Cousin Ermengarde.

ERMENGARDE [*in a flutter*]. I certainly will, my dear boy.

CHARLES. If you need any money, we have agents in Paris and London, remember.

SAM. Well, goodbye...

[*SAM goes briskly out through the dark portal, tossing his unneeded white hair through the door before him.*

LUCIA *sits down at the table with lowered eyes.*

ERMENGARDE [*after a slight pause, in a low, constrained voice, making conversation*]. I spoke to Mrs. Fairchild for a moment coming out of church. Her rheumatism's a little better, she says. She sends you her warmest thanks for the Christmas present. The workbasket, wasn't it?—It was an admirable sermon. And our stained-glass window looked so beautiful, Leonora, so beautiful. Everybody spoke of it and so affectionately of Sammy. [*LEONORA's hand goes to her mouth*]. Forgive me, Leonora, but it's better to speak of him than not to speak of him when we're all thinking of him so hard.

LEONORA [*rising, in anguish*]. He was a mere boy. He was a mere boy, Charles.

CHARLES. My dear, my dear.

LEONORA. I want to tell him how wonderful he was. We let him go so casually. I want to tell him how we all feel about him.—Forgive me, let me walk about a minute.—Yes, of course, Ermengarde—it's best to speak of him.

LUCIA [*in a low voice to* GENEVIEVE]. Isn't there anything I can do?

GENEVIEVE. No, no. Only time, only the passing of time can help in these things.

[*LEONORA, straying about the room finds herself near the door to the hall at the moment that her son RODERICK enters. He links his arm with hers and leads her back to the table.*

RODERICK. What's the matter, anyway? What are you all so glum about? The skating was fine today.

CHARLES. Sit down, young man. I have something to say to you.

RODERICK. Everybody was there. Lucia skated in the corners with Dan Creighton the whole time. When'll it be, Lucia, when'll it be?

LUCIA. I don't know what you mean.

RODERICK. Lucia's leaving us soon, Mother. Dan Creighton, of all people.

CHARLES [*ominously*]. Roderick, I have something to say to you.

RODERICK. Yes, Father.

CHARLES. Is it true, Roderick, that you made yourself conspicuous last night at the Country Club— at a Christmas Eve dance, too?

LEONORA. Not now, Charles, I beg of you. This is Christmas dinner.

RODERICK [loudly]. No, I didn't.

LUCIA. Really, Father, he didn't. It was that dreadful Johnny Lewis.

CHARLES. I don't want to hear about Johnny Lewis. I want to know whether a son of mine...

LEONORA. Charles, I beg of you...

CHARLES. The first family of this city!

RODERICK [rising]. I hate this town and everything about it. I always did.

CHARLES. You behaved like a spoiled puppy, sir, an ill-bred spoiled puppy.

RODERICK. What did I do? What did I do that was wrong?

CHARLES. You were drunk and you were rude to the daughters of my best friends.

GENEVIEVE [striking the table]. Nothing in the world deserves an ugly scene like this. Charles, I'm ashamed of you.

RODERICK. Great God, you gotta get drunk in this town to forget how dull it is. Time passes so slowly here that it stands still, that's what's the trouble.

CHARLES. Well, young man, we can employ your time. You will leave the university and you will come into the Bayard factory on January second.

RODERICK [at the door into the hall]. I have better things to do than to go into your old factory. I'm going somewhere where time passes, my God!

[He goes out into the hall.

LEONORA [rising]. Roderick, Roderick, come here just a moment.—Charles where can he go?

LUCIA [rising]. Sh, Mother. He'll come back. Now I have to go upstairs and pack my trunk.

LEONORA. I won't have any children left!

LUCIA. Sh, Mother. He'll come back. He's only gone to California or somewhere.—Cousin Ermengarde has done most of my packing—thanks a thousand times, Cousin Ermengarde. [She kisses her mother.] I won't be long.

[She runs out into the hall.
GENEVIEVE and LEONORA put on their white hair.

ERMENGARDE. It's a very beautiful day. On the way home from church I stopped and saw Mrs. Foster a moment. Her arthritis comes and goes.

LEONORA. Is she actually in pain, dear?

ERMENGARDE. Oh, she says it'll all be the same in a hundred years!

LEONORA. Yes, she's a brave little stoic.

CHARLES. Come now, a little white meat, Mother— Mary, pass my cousin's plate.

LEONORA. What is it, Mary?—Oh, here's a telegram from them in Paris! "Love and Christmas greetings to all." I told them we'd be eating some of their wedding cake and thinking about them today. It seems to be all decided that they will settle down in the East, Ermengarde. I can't even have my daughter for a neighbor. They hope to build before long somewhere on the shore north of New York.

GENEVIEVE. There is no shore north of New York.

LEONORA. Well, East or West or whatever it is.

[Pause.
CHARLES. My, what a dark day.

[He puts on his white hair. Pause.
How slowly time passes without any young people in the house.

LEONORA. I have three children somewhere.

CHARLES [blunderingly offering comfort]. Well, one of them gave his life for his country.

LEONORA [sadly]. And one of them is selling aluminum in China.

GENEVIEVE [slowly working herself up to a hysterical crisis]. I can stand everything but this terrible soot everywhere. We should have moved long ago. We're surrounded by factories. We have to change the window curtains every week.

LEONORA. Why, Genevieve!

GENEVIEVE. I can't stand it. I can't stand it any more. I'm going abroad. It's not only the soot that comes through the very walls of this house; it's the thoughts, it's the thought of what has been and what might have been here. And the feeling about this house of the years grinding away. My mother died yesterday—not twenty-five years ago. Oh, I'm going to live and die abroad! Yes, I'm going to be the American old maid living and dying in a pension in Munich or Florence.

ERMENGARDE. Genevieve, you're tired.

CHARLES. Come, Genevieve, take a good drink of cold water. Mary, open the window a minute.

GENEVIEVE. I'm sorry. I'm sorry.

[*She hurries tearfully out into the hall.*

ERMENGARDE. Dear Genevieve will come back to us, I think.

[*She rises and starts toward the dark portal.*

You should have been out today, Leonora. It was one of those days when everything was encircled with ice. Very pretty, indeed.

[CHARLES *rises and starts after her.*

CHARLES. Leonora, I used to go skating with Father on mornings like this.—I wish I felt a little better.

LEONORA. What! Have I got two invalids on my hands at once? Now, Cousin Ermengarde, you must get better and help me nurse Charles.

ERMENGARDE. I'll do my best.

[ERMENGARDE *turns at the very portal and comes back to the table.*

CHARLES. Well, Leonora, I'll do what you ask. I'll write the puppy a letter of forgiveness and apology. It's Christmas day. I'll cable it. That's what I'll do.

[*He goes out the dark door.*

LEONORA [*drying her eyes*]. Ermengarde, it's such a comfort having you here with me. Mary, I really can't eat anything. Well, perhaps, a sliver of white meat.

ERMENGARDE [*very old*]. I spoke to Mrs. Keene for a moment coming out of church. She asked after the young people.—At church I felt very proud sitting under our windows, Leonora, and our brass tablets. The Bayard aisle,—it's a regular Bayard aisle and I love it.

LEONORA. Ermengarde, would you be very angry with me if I went and stayed with the young people a little this Spring?

ERMENGARDE. Why, no. I know how badly they want you and need you. Especially now that they're about to build a new house.

LEONORA. You wouldn't be angry? This house is yours as long as you want it, remember.

ERMENGARDE. I don't see why the rest of you dislike it. I like it more than I can say.

LEONORA. I won't be long. I'll be back in no time and we can have some more of our readings-aloud in the evening.

[*She kisses her and goes into the hall.* ERMENGARDE *left alone, eats slowly and talks to* MARY.

ERMENGARDE. Really, Mary, I'll change my mind. If you'll ask Bertha to be good enough to make me a little eggnog. A dear little eggnog. —Such a nice letter this morning from Mrs. Bayard, Mary. Such a nice letter. They're having their first Christmas dinner in the new house. They must be very happy. They call her Mother Bayard, she says, as though she were an old lady. And she says she finds it more comfortable to come and go in a wheel chair.—Such a dear letter....And Mary, I can tell you a secret. It's still a great secret, mind! They're expecting a grandchild. Isn't that good news! Now I'll read a little.

[*She props a book up before her, still dipping a spoon into a custard from time to time. She grows from very old to immensely old. She sighs. The book falls down. She finds a cane beside her, and soon totters into the dark portal, murmuring:*

"Dear little Roderick and little Lucia."

Questions

1. As a play, *The Long Christmas Dinner* throws aside many established conventions: a straightforward time-sequence; the physical presence of sets and props; actors carefully costuming themselves off-stage before making their appearance, and so on. Does Wilder lose the appearance of "reality" by violating these conventions? What kind of reality is he trying to achieve? Does he succeed?

2. Wilder's use of the Christmas dinner as a dramatic device is similar to Chekhov's use of the wedding feast. Compare and contrast the two plays in their dramatic handling of the banquet. Also compare Wilder's banquet to Plato's (p. 190f.) and Nathaniel Hawthorne's *The Christmas Banquet* (p. 454). How does his purpose, thus technique, differ from theirs? Which of them does Wilder most resemble?

3. The handling of chronology is the most obvious technical device in Wilder's drama. Why is time compressed in this way? How is the compression connected with the theme(s) of the play?

4. How important is characterization in Wilder's play? How is dialogue used to convey the aspects of character that are of interest to the playwright?

5. What is the purpose of repetition in action and words in *The Long Christmas Dinner*? Are the actions lifelike or not? Is the dialogue?

6. What is Wilder's tone in the play? Is the view of human life happy, sad, optimistic, pessimistic? Is the play clearly "comic" or "tragic"? Are the people in this play representative of human beings as a whole or of a small, particularized group?

7. Notice all the references to time in the play and the attitudes toward it implicit in each. Is time shown as the enemy of man, a friend, a biological process, an emotional process, a simple "fact"? Is Wilder's view of time essentially that of the anthropologist (e.g., Frazer); the reporter; the historian; the social scientist? How does this viewpoint affect his use of the play as a means of commenting on human existence?

MARIA IRENE FORNÉS

Tango Palace

Cast of Characters

ISIDORE, *an androgynous clown*

LEOPOLD, *an earnest youth*

THE SCENE: [*A room, the same throughout the play. The floor is carpeted. The door is bolted with an*

oversize padlock. There is a big filing cabinet, an armchair, a secretary, a wall mirror, a water jug, a radio, three porcelain teapots, a large vase, a blackboard. There is a large canvas sack on the floor. A recess in the back wall serves as a shrine. Within the recess, hanging from nails, are a guitar, a whip, a toy parrot, a Persian helmet, two swords, a cape, a compass, a muleta, a pair of bulls horns, six banderillas, two masks in the form of beetles' faces. The shrine is decorated with a string of flower-shaped light bulbs. ISIDORE *sits in the shrine. His appearance is a mixture of man and woman. He is stout, has long hair, and is wearing rouge and lipstick; he wears a man's hat and pants, high-heeled shoes, and a silk shirt. There is a corsage of flowers pinned on his shirt. Sometimes his behavior is clearly masculine; other times he could be thought a woman.* LEOPOLD *is inside the canvas sack. He is in his late twenties. He is handsome, and his movements are simple. He wears a business suit. Each time* ISIDORE *feels he has said something important, he takes a card from his pocket or from a drawer and flips it across the room in any direction. [The word "card" in the script indicates when a card should be flipped.] This action is automatic.*

SCENE 1

[ISIDORE *makes a gesture and his shrine is lit. He makes another gesture and chimes sound. One more gesture and the bulbs on his shrine light up.* LEOPOLD *begins to move inside the canvas sack.* ISIDORE *notices the sack and cautiously approaches it.*

ISIDORE. Look what the stork has brought me. [ISIDORE *opens the sack.* LEOPOLD *begins to emerge. They stare at each other for a while.* ISIDORE *is delighted with what he has found. He goes to the shrine, takes the guitar and begins to sing "A Sleepy Lagoon" in an attempt to charm* LEOPOLD.] Song and guitar accompaniment by Isidore. [*card*] [LEOPOLD *has gotten out of the sack and walks curiously about the room. He stops in front of the armchair.* ISIDORE, *noticing* LEOPOLD's *interest in the furniture, addresses him in the affected tones of a salesman in an exclusive shop.*] Queen Anne walnut armchair. Representing the acme of artistic craftsmanship of the Philadelphia school. Circa 1740. Original condition and finish. [*card*] [ISIDORE *steps down from the shrine, walks ostentatiously past* LEOPOLD, *and runs his hand along the surface of the secretary*] Very rare, small, Louis Quinze secretary, representing the acme of artistic craftsmanship of the Parisian school. A pure Louis Quinze leg was never, under any conditions, straight. It was always curvilinear, generally in that shaping which we have come to know as the "cabriole." [*card*] [*taking little steps to the mirror*] Louis Quatorze carved and gilded mirror. [*card*] Bearing sprays of leafage and flowers. Circa 1700. Height sixty-four inches. Width thirty-six inches. [ISIDORE *walks close to* LEOPOLD *and looks him over*] The choice of the examples here is influenced by their significance as distinct types representative of the best tradition, not only in the style and execution but in the choice of subject. [*card*] [ISIDORE *walks toward the shelf containing the porcelain objects*] Tea-pots of rarest Chinese export porcelain with American marine decoration. Circa 1740–1750. Left one shows American flag, right one American admiral's insignia. The one in the center depicts the so-called "Governor Duff," actually Diedrick Durven, governor general of the Dutch East India Company. Exquisite, isn't it? This collection has been formed throughout a period of many years, and it is probably not an exaggeration to say that such a collection could not be formed again. [ISIDORE *waits for a reaction*] Did you say something?…Oh, well…Listen…Music… A tango…[*card*] [ISIDORE *begins to dance*] Do you know this step? Stomach in. Derrière out. Fingers gracefully curved. [*card*] A smile on your lips. Eyes full of stars. Dancing has well been called the poetry of motion. It is the art whereby the feelings of the mind are expressed by measured steps, regulated motions of the body, and graceful gestures. The German waltz, the Spanish fandango, the Polish mazurka, and last but not least the Argentine tango. One…two…three …dip and turn your head to show your profile. One…two…three…dip and swing your little foot back and forth. [LEOPOLD *begins to imitate* ISIDORE] One…two…three…and rotate on one foot, taking little steps with the other. Watch me first. Now you made me lose my step. And a one and a two and a three. Stomach in. Derrière out. Fingers gracefully curved. A smile on your lips. Eyes full of stars. One… two…three…dip and profile. One…two…three …dip and swing your little foot. One…two…three …and rotate. [LEOPOLD's *attention is drawn by the shrine; he moves closer to it*] Don't look there yet. Watch me…watch me. [LEOPOLD *watches for a moment, then he turns to the shrine again and reaches for the whip.* ISIDORE *takes the whip and demonstrates its use.*] This is my whip. [*lashing* LEOPOLD] And that is pain. [*card*] A souvenir of love. I loved her. She loved me.

I gave her the whip. She gave me her cherry…All is fair in love and war. [*card*] [*taking the parrot*] This is my talking parrot. [*to the parrot*] Pretty parrot.

PARROT. Pretty parrot.

ISIDORE. Very smart. He know everything.

PARROT. Very smart. He knows everything.

ISIDORE. Thank you.

PARROT. Thank you.

ISIDORE. [*putting on the Persian helmet*]. And this is the genuine Persian helmet I wore when I fought in Salamis. [*card*] I killed two hundred and fifteen Athenians. Fourteen were captains, three were generals, and the rest foot soldiers. I'll show you. [ISIDORE *takes the sword and swings it while he screams, grunts, whirls, and hops.* LEOPOLD *becomes frightened.*] That's how I killed them. Don't be afraid, I won't hurt you. [*touching* LEOPOLD's *chest with the tip of the sword*] Do you have something to show me?

LEOPOLD. No. I don't have anything.

ISIDORE. Nothing at all?

LEOPOLD. No.

ISIDORE. Oh, that's too bad. Here, I'll show you my flying cape. [ISIDORE *puts on the cape, climbs on a chair, flips his arms, and jumps to the floor*] Extraordinary, isn't it? Would you like to see my joy compass? [*showing joy compass*] It's magic. I sent for it…It points to joy. Now you show me something.

LEOPOLD. I don't own anything.

ISIDORE. Were your things taken away?

LEOPOLD. No, I never had anything, except…

ISIDORE. What?

LEOPOLD. A tattoo.

[*Leopold opens his shirt*

ISIDORE. Oh. How beautiful. [*reading*] "This is man. Heaven or bust." Oh, that's in bad taste. That's in terrible taste. [*card*] Just for that you can't touch any of my things. The only things you can touch are those cards. Those cards are yours. [*card*]

LEOPOLD [*picking up a card*]. These cards are mine? [*reading*] "A tattoo." "Oh. How beautiful. This is man. Heaven or bust. Oh, that's in bad taste."

ISIDORE. You can put them there in that filing cabinet.

LEOPOLD [*disturbed*]. Why do you write what I say?

ISIDORE. First of all, I write what *we* say. And then I don't write, I print...with my magic printing press...if you'd like to know. File them in your filing cabinet. That cabinet is yours too.

LEOPOLD. What for?

ISIDORE. So you can find them when you need them. These cards contain wisdom. File them away. [*card*] Know where they are. [*card*] Have them at hand. [*card*] Be one upon whom nothing is lost. [*card*] Memorize them and you'll be where you were. [*card*] Be where you are. Then and now. Pick them up.

LEOPOLD [*reading a card*]. "All is fair in love and war."

ISIDORE. That's a good one.

LEOPOLD. Why?

ISIDORE. Because it teaches you that all is fair in love and war, and it teaches you that when someone is telling you a story about love and war, you are not to stand there and say...That's not fair...or you'll be considered a perfect fool. [*card*]

LEOPOLD [*still disturbed*]. I don't see why love in war should be different from love in anything else.

ISIDORE [*pulling LEOPOLD's ear and shouting*]. Not love *in* war. Love *and* war! It has taken centuries... [*smack*] centuries, to arrive at this ethical insight and you say it isn't fair. [*smack*] All is fair. You hear? All is fair in love... [*smack*] and war. [*smack*]

LEOPOLD. I don't want your cards. I don't want to have anything to do with them.

ISIDORE. These are not my cards. They are yours. It's you who need learning, not me. I've learned already. [*card*] I know all my cards by heart. [*card*] And I have never forgotten one of them. [*card*] I can recite them in chronological order and I don't leave one word out. [*card*] What's more I never say a thing which is not an exact quotation from one of my cards. [*card*] That's why I never hesitate. [*card*] I'm never short of an answer. [*card*] Or a question. [*card*] Or a remark [*card*] if a remark is more appropriate.

LEOPOLD. I don't want to learn that way.

ISIDORE. There is no other way.

LEOPOLD. Yes, there is. I hear a voice.

ISIDORE. What voice? That's me you hear. I am the only voice.

LEOPOLD. No, it's not you.

ISIDORE. It is so. [*in a falsetto voice*] Listen to me

and always obey me...It's me...me...It's me...and only me...Leopold...Lippy...me...me...

LEOPOLD. No.

ISIDORE. Well, *Dime con quien andas y te dire quien eres...* [*card*] Spanish proverb meaning...You know what it means, and if you don't, go and ask that voice of yours...What does your voice say?

LEOPOLD. You speak like a parrot.

ISIDORE. No, I don't. [ISIDORE *considers for a moment*] My diction is better. Sally says she sells sea shells at the seashore. Have you ever heard a parrot say: Sally says she sells sea shells at the seashore?

LEOPOLD. That's not what I mean.

[ISIDORE *considers for a moment.*

ISIDORE. I talk like a wise parrot. Study hard, learn your cards, and one day you too will be able to talk like a parrot.

LEOPOLD [*imitating a parrot*]. Study hard, learn your cards, and one day you too will be able to talk like a parrot.

ISIDORE. What are you, a parrot? Do you want to be a moron for the rest of your life? Always being pushed around? [ISIDORE *pushes* LEOPOLD] Are you mentally retarded? Do I have to tell you what should be obvious to a half-wit. [*smack*] It should be obvious [*smack*] even [*smack*] to a half-wit. [LEOPOLD *throws a punch at* ISIDORE. ISIDORE *ducks, and kicks* LEOPOLD. LEOPOLD *falls.* ISIDORE *turns and thrusts his buttocks out.*] You bad, bad boy. You'll have to be punished. You tried to hit your loving teacher. Come. [ISIDORE *picks* LEOPOLD *up*]

LEOPOLD [*freeing himself from* ISIDORE]. Take your hands off me.

[LEOPOLD *executes each of* ISIDORE's *commands at the same time as they are spoken, but as if he were acting spontaneously rather than obeying.*

ISIDORE. Walk to the door. [*card*] Notice the padlock. [*card*] Push the door. [*card*] You're locked in. [*card*] Stand there and think. [*card*] Why are you locked in? [*card*] Where are you locked in? [*card*] Turn to the door. [*card*] You know what to do. [*card*] Pull the padlock. [*card*] Push the door. [*card*] Force the padlock. [*card*] You are locked in. [*card*] Kick the door. [*card*] Bang the door. [*card*] Scream.

ISIDORE AND LEOPOLD. Anybody there! Anybody there! [*card*] Let me out. [*card*] Open up! [*card*]

ISIDORE. Kick the door. [*card*] Walk around the room restlessly. [*card*] Bite your thumbnails. [*card*] Get an idea. [*card*] You got an idea. [*card*] [LEOPOLD *charges toward* ISIDORE] Violence does not pay. [*card*] Be sensible, stand still a moment being sensible. Have sensible thought. For every door there's a key. [*card*] The key must be in the room. Look for it in the obvious place first. Under the rare seventeenth-century needlework carpet depicting Elijah in the desert fed by ravens. It's not there. Look in Louis Quinze secretary, mahogany wood. Look in less obvious places. Magnificent marked Wedgwood vase in Rosso Antico ground. In flyleaf of my Gutenberg Bible. Look in places which are not obvious at all. Correction. All places are obvious places. [*card*] Look again in drawer of very rare, small, Louis Quinze secretary, representing the acme of artistic craftsmanship. Fall exhausted on Queen Anne chair. Have desperate thoughts.

[LEOPOLD *kicks the chair.* ISIDORE *speaks soothingly,
to regain control.*

Collect yourself, darling. You must collect yourself.

LEOPOLD. I must collect myself.

ISIDORE. You must collect yourself. You must think, dear. Let's think. Could you have enemies? Perhaps business associates? Perhaps people who envy you? Or could it be the others? The angry husbands? The spinsters? The barking dogs? The man whose toilet you dirtied?

LEOPOLD. Could it be you?

ISIDORE. Could it be you? It doesn't really matter. You might as well stay. Just tidy up your things, darling. Do as I said. File them away. [LEOPOLD *picks up a card and reads it*]

LEOPOLD. And that is pain.

ISIDORE. Be where you were.

[*card*

LEOPOLD [*reading another card*]. Pretty parrot. Very smart. He knows everything.

ISIDORE. Then and now.

[*card*

LEOPOLD [*reading another card*]. Were your things taken away?

ISIDORE. Nothing is lost.

[*card*

LEOPOLD. Nothing is lost?

ISIDORE. Nothing. Come, it's time for your drawing lesson. [ISIDORE *rings the bell and walks to the blackboard to illustrate the lesson*] How to draw a portrait. [*making a mark at the top of the blackboard*] This is the divine. Cleopatra for example. [*making a mark at the bottom of the blackboard*] This down here is the despicable. The werewolf. Now we're going to place the person whose portrait we're drawing. Where shall we put him? Close to the divine? Not so close. Halfway down? Close to the despicable? No. Here. [ISIDORE *makes a mark to the left and halfway between the other two marks*] Now you join the points with lines. This is the portrait of a mediocre person. You can draw a mouth on it. And an eye. But it isn't necessary. Because what counts is the nose.

[*The figure* ISIDORE *has drawn looks like this:*

LEOPOLD. Draw my portrait.

ISIDORE. Unfortunately this system doesn't do you any good, since all we can establish is that I am at the top. And way down at the bottom is you. There is no other point. We therefore can't have an angle. We only have a vertical line. The space around us is infinite, enclosed as it may be, because there is not a third person. And if the space around us is infinite, so is, necessarily, the space between us.

LEOPOLD. Who says you're at the top?

ISIDORE. I.

LEOPOLD. I say you're not at the top.

ISIDORE. But I am.

LEOPOLD. How do you know?

ISIDORE. Because I know everything. I know my cards. I know everything.

LEOPOLD. I'm going to burn those cards.

ISIDORE. You'll die if you burn them....Don't take my word for it. Try it. [LEOPOLD *sets fire to a card*] What in the world are you doing? Are you crazy? [ISIDORE *puts the fire out*] Are you out of your mind? You're going to die. Are you dying? Do you feel awful? [ISIDORE *trips* LEOPOLD] There! You died.

LEOPOLD [*springing to his feet*]. No, I tripped. I think I tripped.

ISIDORE. See? You tripped because you burned that card. If I hadn't put the fire out you would have died.

LEOPOLD. I don't believe you.

ISIDORE. You don't believe me? You could have broken your neck. All right, I don't care what you think. You just stop burning things.

LEOPOLD. You're lying to me, aren't you?

ISIDORE. Go on, burn them if you want to. I won't stop you. [LEOPOLD *moves to burn a card but then stops himself.* ISIDORE *flips a card at Leopold.*] Wisdom. [*card*]

[ISIDORE *begins to dance.*

LEOPOLD [*holding* ISIDORE *to stop him from dancing*]. I beg you.

ISIDORE. Don't put your hands on me, ever, ever, ever, *ari, ari, ari.* That's Bengali, you know. [*card*] It's you who need learning. [*card*] Very smart. He knows everything. [*card*] A souvenir of love. She gave me her cherry. [*card*] I killed two hundred and fifteen Athenians. [*card*] That's a good one. [*card*] A sleepy lagoon. [*card*] What does your voice say? [*card*]

LEOPOLD. Stop flipping those things at me...I beg you...Don't...Please...I beg you. [*kneels at* ISIDORE's *feet*]

ISIDORE. And a one and a two. One, two, three, dip and turn...You still have to be punished. Don't think I forgot. [ISIDORE *takes* LEOPOLD *by the hand and walks him to a corner.* LEOPOLD *leans against the wall.*] Straighten yourself up. Are you hearing things again? I'm jealous. I want to hear too. [*putting his ear against* LEOPOLD's *ear*] Where is it? I can't hear a thing. [*talking into* LEOPOLD's *ear*] Yoo hoo. Where are you? Say something. Talk to me. It won't talk to me. [*to* LEOPOLD] Tell me what it says. I'm angry. [ISIDORE *sits on the shrine, crosses his legs and his arms, and turns his head away from* LEOPOLD] I'm angry. Don't talk to me. I said don't talk to me. Don't you see I'm in the typical position of anger?...Do you want to say something to me?

LEOPOLD. No.

ISIDORE. Well, I want you to tell me what that awful voice was telling you.

LEOPOLD. It said, "Isidore deceives you." It said, "Don't listen to Isidore."

ISIDORE. Oh. Horrible. Horrible. Treason in my own house.

LEOPOLD. Let me tell you...

ISIDORE. Oh. Don't say any more, treason. Oh.

LEOPOLD. Let me tell you what I think, Isidore.

ISIDORE. No.

LEOPOLD. Please.

ISIDORE. You've said enough.

LEOPOLD. I haven't said...

ISIDORE. Treason!

LEOPOLD. Isidore!

ISIDORE [*in a whisper*]. Don't talk so loud.

LEOPOLD [*in a whisper*]. I haven't said...

ISIDORE. I heard you already. Treason!

LEOPOLD. I want to leave.

ISIDORE. Bye, bye, butterfly.

LEOPOLD. I want to get out.

ISIDORE. See you later, alligator.

LEOPOLD. Give me the key.

ISIDORE. Pretty parrot.

PARROT. Pretty parrot.

LEOPOLD. I want the key.

ISIDORE. He wants the key.

PARROT. He wants the key.

ISIDORE. There is no key.

PARROT. No key.

LEOPOLD. You're lying.

ISIDORE. I always tell the truth. I worship truth and truth worships me. Don't be so stubborn. There is no key.

LEOPOLD. There must be a key.

ISIDORE. I see what possesses you. It's faith!

LEOPOLD. So what?

ISIDORE. Faith is a disgusting thing. It's treacherous and destructive. Mountains are moved from place to place. You can't find them. I won't have any of that.

LEOPOLD. Well, I do have faith.

ISIDORE. Infidel. I'm too upset. I can't take any more of this. [*covering his face*] It's the devil. I can't look at you. Tell me you'll give it up. Tell me you have no faith.

LEOPOLD. But I do.

ISIDORE. Well, I'm a mountain. *Move me.*

LEOPOLD. I know there is a way out because there have been moments when I have been away from here.

ISIDORE. That's not true. You get ten demerits for telling lies.

LEOPOLD. It is true. There are moments when you have just vanished...

ISIDORE. Vanished? I have never vanished.

LEOPOLD. I don't mean vanished...exactly...I mean there are moments when I've felt this is not all there is.

ISIDORE. What else is there?

LEOPOLD. Close your eyes... Imagine... that all is calm.

ISIDORE. I don't like playing childish games. I'm supposed to sit there imagining a field of orange blossoms and then you're going to pour a bucket of water on my head. Let me tell, you, young man, that I played that game when I was five. Let me tell you that it was I who invented that game. And let me tell you that I didn't invent it to sit there like a fool and get the water on *my* head. I invented it to pour the water on the fool's head. Let me tell you that. You're not smart enough... not for old Izzy. [*card*]

LEOPOLD. I wasn't going to throw water on you.

ISIDORE. You weren't? Hm... All right. Go on.

LEOPOLD. Don't imagine anything in particular. Don't imagine orange groves or anything. Make your mind a blank. Just imagine that you are in perfect harmony with everything around you...

ISIDORE. Wait, I have to erase the orange grove.

LEOPOLD. Forget about the orange grove.

ISIDORE. I can't forget the orange grove. It's planted in my mind. I have to uproot it. You put things in my mind and then it's I who have to get rid of them. At least leave me in peace for a moment, while I do the work.

LEOPOLD. I didn't put anything in your mind.

ISIDORE. You said, "Don't think of an orange grove." You did, didn't you?

LEOPOLD. Yes...

ISIDORE. Well, the moment you said that, an orange grove popped into my head. Now give me time while I get rid of it. [ISIDORE *moves about the room as if he were picking up oranges and throwing them over a fence with his eyes closed.* LEOPOLD's *impatience increases.*] First I'll throw this orange over the fence. Then, this little orange. Then this orange orange. Now this rotten orange. Now I pull this whole branch off the tree. Oh, oh, it's hard. Now I pull this other orange off the tree. Oh, oh, there are so many. There are thousands and thousands and I think millions and trillions. Oh, I'm tired. No, no, I must not rest. I can't take a moment's rest until I clear away all this mess of oranges. Thousands and thousands of acres, and then I have to clear the other side of the fence, and then the other, and then the other, and then dismantle the fence, and then the other fence, and

then.... [LEOPOLD *reaches for the pitcher of water and empties it on* ISIDORE. *They remain motionless for a moment.* ISIDORE *goes to his shrine and sits in his typical angry position.* LEOPOLD *walks to the opposite end of the room and sits down.*] I'll never trust you again. [*The lights fade out.* ISIDORE *laughs out loud as the curtain falls.*]

SCENE 2

[*The curtain rises with* ISIDORE *and* LEOPOLD *in the same position as at the end of the first scene.*]

ISIDORE.

Isidore I beg you.
Have you no heart?
You play games,
And I'm so earnest.
Isidore I beg you.
Can't you see
You're breaking my heart?
'Cause while I'm so earnest,
You're still playing games.

Sung and composed by Isidore. Sixteen years old. [*card*] [LEOPOLD *looks at* ISIDORE] Stop looking at me like that.

LEOPOLD. Like what?

ISIDORE [*accompanying himself with the guitar*]. Like a lover. Transfigured by the presence of the beloved. Looking as though you want to breathe the minute bubbles of air imprisoned in each of my pores. [*card*] Or like a drug addict who imagines specks of heroin concealed in those beloved dimples. [*card*]

LEOPOLD. And you think that's how I'm looking at you, you slob?

ISIDORE. I'm offended. [*pause*] Come and make up with old Isidore.

LEOPOLD. Leave me alone.

ISIDORE. You'd die of boredom if I left you alone... [*pause*] You'd have to come to me sooner or later. Come now. [*pause*] What if I don't take you later?

LEOPOLD. The better for me.

ISIDORE. I'll count up to ten.

LEOPOLD. Count up to ten.

ISIDORE. Don't be a stubborn brat.

LEOPOLD. Leave me alone.

ISIDORE [*takes the Persian helmet and sets it on*

LEOPOLD's *head*]. I'll let you wear it for a while. There's my baby. Isn't he cute? [LEOPOLD *takes the helmet off*] See how contradictory you are? When I wouldn't lend it to you, you wanted it. Now that I'm willing to lend it to you, you don't want it.

LEOPOLD. Oh, go to hell. You twist everything.

ISIDORE. Now you're being rude.

LEOPOLD. Go back to your hole.

[LEOPOLD *picks up some cards and begins to sort them.*

ISIDORE. My hole. My hole? [ISIDORE *looks through his cards*] He means my shrine. I think I will. [ISIDORE *goes to the shrine doing a dance step*] Peekaboo. [LEOPOLD *stands in front of* ISIDORE.

LEOPOLD. Listen to me.

ISIDORE. Yes.

LEOPOLD. You're going to start behaving from now on. [ISIDORE *nods in consent*] OK. That's all. [LEOPOLD *goes back to the cards.* ISIDORE *passes wind through his lips.*]

ISIDORE. So I'm going to start behaving from now on. Then what?... Stop being silly. What is the matter with you, young man? You should be ashamed of yourself. What is life without humor here and there? A little bit of humor... Look at him sorting out his little cards. He's a good boy.

LEOPOLD. I'm not sorting them. I just don't want to listen to you.

ISIDORE. You can't tear yourself away from them. Can you?... You think I haven't seen you running to your cards the moment you think I'm not looking?

LEOPOLD. That's a lie. I've never...

ISIDORE. I never lie. I have never lied in my life. [*card*] [ISIDORE *crosses himself, then covers his head as if to protect himself from lightning*] So what if I'm a liar? Do you think truth matters? Well, it doesn't. [*card*] Does that confound your infantile mind? It is order that matters, whether there's order or disorder. [*card*] A sloppy liar is despicable [*card*], as despicable as a sloppy truth teller. [*card*] Now, what do you deduce from that?

LEOPOLD. That you're rotten.

[LEOPOLD *flips a card to Isidore.* ISIDORE *sniffs himself.*

ISIDORE. A systematic liar, a man with a goal, a man with a style is the best sort. [*card*] The most reliable. You'll never amount to anything until you learn that.

No, you'll never amount to anything. You'll never make it in the army, the navy, politics, business, stardom. You're worthless. I'm almost tempted to give you the key.

LEOPOLD. Give it to me.

ISIDORE. Never mind that. Come here. I'm about to forgive you... Come now. You really don't want me to forgive you?

LEOPOLD. Where is it, Isidore?

ISIDORE. Oh, here, in my heart.

LEOPOLD. Where is it?

ISIDORE. Oh, you're so insistent. I'll tell you what. [ISIDORE *takes the horns and the cape*] I'll answer all the questions you want if you do a little thing for me. Be a good bull and charge. Then I'll answer your question.

LEOPOLD. You'll tell me where the key is?

ISIDORE. Yes. Charge six times and I'll give you the key... But you won't be satisfied with the key. On the contrary, it's when you have the key that you'll start asking questions. You'll start wondering about the mysteries of the universe. [*counting the banderillas*] One, two, three, four, five, six mysteries has the universe. As I stick each banderilla on your back I'll reveal the answer to a mystery. And then... [*taking the sword*] the moment of truth. Right through the back of your neck... Oh, beautiful transgressions. While I'm answering your last question you'll be expiring your last breath. As eternal verity is revealed to you, darkness will come upon your eyes... Fair? Fair. Charge.

LEOPOLD. Are you kidding?

ISIDORE. I am not kidding. I am proposing the most poetic diversion ever enjoyed by man. You mean to say you're not willing to die for the truth? [ISIDORE *rubs his fingers to indicate* "*shame*"]

LEOPOLD. And when I'm crawling and bleeding to death begging you to answer my questions you'll say something like... Ha, ha.

ISIDORE. You want to play or you don't want to play?

LEOPOLD. I'll play. But I'll only charge six times. Six passes. I only want one answer. No mysteries.

ISIDORE. All right. Ask your question.

LEOPOLD. Where is the key?

ISIDORE. Charge.

LEOPOLD. Answer first.

ISIDORE. The answer after you charge. [*Leopold begins to charge*] Wait. I lost the mood. I need preparation.

[ISIDORE *kneels in front of the shrine and crosses himself. He makes a trumpet with his hand and toots a bullfighter's march.* ISIDORE *performs the passes as he calls out the passes' names.*

Toro and bull. Fearless, confident, and dominant, without altering the composure of his figure. Isidore lifts the spectators from their seats as he receives his enemy with "Veronica."

LEOPOLD. One.

[ISIDORE *turns his back towards the audience.*

ISIDORE. Turning his back to the planks below the box occupied by the Isidore Fan Club to whom he has dedicated this bull. He performs a dangerous "Revolera." Marvelous both in its planning and development.

LEOPOLD. Two.

ISIDORE. "Faroles." And the embellishment.

LEOPOLD. Four.

ISIDORE. Three. A punishing pass. "Pase de castigo." All of Isidore's passes have identical depth and majestic sobriety.

LEOPOLD. Four.

ISIDORE. "Manoletina." Astounding elegance and smoothness. The music breaks out and competes with the deafening clamor of the multitude.

LEOPOLD. Five. [ISIDORE *bows,* LEOPOLD *charges.*

ISIDORE. Then, with authentic domination, he performs the "Isidorina." [ISIDORE *circles the stage and bows*] Ovation. One ear. Turn. And cheers.

LEOPOLD. Six. Answer.

ISIDORE. Gore me.

LEOPOLD. Answer.

ISIDORE. Gore me. That's the answer. [*Leopold charges against* ISIDORE, *this time determined to get him.* ISIDORE *avoids him with a banderillero's turn while he thrusts a banderilla into* LEOPOLD's *back.*] Saint Sebastian! [LEOPOLD *falls to the floor.* ISIDORE *kneels beside him and holds him in his arms.*] Good bull. He attacked nobly and bravely. His killer made him take fifty-one passes and he would have continued charging, following docilely the course marked by deceit. He was cheered

as he was hauled out, but less than he deserved. [ISIDORE *pulls out the banderilla from* LEOPOLD's *back and caresses him tenderly.* LEOPOLD *looks at* ISIDORE *imploringly.* ISIDORE *kisses* LEOPOLD.] I have no alternative.

LEOPOLD. Don't tell me that, Isidore. I can't believe that.

ISIDORE. I have no alternative, Leopold.

LEOPOLD. No alternative? The alternative is simple.

ISIDORE. It isn't simple. I can't be good to you.

LEOPOLD. Just try.

ISIDORE. It's not within my power.

LEOPOLD. Have you no will then?

ISIDORE. No, I don't will it.

LEOPOLD. Who wills it?

ISIDORE. You, Leopold.

LEOPOLD. Me? It is not me, Isidore. You can't be right.

ISIDORE. It is you, Leopold.

LEOPOLD. I have never provoked you. I have never wished for anything but kindness from you. I have never tried but for your love.

ISIDORE. Yes, and maybe it is just that. Maybe you have been too patient, too good-natured.

[LEOPOLD *is astounded. There is a moment's pause. He then struggles with Isidore to break from his embrace.*

LEOPOLD. You are rotten...What are you? What are you that you must have rottenness around you? I am too patient? Too good-natured? I will not become rotten for you. I will not become rotten for you.

[LEOPOLD *holds* ISIDORE *by the neck and tries to strangle him*

ISIDORE. [*gasping for air*]. Son...son...let me tell you...let me tell you...a story...There was once a man...who... [LEOPOLD *covers his ears*] It's very important. You must listen. There was once a man whose only companion was a white rat. He loved this white rat dearly. And one day the rat disappeared. The rat couldn't have left the room, because there were no doors, or windows, or even cracks on the walls or floor. Then the man, thinking that the rat could have hidden in some nook or cranny unknown to him, took his axe and wrecked everything he owned... The rat was nowhere in the room. He then turned to a picture of the rat which was hanging on the wall, and was about to wield his axe against it...but he stopped himself...He said, "This is the only thing I have left of my rat. If I destroy the picture, I will have nothing to remind me of him." And from that moment on, he began to speak to the picture of the rat and to caress it, and even feed it. Eventually, though, his loneliness brought him to such a state of melancholia that he no longer cared whether he was happy or not. He did not even care whether he lived or died. And as if he were summoning his own death, he picked up his axe and smashed the picture of the rat. There, trapped in the wires that supported the picture, was his beloved rat, who had died of starvation. The dead rat turned his head to face the man and said [*as if imitating a ghost*] "If you had not been satisfied with my picture you could have had me. You chicken-hearted bastard," and then disintegrated into dust.

LEOPOLD. [*frightened*]. A fairytale.

ISIDORE. There is a moral to it, Leopold. Try to understand it.

LEOPOLD. The dead don't speak.

ISIDORE. Yes, they do. You'll see, you'll see. Understand the story, Leopold. You must relinquish what you want or you will never have it.

LEOPOLD. I understand one thing. There is something that moves you. There is something that makes you tender and loving, only one thing: nastiness... and meanness and abuse.

ISIDORE. Those are three things, Leopold.

LEOPOLD. They're all the same.

ISIDORE. It's our fate.

LEOPOLD. Not mine...I love...

ISIDORE. You don't love. Don't you see that all you do is whine? [LEOPOLD *cries*] I had to tell you.

LEOPOLD. It's time you answer my question, Isidore.

ISIDORE. I answered it.

LEOPOLD. You told me to gore you.

ISIDORE. Yes, I did.

LEOPOLD. Is that the answer?

ISIDORE. That was my answer.

LEOPOLD. You stabbed me. I want my answer.

ISIDORE. There is a way, Leopold, but only one. You must find it yourself.

LEOPOLD. That's no answer. You wounded me.

ISIDORE. You tried to gore me. I had to defend myself.

LEOPOLD. You told me to gore you.

ISIDORE. That was part of the game.

LEOPOLD. Stinking bastard. Can you bear your own rottenness? You must atone for your wickedness sometime. You cannot go on and on without a purge. Do you ever pray? Do you beat your fist against your chest and ask for forgiveness? If not to redeem yourself, at least to be able to go on with your viciousness. You could not endure it without a purge...Do you spend your nights covering your ears to keep away the sound of my moans? Do you cry then?...Could it be that you do it out of stupidity, that you don't know the difference between right and wrong? Oh no. Let it be anything but that. Let it be malice. If you do it out of a decision to be harmful, I can convince you that it's best to be good. But if you don't know the difference between right and wrong, is there anything I can do? Maybe you must be vicious in spite of yourself. Maybe you have to do it...to protect me from something worse?...for my own good? [LEOPOLD *throws himself on his knees with his head on* ISIDORE's *lap*] Give me a sign, a smile, a look. Tell me you love me.

[ISIDORE *pouts innocently. He makes a circle with his arm and places his hand on* LEOPOLD's *head.*
The lights fade.

SCENE 3

[ISIDORE *and* LEOPOLD *are in the same position.* ISIDORE *stretches himself and yawns. He jerks his thighs slightly to make* LEOPOLD's *head roll and fall to the floor.* ISIDORE *looks at* LEOPOLD *who is waking up and smiles.* ISIDORE *stands up, stretches again, and does a dance step.*

ISIDORE. Cheery-uppy, Leopold.

[*The following scene is to have a nightmarish quality.* ISIDORE *and* LEOPOLD *dance in a ritualistic manner.* ISIDORE *puts on one of the two beetle masks, the one which is wingless, and gives the other to* LEOPOLD.
LEOPOLD *should behave like a sleepwalker.*
Beetles are versatile little animals. For great numbers, the end of autumn does not mean the end of their

lives. There are more beetles by far than any other kind of insect. Over a quarter of a million beetle species have been described. Beetles are in constant conflict with man because there are few of the organic commodities that man has learned to use that do not also interest some beetle. Some spend their life in the thick flesh of century-plant leaves and when caught make an excellent salad, tasting something like shrimp salad. Other notable varieties are: The Clavicornia, the segments of whose tarse are variable in number and whose antennae are equipped with a more or less [ISIDORE *does a bump and grind*] distinct club, the terminal segments being broader than the others. The Hydrophilidae [ISIDORE *places his arms in arabesque position*], Silphidae, Staphylinidae, Nitiduli-dae [*convulsing*], Histeridae, Coccinellidae, Ebdon-nychidae [*holding his breasts*], Erotylidae, Languiridae, and Dermestidae…The literature of beetles is enormous.

LEOPOLD [*crawling on the floor*]. When things are in disorder and I move, I feel like I'm crawling. As if with every movement I have to drag along with me the things that are in disorder. As if I had grown brooms on my sides that extend as far as the wall, to sweep the junk…the dust.

[LEOPOLD *picks up some of the cards. Looks at* ISIDORE *and smiles sadly.*

ISIDORE. They are for your own good. Ingrate. Don't you know? Come, do me a pretty beetle.

LEOPOLD. Dirt, my dear sir, comes to us from everywhere. And it comes out from within us. It comes out through each pore. Then we wash it away, we flush it away, we drown it, we bury it, we in-cinerate it, and then we perfume ourselves. We put odors in our toilets, medicinal odors, terrible odors, but all these odors seem sweet next to our own. What I want, sir, is to live with that loathsomeness near me, not to flush it away. To live with it for all those who throw perfume on it. To be so dirty for those who want to be so clean. To do them that favor. I wanted to drop it in the pot and leave it there for days, and live with it.

ISIDORE. Sometimes you touch the realm of romance.

LEOPOLD. In the latter part of the afternoon I feel cold. I feel the stuff in my bowels. And I feel downcast. The open air is in my mind, but my eyes wander around this cave. I feel such pain for being here.

ISIDORE. The contrast between your poet's taste for languid amusement and my unconventional pageant-ry sends such fresh impetus throbbing through my veins…

LEOPOLD. I see a light in you. The only light. I see it through a tunnel lower than myself. Attempting to go through it and hoping to be invited, I crawl.

ISIDORE. Crawl then. Crawl then.

[LEOPOLD *crawls.*

LEOPOLD. I liked to think I was an exception, of course, I pretended I was not one more snake. And to prove I was an exception, I tried to stand erect, and to stand erect I needed you to support me, and when you refused me I had to beg, and to beg I had to crawl, and snakes crawl, and I am a snake. When crawling tires me, I stand erect. It is to exhaustion and disillusion that I owe my dignity…not to pride… Oh…I cannot make your eyes turn to me with love.

ISIDORE. Give me a pretty smile, pretty beetle.

[LEOPOLD *opens his mouth wide.*

LEOPOLD. To make dirt come out through the mouth you have to close your holes very tight, and let the dirt rot inside. Then it will come out through any opening.

ISIDORE. The prophet, the prophet. Come and hear the dirty prophet.

LEOPOLD [*taking off his mask*]. Oh, Isidore, you are my enemy and yet I love you.

ISIDORE. I am not your enemy.

LEOPOLD. Come here. Let me see you. [ISIDORE *moves near* LEOPOLD] Take that mask off. [ISIDORE *takes the mask off*] You *are* my enemy.

ISIDORE. What makes you say that?

LEOPOLD. Your smell…

ISIDORE. How do I smell?

LEOPOLD. You stink.

ISIDORE. Not true. What you smell is your own stink. You are putrid.

LEOPOLD. I'm going to kill you.

ISIDORE. Don't, you're trying to scare me. You're trying to scare me so I'll be good to you.

LEOPOLD. No…I know nothing can make you change. No…If I were to frighten you you'd behave for a while, but then you would get to like it, and you'd want more and more of it.

ISIDORE. And you wouldn't do it just to please your old friend?

LEOPOLD. No, I wouldn't. I have already played too many of your games. I have become as corrupt as you intended me to be. But...no more.

ISIDORE. You can't stop now. It's too late.

LEOPOLD. I know. That's why I've decided to kill you.

ISIDORE. You have?

[LEOPOLD *goes to the shrine and gets the knife.* ISIDORE *hides behind a piece of furniture and begins to tremble.*

LEOPOLD. Where are you?

ISIDORE [*waving a white handkerchief*]. Here.

LEOPOLD. Get up, Isidore.

ISIDORE. No.

[LEOPOLD *lifts the knife and holds it up for a moment, then lowers it slowly.*

LEOPOLD. If I killed you what would I be?

ISIDORE. A murderer...that's what you'd be...a murderer. A dirty ratty murderer.

LEOPOLD. There will be no one to judge me.

ISIDORE. Yourself...you'll judge yourself. You'll die of guilt.

LEOPOLD. Guilt...? Is that what it is?

ISIDORE. Yes. And then you'll be all alone. You don't know what it is to be alone. It's horribly... lonely.

LEOPOLD. I am afraid of my own death. I see myself dead.

ISIDORE. You're not going to do it then?

LEOPOLD. You're disappointed.

ISIDORE. Yes, I thought I was going to have some thrills and suspense, never knowing when you would strike...having to sleep with one eye open. But as usual you are a party pooper...You could never kill me, Leopold. Don't you see? You are just what I want you to be. You only know what I have taught you. And I haven't taught you how to kill.

LEOPOLD. You have offended me. If you died I still would be offended.

ISIDORE. I have offended you and you haven't challenged me to a duel? Challenge me to a duel immediately...What kind of mouse are you...I have

offended you. I am offending you right now. You mouse. [*smack*] You mouse. [*smack*] You misbegotten mouse. You misbegotten lifeless mouse.

LEOPOLD. If I killed you the offense would not be undone. If you died, you would not be able to atone for it.

ISIDORE. Don't worry, there isn't a chance of that. I'll kill you and be done with you.

[ISIDORE *puts the sword in* LEOPOLD's *hand.*

LEOPOLD. If you killed me you would be convinced that you had the right to offend me.

ISIDORE. Beautiful, beautiful. Let's duel. You'll fight for your offended pride. I, for the right to offend you. Come on. Come on.

LEOPOLD. Please stop, Isidore.

ISIDORE. No, this is fun. It's fun. *En garde.*

LEOPOLD [*poking different objects with his sword*]. What are these things...Leopold? Leopold? Are you Leopold? Are you...They don't strike back. You are Leopold.

ISIDORE. Too much reflection.

[ISIDORE *pokes* LEOPOLD *with the sword.* LEOPOLD *shrinks back.*

LEOPOLD. Each time I hold back I die a little.

ISIDORE. That's why you stink, you're putrid with death. Cleanliness is close to godliness. [*card*] I still have a lot to teach you.

LEOPOLD [*swaying*]. I feel faint. If only I could find a spot to fix on and steady myself.

ISIDORE [*swaying and lurching*]. Look at me. Let me be the spot. Look, everything is moving. But I am steady as a rock.

LEOPOLD. Come here, Isidore. [ISIDORE *obeys*] Open your arms.

[ISIDORE *obeys.* LEOPOLD *lifts the sword slowly, points it to* ISIDORE's *heart, and pushes it into his body.* ISIDORE *falls to the floor.*

ISIDORE. How could you do this? [LEOPOLD *holds* ISIDORE *in his arms. He doesn't answer.*] Say you're sorry and my wound will heal.

LEOPOLD. I know.

ISIDORE. Say you're sorry.

LEOPOLD. If I do you'll curse me.

ISIDORE. I beg you, Leopold. I'm dying.

LEOPOLD. Die, Isidore...I understand now...You made it clear enough...[ISIDORE *dies*] It is done. All the thought and preparation did not help me do it. It is done. And I don't know what made me do it. The moment came. The only moment when it could be done. It possessed me and I let it take me.

[*The stage darkens. The door opens. The sound of harps is heard outside. There is a blue sky. ISIDORE appears among the clouds dressed as an angel. He carries stacks of cards. He beckons LEOPOLD to follow him. LEOPOLD picks up a few cards, then the sword, then a few more cards. ISIDORE shakes his head, and shows LEOPOLD the cards he carries. LEOPOLD walks through the door slowly, but with determination. He is ready for the next stage of their battle.*]

THE END

Questions

1. *Tango Palace* is a contemporary experimental play by a young playwright. Compared with the other playwrights here, how does Miss Fornés use established dramatic conventions: setting, dialogue, and so on? Does she dispense with these entirely? Why does she modify them as she does?

2. What is the purpose of showing Isidore as an androgyne (half man-half woman)? Is he supposed to be a sexual freak, inhuman, a composite character? Why is he a "clown"?

3. What is the central intention of this play? What response in her audience does the author try to provoke and how does she go about doing this?

4. What attitude(s) toward "factual" knowledge are shown in this drama? What kind of knowledge does the interaction between Isidore and Leopold display or convey to the audience?

5. What is the significance of the little cards? The tango? The shrine? The background music? The scenic view of Isidore in heaven?

6. What kind of human relationships are shown in *Tango Palace*? Are these subject to examination for the social scientist or psychologist? To the psychiatrist? Can a play deal with these relationships more effectively than other kinds of writing?

General Exercises and Questions

1. The plays given here arise from "social" situations: a wedding, a death and funeral, a drinking reunion in a hotel room, a Christmas feast. Must a play be based on events of a social character? Is there any sort of action or situation that literally cannot be treated in dramatic form? Would "unpresentable" aspects of life be due to social taboos, the abstract nature of those aspects, their limited significance, or something else?

2. Is it necessary—or even possible—to find within a play the beliefs of the playwright; to say, for example, that Synge is superstitious or Williams is racially prejudiced or that Wilder disapproves of drinking wine? What does a play present if not the personal values of its author?

3. There are many ways in which a dramatist can show conflict: between two people; between a man and his environment; between a man and society at large; or internal conflict in the single man. The conflict, furthermore, may be of a physical or emotional or intellectual sort. Identify the varieties of conflict and the resulting tensions in the plays included above.

4. Is it possible for the spectator to believe totally in the dramatic presentation of a play: that the sets are real or the actors are the persons they pretend to be or the action is literal? How are the reactions of the spectator to drama best described?

5. If a play is not historically or empirically "real," what kind of "truth" does it convey, if any? Is this truth practicable in any fashion?

SECTION FOUR

Narrative Fictions

A narrative, or "story," is a sequence of events in time recounted by a narrator, or storyteller. There are many varieties of factual writing that are essentially narrative forms, among them the autobiography, the biography, the journalistic report, and the history. The empirical record that stresses causal occurrences in a chronological pattern is a factual narrative or "true story." The teller of an invented "story" uses many of the same devices—point of view, narrative technique, diction—often for the sake of verisimilitude, or appearance of testable reality. But the fictional narrator also employs narrative techniques that may emphasize the literal impossibility of the events he relates: he can describe simultaneous happenings in places far apart or peer into peoples' minds or throw away chronology and causation as they are ordinarily conceived. In doing so, he assumes only one duty: to convince the reader of the validity of the story by engrossing him with a self-contained if imaginary world.

Those who have studied the techniques of fictional narration, including many novelists and short story writers, believe that the most important element in the form is the point of view from which the events are told. A narrative must be told by someone; and the chief fictional elements will depend upon the central authority, or narrator, of the events. This narrator himself is an imagined being, a *persona,* invented by the author as the most appropriate kind of central intelligence or emotional focus for the configurations of experience that the author wants to frame. There are four basic kinds of fictional narrator or narrative points of view. These are given various designations; but if they

446

are termed the Autobiographical, the Biographical, the Reporter, and the Historical Narrators, their fundamental devices are understandable as analogous to the methods of factual writers and their possibilities (as well as limitations) become apparent to the reader.

Fictional narratives may concentrate on one limited occurrence, involving a single character, or deal with a complex of actions involving hundreds of characters. From the anecdote to the epic or novel, whether in verse or prose, the writers of narrative fiction construct their patterns of imagined events not to reflect the surface reality of objects and processes but to penetrate the innermost, often pre-logical reality of human consciousness.

PERCY BYSSHE SHELLEY

Ozymandias

SONNET

I met a traveler from an antique land
Who said: Two vast and trunkless legs of stone
Stand in the desert. Near them, on the sand,
Half sunk, a shattered visage lies, whose frown,
And wrinkled lip, and sneer of cold command,   5
Tell that its sculptor well those passions read
Which yet survive, stamped on these lifeless things,
The hand that mocked them and the heart that fed;
And on the pedestal these words appear:
"My name is Ozymandias, king of kings: 10
Look on my works, ye Mighty, and despair!"
Nothing beside remains. Round the decay
Of that colossal wreck, boundless and bare
The lone and level sands stretch far away.

Commentary

Ozymandias was a great, legendary king of Egypt (or Nubia), the "antique land" of the poem. In what sense is this poem concerned

with history? How does the poetic treatment of history differ from that of historians? Compare Shelley's view of the ruins of Ozymandias's statue (and presumably palace) with Eleanor Clark's view of Hadrian's villa.

GEORGE MEREDITH

Lucifer in Starlight

On a starred night Prince Lucifer uprose.
Tired of his dark dominion, swung the fiend
Above the rolling ball in cloud part screened,
Where sinners hugged their specter of repose.
Poor prey to his hot fit of pride were those.   5
And now upon his western wing he leaned,
Now his huge bulk o'er Afric's sands careened.
Now the black planet shadowed Arctic snows.
Soaring through wider zones that pricked his scars
With memory of the old revolt from Awe,   10
He reached a middle height, and at the stars,
Which are the brain of heaven, he looked, and sank.
Around the ancient track marched, rank on rank,
The army of unalterable law.

WALT WHITMAN

When I Heard the
Learn'd Astronomer

When I heard the learn'd astronomer,
When the proofs, the figures, were ranged in columns before me,
When I was shown the charts and diagrams, to add, divide, and measure them,
When I sitting heard the astronomer where he lectured with much applause in the
    lecture-room,
How soon unaccountable I became tired and sick,   5
Till rising and gliding out I wander'd off by myself,
In the mystical moist night-air, and from time to time,
Look'd up in perfect silence at the stars.

ANONYMOUS

Questions

1. Meredith's sonnet, "Lucifer in Starlight," makes certain assumptions about the stars. Do they correspond to those of Gamow's *Galaxies in Flight*? Does this fact affect the meaning of Meredith's poem?
2. Compare Meredith's poem with Mac-Leish's "Epistle to Be Left in the Earth" on p. 527. Which is the more "scientifically true"? Do the poems agree with or contradict each other in their views of the universe?
3. How does Whitman's "When I Heard the Learn'd Astronomer" resemble Meredith's poem? Is his interest in stars the same as Meredith's? Is it the same as Gamow's?
4. W. H. Auden's "A Walk after Dark" bears some close resemblances to the situation shown in the Meredith, Whitman, and MacLeish poems (See p. 548). What astronomical assumptions does Auden make? Are they scientifically correct? Is it important for poems to be scientifically correct?

Barbara Allen

It was in and about the Martinmas time,
    When the green leaves were a falling,
That Sir John Graeme, in the West Country,
    Fell in love with Barbara Allen.

He sent his man down through the town,   5
    To the place where she was dwelling:
"O haste and come to my master dear,
    Gin ye be Barbara Allen."

O hooly, hooly rose she up,
    To the place where he was lying,   10
And when she drew the curtain by,
    "Young man, I think you're dying."

"O it's I'm sick, and very, very sick,
    And 'tis a' for Barbara Allen";
"O the better for me ye's never be,   15
    Tho your heart's blood were a spilling."

"O dinna ye mind, young man," said she,
  "When ye was in the tavern a drinking,
That ye made the healths gae round and round,
  And slighted Barbara Allen?"   20

He turned his face unto the wall,
  And death was with him dealing:
"Adieu, adieu, my dear friends all,
  And be kind to Barbara Allen."

And slowly, slowly raise she up,   25
  And slowly, slowly left him,
And sighing said, she could not stay,
  Since death of life had reft him.

She had not gane a mile but twa,
  When she heard the dead-bell ringing,   30
And every jow that the dead-bell geid,
  It cry'd, Woe to Barbara Allen!

"O Mother, mother, make my bed!
  O make it saft and narrow!
Since my love died for me to-day,   35
  I'll die for him to-morrow."

ANONYMOUS

The Wife of Usher's Well

There lived a wife at Usher's Well,
  And a wealthy wife was she;
She had three stout and stalwart sons,
  And sent them oer the sea.

They hadna been a week from her,   5
  A week but barely ane,
Whan word came to the carlin wife
  That her three sons were gane.

They hadna been a week from her,
  A week but barely three,   10
Whan word came to the carlin wife
  That her sons she'd never see.

"I wish the wind may never cease,
  Nor fashes in the flood,
Till my three sons come hame to me,   15
  In earthly flesh and blood."

It fell about the Martinmass,
  When nights are lang and mirk,
The carlin wife's three sons came hame,
  And their hats were o the birk.   20

It neither grew in syke nor ditch,
  Nor yet in ony sheugh;
But at the gates o Paradise,
  That birk grew fair eneugh.

         *   *   *

"Blow up the fire, my maidens,   25
  Bring water from the well;
For a' my house shall feast this night,
  Since my three sons are well."

And she has made to them a bed,
  She's made it large and wide,   30
And she's taen her mantle her about,
  Sat down at the bed-side.

         *   *   *

Up then crew the red, red cock,
  And up and crew the gray;
The eldest to the youngest said,   35
  'Tis time we were away.

The cock he hadna crawd but once,
  And clapped his wings at a',
When the youngest to the eldest said,
  Brother, we must awa.   40

"The cock doth craw, the day doth daw,
  The channerin worm doth chide;
Gin we be mist out o our place,
  A sair pain we maun bide."

"Fare ye weel, my mother dear!   45
  Fareweel to barn and byre!
And fare ye weel, the bonny lass
  That kindles my mother's fire!"

Commentary

"The Wife of Usher's Well" is very like Synge's *Riders to the Sea* in its setting, events, characters, tone, and overall view of life and death. Compare the two works closely, then answer these questions:

1. Which work—the play or the ballad—has the greatest emotional impact? Is this due to the vividness of single details or the cumulative effect of many details?
2. What is the narrative point of view in the ballad; i.e., who is telling us of these events? Is the ballad more or less objective and impersonal in tone than the play because of this point of view?
3. Does the ballad convey any attitudes, values, or insights that the play does not, and vice versa? Could the dimensions of insight in the one have been successfully included in the other, or does the form of the work limit what each can accomplish?
4. Does the unscientific—or anti-scientific—nature of the events described in these two works (omens, visions, ghosts) keep them from meaning very much to the modern reader? Can the sort of experience contained in them be explained by reference to twentieth-century psychological theories or scientific proof? If not, what can they convey to the twentieth-century mind?
5. A "ballad" is a very old form of folk-narrative, often based on real events; it was an early form of journalism. Judging from "The Wife" and "Barbara Allen", what are the chief characteristics of ballads in form, interest, and techniques? Does the ballad show any implicit attitudes towards current events or time or social experience?

EDGAR ALLAN POE

The Masque of the Red Death

The "Red Death" had long devastated the country. No pestilence had ever been so fatal, or so hideous. Blood was its Avatar and its seal—the redness and the horror of blood. There were sharp pains, and sudden dizziness, and then profuse bleeding at the pores, with dissolution. The scarlet stains upon the body and especially upon the face of the victim, were the pest ban which shut him out from the aid and from the sympathy of his fellow-men. And the whole seizure, progress, and termination of the disease, were the incidents of half an hour.

But the Prince Prospero was happy and dauntless and sagacious. When his dominions were half depopulated, he summoned to his presence a thousand hale and lighthearted friends from among the knights and dames of his court, and with these retired to the deep seclusion of one of his castellated abbeys. This was an extensive and magnificent structure, the creation of the prince's own eccentric yet august taste. A strong and lofty wall girdled it in. This wall had gates of iron. The courtiers, having entered, brought furnaces and massy hammers and welded the bolts. They resolved to leave means neither of ingress or egress to the sudden impulses of despair or of frenzy from within. The abbey was amply provisioned. With such precautions the courtiers might bid defiance to contagion. The external world could take care of itself. In the meantime it was folly to grieve, or to think. The prince had provided all the appliances of pleasure. There were buffoons, there were improvisatori, there were ballet-dancers, there were musicians, there was Beauty, there was wine. All these and security were within. Without was the "Red Death."

It was toward the close of the fifth or sixth month of his seclusion, and while the pestilence raged most furiously abroad, that the Prince Prospero entertained his thousand friends at a masked ball of the most unusual magnificence.

It was a voluptuous scene, that masquerade. But first let me tell of the rooms in which it was held. There were seven—an imperial suite. In many palaces, however, such suites form a long and straight vista, while the folding doors slide back nearly to the walls on either hand, so that the view of the whole extent is scarcely impeded.

Here the case was very different; as might have been expected from the duke's love of the *bizarre*. The apartments were so irregularly disposed that the vision embraced but little more than one at a time. There was a sharp turn at every twenty or thirty yards, and at each turn a novel effect. To the right and left, in the middle of each wall, a tall and narrow Gothic window looked out upon a closed corridor which pursued the windings of the suite. These windows were of stained glass whose color varied in accordance with the prevailing hue of the decorations of the chamber into which it opened. That at the eastern extremity was hung, for example, in blue —and vividly blue were its windows. The second chamber was purple in its ornaments and tapestries, and here the panes were purple. The third was green throughout, and so were the casements. The fourth was furnished and lighted with orange—the fifth with white—the sixth with violet. The seventh apartment was closely shrouded in black velvet tapestries that hung all over the ceiling and down the walls, falling in heavy folds upon a carpet of the same material and hue. But in this chamber only, the color of the windows failed to correspond with the decorations. The panes here were scarlet—a deep blood color. Now in no one of the seven apartments was there any lamp or candelabrum, amid the profusion of golden ornaments that lay scattered to and fro or depended from the roof. There was no light of any kind emanating from the lamp or candle within the suite of chambers. But in the corridors that followed the suite, there stood, opposite to each window, a heavy tripod, bearing a brazier of fire, that projected its rays through the tinted glass and so glaringly illuminated the room. And thus were produced a multitude of gaudy and fantastic appearances. But in the western or black chamber the effect of the firelight that streamed upon the dark hangings through the blood-tinted panes was ghastly in the extreme, and produced so wild a look upon the countenances of those who entered, that there were few of the company bold enough to set foot within its precincts at all.

It was in this apartment, also, that there stood against the western wall, a gigantic clock of ebony. Its pendulum swung to and fro with a dull, heavy, monotonous clang; and when the minute-hand made the circuit of the face, and the hour was to be stricken, there came from the brazen lungs of the clock a sound which was clear and loud and deep and exceedingly musical, but of so peculiar a note and emphasis that, at each lapse of an hour, the musicians of the orchestra were constrained to pause, momentarily, in their performance, to hearken to the sound; and thus the waltzers perforce ceased their evolutions; and there was a brief disconcert of the whole gay company; and, while the chimes of the clock yet rang, it was observed that the giddiest grew pale, and the more aged and sedate passed their hands over their brows as if in confused revery or meditation. But when the echoes had fully ceased, a light laughter at once pervaded the assembly; the musicians looked at each other and smiled as if at their own nervousness and folly, and made whispering vows, each to the other, that the next chiming of the clock should produce in them no similar emotion; and then, after the lapse of sixty minutes (which embrace three thousand and six hundred seconds of the Time that flies), there came yet another chiming of the clock, and then were the same disconcert and tremulousness and meditation as before.

But, in spite of these things, it was a gay and magnificent revel. The tastes of the duke were peculiar. He had a fine eye for colors and effects. He disregarded the *decora* of mere fashion. His plans were bold and fiery, and his conceptions glowed with barbaric lustre. There are some who would have thought him mad. His followers felt that he was not. It was necessary to hear and see and touch him to be *sure* that he was not.

He had directed, in great part, the movable embellishments of the seven chambers, upon occasion of this great *fête*; and it was his own guiding taste which had given character to the masqueraders. Be sure they were grotesque. There were much glare and glitter and piquancy and phantasm—much of what has been since seen in "Hernani." There were arabesque figures with unsuited limbs and appointments.

There were delirious fancies such as the madman fashions. There were much of the beautiful, much of the wanton, much of the *bizarre,* something of the terrible, and not a little of that which might have excited disgust. To and fro in the seven chambers there stalked, in fact, a multitude of dreams. And these—the dreams— writhed in and about, taking hue from the rooms, and causing the wild music of the orchestra to seem as the echo of their steps. And, anon, there strikes the ebony clock which stands in the hall of the velvet. And then, for a moment, all is still, and all is silent save the voice of the clock. The dreams are stiff-frozen as they stand. But the echoes of the chime die away—they have endured but an instant—and a light, half-subdued laughter floats after them as they depart. And now again the music swells, and the dreams live, and writhe to and fro more merrily than ever, taking hue from the many-tinted windows through which stream the rays from the tripods. But to the chamber which lies most westwardly of the seven there are now none of the maskers who venture; for the night is waning away; and there flows a ruddier light through the blood-colored panes; and the blackness of the sable drapery appalls; and to him whose foot falls upon the sable carpet, there comes from the near clock of ebony a muffled peal more solemnly emphatic than any which reaches *their* ears who indulge in the more remote gaieties of the other apartments.

But these other apartments were densely crowded, and in them beat feverishly the heart of life. And the revel went whirlingly on, until at length there commenced the sounding of midnight upon the clock. And then the music ceased, as I have told; and the evolutions of the waltzers were quieted; and there was an uneasy cessation of all things as before. But now there were twelve strokes to be sounded by the bell of the clock; and thus it happened, perhaps that more of thought crept, with more of time, into the meditations of the thoughtful among those who revelled. And thus too, it happened, perhaps, that before the last echoes of the last chime had utterly sunk into silence, there were many individuals in the crowd who had found leisure to become aware of the presence of a masked figure which had arrested the attention of no single individual before. And the rumor of this new presence having spread itself whisperingly around, there arose at length from the whole company a buzz, or murmur, expressive of disapprobation and surprise—then, finally, of terror, of horror, and of disgust.

In an assembly of phantasms such as I have painted, it may well be supposed that no ordinary appearance could have excited such sensation. In truth the masquerade license of the night was nearly unlimited; but the figure in question had out-Heroded Herod, and gone beyond the bounds of even the prince's indefinite decorum. There are chords in the hearts of the most reckless which cannot be touched without emotion.

Even with the utterly lost, to whom life and death are equally jests, there are matters of which no jest can be made. The whole company, indeed, seemed now deeply to feel that in the costume and bearing of the stranger neither wit nor propriety existed. The figure was tall and gaunt, and shrouded from head to foot in the habiliments of the grave. The mask which concealed the visage was made so nearly to resemble the countenance of a stiffened corpse that the closest scrutiny must have had difficulty in detecting the cheat. And yet all this might have been endured, if not approved, by the mad revellers around. But the mummer had gone so far as to assume the type of the Red Death. His vesture was dabbled in *blood*—and his broad brow, with all the features of the face, was besprinkled with the scarlet horror.

When the eyes of Prince Prospero fell upon this spectral image (which, with a slow and solemn movement, as if more fully to sustain its *rôle*, stalked to and fro among the waltzers) he was seen to be convulsed, in the first moment with a strong shudder either of terror or distaste; but, in the next, his brow reddened with rage.

"Who dares"—he demanded hoarsely of the courtiers who stood near him—"who dares insult us with this blasphemous mockery? Seize him and unmask him—that we may know whom we have to hang, at sunrise, from the battlements!"

It was in the eastern or blue chamber in which stood the Prince Prospero as he uttered these words. They rang throughout the seven rooms loudly and clearly, for the prince was a bold and robust man, and the music had become hushed at the waving of his hand.

It was in the blue room where stood the prince, with a group of pale courtiers by his side. At first, as he spoke, there was a slight rushing movement of this group in the direction of the intruder, who, at the moment was also near at hand, and now, with deliberate and stately step, made closer approach to the speaker. But from a certain nameless awe with which the mad assumptions of the mummer had inspired the whole party, there were found none who put forth hand to seize him; so that, unimpeded, he passed within a yard of the prince's person; and, while the vast assembly, as if with one impulse, shrank from the centers of the rooms to the walls, he made his way uninterruptedly, but with the same solemn and measured step, which had distinguished him from the first, through the blue chamber to the purple—through the purple to the green—through the green to the orange— through this again to the white—and even thence to the violet, ere a decided movement had been made to arrest him. It was then, however, that the Prince Prospero, maddening with rage and the shame of his own momentary cowardice, rushed hurriedly through the six chambers, while none followed him on account of a deadly terror that had seized upon all. He bore aloft a drawn dagger, and had approached, in rapid impetuosity, to within three or four feet of the retreating figure, when the latter, having attained the extremity of the velvet apartment, turned suddenly and confronted his pursuer.

There was a sharp cry—and the dagger dropped gleaming upon the sable carpet, upon which, instantly afterward, fell prostrate in death the Prince Prospero. Then, summoning the wild courage of despair, a throng of the revellers at once threw themselves into the black apartment, and, seizing the mummer, whose tall figure stood erect and motionless within the shadow of the ebony block, gasped in unutterable horror at finding the grave-cerements and corpse-like mask, which they handled with so violent a rudeness, untenanted by any tangible form.

And now was acknowledged the presence of the Red Death. He had come like a thief in the night. And one by one dropped the revellers in the blood-bedewed halls of their revel, and died each in the despairing posture of his fall. And the life of the ebony clock went out with that of the last of the gay. And the flames of the tripods expired. And Darkness and Decay and the Red Death held illimitable dominion over all.

Questions

1. Although Edgar Allan Poe uses the first-person "I" in narrating *The Masque of the Red Death,* is the point of view really that of the Autobiographical Narrator? What evidence indicates that Poe's Narrator is an Historical one? (Compare Poe's use of "I" with that of Thucydides, Gibbon, and Carlyle.)

2. In what ways does the account of the events in this story resemble the catastrophes described in *R.M.S. Titanic* by Hanson W. Baldwin and *The Fall of Constantinople* by Gibbon? Does Poe as a storyteller share the same interest and beliefs as the reporter and the historian? Does he create the same effect with his account?

3. Which is the most effective account of the ravages of plague: Thucydides's, Defoe's, Zinsser's, or Poe's?

4. Point out the ways that Poe "alters" or "heightens" factual details to gain his

aesthetic effects. Does he intend only to cause the reader to feel strong emotions or to affect the reader's attitudes and opinions as well?

5. What poetic devices does Poe use to create his effects? Why are there seven rooms in the suite? What significance do the colors have, if any? Does the Duke's name suggest anything? What is the importance of the clock; why is it ebony?

6. *Allegory* has been defined as a form of extended metaphor in which objects and persons in a narrative, either in verse or prose, are equated with meanings that lie outside the narrative itself; thus it represents one thing in the guise of another, often an abstraction in the form of concrete images. Is *The Masque of the Red Death* an allegory? If so, what do the concrete details represent? Does the overall narrative have allegorical meaning, or is it only a series of symbolic details? Compare Poe's story with Hawthorne's *The Christmas Banquet* below. Is one more clearly allegorical than the other?

NATHANIEL HAWTHORNE

The Christmas Banquet

"I have here attempted," said Roderick, unfolding a few sheets of manuscript, as he sat with Rosina and the sculptor in the summerhouse; "I have attempted to seize hold of a personage who glides past me occasionally in my walk through life. My former sad experience, as you know, has gifted me with some degree of insight into the gloomy mysteries of the human heart, through which I have wandered like one astray in a dark cavern with his torch fast flickering to extinction. But this man—this class of men—is a hopeless puzzle."

"Well, but propound him," said the sculptor. "Let us have an idea of him, to begin with."

"Why, indeed," replied Roderick, "he is such a being as I could conceive you to carve out of marble, and some yet unrealized perfection of human science to endow with an exquisite mockery of intellect; but still there lacks the last inestimable touch of a divine Creator. He looks like a man, and perchance like a better specimen of man than you ordinarily meet. You might esteem him wise—he is capable of cultivation and refinement, and has at least an external conscience—but the demands that spirit makes upon spirit are precisely those to which he cannot respond. When, at last, you are come close to him, you find him chill and unsubstantial—a mere vapor."

"I believe," said Rosina, "I have a glimmering idea of what you mean."

"Then be thankful," answered her husband, smiling, "but do not anticipate any further illumination from what I am about to read. I have here imagined such a man to be—what, probably, he never is—conscious of the deficiency in his spiritual organization. Methinks the result would be a sense of cold unreality wherewith he would go shivering through the world, longing to exchange his load of ice for any burden of real grief that fate could fling upon a human being."

Contenting himself with this preface Roderick began to read.

"In a certain old gentleman's last will and testament there appeared a bequest which, as his final thought and deed, was singularly in keeping with a long life of melancholy and eccentricity. He devised a considerable sum for establishing a fund the interest of which was to be expended annually forever in preparing a Christian banquet for ten of the most miserable persons that could be found. It seemed not to be the testator's purpose to make these half a score of sad hearts merry, but to provide that the stern or fierce expression of human discontent should not be drowned, even for that one holy and joyful day, amid the acclamations of festal gratitude which all Christendom sends up. And he desired, likewise, to perpetuate his own remonstrance against the earthly course of Providence and his sad and sour dissent from those systems of religion or philosophy which either find sunshine in the world or draw it down from heaven.

"The task of inviting the guests or of selecting among such as might advance their claims to partake of this dismal hospitality was confided to the two trustees, or stewards, of the fund. These gentlemen, like their deceased friend, were somber humorists who made it their principal occupation to number the sable threads in the web of human life and drop all the golden ones out of the reckoning. They performed their present office with integrity and judgment. The aspect of the assembled company on the day of the first festival might not, it is true, have satisfied every beholder that these were especially the individuals, chosen forth from all the world, whose griefs were worthy to stand as indicators of the mass of human suffering. Yet, after due consideration, it could not be disputed that here was a variety of hopeless discomforts which, if it sometimes arose from causes apparently inadequate, was thereby only the shrewder imputation against the nature and mechanism of life.

"The arrangements and decorations of the banquet were probably intended to signify that death in life which had been the testator's definition of existence. The hall, illuminated by torches, was hung round with curtains of deep and dusky purple and adorned with branches of cypress and wreaths of artificial flowers imitative of such as used to be strewn over the dead. A sprig of parsley was laid by every plate. The main reservoir of wine was a sepulchral urn of silver, whence the liquor was distributed around the table in small vases accurately copied from those that held the tears of ancient mourners. Neither had the stewards—if it were their taste that arranged these details—forgotten the fantasy of the old Egyptians, who seated a skeleton at every festive board and mocked their own merriment with the imper-

turbable grin of a death's head. Such a fearful guest, shrouded in a black mantle, sat now at the head of the table. It was whispered—I know not with what truth—that the testator himself had once walked the visible world with the machinery of that same skeleton, and that it was one of the stipulations of his will that he should thus be permitted to sit, from year to year, at the banquet which he had instituted. If so, it was perhaps covertly implied that he had cherished no hopes of bliss beyond the grave to compensate for the evils which he felt or imagined here. And if, in their bewildered conjectures as to the purpose of earthly existence, the banqueters should throw aside the veil and cast an inquiring glance at this figure of Death, as seeking thence the solution otherwise unattainable, the only reply would be a stare of the vacant eye-caverns and a grin of the skeleton jaws. Such was the response that the dead man had fancied himself to receive when he asked of Death to solve the riddle of his life, and it was his desire to repeat it when the guests of his dismal hospitality should find themselves perplexed with the same question.

" 'What means that wreath?' asked several of the company while viewing the decorations of the table. They alluded to a wreath of cypress which was held on high by a skeleton arm protruding from within the black mantle.

" 'It is a crown,' said one of the stewards, 'not for the worthiest, but for the wofulest when he shall prove his claim to it.'

"The guest earliest bidden to the festival was a man of soft and gentle character who had not energy to struggle against the heavy despondency to which his temperament rendered him liable, and therefore, with nothing outwardly to excuse him from happiness, he had spent a life of quiet misery that made his blood torpid, and weighed upon his breath, and sat like a ponderous night-fiend upon every throb of his unresisting heart; his wretchedness seemed as deep as his original nature, if not identical with it. It was the misfortune of a second guest to cherish within his bosom a diseased heart which had become so wretchedly sore that the continual and unavoidable rubs of the world, the blow of an enemy, the careless jostle of a stranger, and even the faithful and loving touch of a friend, alike made ulcers in it; as is the habit of people thus afflicted, he found his chief employment in exhibiting these miserable sores to any who would give themselves the pain of viewing them. A third guest was a hypochondriac whose imagination wrought necromancy in his outward and inward world, and caused him to see monstrous faces in the household fire, and dragons in the clouds of sunset, and fiends in the guise of beautiful women, and something ugly or wicked beneath all the pleasant surfaces of nature. His neighbor at table was one who in his early youth had trusted mankind too much and hoped too highly in their behalf, and, meeting with many disappointments, had become desperately soured; for several years back this misanthrope had employed himself in accumulating motives for hating and despising his race, such as murders, lust, treachery, ingratitude, faithlessness of trusted friends, instinctive vices of children, impurity of women, hidden guilt in men of saintlike aspect, and, in short, all manner of black realities that sought to decorate themselves with outward grace or glory. But at every atrocious fact that was added to his catalogue—at every increase of the sad knowledge which he spent his life to collect—the native impulses of the poor man's loving and confident heart made him groan with anguish. Next, with his heavy brow bent downward, there stole into the hall a man naturally earnest and impassioned who from his immemorial infancy had felt the consciousness of a high message to the world, but, essaying to deliver it, had found either no voice or form of speech, or else no ears to listen; therefore his whole life was a bitter questioning of himself: 'Why have not men acknowledged my mission? Am I not a self-deluding fool? What business have I on earth? Where is my grave?' Throughout the festival he quaffed frequent draughts from the sepulchral urn of wine, hoping thus to quench the celestial fire that tortured his own breast and could not benefit his race. Then there entered, having flung away a ticket for a ball, a gay gallant of yesterday who had found four or five wrinkles in his brow, and more gray hairs than he could well number on his head. Endowed with sense and feeling, he had nevertheless spent his youth in folly, but had reached at last that dreary point in life where Folly quits us of her own accord, leaving us to make friends with Wisdom if we can. Thus, cold and desolate, he had come to seek Wisdom at the banquet, and wondered if the skeleton was she. To eke out the company, the steward had invited a distressed poet from his home in the almshouse and a melancholy idiot from the street-corner. The latter had just the glimmering of sense that was sufficient to make him conscious of a vacancy which the poor fellow all his life long had mistily sought to fill up with intelligence, wandering up and down the streets and groaning miserably because his attempts were ineffectual. The only lady in the hall was one who had fallen short of absolute and perfect beauty merely by the trifling defect of a slight cast in her left eye; but this blemish, minute as it was, so shocked the pure ideal of her soul, rather than her vanity, that she passed her life in solitude and veiled her countenance even from her own gaze. So the skeleton sat shrouded at one end of the table, and this poor lady at the other.

"One other guest remains to be described. He was a young man of smooth brow, fair cheek and fashionable mien. So far as his exterior developed him, he might much more suitably have found a place at some merry Christmas table than have been numbered among the blighted fate-stricken, fancy-tortured set of ill-starred banqueters. Murmurs arose among the guests as they noted the glance of general scrutiny which the intruder threw over his companions. What had he to do among them? Why did not the skeleton of the dead founder of the feast unbend its rattling joints, arise and motion the unwelcome stranger from the board?

" 'Shameful!' said the morbid man, while a

new ulcer broke out in his heart. 'He comes to mock us; we shall be the jest of his tavern friends. He will make a farce of our miseries and bring it out upon the stage.'

" 'Oh, never mind him,' said the hypochondriac, smiling sourly. 'He shall feast from yonder tureen of viper-soup; and if there is a fricassee of scorpions on the table, pray let him have his share of it. For the dessert he shall taste the apples of Sodom. Then, if he like our Christmas fare, let him return again next year.'

" 'Trouble him not,' murmured the melancholy man, with gentleness. 'What matters it whether the consciousness of misery come a few years sooner or later? If this youth deem himself happy now, yet let him sit with us, for the sake of the wretchedness to come.'

"The poor idiot approached the young man with that mournful aspect of vacant inquiry which his face continually wore, and which caused people to say that he was always in search of his missing wits. After no little examination he touched the stranger's hand, but immediately drew back his own, shaking his head and shivering.

" 'Cold! cold!' muttered the idiot.

"The young man shivered too, and smiled.

" 'Gentlemen—and you, madam,' said one of the stewards of the festival—'do not conceive so ill either of our caution or judgment as to imagine that we have admitted this young stranger—Gervayse Hastings by name—without a full investigation and thoughtful balance of his claims. Trust me, not a guest at the table is better entitled to his seat.'

"The steward's guaranty was perforce satisfactory. The company, therefore, took their places and addressed themselves to the serious business of the feast, but were soon disturbed by the hypochondriac, who thrust back his chair, complaining that a dish of stewed toads and vipers was set before him, and that there was green ditch-water in his cup of wine. This mistake being amended, he quietly resumed his seat. The wine, as it flowed freely from the sepulchral urn, seemed to come imbued with all gloomy inspirations; so that its influence was not to cheer, but either to sink the revelers into a deeper melancholy or elevate their spirits to an enthusiasm of wretchedness. The conversation was various. They told sad stories about people who might have been worthy guests at such a festival as the present. They talked of grizzly incidents in human history—of strange crimes which, if truly considered, were but convulsions of agony; of some lives that had been altogether wretched, and of others which, wearing a general semblance of happiness, had yet been deformed sooner or later by misfortune as by the intrusion of a grim face at a banquet; of deathbed scenes and what dark intimations might be gathered from the words of dying men; of suicide, and whether the more eligible mode were by halter, knife, poison, drowning, gradual starvation, or the fumes of charcoal. The majority of the guests, as is the custom with people thoroughly and profoundly sick at heart, were anxious to make their own woes the theme of discussion and prove themselves most excellent in anguish. The misanthropist went deep into the philosophy of evil, and wandered about in the darkness with now and then a gleam of discolored light hovering on ghastly shapes and horrid scenery. Many a miserable thought such as men have stumbled upon from age to age did he now rake up again, and gloat over it as an inestimable gem, a diamond, a treasure far preferable to those bright, spiritual revelations of a better world which are like precious stones from heaven's pavement. And then, amid his lore of wretchedness, he hid his face and wept.

"It was a festival at which the woful man of Uz might suitably have been a guest, together with all in each succeeding age who have tasted deepest of the bitterness of life. And be it said, too, that every son or daughter of woman, however favored with happy fortune, might at one sad moment or another have claimed the privilege of a stricken heart to sit down at this table. But throughout the feast it was remarkable that the young stranger, Gervayse Hastings, was unsuccessful in his attempts to catch its pervading spirit. At any deep, strong thought that found utterance, and which was torn out, as it were, from the saddest recesses of human consciousness, he looked mystified and bewildered—even more than the poor idiot, who seemed to grasp at such things with his earnest heart, and thus occasionally to comprehend them. The young man's conversation was of a colder and lighter kind, often brilliant, but lacking the powerful characteristics of a nature that had been developed by suffering.

" 'Sir,' said the misanthropist, bluntly, in reply to some observation by Gervayse Hastings, 'pray do not address me again. We have no right to talk together; our minds have nothing in common. By what claim you appear at this banquet I cannot guess, but methinks, to a man who could say what you have just said now, my companions and myself must seem no more than shadows flickering on the wall. And precisely such a shadow are you to us.'

"The young man smiled and bowed, but, drawing himself back in his chair, he buttoned his coat over his breast, as if the banqueting-hall were growing chill. Again the idiot fixed his melancholy stare upon the youth and murmured 'Cold! cold! cold!'

"The banquet drew to its conclusion, and the guests departed. Scarcely had they stepped across the threshold of the hall, when the scene that had there passed seemed like the vision of a sick fancy or an exhalation from a stagnant heart. Now and then, however, during the year that ensued, these melancholy people caught glimpses of one another—transient, indeed, but enough to prove that they walked the earth with the ordinary allotment of reality. Sometimes a pair of them came face to face while stealing through the evening twilight enveloped in the sable cloaks. Sometimes they casually met in church-yards. Once, also, it happened that two of the dismal banqueters mutually started at recognizing each other in the noonday sunshine of a crowded street, stalking there like ghosts astray. Doubtless they wondered why

the skeleton did not come abroad at noonday, too.

"But, whenever the necessity of their affairs compelled these Christmas guests into the bustling world, they were sure to encounter the young man who had so unaccountably been admitted to the festival. They saw him among the gay and fortunate, they caught the sunny sparkle of his eye, they heard the light and careless tones of his voice, and muttered to themselves with such indignation as only the aristocracy of wretchedness could kindle: 'The traitor! The vile impostor! Providence in its own good time may give him a right to feast among us.' But the young man's unabashed eye dwelt upon their gloomy figures as they passed him, seeming to say, perchance with somewhat of a sneer. 'First know my secret, then measure your claims with mine.'

"The step of time stole onward, and soon brought merry Christmas round again, with glad and solemn worship in the churches, and sports, games, festivals, and everywhere the bright face of Joy beside the household fire. Again, likewise, the hall, with its curtains of dusky purple, was illuminated by the death-torches gleaming on the sepulchral decorations of the banquet. The veiled skeleton sat in state, lifting the cypress-wreath above its head as the guerdon of some guest illustrious in the qualifications which there claimed precedence. As the stewards deemed the world inexhaustible in misery and were desirous of recognizing it in all its forms, they have not seen fit to reassemble the company of the former year. New faces now threw their gloom across the table.

"There was a man of nice conscience who bore a bloodstain in his heart—the death of a fellow-creature—which for his more exquisite torture had chanced with such a peculiarity of circumstances that he could not absolutely determine whether his will had entered into the deed or not. Therefore his whole life was spent in the agony of an inward trial for murder, with a continual sifting of the details of his terrible calamity, until his mind had no longer any thought nor his soul any emotion disconnected with it. There was a mother, too—a mother once, but a desolation now—who many years before had gone out on a pleasure-party, and, returning, found her infant smothered in its little bed, and ever since she has been tortured with the fantasy that her buried baby lay smothering in its coffin. Then there was an aged lady who had lived from time immemorial with a constant tremor quivering through her frame. It was terrible to discern her dark shadow tremulous upon the wall. Her lips, likewise, were tremulous, and the expression of her eye seemed to indicate that her soul was trembling too. Owing to the bewilderment and confusion which made almost a chaos of her intellect, it was impossible to discover what dire misfortune had thus shaken her nature to its depths; so that the stewards had admitted her to the table, not from any acquaintance with her history, but on the safe testimony of her miserable aspect. Some surprise was expressed at the presence of a bluff, red-faced gentleman, a certain Mr. Smith, who had evidently the fat of many a rich feast within him, and the habitual twinkle of whose eye betrayed a disposition to break forth into uproarious laughter for little cause, or none. It turned out, however, that with the best possible flow of spirits our poor friend was afflicted with a physical disease of the heart which threatened instant death on the slightest cachinnatory indulgence, or even that titillation of the bodily frame produced by merry thoughts. In this dilemma he had sought admittance to the banquet on the ostensible plea of his irksome and miserable state, but, in reality, with the hope of imbibing a life-preserving melancholy.

"A married couple had been invited from a motive of bitter humor, it being well understood that they rendered each other unutterably miserable whenever they chanced to meet, and therefore must necessarily be fit associates at the festival. In contrast with these was another couple, still unmarried, who had interchanged their hearts in early life, but had been divided by circumstances as impalpable as morning mist, and kept apart so long that their spirits now found it impossible to meet. Therefore, yearning for communion, yet shrinking from one another, and choosing none besides, they felt themselves companionless in life and looked upon eternity as a boundless desert. Next to the skeleton sat a mere son of earth—a hunter of the Exchange, a gatherer of shining dust, a man whose life's record was in his ledger, and whose soul's prison-house the vaults of the bank where he kept his deposits. This person had been greatly perplexed at his invitation, deeming himself one of the most fortunate men in the city; but the stewards persisted in demanding his presence, assuring him that he had no conception how miserable he was.

"And now appeared a figure which we must acknowledge as our acquaintance of the former festival. It was Gervayse Hastings, whose presence had then caused so much question and criticism, and who now took his place with the composure of one whose claims were satisfactory to himself and must needs be allowed by others. Yet his easy and unruffled face betrayed no sorrow. The well-skilled beholders gazed a moment into his eyes and shook their heads to miss the unuttered sympathy—the counter-sign never to be falsified, of those whose hearts are cavern-mouths through which they descend into a region of illimitable woe and recognize other wanderers there.

" 'Who is this youth?' asked the man with a blood-stain on his conscience. 'Surely he has never gone down into the depths? I know all the aspects of those who have passed through the dark valley. By what right he is among us?'

" 'Ah! it is a sinful thing to come hither without a sorrow,' murmured the aged lady, in accents that partook of the eternal tremor which pervaded her whole being. "Depart, young man! Your soul has never been shaken, and therefore I tremble so much the more to look at you.'

" 'His soul shaken! No; I'll answer for it', said bluff Mr. Smith, pressing his hand upon his heart and making himself as melancholy as he could, for fear of a fatal explosion of laughter. 'I know the lad well; he has as fair prospects as any young man about town, and has no more right among us miserable creatures than the child unborn. He never was miserable, and probably never will be.'

" 'Our honored guests,' interposed the stewards, 'pray have patience with us, and believe, at least, that our deep veneration for the sacredness of this solemnity would preclude any willful violation of it. Receive this young man to your table. It may not be too much to say that no guest here would exchange his own heart for the one that beats within that youthful bosom.'

" 'I'd call it a bargain, and gladly, too,' muttered Mr. Smith, with a perplexing mixture of sadness and mirthful conceit. 'A plague upon their nonsense! My own heart is the only really miserable one in the company. It will certainly be the death of me at last.'

"Nevertheless, as on the former occasion, the judgment of the stewards being without appeal, the company sat down. The obnoxious guest made no more attempt to obtrude his conversation on those about him, but appeared to listen to the table-talk with peculiar assiduity, as if some inestimable secret, otherwise beyond his reach, might be conveyed in a casual word. And, in truth, to those who could understand and value it, there was rich matter in the upgushings and outpourings of these initiated souls to whom sorrow had been a talisman admitting them into spiritual depths which no other spell can open. Sometimes out of the midst of densest gloom there flashed a momentary radiance pure as crystal, bright as the flame of stars and shedding such a glow upon the mysteries of life that the guests were ready to exclaim: 'Surely the riddle is on the point of being solved!' At such illuminated intervals the saddest mourners felt it to be revealed that mortal griefs are but shadowy and external—no more than the sable robes voluminously shrouding a certain divine reality, and thus indicating what might otherwise be altogether invisible to mortal eye.

" 'Just now,' remarked the trembling old woman, 'I seemed to see beyond the outside, and then my everlasting tremor passed away.'

" 'Would that I could dwell always in these momentary gleams of light!' said the man of stricken conscience. 'Then the blood-stain in my heart would be washed clean away.'

"This strain of conversation appeared so unintelligibly absurd to good Mr. Smith that he burst into precisely the fit of laughter which his physicians had warned him against as likely to prove instantaneously fatal. In effect, he fell back in his chair a corpse with a broad grin upon his face, while his ghost, perchance, remained beside it, bewildered at its unpremeditated exit. This catastrophe, of course, broke up the festival.

" 'How is this? You do not tremble,' observed the tremulous old woman to Gervayse Hastings, who was gazing at the dead man with singular intentness. 'Is it not awful to see him so suddenly vanish out of the midst of life—this man of flesh and blood whose earthly nature was so warm and strong? There is a never-ending tremor in my soul, but it trembles afresh at this. And you are calm!'

" 'Would that he could teach me somewhat!' said Gervayse Hastings, drawing a long breath. 'Men pass before me like shadows on the wall; their actions, passions, feelings, are flickerings of the light, and then they vanish! Neither the corpse nor yonder skeleton nor this old woman's everlasting tremor can give me what I seek.'

"And then the company departed.

"We cannot linger to narrate in such detail more circumstances of these singular festivals, which, in accordance with the founder's will, continued to be kept with the regularity of an established institution. In process of time the stewards adopted the custom of inviting from far and near those individuals whose misfortunes were prominent above other men's, and whose mental and moral development might, therefore, be supposed to possess a corresponding interest. The exiled noble of the French Revolution and the broken soldier of the Empire were alike represented at the table. Fallen monarchs wandering about the earth have found places at that forlorn and miserable feast. The statesman, when his party flung him off, might, if he chose it, be once more a great man for the space of a single banquet. Aaron Burr's name appears on the record at a period when his ruin—the profoundest and most striking, with more of moral circumstance in it than that of almost any other man—was complete, in his lonely age. Stephen Girard, when his wealth weighed upon him like a mountain, once sought admittance of his own accord. It is not probable, however, that these men had any lesson to teach in the lore of discontent and misery which might not equally well have been studied in the common walks of life. Illustrious unfortunates attract a wider sympathy, not because their griefs are more intense, but because, being set on lofty pedestals, they the better serve mankind as instances and by-words of calamity.

"It concerns our present purpose to say that at each successive festival Gervayse Hastings showed his face gradually changing from the smooth beauty of his youth to the thoughtful comeliness of manhood, and thence to the bald, impressive dignity of age. He was the only individual invariably present, yet on every occasion there were murmurs, both from those who knew his character and position and from them whose hearts shrunk back, as denying his companionship in their mystic fraternity.

" 'Who is this impassive man?' had been asked a hundred times. 'Has he suffered? Has he sinned? There are no traces of either. Then wherefore is he here?'

" 'You must inquire of the stewards or of himself,' was the constant reply. 'We seem to know him well here in our city, and know nothing of him but what is creditable and fortunate. Yet hither he comes, year after year, to this gloomy banquet, and sits among the guests like a marble statue. Ask yonder skeleton; perhaps that may solve the riddle.'

"It was, in truth, a wonder. The life of Gervayse Hastings was not merely a prosperous but a brilliant one. Everything had gone well

with him. He was wealthy far beyond the expenditure that was required by habits of magnificence, a taste of rare purity and cultivation, a love of travel, a scholar's instinct to collect a splendid library, and, moreover, what seemed a munificent liberality to the distressed. He had sought domestic happiness, and not vainly if a lovely and tender wife and children of fair promise could insure it. He had, besides, ascended above the limit which separates the obscure from the distinguished, and had won a stainless reputation in affairs of the wildest public importance. Not that he was a popular character or had within him the mysterious attributes which are essential to that species of success. To the public he was a cold abstraction wholly destitute of those rich hues of personality, that living warmth and the peculiar faculty of stamping his own heart's impression on a multitude of hearts by which the people recognize their favorites. And it must be owned that, after his most intimate associates had done their best to know him thoroughly and love him warmly, they were startled to find how little hold he had upon their affections. They approved, they admired, but still, in those moments when the human spirit most craves reality, they shrunk back from Gervayse Hastings as powerless to give them what they sought. It was the feeling of distrustful regret with which we should draw back the hand after extending it in an illusive twilight to grasp the hand of a shadow upon the wall.

"As the superficial fervency of youth decayed, this peculiar effect of Gervayse Hastings's character grew more perceptible. His children, when he extended his arms, came coldly to his knees, but never climbed them of their own accord. His wife wept secretly and almost adjudged herself a criminal because she shivered in the chill of his bosom. He, too, occasionally appeared not unconscious of the chilliness of his normal atmosphere, and willing, if it might be so, to warm himself at a kindly fire. But age stole onward and benumbed him more and more. As the hoar frost began to gather on him his wife went to her grave, and was doubtless warmer there; his children either died or were scattered to different homes of their own; and old Gervayse Hastings—unscathed by grief, alone, but needing no companionship—continued his steady walk through life and still on every Christmas day attended at the dismal banquet. His privilege as a guest had become prescriptive now. Had he claimed the head of the table, even the skeleton would have been rejected from its seat.

"Finally, at the merry Christmas-tide when he had numbered fourscore years complete, this pale, high-browed, marble-featured old man once more entered the long-frequented hall with the same impassive aspect that had called forth so much dissatisfied remark at his first attendance. Time, except in matters merely external, had done nothing for him, either of good or evil. As he took his place he threw a calm inquiring glance around the table, as if to ascertain whether any guest had yet appeared, after so many unsuccessful banquets, who might impart to him the mystery, the deep warm secret, the life within the life, which, whether manifested in joy or sorrow, is what gives substance to a world of shadows.

" 'My friends,' said Gervayse Hastings, assuming a position which his long conversance with the festival caused to appear natural, 'you are welcome! I drink to you all in this cup of sepulchral wine.'

"The guests replied courteously, but still in a manner that proved them unable to receive the old man as a member of their sad fraternity.

"It may be well to give the reader an idea of the present company at the banquet. One was formerly a clergyman enthusiastic in his profession, and apparently of the genuine dynasty of these old Puritan divines whose faith in their calling and stern exercise of it had placed them among the mighty of the earth. But, yielding to the speculative tendency of the age, he had gone astray from the firm foundation of an ancient faith and wandered into a cloud-region where everything was misty and deceptive, ever mock-

ing him with a semblance of reality, but still dissolving when he flung himself upon it for support and rest. His instinct and early training demanded something steadfast, but, looking forward, he beheld vapors piled on vapors, and behind him an impassable gulf between the man of yesterday and to-day, on the borders of which he paced to and fro sometimes wringing his hands in agony and often making his own woe a theme of scornful merriment. This surely was a miserable man. Next, there was a theorist, one of a numerous tribe, although he deemed himself unique since the creation—a theorist who had conceived a plan by which all the wretchedness of earth, moral and physical, might be done away and the bliss of the millennium at once accomplished. But, the incredulity of mankind debarring him from action, he was smitten with as much grief as if the whole mass of woe which he was denied the opportunity to remedy were crowded into his own bosom. A plain old man in black attracted much of the company's notice on the supposition that he was no other than Father Miller, who, it seemed, had given himself up to despair at the tedious delay of the final conflagration. Then there was a man distinguished for native pride and obstinacy who a little while before had possessed immense wealth and held the control of a vast moneyed interest, which he had wielded in the same spirit as a despotic monarch would wield the power of his empire, carrying on a tremendous moral warfare the roar and tremor of which was felt at every fireside in the land. At length came a crushing ruin—a total overthrow of fortune, power and character—the effect of which on his imperious and in many respects noble and lofty nature might have entitled him to a place not merely at our festival, but among the peers of Pandemonium. There was a modern philanthropist who had become so deeply sensible of the calamities of thousands and millions of his fellow-creature, and of the impracticableness of any general measures for their relief, that he had no heart to do what little good lay immediately within his power, but contented himself with being miserable for sympathy. Near him sat a gentleman in a predicament hitherto unprecedented, but of which the present epoch probably affords numerous examples. Ever since he was of capacity to read a newspaper this person had prided himself on his consistent adherence to one political party, but in the confusion of these latter days had got bewildered, and knew not whereabouts his party was. This wretched condition, so morally desolate and disheartening to a man who has long accustomed himself to merge his individuality in the mass of a great body, can only be conceived by such as have experienced it. His next companion was a popular orator who had lost his voice, and, as it was pretty much all that he had to lose, had fallen into a state of hopeless melancholy. The table was likewise graced by two of the gentler sex—one, a half-starved, consumptive seamstress, the representative of thousands just as wretched; the other, a woman of unemployed energy who found herself in the world with nothing to achieve, nothing to enjoy and nothing even to suffer. She had, therefore, driven herself to the verge of madness by dark broodings over the wrongs of her sex and its exclusion from a proper field of action. The roll of guests being thus complete, a side-table had been set for three or four disappointed office-seekers, with hearts as sick as death, whom the stewards had admitted, partly because their calamities really entitled them to entrance here and partly that they were in especial need of a good dinner. There was likewise a homeless dog, with his tail between his legs, licking up the crumb and gnawing the fragments of the feast—such a melancholy cur as one sometimes sees about the streets without a master and willing to follow the first that will accept his service.

"In their own way these were as wretched a set of people as ever had assembled at the festival. There they sat, with the veiled skeleton of the founder holding aloft the cypress-wreath at one end of the table, and at the other, wrapped in furs, the withered figure of Gervayse Hastings, stately, calm and cold, impressing the

company with awe, yet so little interesting their sympathy that he might have vanished into thin air without their once exclaiming: 'Whither is he gone?'

" 'Sir,' said the philanthropist, addressing the old man, 'you have been so long a guest at this annual festival, and have thus been conversant with so many varieties of human affliction, that not improbably you have thence derived some great and important lessons. How blessed were your lot could you reveal a secret by which all this mass of woe might be removed!'

" 'I know of but one misfortune,' answered Gervayse Hastings, quietly, 'and that is my own.'

" 'Your own!' rejoined the philanthropist. 'And, looking back on your serene and prosperous life, how can you claim to be the sole unfortunate of the human race?'

" 'You will not understand it,' replied Gervayse Hastings, feebly and with a singular inefficiency of pronounciation, and sometimes putting one word for another. 'None have understood it—not even those who experience the like. It is a chilliness, a want of earnestness, a feeling as if what should be my heart were a thing of vapor, a haunting perception of unreality. Thus, seeming to possess all that other men have—all that men aim at—I have really possessed nothing—neither joy nor griefs. All things, all persons—as was truly said to me at this table long and long ago—have been like shadows flickering on the wall. It was so with my wife and children, with those who seemed my friends; it is so with yourselves, whom I see now before me. Neither have I myself any real existence, but am a shadow like the rest.'

" 'And how is it with your views of a future life?' inquired the speculative clergymen.

" 'Worse than with you,' said the old man, in a hollow and feeble tone, 'for I cannot conceive it earnestly enough to feel either hope or fear. Mine—mine is the wretchedness! This cold heart—this unreal life! Ah! it grows colder still.

"It so chanced that at this juncture the decayed ligaments of the skeleton gave way and the dry bones fell together in a heap, thus causing the dusty wreath of cypress to drop upon the table. The attention of the company being thus diverted for a single instant from Gervayse Hastings, they perceived, on turning again toward him, that the old man had undergone a change; his shadow had ceased to flicker on the wall."

"Well, Rosina, what is your criticism?" asked Roderick, as he rolled up the manuscript.

"Frankly, your success is by no means complete," replied she. "It is true I have an idea of the character you endeavour to describe, but it is rather by dint of my own thought than your expression."

"That is unavoidable," observed the sculptor, "because the characteristics are all negative. If Gervayse Hastings could have imbibed one human grief at the gloomy banquet, the task of describing him would have been infinitely easier. Of such persons—and we do meet with these moral monsters now and then—it is difficult to conceive how they came to exist here or what there is in them capable of existence hereafter. They seem to be on the outside of everything, and nothing wearies the soul more than an attempt to comprehend them within its grasp."

Questions

1. *The Christmas Banquet* is actually a narrative within a framework of a narrative: a Reporter Narrator describes the summer house and reports the conversation of its inhabitants; then Roderick, as a Historian Narrator, tells the history of the annual banquet and Gervayse Hastings; finally the Reporter Narrator gives the concluding dialogue in the summer house. Why does Hawthorne use this sort of narrative method for his story? Is it necessary? By what other method might the story have been told? What would have been lost by doing so?

2. *The Christmas Banquet* is obviously like *The Long Christmas Dinner:* both focus on the annual event; both are concerned with the pattern and meaning of human life, etc. In what important ways do they differ?

3. Discuss the use of symbols by Hawthorne (the skeleton, the wreath, the missing shadow, Christmas as a religious holiday). Is the story a consistent allegory? If so, what is the abstract parallel meaning to the events described? What intangible truths is Hawthorne concerned with?

4. Read E. A. Robinson's "Richard Cory" (p. 542 below). Are Richard Cory and Gervayse Hastings the same man or not? What differences, if any, are there between the two characterizations? Are these the result of different points of view in narration or something else?

5. What is the central theme of *The Christmas Banquet:* human misery; the futility of life; the emptiness of existence without a belief in the afterlife; isolation and its effects; none of these; all of these and more?

FRANZ KAFKA

The Judgment

It was a Sunday morning in the very height of spring. Georg Bendemann, a young merchant, was sitting in his own room on the first floor of one of a long row of small, ramshackle houses stretching beside the river which were scarcely distinguishable from each other except in height and coloring. He had just finished a letter to an old friend of his who was now living abroad, had put it into its envelope in a slow and dreamy fashion, and with his elbows propped on the writing table was gazing out of the window

THE JUDGMENT: Reprinted by permission of Schocken Books Inc. from *The Penal Colony* by Franz Kafka. Copyright © 1948 by Schocken Books Inc.

at the river, the bridge and the hills on the farther bank with their tender green.

He was thinking about his friend, who had actually run away to Russia some years before, being dissatisfied with his prospects at home. Now he was carrying on a business in St. Petersburg, which had flourished to begin with but had long been going downhill, as he always complained on his increasingly rare visits. So he was wearing himself out to no purpose in a foreign country; the unfamiliar full beard he wore did not quite conceal the face Georg had known so well since childhood, and his skin was growing so yellow as to indicate some latent disease. By his own account he had no regular connection with the colony of his fellow countrymen out there and almost no social intercourse with Russian families, so that he was resigning himself to becoming a permanent bachelor.

What could one write to such a man, who had obviously run off the rails, a man one could be sorry for but could not help? Should one advise him to come home, to transplant himself and take up his old friendships again—there was nothing to hinder him—and in general to rely on the help of his friends? But that was as good as telling him, and the more kindly the more offensively, that all his efforts hitherto had miscarried, that he should finally give up, come back home, and be gaped at by everyone as a returned prodigal, that only his friends knew what was what and that he himself was just a big child who should do what his successful and home-keeping friends prescribed. And was it certain, besides, that all the pain one would have to inflict on him would achieve its object? Perhaps it would not even be possible to get him to come home at all—he said himself that he was now out of touch with commerce in his native country—and then he would still be left an alien in a foreign land embittered by his friends' advice and more than ever estranged from them. But if he did follow their advice and then didn't fit in at home—not out of malice, of course, but through force of circumstances—couldn't get on with his friends or without them, felt humiliated,

couldn't be said to have either friends or a country of his own any longer, wouldn't it have been better for him to stay abroad just as he was? Taking all this into account, how could one be sure that he would make a success of life at home?

For such reasons, supposing one wanted to keep up correspondence with him, one could not send him any real news such as could frankly be told to the most distant acquaintance. It was more than three years since his last visit, and for this he offered the lame excuse that the political situation in Russia was too uncertain, which apparently would not permit even the briefest absence of a small business man while it allowed hundreds of thousands of Russians to travel peacefully abroad. But during these three years Georg's own position in life had changed a lot. Two years ago his mother had died, since when he and his father had shared the household together, and his friend had of course been informed of that and had expressed his sympathy in a letter phrased so dryly that the grief caused by such an event, one had to conclude, could not be realized in a distant country. Since that time, however, Georg had applied himself with greater determination to the business as well as to everything else.

Perhaps during his mother's lifetime his father's insistence on having everything his own way in the business had hindered him from developing any real activity of his own, perhaps since her death his father had become less aggressive, although he was still active in the business, perhaps it was mostly due to an accidental run of good fortune—which was very probable indeed—but at any rate during those two years the business had developed in a most unexpected way, the staff had had to be doubled, the turnover was five times as great, no doubt about it, further progress lay just ahead.

But Georg's friend had no inkling of this improvement. In earlier years, perhaps for the last time in that letter of condolence, he had tried to persuade Georg to emigrate to Russia and had enlarged upon the prospects of success for precisely Georg's branch of trade. The figures quoted were microscopic by comparison with the range of Georg's present operations. Yet he shrank from letting his friend know about his business success, and if he were to do it now retrospectively that certainly would look peculiar.

So Georg confined himself to giving his friend unimportant items of gossip such as rise at random in the memory when one is idly thinking things over on a quiet Sunday. All he desired was to leave undisturbed the idea of the home town which his friend must have built up to his own content during the long interval. And so it happened to Georg that three times in three fairly widely separated letters he had told his friend about the engagement of an unimportant man to an equally unimportant girl, until indeed, quite contrary to his intentions, his friend began to show some interest in this notable event.

Yet Georg preferred to write about things like these rather than to confess that he himself had got engaged a month ago to a Fräulein Frieda Brandenfeld, a girl from a well-to-do family. He often discussed this friend of his with his fiancée and the peculiar relationship that had developed between them in their correspondence. "So he won't be coming to our wedding," said she, "and yet I have a right to get to know all your friends." "I don't want to trouble him," answered Georg. "Don't misunderstand me, he would probably come, at least I think so, but he would feel that his hand had been forced and he would be hurt, perhaps he would envy me and certainly he'd be discontented and without being able to do anything about his discontent he'd have to go away again alone. Alone—do you know what that means?" "Yes, but may he not hear about our wedding in some other fashion?" "I can't prevent that, of course, but it's unlikely, considering the way he lives." "Since your friends are like that, Georg, you shouldn't ever have got engaged at all." "Well, we're both to blame for that; but I wouldn't have it any other way now." And when, breathing quickly under his kisses, she still

brought out: "All the same, I do feel upset," he thought it could not really involve him in trouble were he to send the news to his friend. "That's the kind of man I am and he'll just have to take me as I am," he said to himself, "I can't cut myself to another pattern that might make a more suitable friend for him."

And in fact he did inform his friend, in the long letter he had been writing that Sunday morning, about his engagement, with these words: "I have saved my best news to the end. I have got engaged to a Fräulein Frieda Brandenfeld, a girl from a well-to-do family, who only came to live here a long time after you went away, so that you're hardly likely to know her. There will be time to tell you more about her later, for today let me just say that I am very happy and as between you and me the only difference in our relationship is that instead of a quite ordinary kind of friend you will now have in me a happy friend. Besides that, you will acquire in my fiancée, who sends her warm greetings and will soon write you herself, a genuine friend of the opposite sex, which is not without importance to a bachelor. I know that there are many reasons why you can't come to see us, but would not my wedding be precisely the right occasion for giving all obstacles the go-by? Still, however that may be, do just as seems good to you without regarding any interests but your own."

With this letter in his hand, Georg had been sitting a long time at the writing table, his face turned towards the window. He had barely acknowledged, with an absent smile, a greeting waved to him from the street by a passing acquaintance.

At last he put the letter in his pocket and went out of his room across a small lobby into his father's room, which he had not entered for months. There was in fact no need for him to enter it, since he saw his father daily at business and they took their midday meal together at an eating house; in the evening, it was true, each did as he pleased, yet even then, unless Georg—as mostly happened—went out with friends or, more recently, visited his fiancée, they always sat for a while, each with his newspaper, in their common sitting room.

It surprised Georg how dark his father's room was even on this sunny morning. So it was overshadowed as much as that by the high wall on the other side of the narrow courtyard. His father was sitting by the window in a corner hung with various mementoes of Georg's dead mother, reading a newspaper which he held to one side before his eyes in an attempt to overcome a defect of vision. On the table stood the the remains of his breakfast, not much of which seemed to have been eaten.

"Ah, Georg," said his father, rising at once to meet him. His heavy dressing gown swung open as he walked and the skirts of it fluttered round him.—"My father is still a giant of a man," said Georg to himself.

"It's unbearably dark here," he said aloud.

"Yes, it's dark enough," answered his father.

"And you've shut the window, too?"

"I prefer it like that."

"Well, it's quite warm outside," said Georg, as if continuing his previous remark, and sat down.

His father cleared away the breakfast dishes and set them on a chest.

"I really only wanted to tell you," went on Georg, who had been vacantly following the old man's movements, "that I am now sending the news of my engagement to St. Petersburg." He drew the letter a little way from his pocket and let it drop back again.

"To St. Petersburg?" asked his father.

"To my friend there," said Georg, trying to meet his father's eye. In business hours he's quite different, he was thinking. How solidly he sits here with his arms crossed.

"Oh, yes. To your friend," said his father, with peculiar emphasis.

"Well, you know, Father, that I wanted not to tell him about my engagement at first. Out of consideration for him, that was the only reason. You know yourself he's a difficult man. I said to myself that some one else might tell him about

my engagement, although he's such a solitary creature that that was hardly likely—I couldn't prevent that—but I wasn't ever going to tell him myself."

"And now you've changed your mind?" asked his father, laying his enormous newspaper on the window sill and on top of it his spectacles, which he covered with one hand.

"Yes, I've been thinking it over. If he's a good friend of mine, I said to myself, my being happily engaged should make him happy too. And so I wouldn't put off telling him any longer. But before I posted the letter I wanted to let you know."

"Georg," said his father, lengthening his toothless mouth, "listen to me! You've come to me about this business, to talk it over with me. No doubt that does you honor. But it's nothing, it's worse than nothing, if you don't tell me the whole truth. I don't want to stir up matters that shouldn't be mentioned here. Since the death of our dear mother certain things have been done that aren't right. Maybe the time will come for mentioning them, and maybe sooner than we think. There's many a thing in the business I'm not aware of, maybe it's not done behind my back—I'm not going to say that it's done behind my back—I'm not equal to things any longer, my memory's failing, I haven't an eye for so many things any longer. That's the course of nature in the first place, and in the second place the death of our dear mother hit me harder than it did you. But since we're talking about it, about this letter, I beg you, Georg, don't deceive me. It's a trivial affair, it's hardly worth mentioning, so don't deceive me. Do you really have this friend in St. Petersburg?"

Georg rose in embarrassment. "Never mind my friends. A thousand friends wouldn't make up to me for my father. Do you know what I think? You're not taking enough care of yourself. But old age must be taken care of. I can't do without you in the business, you know that very well, but if the business is going to undermine your health, I'm ready to close it down tomorrow forever. And that won't do. We'll have to make a change in your way of living. But a radical change. You sit here in the dark, and in the sitting room you would have plenty of light. You just take a bite of breakfast instead of properly keeping up your strength. You sit by a closed window, and the air would be so good for you. No, Father! I'll get the doctor to come, and we'll follow his orders. We'll change your room, you can move into the front room and I'll move in here. You won't notice the change, all your things will be moved with you. But there's time for all that later. I'll put you to bed now for a little; I'm sure you need to rest. Come, I'll help you to take off your things, you'll see I can do it. Or if you would rather go into the front room at once, you can lie down in my bed for the present. That would be the most sensible thing."

Georg stood close beside his father, who had let his head with its unkempt white hair sink on his chest.

"Georg," said his father in a low voice, without moving.

Georg knelt down at once beside his father. In the old man's weary face he saw the pupils, over-large, fixedly looking at him from the corners of the eyes.

"You have a friend in St. Petersburg. You've always been a leg-puller and you haven't even shrunk from pulling my leg. How could you have a friend out there! I can't believe it."

"Just think back a bit, Father," said Georg, lifting his father from the chair and slipping off his dressing gown as he stood feebly enough, "it'll soon be three years since my friend came to see us last. I remember that you used not to like him very much. At least twice I kept you from seeing him, although he was actually sitting with me in my room. I could quite well understand your dislike of him, my friend has his peculiarities. But then, later, you got on with him very well. I was proud because you listened to him and nodded and asked him questions. If you think back you're bound to remember. He used to tell us the most incredible stories of the Russian Revolution. For instance, when he was on a business trip to Kiev and ran into a riot,

and saw a priest on a balcony who cut a broad cross in blood on the palm of his hand and held the hand up and appealed to the mob. You've told that story yourself once or twice since."

Meanwhile Georg had succeeded in lowering his father down again and carefully taking off the woolen drawers he wore over his linen underpants and his socks. The not particularly clean appearance of this underwear made him reproach himself for having been neglectful. It should have certainly been his duty to see that his father had clean changes of underwear. He had not yet explicitly discussed with his bride-to-be what arrangements should be made for his father in the future, for they had both of them silently taken it for granted that the old man would go on living alone in the old house. But now he made a quick, firm decision to take him into his own future establishment. It almost looked, on closer inspection, as if the care he meant to lavish there on his father might come too late.

He carried his father to bed in his arms. It gave him a dreadful feeling to notice that while he took the few steps towards the bed the old man on his breast was playing with his watch chain. He could not lay him down on the bed for a moment, so firmly did he hang on to the watch chain.

But as soon as he was laid in bed, all seemed well. He covered himself up and even drew the blankets farther than usual over his shoulders. He looked up at Georg with a not unfriendly eye.

"You begin to remember my friend, don't you?" asked Georg, giving him an encouraging nod.

"Am I well covered up now?" asked his father, as if he were not able to see whether his feet were properly tucked in or not.

"So you find it snug in bed already," said Georg, and tucked the blankets more closely round him.

"Am I well covered up?" asked the father once more, seeming to be strangely intent upon the answer.

"Don't worry, you're well covered up."

"No!" cried his father, cutting short the answer, threw the blankets off with a strength that sent them all flying in a moment and sprang erect in bed. Only one hand lightly touched the ceiling to steady him.

"You wanted to cover me up, I know, my young sprig, but I'm far from being covered up yet. And even if this is the last strength I have, it's enough for you, too much for you. Of course I know your friend. He would have been a son after my own heart. That's why you've been playing him false all these years. Why else? Do you think I haven't been sorry for him? And that's why you had to lock yourself up in your office—the Chief is busy, mustn't be disturbed—just so that you could write your lying little letters to Russia. But thank goodness a father doesn't need to be taught how to see through his son. And now that you thought you'd got him down, so far down that you could set your bottom on him and sit on him and he wouldn't move, then my fine son makes up his mind to get married!"

Georg stared at the bogey conjured up by his father. His friend in St. Petersburg, whom his father suddenly knew too well, touched his imagination as never before. Lost in the vastness of Russia he saw him. At the door of an empty, plundered warehouse he saw him. Among the wreckage of his showcases, the slashed remnants of his wares, the falling gas brackets, he was just standing up. Why did he have to go so far away!

"But attend to me!" cried his father, and Georg, almost distracted, ran towards the bed to take everything in, yet came to a stop halfway.

"Because she lifted up her skirts," his father began to flute, "because she lifted her skirts like this, the nasty creature," and mimicking her he lifted his shirt so high that one could see the scar on his thigh from his war wound, "because she lifted her skirts like this and this you made up to her, and in order to make free with her undisturbed you have disgraced your mother's memory, betrayed your friend and stuck your father into bed so that he can't move. But he can move, or can't he?"

And he stood up quite unsupported and kicked his legs out. His insight made him radiant.

Georg shrank into a corner, as far away from his father as possible. A long time ago he had firmly made up his mind to watch closely every least movement so that he should not be surprised by any indirect attack, a pounce from behind or above. At this moment he recalled this long-forgotten resolve and forgot it again, like a man drawing a short thread through the eye of a needle.

"But your friend hasn't been betrayed after all!" cried his father, emphasizing the point with stabs of his forefinger. "I've been representing him here on the spot."

"You comedian!" Georg could not resist the retort, realized at once the harm done and, his eyes starting in his head, bit his tongue back, only too late, till the pain made his knees give.

"Yes, of course I've been playing a comedy! A comedy! That's a good expression! What other comfort was left to a poor old widower? Tell me—and while you're answering me be you still my living son—what else was left to me, in my back room, plagued by a disloyal staff, old to the marrow of my bones? And my son strutting through the world, finishing off deals that I had prepared for him, bursting with triumphant glee and stalking away from his father with the closed face of a respectable business man! Do you think I didn't love you, I, from whom you are sprung?"

Now he'll lean forward, thought Georg. What if he topples and smashes himself! These words went hissing through his mind.

His father leaned forward but did not topple. Since Georg did not come any nearer, as he had expected, he straightened himself again.

"Stay where you are, I don't need you! You think you have strength enough to come over here and that you're only hanging back of your own accord. Don't be too sure! I am still much the stronger of us two. All by myself I might have had to give way, but your mother has given me so much of her strength that I've established a fine connection with your friend and I have your customers here in my pocket!"

"He has pockets even in his shirt!" said Georg to himself, and believed that with this remark he could make him an impossible figure for all the world. Only for a moment did he think so, since he kept on forgetting everything.

"Just take your bride on your arm and try getting in my way! I'll sweep her from your very side, you don't know how!"

Georg made a grimace of disbelief. His father only nodded, confirming the truth of his words, towards Georg's corner.

"How you amused me today, coming to ask me if you should tell your friend about your engagement. He knows it already, you stupid boy, he knows it all! I've been writing to him, for you forgot to take my writing things away from me. That's why he hasn't been here for years, he knows everything a hundred times better than you do yourself, in his left hand he crumples your letters unopened while in his right hand he holds up my letters to read through!"

In his enthusiasm he waved his arm over his head. "He knows everything a thousand times better!" he cried.

"Ten thousand times!" said Georg, to make fun of his father, but in his very mouth the words turned into deadly earnest.

"For years I've been waiting for you to come with some such question! Do you think I concern myself with anything else? Do you think I read my newspaper? Look!" and he threw Georg a newspaper sheet which he had somehow taken to bed with him. An old newspaper, with a name entirely unknown to Georg.

"How long a time you've taken to grow up! Your mother had to die, she couldn't see the happy day, your friend is going to pieces in Russia, even three years ago he was yellow enough to be thrown away, and as for me, you see what condition I'm in. You have eyes in your head for that!"

"So you've been lying in wait for me!" cried Georg.

His father said pityingly, in an offhand manner: "I suppose you wanted to say that sooner. But now it doesn't matter." And in a louder voice: "So now you know what else there was in the world besides yourself, till now you've known only about yourself! An innocent child, yes, that you were, truly, but still more truly have you been a devilish human being!— And therefore take note: I sentence you now to death by drowning!"

Georg felt himself urged from the room. The crash with which his father fell on the bed behind him was still in his ears as he fled. On the staircase, which he rushed down as if its steps were an inclined plane, he ran into his charwoman on her way up to do the morning cleaning of the room. "Jesus!" she cried, and covered her face with her apron, but he was already gone. Out of the front door he rushed, across the roadway, driven towards the water. Already he was grasping at the railings as a starving man clutches food. He swung himself over, like the distinguished gymnast he had once been in his youth, to his parents' pride. With weakening grip he was still holding on when he spied between the railings a motor-bus coming which would easily cover the noise of his fall, called in a low voice: "Dear parents, I have always loved you, all the same," and let himself drop.

At this moment an unending stream of traffic was just going over the bridge.

Questions

1. From what point of view is *The Judgment* narrated? Is this the best narrative method for the story or not? Could Georg have acted as an Autobiographical Narrator in *The Judgment*? If he had, would *The Judgment* have been just another version of *Dear Father* (see p. 102)? Does Georg have characteristics that Kafka does not, or vice-versa?

2. Obviously, *The Judgment* is based on Kafka's personal relationship with his father. Does this factual basis make it

more or less convincing? Does Kafka's story depend for its meaning on biographical knowledge about him? Upon what does the "reality" of *The Judgment* depend?

3. Is there anything in this story that could not happen literally? Is the story an allegory?

4. What is the meaning of such details as the father's defect in vision, his dark room, the yellow newspaper, the war wound in the thigh? What is the significance of the friend in distant Russia? Of the title of the story? Are all of these related or are they independent symbols?

5. Review these father-son relationships briefly in works read earlier: Lord Chesterfield and his son; Boswell and his father; Proust and his father. What relationship does this story have to them? Does the fictional relationship convey more to the reader than the factual ones or not?

JAMES THURBER

The Secret Life
of Walter Mitty

"We're going through!" The Commander's voice was like thin ice breaking. He wore his full-dress uniform, with the heavily braided white cap pulled down rakishly over one cold gray eye. "We can't make it, sir. It's spoiling for a hurricane, if you ask me." "I'm not asking you, Lieutenant Berg," said the Commander. "Throw on the power lights! Rev her up to 8,500! We're going through!" The pounding of the cylinders increased: ta-pocketa-pocketa-pocketa-*pocketa-pocketa*. The Commander stared at the ice forming on the pilot window. He

THE SECRET LIFE OF WALTER MITTY: Copr. © 1942 James Thurber. From *My World—And Welcome To It*, published by Harcourt, Brace and World. Originally printed in *The New Yorker*.

walked over and twisted a row of complicated dials. "Switch on No. 8 auxiliary!" he shouted. "Switch on No. 8 auxiliary!" repeated Lieutenant Berg. "Full strength in No. 3 turret!" shouted the Commander. "Full strength in No. 3 turret!" The crew, bending to their various tasks in the huge, hurtling eight-engined Navy hydroplane, looked at each other and grinned. "The Old Man'll get us through," they said to one another. "The Old Man ain't afraid of Hell!"...

"Not so fast! You're driving too fast!" said Mrs. Mitty. "What are you driving so fast for?"

"Hmm?" said Walter Mitty. He looked at his wife, in the seat beside him, with shocked astonishment. She seemed grossly unfamiliar, like a strange woman who had yelled at him in a crowd. "You were up to fifty-five," she said. "You know I don't like to go more than forty. You were up to fifty-five." Walter Mitty drove on toward Waterbury in silence, the roaring of the SN202 through the worst storm in twenty years of Navy flying fading in the remote, intimate airways of his mind. "You're tensed up again," said Mrs. Mitty. "It's one of your days. I wish you'd let Dr. Renshaw look you over."

Walter Mitty stopped the car in front of the building where his wife went to have her hair done. "Remember to get those overshoes while I'm having my hair done," she said. "I don't need overshoes," said Mitty. She put her mirror back into her bag. "We've been all through that," she said, getting out of the car. "You're not a young man any longer." He raced the engine a little. "Why don't you wear your gloves? Have you lost your gloves?" Walter Mitty reached in a pocket and brought out the gloves. He put them on, but after she had turned and gone into the building and he had driven on to a red light, he took them off again. "Pick it up, brother!" snapped a cop as the light changed, and Mitty hastily pulled on his gloves and lurched ahead. He drove around the streets aimlessly for a time, and then he drove past the hospital on his way to the parking lot.

..."It's the millionaire banker, Wellington

McMillan," said the pretty nurse. "Yes?" said Walter Mitty, removing his gloves slowly. "Who has the case?" "Dr. Renshaw and Dr. Benbow, but there are two specialists here, Dr. Remington from New York and Mr. Pritchard-Mitford from London. He flew over." A door opened down a long, cool corridor and Dr. Renshaw came out. He looked distraught and haggard. "Hello Mitty," he said "We're having the devil's own time with McMillan, the millionaire banker and close personal friend of Roosevelt. Obstreosis of the ductal tract. Tertiary. Wish you'd take a look at him." "Glad to," said Mitty.

In the operating room there were whispered introductions: "Dr. Remington, Dr. Mitty. Mr. Pritchard-Mitford, Dr. Mitty." "I've read your book on streptothricosis," said Pritchard-Mitford, shaking hands. "A brilliant performance, sir." "Thank you," said Walter Mitty. "Didn't know you were in the States, Mitty," grumbled Remington. "Coals to Newcastle, bringing Mitford and me up here for a tertiary," "You are very kind," said Mitty. A huge, complicated machine, connected to the operating table, with many tubes and wires, began at this moment to go pocketa-pocketa-pocketa. "The new anesthetizer is giving way!" shouted an intern. "There is no one in the East who knows how to fix it!" "Quiet, man!" said Mitty, in a low, cool voice. He sprang to the machine, which was now going pocketa-pocketa-queep-pocketa-queep. He began fingering delicately a row of glistening dials. "Give me a fountain pen!" he snapped. Someone handed him a fountain pen. He pulled a faulty piston out of the machine and inserted the pen in its place. "That will hold for ten minutes," he said. "Get on with the operation." A nurse hurried over and whispered to Renshaw and Mitty saw the man turn pale. "Coreopsis has set in," said Renshaw nervously. "If you would take over, Mitty?" Mitty looked at him and at the craven figure of Benbow, who drank, and at the grave, uncertain faces of the two great specialists. "If you wish," he said. They slipped a white gown

on him; he adjusted a mask and drew on thin gloves; nurses handed him shining…

"Back it up, Mac! Look out for that Buick!" Walter Mitty jammed on the brakes. "Wrong lane, Mac," said the parking-lot attendant, looking at Mitty closely. "Gee. Heh," muttered Mitty. He began cautiously to back out of the lane marked "Exit Only." "Leave her sit there," said the attendant. "I'll put her away." Mitty got out of the car. "Hey, better leave the key." "Oh," said Mitty, handing the man the ignition key. The attendant vaulted into the car, backed it up with insolent skill, and put it where it belonged.

They're so damn cocky, thought Walter Mitty, walking along Main Street; they think they know everything. Once he had tried to take his chains off, outside New Milford, and he had got them wound around the axles. A man had had to come out in a wrecking car and unwind them, a young, grinning garageman. Since then Mrs. Mitty always made him drive to a garage to have the chains taken off. The next time, he thought, I'll wear my right arm in a sling; they won't grin at me then. I'll have my right arm in a sling and they'll see I couldn't possibly take the chains off myself. He kicked at the slush on the sidewalk. "Overshoes," he said to himself, and he began looking for a shoe store.

When he came out into the street again, with the overshoes in a box under his arm, Walter Mitty began to wonder what the other thing was his wife had told him to get. She had told him, twice, before they set out from their house for Waterbury. In a way he hated these weekly trips to town—he was always getting something wrong. Kleenex, he thought, Squibb's, razor blades? No. Toothpaste, toothbrush, bicarbonate, carborundum, initiative and referendum? He gave it up. But she would remember it. "Where's the what's-its-name?" she would ask. "Don't tell me you forgot the what's-its-name." A newsboy went by shouting something about the Waterbury trial.

…"Perhaps this will refresh your memory." The District Attorney suddenly thrust a heavy automatic at the quiet figure on the witness stand. "Have you ever seen this before?" Walter Mitty took the gun and examined it expertly. "This is my Webley-Vickers 50.80," he said calmly. An excited buzz ran around the courtroom. The Judge rapped for order. "You are a crack shot with any sort of firearms, I believe?" said the District Attorney, insinuatingly. "Objection!" shouted Mitty's attorney. "We have shown that the defendant could not have fired the shot. We have shown that he wore his right arm in a sling on the night of the fourteenth of July." Walter Mitty raised his hand briefly and the bickering attorneys were stilled. "With any known make of gun," he said evenly, "I could have killed Gregory Fitzhurst at three hundred feet *with my left hand*." Pandemonium broke loose in the courtroom. A woman's scream rose above the bedlam and suddenly a lovely, dark haired girl was in Walter Mitty's arms. The District Attorney struck at her savagely. Without rising from his chair, Mitty let the man have it on the point of the chin. "You miserable cur!" ...

"Puppy biscuit," said Walter Mitty. He stopped walking and the buildings of Waterbury rose up out of the misty courtroom and surrounded him again. A woman who was passing laughed. "He said 'Puppy biscuit,'" she said to her companion. "That man said 'Puppy biscuit' to himself." Walter Mitty hurried on. He went into an A. & P., not the first one he came to but a smaller one farther up the street. "I want some biscuit for small, young dogs," he said to the clerk. "Any special brand, sir?" The greatest pistol shot in the world thought a moment. "It says 'Puppies Bark for It' on the box," said Walter Mitty.

His wife would be through at the hairdresser's in fifteen minutes, Mitty saw in looking at his watch, unless they had trouble drying it: sometimes they had trouble drying it. She didn't like to get to the hotel first; she would want him to be there waiting for her as usual. He found a big leather chair in the lobby, facing a window, and he put the overshoes and the puppy biscuit on the floor beside it. He picked up an old copy of *Liberty* and sank down into the chair. "Can Germany Conquer the World Through the Air?" Walter Mitty looked at the pictures of bombing planes and of ruined streets.

... "The cannonading has got the wind up in young Raleigh, sir," said the sergeant. Captain Mitty looked up at him through tousled hair. "Get him to bed," he said wearily. "With the others, I'll fly alone." "But you can't, sir," said the sergeant anxiously. "It takes two men to handle that bomber and the Archies are pounding hell out of the air. Von Richtman's circus is between here and Saulier." "Somebody's got to get that ammunition dump," said Mitty. "I'm going over. Spot of brandy?" He poured a drink for the sergeant and one for himself. War thundered and whined around the dugout and battered at the door. There was a rending of wood and splinters flew through the room. "A bit of a near thing," said Captain Mitty carelessly. "The box barrage is closing in," said the sergeant. "We only live once, Sergeant," said Mitty, with his faint, fleeting smile. "Or do we?" He poured another brandy and tossed it off. "I never see a man could hold his brandy like you sir," said the sergeant. "Begging your pardon, sir." Captain Mitty stood up and strapped on his huge Webley-Vickers automatic. "It's forty kilometers through hell, sir," said the sergeant. Mitty finished one last brandy. "After all," he said softly, "what isn't?" The pounding of the cannon increased; there was the rat-tat-tatting of machine guns, and from somewhere came the menacing pocketa-pocketa-pocketa of the new flame-throwers. Walter Mitty walked to the door of the dugout humming "Auprès de Ma Blonde." He turned and waved to the sergeant. "Cheerio!" he said ...

Something struck his shoulder. "I've been looking all over this hotel for you," said Mrs. Mitty. "Why do you have to hide in this old chair? How did you expect me to find you?" "Things close in," said Walter Mitty vaguely.

"What?" Mrs. Mitty said. "Did you get the what's-its-name? The puppy biscuit? What's in that box?" "Overshoes," said Mitty. "Couldn't you have put them on in the store?" "I was thinking," said Walter Mitty. "Does it ever occur to you that I am sometimes thinking?" She looked at him. "I'm going to take your temperature when I get you home," she said.

They went out through the revolving doors that made a faintly derisive whistling sound when you pushed them. It was two blocks to the parking lot. At the drugstore on the corner she said, "Wait here for me. I forgot something. I won't be a minute." She was more than a minute. Walter Mitty lighted a cigarette. It began to rain, rain with sleet in it. He stood up against the wall of the drugstore, smoking.... He put his shoulders back and his heels together. "To hell with the handkerchief," said Walter Mitty scornfully. He took one last drag on his cigarette and snapped it away. Then, with the faint, fleeting smile playing about his lips, he faced the firing squad; erect and motionless, proud and disdainful, Walter Mitty the Undefeated, inscrutable to the last.

Questions

1. Which group of factual essays treats the same general aspect of human life as Thurber's story? How do the treatments differ? Which do you find the more convincing?
2. From what point of view does Thurber have the story told? How is this perspective related to the chief theme of the story?
3. How much time lapses during the events in the story? Are there any periods unaccounted for by the recounted events? Is this a weakness in the story or a strength?
4. Are the events shown here causally connected in any way? Explain.
5. In some ways, *The Secret Life of Walter Mitty* resembles "The Love Song of J. Alfred Prufrock." Compare and contrast the two works in terms of form, techniques,

and especially characterization, theme, and tone.
6. What areas of factual, or scientific, knowledge (medicine, history, etc.) are referred to in this story? How accurate are the data used? (Notice the reference to coreopsis on p. 472. What *is* coreopsis?) Is the use of such data merely a humorous device or is it an aspect of characterization?
7. Both *The Judgment* and *Walter Mitty* deal with the domination of a weak, passive person by a stronger; Georg by his father, Mitty by his wife. One story is pathetic or perhaps tragic; the other is comic. Is the difference in tone the result of basic differences in the materials used, the attitude of the author, the use of details, or other factors?

WILLIAM FAULKNER

That Evening Sun

I

Monday is no different from any other weekday in Jefferson now. The streets are paved now, and the telephone and electric companies are cutting down more and more of the shade trees—the water oaks, the maples and locusts and elms—to make room for iron poles bearing clusters of bloated and ghostly and bloodless grapes, and we have a city laundry which makes the rounds on Monday morning, gathering the bundles of clothes into bright-colored, specially-made motor cars: the soiled wearing of a whole week now flees apparitionlike behind alert and irritable electric horns, with a long diminishing noise of rubber and asphalt like tearing silk, and even the Negro women who still take in white people's washing after the old custom, fetch and deliver it in automobiles.

But fifteen years ago, on Monday morning the quiet, dusty, shady streets would be full of Negro women with, balanced on their steady, turbaned heads, bundles of clothes tied up in sheets, almost as large as cotton bales, carried so without touch of hand between the kitchen door of the white house and the blackened washpot beside a cabin door in Negro Hollow.

Nancy would set her bundle on the top of her head, then upon the bundle in turn she would set the black straw sailor hat which she wore winter and summer. She was tall, with a high, sad face sunken a little where her teeth were missing. Sometimes we would go a part of the way down the lane and across the pasture with her, to watch the balanced bundle and the hat that never bobbed nor wavered, even when she walked down into the ditch and up the other side and stooped through the fence. She would go down on her hands and knees and crawl through the gap, her head rigid, uptilted, the bundle steady as a rock or a balloon, and rise to her feet again and go on.

Sometimes the husbands of the washing women would fetch and deliver the clothes, but Jesus never did that for Nancy, even before father told him to stay away from our house, even when Dilsey was sick and Nancy would come to cook for us.

And then about half the time we'd have to go down the lane to Nancy's cabin and tell her to come on and cook breakfast. We would stop at the ditch, because father told us to not have anything to do with Jesus—he was a short black man, with a razor scar down his face—and we would throw rocks at Nancy's house until she came to the door, leaning her head around it without any clothes on.

"What yawl mean, chunking my house?" Nancy said. "What you little devils mean?"

"Father says for you to come on and get breakfast," Caddy said. "Father says it's over a half an hour now, and you've got to come this minute."

"I aint studying no breakfast," Nancy said. "I going to get my sleep out."

"I bet you're drunk," Jason said. "Father says you're drunk. Are you drunk, Nancy?"

"Who says I is?" Nancy said. "I got to get my sleep out. I aint studying no breakfast."

So after a while we quit chunking the cabin and went back home. When she finally came, it was too late for me to go to school. So we thought it was whisky until that day they arrested her again and they were taking her to jail and they passed Mr. Stovall. He was the cashier in the bank and a deacon in the Baptist church, and Nancy began to say:

"When you going to pay me, white man? When you going to pay me, white man? It's been three times now since you paid me a cent—" Mr. Stovall knocked her down, but she kept on saying. "When you going to pay me, white man? It's been three times now since—" until Mr. Stovall kicked her in the mouth with his heel and the marshal caught Mr. Stovall back, and Nancy lying in the street, laughing. She turned her head and spat out some blood and teeth and said, "It's been three times now since he paid me a cent."

That was how she lost her teeth, and all that day they told about Nancy and Mr. Stovall, and all that night the ones that passed the jail could hear Nancy singing and yelling. They could see her hands holding to the window bars, and a lot of them stopped along the fence, listening to her and to the jailer trying to make her stop. She didn't shut up until almost daylight, when the jailer began to hear a bumping and a scraping upstairs and he went up there and found Nancy hanging from the window bar. He said that it was cocaine and not whisky, because no nigger would try to commit suicide unless he was full of cocaine, because a nigger full of cocaine wasn't a nigger any longer.

The jailer cut her down and revived her; then he beat her, whipped her. She had hung herself with her dress. She had fixed it all right, but when they arrested her she didn't have on anything except a dress and so she didn't have anything to tie her hands with and she couldn't make her hands let go of the window ledge. So the jailer heard the noise and ran up there and found Nancy hanging from the window stark naked, her belly already swelling out a little, like a little balloon.

When Dilsey was sick in her cabin and Nancy was cooking for us, we could see her apron swelling out; that was before father told Jesus to stay away from the house. Jesus was in the kitchen, sitting behind the stove, with his razor scar on his black face like a piece of dirty string. He said it was a watermelon that Nancy had under her dress.

"It never come off your vine, though," Nancy said.

"Off of what vine?" Caddy said.

"I can cut down the vine it did come off of," Jesus said.

"What makes you want to talk like that before these chillen?" Nancy said. "Whyn't you go on to work? You done et. You want Mr. Jason to catch you hanging around his kitchen, talking that way before these chillen?"

"Talking what way?" Caddy said. "What vine?"

"I can't hang around white man's kitchen," Jesus said. "But white man can hang around mine. White man can come in my house, but I can't stop him. When white man want to come in my house, I ain't got no house. I can't stop him, but he can't kick me outen it. He can't do that."

Dilsey was still sick in her cabin. Father told Jesus to stay off our place. Dilsey was still sick. It was a long time. We were in the library after supper.

"Isn't Nancy through in the kitchen yet?" mother said. "It seems to me that she has had plenty of time to have finished the dishes."

"Let Quentin go and see," father said. "Go and see if Nancy is through, Quentin. Tell her she can go on home."

I went to the kitchen. Nancy was through. The dishes were put away and the fire was out. Nancy was sitting in a chair, close to the cold stove. She looked at me.

"Mother wants to know if you are through," I said.

"Yes," Nancy said. She looked at me. "I done finished." She looked at me.

"What is it?" I said. "What is it?"

"I ain't nothing but a nigger," Nancy said. "It ain't none of my fault."

She looked at me, sitting in the chair before the cold stove, the sailor hat on her head. I went back to the library. It was the cold stove and all, when you think of a kitchen being warm and busy and cheerful. And with a cold stove and the dishes all put away, and nobody wanting to eat at that hour.

"Is she through?" mother said.

"Yessum," I said.

"What is she doing?" mother said.

"She's not doing anything. She's through."

"I'll go and see," father said.

"Maybe she's waiting for Jesus to come and take her home," Caddy said.

"Jesus is gone," I said. Nancy told us how one morning she woke up and Jesus was gone.

"He quit me," Nancy said. "Done gone to Memphis, I reckon. Dodging them city *po*-lice for a while, I reckon."

"And a good riddance," father said. "I hope he stays there."

"Nancy's scaired of the dark," Jason said.

"So are you," Caddy said.

"I'm not," Jason said.

"Scairy cat," Caddy said.

"I'm not," Jason said.

"You, Candace!" mother said. Father came back.

"I am going to walk down the lane with Nancy," he said. "She says that Jesus is back."

"Has she seen him?" mother said.

"No. Some Negro sent her word that he was back in town. I won't be long."

"You'll leave me alone, to take Nancy home?" mother said. "Is her safety more precious to you than mine?"

"I won't be long," father said.

"You'll leave these children unprotected, with that Negro about?"

"I'm going too," Caddy said. "Let me go, Father."

"What would he do with them, if he were unfortunate enough to have them?" father said.

"I want to go, too," Jason said.

"Jason!" mother said. She was speaking to father. You could tell that by the way she said the name. Like she believed that all day father had been trying to think of doing the thing she wouldn't like the most, and that she knew all the time that after a while he would think of it. I stayed quiet, because father and I both knew that mother would want him to make me stay with her if she just thought of it in time. So father didn't look at me. I was the oldest. I was nine and Caddy was seven and Jason was five.

"Nonsense," father said. "We won't be long."

Nancy had her hat on. We came to the lane. "Jesus always been good to me." Nancy said. "Whenever he had two dollars, one of them was mine." We walked in the lane. "If I can just get through the lane," Nancy said, "I be all right then."

The lane was always dark. "This is where Jason got scared on Hallowe'en," Caddy said.

"I didn't," Jason said.

"Can't Aunt Rachel do anything with him?" father said. Aunt Rachel was old. She lived in a cabin beyond Nancy's, by herself. She had white hair and she smoked a pipe in the door, all day long; she didn't work any more. They said she was Jesus's mother. Sometimes she said she was and sometimes she said she wasn't any kin to Jesus.

"Yes, you did," Caddy said. "You were scairder than Frony. You were scairder than T. P. even. Scairder than niggers."

"Can't nobody do nothing with him," Nancy said. "He say I done woke up the devil in him and ain't but one thing going to lay it down again."

"Well, he's gone now," father said. "There's nothing for you to be afraid of now. And if you'd just let white men alone."

"Let what white men alone?" Caddy said. "How let them alone?"

"He ain't gone nowhere," Nancy said. "I can feel him. I can feel him now, in this lane. He hearing us talk, every word, hid somewhere, waiting. I ain't seen him, and I ain't going to see him again but once more, with that razor in his mouth. That razor on that string down his back, inside his shirt. And then I ain't going to be even surprised."

"I wasn't scaired," Jason said.

"If you'd behave yourself, you'd have kept out of this," father said. "But it's all right now. He's probably in St. Louis now. Probably got another wife by now and forgot all about you."

"If he has, I better not find out about it," Nancy said. "I'd stand there right over them, and every time he wropped her, I'd cut that arm off. I'd cut his head off and I'd slit her belly and I'd shove—"

"Hush," father said.

"Slit whose belly, Nancy?" Caddy said.

"I wasn't scaired," Jason said. "I'd walk right down this lane by myself."

"Yah," Caddy said. "You wouldn't dare to put your foot down in it if we were not here too."

II

Dilsey was still sick, so we took Nancy home every night until mother said, "How much longer is this going on? I to be left alone in this big house while you take home a frightened Negro?"

We fixed a pallet in the kitchen for Nancy. One night we waked up, hearing the sound. It was not singing and it was not crying, coming up the dark stairs. There was a light in mother's room and we heard father going down the hall, down the back stairs, and Caddy and I went into the hall. The floor was cold. Our toes curled away from it while we listened to the sound. It was like singing and it wasn't like singing, like the sounds that Negroes make.

Then it stopped and we heard father going down the back stairs, and we went to the head of the stairs. Then the sound began again, in the stairway, not loud, and we could see Nancy's eyes halfway up the stairs, against the wall. They looked like cat's eyes do, like a big cat against the wall, watching us. When we came down the steps to where she was, she quit making the sound again, and we stood there until father came back up from the kitchen, with his pistol in his hand. He went back down with Nancy and they came back with Nancy's pallet.

We spread the pallet in our room. After the light in mother's room went off, we could see Nancy's eyes again. "Nancy," Caddy whispered, "are you asleep, Nancy?"

Nancy whispered something. It was oh or no, I don't know which. Like nobody had made it, like it came from nowhere and went nowhere, until it was like Nancy was not there at all; that I had looked so hard at her eyes on the stairs that they had got printed on my eyeballs, like the sun does when you have closed your eyes and there is no sun. "Jesus," Nancy whispered. "Jesus."

"Was it Jesus?" Caddy said. "Did he try to come into the kitchen?"

"Jesus," Nancy said. Like this: Jeeeeeeeeeee-eeeus, until the sound went out, like a match or a candle does.

"It's the other Jesus she means," I said.

"Can you see us, Nancy?" Caddy whispered. "Can you see our eyes too?"

"I ain't nothing but a nigger," Nancy said. "God knows. God knows."

"What did you see down there in the kitchen?" Caddy whispered. "What tried to get in?"

"God knows," Nancy said. We could see her eyes. "God knows."

Dilsey got well. She cooked dinner. "You'd better stay in bed a day or two longer," father said.

"What for?" Dilsey said. "If I had been a day later, this place would be to rack and ruin. Get on out of here now, and let me get my kitchen straight again."

Dilsey cooked supper too. And that night, just before dark, Nancy came into the kitchen.

"How do you know he's back?" Dilsey said. "You ain't seen him."

"Jesus is a nigger," Jason said.

"I can feel him," Nancy said. "I can feel him laying yonder in the ditch."

"Tonight?" Dilsey said. "Is he there tonight?"

"Dilsey's a nigger too," Jason said.

"You try to eat something," Dilsey said.

"I don't want nothing," Nancy said.

"I ain't a nigger," Jason said.

"Drink some coffee," Dilsey said. She poured a cup of coffee for Nancy. "Do you know he's out there tonight? How come you know it's tonight?"

"I know," Nancy said. "He's there, waiting. I know. I done lived with him too long. I know what he is fixing to do fore he know it himself."

"Drink some coffee," Dilsey said. Nancy held the cup to her mouth and blew into the cup. Her mouth pursed out like a spreading adder's, like a rubber mouth, like she had blown all the color out of her lips with blowing the coffee.

"I ain't a nigger," Jason said. "Are you a nigger, Nancy?"

"I hellborn, child," Nancy said. "I won't be nothing soon. I going back where I come from soon."

III

She began to drink the coffee. While she was drinking, holding the cup in both hands, she began to make the sound again. She made the sound into the cup and the coffee sploshed out onto her hands and her dress. Her eyes looked at us and she sat there, her elbows on her knees, holding the cup in both hands, looking at us across the wet cup, making the sound. "Look at Nancy," Jason said. "Nancy can't cook for us now. Dilsey's got well now."

"You hush up," Dilsey said. Nancy held the cup in both hands, looking at us, making the sound, like there were two of them: one looking at us and the other making the sound. "Whyn't you let Mr Jason telefoam the marshal?" Dilsey said. Nancy stopped then, holding the cup in her long brown hands. She tried to drink some coffee again, but it sploshed out of the cup, onto her hands and her dress, and she put the cup down. Jason watched her.

"I can't swallow it," Nancy said. "I swallows but it won't go down me."

"You go down to the cabin," Dilsey said. "Frony will fix you a pallet and I'll be there soon."

"Won't no nigger stop him," Nancy said.

"I ain't a nigger," Jason said. "Am I, Dilsey?"

"I reckon not," Dilsey said. She looked at Nancy. "I don't reckon so. What you going to do, then?"

Nancy looked at us. Her eyes went fast, like she was afraid there wasn't time to look, without hardly moving at all. She looked at us, at all three of us at one time. "You member that night I stayed in yawls' room?" she said. She told about how we waked up early the next morning, and played. We had to play quiet, on her pallet, until father woke up and it was time to get breakfast. "Go and ask your maw to let me stay here tonight," Nancy said. "I won't need no pallet. We can play some more."

Caddy asked mother. Jason went too. "I can't have Negroes sleeping in the bedrooms," mother said. Jason cried. He cried until mother said he couldn't have any dessert for three days if he didn't stop. Then Jason said he would stop if Dilsey would make a chocolate cake. Father was there.

"Why don't you do something about it?" mother said. "What do we have officers for?"

"Why is Nancy afraid of Jesus?" Caddy said. "Are you afraid of father, mother?"

"What could the officers do?" father said. "If Nancy hasn't seen him, how could the officers find him?"

"Then why is she afraid?" mother said.

"She says he is there. She says she knows he is there tonight."

"Yet we pay taxes," mother said. "I must wait here alone in this big house while you take a Negro woman home."

"You know that I am not lying outside with a razor," father said.

"I'll stop if Dilsey will make a chocolate cake," Jason said. Mother told us to go out and father said he didn't know if Jason would get a chocolate cake or not, but he knew what Jason was going to get in about a minute. We went back to the kitchen and told Nancy.

"Father said for you to go home and lock the door, and you'll be all right," Caddy said. "All right from what, Nancy? Is Jesus mad at you?" Nancy was holding the coffee cup in her hands again, her elbows on her knees and her hands holding the cup between her knees. She was looking into the cup. "What have you done that made Jesus mad?" Caddy said. Nancy let the cup go. It didn't break on the floor, but the coffee spilled out, and Nancy sat there with her hands still making the shape of the cup. She began to make the sound again, not loud. Not singing and not unsinging. We watched her.

"Here," Dilsey said. "You quit that, now. You get aholt of yourself. You wait here. I going to get Versh to walk home with you." Dilsey went out.

We looked at Nancy. Her shoulders kept shaking, but she quit making the sound. We watched her. "What's Jesus going to do to you?" Caddy said. "He went away."

Nancy looked at us. "We had fun that night I stayed in yawls' room, didn't we?"

"I didn't," Jason said. "I didn't have any fun."

"You were asleep in mother's room," Caddy said. "You were not there."

"Let's go down to my house and have some more fun," Nancy said.

"Mother won't let us," I said. "It's too late now."

"Don't bother her," Nancy said. "We can tell her in the morning. She won't mind."

"She wouldn't let us," I said.

"Don't ask her now," Nancy said. "Don't bother her now."

"She didn't say we couldn't go," Caddy said.

"We didn't ask," I said.

"If you go, I'll tell," Jason said.

"We'll have fun," Nancy said. "They won't mind, just to my house. I been working for yawl a long time. They won't mind."

"I'm not afraid to go," Caddy said. "Jason is the one that's afraid. He'll tell."

"I'm not," Jason said.

"Yes, you are," Caddy said. "You'll tell."

"I won't tell," Jason said. "I'm not afraid."

"Jason ain't afraid to go with me," Nancy said. "Is you, Jason?"

"Jason is going to tell," Caddy said. The lane was dark. We passed the pasture gate. "I bet if something was to jump out from behind that gate, Jason would holler."

"I wouldn't," Jason said. We walked down the lane. Nancy was talking loud.

"What are you talking so loud for, Nancy?" Caddy said.

"Who; me?" Nancy said. "Listen at Quentin and Caddy and Jason saying I'm talking loud."

"You talk like there was five of us here," Caddy said. "You talk like father was here too."

"Who; me talking loud, Mr. Jason?" Nancy said.

"Nancy called Jason 'Mister,'" Caddy said.

"Listen how Caddy and Quentin and Jason talk," Nancy said.

"We're not talking loud," Caddy said. "You're the one that's talking like father—"

"Hush," Nancy said; "hush, Mr. Jason."

"Nancy called Jason 'Mister' aguh—"

"Hush," Nancy said. She was talking loud when we crossed the ditch and stooped through the fence where she used to stoop through with the clothes on her head. Then we came to her house. We were going fast then. She opened the door. The smell of the house was like the lamp and the smell of Nancy was like the wick, like they were waiting for one another to begin to smell. She lit the lamp and closed the door and put the bar up. Then she quit talking loud, looking at us.

"What're we going to do?" Caddy said.

"What do yawl want to do?" Nancy said.

"You said we would have some fun," Caddy said.

There was something about Nancy's house; something you could smell besides Nancy and the house. Jason smelled it, even. "I don't want to stay here," he said. "I want to go home."

"Go home, then," Caddy said.

"I don't want to go by myself," Jason said.

"We're going to have some fun," Nancy said.

"How?" Caddy said.

Nancy stood by the door. She was looking at us, only it was like she had emptied her eyes, like she had quit using them. "What do you want to do?" she said.

"Tell us a story," Caddy said. "Can you tell a story?"

"Yes," Nancy said.

"Tell it," Caddy said. We looked at Nancy. "You don't know any stories."

"Yes," Nancy said. "Yes, I do."

She came and sat in a chair before the hearth. There was a little fire there. Nancy built it up, when it was already hot inside. She built a good blaze. She told a story. She talked like her eyes looked, like her eyes watching us and her voice talking to us did not belong to her. Like she was living somewhere else, waiting somewhere else. She was outside the cabin. Her voice was inside and the shape of her, the Nancy that could stoop under a barbed wire fence with a bundle of clothes balanced on her head as though without weight, like a balloon, was there. But that was all. "And so this here queen come walking up to the ditch, where that bad man was hiding, She was walking up to the ditch, and she say, 'If I can just get past this here ditch,' was what she say. . . ."

"What ditch?" Caddy said. "A ditch like that one out there? Why did a queen want to go into a ditch?"

"To get to her house," Nancy said. She looked at us. "She had to cross the ditch to get into her house quick and bar the door."

"Why did she want to go home and bar the door?" Caddy said.

IV

Nancy looked at us. She quit talking. She looked at us. Jason's legs stuck straight out of his pants where he sat on Nancy's lap. "I don't think that's a good story," he said. "I want to go home."

"Maybe we had better," Caddy said. She got up from the floor. "I bet they are looking for us right now," She went toward the door.

"No," Nancy said. "Don't open it." She got up quick and passed Caddy. She didn't touch the door, the wooden bar.

"Why not?" Caddy said.

"Come back to the lamp," Nancy said. "We'll have fun. You don't have to go."

"We ought to go," Caddy said. "Unless we have a lot of fun." She and Nancy came back to the fire, the lamp.

"I want to go home," Jason said. "I'm going to tell."

"I know another story," Nancy said. She stood close to the lamp. She looked at Caddy, like when your eyes look up at a stick balanced on your nose. She had to look down to see Caddy, but her eyes looked like that, like when you are balancing a stick.

"I won't listen to it," Jason said. "I'll bang on the floor."

"It's a good one," Nancy said. "It's better than the other one."

"What's it about?" Caddy said. Nancy was standing by the lamp. Her hand was on the lamp, against the light, long and brown.

"Your hand is on that hot globe," Caddy said. "Don't it feel hot to your hand?"

Nancy looked at her hand on the lamp chimney. She took her hand away, slow. She stood there, looking at Caddy, wringing her long hand as though it were tied to her wrist with a string.

"Let's do something else," Caddy said.

"I want to go home," Jason said.

"I got some popcorn," Nancy said. She looked at Caddy and then at Jason and then at me and then at Caddy again. "I got some popcorn."

"I don't like popcorn," Jason said. "I'd rather have candy."

Nancy looked at Jason. "You can hold the popper." She was still wringing her hand; it was long and limp and brown.

"All right," Jason said. "I'll stay a while if I can do that. Caddy can't hold it. I'll want to go home again if Caddy holds the popper."

Nancy built up the fire. "Look at Nancy putting her hands in the fire," Caddy said. "What's the matter with you, Nancy?"

"I got popcorn," Nancy said. "I got some." She took the popper from under the bed. It was broken. Jason began to cry.

"Now we can't have any popcorn," he said.

"We ought to go home, anyway," Caddy said. "Come on, Quentin."

"Wait," Nancy said; "wait. I can fix it. Don't you want to help me fix it?"

"I don't think I want any," Caddy said. "It's too late now."

"You help me, Jason," Nancy said. "Don't you want to help me?"

"No," Jason said. "I want to go home."

'Hush," Nancy said; 'hush. Watch. Watch me. I can fix it so Jason can hold it and pop the corn." She got a piece of wire and fixed the popper.

"It won't hold good," Caddy said.

"Yes, it will," Nancy said. "Yawl watch. Yawl help me shell some corn."

The popcorn was under the bed too. We shelled it into the popper and Nancy helped Jason hold the popper over the fire.

"It's not popping," Jason said. "I want to go home."

"You wait," Nancy said. "It'll begin to pop. We'll have fun then." She was sitting close to the fire. The lamp was turned up so high it was beginning to smoke.

"Why don't you turn it down some?" I said.

"It's all right," Nancy said. "I'll clean it. Yawl wait. The popcorn will start in a minute."

"I don't believe it's going to start." Caddy said. "We ought to start home, anyway. They'll be worried."

"No," Nancy said. "It's going to pop. Dilsey will tell um yawl with me. I been working for yawl long time. They won't mind if yawl at my house. You wait, now. It'll start popping any minute now."

Then Jason got some smoke in his eyes and he began to cry. He dropped the popper into the fire. Nancy got a wet rag and wiped Jason's face, but he didn't stop crying.

"Hush," she said. "Hush." But he didn't hush. Caddy took the popper out of the fire.

"It's burned up," she said. "You'll have to get some more popcorn, Nancy."

"Did you put all of it in?" Nancy said.

"Yes," Caddy said. Nancy looked at Caddy. Then she took the popper and opened it and poured the cinders into her apron and began to sort the grains, her hands long and brown, and we watching her.

"Haven't you got any more?" Caddy said.

"Yes," Nancy said; "yes. Look. This here ain't burnt. All we need to do is—"

"I want to go home," Jason said. "I'm going to tell."

"Hush," Caddy said. We all listened. Nancy's head was already turned toward the barred door, her eyes filled with red lamplight. "Somebody is coming," Caddy said.

Then Nancy began to make that sound again, not loud, sitting there above the fire, her long hands dangling between her knees; all of a sudden water began to come out on her face in big drops, running down her face, carrying in each one a little turning ball of firelight like a spark until it dropped off her chin. "She's not crying," I said.

"I ain't crying," Nancy said. Her eyes were closed. "I ain't crying. Who is it?"

"I don't know," Caddy said. She went to the door and looked out. "We've got to go now," she said. "Here comes father."

"I'm going to tell," Jason said. "Yawl made me come."

The water still ran down Nancy's face. She turned in her chair. "Listen. Tell him. Tell him we going to have fun. Tell him I take good care of

yawl until in the morning. Tell him to let me come home with yawl and sleep on the floor Tell him I won't need no pallet. We'll have fun. You remember last time how we had so much fun?"

"I didn't have fun," Jason said. "You hurt me. You put smoke in my eyes. I'm going to tell."

V

Father came in. He looked at us. Nancy did not get up.

"Tell him," she said.

"Caddy made us come down here," Jason said. "I didn't want to."

Father came to the fire. Nancy looked up at him. "Can't you go to Aunt Rachel's and stay?" he said. Nancy looked up at father, her hands between her knees. "He's not here," father said. "I would have seen him. There's not a soul in sight."

"He in the ditch," Nancy said. "He waiting in the ditch yonder."

"Nonsense," father said. He looked at Nancy. "Do you know he's there?"

"I got the sign," Nancy said.

"What sign?"

"I got it. It was on the table when I come in. It was a hog-bone, with blood meat still on it, laying by the lamp. He's out there. When yawl walk out that door, I gone."

"Gone where, Nancy?" Caddy said.

"I'm not a tattletale," Jason said.

"Nonsense," father said.

"He out there," Nancy said. "He looking through that window this minute, waiting for yawl to go. Then I gone."

"Nonsense," father said. "Lock up your house and we'll take you on to Aunt Rachel's."

" 'Twon't do no good," Nancy said. She didn't look at father now, but he looked down at her, at her long limp, moving hands. "Putting it off won't do no good."

"Then what do you want to do?" father said.

"I don't know," Nancy said. "I can't do nothing. Just put it off. And that don't do no good. I reckon it belong to me. I reckon what I going to get ain't no more than mine."

"Get what?" Caddy said. "What's yours?"

"Nothing," father said. "You all must get to bed."

"Caddy made me come," Jason said.

"Go on to Aunt Rachel's," father said.

"It won't do no good," Nancy said. She sat before the fire, her elbows on her knees, her long hands between her knees. "When even your own kitchen wouldn't do no good. When even if I was sleeping on the floor in the room with your chillen, and the next morning there I am, and blood—"

"Hush," father said. "Lock the door and put out the lamp and go to bed."

"I scared of the dark," Nancy said. "I scared for it to happen in the dark."

"You mean you're going to sit right here with the lamp lighted?" father said. Then Nancy began to make the sound again, sitting before the fire, her long hands between her knees. "Ah, damnation," father said. "Come along, chillen, It's past bedtime."

"When yawl go home, I gone," Nancy said. She talked quieter now, and her face looked quiet, like her hands. "Anyway, I got my coffin money saved up with Mr. Lovelady." Mr. Lovelady was a short, dirty man who collected the Negro insurance, coming around to the cabins or the kitchens every Saturday morning, to collect fifteen cents. He and his wife lived at the hotel. One morning his wife committed suicide. They had a child, a little girl. He and the child went away. After a week or two he came back alone. We would see him going along the lanes and the back streets on Saturday mornings.

"Nonsense," father said. "You'll be the first thing I'll see in the kitchen tomorrow morning."

"You'll see what you'll see, I reckon," Nancy said. "But it will take the Lord to say what that will be."

VI

We left her sitting before the fire.

"Come and put the bar up," father said. But she didn't move. She didn't look at us again, sitting quietly there between the lamp and the fire. From some distance down the lane we could look back and see her through the open door.

"What, Father?" Caddy said. "What's going to happen?"

"Nothing," father said. Jason was on father's back, so Jason was the tallest of all of us. We went down into the ditch. I looked at it, quiet. I couldn't see much where the moonlight and the shadows tangled.

"If Jesus is hid here, he can see us, can't he?" Caddy said.

"He's not there," father said. "He went away a long time ago."

"You made me come," Jason said, high; against the sky it looked like father had two heads, a little one and a big one. "I didn't want to."

We went up out of the ditch. We could still see Nancy's house and the open door, but we couldn't see Nancy now, sitting before the fire with the door open, because she was tired. "I just done got tired," she said. "I just a nigger. It ain't no fault of mine."

But we could hear her, because she began just after we came up out of the ditch, the sound that was not singing and not unsinging. "Who will do our washing now, Father?" I said.

"I'm not a nigger," Jason said, high and close above father's head.

"You're worse," Caddy said, "you are a tattletale. If something was to jump out, you'd be scairder than a nigger."

"I wouldn't," Jason said.

"You'd cry," Caddy said.

"Caddy," father said.

"I wouldn't!" Jason said.

"Scairy cat," Caddy said.

"Candace!" father said.

Commentary

That Evening Sun deals with a past cultural period: the American South of the late nineteenth century. (Williams's play, *The Last of My Solid Gold Watches* deals with the South in the 1930's and Eudora Welty's *Why I Live at the P.O.* takes place in the 1940's. All three works are set in Mississippi.) Faulkner shows the life of the Southern Negro and his relationship to his white master through the recollections of a young man, Quentin Compson, who tells of events that took place when he was nine years old. The story is thus told by an Autobiographical Narrator fifteen years later when he is twenty-four years old, but he carefully uses the diction and narrative style of a child. (Compare James Baldwin's adult reminiscences of his childhood in *My Conversion* and Proust's recreation of his childhood in *My Mother, My Father, and I.*) Why does Faulkner use this involved point of view? Is chronological distance from the described events necessary for any reason? Does the lapse of time weaken the impact of the story or not? Could Caddie or Jason or Mr. Compson have told the story more effectively? Could Nancy? The sequence of events is carefully contrived to build a terrible tension in Nancy—and in the reader. Is the tension lessened at the end of the story or not? Does any doubt about Nancy's fate remain when the narrative ends? Compare Faulkner's interest in the Negro with Warren's and Baldwin's. Is he criticizing, protesting, condemning, or something else?

EUDORA WELTY

Why I Live at the P.O.

I was getting along fine with Mama, Papa-Daddy and Uncle Rondo until my sister Stella-Rondo just separated from her husband and

came back home again. Mr. Whitaker! Of course I went with Mr. Whitaker first, when he first appeared here in China Grove, taking "Pose Yourself" photos, and Stella-Rondo broke us up. Told him I was one-sided. Bigger on one side than the other, which is a deliberate, calculated falsehood: I'm the same. Stella-Rondo is exactly twelve months to the day younger than I am and for that reason she's spoiled.

She's always had anything in the world she wanted and then she'd throw it away. Papa-Daddy gave her this gorgeous Add-a-Pearl necklace when she was eight years old and she threw it away playing baseball when she was nine, with only two pearls.

So as soon as she got married and moved away from home the first thing she did was separate! From Mr. Whitaker! This photographer with the popeyes she said she trusted. Came home from one of those towns up in Illinois and to our complete surprise brought this child of two.

Mamma said she like to made her drop dead for a second. "Here you had this marvelous blonde child and never so much as wrote your mother a word about it," says Mama. "I'm thoroughly ashamed of you." But of course she wasn't.

Stella-Rondo just calmly takes off this *hat,* I wish you could see it. She says, "Why, Mama, Shirley-T.'s adopted, I can prove it."

"How?" says Mama, but all I says was, "H'm!" There I was over the hot stove, trying to stretch two chickens over five people and a completely unexpected child into the bargain, without one moment's notice.

"What do you mean—'H'm!'?" says Stella-Rondo, and Mama says, "I heard that, Sister."

I said that oh, I didn't mean a thing, only that whoever Shirley-T. was, she was the spit-image of Papa-Daddy if he'd cut off his beard, which of course he'd never do in the world. Papa-Daddy's Mama's papa and sulks.

Stella-Rondo got furious! She said, "Sister, I don't need to tell you you got a lot of nerve and always did have and I'll thank you to make no future reference to my adopted child whatsoever."

"Very well," I said. "Very well, very well. Of course I noticed at once she looks like Mr. Whitaker's side too. That frown. She looks like a cross between Mr. Whitaker and Papa-Daddy."

"Well, all I can say is she isn't."

"She looks exactly like Shirley Temple to me," says Mama, but Shirley-T. just ran away from her.

So the first thing Stella-Rondo did at the table was turn Papa-Daddy against me.

"Papa-Daddy," she says. He was trying to cut up his meat. "Papa-Daddy!" I was taken completely by surprise. Papa-Daddy is about a million years old and's got this long-long beard. "Papa-Daddy, Sister says she fails to understand why you don't cut off your beard."

So Papa-Daddy l-a-y-s down his knife and fork! He's real rich. Mama says he is, he says he isn't. So he says, "Have I heard correctly? You don't understand why I don't cut off my beard?"

"Why," I says, "Papa-Daddy, of course I understand, I did not say any such of a thing, the idea!"

He says, "Hussy!"

I says, "Papa-Daddy, you know I wouldn't any more want you to cut off your beard than the man in the moon. It was the farthest thing from my mind! Stella-Rondo sat there and made that up while she was eating breast of chicken."

But he says, "So the postmistress fails to understand why I don't cut off my beard. Which job I got you through my influence with the government. 'Birds' nest'—is that what you call it?"

Not that it isn't the next to smallest P.O. in the entire state of Mississippi.

I says, "Oh, Papa-Daddy," I says, "I didn't say any such of a thing, I never dreamed it was a bird's nest, I have always been grateful though this is the next to smallest P.O. in the state of Mississippi, and I do not enjoy being referred to as a hussy by my own grandfather."

But Stella-Rondo says, "Yes, you did say it too. Anybody in the world could of heard you, that had ears."

"Stop right there," says Mama, looking at *me*.

So I pulled my napkin straight back through the napkin ring and left the table.

As soon as I was out of the room Mama says, "Call her back, or she'll starve to death," but Papa-Daddy says, "This is the beard I started growing on the Coast when I was fifteen years old." He would of gone on till nightfall if Shirley-T. hadn't lost the Milky Way she ate in Cairo.

So Papa-Daddy says, "I am going out and lie in the hammock, and you can all sit here and remember my words: I'll never cut off my beard as long as I live, even one inch, and I don't appreciate it in you at all." Passed right by me in the hall and went straight out and got in the hammock.

It would be a holiday. It wasn't five minutes before Uncle Rondo suddenly appeared in the hall in one of Stella-Rondo's flesh-colored kimonos, all cut on the bias, like something Mr. Whitaker probably thought was gorgeous.

"Uncle Rondo!" I says. "I didn't know who that was! Where are you going?"

"Sister," he says, "get out of my way, I'm poisoned."

"If you're poisoned stay away from Papa-Daddy," I says. "Keep out of the hammock. Papa-Daddy will certainly beat you on the head if you come within forty miles of him. He thinks I deliberately said he ought to cut off his beard after he got me the P.O., and I've told him and told him and told him, and he acts like he just don't hear me, Papa-Daddy must of gone stone deaf."

"He picked a fine day to do it then," says Uncle Rondo, and before you could say "Jack Robinson" flew out in the yard.

What he'd really done, he'd drunk another bottle of that prescription. He does it every single Fourth of July as sure as shooting, and it's horribly expensive. Then he falls over in the hammock and snores. So he insisted on zigzagging right on out to the hammock, looking like a half-wit.

Papa-Daddy woke up with this horrible yell

and right there without moving an inch he tried to turn Uncle Rondo against me. I heard every word he said. Oh, he told Uncle Rondo I didn't learn to read till I was eight years old and he didn't see how in the world I ever got the mail put up at the P.O., much less read it all, and he said if Uncle Rondo could only fathom the lengths he had gone to to get me that job! And he said on the other hand he thought Stella-Rondo had a brilliant mind and deserved credit for getting out of town. All the time he was just lying there swinging as pretty as you please and looping out his beard, and poor Uncle Rondo was *pleading* with him to slow down the hammock, it was making him as dizzy as a witch to watch it. But that's what Papa-Daddy likes about a hammock. So Uncle Rondo was too dizzy to get turned against me for the time being. He's Mama's only brother and is a good case of a one-track mind. Ask anybody. A certified pharmacist.

Just then I heard Stella-Rondo raising the upstairs window. While she was married she got this peculiar idea that it's cooler with the windows shut and locked. So she has to raise the window before she can make a soul hear her outdoors.

So she raises the window and says, "*Oh!*" You would have thought she was mortally wounded.

Uncle Rondo and Papa-Daddy didn't even look up, but kept right on with what they were doing. I had to laugh.

I flew up the stairs and threw the door open! I says, "What in the wide world's the matter, Stella-Rondo? You mortally wounded?"

"No," she says, "I am not mortally wounded but I wish you would do me the favor of looking out that window there and telling me what you see."

So I shade my eyes and look out the window.

"I see the front yard," I says.

"Don't you see any human beings?" she says.

"I see Uncle Rondo trying to run Papa-Daddy out of the hammock," I says. "Nothing more. Naturally, it's so suffocating-hot in the house, with all the windows shut and locked, everybody

who cares to stay in their right mind will have to go out and get in the hammock before the Fourth of July is over."

"Don't you notice anything different about Uncle Rondo?" asks Stella-Rondo.

"Why, no, except he's got on some terrible-looking flesh-colored contraption I wouldn't be found dead in, is all I can see," I says.

"Never mind, you won't be found dead in it, because it happens to be part of my trousseau, and Mr. Whitaker took several dozen photographs of me in it," says Stella-Rondo. "What on earth could Uncle Rondo *mean* by wearing part of my trousseau out in the broad open daylight without saying so much as 'Kiss my foot,' *knowing* I only got home this morning after my separation and hung my negligee up on the bathroom door, just as nervous as I could be?"

"I'm sure I don't know, and what do you expect me to do about it?" I says. "Jump out the window?"

"No, I expect nothing of the kind. I simply declare that Uncle Rondo looks like a fool in it, that's all," she says. "It makes me sick to my stomach."

"Well, he looks as good as he can," I says. "As good as anybody in reason could." I stood up for Uncle Rondo, please remember. And I said to Stella-Rondo, "I think I would do well not to criticize so freely if I were you and came home with a two-year-old child I had never said a word about, and no explanation whatever about my separation."

"I asked you the instant I entered this house not to refer one more time to my adopted child, and you gave me your word of honor you would not," was all Stella-Rondo would say, and started pulling out every one of her eyebrows with some cheap Kress tweezers.

So I merely slammed the door behind me and went down and made some green-tomato pickle. Somebody had to do it. Of course Mama had turned both the niggers loose; she always said no earthly power could hold one anyway on the Fourth of July, so she wouldn't even try. It turned out that Jaypan fell in the lake and came within a very narrow limit of drowning.

So Mama trots in. Lifts up the lid and says. "H'm! Not very good for your Uncle Rondo in his precarious condition, I must say. Or poor little adopted Shirley T. Shame on you!"

That made me tired. I says, "Well, Stella-Rondo had better thank her lucky stars it was her instead of me came trotting in with that very peculiar-looking child. Now if it had been me that trotted in from Illinois and brought a peculiar-looking child of two, I shudder to think of the reception I'd of got, much less controlled the diet of an entire family."

"But you must remember, Sister, that you were never married to Mr. Whitaker in the first place and didn't go up to Illinois to live," says Mama, shaking a spoon in my face. "If you had I would of been just as overjoyed to see you and your little adopted girl as I was to see Stella-Rondo, when you wound up with your separation and came on back home."

"You would not," I says.

"Don't contradict me, I would," says Mama.

But I said she couldn't convince me though she talked till she was blue in the face. Then I said, "Besides, you know as well as I do that that child is not adopted."

"She most certainly is adopted," says Mama, stiff as a poker.

I says, "Why, Mama, Stella-Rondo had her just as sure as anything in this world, and just too stuck up to admit it."

"Why, Sister," said Mama. "Here I thought we were going to have a pleasant Fourth of July, and you start right out not believing a word your own baby sister tells you!"

"Just like Cousin Annie Flo. Went to her grave denying the facts of life," I remind Mama.

"I told you if you ever mentioned Annie Flo's name I'd slap your face," says Mama, and slaps my face.

"All right, you wait and see," I says.

"I," says Mama, *I* prefer to take my children's word for anything when it's humanly possible." You ought to see Mama, she weighs two hundred pounds and has real tiny feet.

Just then something perfectly horrible occurred to me.

"Mama," I says, "can that child talk?" I simply had to whisper! "Mama, I wonder if that child can be—you know—in any way? Do you realize," I says, "that she hasn't spoken one single, solitary word to a human being up to the minute? This is the way she looks," I says, and I looked like this.

Well, Mama and I just stood there and stared at each other. It was horrible!

"I remember well that Joe Whitaker frequently drank like a fish," says Mama. "I believed to my soul he drank *chemicals*." And without another word she marches to the foot of the stairs and calls Stella-Rondo.

"Stella-Rondo? O-o-o-o-o! Stella-Rondo!"

"What?" says Stella-Rondo from upstairs. Not even the grace to get up off the bed.

"Can that child of yours talk?" asks Mama. Stella-Rondo says, "Can she what?"

"Talk! Talk!" says Mama. "Burdyburdy-burdyburdy!"

So Stella-Rondo yells back, "Who says she can't talk?"

"Sister says so," says Mama.

"You didn't have to tell me, I know whose word of honor don't mean a thing in this house," says Stella-Rondo.

And in a minute the loudest Yankee voice I ever heard in my life yells out, "OE'm Pop-OE the Sailor-r-r-r Ma-a-an!" and then somebody jumps up and down in the upstairs hall. In another second the house would of fallen down.

"Not only talks, she can tap-dance!" calls Stella-Rondo. "Which is more than some people I won't name can do."

"Why, the little precious darling thing!" Mama says, so surprised. "Just as smart as she can be!" Starts talking baby talk right there. Then she turns on me. "Sister, you ought to be thoroughly ashamed! Run upstairs this instant and apologize to Stella-Rondo and Shirley-T."

"Apologize for what?" I says. "I merely wondered if the child was normal, that's all.

Now that she's proved she is, why, I have nothing further to say."

But Mama just turned on her heel and flew out, furious. She ran right upstairs and hugged the baby. She believed it was adopted. Stella-Rondo hadn't done a thing but turn her against me from upstairs while I stood there helpless over the hot stove. So that made Mama, Papa-Daddy and the baby all on Stella-Rondo's side.

Next, Uncle Rondo.

I must say that Uncle Rondo has been marvelous to me at various times in the past and I was completely unprepared to be made to jump out of my skin, the way it turned out. Once Stella-Rondo did something perfectly horrible to him—broke a chain letter from Flanders Field—and he took the radio back he had given her and gave it to me. Stella-Rondo was furious! For six months we all had to call her Stella instead of Stella-Rondo, or she wouldn't answer. I always thought Uncle Rondo had all the brains of the entire family. Another time he sent me to Mammoth Cave, with all expenses paid.

But this would be the day he was drinking that prescription, the Fourth of July.

So at supper Stella-Rondo speaks up and says she thinks Uncle Rondo ought to try to eat a little something. So finally Uncle Rondo said he would try a little cold biscuits and ketchup, but that was all. So *she* brought it to him.

"Do you think it wise to disport with ketchup in Stella-Rondo's flesh-colored kimono?" I says. Trying to be considerate! If Stella-Rondo couldn't watch out for her trousseau, somebody had to.

"Any objections?" asks Uncle Rondo, just about to pour out all the ketchup.

"Don't mind what she says, Uncle Rondo," says Stella-Rondo. "Sister has been devoting this solid afternoon to sneering out my bedroom window at the way you look."

"What's that?" says Uncle Rondo. Uncle Rondo has got the most terrible temper in the world. Anything is liable to make him tear the house down if it comes at the wrong time.

So Stella-Rondo says, "Sister says, 'Uncle Rondo certainly does look like a fool in that pink kimono!'"

Do you remember who it was really said that?

Uncle Rondo spills out all the ketchup and jumps out of his chair and tears off the kimono and throws it down on the dirty floor and puts his foot on it. It had to be sent all the way to Jackson to the cleaners and re-pleated.

"So that's your opinion of your Uncle Rondo, is it?" he says. "I look like a fool, do I? Well, that's the last straw. A whole day in this house with nothing to do, and then to hear you come out with a remark like that behind my back!"

"I didn't say any such of a thing, Uncle Rondo," I says, "and I'm not saying who did, either. Why, I think you look all right. Just try to take care of yourself and not talk and eat at the same time," I says. "I think you better go lie down."

"Lie down my foot," says Uncle Rondo. I ought to of known by that he was fixing to do something perfectly horrible.

So he didn't do anything that night in the precarious state he was in—just played Casino with Mama and Stella-Rondo and Shirley-T. and gave Shirley-T. a nickel with a head on both sides. It tickled her nearly to death, and she called him "Papa." But at 6:30 A.M. the next morning, he threw a whole five-cent package of some unsold one-inch firecrackers from the store as hard as he could into my bedroom and they every one went off. Not one bad one in the string. Anybody else, there'd be one that wouldn't go off.

Well, I'm just terribly susceptible to noise of any kind, the doctor has always told me I was the most sensitive person he had ever seen in his whole life, and I was simply prostrated. I couldn't eat! People tell me they heard it as far as the cemetery, and old Aunt Jep Patterson, that had been holding her own so good, thought it was Judgment Day and she was going to meet her whole family. It's usually so quiet here.

And I'll tell you it didn't take me any longer than a minute to make up my mind what to do. There I was with the whole entire house on Stella-Rondo's side and turned against me. If I have anything at all I have pride.

So I just decided I'd go straight down to the P.O. There's plenty of room there in the back, I says to myself.

Well! I made no bones about letting the family catch on to what I was up to. I didn't try to conceal it.

The first thing they knew, I marched in where they were all playing Old Maid and pulled the electric oscillating fan out by the plug, and everything got real hot. Next I snatched the pillow I'd done the needlepoint on right off the davenport from behind Papa-Daddy. He went "Ugh!" I beat Stella-Rondo up the stairs and finally found my charm bracelet in her bureau drawer under a picture of Nelson Eddy.

"So that's the way the land lies," says Uncle Rondo. There he was, piecing on the ham. "Well, Sister, I'll be glad to donate my army cot if you got any place to set it up, providing you'll leave right this minute and let me get some peace." Uncle Rondo was in France.

"Thank you kindly for the cot and 'peace' is hardly the word I would select if I had to resort to firecrackers at 6:30 A.M. in a young girl's bedroom," I says back to him. "And as to where I intend to go, you seem to forget my position as postmistress of China Grove, Mississippi," I says. "I've always got the P.O."

Well, that made them all sit up and take notice.

I went out front and started digging up some four-o'clocks to plant around the P.O.

"Ah-ah-ah!" says Mama, raising the window. "Those happen to be my four-o'clocks. Everything planted in that star is mine. I've never known you to make anything grow in your life."

"Very well," I says. "But I take the fern. Even you, Mama, can't stand there and deny that I'm the one watered that fern. And I happen to know where I can send in a box top and

get a packet of one thousand mixed seeds, no two the same kind, free."

"Oh, where?" Mama wants to know.

But I says, "Too late. You 'tend to your house, and I'll 'tend to mine. You hear things like that all the time if you know how to listen to the radio. Perfectly marvelous offers. Get anything you want free."

So I hope to tell you I marched in and got that radio, and they could of all bit a nail in two, especially Stella-Rondo, that it used to belong to, and she well knew she couldn't get it back, I'd sue for it like a shot. And I very politely took the sewing-machine motor I helped pay the most on to give Mama for Christmas back in 1929, and a good big calendar, with the first-aid remedies on it. The thermometer and the Hawaiian ukulele certainly were rightfully mine, and I stood on the stepladder and got all my watermelon-rind preserves and every fruit and vegetable I'd put up, every jar. Then I began to pull the tacks out of the bluebird wall vases on the archway to the dining room.

"Who told you you could have those, Miss Priss?" says Mama, fanning as hard as she could.

"I bought 'em and I'll keep track of 'em," I says. "I'll tack 'em up one on each side of the post-office window, and you can see 'em when you come to ask me for your mail, if you're so dead to see 'em."

"Not I! I'll never darken the door to that post office again if I live to be a hundred," Mama says. "Ungrateful child! After all the money we spent on you at the Normal."

"Me either," says Stella-Rondo. "You can just let my mail lie there and *rot*, for all I care. I'll never come and relieve you of a single, solitary piece."

"I should worry," I says. "And who you think's going to sit down and write you all those big fat letters and postcards, by the way? Mr. Whitaker? Just because he was the only man ever dropped down in China Grove and you got him—unfairly—is he going to sit down and write you a lengthy correspondence after you come home giving no rhyme nor reason what-soever for your separation and no explanation for the presence of that child? I may not have your brilliant mind, but I fail to see it."

So Mama says, "Sister, I've told you a thousand times that Stella-Rondo simply got homesick, and this child is far too big to be hers," and she says, "Now, why don't you all just sit down and play Casino?"

Then Shirley-T. sticks out her tongue at me in this perfectly horrible way. She has no more manners than the man in the moon. I told her she was going to cross her eyes like that some day and they'd stick.

"It's too late to stop me now," I says. "You should have tried that yesterday. I'm going to the P.O. and the only way you can possibly see me is to visit me there."

So Papa-Daddy says, "You'll never catch me setting foot in that post office, even if I should take a notion into my head to write a letter some place." He says, "I won't have you reachin' out of that little old window with a pair of shears and cuttin' off any beard of mine. I'm too smart for you!"

"We all are," says Stella-Rondo.

But I said, "If you're so smart, where's Mr. Whitaker?"

So then Uncle Rondo says, "I'll thank you from now on to stop reading all the orders I get on postcards and telling everybody in China Grove what you think is the matter with them," but I says, "I draw my own conclusions and will continue in the future to draw them." I says, "If people want to write their inmost secrets on penny postcards, there's nothing in the wide world you can do about it, Uncle Rondo."

"And if you think we'll ever write another postcard you're sadly mistaken," says Mama.

"Cutting off your nose to spite your face then," I says. "But if you're all determined to have no more to do with the U.S. mail, think of this: What will Stella-Rondo do now, if she wants to tell Mr. Whitaker to come after her?"

"Wah!" says Stella-Rondo. I knew she'd cry. She had a conniption fit right there in the kitchen.

"It will be interesting to see how long she holds out," I says. "And now—I am leaving."

"Good-bye," says Uncle Rondo.

"Oh, I declare," says Mama, "to think that a family of mine should quarrel on the Fourth of July, or the day after, over Stella-Rondo leaving old Mr. Whitaker and having the sweetest little adopted child! It looks like we'd all be glad!"

"Wah!" says Stella-Rondo, and has a fresh conniption fit.

"*He* left *her*—you mark my words," I says. "That's Mr. Whitaker. I know Mr. Whitaker. After all, I knew him first. I said from the beginning he'd up and leave her. I foretold every single thing that's happened."

"Where did he go?" asks Mamma.

"Probably to the North Pole, if he knows what's good for him," I says.

But Stella-Rondo just bawled and wouldn't say another word. She flew to her room and slammed the door.

"Now look what you've gone and done, Sister," says Mama. "You go apologize."

"I haven't got time, I'm leaving," I says.

"Well, what are you waiting around for?" asks Uncle Rondo.

So I just picked up the kitchen clock and marched off, without saying "Kiss my foot" or anything, and never did tell Stella-Rondo good-bye.

There was a nigger girl going along on a little wagon right in front.

"Nigger girl," I says, "come help me haul these things down the hill, I'm going to live in the post office."

Took her nine trips in her express wagon. Uncle Rondo came out on the porch and threw her a nickel.

And that's the last I've laid eyes on any of my family or my family laid eyes on me for five solid days and nights. Stella-Rondo may be telling the most horrible tales in the world about Mr. Whitaker, but I haven't heard them. As I tell everybody, I draw my own conclusions.

But oh, I like it here. It's ideal, as I've been saying. You see, I've got everything cater-cornered, the way I like it. Hear the radio? All the war news. Radio, sewing machine, book ends, ironing board and that great big piano lamp— peace, that's what I like. Butter-bean vines planted all along the front where the strings are.

Of course, there's not much mail. My family are naturally the main people in China Grove, and if they prefer to vanish from the face of the earth, for all the mail they get or the mail they write, why, I'm not going to open my mouth. Some of the folks here in town are taking up for me and some turned against me. I know which is which. There are always people who will quit buying stamps just to get on the right side of Papa-Daddy.

But here I am, and here I'll stay. I want the world to know I'm happy.

And if Stella-Rondo should come to me this minute, on bended knees, and *attempt* to explain the incidents of her life with Mr. Whitaker, I'd simply put my fingers in both my ears and refuse to listen.

Questions

1. Like Faulkner, Eudora Welty writes about the people, white and black, of Mississippi. Are the characters in *Why I Live at the P.O.* and *That Evening Sun* similar in any way or not? Are their differences due to class, education, period of time, or something else?
2. Both Faulkner and Miss Welty use Autobiographical Narrators. Compare and contrast their spokesmen as characters as well as in terms of their roles in the events they describe, their diction, their intellects.
3. "Sister" and the other characters use colloquialisms: terms indigenous to local regions. Such language can be realistic and colorful, but it may be difficult to understand for people who live elsewhere. Does the dialogue in *Why I Live at the P.O.* convince you that it is real talk between real people? What effect does the hyperbolic and figurative language of

rural Southerners have on the characterizations of this story?
4. What kind of person is Sister; how would you describe her character? How does her character affect the truth of her narrative? Is she abnormal in any way? Is she what she thinks she is (a sweet young girl victimized by her calculating, selfish sister) or something else?
5. Is *Why I Live at the P.O.* an entirely light-hearted, funny story or does it present some basically serious views of people and behaviour? Is its conflict without consequence or is it significant? Compare Sister's relations with her family to Anne Frank's. Is a comparison illuminating or not?

LIONEL TRILLING

Of This Time,
Of That Place

It was a fine September day. By noon it would be summer again, but now it was true autumn with a touch of chill in the air. As Joseph Howe stood on the porch of the house in which he lodged, ready to leave for his first class of the year, he thought with pleasure of the long indoor days that were coming. It was a moment when he could feel glad of his profession.

On the lawn the peach tree was still in fruit and young Hilda Aiken was taking a picture of it. She held the camera tight against her chest. She wanted the sun behind her, but she did not want her own long morning shadow in the foreground. She raised the camera, but that did not help, and she lowered it, but that made things worse. She twisted her body to the left, then to the right. In the end she had to step

Of This Time, Of That Place: by Lionel Trilling. Copyright 1945 by Lionel Trilling. Reprinted by permission of The Viking Press, Inc.

---

out of the direct line of the sun. At last she snapped the shutter and wound the film with intense care.

Howe, watching her from the porch, waited for her to finish and called good morning. She turned, startled, and almost sullenly lowered her glance. In the year Howe had lived at the Aikens', Hilda had accepted him as one of her family, but since his absence of the summer she had grown shy. Then suddenly she lifted her head and smiled at him, and the humorous smile confirmed his pleasure in the day. She picked up her bookbag and set off for school.

The handsome houses on the streets to the college were not yet fully awake, but they looked very friendly. Howe went by the Bradby house where he would be a guest this evening at the first dinner party of the year. When he had gone the length of the picket fence, the whitest in town, he turned back. Along the path there was a fine row of asters and he went through the gate and picked one for his buttonhole. The Bradbys would be pleased if they happened to see him invading their lawn and the knowledge of this made him even more comfortable.

He reached the campus as the hour was striking. The students were hurrying to their classes. He himself was in no hurry. He stopped at his dim cubicle of an office and lit a cigarette. The prospect of facing his class had suddenly presented itself to him and his hands were cold; the lawful seizure of power he was about to make seemed momentous. Waiting did not help. He put out his cigarette, picked up a pad of theme paper, and went to his classroom.

As he entered, the rattle of voices ceased, and the twenty-odd freshmen settled themselves and looked at him appraisingly. Their faces seemed gross, his heart sank at their massed impassivity, but he spoke briskly.

"My name is Howe," he said, and turned and wrote it on the blackboard. The carelessness of the scrawl confirmed his authority. He went on, "My office is 412 Slemp Hall, and my office-hours are Monday, Wednesday and Friday from eleven-thirty to twelve-thirty."

He wrote, "M., W., F., 11:30-12:30." He said, "I'll be very glad to see any of you at that time. Or if you can't come then, you can arrange with me for some other time."

He turned again to the blackboard and spoke over his shoulder. "The text for the course is Jarman's *Modern Plays,* revised edition. The Co-op has it in stock." He wrote the name, underlined "revised edition" and waited for it to be taken down in the new notebooks.

When the bent heads were raised again he began his speech of prospectus. "It is hard to explain—" he said, and paused as they composed themselves. "It is hard to explain what a course like this is intended to do. We are going to try to learn something about modern literature and something about prose composition."

As he spoke, his hands warmed and he was able to look directly at the class. Last year on the first day the faces had seemed just as cloddish, but as the term wore on they became gradually alive and quite likable. It did not seem possible that the same thing could happen again.

"I shall not lecture in this course," he continued. "Our work will be carried on by discussion and we will try to learn by an exchange of opinion. But you will soon recognize that my opinion is worth more than anyone else's here."

He remained grave as he said it, but two boys understood and laughed. The rest took permission from them and laughed too. All Howe's private ironies protested the vulgarity of the joke, but the laughter made him feel benign and powerful.

When the little speech was finished, Howe picked up the pad of paper he had brought. He announced that they would write an extemporaneous theme. Its subject was traditional, "Who I am and why I came to Dwight College." By now the class was more at ease and it gave a ritualistic groan of protest. Then there was a stir as fountain pens were brought out and the writing-arms of the chairs were cleared, and the paper was passed about. At last, all the heads bent to work, and the room became still.

Howe sat idly at his desk. The sun shone through the tall clumsy windows. The cool of the morning was already passing. There was a scent of autumn and of varnish and the stillness of the room was deep and oddly touching. Now and then a student's head was raised and scratched in the old, elaborate students' pantomime that calls the teacher to witness honest intellectual effort.

Suddenly a tall boy stood within the frame of the open door. "Is this," he said, and thrust a large nose into a college catalogue, "is this the meeting place of English 1A? The section instructed by Dr. Joseph Howe?"

He stood on the very sill of the door, as if refusing to enter until he was perfectly sure of all his rights. The class looked up from work, found him absurd and gave a low mocking cheer.

The teacher and the new student, with equal pointedness, ignored the disturbance. Howe nodded to the boy, who pushed his head forward and then jerked it back in a wide elaborate arc to clear his brow of a heavy lock of hair. He advanced into the room and halted before Howe, almost at attention. In a loud, clear voice he announced, "I am Tertan, Ferdinand R., reporting at the direction of Head of Department Vincent."

The heraldic formality of this statement brought forth another cheer. Howe looked at the class with a sternness he could not really feel, for there was indeed something ridiculous about this boy. Under his displeased regard the rows of heads dropped to work again. Then he touched Tertan's elbow, led him up to the desk and stood so as to shield their conversation from the class.

"We are writing an extemporaneous theme," he said. "The subject is, 'Who I am and why I came to Dwight College.'"

He stripped a few sheets from the pad and offered them to the boy. Tertan hesitated and then took the paper, but he held it only tentatively. As if with the effort of making something clear, he gulped, and a slow smile fixed itself on his face. It was at once knowing and shy.

"Professor," he said, "to be perfectly fair to my classmates"—he made a large gesture over the room—"and to you"—he inclined his head to Howe—"this would not be for me an extemporaneous subject."

Howe tried to understand. "You mean you've already thought about it—you've heard we always give the same subject? That doesn't matter."

Again the boy ducked his head and gulped. It was the gesture of one who wishes to make a difficult explanation with perfect candor. "Sir," he said, and made the distinction with great care, "the topic I did not expect, but I have given much ratiocination to the subject."

Howe smiled and said, "I don't think that's an unfair advantage. Just go ahead and write."

Tertan narrowed his eyes and glanced sidewise at Howe. His strange mouth smiled. Then in quizzical acceptance, he ducked his head, threw back the heavy, dank lock, dropped into a seat with a great loose noise and began to write rapidly.

The room fell silent again and Howe resumed his idleness. When the bell rang, the students who had groaned when the task had been set now groaned again because they had not finished. Howe took up the papers, and held the class while he made the first assignment. When he dismissed it, Tertan bore down on him, his slack mouth held ready for speech.

"Some professors," he said, "are pedants. They are Dryasdusts. However, some professors are free souls and creative spirits. Kant, Hegel and Nietzsche were all professors." With this pronouncement he paused. "It is my opinion," he continued, "that you occupy the second category."

Howe looked at the boy in surprise and said with good-natured irony, "With Kant, Hegel and Nietzsche?"

Not only Tertan's hand and head but his whole awkward body waved away the stupidity. "It is the kind and not the quantity of the kind," he said sternly.

Rebuked, Howe said as simply and seriously

as he could, "It would be nice to think so." He added, "Of course I am not a professor."

This was clearly a disappointment but Tertan met it. "In the French sense," he said with composure. "Generically, a teacher."

Suddenly he bowed. It was such a bow, Howe fancied, as a stage-director might teach an actor playing a medieval student who takes leave of Abelard—stiff, solemn, with elbows close to the body and feet together. Then, quite as suddenly, he turned and left.

A queer fish, and as soon as Howe reached his office, he sifted through the batch of themes and drew out Tertan's. The boy had filled many sheets with his unformed headlong scrawl. "Who am I?" he had begun. "Here, in a mundane, not to say commercialized academe, is asked the question which from time long immemorably out of mind has accreted doubts and thoughts in the psyche of man to pester him as a nuisance. Whether in St. Augustine (or Austin as sometimes called) or Miss Bashkirtsieff or Frederic Amiel or Empedocles, or in less lights of the intellect than these, this posed question has been ineluctable."

Howe took out his pencil. He circled "academe" and wrote "vocab." in the margin. He underlined "time long immemorably out of mind" and wrote "Diction!" But this seemed inadequate for what was wrong. He put down his pencil and read ahead to discover the principle of error in the theme. "Today as ever, in spite of gloomy prophets of the dismal science (economics) the question is uninvalidated. Out of the starry depths of heaven hurtles this spear of query demanding to be caught on the shield of the mind ere it pierces the skull and the limbs be unstrung."

Baffled but quite caught, Howe read on. "Materialism, by which is meant the philosophic concept and not the moral idea, provides no aegis against the question which lies beyond the tangible (metaphysics). Existence without alloy is the question presented. Environment and heredity relegated aside, the rags and old clothes of practical life discarded, the name and the instrumentality of livelihood do not, as the prophets of the dismal science insist on in this connection, give solution to the interrogation which not from the professor merely but veritably from the cosmos is given. I think, therefore I am (cogito etc.) but who am I? Tertan I am, but what is Tertan? Of this time, of that place, of some parentage, what does it matter?'

Existence without alloy: The phrase established itself. Howe put aside Tertan's paper and at random picked up another. "I am Arthur J. Casebeer, Jr.," he read. "My father is Arthur J. Casebeer and my grandfather was Arthur J. Casebeer before him. My mother is Nina Wimble Casebeer. Both of them are college graduates and my father is in insurance. I was born in St. Louis eighteen years ago and we still make our residence there."

Arthur J. Casebeer, who knew who he was, was less interesting than Tertan, but more coherent. Howe picked up Tertan's paper again. It was clear that none of the routine marginal comments, no "sent. str." or "punct." or "vocab." could cope with this torrential rhetoric. He read ahead, contenting himself with underscoring the errors against the time when he should have the necessary "conference" with Tertan.

It was a busy and official day of cards and sheets, arrangements and small decisions, and it gave Howe pleasure. Even when it was time to attend the first of the weekly Convocations he felt the charm of the beginning of things when intention is still innocent and uncorrupted by effort. He sat among the young instructors on the platform, and joined in their humorous complaints at having to assist at the ceremony, but actually he got a clear satisfaction from the ritual of prayer, and prosy speech, and even from wearing his academic gown. And when the Convocation was over the pleasure continued as he crossed the campus, exchanging greetings with men he had not seen since the spring. They were people who did not yet, and perhaps never would, mean much to him, but in a year they had grown amiably to be part of his life. They were his fellow-townsmen.

The day had cooled again at sunset, and there was a bright chill in the September twilight. Howe carried his voluminous gown over his arm, he swung his doctoral hood by its purple neckpiece, and on his head he wore his mortarboard with its heavy gold tassel bobbing just over his eye. These were the weighty and absurd symbols of his new profession and they pleased him. At twenty-six Joseph Howe had discovered that he was neither so well off nor so bohemian as he had once thought. A small income, adequate when supplemented by a sizable cash legacy, was genteel poverty when the cash was all spent. And the literary life—the room at the Lafayette, or the small apartment without a lease, the long summers on the Cape, the long afternoons and the social evenings—began to weary him. His writing filled his mornings, and should perhaps have filled his life, yet it did not. To the amusement of his friends, and with a certain sense that he was betraying his own freedom, he had used the last of his legacy for a year at Harvard. The small but respectable reputation of his two volumes of verse had proved useful—he continued at Harvard on a fellowship and when he emerged as Doctor Howe he received an excellent appointment, with prospects, at Dwight.

He had his moments of fear when all that had ever been said of the dangers of the academic life had occurred to him. But after a year in which he had tested every possibility of corruption and seduction he was ready to rest easy. His third volume of verse, most of it written in his first years of teaching, was not only ampler but, he thought, better than its predecessors.

There was a clear hour before the Bradbury dinner party, and Howe looked forward to it. But he was not to enjoy it, for lying with his mail on the hall table was a copy of this quarter's issue of *Life and Letters*, to which his landlord subscribed. Its severe cover announced that its editor, Frederic Woolley, had this month contributed an essay called 'Two Poets,' and

Howe, picking it up, curious to see who the two poets might be, felt his own name start out at him with cabalistic power—Joseph Howe. As he continued to turn the pages his hand trembled.

Standing in the dark hall, holding the neat little magazine, Howe knew that his literary contempt for Frederic Woolley meant nothing, for he suddenly understood how he respected Woolley in the way of the world. He knew this by the trembling of his hand. And of the little world as well as the great, for although the literary groups of New York might dismiss Woolley, his name carried high authority in the academic world. At Dwight it was even a revered name, for it had been here at the college that Frederic Woolley had made the distinguished scholarly career from which he had gone on to literary journalism. In middle life he had been induced to take the editorship of *Life and Letters,* a literary monthly not widely read but heavily endowed, and in its pages he had carried on the defense of what he sometimes called the older values. He was not without wit, he had great knowledge and considerable taste, and even in the full movement of the "new" literature he had won a certain respect for his refusal to accept it. In France, even in England, he would have been connected with a more robust tradition of conservatism, but America gave him an audience not much better than genteel. It was known in the college that to the subsidy of *Life and Letters* the Bradbys contributed a great part.

As Howe read, he saw that he was involved in nothing less than an event. When the Fifth Series of *Studies in Order and Value* came to be collected, this latest of Frederic Woolley's essays would not be merely another step in the old direction. Clearly and unmistakably, it was a turning point. All his literary life Woolley had been concerned with the relation of literature to morality, religion, and the private and delicate pieties, and he had been unalterably opposed to all that he had called "inhuman humanitarianism." But here, suddenly, dramatically late, he had made an about-face, turning to the public life and to the humanitarian politics he had so long despised. This was the kind of incident the histories of literature make much of. Frederic Woolley was opening for himself a new career and winning a kind of new youth. He contrasted the two poets, Thomas Wormser, who was admirable, Joseph Howe, who was almost dangerous. He spoke of the "precious subjectivism" of Howe's verse. "In times like ours," he wrote, "with millions facing penury and want, one feels that the qualities of the *tour d'ivoire* are well-nigh inhuman, nearly insulting. The *tour d'ivoire* becomes the *tour d'ivresse,* and it is not self-intoxicated poets that our people need." The essay said more: "The problem is one of meaning. I am not ignorant that the creed of the esoteric poets declares that a poem does not and should not *mean* anything, that it *is* something. But poetry is what the poet makes it, and if he is a true poet he makes what his society needs. And what is needed now is the tradition in which Mr. Wormser writes, the true tradition of poetry. The Howes do no harm, but they do no good when positive good is demanded of all responsible men. Or do the Howes indeed do no harm? Perhaps Plato would have said they do, that in some ways theirs is the Phrygian music that turns men's minds from the struggle. Certainly it is true that Thomas Wormser writes in the lucid Dorian mode which sends men into battle with evil."

It was easy to understand why Woolley had chosen to praise Thomas Wormser. The long, lilting lines of *Corn Under Willows* hymned, as Woolley put it, the struggle for wheat in the Iowa fields, and expressed the real lives of real people. But why out of the dozen more notable examples he had chosen Howe's little volume as the example of "precious subjectivism" was hard to guess. In a way it was funny, this multiplication of himself into "the Howes." And yet this becoming the multiform political symbol by whose creation Frederic Woolley gave the sign of a sudden new life, this use of him as a sacrifice whose blood was necessary for the rites of rejuvenation, made him feel oddly unclean.

Nor could Howe get rid of a certain practical resentment. As a poet he had a special and respectable place in the college life. But it might be another thing to be marked as the poet of a wilful and selfish obscurity.

As he walked to the Bradbys', Howe was a little tense and defensive. It seemed to him that all the world knew of the "attack" and agreed with it. And, indeed, the Bradbys had read the essay but Professor Bradby, a kind and pretentious man, said, "I see my old friend knocked you about a bit, my boy," and his wife Eugenia looked at Howe with her child-like blue eyes and said, "I shall *scold* Frederic for the untrue things he wrote about you. You aren't the least obscure." They beamed at him. In their genial snobbery they seemed to feel that he had distinguished himself. He was the leader of Howeism. He enjoyed the dinner party as much as he had thought he would.

And in the following days, as he was more preoccupied with his duties, the incident was forgotten. His classes had ceased to be mere groups. Student after student detached himself from the mass and required or claimed a place in Howe's awareness. Of them all it was Tertan who first and most violently signaled his separate existence. A week after classes had begun Howe saw his silhouette on the frosted glass of his office door. It was motionless for a long time, perhaps stopped by the problem of whether or not to knock before entering. Howe called, "Come in!" and Tertan entered with his shambling stride.

He stood beside the desk, silent and at attention. When Howe asked him to sit down, he responded with a gesture of head and hand, as if to say that such amenities were beside the point. Nevertheless, he did take the chair. He put his ragged, crammed briefcase between his legs. His face, which Howe now observed fully for the first time, was confusing, for it was made up of florid curves, the nose arched in the bone and voluted in the nostril, the mouth loose and soft and rather moist. Yet the face was so thin and narrow as to seem the very type of asceticism. Lashes of unusual length veiled the eyes and, indeed, it seemed as if there were a veil over the whole countenance. Before the words actually came, the face screwed itself into an attitude of preparation for them.

"You can confer with me now?" Tertan said.

"Yes, I'd be glad to. There are several things in your two themes I want to talk to you about." Howe reached for the packet of themes on his desk and sought for Tertan's. But the boy was waving them away.

"These are done perforce," he said. "Under the pressure of your requirement. They are not significant; mere duties." Again his great hand flapped vaguely to dismiss his themes. He leaned forward and gazed at his teacher.

"You are," he said, "a man of letters? You are a poet?" It was more declaration than question.

"I should like to think so," Howe said.

At first Tertan accepted the answer with a show of appreciation, as though the understatement made a secret between himself and Howe. Then he chose to misunderstand. With his shrewd and disconcerting control of expression, he presented to Howe a puzzled grimace. "What does that mean?" he said.

Howe retracted the irony. "Yes. I am a poet." It sounded strange to say.

"That," Tertan said, "is a wonder." He corrected himself with his ducking head. "I mean that is wonderful."

Suddenly, he dived at the miserable briefcase between his legs, put it on his knees, and began to fumble with the catch, all intent on the difficulty it presented. Howe noted that his suit was worn thin, his shirt almost unclean. He became aware, even, of a vague and musty odor of garments worn too long in unaired rooms. Tertan conquered the lock and began to concentrate upon a search into the interior. At last he held in his hand what he was after, a torn and crumpled copy of *Life and Letters*.

"I learned it from here," he said, holding it out.

Howe looked at him sharply, his hackles a little up. But the boy's face was not only perfectly innocent, it even shone with a conscious admiration. Apparently nothing of the import of the essay had touched him except the wonderful fact that his teacher was a "man of letters." Yet this seemed too stupid, and Howe, to test it, said, "The man who wrote that doesn't think it's wonderful."

Tertan made a moist hissing sound as he cleared his mouth of saliva. His head, oddly loose on his neck, wove a pattern of contempt in the air. "A critic," he said, "who admits *prima facie* that he does not understand." Then he said grandly, "It is the inevitable fate."

It was absurd, yet Howe was not only aware of the absurdity but of a tension suddenly and wonderfully relaxed. Now that the "attack" was on the table between himself and this strange boy, and subject to the boy's funny and absolutely certain contempt, the hidden force of his feeling was revealed to him in the very moment that it vanished. All unsuspected, there had been a film over the world, a transparent but discoloring haze of danger. But he had no time to stop over the brightened aspect of things. Tertan was going on. "I also am a man of letters. Putative."

"You have written a good deal?" Howe meant to be no more than polite, and he was surprised at the tenderness he heard in his words.

Solemnly the boy nodded, threw back the dank lock, and sucked in a deep, anticipatory breath. "First, a work of homiletics, which is a defense of the principles of religious optimism against the pessimism of Schopenhauer and the humanism of Nietzsche."

"Humanism? Why do you call it humanism?"

"It is my nomenclature for making a deity of man," Tertan replied negligently. "Then three fictional works, novels. And numerous essays in science, combating materialism. Is it your duty to read these if I bring them to you?"

Howe answered simply, "No, it isn't exactly my duty, but I shall be happy to read them."

Tertan stood up and remained silent. He rested his bag on the chair. With a certain compunction—for it did not seem entirely proper that, of two men of letters, one should have the right to blue-pencil the other, to grade him or to question the quality of his "sentence structure"—Howe reached for Tertan's papers. But before he could take them up, the boy suddenly made his bow-to-Abelard, the stiff inclination of the body with the hands seeming to emerge from the scholar's gown. Then he was gone.

But after his departure something was still left of him. The timbre of his curious sentences, the downright finality of so quaint a phrase as "It is the inevitable fate" still rang in the air. Howe gave the warmth of his feeling to the new visitor who stood at the door announcing himself with a genteel clearing of the throat.

"Doctor Howe, I believe?" the student said. A large hand advanced into the room and grasped Howe's hand. "Blackburn, sir, Theodore Blackburn, vice-president of the Student Council. A great pleasure, sir."

Out of a pair of ruddy cheeks a pair of small eyes twinkled good-naturedly. The large face, the large body were not so much fat as beefy and suggested something "typical"—monk, politician, or innkeeper.

Blackburn took the seat beside Howe's desk. "I may have seemed to introduce myself in my public capacity, sir," he said. "But it is really as an individual that I came to see you. That is to say, as one of your students to be."

He spoke with an English intonation and he went on, "I was once an English major, sir."

For a moment Howe was startled, for the roastbeef look of the boy and the manner of his speech gave a second's credibility to one sense of his statement. Then the collegiate meaning of the phrase asserted itself, but some perversity made Howe say what was not really in good taste even with so forward a student, "Indeed? What regiment?"

Blackburn stared and then gave a little pouf-pouf of laughter. He waved the misapprehension away. "*Very* good, sir. It certainly is an ambiguous term." He chuckled in appreciation of Howe's joke, then cleared his throat to put it

aside. "I look forward to taking your course in the romantic poets, sir," he said earnestly. "To me the romantic poets are the very crown of English literature."

Howe made a dry sound, and the boy, catching some meaning in it, said, "Little as I know them, of course. But even Shakespeare who is so dear to us of the Anglo-Saxon tradition is in a sense but the preparation for Shelley, Keats and Byron. And Wadsworth."

Almost sorry for him, Howe dropped his eyes. With some embarrassment, for the boy was not actually his student, he said softly, "Wordsworth."

"Sir?"

"Wordsworth, not Wadsworth. You said Wadsworth."

"Did I, sir?" Gravely he shook his head to rebuke himself for the error. "Wordsworth, of course—slip of the tongue." Then, quite in command again, he went on. "I have a favor to ask of you, Doctor Howe. You see, I began my college course as an English major,"—he smiled—"as I said."

"Yes?"

"But after my first year I shifted. I shifted to the social sciences. Sociology and government—I find them stimulating and very *real*." He paused, out of respect for reality. "But now I find that perhaps I have neglected the other side."

"The other side?" Howe said.

"Imagination, fancy, culture. A well-rounded man." He trailed off as if there were perfect understanding between them. "And so, sir, I have decided to end my senior year with your course in the romantic poets."

His voice was filled with an indulgence which Howe ignored as he said flatly and gravely, "But that course isn't given until the spring term."

"Yes, sir, and that is where the favor comes in. Would you let me take your romantic prose course? I can't take it for credit, sir, my program is full, but just for background it seems to me that I ought to take it. I do hope," he concluded in a manly way, "that you will consent."

"Well, it's no great favor, Mr. Blackburn. You can come if you wish, though there's not much point in it if you don't do the reading."

The bell rang for the hour and Howe got up.

"May I begin with this class, sir?" Blackburn's smile was candid and boyish.

Howe nodded carelessly and together, silently, they walked to the classroom down the hall. When they reached the door Howe stood back to let his student enter, but Blackburn moved adroitly behind him and grasped him by the arm to urge him over the threshold. They entered together with Blackburn's hand firmly on Howe's biceps, the student inducting the teacher into his own room. Howe felt a surge of temper rise in him and almost violently he disengaged his arm and walked to the desk, while Blackburn found a seat in the front row and smiled at him.

II

The question was, At whose door must the tragedy be laid?

All night the snow had fallen heavily and only now was abating in sparse little flurries. The windows were valanced high with white. It was very quiet; something of the quiet of the world had reached the class, and Howe found that everyone was glad to talk or listen. In the room there was a comfortable sense of pleasure in being human.

Casebeer believed that the blame for the tragedy rested with heredity. Picking up the book he read, "The sins of the fathers are visited on their children." This opinion was received with general favor. Nevertheless, Johnson ventured to say that the fault was all Pastor Manders's because the Pastor had made Mrs. Alving go back to her husband and was always hiding the truth. To this Hibbard objected with logic enough, "Well then, it was really all her husband's fault. He *did* all the bad things." De Witt, his face bright with an impatient idea, said that the fault was all society's. "By society I don't mean upper-crust society," he said. He

looked around a little defiantly, taking in any members of the class who might be members of upper-crust society. "Not in that sense. I mean the social unit."

Howe nodded and said, "Yes, of course."

"If the society of the time had progressed far enough in science," De Witt went on, "then there would be no problem for Mr. Ibsen to write about. Captain Alving plays around a little, gives way to perfectly natural biological urges, and he gets a social disease, a venereal disease. If the disease is cured, no problem. Invent salvarsan and the disease is cured. The problem of heredity disappears and li'l Oswald just doesn't get paresis. No paresis, no problem— no problem, no play."

This was carrying the ark into battle, and the class looked at De Witt with respectful curiosity. It was his usual way and on the whole they were sympathetic with his struggle to prove to Howe that science was better than literature. Still, there was something in his reckless manner that alienated them a little.

"Or take birth-control, for instance," De Witt went on. "If Mrs. Alving had some knowledge of contraception, she wouldn't have had to have li'l Oswald at all. No li'l Oswald, no play."

The class was suddenly quieter. In the back row Stettenhover swung his great football shoulders in a righteous sulking gesture, first to the right, then to the left. He puckered his mouth ostentatiously. Intellect was always ending up by talking dirty.

Tertan's hand went up, and Howe said, "Mr. Tertan." The boy shambled to his feet and began his long characteristic gulp. Howe made a motion with his fingers, as small as possible, and Tertan ducked his head and smiled in apology. He sat down. The class laughed. With more than half the term gone, Tertan had not been able to remember that one did not rise to speak. He seemed unable to carry on the life of the intellect without this mark of respect for it. To Howe the boy's habit of rising seemed to accord with the formal shabbiness of his dress.

He never wore the casual sweaters and jackets of his classmates. Into the free and comfortable air of the college classroom he brought the stuffy sordid strictness of some crowded, metropolitan high school.

"Speaking from one sense," Tertan began slowly, "there is no blame ascribable. From the sense of determinism, who can say where the blame lies? The preordained is the preordained and it cannot be said without rebellion against the universe, a palpable absurdity."

In the back row Stettenhover slumped suddenly in his seat, his heels held out before him, making a loud, dry, disgusted sound. His body sank until his neck rested on the back of his chair. He folded his hands across his belly and looked significantly out of the window, exasperated not only with Tertan, but with Howe, with the class, with the whole system designed to encourage this kind of thing. There was a certain insolence in the movement and Howe flushed. As Tertan continued to speak, Howe stalked casually toward the window and placed himself in the line of Stettenhover's vision. He stared at the great fellow, who pretended not to see him. There was so much power in the big body, so much contempt in the Greek-athlete face under the crisp Greek-athlete curls, that Howe felt almost physical fear. But at last Stettenhover admitted him to focus and under his disapproving gaze sat up with slow indifference. His eyebrows raised high in resignation, he began to examine his hands. Howe relaxed and turned his attention back to Tertan.

"Flux of existence," Tertan was saying, "produces all things, so that judgment wavers. Beyond the phenomena, what? But phenomena are adumbrated and to them we are limited."

Howe saw it for a moment as perhaps it existed in the boy's mind—the world of shadows which are cast by a great light upon a hidden reality as in the old myth of the Cave. But the little brush with Stettenhover had tired him, and he said irritably, "But come to the point, Mr. Tertan."

He said it so sharply that some of the class looked at him curiously. For three months he had gently carried Tertan through his verbosities, to the vaguely respectful surprise of the other students, who seemed to conceive that there existed between this strange classmate and their teacher some special understanding from which they were content to be excluded. Tertan looked at him mildly, and at once came brilliantly to the point. "This is the summation of the play," he said and took up his book and read, " 'Your poor father never found any outlet for the overmastering joy of life that was in him. And I brought no holiday into his home, either. Everything seemed to turn upon duty and I am afraid I made your poor father's home unbearable to him, Oswald.' Spoken by Mrs. Alving."

Yes that was surely the "summation" of the play and Tertan had hit it, as he hit, deviously and eventually, the literary point of almost everything. But now, as always, he was wrapping it away from sight. "For most mortals," he said, "there are only joys of biological urgings, gross and crass, such as the sensuous Captain Alving. For certain few there are the transmutations beyond these to a contemplation of the utter whole."

Oh, the boy was mad. And suddenly the word, used in hyperbole, intended almost for the expression of exasperated admiration, became literal. Now that the word was used, it became simply apparent to Howe that Tertan was mad.

It was a monstrous word and stood like a bestial thing in the room. Yet it so completely comprehended everything that had puzzled Howe, it so arranged and explained what for three months had been perplexing him that almost at once its horror became domesticated. With this word Howe was able to understand why he had never been able to communicate to Tertan the value of a single criticism or correction of his wild, verbose themes. Their conferences had been frequent and long but had done nothing to reduce to order the splendid confusion of the boy's ideas. Yet, impossible though its expression was, Tertan's incandescent mind could always strike for a moment into some dark corner of thought.

And now it was suddenly apparent that it was not a faulty rhetoric that Howe had to contend with. With his new knowledge he looked at Tertan's face and wondered how he could have so long deceived himself. Tertan was still talking, and the class had lapsed into a kind of patient unconsciousness, a coma of respect for words which, for all that most of them knew, might be profound. Almost with a suffusion of shame, Howe believed that in some dim way the class had long ago had some intimation of Tertan's madness. He reached out as decisively as he could to seize the thread of Tertan's discourse before it should be entangled further.

"Mr. Tertan says that the blame must be put upon whoever kills the joy of living in another. We have been assuming that Captain Alving was a wholly bad man, but what if we assume that he became bad only because Mrs. Alving, when they were first married, acted toward him in the prudish way she says she did?"

It was a ticklish idea to advance to freshmen and perhaps not profitable. Not all of them were following.

"That would put the blame on Mrs. Alving herself, whom most of you admire. And she herself seems to think so." He glanced at his watch. The hour was nearly over. "What do you think, Mr. De Witt?"

De Witt rose to the idea; he wanted to know if society couldn't be blamed for educating Mrs. Alving's temperament in the wrong way. Casebeer was puzzled. Stettenhover continued to look at his hands until the bell rang.

Tertan, his brows louring in thought, was making as always for a private word. Howe gathered his books and papers to leave quickly. At this moment of his discovery and with the knowledge still raw, he could not engage himself with Tertan. Tertan sucked in his breath to prepare for speech and Howe made ready for the pain and confusion. But at that moment Casebeer detached himself from the group with

which he had been conferring and which he seemed to represent. His constituency remained at a tactful distance. The mission involved the time of an assigned essay. Casebeer's presentation of the plea—it was based on the freshmen's heavy duties at the fraternities during Carnival Week—cut across Tertan's preparations for speech. "And so some of us fellows thought," Casebeer concluded with heavy solemnity, "that we could do a better job, give our minds to it more, if we had more time."

Tertan regarded Casebeer with mingled curiosity and revulsion. Howe not only said that he would postpone the assignment but went on to talk about the Carnival, and even drew the waiting constituency into the conversation. He was conscious of Tertan's stern and astonished stare, then of his sudden departure.

Now that the fact was clear, Howe knew that he must act on it. His course was simple enough. He must lay the case before the Dean. Yet he hesitated. His feeling for Tertan must now, certainly, be in some way invalidated. Yet could he, because of a word, hurry to assign to official and reasonable solicitude what had been, until this moment, so various and warm? He could at least delay and, by moving slowly, lend a poor grace to the necessary, ugly act of making his report.

It was with some notion of keeping the matter in his own hands that he went to the Dean's office to look up Tertan's records. In the outer office the Dean's secretary greeted him brightly, and at his request brought him the manila folder with the small identifying photograph pasted in the corner. She laughed. "He was looking for the birdie in the wrong place," she said.

Howe leaned over her shoulder to look at the picture. It was as bad as all the Dean's-office photographs were, but it differed from all that Howe had ever seen. Tertan, instead of looking into the camera, as no doubt he had been bidden, had, at the moment of exposure, turned his eyes upward. His mouth, as though conscious of the trick played on the photographer, had the sly superior look that Howe knew.

The secretary was fascinated by the picture. "What a funny boy," she said. "He looks like Tartuffe!"

And so he did, with the absurd piety of the eyes and the conscious slyness of the mouth and the whole face bloated by the bad lens.

"Is he *like* that?" the secretary said.

"Like Tartuffe? No."

From the photograph there was little enough comfort to be had. The records themselves gave no clue to madness, though they suggested sadness enough. Howe read of a father, Stanislaus Tertan, born in Budapest and trained in engineering in Berlin, once employed by the Hercules Chemical Corporation—this was one of the factories that dominated the sound end of the town—but now without employment. He read of a mother Erminie (Youngfellow) Tertan, born in Manchester, educated at a Normal School at Leeds, now housewife by profession. The family lived on Greenbriar Street which Howe knew as a row of once elegant homes near what was now the factory district. The old mansion had long ago been divided into small and primitive apartments. Of Ferdinand himself there was little to learn. He lived with his parents, had attended a Detroit high school and had transferred to the local school in his last year. His rating for intelligence, as expressed in numbers, was high, his scholastic record was remarkable, he held a college scholarship for his tuition.

Howe laid the folder on the secretary's desk. "Did you find what you wanted to know?" she asked.

The phrases from Tertan's momentous first theme came back to him. "Tertan I am, but what is Tertan? Of this time, of that place, of some parentage, what does it matter?"

"No, I didn't find it," he said.

Now that he had consulted the sad, half-meaningless record he knew all the more firmly that he must not give the matter out of his own hands. He must not release Tertan to authority. Not that he anticipated from the Dean anything but the greatest kindness for Tertan. The Dean would have the experience and skill which he himself could not have. One way or another the Dean could answer the question, "What is Tertan?" Yet this was precisely what he feared. He alone could keep alive—not forever but for a somehow important time—the question, "What is Tertan?" He alone could keep it still a question. Some sure instinct told him that he must not surrender the question to a clean official desk in a clear official light to be dealt with, settled and closed.

He heard himself saying, "Is the Dean busy at the moment? I'd like to see him."

His request came thus unbidden, even forbidden, and it was one of the surprising and startling incidents of his life. Later when he reviewed the events, so disconnected in themselves, or so merely odd, of the story that unfolded for him that year, it was over this moment, on its face the least notable, that he paused longest. It was frequently to be with fear and never without a certainty of its meaning in his own knowledge of himself that he would recall this simple, routine request, and the feeling of shame and freedom it gave him as he sent everything down the official chute. In the end, of course, no matter what he did to "protect" Tertan, he would have had to make the same request and lay the matter on the Dean's clean desk. But it would always be a landmark of his life that, at the very moment when he was rejecting the official way, he had been, without will or intention, so gladly drawn to it.

After the storm's last delicate flurry, the sun had come out. Reflected by the new snow, it filled the office with a golden light which was almost musical in the way it made all the commonplace objects of efficiency shine with a sudden sad and noble significance. And the light, now that he noticed it, made the utterance of his perverse and unwanted request even more momentous.

The secretary consulted the engagement pad. "He'll be free any minute. Don't you want to wait in the parlor?"

She threw open the door of the large and

pleasant room in which the Dean held his Committee meetings, and in which his visitors waited. It was designed with a homely elegance on the masculine side of the eighteenth-century manner. There was a small coal fire in the grate and the handsome mahogany table was strewn with books and magazines. The large windows gave on the snowy lawn, and there was such a fine width of window that the white casements and walls seemed at this moment but a continuation of the snow, the snow but an extension of casement and walls. The outdoors seemed taken in and made safe, the indoors seemed luxuriously freshened and expanded.

Howe sat down by the fire and lighted a cigarette. The room had its intended effect upon him. He felt comfortable and relaxed, yet nicely organized, some young diplomatic agent of the eighteenth century, the newly fledged Swift carrying out Sir William Temple's business. The rawness of Tertan's case quite vanished. He crossed his legs and reached for a magazine.

It was that famous issue of *Life and Letters* that his idle hand had found and his blood raced as he sifted through it, and the shape of his own name, Joseph Howe, sprang out at him, still cabalistic in its power. He tossed the magazine back on the table as the door of the Dean's office opened and the Dean ushered out Theodore Blackburn.

"Ah, Joseph!" the Dean said.

Blackburn said, "Good morning, Doctor." Howe winced at the title and caught the flicker of amusement over the Dean's face. The Dean stood with his hand high on the door-jamb and Blackburn, still in the doorway, remained standing almost under the long arm.

Howe nodded briefly to Blackburn, snubbing his eager deference. "Can you give me a few minutes?" he said to the Dean.

"All the time you want. Come in." Before the two men could enter the office, Blackburn claimed their attention with a long full "er." As they turned to him, Blackburn said, "Can *you* give *me* a few minutes, Doctor Howe?" His eyes sparkled at the little audacity he had

committed, the slightly impudent play with hierarchy. Of the three of them Blackburn kept himself the lowest, but he reminded Howe of his subaltern relation to the Dean.

"I mean, of course," Blackburn went on easily, "when you've finished with the Dean."

"I'll be in my office shortly," Howe said, turned his back on the ready "Thank you, sir," and followed the Dean into the inner room.

"Energetic boy," said the Dean. "A bit beyond himself but very energetic. Sit down."

The Dean lighted a cigarette, leaned back in his chair, sat easy and silent for a moment, giving Howe no signal to go ahead with business. He was a young Dean, not much beyond forty, a tall handsome man with sad, ambitious eyes. He had been a Rhodes scholar. His friends looked for great things from him, and it was generally said that he had notions of education which he was not yet ready to try to put into practice.

His relaxed silence was meant as a compliment to Howe. He smiled and said, "What's the business, Joseph?"

"Do you know Tertan—Ferdinand Tertan, a freshman?"

The Dean's cigarette was in his mouth and his hands were clasped behind his head. He did not seem to search his memory for the name. He said, "What about him?"

Clearly the Dean knew something, and he was waiting for Howe to tell him more. Howe moved only tentatively. Now that he was doing what he had resolved not to do, he felt more guilty at having been so long deceived by Tertan and more need to be loyal to his error.

"He's a strange fellow," he ventured. He said stubbornly, "In a strange way he's very brilliant." He concluded. "But very strange."

The springs of the Dean's swivel chair creaked as he came out of his sprawl and leaned forward to Howe. "Do you mean he's so strange that it's something you could give a name to?"

Howe looked at him stupidly. "What do you mean?" he said.

"What's his trouble?" the Dean said more neutrally.

"He's very brilliant, in a way. I looked him up and he has a top intelligence rating. But somehow, and it's hard to explain just how, what he says is always on the edge of sense and doesn't quite make it."

The Dean looked at him and Howe flushed up. The Dean had surely read Woolley on the subject of "the Howes" and the *tour d'ivresse.* Was that quick glance ironical?

The Dean picked up some papers from his desk, and Howe could see that they were in Tertan's impatient scrawl. Perhaps the little gleam in the Dean's glance had come only from putting facts together.

"He sent me this yesterday," the Dean said. "After an interview I had with him. I haven't been able to do more than glance at it. When you said what you did, I realized there was something wrong."

Twisting his mouth, the Dean looked over the letter. "You seem to be involved," he said without looking up. "By the way, what did you give him at mid-term?"

Flushing, setting his shoulders. Howe said firmly, "I gave him A-minus."

The Dean chuckled. "Might be a good idea if some of our nicer boys went crazy—just a little." He said, "Well," to conclude the matter and handed the papers to Howe. "See if this is the same thing you've been finding. Then we can go into the matter again."

Before the fire in the parlor, in the chair that Howe had been occupying, sat Blackburn. He sprang to his feet as Howe entered.

"I said my office, Mr. Blackburn." Howe's voice was sharp. Then he was almost sorry for the rebuke, so clearly and naively did Blackburn seem to relish his stay in the parlor, close to authority.

"I'm in a bit of a hurry, sir," he said, "and I did want to be sure to speak to you, sir."

He was really absurd, yet fifteen years from now he would have grown up to himself, to the assurance and mature beefiness. In banks, in consular offices, in brokerage firms, on the bench, more seriously affable, a little sterner, he would make use of his ability to be administered by his job. It was almost reassuring. Now he was exercising his too-great skill on Howe. "I owe you an apology, sir," he said.

Howe knew that he did, but he showed surprise.

"I mean, Doctor, after your having been so kind about letting me attend your class, I stopped coming." He smiled in deprecation. "Extracurricular activities take up so much of my time. I'm afraid I undertook more than I could perform."

Howe had noticed the absence and had been a little irritated by it after Blackburn's elaborate plea. It was an absence that might be interpreted as a comment on the teacher. But there was only one way for him to answer. "You've no need to apologize," he said. "It's wholly your affair."

Blackburn beamed. "I'm so glad you feel that way about it, sir. I was worried you might think I had stayed away because I was influenced by—" he stopped and lowered his eyes.

Astonished, Howe said, "Influenced by what?"

"Well, by—" Blackburn hesitated and for answer pointed to the table on which lay the copy of *Life and Letters.* Without looking at it, he knew where to direct his hand. "By the unfavorable publicity, sir." He hurried on. "And that brings me to another point, sir. I am secretary of Quill and Scroll, sir, the student literary society, and I wonder if you would address us. You could read your own poetry, sir, and defend your own point of view. It would be very interesting."

It was truly amazing. Howe looked long and cruelly into Blackburn's face, trying to catch the secret of the mind that could have conceived this way of manipulating him, this way so daring and inept—but not entirely inept—with its malice so without malignity. The face did not yield its secret. Howe smiled broadly and said, "Of course I don't think you were influenced by the unfavorable publicity."

"I'm still going to take—regularly, for

credit—your romantic poets course next term," Blackburn said.

"Don't worry, my dear fellow, don't worry about it."

Howe started to leave and Blackburn stopped him with, "But about Quill, sir?"

"Suppose we wait until next term? I'll be less busy then."

And Blackburn said, "Very good, sir, and thank you."

In his office the little encounter seemed less funny to Howe, was even in some indeterminate way disturbing. He made an effort to put it from his mind by turning to what was sure to disturb him more, the Tertan letter read in the new interpretation. He found what he had always found, the same florid leaps beyond fact and meaning, the same headlong certainty. But as his eye passed over the familiar scrawl it caught his own name, and for the second time that hour he felt the race of his blood.

"The Paraclete," Tertan had written to the Dean, "from a Greek word meaning to stand in place of, but going beyond the primitive idea to mean traditionally the helper, the one who comforts and assists, cannot without fundamental loss be jettisoned. Even if taken no longer in the supernatural sense, the concept remains deeply in the human consciousness inevitably. Humanitarianism is no reply, for not every man stands in the place of every other man for this other comrade's comfort. But certain are chosen out of the human race to be the consoler of some other. Of these, for example, is Joseph Barker Howe, Ph.D. Of intellects not the first yet of true intellect and lambent instructions, given to that which is intuitive and irrational, not to what is logical in the strict word, what is judged by him is of the heart and not the head. Here is one chosen, in that he chooses himself to stand in the place of another for comfort and consolation. To him more than another I give my gratitude, with all respect to our Dean who reads this, a noble man, but merely dedicated, not consecrated. But not in the aspect of the Paraclete only is Dr. Joseph Barker Howe

established, for he must be the Paraclete to another aspect of himself, that which is driven and persecuted by the lack of understanding in the world at large, so that he in himself embodies the full history of man's tribulations and, overflowing upon others, notably the present writer, is the ultimate end."

This was love. There was no escape from it. Try as Howe might to remember that Tertan was mad and all his emotions invalidated, he could not destroy the effect upon him of his student's stern, affectionate regard. He had betrayed not only a power of mind but a power of love. And, however firmly he held before his attention the fact of Tertan's madness, he could do nothing to banish the physical sensation of gratitude he felt. He had never thought of himself as "driven and persecuted" and he did not now. But still he could not make meaningless his sensation of gratitude. The pitiable Tertan sternly pitied him, and comfort came from Tertan's never-to-be-comforted mind.

III

In an academic community, even an efficient one, official matters move slowly. The term drew to a close with no action in the case of Tertan, and Joseph Howe had to confront a curious problem. How should he grade his strange student, Tertan?

Tertan's final examination had been no different from all his other writing, and what did one "give" such a student? De Witt must have his *A*, that was clear. Johnson would get a *B*. With Casebeer it was a question of a *B*-minus or a *C*-plus, and Stettenhover, who had been crammed by the team tutor to fill half a blue-book with his thin feminine scrawl, would have his *C*-minus which he would accept with mingled indifference and resentment. But with Tertan it was not so easy.

The boy was still in the college process and his name could not be omitted from the grade sheet. Yet what should a mind under suspicion of madness be graded? Until the medical verdict was given, it was for Howe to continue as Tertan's teacher and to keep his judgment pedagogical. Impossible to give him an *F*: He had not failed. *B* was for Johnson's stolid mediocrity. He could not be put on the edge of passing with Stettenhover, for he exactly did not pass. In energy and richness of intellect he was perhaps even De Witt's superior, and Howe toyed grimly with the notion of giving him an *A*, but that would lower the value of the *A* De Witt had won with his beautiful and clear, if still arrogant, mind. There was a notation which the Registrar recognized—*Inc.*, for Incomplete, and in the horrible comedy of the situation, Howe considered that. But really only a mark of *M* for Mad would serve.

In his perplexity, Howe sought the Dean, but the Dean was out of town. In the end, he decided to maintain the *A*-minus he had given Tertan at midterm. After all, there had been no falling away from that quality. He entered it on the grade sheet with something like bravado.

Academic time moves quickly. A college year is not really a year, lacking as it does three months. And it is endlessly divided into units which, at their beginning, appear larger than they are—terms, half-terms, months, weeks. And the ultimate unit, the hour, is not really an hour, lacking as it does ten minutes. And so the new term advanced rapidly, and one day the fields about the town were all brown, cleared of even the few thin patches of snow which had lingered so long.

Howe, as he lectured on the romantic poets, became conscious of Blackburn emanating wrath. Blackburn did it well, did it with enormous dignity. He did not stir in his seat, he kept his eyes fixed on Howe in perfect attention, but he abstained from using his notebook, there was no mistaking what he proposed to himself as an attitude. His elbow on the writing-wing of the chair, his chin on the curled fingers of his hand, he was the embodiment of intellectual indignation. He was thinking his own thoughts, would give no

public offense, yet would claim his due, was not to be intimidated. Howe knew that he would present himself at the end of the hour.

Blackburn entered the office without invitation. He did not smile; there was no cajolery about him. Without invitation he sat down beside Howe's desk. He did not speak until he had taken the blue-book from his pocket. He said, "What does this mean, sir?"

It was a sound and conservative student tactic. Said in the usual way it meant, "How could you have so misunderstood me?" or "What does this mean for my future in the course?" But there were none of the humbler tones in Blackburn's way of saying it.

Howe made the established reply, "I think that's for you to tell me."

Blackburn continued icy. "I'm sure I can't, sir."

There was a silence between them. Both dropped their eyes to the blue-book on the desk. On its cover Howe had penciled: "*F*. This is very poor work."

Howe picked up the blue-book. There was always the possibility of injustice. The teacher may be bored by the mass of papers and not wholly attentive. A phrase, even the student's handwriting, may irritate him unreasonably. "Well," said Howe, "Let's go through it."

He opened the first page. "Now here: you write, 'In *The Ancient Mariner*, Coleridge lives in and transports us to a honey-sweet world where all is rich and strange, a world of charm to which we can escape from the humdrum existence of our daily lives, the world of romance. Here, in this warm and honey-sweet land of charming dreams we can relax and enjoy ourselves.'"

Howe lowered the paper and waited with a neutral look for Blackburn to speak. Blackburn returned the look boldly, did not speak, sat stolid and lofty. At last Howe said, speaking gently, "Did you mean that, or were you just at a loss for something to say?"

"You imply that I was just 'bluffing'?" The quotation marks hung palpable in the air about the word.

"I'd like to know. I'd prefer believing that you were bluffing to believing that you really thought this."

Blackburn's eyebrows went up. From the height of a great and firm-based idea he looked at his teacher. He clasped the crags for a moment and then pounced, craftily, suavely, "Do you mean, Doctor Howe, that there aren't two opinions possible?"

It was superbly done in its air of putting all of Howe's intellectual life into the balance. Howe remained patient and simple. "Yes, many opinions are possible, but not this one. Whatever anyone believes of *The Ancient Mariner,* no one can in reason believe that it represents a—a honey-sweet world in which we can relax."

"But that is what I *feel,* sir."

This was well-done, too. Howe said, "Look, Mr. Blackburn. Do you really relax with hunger and thirst, the heat and the sea-serpents, the dead men with staring eyes, Life in Death and the skeletons? Come now, Mr. Blackburn."

Blackburn made no answer, and Howe pressed forward. "Now, you say of Wordsworth, 'Of peasant stock himself, he turned from the effete life of the salons and found in the peasant the hope of a flaming revolution which would sweep away all the old ideas. This is the subject of his best poems.' "

Beaming at his teacher with a youthful eagerness, Blackburn said, "Yes, sir, a rebel, a bringer of light to suffering mankind. I see him as a kind of Prothemeus."

"A kind of what?"

"Prothemeus, sir."

"Think, Mr. Blackburn. We were talking about him only today and I mentioned his name a dozen times. You don't mean Prothemeus. You mean—" Howe waited, but there was no response.

"You mean Prometheus."

Blackburn gave no assent, and Howe took the reins. "You've done a bad job here, Mr. Blackburn, about as bad as could be done." He saw Blackburn stiffen and his genial face harden again. "It shows either a lack of preparation or a complete lack of understanding." He saw Blackburn's face begin to go to pieces and he stopped.

"Oh, sir," Blackburn burst out, "I've never had a mark like this before, never anything below a *B,* never. A thing like this has never happened to me before."

It must be true, it was a statement too easily verified. Could it be that other instructors accepted such flaunting nonsense? Howe wanted to end the interview. "I'll set it down to lack of preparation," he said. "I know you're busy. That's not an excuse, but it's an explanation. Now, suppose you really prepare, and then take another quiz in two weeks. We'll forget this one and count the other."

Blackburn squirmed with pleasure and gratitude. "Thank you, sir. You're really very kind, very kind."

Howe rose to conclude the visit. "All right, then—in two weeks."

It was that day that the Dean imparted to Howe the conclusion of the case of Tertan. It was simple and a little anti-climactic. A physician had been called in, and had said the word, given the name.

"A classic case, he called it," the Dean said. "Not a doubt in the world," he said. His eyes were full of miserable pity, and he clutched at a word. "A classic case, a classic case." To his aid and to Howe's there came the Parthenon and the form of the Greek drama, the Aristotelian logic, Racine and the Well-Tempered Clavichord, the blueness of the Aegean and its clear sky. Classic—that is to say, without a doubt, perfect in its way, a veritable model, and, as the Dean had been told, sure to take a perfectly predictable and inevitable course to a foreknown conclusion.

It was not only pity that stood in the Dean's eyes. For a moment there was fear too. "Terrible," he said, "it is simply terrible."

Then he went on briskly. "Naturally, we've told the boy nothing. And, naturally, we won't. His tuition's paid by his scholarship, and we'll continue him on the rolls until the end of the year. That will be kindest. After that the matter will be out of our control. We'll see, of course, that he gets into the proper hands. I'm told there will be no change, he'll go on like this, be as good as this, for four to six months. And so we'll just go along as usual."

So Tertan continued to sit in Section 5 of English 1A, to his classmates still a figure of curiously dignified fun, symbol to most of them of the respectable but absurd intellectual life. But to his teacher he was now very different. He had not changed—he was still the greyhound casting for the scent of ideas, and Howe could see that he was still the same Tertan, but he could not feel it. What he felt as he looked at the boy sitting in his accustomed place was the hard blank of a fact. The fact itself was formidable and depressing. But what Howe was chiefly aware of was that he had permitted the metamorphosis of Tertan from person to fact.

As much as possible he avoided seeing Tertan's upraised hand and eager eye. But the fact did not know of its mere factuality, it continued its existence as if it were Tertan, hand up and eye questioning, and one day it appeared in Howe's office with a document.

"Even the spirit who lives egregiously, above the herd, must have its relations with the fellow-man," Tertan declared. He laid the document on Howe's desk. It was headed "Quill and Scroll Society of Dwight College. Application for Membership."

"In most ways these are crass minds," Tertan said, touching the paper. "Yet as a whole, bound together in their common love of letters, they transcend their intellectual lacks since it is not a paradox that the whole is greater than the sum of its parts."

"When are the elections?" Howe asked.

"They take place tomorrow."

"I certainly hope you will be successful."

"Thank you. Would you wish to implement that hope?" A rather dirty finger pointed to the bottom of the sheet. "A faculty recommender is necessary." Tertan said stiffly, and waited.

"And you wish me to recommend you?"

"It would be an honor."

"You may use my name."

Tertan's finger pointed again. "It must be a written sponsorship, signed by the sponsor." There was a large blank space on the form under the heading, "Opinion of Faculty Sponsor."

This was almost another thing and Howe hesitated. Yet there was nothing else to do and he took out his fountain pen. He wrote, "Mr. Ferdinand Tertan is marked by his intense devotion to letters and by his exceptional love of all things of the mind." To this he signed his name, which looked bold and assertive on the white page. It disturbed him, the strange affirming power of a name. With a business-like air, Tertan whipped up the paper, folding it with decision, and put it into his pocket. He bowed and took his departure, leaving Howe with the sense of having done something oddly momentous.

And so much now seemed odd and momentous to Howe that should not have seemed so. It was odd and momentous, he felt, when he sat with Blackburn's second quiz before him, and wrote in an excessively firm hand the grade of C-minus. The paper was a clear, an indisputable failure. He was carefully and consciously committing a cowardice. Blackburn had told the truth when he had pleaded his past record. Howe had consulted it in the Dean's office. It showed no grade lower than a B-minus. A canvass of some of Blackburn's previous instructors had brought vague attestations to the adequate powers of a student imperfectly remembered, and sometimes surprise that his abilities could be questioned at all.

As he wrote the grade, Howe told himself that his cowardice sprang from an unwillingness to have more dealings with a student he disliked. He knew it was simpler than that. He knew he feared Blackburn; that was the absurd truth. And cowardice did not solve the matter after all. Blackburn, flushed with a first success, attacked at once. The minimal passing grade had not assuaged his feelings and he sat at Howe's desk and again the blue-book lay between them. Blackburn said nothing. With an enormous impudence, he was waiting for Howe to speak and explain himself.

At last Howe said sharply and rudely, "Well?" His throat was tense and the blood was hammering in his head. His mouth was tight with anger at himself for his disturbance.

Blackburn's glance was almost baleful. "This is impossible, sir."

"But there it is," Howe answered.

"Sir?" Blackburn had not caught the meaning but his tone was still haughty.

Impatiently Howe said, "There it is, plain as day. Are you here to complain again?"

"Indeed I am, sir." There was surprise in Blackburn's voice that Howe should ask the question.

"I shouldn't complain if I were you. You did a thoroughly bad job on your first quiz. This one is a little, only a very little, better." This was not true. If anything, it was worse.

"That might be a matter of opinion, sir."

"It is a matter of opinion. Of my opinion."

"Another opinion might be different, sir."

"You really believe that?" Howe said.

"Yes." The omission of the "sir" was monumental.

"Whose, for example?"

"The Dean's, for example." Then the fleshy jaw came forward a little. "Or a certain literary critic's, for example."

It was colossal and almost too much for Blackburn himself to handle. The solidity of his face almost crumpled under it. But he withstood his own audacity and went on. "And the Dean's opinion might be guided by the knowledge that the person who gave me this mark is the man whom a famous critic, the most eminent judge of literature in this country, called a drunken man. The Dean might think twice about whether such a man is fit to teach Dwight students."

Howe said in quiet admonition, "Blackburn, you're mad," meaning no more than to check the boy's extravagance.

But Blackburn paid no heed. He had another shot in the locker. "And the Dean might be guided by the information, of which I have evidence, documentary evidence,"—he slapped his breast pocket twice—"that this same person personally recommended to the college literary society, the oldest in the country, that he personally recommended a student who is crazy, who threw the meeting into an uproar—a psychiatric case. The Dean might take that into account."

Howe was never to learn the details of that "uproar." He had always to content himself with the dim but passionate picture which at that moment sprang into his mind, of Tertan standing on some abstract height and madly denouncing the multitude of Quill and Scroll who howled him down.

He sat quiet a moment and looked at Blackburn. The ferocity had entirely gone from the student's face. He sat regarding his teacher almost benevolently. He had played a good card and now, scarcely at all unfriendly, he was waiting to see the effect. Howe took up the bluebook and negligently sifted through it. He read a page, closed the book, struck out the *C*-minus and wrote an *F*.

"Now you may take the paper to the Dean," he said. "You may tell him that after reconsidering it, I lowered the grade."

The gasp was audible. "Oh, sir!" Blackburn cried. "Please!" His face was agonized. "It means my graduation, my livelihood, my future. Don't do this to me."

"It's done already."

Blackburn stood up. "I spoke rashly, sir, hastily. I had no intention, no real intention, of seeing the Dean. It rests with you—entirely, entirely. I *hope* you will restore the first mark."

"Take the matter to the Dean or not, just as you choose. The grade is what you deserve and it stands."

Blackburn's head dropped. "And will I be failed at mid-term, sir?"

"Of course."

From deep out of Blackburn's great chest rose a cry of anguish. "Oh, sir, if you want me to go down on my knees to you, I will, I will."

Howe looked at him in amazement.

"I will, I will. On my knees, sir. This mustn't, mustn't happen."

He spoke so literally, meaning so very truly that his knees and exactly his knees were involved and seeming to think that he was offering something of tangible value to his teacher, that Howe, whose head had become icy clear in the nonsensical drama, thought, "The boy is mad," and began to speculate fantastically whether something in himself attracted or developed aberration. He could see himself standing absurdly before the Dean and saying, "I've found another. This time it's the vice-president of the Council, the manager of the debating team and secretary of Quill and Scroll."

One more such discovery, he thought, and he himself would be discovered! And there, suddenly, Blackburn was on his knees with a thump, his huge thighs straining his trousers, his hand oustretched in a great gesture of supplication.

With a cry, Howe shoved back his swivel chair and it rolled away on its casters half across the little room. Blackburn knelt for a moment to nothing at all, then got to his feet.

Howe rose abruptly. He said, "Blackburn, you will stop acting like an idiot. Dust your knees off, take your paper and get out. You've behaved like a fool and a malicious person. You have half a term to do a decent job. Keep your silly mouth shut and try to do it. Now get out."

Blackburn's head was low. He raised it and there was a pious light in his eyes. "Will you shake hands, sir?" he said. He thrust out his hand.

"I will not," Howe said.

Head and hand sank together. Blackburn picked up his blue-book and walked to the door. He turned and said, "Thank you, sir." His back, as he departed, was heavy with tragedy and stateliness.

IV

After years of bad luck with the weather, the College had a perfect day for Commencement. It was wonderfully bright, the air so transparent, the wind so brisk that no one could resist talking about it.

As Howe set out for the campus he heard Hilda calling from the back yard. She called, "Professor, professor," and came running to him.

Howe said, "What's this 'professor' business?"

"Mother told me," Hilda said. "You've been promoted. And I want to take your picture."

"Next year," said Howe. "I won't be a professor until next year. And you know better than to call anybody 'professor.'"

"It was just in fun," Hilda said. She seemed disappointed.

"But you can take my picture if you want. I won't look much different next year." Still, it was frightening. It might mean that he was to stay in this town all his life.

Hilda brightened. "Can I take it in this?" she said, and touched the gown he carried over his arm.

Howe laughed. "Yes, you can take it in this."

"I'll get my things and meet you in front of Otis," Hilda said. "I have the background all picked out."

On the campus the Commencement crowd was already large. It stood about in eager, nervous little family groups. As he crossed, Howe was greeted by a student, capped and gowned, glad of the chance to make an event for his parents by introducing one of his teachers. It was while Howe stood there chatting that he saw Tertan.

He had never seen anyone quite so alone, as though a circle had been woven about him to separate him from the gay crowd on the campus. Not that Tertan was not gay, he was the gayest of all. Three weeks had passed since Howe had last seen him, the weeks of examination, the lazy week before Commencement, and this was now a different Tertan. On his head he wore a panama hat, broad-brimmed and fine, of the shape associated with South American planters. He wore a suit of raw silk, luxurious, but yellowed with age and much too tight, and he sported a whangee cane. He walked sedately, the hat tilted at a devastating angle, the stick coming up and down in time to his measured tread. He had, Howe guessed, outfitted himself to greet the day in the clothes of that ruined father whose existence was on record in the Dean's office. Gravely and arrogantly he surveyed the scene—in it, his whole bearing seemed to say, but not of it. With his haughty step, with his flashing eye, Tertan was coming nearer. Howe did not wish to be seen. He shifted his position slightly. When he looked again, Tertan was not in sight.

The chapel clock struck the quarter hour. Howe detached himself from his chat and hurried to Otis Hall at the far end of the campus. Hilda had not yet come. He went up into the high portico and, using the glass of the door for a mirror, put on his gown, adjusted the hood on his shoulders and set the mortarboard on his head. When he came down the steps, Hilda had arrived.

Nothing could have told him more forcibly that a year had passed than the development of Hilda's photographic possessions from the box camera of the previous fall. By a strap about her neck was hung a leather case, so thick and strong, so carefully stitched and so molded to its contents that it could only hold a costly camera. The appearance was deceptive, Howe knew, for he had been present at the Aikens' pre-Christmas conference about its purchase. It was only a fairly good domestic camera. Still, it looked very impressive. Hilda carried another leather case from which she drew a collapsible tripod. Decisively she extended each of its gleaming legs and set it up on the path. She removed the camera from its case and fixed it to the tripod. In its compact efficiency the camera almost had a life of its own, but Hilda treated it with easy familiarity, looked into its eye, glanced casually at its gauges. Then from a pocket she took still another leather case and drew from it a small instrument through which she looked first at Howe, who began to feel inanimate and lost, and then at the sky. She made some adjustment on the instrument, then some adjustment on the camera. She swept the scene with her eye, found

a spot and pointed the camera in its direction. She walked to the spot, stood on it and beckoned to Howe. With each new leather case, with each new instrument, and with each new adjustment she had grown in ease and now she said, "Joe, will you stand here?"

Obediently Howe stood where he was bidden. She had yet another instrument. She took out a tape-measure on a mechanical spool. Kneeling down before Howe, she put the little metal ring of the tape under the tip of his shoe. At her request, Howe pressed it with his toe. When she had measured her distance, she nodded to Howe who released the tape. At a touch, it sprang back into the spool. "You have to be careful if you're going to get what you want," Hilda said. "I don't believe in all this snap-snap-snapping," she remarked loftily. Howe nodded in agreement, although he was beginning to think Hilda's care excessive.

Now at last the moment had come. Hilda squinted into the camera, moved the tripod slightly. She stood to the side, holding the plunger of the shutter-cable. "Ready," she said. "Will you relax, Joseph, please?" Howe realized that he was standing frozen. Hilda stood poised and precise as a setter, one hand holding the little cable, the other extended with curled dainty fingers like a dancer's, as if expressing to her subject the precarious delicacy of the moment. She pressed the plunger and there was the click. At once she stirred to action, got behind the camera, turned a new exposure. "Thank you," she said. "Would you stand under that tree and let me do a character study with light and shade?"

The childish absurdity of the remark restored Howe's ease. He went to the little tree. The pattern the leaves made on his gown was what Hilda was after. He had just taken a satisfactory position when he heard in the unmistakable voice, "Ah, Doctor! Having your picture taken?"

Howe gave up the pose and turned to Blackburn who stood on the walk, his hands behind his back, a little too large for his bachelor's gown. Annoyed that Blackburn should see him posing for a character study in light and shade, Howe said irritably, "Yes, having my picture taken."

Blackburn beamed at Hilda. "And the little photographer?" he said. Hilda fixed her eyes on the ground and stood closer to her brilliant and aggressive camera. Blackburn, teetering on his heels, his hands behind his back, wholly prelatical and benignly patient, was not abashed at the silence. At last Howe said, "If you'll excuse us, Mr. Blackburn, we'll go on with the picture."

"Go right ahead, sir. I'm running along." But he only came closer. "Doctor Howe," he said fervently, "I want to tell you how glad I am that I was able to satisfy your standards at last."

Howe was surprised at the hard, insulting brightness of his own voice, and even Hilda looked up curiously as he said, "Nothing you have ever done has satisfied me, and nothing you could ever do would satisfy me, Blackburn."

With a glance at Hilda, Blackburn made a gesture as if to hush Howe—as though all his former bold malice had taken for granted a kind of understanding between himself and his teacher, a secret which must not be betrayed to a third person. "I only meant, sir," he said, "that I was able to pass your course after all."

Howe said, "You didn't pass my course, I passed you out of my course, I passed you without even reading your paper. I wanted to be sure the college would be rid of you. And when all the grades were in and I did read your paper, I saw I was right not to have read it first."

Blackburn presented a stricken face. "It was very bad, sir?"

But Howe had turned away. The paper had been fantastic. The paper had been, if he wished to see it so, mad. It was at this moment that the Dean came up behind Howe and caught his arm. "Hello, Joseph," he said. "We'd better be getting along, it's almost late."

He was not a familiar man, but when he saw Blackburn, who approached to greet him, he took Blackburn's arm, too. "Hello, Theodore," he said. Leaning forward on Howe's arm and on Blackburn's, he said, "Hello, Hilda dear." Hilda replied quietly, "Hello, Uncle George."

Still clinging to their arms, still linking Howe and Blackburn, the Dean said, "Another year gone, Joe, and we've turned out another crop. After you've been here a few years, you'll find it reasonably upsetting—you wonder how there can be so many graduating classes while you stay the same. But of course you don't stay the same." Then he said, "Well," sharply, to dismiss the thought. He pulled Blackburn's arm and swung him around to Howe. "Have you heard about Teddy Blackburn?" he asked. "He has a job already, before graduation—the first man of his class to be placed." Expectant of congratulations, Blackburn beamed at Howe. Howe remained silent.

"Isn't that good?" the Dean said. Still Howe did not answer and the Dean, puzzled and put out, turned to Hilda. "That's a very fine-looking camera, Hilda." She touched it with affectionate pride.

"Instruments of precision," said a voice. "Instruments of precision." Of the three with joined arms, Howe was the nearest to Tertan, whose gaze took in all the scene except the smile and the nod which Howe gave him. The boy leaned on his cane. The broad-brimmed hat, canting jauntily over his eye, confused the image of his face that Howe had established, suppressed the rigid lines of the ascetic and brought out the baroque curves. It made an effect of perverse majesty.

"Instruments of precision," said Tertan for the last time, addressing no one, making a casual comment to the universe. And it occurred to Howe that Tertan might not be referring to Hilda's equipment. The sense of the thrice-woven circle of the boy's loneliness smote him fiercely. Tertan stood in majestic jauntiness, superior to all the scene, but his isolation made Howe ache with a pity of which Tertan was more the cause than the object, so general and indiscriminate was it.

Whether in his sorrow he made some unintended movement toward Tertan which the Dean checked, or whether the suddenly tightened grip on his arm was the Dean's own sorrow and fear, he did not know. Tertan watched them in the incurious way people watch a photograph being taken, and suddenly the thought that, to the boy, it must seem that the three were posing for a picture together made Howe detach himself almost rudely from the Dean's grasp.

"I promised Hilda another picture," he announced—needlessly, for Tertan was no longer there, he had vanished in the last sudden flux of visitors who, now that the band had struck up, were rushing nervously to find seats.

"You'd better hurry," the Dean said. "I'll go along, it's getting late for me." He departed and Blackburn walked stately by his side.

Howe again took his position under the little tree which cast its shadow over his face and gown. "Just hurry, Hilda, won't you?" he said. Hilda held the cable at arm's length, her other arm crooked and her fingers crisped. She rose on her toes and said "Ready," and pressed the release. "Thank you," she said gravely and began to dismantle her camera as he hurried off to join the procession.

Questions

1. Since *Of This Time, Of That Place* is a comparatively long story, its author faces certain problems that writers of shorter pieces do not. What particular problems in point of view, time-sequence, characterization, and plot are solved in this story by Lionel Trilling?
2. What kind of Narrator is used in the story? Why was an Historical Narrator not used, since the time and scope of the events are so extensive?
3. Are there more subjects or themes treated within *Of This Time, Of That Place* than in *That Evening Sun* or *The Christmas Banquet*? Are its themes more complex than theirs? Is the length of a story due to its complexity or to something else?

4. Trilling's story makes many of the same comments on formal education that Henry Adams' autobiography does (p. 135 above). Compare these views and the manner in which each author presents them. Which is the more thoughtful and persuasive? What dimensions are there in the Trilling story beyond those in Adams's account?
5. From your own experience in college, are the characters and dialogue in this story believable? What about the events of the plot? Does the story have verisimilitude?
6. Ibsen's *Ghosts*, the play discussed in Howe's class, deals with the increasing insanity of a young man because he has inherited syphilis from a dissolute father. Does this information have any bearing on the story?
7. Contemporary writers often use symbols to suggest factual or emotional values. In this story what symbolic uses have Hilda's camera, Peter Abelard, flowers, Casebeer, Stettenhover, the academic gown and procession? Compare Trilling's use of symbolism with Hawthorne's or Poe's.
8. Point out instances of irony in the story: in plot, characters, tone, dialogue. Is the story as a whole an ironic criticism of academic life and the educational process?
9. As the author of *Art and Neurosis* (p. 17f. above), Lionel Trilling has revealed his knowledge of Freudian psychology. Does his fictional narrative use that knowledge? Does the fact that he writes fiction himself affect Trilling's views on art and neurosis? Discuss.

SHIRLEY JACKSON

The Lottery

The morning of June 27th was clear and sunny, with the fresh warmth of a full-summer day; the flowers were blossoming profusely and the grass

THE LOTTERY: Reprinted with permission of Farrar, Straus & Giroux, Inc. from *The Lottery* by Shirley Jackson. Copyright 1948, 1949 by Shirley Jackson. First appeared in *The New Yorker*.

was richly green. The people of the village began to gather in the square, between the post office and the bank, around ten o'clock; in some towns there were so many people that the lottery took two days and had to be started on June 26th, but in this village, where there were only about three hundred people, the whole lottery took less than two hours, so it could begin at ten o'clock in the morning and still be through in time to allow the villagers to get home for noon dinner.

The children assembled first, of course. School was recently over for the summer, and the feeling of liberty sat uneasily on most of them; they tended to gather together quietly for a while before they broke into boisterous play, and their talk was still of the classroom and the teacher, of books and reprimands. Bobby Martin had already stuffed his pockets full of stones, and the other boys soon followed his example, selecting the smoothest and roundest stones; Bobby and Harry Jones and Dickie Delacroix—the villagers pronounced this name "Dellacroy"—eventually made a great pile of stones in one corner of the square and guarded it against the raids of the other boys. The girls stood aside, talking among themselves, looking over their shoulders at the boys, and the very small children rolled in the dust or clung to the hands of their older brothers or sisters.

Soon the men began to gather, surveying their own children, speaking of planting and rain, tractors and taxes. They stood together, away from the pile of stones in the corner, and their jokes were quiet and they smiled rather than laughed. The women, wearing faded house dresses and sweaters, came shortly after their menfolk. They greeted one another and exchanged bits of gossip as they went to join their husbands. Soon the women, standing by their husbands, began to call to their children, and the children came reluctantly, having to be called four or five times. Bobby Martin ducked under his mother's grasping hand and ran, laughing, back to the pile of stones. His father spoke up sharply, and Bobby came quickly and

took his place between his father and his oldest brother.

The lottery was conducted—as were the square dances, the teen-age club, the Halloween program—by Mr. Summers, who had time and energy to devote to civic activities. He was a round-faced, jovial man and he ran the coal business, and people were sorry for him, because he had no children and his wife was a scold. When he arrived in the square, carrying the black wooden box, there was a murmur of conversation among the villagers, and he waved and called, "Little late today, folks." The postmaster, Mr. Graves, followed him, carrying a three-legged stool, and the stool was put in the center of the square and Mr. Summers set the black box down on it. The villagers kept their distance, leaving a space between themselves and the stool, and when Mr. Summers said, "Some of you fellows want to give me a hand?" there was a hesitation before two men, Mr. Martin and his oldest son, Baxter, came forward to hold the box steady on the stool while Mr. Summers stirred up the papers inside it.

The original paraphernalia for the lottery had been lost long ago, and the black box now resting on the stool had been put into use even before Old Man Warner, the oldest man in town, was born. Mr. Summers spoke frequently to the villagers about making a new box, but no one liked to upset even as much tradition as was represented by the black box. There was a story that the present box had been made with some pieces of the box that had preceded it, the one that had been constructed when the first people settled down to make a village here. Every year, after the lottery, Mr. Summers began talking again about a new box, but every year the subject was allowed to fade off without anything's being done. The black box grew shabbier each year; by now it was no longer completely black but splintered badly along one side to show the original wood color, and in some places faded or stained.

Mr. Martin and his oldest son, Baxter, held the black box securely on the stool until Mr.

Summers had stirred the papers thoroughly with his hand. Because so much of the ritual had been forgotten or discarded, Mr. Summers had been successful in having slips of paper substituted for the chips of wood that had been used for generations. Chips of wood, Mr. Summers had argued, had been all very well when the village was tiny, but now that the population was more than three hundred and likely to keep on growing, it was necessary to use something that would fit more easily into the black box. The night before the lottery, Mr. Summers and Mr. Graves made up the slips of paper and put them in the box, and it was then taken to the safe of Mr. Summer's coal company and locked up until Mr. Summers was ready to take it to the square next morning. The rest of the year, the box was put away, sometimes one place, sometimes another; it had spent one year in Mr. Graves's barn and another year underfoot in the post office, and sometimes it was set on a shelf in the Martin grocery and left there.

There was a great deal of fussing to be done before Mr. Summers declared the lottery open. There were the lists to make up—of heads of families, heads of households in each family, members of each household in each family. There was the proper swearing-in of Mr. Summers by the postmaster, as the official of the lottery; at one time, some people remembered, there had been a recital of some sort, performed by the official of the lottery, a perfunctory, tuneless chant that had been rattled off dully each year; some people believed that the official of the lottery used to stand just so when he said or sang it, others believed that he was supposed to walk among the people, but years and years ago this part of the ritual had been allowed to lapse. There had been, also, a ritual salute, which the official of the lottery had had to use in addressing each person who came up to draw from the box, but this also had changed with time, until now it was felt necessary only for the official to speak to each person approaching. Mr. Summers was very good at all this; in his clean white shirt and blue jeans, with one hand resting carelessly on the black box, he seemed very proper and important as he talked interminably to Mr. Graves and the Martins.

Just as Mr. Summers finally left off talking and turned to the assembled villagers, Mrs. Hutchinson came hurriedly along the path to the square, her sweater thrown over her shoulders, and slid into place in the back of the crowd. "Clean forgot what day it was," she said to Mrs. Delacroix, who stood next to her, and they both laughed softly. "Thought my old man was out back stacking wood," Mrs. Hutchinson went on, "and then I looked out the window and the kids was gone, and then I remembered it was the twenty-seventh and came a-running." She dried her hands on her apron, and Mrs. Delacroix said, "You're in time, though. They're still talking away up there."

Mrs. Hutchinson craned her neck to see through the crowd and found her husband and children standing near the front. She tapped Mrs. Delacroix on the arm as a farewell and began to make her way through the crowd. The people separated good-humoredly to let her through; two or three people said, in voices just loud enough to be heard across the crowd, "Here comes your Missus, Hutchinson," and "Bill, she made it after all." Mrs. Hutchinson reached her husband, and Mr. Summers, who had been waiting, said cheerfully, "Thought we were going to have to get on without you, Tessie." Mrs. Hutchinson said, grinning, "Wouldn't have me leave m'dishes in the sink, now, would you, Joe?", and soft laughter ran through the crowd as the people stirred back into position after Mrs. Hutchinson's arrival.

"Well, now," Mr. Summers said soberly, "guess we better get started, get this over with, so's we can go back to work. Anybody ain't here?"

"Dunbar," several people said. "Dunbar, Dunbar."

Mr. Summers consulted his list. "Clyde Dunbar," he said. "That's right. He's broke his leg, hasn't he? Who's drawing for him?"

"Me, I guess," a woman said, and Mr. Summers turned to look at her. "Wife draws for her husband," Mr. Summers said. "Don't you have a grown boy to do it for you, Janey?" Although Mr. Summers and everyone else in the village knew the answer perfectly well, it was the business of the official of the lottery to ask such questions formally. Mr. Summers waited with an expression of polite interest while Mrs. Dunbar answered.

"Horace's not but sixteen yet," Mrs. Dunbar said regretfully. "Guess I gotta fill in for the old man this year."

"Right," Mr. Summers said. He made a note on the list he was holding. Then he asked, "Watson boy drawing this year?"

A tall boy in the crowd raised his hand. "Here," he said. "I'm drawing for m'mother and me." He blinked his eyes nervously and ducked his head as several voices in the crowd said things like "Good fellow, Jack," and "Glad to see your mother's got a man to do it."

"Well," Mr. Summers said, "guess that's everyone. Old Man Warner make it?"

"Here," a voice said, and Mr. Summers nodded.

A sudden hush fell on the crowd as Mr. Summers cleared his throat and looked at the list. "All ready?" he called. "Now, I'll read the names—heads of families first—and the men come up and take a paper out of the box. Keep the paper folded in your hand without looking at it until everyone has had a turn. Everything clear?"

The people had done it so many times that they only half listened to the directions; most of them were quiet, wetting their lips, not looking around. Then Mr. Summers raised one hand high and said, "Adams." A man disengaged himself from the crowd and came forward. "Hi, Steve," Mr. Summers said, and Mr. Adams said, "Hi, Joe." They grinned at one another humorlessly and nervously. Then Mr. Adams reached into the black box and took out a folded paper. He held it firmly by one corner as

he turned and went hastily back to his place in the crowd, where he stood a little apart from his family, not looking down at his hand.

"Allen," Mr. Summers said. "Anderson.... Bentham."

"Seems like there's no time at all between lotteries any more," Mrs. Delacroix said to Mrs. Graves in the back row. "Seems like we got through with the last one only last week."

"Time sure goes fast," Mrs. Graves said.

"Clark.... Delacroix."

"There goes my old man," Mrs. Delacroix said. She held her breath while her husband went forward.

"Dunbar," Mr. Summers said, and Mrs. Dunbar went steadily to the box while one of the women said, "Go on, Janey," and another said, "There she goes."

"We're next," Mrs. Graves said. She watched while Mr. Graves came around from the side of the box, greeted Mr. Summers gravely, and selected a slip of paper from the box. By now, all through the crowd there were men holding the small folded papers in their large hands, turning them over and over nervously. Mrs. Dunbar and her two sons stood together, Mrs. Dunbar holding the slip of paper.

"Harburt.... Hutchinson."

"Get up there, Bill," Mrs. Hutchinson said, and the people near her laughed.

"Jones."

"They do say," Mr. Adams said to Old Man Warner, who stood next to him, "that over in the north village they're talking of giving up the lottery."

Old Man Warner snorted. "Pack of crazy fools," he said. "Listening to the young folks, nothing's good enough for *them*. Next thing you know, they'll be wanting to go back to living in caves, nobody work any more, live *that* way for a while. Used to be a saying about 'Lottery in June, corn be heavy soon.' First thing you know, we'd all be eating stewed chickweed and acorns. There's *always* been a lottery," he added petulantly. "Bad enough to see young Joe Summers up there joking with everybody."

"Some places have already quit lotteries," Mrs. Adams said.

"Nothing but trouble in *that*," Old Man Warner said stoutly. "Pack of young fools."

"Martin." And Bobby Martin watched his father go forward. "Overdyke.... Percy."

"I wish they'd hurry," Mrs. Dunbar said to her older son. "I wish they'd hurry."

"They're almost through," her son said.

"You get ready to run tell Dad," Mrs. Dunbar said.

Mr. Summers called his own name and then stepped forward precisely and selected a slip from the box. Then he called, "Warner."

"Seventy-seventh year I been in the lottery," Old Man Warner said as he went through the crowd. "Seventy-seventh time."

"Watson." The tall boy came awkwardly through the crowd. Someone said, "Don't be nervous, Jack," and Mr. Summers said, "Take your time, son."

"Zanini."

After that, there was a long pause, a breathless pause, until Mr. Summers, holding his slip of paper in the air, said, "All right, fellows." For a minute, no one moved, and then all the slips of paper were opened. Suddenly, all the women began to speak at once, saying, "Who is it?," "Who's got it?," "Is it the Dunbars?," "Is it the Watsons?" Then the voices began to say, "It's Hutchinson. It's Bill," "Bill Hutchinson's got it."

"Go tell your father," Mrs. Dunbar said to her older son.

People began to look around to see the Hutchinsons. Bill Hutchinson was standing quiet, staring down at the paper in his hand. Suddenly, Tessie Hutchinson shouted to Mr. Summers, "You didn't give him time enough to take any paper he wanted. I saw you. It wasn't fair!"

"Be a good sport, Tessie," Mrs. Delacroix called, and Mrs. Graves said, "All of us took the same chance."

"Shut up, Tessie," Bill Hutchinson said.

"Well, everyone," Mr. Summers said, "that was done pretty fast, and now we've got to be hurrying a little more to get done in time." He consulted his next list. "Bill," he said, "you draw for the Hutchinson family. You got any other households in the Hutchinsons?"

"There's Don and Eva," Mrs. Hutchinson yelled. "Make *them* take their chance!"

"Daughters draw with their husbands' families, Tessie," Mr. Summers said gently. "You know that as well as anyone else."

"It wasn't *fair*," Tessie said.

"I guess not, Joe," Bill Hutchinson said regretfully. "My daughter draws with her husband's family, that's only fair. And I've got no other family except the kids."

"Then, as far as drawing for families is concerned, it's you," Mr. Summers said in explanation, "and as far as drawing for households is concerned, that's you, too. Right?"

"Right," Bill Hutchinson said.

"How many kids, Bill?" Mr. Summers asked formally.

"Three," Bill Hutchinson said. "There's Bill, Jr., and Nancy, and little Dave. And Tessie and me."

"All right, then," Mr. Summers said. "Harry, you got their tickets back?"

Mr. Graves nodded and held up the slips of paper. "Put them in the box then," Mr. Summers directed. "Take Bill's and put it in."

"I think we ought to start over," Mrs. Hutchinson said, as quietly as she could. "I tell you it wasn't *fair*. You didn't give him time enough to choose. *Everybody* saw that."

Mr. Graves had selected the five slips and put them in the box, and he dropped all the papers but those onto the ground, where the breeze caught them and lifted them off.

"Listen, everybody," Mrs. Hutchinson was saying to the people around her.

"Ready, Bill?" Mr. Summers asked, and Bill Hutchinson, with one quick glance around at his wife and children, nodded.

"Remember," Mr. Summers said, "take the slips and keep them folded until each person has taken one. Harry, you help little Dave." Mr. Graves took the hand of the little boy, who came willingly with him up to the box. "Take a paper out of the box, Davy," Mr. Summers said. Davy put his hand into the box and laughed. "Take just *one* paper," Mr. Summers said. "Harry, you hold it for him." Mr. Graves took the child's hand and removed the folded paper from the tight fist and held it while little Dave stood next to him and looked up at him wonderingly.

"Nancy next," Mr. Summers said. Nancy was twelve, and her school friends breathed heavily as she went forward, switching her skirt, and took a slip daintily from the box. "Bill, Jr.," Mr. Summers said, and Billy, his face red and his feet overlarge, nearly knocked the box over as he got a paper out. "Tessie," Mr. Summers said. She hesitated for a minute, looking around defiantly, and then set her lips and went up to the box. She snatched a paper out and held it behind her.

"Bill," Mr. Summers said, and Bill Hutchinson reached into the box and felt around, bringing his hand out at last with the slip of paper in it.

The crowd was quiet. A girl whispered, "I hope it's not Nancy," and the sound of the whisper reached the edges of the crowd.

"It's not the way it used to be," Old Man Warner said clearly. "People ain't the way they used to be."

"All right," Mr. Summers said. "Open the papers. Harry, you open little Dave's."

Mr. Graves opened the slip of paper and there was a general sigh through the crowd as he held it up and everyone could see that it was blank. Nancy and Bill, Jr., opened theirs at the same time, and both beamed and laughed, turning around to the crowd and holding their slips of paper above their heads.

"Tessie," Mr. Summers said. There was a pause, and then Mr. Summers looked at Bill Hutchinson, and Bill unfolded his paper and showed it. It was blank.

"It's Tessie," Mr. Summers said, and his voice was hushed. "Show us her paper, Bill."

Bill Hutchinson went over to his wife and forced the slip of paper out of her hand. It had a black spot on it, the black spot Mr. Summers had made the night before with the heavy pencil in the coal-company office. Bill Hutchinson held it up, and there was a stir in the crowd.

"All right, folks," Mr. Summers said. "Let's finish quickly."

Although the villagers had forgotten the ritual and lost the original black box, they still remembered to use stones. The pile of stones the boys had made earlier was ready; there were stones on the ground with the blowing scraps of paper that had come out of the box. Mrs. Delacroix selected a stone so large she had to pick it up with both hands and turned to Mrs. Dunbar. "Come on," she said. "Hurry up."

Mrs. Dunbar had small stones in both hands, and she said, gasping for breath, "I can't run at all. You'll have to go ahead and I'll catch up with you."

The children had stones already, and someone gave little Davy Hutchinson a few pebbles.

Tessie Hutchinson was in the center of a cleared space by now, and she held her hands out desperately as the villagers moved in on her. "It isn't fair," she said. A stone hit her on the side of the head.

Old Man Warner was saying, "Come on, come on, everyone." Steve Adams was in front of the crowd of villagers, with Mrs. Graves beside him.

"It isn't fair, it isn't right," Mrs. Hutchinson screamed, and then they were upon her.

Commentary

The Lottery is a story with many undertones. It begins as though it is to be a report of a New England town meeting, commonly viewed as one of the noblest forms of the democratic process; it ends as the hideous enactment in modern terms of a primitive ritual. Mrs. Hutchinson becomes a ritual scapegoat like the

Aztec Corn Goddess, the victim of a time-honored custom originating in forgotten superstitions about fertility and death. But Miss Jackson is not simply modernizing a hideous custom to disgust her reader; she is saying that people remain primitive under the surface of civilization. Like Faulkner's Nancy, Mrs. Hutchinson is the blood sacrifice that society makes to preserve its sense of order and fitness. *The Lottery* says a great deal about American society in particular as well as human civilization in general. To what extent does *The Lottery* support the views in Robert Penn Warren's essay on p. 370f.? Do its insights help to explain the historical events in Gibbon's account of the fall of Constantinople? Is Miss Jackson's world the same world John Hersey shows in *A Noiseless Flash*? Do Freud's theories of repression and violence stand confirmed by *The Lottery* as well as *The Death of the Corn Goddess*? Is the plot of Miss Jackson's story a Jungean archetypal situation? Could the events in *The Lottery* be literally true or not? Like other storytellers, Miss Jackson refuses to take a simple, one-dimensional view of reality—such as the biologist's or the journalist's. Consequently, this story presents a "truth" that is confirmed by a number of separate intellectual disciplines but makes its impact on us largely through our emotions.

SECTION FOUR

Lyrical Fictions

Of the three broad categories of "creative" literature, the lyric is that which is almost entirely comprised of poetry rather than prose. In fact, "poetry" and "lyric" are considered synonymous by some critics, who emphasize the qualities of rhythm and figurative language as the categorical principles of the lyric. The word "lyric" itself refers to the musical accompaniment by a lyre for the words of this form of literature; and though most lyric poetry since 1600 has been composed to be read rather than sung or chanted, in employing intense rhythmic patterns of sound and accents, the lyric retains evidence of its melodic origins. Since accent and sound are aspects of language, it is in the ways lyric writing utilizes language that its nature is initially defined. Whereas the language of drama is mimetic (or imitative) and the language of narrative is mnemonic (or memorable), the language of lyricism is expressive, actually *containing* as well as representing the sensations which are its sources and subjects. The lyric is probably the most completely aesthetic species of literature, in its devices and intent.

Although a lyric poem can treat any topic at all, it is the manner of focusing that topic through the personal sensibility of the poet that immediately impresses the reader. The writer of lyric poetry perceives and feels with a degree of awareness beyond that of most men; but if his experiences are due to his greater sentience, he is able to focus these through emotions known to us all and to express both his perceptions and feelings in a language that creates them anew for the reader. By reading the lyric, one can undergo essentially the same process of perception that the poet himself has experienced.

J. S. Mill defined the lyric poem as "the utterance that is overheard." This pithy description suggests many of the qualities characteristic of lyricism: the intensity of the poet's emotion; the basically personal or private quality of lyric perception; the similarity of the reader's nature as a human being to the poet's despite their separateness as individuals; the inevitability of the verbal expression of the poet's "feelings"; the spontaneity of lyricism. Not all lyric poetry is spontaneous and private, of course. Such varieties of lyric as hymns, odes, and dirges clearly have a collective and public function. But whatever its uses or modes of transmission, lyric poetry seems to touch most deeply the inner states of being and the processes of consciousness that make up life's meaning. Like the diarist, the writer of lyric forms seeks to capture the essence of himself in words. When he succeeds, his most private and personal experiences are transformed into a literature that captures the essential humanity of his readers as well.

Because it is infinite in variety, lyrical poetry can be categorized according to numerous basic criteria: its metrical structure (sonnets, villanelles, sestinas, rondeaux, and so forth), its frames of reference (pastoral, Metaphysical, Romantic), its subject-matter (love, marriage, death), its occasion (prothalamium, elegy, triumph), its recipient or honoree (paean, Pindaric Ode), its author (Sapphics, Anacreontics), or a combination of these. A specific lyric poem, for example, may be a Virgilian pastoral eclogue or a Shakespearean love sonnet. These elaborate categories are descriptions rather than generic distinctions in many instances; but they are helpful as a way of identifying the traditional elements in a particular poem or as a way of relating it to its cultural and literary context.

The lyric poems contained here are grouped not according to formal or structural principles, however, but by theme. The subjects that are lyrically expressed below have been treated in other literary forms in previous portions of this anthology. By comparing the way a lyric poem expresses its author's perception of stars or death by drowning or ants or Rome with the treatment of these topics by writers of other persuasions, you, the reader, can appreciate the perspectives and methods that typify lyricism. You will also be able to complete the full literary circle from the most subjectively oriented factual composition through the orders of public writing, factual and fictional, to the lyrical fiction, which bears provocative resemblances to the journals with which this collection began.

Section A

Man in the Universe

ROBERT HERRICK

To Daffodils

WILLIAM SHAKESPEARE

Fair daffodils, we weep to see
   You haste away so soon:
As yet the early-rising sun
   Has not attain'd his noon.
     Stay, stay,   5
   Until the hasting day
     Has run
   But to the Even-song;
And, having pray'd together, we
   Will go with you along.   10

We have short time to stay, as you,
   We have as short a spring;
As quick a growth to meet decay,
   As you, or any thing.
     We die,   15
As your hours do, and dry
     Away,
   Like to the summer's rain;
Or as the pearls of morning's dew
   Ne'er to be found again.   20

Full Fathom Five

Full fathom five thy father lies,
   Of his bones are coral made;
Those are pearls that were his eyes;
   Nothing of him that doth fade,
But doth suffer a sea change   5
Into something rich and strange.
Sea-nymphs hourly ring his knell:
          Ding, dong.
Hark! Now I hear them—Ding, dong, bell.

FROM *The Tempest* (I, ii, 394)

Commentary

This song from Shakespeare's play, *The Tempest*, is sung to Ferdinand after his father has supposedly perished in a shipwreck. The song is very like Thomas Hardy's *Convergence of the Twain* in its picture of the changes undergone by sunken ships and drowned passengers. Note the contrasts in tone and imagery between the two poems, however. In its note of calm and its view of the beauty of change, Shakespeare's song seems very unlike Hardy's brooding on the irony of destiny. Is Shakespeare's view of death by drowning logically antithetical to that of Hanson Baldwin in *R.M.S. Titanic*? Can Shakespeare's described attitude toward the drowned father apply to the men and women who went down on the *Titanic*? What relationship has the aesthetic truth of this poem to the historical truth about the *Titanic's* passengers?

Commentary

Compare Herrick's use of the daffodils as symbols to Wordsworth's use of them in his poem on p. 393. What effect has Herrick's use of the "we" point of view to the theme of this poem? How does it compare with Wordsworth's "I"? Does Herrick agree with Shakespeare about the emotions attached to man's fleeting life and his eventual decay into nature? Which is true?

ALEXANDER POPE

Man

Know then thyself, presume not God to scan;
The proper study of Mankind is Man.
Plac'd on this isthmus of a middle state,
A Being darkly wise, and rudely great:
With too much knowledge for the Skeptic side,   5
With too much weakness for the Stoic's pride,
He hangs between; in doubt to act, or rest;
In doubt to deem himself a God, or Beast;
In doubt his Mind or Body to prefer;
Born but to die, and reas'ning but to err;   10
Alike in ignorance, his reason such,
Whether he thinks too little, or too much:
Chaos of Thought and Passion, all confus'd;
Still by himself abus'd, or disabus'd;
Created half to rise, and half to fall;   15
Great lord of all things, yet a prey to all;
Sole judge of Truth, in endless Error hurl'd:
The glory, jest, and riddle of the world!
   Go, wond'rous creature! mount where Science
     guides,
Go, measure earth, weigh air, and state the tides;   20
Instruct the planets in what orbs to run,
Correct old Time, and regulate the Sun.
Go, soar with Plato to th' empyreal sphere,
To the first good, first perfect, and first fair;
Or tread the mazy round his follow'rs trod,   25
And quitting sense call imitating God;
As Eastern priests in giddy circles run,
And turn their heads to imitate the Sun.
Go, teach Eternal Wisdom how to rule—
Then drop into thyself, and be a fool!   30

JOHN KEATS

Bright Star

Bright star! would I were steadfast as thou art—
Not in lone splendour hung aloft the night,
And watching, with eternal lids apart,

MAN: From *An Essay on Man*, II. 1–30.

Like Nature's patient sleepless Eremite,
The moving waters at their priestlike task   5
Of pure ablution round earth's human shores,
Or gazing on the new soft-fallen mask
Of snow upon the mountains and the moors—
No—yet still steadfast, still unchangeable,
Pillowed upon my fair love's ripening breast,   10
To feel for ever its soft fall and swell,
Awake for ever in a sweet unrest,
Still, still to hear her tender-taken breath,
And so live ever—or else swoon to death.

ROBERT FROST

Once by the Pacific

The shattered water made a misty din.
Great waves looked over others coming in,
And thought of doing something to the shore
That water never did to land before.
The clouds were low and hairy in the skies,   5
Like locks blown forward in the gleam of eyes.
You could not tell, and yet it looked as if
The shore was lucky in being backed by cliff,
The cliff in being backed by continent;
It looked as if a night of dark intent   10
Was coming, and not only a night, an age.
Someone had better be prepared for rage.
There would be more than ocean-water broken
Before God's last *Put out the Light* was spoken.

Commentary

Is this poem a statement of religious faith? Is Frost's system of beliefs, as this poem shows it, like or unlike that of Saint Augustine (p. 114f.)? Compare Frost's attitudes toward infinity with Gibbon's (p. 122). Compare it with *The Second Coming* (p. 534). Are they about the same or different experiences?

Departmental

An ant on the table cloth
Ran into a dormant moth
Of many times his size.
He showed not the least surprise.
His business wasn't with such.   5
He gave it scarcely a touch,
And was off on his duty run.
Yet if he encountered one
Of the hive's enquiry squad
Whose work is to find out God   10
And the nature of time and space,
He would put him onto the case.
Ants are a curious race;
One crossing with hurried tread
The body of one of their dead   15
Isn't given a moment's arrest—
Seems not even impressed.
But he no doubt reports to any
With whom he crosses antennae,
And they no doubt report   20
To the higher up at court.
Then word goes forth in Formic:
"Death's come to Jerry McCormic,
Our selfless forager Jerry.
Will the special Janizary   25
Whose office it is to bury
The dead of the commissary
Go bring him home to his people.
Lay him in state on a sepal.
Wrap him for shroud in a petal.   30
Embalm him with ichor of nettle.
This is the word of your Queen."
And presently on the scene
Appears a solemn mortician;
And taking formal position   35
With feelers calmly atwiddle,
Seizes the dead by the middle,
And heaving him high in air,
Carries him out of there.
No one stands round to stare.   40
It is nobody else's affair.

It couldn't be called ungentle.
But how thoroughly departmental.

Commentary

In what ways is Frost's attitude toward ants like Petrunkevitch's attitude toward wasps and spiders? Is this poem about something more than the behavior of ants?

ROBERT GRAVES

To Juan at the Winter Solstice

There is one story and one story only
That will prove worth your telling,
Whether as learned bard or gifted child;
To it all lines or lesser gauds belong
That startle with their shining   5
Such common stories as they stray into.

Is it of trees you tell, their months and virtues,
Or strange beasts that beset you,
Of birds that croak at you the Triple will?
Or of the Zodiac and how slow it turns   10
Below the Boreal Crown,
Prison of all true kings that ever reigned?

Water to water, ark again to ark,
From woman back to woman:
So each new victim treads unfalteringly   15
The never altered circuit of his fate,
Bringing twelve peers as witness
Both to his starry rise and starry fall.

Or is it of the Virgin's silver beauty,
All fish below the thighs?   20
She in her left hand bears a leafy quince;
When with her right she crooks a finger, smiling,
How may the King hold back?
Royally then he barters life for love.

Or of the undying snake from chaos hatched, 25
Whose coils contain the ocean,
Into whose chops with naked sword he springs,

Then in black water, tangled by the reeds,
Battles three days and nights,
To be spewed up beside her scalloped shore?   30

Much snow is falling, winds roar hollowly,
The owl hoots from the elder,
Fear in your heart cries to the loving-cup:
Sorrow to sorrow as the sparks fly upward.
The log groans and confesses: 35
There is one story and one story only.

Dwell on her graciousness, dwell on her smiling,
Do not forget what flowers
The great boar trampled down in ivy time.
Her brow was creamy as the crested wave,   40
Her sea-blue eyes were wild
But nothing promised that is not performed.

Commentary

This is a poetical treatment of the subject matter that Jung and Frazer treat: the recurrent myths and rituals of the human race. Juan is Graves's own son. The winter solstice is the shortest day of the year, December 22, a traditional date of religious significance because of the nadir of the sun's brightness. Graves summarizes many myths in this poem, asserting that they are all the same myth. What is his attitude toward the universal myth and its effects? Does his poem say anything that Jung and Frazer do not or cannot? Compare Graves's treatment of old religious rituals with Stevens's use in *Sunday Morning* below.

WALLACE STEVENS

Sunday Morning

I

Complacencies of the peignoir, and late
Coffee and oranges in a sunny chair,
And the green freedom of a cockatoo

Upon a rug mingle to dissipate
The holy hush of ancient sacrifice.   5
She dreams a little, and she feels the dark
Encroachment of that old catastrophe,
As a calm darkens among water-lights.
The pungent oranges and bright, green wings
Seem things in some procession of the dead,   10
Winding across wide water, without sound.
The day is like wide water, without sound,
Stilled for the passing of her dreaming feet
Over the seas, to silent Palestine,
Dominion of the blood and sepulchre.   15

II

Why should she give her bounty to the dead?
What is divinity if it can come
Only in silent shadows and in dreams?
Shall she not find in comforts of the sun,
In pungent fruit and bright, green wings, or else   20
In any balm or beauty of the earth,
Things to be cherished like the thought of heaven?
Divinity must live within herself:
Passions of rain, or moods in falling snow;
Grievings in loneliness, or unsubdued   25
Elations when the forest blooms; gusty
Emotions on wet roads on autumn nights;
All pleasures and all pains, remembering
The bough of summer and the winter branch.
These are the measures destined for her soul.   30

III

Jove in the clouds had his inhuman birth.
No mother suckled him, no sweet land gave
Large-mannered motions to his mythy mind.
He moved among us, as a muttering king,
Magnificent, would move among his hinds,   35
Until our blood, commingling, virginal,
With heaven, brought such requital to desire
The very hinds discerned it, in a star.
Shall our blood fail? Or shall it come to be
The blood of paradise? And shall the earth   40
Seem all of paradise that we shall know?
The sky will be much friendlier then than now,
A part of labor and a part of pain,
And next in glory to enduring love,
Not this dividing and indifferent blue.   45

IV

She says, "I am content when wakened birds,
Before they fly, test the reality

Of misty fields, by their sweet questionings;
But when the birds are gone, and their warm fields
Return no more, where, then, is paradise?" 50
There is not any haunt of prophecy,
Nor any old chimera of the grave,
Neither the golden underground, nor isle
Melodious, where spirits gat them home,
Nor visionary south, nor cloudy palm
Remote on heaven's hill, that has endured 55
As April's green endures; or will endure
Like her remembrance of awakened birds,
Or her desire for June and evening, tipped
By the consummation of the swallow's wings. 60

V

She says, "But in contentment I still feel
The need of some imperishable bliss."
Death is the mother of beauty; hence from her,
Alone, shall come fulfilment to our dreams
And our desires. Although she strews the leaves 65
Of sure obliteration on our paths,
The path sick sorrow took, the many paths
Where triumph rang its brassy phrase, or love
Whispered a little out of tenderness,
She makes the willow shiver in the sun 70
For maidens who were wont to sit and gaze
Upon the grass, relinquished to their feet.
She causes boys to pile new plums and pears
On disregarded plate. The maidens taste
And stray impassioned in the littering leaves. 75

VI

Is there no change of death in paradise?
Does ripe fruit never fall? Or do the boughs
Hang always heavy in that perfect sky,
Unchanging, yet so like our perishing earth,
With rivers like our own that seek for seas 80
They never find, the same receding shores
That never touch with inarticulate pang?
Why set the pear upon those river-banks
Or spice the shores with odors of the plum?
Alas, that they should wear our colors there, 85
The silken weavings of our afternoons,
And pick the strings of our insipid lutes!
Death is the mother of beauty, mystical,
Within whose burning bosom we devise
Our earthly mothers waiting, sleeplessly. 90

VII

Supple and turbulent, a ring of men
Shall chant in orgy on a summer morn

Their boisterous devotion to the sun,
Not as a god, but as a god might be,
Naked among them, like a savage source. 95
Their chant shall be a chant of paradise,
Out of their blood, returning to the sky;
And in their chant shall enter, voice by voice,
The windy lake wherein their lord delights,
The trees, like serafim, and echoing hills, 100
That choir among themselves long afterward.
They shall know well the heavenly fellowship
Of men that perish and of summer morn.
And whence they came and whither they shall go
The dew upon their feet shall manifest. 105

VIII

She hears, upon that water without sound,
A voice that cries, "The tomb in Palestine
Is not the porch of spirits lingering.
It is the grave of Jesus, where he lay."
We live in an old chaos of the sun, 110
Or old dependency of day and night,
Or island solitude, unsponsored, free,
Of that wide water, inescapable.
Deer walk upon our mountains, and the quail
Whistle about us their spontaneous cries; 115
Sweet berries ripen in the wilderness;
And, in the isolation of the sky,
At evening, casual flocks of pigeons make
Ambiguous undulations as they sink,
Downward to darkness, on extended wings. 120

WILLIAM EMPSON

Missing Dates

Slowly the poison the whole blood stream fills.
It is not the effort nor the failure tires.
The waste remains, the waste remains and kills.

It is not your system or clear sight that mills
Down small to the consequence a life requires; 5
Slowly the poison the whole blood stream fills.

They bled an old dog dry yet the exchange rills
Of young dog blood gave but a month's desires;
The waste remains, the waste remains and kills.

It is the Chinese tombs and the slag hills   10
Usurp the soil, and not the soil retires.
Slowly the poison the whole blood stream fills.

Not to have fire is to be a skin that shrills.
The complete fire is death. From partial fires
The waste remains, the waste remains and kills.   15

It is the poems you have lost, the ills
From missing dates, at which the heart expires.
Slowly the poison the whole blood stream fills.
The waste remains, the waste remains and kills.

ARCHIBALD MACLEISH

Epistle to Be Left in the Earth

... It is colder now,
                there are many stars,
                            we are drifting
North by the Great Bear,
                        the leaves are falling,   5
The water is stone in the scooped rocks,
                            to southward
Red sun grey air:
                the crows are
Slow on their crooked wings,   10
                        the jays have left us:
Long since we passed the flares of Orion.
Each man believes in his heart he will die.
Many have written last thoughts and last
    letters.
None know if our deaths are now or forever: 15
None know if this wandering earth will be
    found.

We lie down and the snow covers our garments.
I pray you,
        you (if any open this writing)
Make in your mouths the words that were
    our names.   20
I will tell you all we have learned,
                    I will tell you everything:

The earth is round,
                there are springs under the orchards,
The loam cuts with a blunt knife,   25
                        beware of
Elms in thunder,
                    the lights in the sky are stars—
We think they do not see,
                    we think also   30
The trees do not know nor the leaves of the
    grasses hear us:
The birds too are ignorant.
                        Do not listen.
Do not stand at dark in the open windows.
We before you have heard this: 35
                        they are voices:
They are not words at all but the wind rising.
Also none among us has seen God.
... We have thought often
The flaws of sun in the late and driving
    weather   40
Pointed to one tree (but it was not so.)
As for the nights I warn you the nights are
    dangerous:
The wind changes at night and the dreams come.

It is very cold,
            there are strange stars near Arcturus,   45
Voices are crying an unknown name in the sky.

E. E. CUMMINGS

Space being (don't forget to remember) Curved

Space being(don't forget to remember)
    Curved
(and that reminds me who said o yes Frost
Something there is which isn't fond of walls)

an electromagnetic(now I've lost
the)Einstein expanded Newton's law
    preserved   5
conTinuum(but we read that beFore)

of Course life being just a Reflex you
know since Everything is Relative or

to sum it All Up god being Dead(not to

mention in Terred)   10
        LONG LIVE that Upwardlooking
Serene Illustrious and Beatific
Lord of Creation,MAN:
           at a least crooking
of Whose compassionate digit,earth's most
  terrific   15

quadruped swoons into billiardBalls!

Section B

Man in History

WILLIAM SHAKESPEARE

When I Have Seen by Time's Fell Hand

When I have seen by Time's fell hand defaced
The rich-proud cost of outworn buried age;
When sometime lofty towers I see down-razed,
And brass eternal slave to mortal rage;
When I have seen the hungry ocean gain   5
Advantage on the kingdom of the shore,
And the firm soil win of the watery main,
Increasing store with loss, and loss with store;
When I have seen such interchange of state,
Or state itself confounded to decay,   10
Ruin hath taught me thus to ruminate:
That Time will come and take my love away.
This thought is as a death, which cannot choose
But weep to have that which it fears to lose.

JOHN KEATS

Ode on a Grecian Urn

1

Thou still unravish'd bride of quietness,
  Thou foster-child of silence and slow time,
Sylvan historian, who canst thus express
  A flowery tale more sweetly than our rhyme:
What leaf-fring'd legend haunts about thy shape   5
  Of deities or mortals, or of both,
    In Tempe or the dales of Arcady?
  What men or gods are these? What maidens
    loth?
What mad pursuit? What struggle to escape?
  What pipes and timbrels? What wild ecstasy?   10

2

Heard melodies are sweet, but those unheard
  Are sweeter; therefore, ye soft pipes, play on;
Not to the sensual ear, but, more endear'd,
  Pipe to the spirit ditties of no tone:
Fair youth, beneath the trees, thou canst not
    leave   15
  Thy song, nor ever can those trees be bare;
    Bold Lover, never, never canst thou kiss,
Though winning near the goal—yet, do not
    grieve;
    She cannot fade, though thou hast not thy
    bliss,
  For ever wilt thou love, and she be fair!   20

3

Ah, happy, happy boughs! that cannot shed
  Your leaves, nor ever bid the Spring adieu;
And, happy melodist, unwearied,
  For ever piping songs for ever new;
More happy love! more happy, happy love!   25
  For ever warm and still to be enjoy'd,
    For ever panting, and for ever young;
All breathing human passion far above,
  That leaves a heart high-sorrowful and
    cloy'd,
    A burning forehead, and a parching tongue.   30

4

Who are these coming to the sacrifice?
  To what green altar, O mysterious priest,
Lead'st thou that heifer lowing at the skies,
  And all her silken flanks with garlands drest?
What little town by river or sea shore, 35
  Or mountain-built with peaceful citadel,
    Is emptied of this folk, this pious morn?
And, little town, thy streets for evermore
  Will silent be; and not a soul to tell
    Why thou are desolate, can e'er return. 40

5

O Attic shape! Fair attitude! with brede
  Of marble men and maidens overwrought,
With forest branches and the trodden weed;
  Thou, silent form, dost tease us out of thought
As doth eternity: Cold Pastoral! 45
  When old age shall this generation waste,
    Thou shalt remain, in midst of other woe
Than ours, a friend to man, to whom thou say'st,
  Beauty is truth, truth beauty,—that is all
    Ye know on earth, and all ye need to know. 50

GEORGE GORDON, LORD BYRON

The Isles of Greece

I

The isles of Greece, the isles of Greece!
  Where burning Sappho loved and sung,
Where grew the arts of war and peace,
  Where Delos rose, and Phoebus sprung!
Eternal summer gilds them yet, 5
But all, except their sun, is set.

II

The Scian and the Teian muse,
  The hero's harp, the lover's lute,
Have found the fame your shores refuse:
  Their place of birth alone is mute 10
To sounds which echo further west
Than your sires' 'Islands of the Blest.'

III

The mountains look on Marathon—
  And Marathon looks on the sea;
And musing there an hour alone, 15
  I dream'd that Greece might still be free;
For standing on the Persians' grave,
I could not deem myself a slave.

IV

A king sate on the rocky brow
  Which looks o'er sea-born Salamis; 20
And ships, by thousands, lay below,
  And men in nations;—all were his!
He counted them at break of day—
And when the sun set where were they?

V

And where are they? and where art thou, 25
  My country? On thy voiceless shore
The heroic lay is tuneless now—
  The heroic bosom beats no more!
And must thy lyre, so long divine,
Degenerate into hands like mine? 30

VI

'Tis something, in the dearth of fame,
  Though link'd among a fetter'd race,
To feel at least a patriot's shame,
  Even as I sing, suffuse my face;
For what is left the poet here? 35
For Greeks a blush—for Greece a tear.

VII

Must *we* but weep o'er days more blest?
  Must *we* but blush?—Our fathers bled.
Earth! render back from out thy breast
  A remnant of our Spartan dead! 40
Of the three hundred grant but three,
To make a new Thermopylae!

VIII

What, silent still? and silent all?
  Ah! no;—the voices of the dead
Sound like a distant torrent's fall, 45
  And answer, 'Let one living head,
But one arise,—we come, we come!'
'Tis but the living who are dumb.

IX

In vain—in vain: strike other chords;
   Fill high the cup with Samian wine!   50
Leave battles to the Turkish hordes,
   And shed the blood of Scio's vine!
Hark! rising to the ignoble call—
How answers each bold Bacchanal!

X

You have the Pyrrhic dance as yet;   55
   Where is the Pyrrhic phalanx gone?
Of two such lessons, why forget
   The nobler and the manlier one?
You have the letters Cadmus gave—
Think ye he meant them for a slave?   60

XI

Fill high the bowl with Samian wine!
   We will not think of themes like these!
It made Anacreon's song divine:
   He served—but served Polycrates—
A tyrant; but our masters then   65
Were still, at least, our countrymen.

XII

The tyrant of the Chersonese
   Was freedom's best and bravest friend;
That tyrant was Miltiades!
   Oh! that the present hour would lend   70
Another despot of the kind!
Such chains as his were sure to bind.

XIII

Fill high the bowl with Samian wine!
   On Suli's rock, and Parga's shore,
Exists the remnant of a line   75
   Such as the Doric mothers bore;
And there, perhaps, some seed is sown,
The Heracleidan blood might own.

XIV

Trust not for freedom to the Franks—
   They have a king who buys and sells;   80
In native swords, and native ranks,
   The only hope of courage dwells:
But Turkish force, and Latin fraud,
Would break your shield, however broad.

XV

Fill high the bowl with Samian wine!   85
   Our virgins dance beneath the shade—
I see their glorious black eyes shine;
   But gazing on each glowing maid,
My own the burning tear-drop laves,
To think such breasts must suckle slaves.   90

XVI

Place me on Sunium's marbled steep,
   Where nothing, save the waves and I,
May hear our mutual murmurs sweep;
   There, swan-like, let me sing and die:
A land of slaves shall ne'er be mine—
Dash down yon cup of Samian wine!   95

Rome

LXXVIII

Oh Rome! my Country! City of the Soul!
The orphans of the heart must turn to thee,
Lone Mother of dead Empires! and control
In their shut breasts their petty misery.
What are our woes and sufferance? Come and
   see   5
The cypress, hear the owl, and plod your way
O'er steps of broken thrones and temples—Ye!
Whose agonies are evils of a day—
A world is at our feet as fragile as our clay.

LXXIX

The Niobe of nations! there she stands,   10
Childless and crownless, in her voiceless woe;
An empty urn within her wither'd hands,
Whose holy dust was scatter'd long ago;
The Scipios' Tomb contains no ashes now;
The very sepulchres lie tenantless   15
Of their heroic dwellers: dost thou flow,
Old Tiber! through a marble wilderness?
Rise, with thy yellow waves, and mantle her
   distress.

From *Childe Harold's Pilgrimage*, Canto IV.

LXXX

The Goth, the Christian, Time, War, Flood,
   and Fire,
Have dealt upon the seven-hill'd city's pride;   20
She saw her glories star by star expire,
And up the steep barbarian monarchs ride,
Where the car climb'd the Capitol; far and
   wide
Temple and tower went down, nor left a site:—
Chaos of ruins! who shall trace the void,   25
O'er the dim fragments cast a lunar light,
And say, "here was, or is," where all is doubly
   night?

LXXXI

The double night of ages, and of her,
Night's daughter, Ignorance, hath wrapt and
   wrap
All round us; we but feel our way to err: 30
The ocean hath his chart, the stars their map,
And Knowledge spreads them on her ample
   lap;
But Rome is as the desert, where we steer
Stumbling o'er recollections; now we clap
Our hands, and cry "Eureka!" "it is clear"—   35
When but some false mirage of ruin rises near.

. . .

CXLIII

A ruin—yet what ruin! from its mass
Walls, palaces, half-cities, have been rear'd;
Yet oft the enormous skeleton ye pass,
And marvel where the spoil could have
   appear'd.   40
Hath it indeed been plunder'd, or but clear'd?
Alas! developed, opens the decay,
When the colossal fabric's form is near'd:
It will not bear the brightness of the day,
Which streams too much on all, years, man, have
   reft away.   45

CXLIV

But when the rising moon begins to climb
Its topmost arch, and gently pauses there;
When the stars twinkle through the loops of
   time,
And the low night-breeze waves along the air
The garland-forest, which the gray walls wear,   50
Like laurels on the bald first Caesar's head;

When the light shines serene but doth not
   glare,
Then in this magic circle raise the dead:
Heroes have trod this spot—'tis on their dust ye
   tread.

CXLV

"While stands the Coliseum, Rome shall
   stand;   55
When falls the Coliseum, Rome shall fall;
And when Rome falls—the World." From our
   own land
Thus spake the pilgrims o'er this mighty wall
In Saxon times, which we are wont to call
Ancient; and these three mortal things are
   still   60
On their foundations, and unalter'd all;
Rome and her Ruin past Redemption's skill,
The World, the same wide den—of thieves, or
   what ye will.

Commentary

Byron greatly admired the history of Rome as
Gibbon had written it. Compare and contrast
the use of Roman history by the two writers,
noting especially differences in tone and style. In
what ways are Byron's interests in Rome (and
Greece) different from those of Zinsser? Of
Anthony Hecht (p. 405) and A. E. Housman
(below). Are the differences matters of emotion,
idea, or expression?

A. E. HOUSMAN

On Wenlock Edge

On Wenlock Edge the wood's in trouble;
   His forest fleece the Wrekin heaves;
The gale, it plies the saplings double,
   And thick on Severn snow the leaves.

'Twould blow like this through holt and hanger   5
  When Uricon the city stood:
'Tis the old wind in the old anger,
  But then it threshed another wood.

Then, 'twas before my time, the Roman
  At yonder heaving hill would stare: 10
The blood that warms an English yeoman,
  The thoughts that hurt him, they were there.

There, like the wind through woods in riot,
  Through him the gale of life blew high;
The tree of man was never quiet: 15
  Then 'twas the Roman, now 'tis I.

The gale, it plies the saplings double,
  It blows so hard, 'twill soon be gone:
To-day the Roman and his trouble
  Are ashes under Uricon.   20

THOMAS HARDY

Convergence of the Twain

LINES ON THE LOSS OF THE "TITANIC"

I

In a solitude of the sea
Deep from human vanity,
And the Pride of Life that planned her,
                stilly couches she.

II

Steel chambers, late the pyres
Of her salamandrine fires,   5
Cold currents thrid, and turn to rhythmic
                tidal lyres.

III

Over the mirrors meant
To glass the opulent
The sea-worm crawls—grotesque, slimed,
                dumb, indifferent.

IV

Jewels in joy designed   10
To ravish the sensuous mind
Lie lightless, all their sparkles bleared and
                black and blind.

V

Dim moon-eyed fishes near
Gaze at the gilded gear
And query: "What does this vaingloriousness
                down here?"...   15

VI

Well: while was fashioning
This creature of cleaving wing,
The Immanent Will that stirs and urges
                everything

VII

Prepared a sinister mate
For her—so gaily great—   20
A Shape of Ice, for the time far and
                dissociate.

VIII

And as the smart ship grew
In stature, grace, and hue,
In shadowy silent distance grew the Iceberg
                too.

IX

Alien they seemed to be: 25
No mortal eye could see
The intimate welding of their later history.

X

Or sign that they were bent
By paths coincident
On being anon twin halves of one august
                event,   30

XI

Till the Spinner of the Years
Said "Now!" And each one hears,
And consummation comes, and jars two
                hemispheres.

Channel Firing

That night your great guns, unawares,
Shook all our coffins as we lay,
And broke the chancel window-squares,
We thought it was the Judgment-day

And sat upright. While drearisome   5
Arose the howl of wakened hounds:
The mouse let fall the altar-crumb,
The worms drew back into the mounds,

The glebe cow drooled. Till God called, "No;
It's gunnery practice out at sea   10
Just as before you went below;
The world is as it used to be:

"All nations striving strong to make
Red war yet redder. Mad as hatters
They do no more for Christés sake   15
Than you who are helpless in such matters.

"That this is not the judgment-hour
For some of them's a blessed thing,
For if it were they'd have to scour
Hell's floor for so much threatening. . . .   20

"Ha, ha. It will be warmer when
I blow the trumpet (if indeed
I ever do; for you are men,
And rest eternal sorely need)."

So down we lay again. "I wonder,   25
Will the world ever saner be,"
Said one, "than when He sent us under
In our indifferent century!"

And many a skeleton shook his head.
"Instead of preaching forty year,"   30
My neighbour Parson Thirdly said,
"I wish I had stuck to pipes and beer."

Again the guns disturbed the hour,
Roaring their readiness to avenge,
As far inland as Stourton Tower,   35
And Camelot, and starlit Stonehenge.

Commentary

Hardy's poem takes place during a naval battle in the English Channel at the time of World War I. Notice the difference in his approach to that historical era from that of Mrs. Tuchman (p. 272), the historian, and that of e. e. cummings (See below), the lyrical spokesman for the foot-soldier.

E. E. CUMMINGS

my sweet old etcetera

my sweet old etcetera
aunt lucy during the recent

war could and what
is more did tell you just
what everybody was fighting   5

for,
my sister
isabel created hundreds
(and
hundreds)of socks not to   10
mention shirts fleaproof earwarmers

etcetera wristers etcetera,my
mother hoped that

i would die etcetera
bravely of course my father used   15
to become hoarse talking about how it was
a privilege and if only he
could meanwhile my

self etcetera lay quietly
in the deep mud et   20

cetera
(dreaming,
et
    cetera,of
Your smile   25
eyes knees and of your Etcetera)

WILLIAM BUTLER YEATS

The Second Coming

Turning and turning in the widening gyre
The falcon cannot hear the falconer;
Things fall apart; the centre cannot hold;
Mere anarchy is loosed upon the world,
The blood-dimmed tide is loosed, and
    everywhere   5
The ceremony of innocence is drowned;
The best lack all conviction, while the worst
Are full of passionate intensity.

Surely some revelation is at hand;
Surely the Second Coming is at hand.   10
The Second Coming! Hardly are those words out
When a vast image out of *Spiritus Mundi*
Troubles my sight: somewhere in sands of the
    desert
A shape with lion body and the head of a man,
A gaze blank and pitiless as the sun,   15
Is moving its slow thighs, while all about it
Reel shadows of the indignant desert birds.
The darkness drops again; but now I know
That twenty centuries of stony sleep
Were vexed to nightmare by a rocking cradle, 20
And what rough beast, its hour come round at
    last,
Slouches towards Bethlehem to be born?

Commentary

This short poem is a fine example of the way a lyric poet can fuse into a limited number of words and tropes a complexity of attitudes and ideas. Yeats is commenting on twentieth-century society; setting forth his theories of time and historical movement; commenting on religious ritual; suggesting certain psychological premises; remarking on past historical events; and implying how the poetic mind operates. He draws upon the interests of psychology, sociology, historiography, mathematics, and several other disciplines. Read the poem closely and show what branches of knowledge Yeats calls upon, explain how he structures his concepts into a unified poem, and suggest the most important ways the poem differs from other approaches in its emphasis and effect.

ANTHONY HECHT

It Out-Herods Herod. Pray You, Avoid It

Tonight my children hunch
Toward their Western, and are glad
As, with a Sunday punch,
The Good casts out the Bad.

And in their fairy tales   5
The warty giant and witch
Get sealed in doorless jails
And the match-girl strikes it rich.

I've made myself a drink.
The giant and witch are set   10
To bust out of the clink
When my children have gone to bed.

All frequencies are loud
With signals of despair;
In flash and morse they crowd   15
The rondure of the air.

For the wicked have grown strong,
Their numbers mock at death,
Their cow brings forth its young,
Their bull engendereth.   20

Their very fund of strength,
Satan, bestrides the globe;
He stalks its breadth and length
And finds out even Job.

Yet by quite other laws   25
My children make their case;
Half God, half Santa Claus,
But with my voice and face,

A hero comes to save
The poorman, beggarman, thief,   30
And make the world behave
And put an end to grief.

And that their sleep be sound
I say this childermas
Who could not, at one time,   35
Have saved them from the gas.

Commentary

Although the title of this poem is taken from *Hamlet* and refers to the over-exaggerated acting of a character in the old morality plays of the fifteenth century, more directly the "Herod" is a king who was dramatically represented. Herod was the tyrant who caused the slaughter of all young children in Israel in an attempt to exterminate the newly born Jesus. Thus, insanely destructive and inhuman though he was, Herod was historically real—just as Adolf Hitler was real and caused children like Anne Frank to die by the thousands. Hecht's poem about his two sons watching the make-believe world of television with its clearcut simplification of Good and Evil shows a father distressed at a world where the myths of goodness do not operate, where he is helpless to keep his children out of the gas chambers if they are born at the wrong time. Read this poem carefully, noticing how the poet uses mythology, religion, ethics, and history to make a strong, personal emotion out of the same vision of the Beast at Large to be found in Yeats's *The Second Coming*.

G. S. FRASER

Instead of an Elegy

Bullets blot out the Life-Time smile,
Apollo of the picture-page,
Blunt-faced young lion
          Caught by vile
Death in an everlasting cage: 5

And, no more young men in the world,
The old men troop to honour him,
The drums beat glum,
          Slight snow is swirled
In dazzling sun, pale requiem.   10

And pale dark-veiled Persephone,
A golden child in either hand,
Stands by white pillars;
          Silently,
It seems she might for ever stand.   15

In bright grey sun, processionals
Of pomp and honour, and of grief,
Crown that dead head
          With coronals.
Some stony hearts feel some relief: 20

But not your heart, America,
Beating so slow and sure and strong,
Stricken in his
          Triumphal car,
Guard Caesar's bitter laurels long   25

With soldiers' music, rites of war:
He had proved bravely when put on!
The soldiers shoot.
          Waste echoes far
Above the grave at Arlington.   30

Commentary

The subject of Fraser's poem is, of course, the assassination and funeral of John F. Kennedy. Compare Fraser's poem with *A Funeral* in its tone and emphasis. Is the poem historically oriented in any way? Why does Fraser refer to Apollo, Persephone, and other mythological figures to convey his feelings about Kennedy's death? What are these feelings? How would you differentiate this poetic account from those of the historian, journalist, biographer, and sociologist? From the cultural anthropologist? From your own experience, does this poem effectively interpret the scenes it presents? Are they "real"? Are they "true"?

Section C
Man Among His Kind

GEOFFREY CHAUCER

Four Pilgrims

A KNIGHT ther was, and that a worthy man
That fro the tyme that he first bigan
To ryden out, he loved chivalrye,
Trouthe and honour, fredom and curteisye.
Ful worthy was he in his lordes werre,   5
And therto hadde he riden (no man ferre)
As wel in Christendom as hethenesse,
And ever honoured for his worthinesse.

  At Alisaundre he was, whan it was wonne;
Ful ofte tyme he hadde the bord bigonne   10
Aboven alle naciouns in Pruce.
In Lettow hadde he reysed and in Ruce,
No Cristen man so ofte of his degree.
In Gernade at the sege eek hadde he be
Of Algezir, and riden in Belmarye.   15
At Lyeys was he, and at Satalye,
Whan they were wonne; and in the Grete See
At many a noble aryve hadde he be.
At mortal batailles hadde he been fiftene,
And foughten for our feith at Tramissene   20
In listes thryes, and ay slayn his fo.
This ilke worthy knight had been also
Somtyme with the lord of Palatye,
Ageyn another hethen in Turkye:
And evermore he hadde a sovereyn prys.   25
And though that he were worthy, he was wys,
And of his port as meke as is a mayde.
He never yet no vileinye ne sayde
In al his lyf, un-to no maner wight.
He was a verray parfit gentil knight.   30
But for to tellen yow of his array,
His hors were gode, but he was nat gay.
Of fustian he wered a gipoun
Al bismotered with his habergeoun;
For he was late y-come from his viage,   35
And wente for to doon his pilgrimage.

  With him ther was his sone, a yong SQUYER,

A lovyere, and a lusty bacheler,
With lokkes crulle, as they were leyd in presse,
Of twenty yeer of age he was, I gesse.   40
Of his stature he was of evene lengthe,
And wonderly deliver, and greet of strengthe.
And he had been somtyme in chivachye,
In Flaundres, in Artoys, and Picardye,
And born him wel, as of so litel space,   45
In hope to stonden in his lady grace.
Embrouded was he, as it were a mede
Al ful of fresshe floures, whyte and rede.
Singinge he was, or floytinge, all the day;
He was as fresh as is the month of May.   50
Short was his goune, with sleves longe and wyde.
Wel coude he sitte on hors, and faire ryde.
He coude songes make and wel endyte,
Juste and eek daunce, and wel purtreye and wryte.
So hote he lovede, that by nightertale   55
He sleep namore than dooth a nightingale.
Curteys he was, lowly, and servisable,
And carf biforn his fader at the table....

  Ther was also a Nonne, a PRIORESSE,
That of hir smyling was ful simple and coy: 60
Hir gretteste ooth was but by sëynt Loy;
And she was cleped madame Eglentyne.
Ful wel she song the service divyne,
Entuned in hir nose ful semely;
And Frensh she spak ful faire and fetisly,   65
After the scole of Stratford atte Bowe,
For Frensh of Paris was to hir unknowe.
At mete wel y-taught was she with-alle;
She leet no morsel from hir lippes falle,
Ne wette hir fingres in hir sauce depe.   70
Wel coude she carie a morsel, and wel kepe,
That no drope ne fille up-on hir brest.
In curteisye was set ful muche hir lest.
Hir over lippe wyped she so clene,
That in hir coppe was no ferthing sene   75
Of grece, whan she dronken hadde hir draughte.
Ful semely after hir mete she raughte,
And sikerly she was of greet disport,
And ful plesaunt, and amiable of port,
And peyned hir to countrefete chere   80
Of court, and been estatlich of manere,
And to ben holden digne of reverence.
But, for to speken of hir conscience,
She was so charitable and so pitous,
She wolde wepe, if that she sawe a mous   85
Caught in a trappe, if it were deed or bledde.

Of smale houndes had she, that she fedde
With rosted flesh, or milk and wastel-breed,
But sore weep she if oon of hem were deed,
Or if men smoot it with a yerde smerte: 90
And al was conscience and tendre herte.
Ful semely hir wimpel pinched was;
Hir nose tretys; hir eyen greye as glas;
Hir mouth ful smal, and ther-to softe and reed;
But sikerly she hadde a fair forheed;   95
It was almost a spanne brood, I trowe;
For, hardily, she was nat undergrowe.
Ful fetis was hir cloke, as I was war.
Of smal coral aboute hir arm she bar
A peire of bedes, gauded al with grene;   100
And ther-on heng a broche of gold ful shene,
On which ther was first write a crowned A,
And after, *Amor vincit omnia*....

    A good WYF was ther of bisyde BATHE,
But she was som-del deef, and that was scathe.   105
Of clooth-making she hadde swiche an haunt,
She passed hem of Ypres and of Gaunt.
In al the parisshe wyf ne was ther noon
That to th' offring bifore hir sholde goon;
And if ther dide, certeyn, so wrooth was she,   110
That she was out of alle charitee.
Hir coverchiefs ful fyne were of ground;
I dorste swere they weyeden ten pound
That on a Sonday were upon hir heed.
Hir hosen weren of fyn scarlet reed,   115
Ful streite y-teyd, and shoos ful moiste and newe.
Bold was hir face, and fair, and reed of hewe.
She was a worthy womman al hir lyve,
Housbondes at chirche-dore she hadde fyve,
Withouten other companye in youthe;   120
But therof nedeth nat to speke as nouthe.
And thryes hadde she been at Jerusalem;
She hadde passed many a straunge streem;
At Rome she hadde been, and at Boloigne,
In Galice at seint Jame, and at Coloigne.   125
She coude muche of wandring by the weye:
Gat-tothed was she, soothly for to seye.
Up-on an amblere esily she sat,
Y-wimpled wel, and on hir heed an hat
As brood as is a bokeler or a targe;   130
A foot-mantel aboute hir hipes large,
And on hir feet a paire of spores sharpe.
In felawschip wel coude she laughe and carpe.
Of remedyes of love she knew perchaunce,
For she coude of that art the olde daunce.   135

Commentary

In presenting his fictional people, does Chaucer employ any of the techniques of the prose biographer? Does he use any additional techniques peculiar to poetry? Is the poetic form a good one or not for conveying a man's inner qualities?

JOHN WILMOT, EARL OF ROCHESTER

Impromptus on the Court of Charles II

I

Here's Monmouth the witty,
Laurendine the pritty,
    And Frazier the great physitian;
But as for the rest,
Take York for a jest,   5
    And yourself for a great politician.

II

We have a pritty witty king
    And whose word no man relys on:
He never said a foolish thing,
    And never did a wise one.   10

Commentary

John Wilmot, himself a brilliant member of the court of King Charles II of England (1660–1685), was notorious for his ability to hit at a man's weakness in a sharp phrase. The Duke of Monmouth was the handsome, libertine bastard son of King Charles who tried to succeed to the throne illegally after his father's death. The Duke of York, later King James II, was the king's brother and the heir to the throne. When he became king, he beheaded Monmouth. Frazier, the Court doctor, presided over the

death of Charles and was rumored to have
poisoned him, at James's urging. Laurendine
was a handsome but vacuous member of
Charles's circle; and the "pritty witty king" was
Charles himself. These offhand character
sketches were written at least fifteen years
before these power struggles. How astutely did
Rochester sum up his victims?

SAMUEL JOHNSON

The Vanity
of Human Wishes

Let Observation, with extensive view,
Survey mankind, from China to Peru;
Remark each anxious toil, each eager strife,
And watch the busy scenes of crowded life;
Then say how hope and fear, desire and hate   5
O'erspread with snares the clouded maze of fate,
Where wav'ring man, betray'd by vent'rous pride
To tread the dreary paths without a guide,
As treach'rous phantoms in the mist delude,
Shuns fancied ills, or chases airy good;   10
How rarely Reason guides the stubborn choice,
Rules the bold hand, or prompts the suppliant
     voice;
How nations sink, by darling schemes oppress'd,
When Vengeance listens to the fool's request.
Fate wings with ev'ry wish th' afflictive dart,   15
Each gift of nature, and each grace of art;
With fatal heat impetuous courage glows,
With fatal sweetness elocution flows,
Impeachment stops the speaker's powerful breath,
And restless fire precipitates on death.   20
     But scarce observ'd, the knowing and the bold
Fall in the gen'ral massacre of gold;
Wide-wasting pest! that rages unconfin'd,
And crowds with crimes the records of mankind;
For gold his sword the hireling ruffian draws,   25
For gold the hireling judge distorts the laws;
Wealth heap'd on wealth, nor truth nor safety
     buys,
The dangers gather as the treasures rise.
     Let Hist'ry tell where rival kings command,

And dubious title shakes the madded land,   30
When statutes glean the refuse of the sword,
How much more safe the vassal than the lord,
Low skulks the hind beneath the rage of power,
And leaves the wealthy traitor in the Tower,
Untouch'd his cottage, and his slumbers sound,   35
Tho' confiscation's vultures hover round.
     The needy traveller, serene and gay,
Walks the wild heath, and sings his toil away.
Does envy seize thee? crush th' upbraiding joy,
Increase his riches and his peace destroy;   40
New fears in dire vicissitude invade,
The rustling brake alarms, and quiv'ring shade,
Nor light nor darkness bring his pain relief,
One shews the plunder, and one hides the thief.
     Yet still one gen'ral cry the skies assails,   45
And gain and grandeur load the tainted gales;
Few know the toiling statesman's fear or care,
Th' insidious rival and the gaping heir.
     Once more, Democritus, arise on earth,
With cheerful wisdom and instructive mirth,   50
See motley life in modern trappings dress'd,
And feed with varied fools th' eternal jest:
Thou who couldst laugh where want enchain'd
     caprice,
Toil crush'd conceit, and man was of a piece;
Where wealth unlov'd without a mourner dy'd;   55
And scarce a sycophant was fed by pride;
Where ne'er was known the form of mock debate,
Or seen a new-made mayor's unwieldy state;
Where change of fav'rites made no change of laws,
And senates heard before they judg'd a cause;   60
How wouldst thou shake at Britain's modish tribe,
Dart the quick taunt, and edge the piercing gibe?
Attentive truth and nature to descry,
And pierce each scene with philosophic eye,
To thee were solemn toys or empty show   65
The robes of pleasures and the veils of woe:
All aid the farce, and all thy mirth maintain,
Whose joys are causeless, or whose griefs are vain.
     Such was the scorn that fill'd the sage's mind,
Renew'd at ev'ry glance on human kind;   70
How just that scorn ere yet thy voice declare,
Search ev'ry state, and canvass ev'ry pray'r.
     Unnumber'd suppliants crowd Preferment's
     gate,
Athirst for wealth, and burning to be great;
Delusive Fortune hears th' incessant call,   75
They mount, they shine, evaporate, and fall.
On ev'ry stage the foes of peace attend,

Hate dogs their flight, and insult mocks their end.
Love ends with hope, the sinking statesman's door
Pours in the morning worshipper no more;   80
For growing names the weekly scribbler lies,
To growing wealth the dedicator flies;
From ev'ry room descends the painted face,
That hung the bright palladium of the place;
And smok'd in kitchens, or in auctions sold,   85
To better features yields the frame of gold;
For now no more we trace in ev'ry line
Heroic worth, benevolence divine:
The form distorted justifies the fall,
And detestation rids th' indignant wall.   90
  But will not Britain hear the last appeal,
Sign her foe's doom, or guard her fav'rites' zeal?
Thro' Freedom's sons no more remonstrance
    rings,
Degrading nobles and controlling kings;
Our supple tribes repress their patriot throats,   95
And ask no questions but the price of votes;
With weekly libels and septennial ale.
Their wish is full to riot and to rail.
  In full-blown dignity, see Wolsey stand,
Law in his voice, and fortune in his hand: 100
To him the church, the realm, their powers
    consign,
Through him the rays of regal bounty shine;
Turn'd by his nod the stream of honour flows,
His smile alone security bestows:
Still to new heights his restless wishes tower,   105
Claim leads to claim, and pow'r advances power;
Till conquest unresisted ceas'd to please,
And rights submitted, left him none to seize.
At length his sov'reign frowns—the train of state
Mark the keen glance, and watch the sign to
    hate.   110
Where'er he turns, he meets a stranger's eye,
His suppliants scorn him, and his followers fly;
At once is lost the pride of awful state,
The golden canopy, the glitt'ring plate,
The regal palace, the luxurious board,   115
The liv'ried army, and the menial lord.
With age, with cares, with maladies oppress'd,
He seeks the refuge of monastic rest.
Grief aids disease, remember'd folly stings,
And his last sighs reproach the faith of kings.   120
  Speak thou, whose thoughts at humble peace
    repine,
Shall Wolsey's wealth, with Wolsey's end be
    thine?

Or liv'st thou now, with safer pride content,
The wisest justices on the banks of Trent?
For why did Wolsey, near the steeps of fate,   125
On weak foundations raise th' enormous
    weight?
Why but to sink beneath misfortune's blow,
With louder ruin to the gulfs below?
  What gave great Villiers to th' assassin's knife,
And fix'd disease on Harley's closing life?   130
What murder'd Wentworth, and what exil'd
    Hyde,
By kings protected and to kings allied?
What but their wish indulg'd in courts to shine,
And pow'r too great to keep or to resign?
  When first the college rolls receive his name,   135
The young enthusiast quits his ease for fame;
Resistless burns the fever of renown
Caught from the strong contagion of the gown:
O'er Bodley's dome his future labours spread,
And Bacon's mansion trembles o'er his head.   140
Are these thy views? proceed, illustrious youth,
And Virtue guard thee to the throne of Truth!
Yet should thy soul indulge the gen'rous heat,
Till captive Science yields her last retreat;
Should Reason guide thee with her brightest
    ray,   145
And pour on misty Doubt resistless day;
Should no false kindness lure to loose delight,
Nor praise relax, nor difficulty fright;
Should tempting Novelty thy cell refrain,
And Sloth effuse her opiate fumes in vain;   150
Should Beauty blunt on fops her fatal dart,
Nor claim the triumph of a letter'd heart;
Should no disease thy torpid veins invade,
Nor Melancholy's phantoms haunt thy shade;
Yet hope not life from grief or danger free,   155
Nor think the doom of man revers'd for thee:
Deign on the passing world to turn thine eyes,
And pause a while from letters, to be wise;
There mark what ills the scholar's life assail,
Toil, envy, want, the patron, and the gaol.   160
See nations slowly wise, and meanly just,
To buried merit raise the tardy bust.
If dreams yet flatter, once again attend,
Hear Lydiat's life, and Galileo's end.
  Nor deem, when Learning her last prize
    bestows,   165
The glitt'ring eminence exempt from foes;
See when the vulgar 'scapes, despis'd or aw'd,
Rebellion's vengeful talons seize on Laud.

From meaner minds though smaller fines content,
The plunder'd palace, or sequester'd rent;   170
Mark'd out by dang'rous parts he meets the
    shock,
And fatal Learning leads him to the block:
Around his tomb let Art and Genius weep,
But hear his death, ye blockheads, hear and
    sleep.
    The festal blazes, the triumphal show,   175
The ravish'd standard, and the captive foe,
The senate's thanks, the gazette's pompous tale,
With force resistless o'er the brave prevail.
Such bribes the rapid Greek o'er Asia whirl'd,
For such the steady Romans shook the world;   180
For such in distant lands the Britons shine,
And strain with blood the Danube or the Rhine;
This pow'r has praise, that virtue scarce can
    warm,
Till fame supplies the universal charm.
Yet Reason frowns on War's unequal game,   185
Where wasted nations raise a single name,
And mortgag'd states their grandsires' wreaths
    regret
From age to age in everlasting debt;
Wreaths which at last the dear-bought right
    convey
To rust on medals, or on stones decay.   190
    On what foundation stands the warrior's pride,
How just his hopes, let Swedish Charles decide;
A frame of adamant, a soul of fire,
No dangers fright him, and no labours tire;
O'er love, o'er fear, extends his wide domain,   195
Unconquer'd lord of pleasure and of pain;
No joys to him pacific sceptres yield,
War sounds the trump, he rushes to the field;
Behold surrounding kings their powers combine,
And one capitulate, and one resign;   200
Peace courts his hand, but spreads her charms
    in vain;
"Think nothing gain'd," he cries, "till naught
    remain,
On Moscow's walls till Gothic standards fly,
And all be mine beneath the polar sky."
The march begins in military state,   205
And nations on his eye suspended wait;
Stern Famine guards the solitary coast,
And Winter barricades the realms of Frost;
He comes, nor want nor cold his course delay;—
Hide, blushing Glory, hide Pultowa's day: 210
The vanquish'd hero leaves his broken bands,

And shows his miseries in distant lands;
Condemn'd a needy supplicant to wait,
While ladies interpose, and slaves debate.
But did not Chance at length her error mend?   215
Did no subverted empire mark his end?
Did rival monarchs give the fatal wound?
Or hostile millions press him to the ground?
His fall was destin'd to a barren strand,
A petty fortress, and a dubious hand;   220
He left the name at which the world grew pale,
To point a moral, or adorn a tale.
    All times their scenes of pompous woes afford,
From Persia's tyrant to Bavaria's lord.
In gay hostility, and barb'rous pride,   225
With half mankind embattled at his side.
Great Xerxes comes to seize the certain prey,
And starves exhausted regions in his way;
Attendant Flatt'ry counts his myriads o'er,
Till counted myriads sooth his pride no more;   230
Fresh praise is tried till madness fires his mind,
The waves he lashes, and enchains the wind;
New pow'rs are claim'd, new pow'rs are still
    bestow'd,
Till rude resistance lops the spreading god;
The daring Greeks deride the martial show,   235
And heap their valleys with the gaudy foe;
Th' insulted sea with humbler thought he gains,
A single skiff to speed his flight remains;
Th' incumber'd oar scarce leaves the dreaded
    coast
Through purple billows and a floating host.   240
    The bold Bavarian, in a luckless hour,
Tries the dread summits of Cæsarean pow'r,
With unexpected legions bursts away,
And sees defenseless realms receive his sway;
Short sway! fair Austria spreads her mournful
    charms,   245
The queen, the beauty, sets the world in arms;
From hill to hill the beacon's rousing blaze
Spreads wide the hope of plunder and of praise;
The fierce Croatian, and the wild Hussar,
With all the sons of ravage crowd the war;   250
The baffled prince, in honour's flatt'ring bloom
Of hasty greatness finds the fatal doom;
His foes' derision, and his subjects' blame,
And steals to death from anguish and from
    shame.
    Enlarge my life with multitude of days!   255
In health, in sickness, thus the suppliant prays;
Hides from himself his state, and shuns to know,

That life protracted is protracted woe.
Time hovers o'er, impatient to destroy,
And shuts up all the passages of joy;   260
In vain their gifts the bounteous seasons pour,
The fruit autumnal, and the vernal flower;
With listless eyes the dotard views the store,
He views, and wonders that they please no
    more;
Now pall the tasteless meats, and joyless
    wines,   265
And Luxury with sighs her slave resigns.
Approach, ye minstrels, try the soothing strain,
Diffuse the tuneful lenitives of pain:
No sounds, alas! would touch th' impervious ear,
Though dancing mountains witness'd Orpheus
    near;   270
Nor lute nor lyre his feeble powers attend,
Nor sweeter music of a virtuous friend,
But everlasting dictates crowd his tongue,
Perversely grave, or positively wrong.
The still returning tale, and ling'ring jest,   275
Perplex the fawning niece and pamper'd guest,
While growing hopes scarce awe the gath'ring
    sneer,
And scarce a legacy can bribe to hear;
The watchful guests still hint the last offence;
The daughter's petulance, the son's expense,   280
Improve his heady rage with treach'rous skill,
And mould his passions till they make his will.
    Unnumber'd maladies his joints invade,
Lay siege to life and press the dire blockade;
But unextinguish'd Av'rice still remains,   285
And dreaded losses aggravate his pains;
He turns, with anxious heart and crippled hands,
His bonds of debt, and mortgages of lands;
Or views his coffers with suspicious eyes,
Unlocks his gold, and counts it till he dies.   290
    But grant, the virtues of a temp'rate prime
Bless with an age exempt from scorn or crime;
An age that melts with unperceiv'd decay,
And glides in modest innocence away;
Whose peaceful day Benevolence endears,   295
Whose night congratulating Conscience cheers;
The gen'ral fav'rite as the gen'ral friend:
Such age there is, and who shall wish its end?
    Yet ev'n on this her load Misfortune flings,
To press the weary minutes' flagging wings;   300
New sorrow rises as the day returns,
A sister sickens, or a daughter mourns.
Now kindred Merit fills the sable bier,

Now lacerated Friendship claims a tear;
Year chases year, decay pursues decay,   305
Still drops some joy from with'ring life away;
New forms arise, and diff'rent views engage,
Superfluous lags the vet'ran on the stage,
Till pitying Nature signs the last release,
And bids afflicted worth retire to peace.   310
    But few there are whom hours like these
    await,
Who set unclouded in the gulfs of Fate.
From Lydia's monarch should the search
    descend,
By Solon caution'd to regard his end,
In life's last scene what prodigies surprise,   315
Fears of the brave, and follies of the wise!
From Marlb'rough's eyes the streams of dotage
    flow,
And Swift expires a driv'ler and a show.
    The teeming mother, anxious for her race,
Begs for each birth the fortune of a face: 320
Yet Vane could tell what ills from beauty spring;
And Sedley curs'd the form that pleas'd a king.
Ye nymphs of rosy lips and radiant eyes,
Whom Pleasure keeps too busy to be wise,
Whom joys with soft varieties invite,   325
By day the frolic, and the dance by night;
Who frown with vanity, who smile with art,
And ask the latest fashion of the heart;
What care, what rules your heedless charms
    shall save,
Each nymph your rival, and each youth your
    slave?   330
Against your fame with fondness hate combines,
The rival batters, and the lover mines.
With distant voice neglected Virtue calls,
Less heard and less, the faint remonstrance falls;
Tir'd with contempt, she quits the slipp'ry
    reign,   335
And Pride and Prudence take her seat in vain.
In crowd at once, where none the pass defend,
The harmless freedom, and the private friend.
The guardians yield, by force superior plied:
To Int'rest, Prudence; and to Flatt'ry, Pride.   340
Now Beauty falls betray'd, despis'd, distress'd,
And hissing Infamy proclaims the rest.
    Where then shall Hope and Fear their objects
    find?
Must dull suspense corrupt the stagnant mind?
Must helpless man, in ignorance sedate,   345
Roll darkling down the torrent of his fate?

Must no dislike alarm, no wishes rise,
No cries invoke the mercies of the skies?
Inquirer, cease; petitions yet remain,
Which Heaven may hear, nor deem Religion
  vain.   350
Still raise for good the supplicating voice,
But leave to Heaven the measure and the
  choice.
Safe in His power, whose eyes discern afar
The secret ambush of a specious prayer.
Implore His aid, in His decisions rest,   355
Secure, whate'er He gives, He gives the best.
Yet when the sense of sacred presence fires,
And strong devotion to the skies aspires,
Pour forth thy fervours for a healthful mind,
Obedient passions, and a will resign'd;   360
For love, which scarce collective man can fill;
For patience sov'reign o'er transmuted ill;
For faith, that panting for a happier seat,
Counts death kind Nature's signal of retreat:
These goods for man the laws of Heaven ordain, 365
These goods He grants, who grants the power
  to gain;
With these celestial Wisdom calms the mind,
And makes the happiness she does not find.

Miniver mourned the ripe renown
    That made so many a name so fragrant;
He mourned Romance, now on the town,   15
    And Art, a vagrant.

Miniver loved the Medici,
    Albeit he had never seen one;
He would have sinned incessantly
    Could he have been one.   20

Miniver cursed the commonplace
    And eyed a khaki suit with loathing;
He missed the mediaeval grace
    Of iron clothing.

Miniver scorned the gold he sought,   25
    But sore annoyed was he without it;
Miniver thought, and thought, and thought,
    And thought about it.

Miniver Cheevy, born too late,
    Scratched his head and kept on thinking; 30
Miniver coughed, and called it fate,
    And kept on drinking.

EDWIN ARLINGTON ROBINSON

Miniver Cheevy

Richard Cory

Miniver Cheevy, child of scorn,
    Grew lean while he assailed the seasons;
He wept that he was ever born,
    And he had reasons.

Miniver loved the days of old   5
    When swords were bright and steeds were
      prancing;
The vision of a warrior bold
    Would set him dancing.

Miniver sighed for what was not,
    And dreamed, and rested from his labors; 10
He dreamed of Thebes and Camelot,
    And Priam's neighbors.

Whenever Richard Cory went down town,
We people on the pavement looked at him:
He was a gentleman from sole to crown,
Clean favored, and imperially slim.

And he was always quietly arrayed,   5
And he was always human when he talked;
But still he fluttered pulses when he said,
"Good morning," and he glittered when he
  walked.

And he was rich—yes, richer than a king—
And admirably schooled in every grace: 10
In fine, we thought that he was everything
To make us wish that we were in his place.

So on we worked, and waited for the light,
And went without the meat, and cursed the
  bread;
And Richard Cory, one calm summer night,   15
Went home and put a bullet through his head.

Commentary

From whose point of view are Miniver Cheevy
and Richard Cory described? How does this
serve to point up the characters of the men?
Are Cheevy and Cory stereotypes or individuals?
Are they eccentrics? Why would a poet write
about these imaginary men?

E. E. CUMMINGS

my father moved through dooms of love

my father moved through dooms of love
through sames of am through haves of give,
singing each morning out of each night
my father moved through depths of height

this motionless forgetful where   5
turned at his glance to shining here;
that if(so timid air is firm)
under his eyes would stir and squirm

newly as from unburied which
floats the first who,his april touch   10
drove sleeping selves to swarm their fates
woke dreamers to their ghostly roots

and should some why completely weep
my father's fingers brought her sleep:
vainly no smallest voice might cry   15
for he could feel the mountains grow.

Lifting the valleys of the sea
my father moved through griefs of joy;
praising a forehead called the moon
singing desire into begin   20

joy was his song and joy so pure
a heart of star by him could steer
and pure so now and now so yes
the wrists of twilight would rejoice

keen as midsummer's keen beyond   25
conceiving mind of sun will stand,
so strictly(over utmost him
so hugely)stood my father's dream

his flesh was flesh his blood was blood:
no hungry man but wished him food;   30
no cripple wouldn't creep one mile
uphill to only see him smile.

Scorning the pomp of must and shall
my father moved through dooms of feel;
his anger was as right as rain   35
his pity was as green as grain

septembering arms of year extend
less humbly wealth to foe and friend
than he to foolish and to wise
offered immeasurable is   40

proudly and(by octobering flame
beckoned)as earth will downward climb,
so naked for immortal work
his shoulders marched against the dark

his sorrow was as true as bread: 45
no liar looked him in the head;
if every friend became his foe
he'd laugh and build a world with snow.

My father moved through theys of we,
singing each new leaf out of each tree   50
(and every child was sure that spring
danced when she heard my father sing)

then let men kill which cannot share,
let blood and flesh be mud and mire,
scheming imagine,passion willed,   55
freedom a drug that's bought and sold

giving to steal and cruel kind,
a heart to fear,to doubt a mind,
to differ a disease of same,
conform the pinnacle of am   60

though dull were all we taste as bright,
bitter all utterly things sweet,
maggoty minus and dumb death
all we inherit,all bequeath

and nothing quite so least as truth   65
—i say though hate were why men breathe—
because my father lived his soul
love is the whole and more than all

objectively portrayed—Cummings's or Proust's? Which are the more complex and unusual personalities? Contrast the stylistic ways used by Cummings and Proust to achieve their character sketches. Which style do you find the more ingenious? Which do you prefer and why?

ROBERT FROST

if there are
any heavens

if there are any heavens my mother will(all by
    herself)have
one. It will not be a pansy heaven nor
a fragile heaven of lilies-of the-valley but
it will be a heaven of blackred roses

my father will be(deep like a rose   5
tall like a rose)

standing near my

swaying over her
silent)
with eyes which are really petals and see   10

nothing with the face of a poet really which
is a flower and not a face with
hands
which whisper
This is my beloved my   15

                    (suddenly in sunlight
he will bow,

& the whole garden will bow)

Commentary

Compare Cummings's presentation of his father and mother with Proust's picture of his parents on p. 143f. above. Which set of parents are more

After Apple-Picking

My long two-pointed ladder's sticking through a
    tree
Toward heaven still,
And there's a barrel that I didn't fill
Beside it, and there may be two or three
Apples I didn't pick upon some bough.   5
But I am done with apple-picking now.
Essence of winter sleep is on the night,
The scent of apples: I am drowsing off.
I cannot rub the strangeness from my sight
I got from looking through a pane of glass   10
I skimmed this morning from the drinking trough
And held against the world of hoary grass.
It melted, and I let it fall and break.
But I was well
Upon my way to sleep before it fell,   15
And I could tell
What form my dreaming was about to take.
Magnified apples appear and disappear,
Stem end and blossom end,
And every fleck of russet showing clear,   20
My instep arch not only keeps the ache,
It keeps the pressure of a ladder-round.
I feel the ladder sway as the boughs bend.
And I keep hearing from the cellar bin
The rumbling sound   25
Of load on load of apples coming in.
For I have had too much
Of apple-picking: I am overtired
Of the great harvest I myself desired.
There were ten thousand thousand fruit to touch,   30
Cherish in hand, lift down, and not let fall.
For all
That struck the earth,

No matter if not bruised or spiked with stubble,
Went surely to the cider-apple heap   35
As of no worth.
One can see what will trouble
This sleep of mine, whatever sleep it is.
Were he not gone,
The woodchuck could say whether it's like his   40
Long sleep, as I describe its coming on,
Or just some human sleep.

Commentary

How does this poem resemble the autobiography? Is the situation developed in this poem
merely one brief episode in a man's life or is it
something more? Why are the "pane of glass"
and the woodchuck brought into the poem?
Compare Frost's tone and view of experience
with those of Henry Adams (p. 135f.) and
Tennessee Williams (p. 420f.).

Section D
Man and Himself

WILLIAM SHAKESPEARE

When to the Sessions of Sweet Silent Thought

When to the sessions of sweet silent thought
I summon up remembrance of things past,
I sigh the lack of many a thing I sought,
And with old woes new wail my dear time's
    waste;
Then can I drown an eye unused to flow   5
For precious friends hid in death's dateless night,
And weep afresh love's long since cancelled woe,
And moan the expense of many a vanished sight;
Then can I grieve at grievances foregone,

And heavily from woe to woe tell o'er   10
The sad account of fore-bemoanèd moan,
Which I new pay as if not paid before.
But if the while I think on thee, dear friend,
All losses are restored and sorrows end.

Poor Soul, the Center of my Sinful Earth

Poor soul, the center of my sinful earth,
Thrall to these rebel powers that thee array,
Why dost thou pine within and suffer dearth,
Painting thy outward walls so costly gay?
Why so large cost, having so short a lease,   5
Dost thou upon thy fading mansion spend?
Shall worms, inheritors of this excess,
Eat up thy charge? Is this thy body's end?
Then, soul, live thou upon thy servant's loss,
And let that pine to aggravate thy store;   10
Buy terms divine in selling hours of dross;
Within be fed, without be rich no more:
So shalt thou feed on Death, that feeds on men,
And Death once dead, there's no more dying then.

JOHN DONNE

The Sun Rising

    Busy old fool, unruly Sun,
        Why dost thou thus,
Through windows and through curtains, call
    on us?
Must to thy motions lovers' seasons run?
        Saucy pedantic wretch, go chide   5
        Late schoolboys and sour 'prentices,
    Go tell court-huntsmen that the King will
        ride,

Call country ants to harvest offices;
Love, all alike, no season knows, nor clime,
Nor hours, days, months, which are the rags of
        time.   10

        Thy beams, so reverend and strong
        Why should'st thou think?
I could eclipse and cloud them with a wink,
But that I would not lose her sight so long.
        If her eyes have not blinded thine,   15
        Look, and tomorrow late, tell me,
Whether both the Indias of spice and mine
Be where thou left'st them, or lie here with
        me.
Ask for those Kings whom thou saw'st yesterday,
And thou shalt hear, All here in one bed lay.   20

        She is all States, and all Princes, I,
        Nothing else is.
Princes do but play us; compared to this,
All honor's mimic, all wealth alchemy.
        Thou, sun, art half as happy as we,   25
        In that the world's contracted thus;
        Thine age asks ease, and since thy duties be
        To warm the world, that's done in warming
        us.
Shine here to us, and thou art everywhere;
This bed thy center, these walls thy sphere.   30

If Poisonous Minerals

If poisonous minerals, and if that tree
Whose fruit threw death on else immortal us,
If lecherous goats, if serpents envious
Cannot be damned, alas, why should I be?
Why should intent or reason, born in me,   5
Make sins, else equal, in me more heinous?
And mercy being easy and glorious
To God, in his stern wrath why threatens He?
But who am I that dare dispute with Thee,
O God? O, of thine only worthy blood   10
And my tears make a heavenly Lethean flood,

And drown it in my sins' black memory.
That thou remember them, some claim as debt;
I think it mercy if thou wilt forget.

Batter My Heart, Three-Personed God

Batter my heart, three-personed God, for you
As yet but knock, breathe, shine, and seek to
        mend;
That I may rise and stand, o'erthrow me, and
        bend
Your force to break, blow, burn and make me
        new.
I, like an usurped town, to another due,   5
Labour to admit you, but oh, to no end;
Reason, your viceroy in me, me should defend,
But is captived, and proves weak or untrue.
Yet dearly I love you, and would be loved fain,
But am betrothed unto your enemy: 10
Divorce me, untie, or break that knot again,
Take me to you, imprison me, for I
Except you enthrall me, never shall be free,
Nor ever chaste, except you ravish me.

Commentary

Compare the passions and desires expressed in
this Holy Sonnet of Donne's with Saint
Augustine's *Confessions* (p. 114f.).

JOHN KEATS

Ode on Melancholy

1

No, no, go not to Lethe, neither twist
    Wolf's-bane, tight-rooted, for its poisonous
        wine;

Nor suffer thy pale forehead to be kiss'd
  By nightshade, ruby grape of Proserpine;
Make not your rosary of yew-berries,   5
  Nor let the beetle, nor the death-moth be
    Your mournful Psyche, nor the downy owl
A partner in your sorrow's mysteries;
  For shade to shade will come too drowsily,
    And drown the wakeful anguish of the soul. 10

2

But when the melancholy fit shall fall
  Sudden from heaven like a weeping cloud,
That fosters the droop-headed flowers all,
  And hides the green hill in an April shroud;
Then glut thy sorrow on a morning rose,   15
  Or on the rainbow of the salt sand-wave,
    Or on the wealth of globéd peonies;
Or if thy mistress some rich anger shows,
  Emprison her soft hand, and let her rave,
    And feed deep, deep upon her peerless eyes. 20

3

She dwells with Beauty—Beauty that must die;
  And Joy, whose hand is ever at his lips
Bidding adieu; and aching Pleasure nigh,
  Turning to poison while the bee-mouth sips:
Ay, in the very temple of Delight   25
  Veil'd Melancholy has her sovran shrine,
    Though seen of none save him whose
      strenuous tongue
Can burst Joy's grape against his palate fine;
His soul shall taste the sadness of her might,
  And be among her cloudy trophies hung. 30

Commentary

Like Boswell, Keats was subject to melancholic depressions; see Boswell's *Journal* and Keats's *Letters* above. Is this reflective poem significantly unlike the factual statements about melancholy in their prose writings? Is this poem a private statement or does it have wider connotations? What are the chief poetic devices used by Keats? Do these make the poem more or less general in application and appeal?

EMILY DICKINSON

Pain Has an Element of Blank

Pain has an element of blank;
It cannot recollect
When it began, or if there were
A day when it was not.

It has no future but itself,   5
Its infinite realms contain
Its past, enlightened to perceive
New periods of pain.

The Bustle in a House

The bustle in a house
The morning after death
Is solemnest of industries
Enacted upon earth,—

The sweeping up of heart,   5
And putting love away
We shall not want to use again
Until eternity.

Commentary

Compare this poetic picture of death and grief with that in Emily Dickinson's letters. Is the poem more or less abstract than the letters? Is it less intense in tone? Which is the more convincing expression for you: the factual or the fictional?

WALLACE STEVENS

The Emperor
of Ice-Cream

Call the roller of big cigars,
The muscular one, and bid him whip
In kitchen cups concupiscent curds.
Let the wenches dawdle in such dress
As they are used to wear, and let the boys   5
Bring flowers in last month's newspapers.
Let be be finale of seem.
The only emperor is the emperor of ice-cream.

Take from the dresser of deal,
Lacking the three glass knobs, that sheet   10
On which she embroidered fantails once
And spread it so as to cover her face.
If her horny feet protrude, they come
To show how cold she is, and dumb.
Let the lamp affix its beam.   15
The only emperor is the emperor of ice-cream.

ROBERT FROST

Acquainted
with the Night

I have been one acquainted with the night.
I have walked out in rain—and back in rain.
I have outwalked the furthest city light.

I have looked down the saddest city lane.
I have passed by the watchman on his beat   5
And dropped my eyes, unwilling to explain.

I have stood still and stopped the sound of feet
When far away an interrupted cry
Came over houses from another street,

But not to call me back or say good-bye;   10
And further still at an unearthly height,
One luminary clock against the sky

Proclaimed the time was neither wrong nor right.
I have been one acquainted with the night.

Commentary

Compare this poem with Frost's *Once by the Pacific*. Are they both versions of the same insight and point of view? Compare *Acquainted with the Night* with Auden's *A Walk after Dark* below.

W. H. AUDEN

A Walk after Dark

A cloudless night like this
Can set the spirit soaring;
After a tiring day
The clockwork spectacle is
Impressive in a slightly boring   5
Eighteenth-century way.

It soothed adolescence a lot
To meet so shameless a stare;
The things I did could not
Be as shocking as they said   10
If that would still be there
After the shocked were dead.

Now, unready to die
But already at the stage
When one starts to dislike the young,   15
I am glad those points in the sky
May also be counted among
The creatures of middle-age.

It's cosier thinking of night
As more an Old People's Home   20
Than a shed for a faultless machine,

That the red pre-Cambrian light
Is gone like Imperial Rome
Or myself at seventeen.

Yet however much we may like   25
The stoic manner in which
The classical authors wrote,
Only the young and the rich
Have the nerve or the figure to strike
The lacrimae rerum note.   30

For the present stalks abroad
Like the past and its wronged again
Whimper and are ignored,
And the truth cannot be hid;
Somebody chose their pain,   35
What needn't have happened did.

Occurring this very night
By no established rule,
Some event may already have hurled
Its first little No at the right   40

Of the laws we accept to school
Our post-diluvian world:

But the stars burn on overhead,
Unconscious of final ends,
As I walk home to bed,   45
Asking what judgment waits
My person, all my friends,
And these United States.

Commentary

Notice the difference in perspective and tone between Auden's look back on his youth and Thomas's retrospective views in *Fern Hill*. Are these "private" poems or autobiographical versions of the private? Compare the use of point of view by Auden and Thomas with the reflections of Gibbon (p. 116f.), Augustine (p. 114f.), and Wordsworth (p. 390f.).

DYLAN THOMAS

Fern Hill

Now as I was young and easy under the apple boughs
About the lilting house and happy as the grass was green,
    The night above the dingle starry,
      Time let me hail and climb
    Golden in the heydays of his eyes,   5
And honoured among wagons I was prince of the apple towns
And once below a time I lordly had the trees and leaves
      Trail with daisies and barley
    Down the rivers of the windfall light.

And as I was green and carefree, famous among the barns   10
About the happy yard and singing as the farm was home,
    In the sun that is young once only,
      Time let me play and be
    Golden in the mercy of his means,
And green and golden I was huntsman and herdsman, the calves   15
Sang to my horn, the foxes on the hills barked clear and cold,
      And the sabbath rang slowly
    In the pebbles of the holy streams.

All the sun long it was running, it was lovely, the hay
Fields high as the house, the tunes from the chimneys, it was air   20
    And playing, lovely and watery
      And fire green as grass.

    And nightly under the simple stars
As I rode to sleep the owls were bearing the farm away,
All the moon long I heard, blessed among stables, the nightjars   25
    Flying with the ricks, and the horses
      Flashing into the dark.

And then to awake, and the farm, like a wanderer white
With the dew, come back, the cock on his shoulder: it was all
    Shining, it was Adam and maiden,   30
      The sky gathered again
    And the sun grew round that very day.
So it must have been after the birth of the simple light
In the first, spinning place, the spellbound horses walking warm
    Out of the whinnying green stable   35
      On to the fields of praise.

And honoured among foxes and pheasants by the gay house
Under the new made clouds and happy as the heart was long,
    In the sun born over and over,
      I ran my heedless ways,   40
      My wishes raced through the house high hay
And nothing I cared, at my sky blue trades, that time allows
In all his tuneful turning so few and such morning songs
    Before the children green and golden
      Follow him out of grace,   45

Nothing I cared, in the lamb white days, that time would take me
Up to the swallow thronged loft by the shadow of my hand,
    In the moon that is always rising,
      Nor that riding to sleep
    I should hear him fly with the high fields   50
And wake to the farm forever fled from the childless land.
Oh as I was young and easy in the mercy of his means,
    Time held me green and dying
    Though I sang in my chains like the sea.